Dictionary of Literary Biography

Dictionary of Literary Biography Documentary Series

Dictionary of Literary Biography Yearbooks

1980 edited by Karen L. Rood, Jean W. Ross, and Richard Ziegfeld (1981)

1981 edited by Karen L. Rood, Jean W. Ross, and Richard Ziegfeld (1982)

1982 edited by Richard Ziegfeld; associate editors: Jean W. Ross and Lynne C. Zeigler (1983)

1983 edited by Mary Bruccoli and Jean W. Ross; associate editor Richard Ziegfeld (1984)

1984 edited by Jean W. Ross (1985)

1985 edited by Jean W. Ross (1986)

1986 edited by J. M. Brook (1987)

1987 edited by J. M. Brook (1988)

1988 edited by J. M. Brook (1989)

1989 edited by J. M. Brook (1990)

1990 edited by James W. Hipp (1991)

1991 edited by James W. Hipp (1992)

1992 edited by James W. Hipp (1993)

1993 edited by James W. Hipp, contributing editor George Garrett (1994)

1994 edited by James W. Hipp, contributing editor George Garrett (1995)

1995 edited by James W. Hipp, contributing editor George Garrett (1996)

1996 edited by Samuel W. Bruce and L. Kay Webster, contributing editor George Garrett (1997)

1997 edited by Matthew J. Bruccoli and George Garrett, with the assistance of L. Kay Webster (1998)

1998 edited by Matthew J. Bruccoli, contributing editor George Garrett, with the assistance of D. W. Thomas (1999)

1999 edited by Matthew J. Bruccoli, contributing editor George Garrett, with the assistance of D. W. Thomas (2000)

2000 edited by Matthew J. Bruccoli, contributing editor George Garrett, with the assistance of George Parker Anderson (2001)

2001 edited by Matthew J. Bruccoli, contributing editor George Garrett, with the assistance of George Parker Anderson (2002)

2002 edited by Matthew J. Bruccoli and George Garrett; George Parker Anderson, Assistant Editor (2003)

Concise Series

Concise Dictionary of American Literary Biography, 7 volumes (1988–1999): *The New Consciousness, 1941–1968; Colonization to the American Renaissance, 1640–1865; Realism, Naturalism, and Local Color, 1865–1917; The Twenties, 1917–1929; The Age of Maturity, 1929–1941; Broadening Views, 1968–1988; Supplement: Modern Writers, 1900–1998.*

Concise Dictionary of British Literary Biography, 8 volumes (1991–1992): *Writers of the Middle Ages and Renaissance Before 1660; Writers of the Restoration and Eighteenth Century, 1660–1789; Writers of the Romantic Period, 1789–1832; Victorian Writers, 1832–1890; Late-Victorian and Edwardian Writers, 1890–1914; Modern Writers, 1914–1945; Writers After World War II, 1945–1960; Contemporary Writers, 1960 to Present.*

Concise Dictionary of World Literary Biography, 4 volumes (1999–2000): *Ancient Greek and Roman Writers; German Writers; African, Caribbean, and Latin American Writers; South Slavic and Eastern European Writers.*

Dictionary of Literary Biography® • Volume Three Hundred Thirty-Six

Eighteenth-Century British Historians

Eighteenth-Century British Historians

Ellen J. Jenkins

Arkansas Tech University

A Bruccoli Clark Layman Book

THOMSON
GALE

Detroit • New York • San Francisco • New Haven, Conn. • Waterville, Maine • London • Munich

Dictionary of Literary Biography
Volume 336: Eighteenth-Century British Historians
Ellen J. Jenkins

Advisory Board
John Baker
William Cagle
Patrick O'Connor
George Garrett
Trudier Harris
Alvin Kernan

Editorial Directors
Matthew J. Bruccoli and Richard Layman

LIBRARY OF CONGRESS CATALOGING-IN-PUBLICATION DATA

Eighteenth-century British historians / edited by Ellen J. Jenkins.
    p. cm. — (Dictionary of literary biography ; v. 336)
"A Bruccoli Clark Layman Book."
Includes bibliographical references and index.
ISBN-13: 978–0–7876–8154–8 (hardcover)
ISBN-10: 0–7876–8154–7 (hardcover)
1. Historians—Great Britain—Biography. 2. Historiography—Great Britain—History—18th century. I. Jenkins, Ellen J.

DA3.A1E44 2007
941.0072'02—dc22
            2007026136

Printed in the United States of America
10 9 8 7 6 5 4 3 2 1

In memory of my parents

Neal Jenkins (1932–1996)
and
Melissa Harwell Jenkins (1934–2004)

Contents

Plan of the Series

. . . Almost the most prodigious asset of a country, and perhaps its most precious possession, is its native literary product—when that product is fine and noble and enduring.

Mark Twain*

The advisory board, the editors, and the publisher of the *Dictionary of Literary Biography* are joined in endorsing Mark Twain's declaration. The literature of a nation provides an inexhaustible resource of permanent worth. Our purpose is to make literature and its creators better understood and more accessible to students and the reading public, while satisfying the needs of teachers and researchers.

To meet these requirements, *literary biography* has been construed in terms of the author's achievement. The most important thing about a writer is his writing. Accordingly, the entries in *DLB* are career biographies, tracing the development of the author's canon and the evolution of his reputation.

The purpose of *DLB* is not only to provide reliable information in a usable format but also to place the figures in the larger perspective of literary history and to offer appraisals of their accomplishments by qualified scholars.

The publication plan for *DLB* resulted from two years of preparation. The project was proposed to Bruccoli Clark by Frederick G. Ruffner, president of the Gale Research Company, in November 1975. After specimen entries were prepared and typeset, an advisory board was formed to refine the entry format and develop the series rationale. In meetings held during 1976, the publisher, series editors, and advisory board approved the scheme for a comprehensive biographical dictionary of persons who contributed to literature. Editorial work on the first volume began in January 1977, and it was published in 1978. In order to make *DLB* more than a dictionary and to compile volumes that individually have claim to status as literary history, it was decided to organize volumes by topic, period, or genre. Each of these freestanding volumes provides a

*From an unpublished section of Mark Twain's autobiography, copyright by the Mark Twain Company

biographical-bibliographical guide and overview for a particular area of literature. We are convinced that this organization—as opposed to a single alphabet method—constitutes a valuable innovation in the presentation of reference material. The volume plan necessarily requires many decisions for the placement and treatment of authors. Certain figures will be included in separate volumes, but with different entries emphasizing the aspect of his career appropriate to each volume. Ernest Hemingway, for example, is represented in *American Writers in Paris, 1920–1939* by an entry focusing on his expatriate apprenticeship; he is also in *American Novelists, 1910–1945* with an entry surveying his entire career, as well as in *American Short-Story Writers, 1910–1945, Second Series* with an entry concentrating on his short fiction. Each volume includes a cumulative index of the subject authors and articles.

Between 1981 and 2002 the series was augmented and updated by the *DLB Yearbooks*. There have also been nineteen *DLB Documentary Series* volumes, which provide illustrations, facsimiles, and biographical and critical source materials for figures, works, or groups judged to have particular interest for students. In 1999 the *Documentary Series* was incorporated into the *DLB* volume numbering system beginning with *DLB 210: Ernest Hemingway.*

We define literature as the *intellectual commerce of a nation:* not merely as belles lettres but as that ample and complex process by which ideas are generated, shaped, and transmitted. *DLB* entries are not limited to "creative writers" but extend to other figures who in their time and in their way influenced the mind of a people. Thus the series encompasses historians, journalists, publishers, book collectors, and screenwriters. By this means readers of *DLB* may be aided to perceive literature not as cult scripture in the keeping of intellectual high priests but firmly positioned at the center of a nation's life.

DLB includes the major writers appropriate to each volume and those standing in the ranks behind them. Scholarly and critical counsel has been sought in deciding which minor figures to include and how full their entries should be. Wherever possible, useful references are made to figures who do not warrant separate entries.

Each *DLB* volume has an expert volume editor responsible for planning the volume, selecting the figures for inclusion, and assigning the entries. Volume editors are also responsible for preparing, where appropriate, appendices surveying the major periodicals and literary and intellectual movements for their volumes, as well as lists of further readings. Work on the series as a whole is coordinated at the Bruccoli Clark Layman editorial center in Columbia, South Carolina, where the editorial staff is responsible for accuracy and utility of the published volumes.

One feature that distinguishes *DLB* is the illustration policy–its concern with the iconography of literature. Just as an author is influenced by his surroundings, so is the reader's understanding of the author enhanced by a knowledge of his environment. Therefore *DLB*

volumes include not only drawings, paintings, and photographs of authors, often depicting them at various stages in their careers, but also illustrations of their families and places where they lived. Title pages are regularly reproduced in facsimile along with dust jackets for modern authors. The dust jackets are a special feature of *DLB* because they often document better than anything else the way in which an author's work was perceived in its own time. Specimens of the writers' manuscripts and letters are included when feasible.

Samuel Johnson rightly decreed that "The chief glory of every people arises from its authors." The purpose of the *Dictionary of Literary Biography* is to compile literary history in the surest way available to us–by accurate and comprehensive treatment of the lives and work of those who contributed to it.

The *DLB* Advisory Board

Introduction

The writing of history is as much about the times in which it is written as about the past. This characteristic is especially true of the eighteenth century, in which many opinions differed from those of previous times, not least in the appraisal of history. The new ideas that characterized the period provided a catalyst for the rational reassessment of all previous centuries, governments, religions, traditions, and cultures. According to the new ideology of the Enlightenment (the belief, particularly in the eighteenth century, that Man could use his powers of reason to make a better world), Man could discover the laws that governed his role in the Universe; he could aim for perfection and achieve the personal, social, and scientific progress to take him there. Because his roles in Society and in the Universe were subject to the laws of Nature, the old lines of authority—church, monarchy, and aristocracy—were no longer justified by their claims upon tradition. Such views meant that everything was subject to fresh scrutiny and revision. They also meant that history must be reexamined for new meaning and understanding.

The impetus for a more rational interpretation of history and historical events had evolved with the Scientific Revolution, which had reached a peak when Sir Isaac Newton published his *Principia Mathematica* in 1687, disclosing that celestial bodies were governed by the law of universal gravitation. If Nature was ruled by scientific laws, then surely there were scientific laws that applied to Man's place in the Universe and, thus, to Man's role in Society. Rationalism, empiricism, skepticism, and progress, all watchwords of the era, also called the concept of Revealed Truth (the use by God of the supernatural or mysteries to demonstrate what the rational mind cannot penetrate entirely through reason) into question. Some intellectuals doubted that God even existed, while others—the deists—argued that if God existed, He had designed the Universe according to rational scientific principles—in other words, he had created a mechanical universe that operated without his constant intervention.

The Enlightenment period, roughly corresponding to the eighteenth century, was the first in which religious ideology did not color all of Mankind's endeavors, and the history written during the era provides much evidence of the change in thought. Countering the destructive religiosity of the seventeenth century, one of the hallmarks of the Enlightenment was an increased secularization in attitudes and explanations, which affected daily life as well as the realm of intellectual activity. The concept that God was the agent of all of Man's endeavors—and, thus, the agent of all history of Man—was no longer clear. Instead, Man appeared to be the agent of his own triumphs and disasters.

France often gets the credit for Enlightenment thought, with Scotland and Germany coming next, and then, as an afterthought, England. The truth, however, is that communications were no longer limited by regional or national boundaries, and as commercial opportunities spread, so did ideas. Britain witnessed a boom in print culture with the first circulating libraries, which began in the 1660s when booksellers allowed people to borrow books for a fee. By the 1780s circulating libraries had become important in Britain. The 1695 end of the Licensing Act that limited the number of printers and required licensing of the press resulted in newspapers becoming abundant. With the advent of a burgeoning popular press, people, no matter where they lived, could read and discuss the works of Voltaire and Charles de Secondat, Baron de Montesquieu, or David Hume and Edward Gibbon. The Enlightenment as an intellectual movement was an amalgamation of thought from across Europe, and it owed a great deal to England, as well as to Scotland. Two recent works that illuminate the roles these countries played in the Enlightenment are Roy Porter's admirable *The Creation of the Modern World: The Untold Story of the British Enlightenment* (2000) and James Buchan's excellent *Crowded with Genius, The Scottish Enlightenment: Edinburgh's Moment of the Mind* (2003).

One of the major thrusts for new theories on Society, Man, and Government was the work of John Locke (1632–1704), who described the relationship as a political contract. If Government violated the rights of its subjects, then those subjects had a right to rebel. England's Civil War of 1640–1649 and the Glorious Revolution of 1688 actually constituted the first of the national revolutions that eventually included those in America and France. In trying and executing their king, Charles I, in 1649, the English had overthrown a despotic government; in deposing his son, James II, in 1688, the English had reiterated the lesson that rulers who did not respond to the interests and welfare of their subjects had broken faith and could be unseated, or, as Locke had written in 1690, in *An Essay Concerning the True Original, Extent, and End of Civil Govern-*

ment, "When any one, or more, shall take upon them to make laws whom the people have not appointed so to do, they make laws without authority, which the people are not therefore bound to obey; by which means they come again to be out of subjection and may constitute to themselves a new legislative, as they think best, being in full liberty to resist the force of those who, without authority, would impose anything upon them." The two Stuart kings who lost their thrones in the seventeenth century had not only appeared ready to restore Catholicism to England but had also deemed themselves above Parliament and the law.

Before the end of the seventeenth century, the English had negotiated the terms by which William III and Mary II ascended the throne, establishing a constitutional monarchy and a bill of rights that clarified the monarch's responsibility to the laws of the realm and limited his/her power over Parliament and his/her subjects. The Bill of Rights required Parliamentary approval for the monarch to levy taxes or maintain a standing army, and he could no longer interfere in parliamentary elections or prosecute members for statements made in parliamentary debate. Thus, England entered the eighteenth century with powerful new ideologies that gave momentum to many political and social changes over the next two hundred years and more.

During the course of the century, which began under William III and ended under George III, the 1701 Act of Settlement provided that the Hanoverian line would succeed the last Stuarts. Other changes occurred. The 1707 Act of Union joined Scotland and England; Protestantism was finally secure in England (although the role of religion in daily life declined); and the Tory Party aimed at the conservation of traditional institutions and privilege, while the Whig Party increasingly allied itself with efforts toward parliamentary and social reform.

For Great Britain, the eighteenth century was an era of colonization, national prosperity, commercial enterprise, and international prestige. With a growing empire, a navy that claimed dominion over the seas, the beginning of industrialization, and an intellectual tradition that ranked among the foremost in Europe, the Briton of the period must have believed that he was at the center of the world. Historians of the age encouraged him in that conceit. Much history was written for the wider reading public, rather than for scholars.

The writing of history had long been an avocation for clergymen or gentlemen scholars, rather than a profession in itself. Indeed, gentlemen specialists in archaeology or the study of antiquities wrote some important historical works during the eighteenth century, breaking new ground in the preparation of local or county histories, in the collection of detailed observations and descriptions, and in encouraging the preservation of ruins. These

include Thomas Hearne and his *Reliquiae Bodleianae: or, Some Genuine Remains of Sir Thomas Bodley* (1703), and Francis Wise, who wrote a compendium on ancient coins in the Bodleian Library, *Nummorum Antiquorum Scriniis Bodleianis Reconditorum Catalogus cum Commentario, Tabulis Aeneis, et Appendice* (1750). Their contemporaries were often quick to dismiss these scholars as mere cranks dabbling in coins and stone circles, according to Rosemary Sweet's excellent book *Antiquaries: The Discovery of the Past in Eighteenth-Century Britain* (2004), but these antiquarians actually created a methodology still followed by modern historians.

One major event in the writing of history was the increased reliance upon primary sources from church and government archives, so that some works, such as those by the clergyman John Strype (1643–1737), whose three-volume *Ecclesiastical Memorials; Chiefly Relating to Religion and the Reformation of It, and the Emergence of the Church of England under King Henry VIII, King Edward VI and Queen Mary the First* appeared in 1721, and by the Bishop of Peterborough, White Kennett, who published *A Register and Chronicle Ecclesiastical and Civil, Containing Matters of Fact . . . with . . . Notes and References towards Discovering and Connecting the True History of England from the Restauration of King Charles II. Faithfully taken from the manuscript collections of the Lord Bishop of Peterborough* in 1728, were criticized for being more compendiums of facts than narratives. George Lyttelton, writer of *The History of the Life of Henry the Second, and the Age in Which He Lived* (1767), and Richard Gough, who contributed to the volumes titled *The History and Antiquities of the County of Dorset: Compiled from the Best and Most Ancient Historians* and *Inquisitiones Post Mortem, and Other Valuable Records and Mss. in the Public Offices, and Libraries, and in Private Hands,* published between 1774 and 1815, made use of manuscripts and government records, and memoirs and private papers for their histories. The work of these scholars, with their devotion to detail, to the collection of information, and to the study of documents, eventually ceased to be a disconnected process from that of historians who wrote narratives, and the combined strengths of both camps created history that was both narrative and based upon evidence.

Adam Ferguson, who wrote *Essay on the History of Civil Society* (1767), John Millar, who wrote *Observations concerning the Distinction of Ranks in Society* (1771), and Adam Smith, whose *An Inquiry into the Nature and Causes of the Wealth of Nations* (1776) made him one of the stars of the Scottish Enlightenment, wrote stadial or conjectural history, arguing the theory that societies must evolve through a progression of stages, passing from hunting to herding to agriculture and, finally, to trade. Along with Smith, Hume was and is the writer most often identified with the Enlightenment in Scotland. That commerce marked the high point of social advancement was also one of Hume's arguments in *Essays, Moral, Political, and Literary* (1742); it explained the high position of England among nations.

Throughout the eighteenth century, the writing of history reflected political divisions. Whig historians, those who decried the tyranny and wrongheadedness in past governments or Catholicism or who lauded the earliest (and often fanciful) proofs of liberty-loving Britons, included John Oldmixon, who published *The Critical History of England: Ecclesiastical and Civil: Wherein the Errors of the Monkish Writers, and Others Before the Reformation, Are Expos'd and Corrected* in 1724; and Kennett, whose *A Seasonable Discourse upon the Rise, Progress, Discovery and Utter Disappointment of the Gunpowder Treason and Rebellion Plotted by the Papists in 1605* was originally delivered as a sermon in 1715. Many on both sides wrote history in the effort to influence political outcomes, including Catherine Macaulay, who in 1767 wrote *Loose Remarks on Certain Positions to Be Found in Mr. Hobbes's Philosophical Rudiments of Government and Society. With a Short Sketch of A Democratical Form of Government, in a Letter to Signior Paoli* on the side of the Whigs and Henry St. John, Viscount Bolingbroke, who in 1735 published *A Dissertation upon Parties* on the Tory side. Bolingbroke claimed that the ancient English constitution had included measures to counteract tyranny, and that, combined with the careful supervision of the propertied classes, it was the most effective in all of history.

Britain's eighteenth century, however, was not accompanied by uninterrupted triumph. Late in the 1700s, the British lost their North American colonies, and revolution in France made any move toward social reform suspect and any outspokenness among the lower classes a matter for distrust. In addition, throughout the century, Parliament had enacted an avalanche of laws protecting property, so that even the smallest thefts might be punishable by hanging or transportation. The poor remained miserably poor, and their crimes met with heavy punishments, even as intellectuals in Britain wrote about and lauded the British subject, in the most general sense, as a paragon of historical virtue. Most of the reforms spawned by the overabundance of progressive views in Enlightenment ideology were not applied until the nineteenth century.

The collection of biographical essays in this volume addresses the lives and works of eighteenth-century British historians. Many modern scholars tend to allow a decade or more of "overlap" before and after the actual dates that mark a century, since the major events in history do not start and stop in a fashion so tidy as to fit neatly inside century bookends. In order to distill the period covered, however, they have found it more efficient to restrict the current selection of historians to those writing and publishing in the century proper, 1700–1799, rather than in the extended era identified as the "long" eighteenth century, from approximately 1688 to 1815.

Some of the great polymaths of the century have been omitted from this collection, having been included in previous volumes of *The Dictionary of Literary Biography,* some of them appearing in several volumes. These include Horace Walpole, James Boswell, Samuel Johnson, and others who wrote history but whose reputations were not based primarily upon the writing of history. Several of those included herein–such as Smith, Hume, and Edmund Burke–were political scientists and philosophers though they remain at the center of eighteenth-century historiography and are, therefore, fundamental to this volume.

–*Ellen J. Jenkins*

Acknowledgments

This book was produced by Bruccoli Clark Layman, Inc. Penelope M. Hope was the in-house editor.

Production manager is Philip B. Dematteis.

Administrative support was provided by Carol A. Cheschi.

Accountant is Ann-Marie Holland.

Copyediting supervisor is Sally R. Evans. The copyediting staff includes Phyllis A. Avant, Caryl Brown, and Rebecca Mayo. Freelance copyeditors are Brenda L. Cabra, Jennifer E. Cooper, and David C. King.

Pipeline manager is James F. Tidd Jr.

Editorial associates are Elizabeth Leverton and Dickson Monk.

Permissions editor is Amber L. Coker.

Office manager is Kathy Lawler Merlette.

Photography editor is Crystal A. Leidy.

Digital photographic copy work was performed by Crystal A. Leidy.

Systems manager is James Sellers.

Typesetting supervisor is Kathleen M. Flanagan. The typesetting staff includes Patricia M. Flanagan.

Library research was facilitated by the following librarians at the Thomas Cooper Library of the University of South Carolina: Elizabeth Sudduth and the rare-book department; Jo Cottingham, interlibrary loan department; circulation department head Tucker Taylor; reference department head Virginia W. Weathers; reference department staff Marilee Birchfield, Karen Brown, Mary Bull, Gerri Corson, Joshua Garris, Beki Gettys, Laura Ladwig, Tom Marcil, Anthony Diana McKissick, Bob Skinder, and Sharon Verba; interlibrary loan department head Marna Hostetler; and interlibrary loan staff Robert Amerson and Timothy Simmons.

Dictionary of Literary Biography® • Volume Three Hundred Thirty-Six

Eighteenth-Century British Historians

Dictionary of Literary Biography

John Aikin
(15 January 1747 – 7 December 1822)

Michael Griffin
University of Limerick

BOOKS: *Observations on the External Use of Preparations of Lead, with Some General Remarks on Topical Medicines* (London: Printed for J. Johnson, 1771);

Thoughts on Hospitals, with Thomas Percival (London: Printed for J. Johnson, 1771);

Essays on Song-Writing (London: Printed for J. Johnson, 1772);

Miscellaneous Pieces: In Prose, by Aikin and Anna Letitia Barbauld (London: Printed for J. Johnson, 1773);

A Specimen of the Medical Biography of Great Britain; With an Address to the Public (London: Printed for J. Johnson, 1775);

An Essay on the Application of Natural History to Poetry (Warrington: Printed for J. Johnson, 1777);

Heads of Chemistry (Warrington: Printed by W. Eyres, 1778);

Biographical Memoirs of Medicine in Great Britain, from the Revival of Literature to the Time of Harvey (London: Printed for J. Johnson, 1780);

The Calendar of Nature: Designed for the Instruction and Entertainment of Young Persons, printed as anonymous (Dublin: printed for H. Chamberlain, 1784; New-York: Printed by Samuel Wood, 1815);

A Manual of Materia Medica, Containing a Brief Account of All the Simples Directed in the London and Edinburgh Dispensatories, with Their Several Preparations and the Principal Compositions into Which They Enter (Yarmouth: Printed by Downes & March, for J. Johnson, London, 1785);

England Delineated; or, A Geographical Description of Every County in England and Wales: With a Concise Account of Its Most Important Products, Natural and Artificial. For the Use of Young Persons (London: Printed by T. Bensley for J. Johnson, 1788);

John Aikin (Engraving by Englehart; 1823, National Portrait Gallery)

An Address to the Dissidents of England on Their Late Defeat (London: Printed for J. Johnson, 1790);

The Spirit of the Constitution and That of the Church of England Compared (London: Printed for J. Johnson, 1790);

Poems (London: Printed for J. Johnson, 1791);

A View of the Character and Public Services of the Late John Howard, Esq. (London: Printed for J. Johnson, 1792; Philadelphia: Printed for John Ormrod, by W. W. Woodward / Boston: Printed by Manning & Loring, for J. White, S. Hall, Thomas & Andrews, D. West, W. Spotswood, E. Larkin, J. West, and the proprietor of the Boston Bookstore [William P. Blake], 1794);

Evenings at Home; or, the Juvenile Budget Opened, 6 volumes, with Anna Letitia Barbauld (London: Printed for J. Johnson, 1792–1796; volumes 1–4, Philadelphia: Printed by T. Dobson, 1797; 6 volumes, second edition, Philadelphia: Printed by A. Bartram, 1802);

Food for National Penitence; or, A Discourse Intended for the Approaching Fast Day (London: Printed for J. Johnson, 1793);

Letters from a Father to His Son, on Various Topics; Relative to Literature and the Conduct of Life, 2 volumes (London: Printed for J. Johnson, 1793, 1800; volume 1, Philadelphia: Printed by Samuel Harrison Smith, 1794);

Proposals for Publishing by Subscription . . . A Description of the Country from Thirty to Forty Miles Round Manchester (London: Printed for John Stockdale, 1793);

General Biography; or, Lives, Critical and Historical, of the Most Eminent Persons of All Ages, Countries, Conditions and Professions, 10 volumes, chiefly composed by Aikin and William Enfield (London: Printed for G. G. & J. Robinson, 1799–1815);

The Arts of Life (London: Printed for J. Johnson, 1802; Boston: Printed by Hosea Sprague, for Samuel H. Parker, 1803);

The Woodland Companion; or, A Brief Description of British Trees (London: Printed for J. Johnson by Taylor & Wilks, 1802);

Poems, Lyrical and Miscellaneous (London: Printed for J. Johnson, 1803);

Letters to a Young Lady on a Course of English Poetry (London: Printed for J. Johnson by R. Taylor, 1804; Newburyport, Mass.: Thomas & Whipple, 1806);

Geographical Delineations; or, A Compendious View of the Natural and Political State of All Parts of the Globe (London: Printed for J. Johnson, 1806; Philadelphia: Printed for F. Nichols, by Kimber, Conrad, 1806);

Essays Literary and Miscellaneous (London: Printed for J. Johnson, 1811);

The Lives of John Selden, Esq., and Archbishop Usher; With Notices of the Principal English Men of Letters with Whom They Were Connected (London: Printed for Mathews & Leigh, 1812);

Annals of the Reign of King George the Third, 2 volumes (London: Printed for Longman, Hurst, Rees, Orme & Brown, 1816; second edition, expanded, 1820).

OTHER: "Essay on the Ligature of Arteries," in Charles White, *Cases in Surgery, with Remarks* (London: W. Johnston, 1770);

"An Essay on the Plan and Character of the Poem," in James Thomson, *The Seasons* (London: Printed for

J. Murray, 1778; New York: Printed by George F. Hopkins, 1802);

William Lewis, *An Experimental History of the Materia Medica,* third edition, with additions and corrections by Aikin (London: Printed for J. Johnson & R. Baldwin, 1784);

John Howard, *An Account of the Principal Lazarettos in Europe: With Various Papers Relative to the Plague: Together with Further Observations on Some Foreign Prisons and Hospitals: With Additional Remarks on the Present State of Those in Great Britain and Ireland,* edited by Aikin (London: Printed for J. Johnson, C. Dilly & T. Cadell, 1791);

"A Critical Essay on the Poem," in John Armstrong, *The Art of Preserving Health* (London: Printed for T. Cadell Jr. & W. Davies, 1795; Boston: Printed by Hosea Sprague, 1802);

Gilbert White, *A Naturalist's Calendar, with Observations in Various Branches of Natural History* (London: Printed for B. & J. White, 1795);

"Introduction," in Alexander Pope, *An Essay on Man* (London: Printed for T. Cadell Jr. & W. Davies, 1796);

"Essay on the Poems of Green," in Matthew Green, *The Spleen, and Other Poems* (London: Printed for T. Cadell Jr. & W. Davies, 1796; Philadelphia: Printed for Benjamin Johnson, J. Johnson & R. Johnson, 1804);

William Somerville, *The Chace. A Poem. New Edition,* with a critical essay by Aikin (London: Printed for T. Cadell Jr. & W. Davies, 1796);

Monthly Magazine, literary editor (1796–1806);

William Enfield, *Sermons on Practical Subjects,* 3 volumes, with memoirs of the author by Aikin (London: Printed for J. Johnson, 1798);

John Milton, *The Poetical Works of John Milton, from the Text of Dr. Newton,* with a critical essay by Aikin, 4 volumes (London: Printed for J. Johnson, 1801; Philadelphia: Benjamin Johnson, 1804);

Oliver Goldsmith, *The Poetical Works of Oliver Goldsmith, with an Account of His Life & Writings to Which Is Added a Critical Dissertation on His Poetry,* by Aikin (London: Printed for Cadell & Davies, 1805; Boston: Hastings, Etheridge & Bliss / Baltimore: Coale & Thomas, 1809);

Poetry for Children (N.p. [ca. 1805]);

Henry Moore, *Poems, Lyrical and Miscellaneous,* edited by Aikin (London, 1806);

The Athenaeum: A Magazine of Literary and Miscellaneous Information, edited by Aikin (1807–1809);

Vocal Poetry; or, A Select Collection of English Songs. To Which Is Prefixed an Essay on Song-Writing, by Aikin (London: Printed for J. Johnson, 1810; Boston: Published by J. Belcher, J. W. Burditt & Thomas & Whipple, 1811);

The Annual Register; or, A View of the History, Politicks and Literature for the Year ___, edited by Aikin (1811–1819?);

Select Works of the British Poets; With Biographical and Critical Prefaces (London: Printed for Longman, Hurst, Rees, Orme & Brown, 1820).

TRANSLATIONS: Publius Cornelius Tacitus, *Cn. Julii Agricolæ vita, The Life of Agricola* (Warrington: Printed by William Eyres, 1774); reprinted in *A Treatise on the Situation, Manners, and Inhabitants of Germany; and The Life of Agricola* (Warrington: Printed for J. Johnson, 1777);

Antoine Baumé, *A Manual of Chemistry; or, A Brief Account of the Operations of Chemistry and Their Products* (Warrington: Printed for J. Johnson, 1778);

Jean Le Rond d'Alembert, *Select Eulogies of Members of the French Academy* (London: Printed by A. Strahan, for T. Cadell Jr. & W. Davies, 1799);

Johann Heinrich D. Zschokke, *The History of Switzerland by the French, and the Destruction of the Democratic Republics of Schwitz, Uri, and Unterwalden* (London, 1803);

Memoirs of the Life of Peter Daniel Huet, Bishop of Avranches, Written by Himself (London: Printed for Longman, Hurst, Rees, Orme, Cadell & Davies, 1810).

The career of John Aikin is best described as that of a prolific, yet miscellaneous, writer. A natural, medical, and political historian, a physician, and a geographer, the range and variety of Aikin's work belies his strong continuity of educational purpose. Immersed in the intellectual environment of radical dissent from an early age, Aikin's engagement with the scientific developments of the eighteenth century stimulated his interests in literature and education. His works are perhaps too miscellaneous to have guaranteed him a reputation in any one branch of writing; the variety of his publications may also account for their not being studied or republished since the nineteenth century. Aside from the historical researches implied in his pioneering compendia of biography, his only major historical work is his *Annals of the Reign of King George the Third,* published in 1816, with a second edition in 1820.

John Aikin was born at Kibworth-Harcourt in Leicestershire on 15 January 1747, the grandson of a Scottish shopkeeper who had settled in London, and the only son of the Reverend John Aikin. His mother, Jane, was the daughter of the Reverend John Jennings, who taught at a dissenting Protestant academy at Kibworth. Aikin senior was a pupil of, and subsequently an assistant to, noted hymn composer Philip Doddridge at

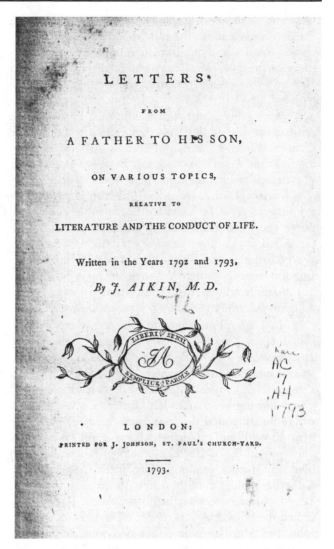

Title page for the first edition of Aikin's letters of advice to his son (Special Collections, Thomas Cooper Library, University of South Carolina)

Kibworth. In 1756 the senior Aikin moved his family to Warrington, in Lancashire, where a liberal dissenting academy was established. Because John Aikin the son, then twelve years old, had a weak voice, he turned away from his intended vocation as a preacher and to medicine. To that end, he was dispatched to study with Maxwell Garthshore, surgeon and apothecary of Uppingham, Rutlandshire.

At the age of eighteen Aikin traveled to Edinburgh to pursue his medical training. Among his distinguished teachers were Joseph Black, Alexander Monro, and William Cullen. Aikin spent two years at Edinburgh before briefly returning to Warrington in May 1766. His father's school there was supplied with illustrious tutors who had a profound intellectual effect on Aikin. Among them were Johann Reinhold Forster, a naturalist who accompanied Captain James Cook on his circumnavigation; the radical Joseph Priestley, who taught classics and modern literature and whose lectures on history were afterward published; and John Holt, who was tutor in natural philosophy and mathematics.

After this short but salubrious break, Aikin returned to his studies later that year, this time under Charles White, a surgeon of note in Manchester. During this time Aikin composed an "Essay on the Ligature of Arteries," which appeared in White's *Cases in Surgery with Remarks* (1770). Meanwhile, Aikin's interest in literary matters grew. He collected English songs and composed verse and prose translations, some of which were published in London newspapers. Aikin spent three years in Manchester. In the winter of 1769 he went to London to study under William Hunter. While in London, Aikin lived with his uncle, Arthur Jennings, whose daughter Martha eventually became Aikin's wife.

In 1770 Aikin moved to Chester, where he published *Observations on the External Use of Preparations of Lead, with Some General Remarks on Topical Medicines* (1771). At this time, Aikin met traveler and naturalist Thomas Pennant, who fostered his interest in natural history. The following year Aikin left Chester for Warrington, where he cultivated the friendships of theologian William Enfield and mathematician George Walker. In 1772 he published his *Essays on Song-Writing*. He also married Martha Jennings. His sister, Anna Laetitia (later Barbauld), published her poems that year with assistance and encouragement from Aikin. They collaborated the following year on *Miscellaneous Pieces: In Prose*. John and Martha Aikin's first two sons, Arthur and Charles Rochemont, were born in 1773 and 1775, respectively.

In 1774 Aikin's translation of Publius Cornelius Tacitus's *Life of Agricola* was first published and then was republished in 1777 with *A Treatise on the Situation, Manners and Inhabitants of Germany*. Aikin then began work on his medical biographies, which were published in 1780 as *Biographical Memoirs of Medicine in Great Britain, from the Revival of Literature to the Time of Harvey*. An *Essay on the Application of Natural History to Poetry,* dedicated to Pennant, appeared in 1777. The research for this work also drew Aikin to write an essay on poet James Thomson, whose poems in *The Seasons* (1730) were inspired by developments in botanical and physical science; Aikin's "An Essay on the Plan and Character of the Poem" was published with Thomson's *The Seasons* in 1778. For the next seven years, Aikin recorded the names, habitats, and flowering periods of plants, compiling the results in *The Calendar of Nature: Designed for the Instruction and Entertainment of Young Persons* (1789), an educational work that included the blank-verse fragment "The Botanic Walk."

In February 1777 Aikin reported to his sister the beginnings of his association with John Howard, who was then printing his critical account of prisons. In 1792 Aikin wrote a biography of Howard, with whom he was friendly and whose political courage he regarded highly.

Though disdainful of the erroneous fabulism of classical natural history, Aikin worked for a time on translating the works of Pliny, all the while teaching courses in chemistry at the Warrington Academy and conducting experiments with students. He published his translation of Antoine Baumé's *Manuel de Chymie* (1763) in 1778. Throughout the following year Aikin continued his work on medical biography. It was the first such compendium of biographies in English and included entries on such eminent British medics as William Gilbert and William Harvey. For the earlier part of the decade, public engagements meant that Aikin had less time to write, though he did translate some verse for an edition of Horatian philosophy. Two more children were born to the Aikins at this time: Edmund in 1780, and Lucy (subsequently her father's biographer) in 1781.

In 1783 the Warrington Academy was dissolved, scattering the various tutors, except for Enfield, with whom Aikin discussed and proposed an "Essay on the Allegorical Personages introduced into Poetry," with particular emphasis on the poetry of Edmund Spenser. Having decided to pursue his doctoral degree, Aikin proceeded to Leyden in July 1784, with thesis in hand. When he returned to England, he moved from Warrington to Yarmouth. In 1784 William Lewis's *Experimental History of the Materia Medica,* corrected and enlarged, appeared, as did, finally, *The Calendar of Nature*. The entertainment and education of his own children and the children of others inspired various works. Specifically, he continued to promote the mutual applicability of natural history and poetry. In the years following, he continued with the geographical and topographical writing that became *England Delineated; or, A Geographical Description of Every County in England and Wales* (1788).

Aikin, always politically informed, was sometimes radical. He welcomed, initially at least, the French Revolution. He wrote to a friend (in correspondence compiled by his daughter) in December 1790 of the "false principles and distorted reasonings" of the Irish anti-Jacobin Edmund Burke and lauded the "fair fabric of French liberty." When an overwhelming majority in the House of Commons rejected the repeal of the Corporation and Test Acts, he wrote two strong pamphlets that, though published anonymously, caused him to be ostracized by less radical friends and patients. Only Enfield stood by him.

In 1792 *A View of the Character and Public Services of the Late John Howard, Esq.* was published, as was a small volume of poems, partly original, partly translated. Aikin moved to London again early in that year, claiming to have been a victim of political bias in Yarmouth. (He was also bored with provincial life.) His "Critical Essay on the Poems of Goldsmith" was published that year, as was the first volume of *Evenings at Home; or, the Juvenile Budget Opened,* a compendium of tales, fables, dialogues, various subjects, and natural history, co-authored with his sister and which by 1796 totaled six volumes. It was perhaps the most popular of his works.

Through 1794 Aikin worked on several projects: a fourth volume of *Evenings at Home;* a "Critical Essay on John Armstrong's 'Art of Preserving Health'"; his "Memoirs of Science and the Arts" was work ongoing, though never published; a new edition of *England Delineated* (1795); a life of his old physician friend John Fothergill for a new edition of *Biographia Brittanica* (which was never published); and a small volume of natural historical observations, *A Naturalist's Calendar, with Observations in Various Branches of Natural History* (1795), which was designed as a sequel to Gilbert White's *The Natural History and Antiquities of Selborne* (1789) and was informed by White's papers. Aikin also published *Letters from a Father to His Son, on Various Topics, Relative to Literature and the Conduct of Life* (1793), which included essays on character, improvement, literature, classicism, religion, bigotry, natural history, medicine, gardening, and the choice of a wife. The following year he wrote an essay on the poems of Matthew Green, author of the well-known poem *The Spleen* (1737).

In 1796 Aikin took up the literary editorship of the *Monthly Magazine,* a periodical that sought to embody liberal thought in the midst of the postrevolutionary schism in England. He stood back from the public affairs of the magazine, inspecting proofs and vetting articles and original correspondences. Along with composing essays on William Somerville's *The Chace* (1735) and Alexander Pope's *Essay on Man* (1733–1734), he began to work with Enfield on the *General Biography; or, Lives, Critical and Historical, of the Most Eminent Persons of All Ages, Countries, Conditions and Professions* (1799–1815). Though Enfield died the following year, and Aikin's own health was not good, the first volume of the *General Biography,* an ambitious compendium that collected the biographies of notable persons from all historical periods and countries, was published in the spring of 1799.

By that time, Aikin had moved to Dorking in Surrey, where he recovered from ill health in the company of his sister and her husband. He translated Jean Le Rond d'Alembert's *Select Eulogies of Members of the French Academy* (1799) and began work on the second volume

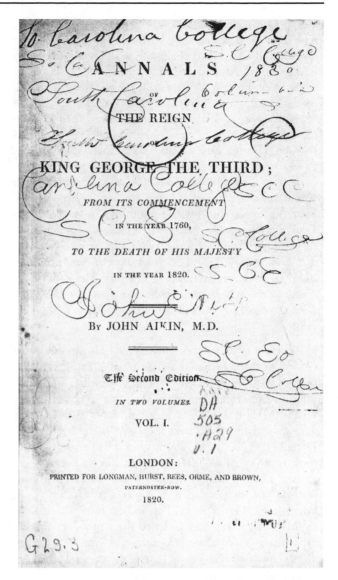

Title page for volume one of Aikin's history of the reign of George III (Special Collections, Thomas Cooper Library, University of South Carolina)

of his *Letters from a Father to His Son* (1800), which included tracts on party, morality, farming, and John Milton. The introductory letter to the second volume demonstrates that, as events in France had developed, Aikin's radicalism had waned. He expressed dismay at the Terror and the new French militarism: "Who but must turn," he writes, "with loathing from successive fields of carnage, and shameless violations of all faith, equity, and humanity!"

Though politically disillusioned, Aikin remained busy in the new century. He oversaw a new edition of Samuel Johnson's *Lives of the Poets* (1779–1781), although it was aborted. He published *The Arts of Life* (1802), in which young readers were advised on matters of food, clothing, and shelter. He wrote *The Woodland Companion; or, A Brief Description of British Trees* (1802) and addressed a poem to Gilbert Wakefield, the Warrington tutor who had been imprisoned (and released in 1801) for "seditious libel" against William Pitt's war policy. The following year Aikin wrote a preface to the poems of Henry Moore, a dissenting minister who had died in obscurity in November of that year. He translated Johann Heinrich D. Zschokke's *The History of Switzerland by the French, and the Destruction of the Democratic Republics of Schwitz, Uri, and Unterwalden* (1803), the preface to which was a timely critique of what he now viewed as the French menace. In 1804 he published *Letters to a Young Lady on a Course of English Poetry* and an essay prefatory to the 1806 edition of John Dryden's *Fables from Boccaccio and Chaucer* (1700), and he worked on new editions of his own early translations of Tacitus. He also began work on his *Geographical Delineations; or, A Compendious View of the Natural and Political State of All Parts of the Globe* (1806).

Aikin's connection with the *Monthly Magazine* ceased in 1806, when he developed plans for a new periodical, *The Athenaeum,* the first number of which appeared on 31 December of that year. It ceased publication in 1809. In 1809, during a hiatus in the *General Biography,* Aikin translated the Latin memoirs of Peter Daniel Huet, Bishop of Avranches. His periodical writings from the *Monthly Magazine* and *The Athanaeum* were gathered in 1811 in *Essays Literary and Miscellaneous.* Most notable and substantial were his essays "On Similes in Poetry" and "On Poetical Personifications." By the end of that year, Aikin had accepted the editorship of Robert Dodsley's *The Annual Register; or, A View of the History, Politicks and Literature for the Year ___ .*

The Lives of John Selden, Esq., and Archbishop Usher; With Notices of the Principal English Men of Letters with Whom They Were Connected was published in 1812; and by 1815 all ten volumes of the *General Biography* were completed, drawing to a close twenty years of research. Aikin was now sixty-eight. He proceeded to publish the *Select Works of the British Poets; With Biographical and Critical Prefaces* (1820) as well as *Annals of the Reign of King George the Third,* the first edition of which ended with the Peace of Paris in 1815, the second with the King's death in 1820. In the preface to the 1820 edition, Aikin claims:

> no other pretensions than those of a summary of the principal events, domestic and foreign, of the late reign. In its composition, the objects in view have been perspicuity and order in narrative, selection of the most important circumstances, and a strict impartiality, exhibited not only in a fair and ungarbled representation of facts, but in the absence of every kind of colouring which might favour the purposes of what may properly be denominated *party.*

Though he does concede that his feelings on moral and constitutional questions might reveal themselves, he declares that "the true philosophy of history" objectively extracts and observes the primary facts in "the great series of human affairs . . . directed by a chain of causes and effects of much superior potency to the efforts of individuals in any station." Equally, he proposes that the political history of George III's reign could not be understood except in the context of broader European and world developments.

At this point a stroke caused Aikin a short-term loss of speech and memory; his weakness in the final two years of his life was compounded by the death of his youngest son, Edmund. He retired to Stoke-Newington, where he died by a stroke of apoplexy on 7 December 1822. He was interred in the churchyard of Stoke-Newington. Lucy Aikin wrote in her biography of "the generally easy tenor" of her father's life, a tenor that belied his impressive and various body of work. Perhaps the extreme variety of his career in writing is what has resulted in the obscuring of his particular capabilities as an historian.

Biography:
Lucy Aikin, *Memoir of John Aikin, M.D., with a Selection of His Miscellaneous Pieces, Biographical, Moral, and Critical,* 2 volumes (London: Printed for Baldwin, Cradock & Joy, 1823).

Papers:
The Aikin Family Papers are at the University of Rochester, River Campus Libraries.

Mary Astell

(6 November 1666 – 14 May 1731)

Aneilya Hancock-Barnes
University of Arkansas

See also the Astell entry in *DLB 252: British Philosophers, 1500–1799.*

BOOKS: *A Serious Proposal to the Ladies, for the Advancement of Their True and Greatest Interest* (London: Printed for Richard Wilkin, 1694; corrected edition, 1695; corrected edition, 1696); reprinted in *A Serious Proposal to the Ladies: For the Advancement of Their True and Greatest Interest. In Two Parts* (London: Printed for Richard Wilkin, 1697);

Letters Concerning the Love of God between the Author of the Proposal to the Ladies [that is, Mary Astell], and Mr. John Norris (London: Printed for Samuel Manship & Richard Wilkin, 1695);

A Serious Proposal to the Ladies, Part II: Wherein a Method Is Offer'd for the Improvement of Their Minds (London: Printed for Richard Wilkin, 1697); reprinted in *A Serious Proposal to the Ladies: For the Advancement of Their True and Greatest Interest. In Two Parts* (London: Printed for Richard Wilkin, 1697);

Some Reflections upon Marriage Occasion'd by the Duke & Dutchess of Mazarine's Case, Which Is Also Considered (London: Printed for John Nutt, 1700);

Moderation Truly Stated; or, A Review of a Late Pamphlet Entitul'd Moderation a Vertue (London: Printed for Richard Wilkin, 1704);

An Impartial Enquiry into the Causes of Rebellion and Civil War in This Kingdom: in an Examination of Dr. Kennett's Sermon, Jan. 31, 1703–4 (London: Printed for Richard Wilkin, 1704);

A Fair Way with the Dissenters and Their Patrons (London: Printed for Richard Wilkin, 1704);

The Christian Religion as Profess'd by a Daughter of the Church of England (London: Printed for Richard Wilkin, 1705);

The Case of Moderation and Occasional Communion Represented by Way of Caution to the True Sons of the Church of England, by Astell and Thomas Wagstaffe (London: Printed for Richard Wilkin, 1705);

Bart'lemy Fair; or, An Enquiry after Wit (London: Printed for Richard Wilkin, 1709).

Editions and Collections: *The First English Feminist: "Reflections Upon Marriage" and Other Writings by Mary Astell,* edited, with an introduction, by Bridget Hill (Aldershot, U.K.: Gower/Maurice Temple Smith, 1986);

Astell, Political Writings, edited by Patricia Springborg (New York & Cambridge: Cambridge University Press, 1996);

A Serious Proposal to the Ladies: Parts I and II, edited, with an introduction, by Springborg (London & Brookfield, Vt.: Pickering & Chatto, 1997);

Mary Astell and John Norris: Letters Concerning the Love of God, edited by E. Derek Taylor and Melvyn New (Aldershot: Ashgate, 2005).

OTHER: "Mary Astell's Preface to the Embassy Letters," in *The Complete Letters of Lady Mary Wortley Montagu,* volume 1, edited by Robert Halsband (New York & Oxford: Oxford University Press, 1965), pp. 466–468.

Mary Astell was an historian, philosopher, devout Anglican, and polemicist who wrote prolifically on the issues of women's plight in society, religion, and politics. Because of the extreme conservatism of her political and religious views, Astell's lifelong active role in the public realm never damaged her reputation as a respectable woman. While she fought vehemently to expand the realm of feminine education, she did so in a manner that upheld traditional Anglican social views.

Unlike many of her contemporaries, Astell did not enthusiastically advocate that women study history. Most of society deemed historical studies a worthwhile endeavor for women because it provided them with moral lessons while they remained within the safety of their respectable homes. Astell, however, argued that the study of history should be reserved for those who had the ability to influence political change in a nation, such as public officials. Astell's later political writings, however, had a great influence in the political realm of her nation and significant historical importance.

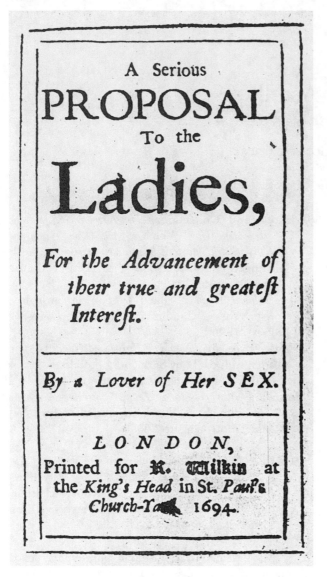

A Serious
PROPOSAL
To the
Ladies,

For the Advancement of
their true and greatest
Interest.

By a Lover of Her SEX.

LONDON,
Printed for R. Wilkin at
the King's Head in St. Paul's
Church-Yard 1694.

Title page for the first edition of Mary Astell's work on education for women (Microforms Collection, Thomas Cooper Library, University of South Carolina)

Astell was one of the first widely read female polemicists in Britain, and she was perhaps the first respectable woman prose writer in her nation, as well. She inspired many of the women intellectuals of her time—such as Elizabeth Thomas, Elizabeth Elstob, and Lady Mary Wortley Montagu—and helped lay the foundation for the so-called Bluestocking Society, an intellectual women's group that emphasized that women pursue literary studies beyond what was traditionally acceptable. As one of Britain's first politically active feminists, she began laying the groundwork for women with intellectual or literary interests, including the Bluestockings of the next generation.

The daughter of a Newcastle coal merchant, Astell is thought to have been educated when young. Some sources claim that she was instructed in philosophy, logic, and mathematics by her uncle Ralph Astell, who was a graduate of Cambridge University and a curate in St. Nicholas Cathedral. Despite her lack of formal education, which was open only to the men of her generation, she read widely on her own. She had a limited background in linguistics, though, and later in life she claimed that her inability to understand classical languages well put her at a great disadvantage when discussing Scripture with the learned. Her philosophical background was her intellectual strength and led to the notoriety of her best-known works.

After the death of her mother, twenty-two-year-old Astell went to London, where she was unable to find a means to provide for herself, as few doors were open to women who did not fit into the traditional roles of wife and mother. The tides of fortune shifted for Astell when Archbishop William Sancroft came to her aid in the absence of friends and family who were able or willing to lend her financial support. By 1692, as a result of the charity of Sancroft and others, she was able to settle in Chelsea, where she remained until her death. Undoubtedly, the difficulty she had finding a niche in society as an unwed woman with intellectual interests played a crucial role in the political views she developed and expressed in her writings.

After arriving at Chelsea, Astell surrounded herself with a group of elite women who shared her literary interests. She quickly forged a long-lasting relationship with the influential Lady Catherine Jones and even dedicated several works to Jones. Among other prominent women, Astell's friends in the emerging Bluestocking group included Lady Elizabeth Hastings and Montagu. Astell carried on a lengthy correspondence with Hastings, but Hastings destroyed the letters. Astell held Montagu in the highest esteem but remained true to her convictions and continually urged Montagu to reject the materialistic focus of upper-class life in favor of contemplating her own mortality, a lifelong pursuit for Astell.

Soon after her arrival in Chelsea, Mary Astell also began correspondence with the Reverend John Norris of Bemerton. Well-versed in neo-Platonist theory, Astell was drawn to the philosophical musings of Norris, who was one of the few remaining so-called Cambridge Platonists. The inspiration of Cartesian philosophical principles was the catalyst for much of her feminist rhetoric, her firm beliefs in the authority of the thinking self, and the equal spiritual and intellectual capacities of the two sexes. Consequently, she argued that society should encourage women to develop their intellectual capacities beyond what was necessary for their roles as wives and mothers.

Over a period of ten months, Astell and Norris discussed how individuals should focus their love on God, debated appropriate responses to the unfortunate events that divine providence often handed down to humanity, and deliberated other spiritual ideas that conflicted with human desires. In the midst of this intellectual discourse, Astell anonymously published the first part of her most important and revolutionary work, *A Serious Proposal to the Ladies, for the Advancement of Their True and Greatest Interest* (1694), the inaugural event in what became her lengthy and public career as an ardent feminist.

In *A Serious Proposal to the Ladies,* Astell advocated the establishment of an institution of higher education for women that would serve as a place for religious retirement but would not require the sort of vows that accompanied entrance into most monastic communities. She proposed that the academy be a place where women could withdraw from the world in favor of devoting themselves to intellectual, religious, and charitable pursuits. While the institution would provide an atmosphere for secular intellectual pursuits, its primary focus would be religious study, which Astell believed should be the primary focus of life in general. Astell maintained that women could only fulfill their duty to God by developing their full intellectual potential in order to understand theological issues better.

Unlike most of her contemporaries, Astell argued that God intended for women to develop to their highest potential rather than to live as secondary citizens. She concluded that women could not achieve their potential by living merely to fulfill the needs of men and that only educated women could serve themselves and society at a higher level. Furthermore, Astell proposed that elite women who did not intend to marry should use the money reserved for their dowries to finance academies for women, thereby creating a niche in society for women beyond the roles of wife and mother. Clearly, the ideas behind Astell's proposal for Protestant academic cloisters stemmed from her own intellectual desires and her previous difficulty in finding some form of financial stability, even though she was a healthy and intelligent young woman.

The publication of *A Serious Proposal to the Ladies* led to immediate public response from several notables, including Anglican scholar and author John Evelyn and author Daniel Defoe, who approved of Astell's proposal for an all-female academic institution. Unlike Astell, however, Defoe suggested that the intellectual emphasis should be on secular training so that the secluded establishment would not so closely mirror a Roman Catholic convent.

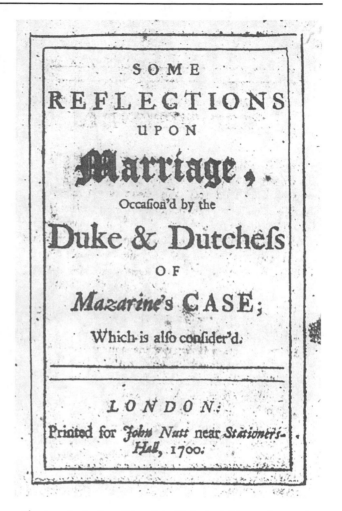

Title page for the first edition of Astell's book advising against unwise marriage (Microforms Collections, Thomas Cooper Library, University of South Carolina)

The public response to the work is indicative of the revolutionary ideas and historical significance of the publication. Despite the open support Astell received from such writers as Defoe and Evelyn, *A Serious Proposal to the Ladies* also drew a great deal of hostility from its audience; Astell's contemporaries feared that she was advocating a return to Roman Catholicism. They thought that her proposal for cloistering women during their education, particularly with an emphasis on religious study, too closely resembled Catholicism. Even those who were sympathetic to the feminine plight, including Defoe, believed that it was a flawed proposal. As a result, Astell did not win the support of the public sphere as a whole. Regardless, the publication is a valuable historical document as it clearly demonstrates the plight of women as second-class citizens during the late seventeenth and early eighteenth centuries. Also, the public's response to the work is indicative of the anti-Catholicism and antifeminist views of the masses, as

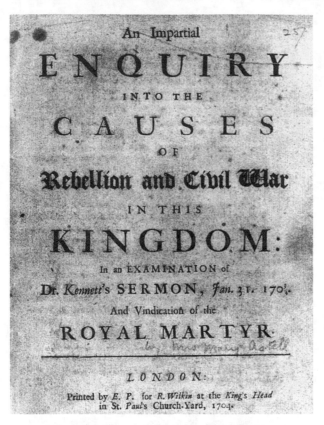

Title page for the first edition of one of Astell's most important political works (from Mary Astell, Political Writings, *Patricia Springborg, ed., 1996; Thomas Cooper Library, University of South Carolina)*

well as evidence of how revolutionary Astell's ideas were.

Following the publication of *A Serious Proposal to the Ladies,* Astell and Norris finally published their correspondence under the title *Letters Concerning the Love of God* (1695). In this collection Astell maintained that humanity could only truly reach an understanding of God through love. While secular and religious studies were necessary for a proper religious life, an understanding through love of God should be the ultimate goal, since it would lead people truly to love one another. Even with her philosophical background and her understanding of Enlightenment principles, Astell staunchly rejected deism, which overstated the value of reason in the understanding of God. Furthermore, she refused to accept that God was indifferent to the affairs of humanity. Despite the controversy surrounding *A Serious Proposal to the Ladies,* its publication and the success of *Letters Concerning the Love of God* quickly established Astell's reputation as an author and an intellectual among a broader literary community.

Astell's next publication, *A Serious Proposal to the Ladies, Part II* (1697), elaborated on her early arguments. Like the first volume, the second one focused on women who were unable to find a means of support in society outside of marriage or to acquire an education equal to those offered to men. Once again drawing from her Cartesian background, she outlined the rules for rational thought and a summation of René Descartes's logic in the text. Soon after its publication, *A Serious Proposal to the Ladies, Part II* was combined with its predecessor, and they were subsequently published together as one book, also in 1697. The second half of the publication added to Astell's importance as an historian, because in it she clearly documented how conservative thinkers, such as herself, combined the ideas of the Enlightenment with their views while rejecting deism.

In 1700 Astell returned to her feminine subjects with the publication of *Some Reflections upon Marriage Occasion'd by the Duke & Dutchess of Mazarine's Case, Which Is Also Considered* (1700). While some critics maintained that Astell's views in the text were staunchly opposed to marriage, Astell only advised against rash marriages. For Astell, these included marriages of convenience for women who sought to ensure their financial or social stability or any other marital arrangements that were not based on love. She claimed that if a woman could neither love nor honor her husband, she was wrong to promise obedience to him. Also, if she lacked the desire to love, honor, and obey, it increased the likelihood that the woman would have a heavy-handed master regulating her every action. Astell argued that when the wife's obedience was based on duty to authority and not on love for the individual or a sense of the justice and reasonableness of the command, the union of marriage was undoubtedly one of uncertain tenure.

Unlike many of her contemporaries, Astell realized that to escape their tenuous position in society was virtually impossible for women. She complained that women were rarely taught that they should have a greater aspiration for themselves in life than to find a husband. She was also aware that the unfortunate consequence of a loveless marriage was a lifelong sentence, because women generally had no hope of liberation from such a situation, as society did not allow it. Because of the difficulty in escaping such a life of misery, Astell concluded that women should be taught that they can find acceptable and respectable alternatives, such as retiring to a life of religious and academic contemplation, rather than accept the lifelong and tyrannical sentence of an unhappy marriage.

Astell succeeded again in recording for future generations the contemporary issues that women were facing. While advising women on their marital decisions, Astell documented the domestic conditions that many women were dealing with at the time, such as living with dictatorial spouses whom they could not escape. When complaining that as young girls women were never taught to aspire for anything more than to marry well, Astell was giving an accurate depiction of contemporary ideology. When describing women's inability to escape a tyrannical relationship without ruining their respectability and social standing, she drew an accurate picture of women's second-class citizenry not only in society, but also in the legal system. Perhaps more importantly, while she advocated women's making wiser marital decisions, she never claimed that the woman should not submit to the authority of her husband, a belief that certainly documented contemporary ideology even among those who advocated more rights for women.

The preface that Astell added to the 1706 edition of *A Serious Proposal to the Ladies* summed up her use of political rhetoric, which she so often applied to the issue of women's rights. Occasionally employing satire, Astell denounced the mindless feminine concern with fashion for the sole purpose of gaining masculine attention, claiming that God had surely created women to fulfill greater purposes in society. She stated that women should learn to pride themselves for something more important than their clothing and the bodies it covered, such as the individual souls they were cultivating for eternity. They could be as ambitious as they chose and should aspire to their greatest intellectual and spiritual potentials. Again, Astell was advocating a somewhat ascetic idea, which encouraged women to deny their worldly desires and be more introspective. Thus, she emphasized her vision of secular training for women that promoted the conventional Anglican traditions of her day.

In 1704 Astell published three political works—*Moderation Truly Stated, A Fair Way with the Dissenters and Their Patrons,* and *An Impartial Enquiry into the Causes of Rebellion and Civil War in This Kingdom*—that launched her into the center of the arena of political controversy. In two of the publications, *Moderation Truly Stated* and *A Fair Way With Dissenters and Their Patrons,* Astell argued in favor of the Occasional Conformity Bill, which was designed to prevent non-Anglicans from holding public office; her plea won her high praises from religious conservatives. In *Moderation Truly Stated,* she proclaimed that the proper public official's job was to eradicate the vices of society while upholding the Anglican Church.

Continuing to uphold the religious conservatism that she believed should be the underlying moral code for both everyday life and the political agenda of the nation, in *An Impartial Enquiry into the Causes of Rebellion and Civil War in This Kingdom* Astell went so far as to claim that the Whig Party and dissenting ideology had sparked England's civil war. Astell candidly stated in *An*

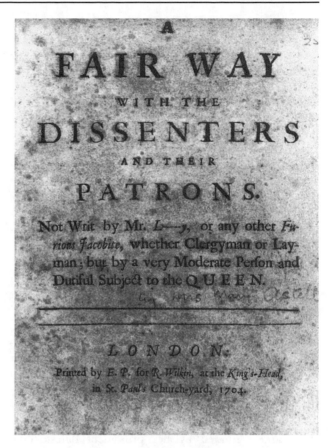

Title page for the first edition of a work in which Astell attacks Daniel Defoe (from Mary Astell, Political Writings, edited by Patricia Springborg [1996]; Thomas Cooper Library, University of South Carolina)

Impartial Enquiry that public officials who did not conform to the Anglican Church were little more than rebellious leaders who were using religion merely to support their political aspirations. Furthermore, she said that kings could be forced to succumb to the public pressures at the hands of such rebels. Therefore, Astell placed the blame for oppression on those who could be deemed disloyal to the nation and its church, such as non-Anglicans. Indeed, her polemical works have as much historical significance as her previous publications because they document important controversial issues surrounding the Anglican Church during the early eighteenth century and the positions advocated by the supporters of that institution.

In 1705 Astell published *The Christian Religion as Profess'd by a Daughter of the Church of England*. In this work she employed Cartesian philosophical principles to progress from the existence of reason to a belief in God. Essentially, *The Christian Religion as Profess'd by a Daughter of the Church of England* combined Astell's religious and educational theories into one publication.

Astell turned to political involvement once again in 1709. Although it was her last book, *Bart'lemy Fair; or, An Enquiry After Wit* (1709) was a vehement attempt to encourage Anglican loyalty among her audience. The work was also written as a reply to *Letter Concerning Enthusiasm* (1708) by Anthony Ashley Cooper, Earl of Shaftesbury. Astell staunchly criticized Shaftesbury's advocacy of civil liberties, claiming that any attack on the Church of England, which was inherent in such dissenting views, was an attack on the moral code of the nation and the people who comprised the nation.

Astell wrote a new preface to *Bart'lemy Fair; or, An Enquiry After Wit* in 1722 and continued to rewrite prefaces for her other publications throughout her remaining years. She also issued new editions of *Letters Concerning the Love of God* and *Some Reflections upon Marriage Occasion'd by the Duke & Duchess of Mazarine's Case* in 1730, but she mostly retired to a contemplative life that focused on the religious meditation she had advocated for so long.

Toward the end of her life, Astell had not abandoned the idea of an all-female institution that had first appeared in *A Serious Proposal to the Ladies,* but she still had not rallied enough public support for such a large endeavor. Therefore, she settled on a much smaller plan—a charity school for the girls of Chelsea, which was largely funded by her prominent Bluestocking friends, including Jones, Hastings, and Lady Ann Coventry, and the school was established in 1729.

In her historical writings Mary Astell brought an awareness of women's social issues to Britain's literary community as she recorded the social dilemmas women faced at the turn of the century. In response to her radical works, she was frequently satirized in contemporary publications, such as *The Tatler*. Nonetheless, her progressive ideas and the style of her language were often imitated, even by the leading male authors of the day, including Daniel Defoe, who clearly respected her even when he disagreed with her.

Astell died after an operation for a breast tumor 14 May 1731 and was buried in the churchyard at Chelsea. In the twenty-first century, she is largely remembered for *A Serious Proposal to the Ladies* and *Some Reflections upon Marriage Occasion'd by the Duke & Dutchess of Mazarine's Case*. While advocating women's rights, emphasizing her conservative political views, and promoting her brand of religion, Astell influenced the ideals of her audience and paved the way for future women authors. Although she may not have strongly advocated the study of history for women, she herself was a strong influence in women's history and played a leading role in recording the events of her time.

References:

Devoney Looser, *British Women Writers and the Writing of History, 1670–1820* (Baltimore: Johns Hopkins University Press, 2000);

Verena E. Neuburger, *Margery Kempe: A Study in Early English Feminism* (Berne: Peter Lang, 1994);

Ruth Perry, *The Celebrated Mary Astell: An Early English Feminist* (Chicago: University of Chicago Press, 1986);

Florene M. Smith, *Mary Astell* (New York: Columbia University Press, 1916);

Hilda L. Smith, *Reason's Disciples: Seventeenth-Century English Feminists* (Urbana: University of Illinois Press, 1982);

Hilda L. Smith, ed., *Women Writers and the Early Modern British Political Tradition* (Cambridge: Cambridge University Press, 1998);

Patricia Springborg, ed., *Astell, Political Writings* (Cambridge: Cambridge University Press, 1996).

Anna Laetitia Barbauld

(20 June 1743 – 9 March 1825)

Aneilya Hancock-Barnes
University of Arkansas

See also the Barbauld entries in *DLB 107: British Romantic Prose Writers, 1789–1832, First Series; DLB 109: Eighteenth-Century British Poets, Second Series; DLB 142: Eighteenth-Century Literary Biographers;* and *DLB 158: British Reform Writers, 1789–1832.*

BOOKS: *Poems* (London: Printed for Joseph Johnson, 1773)—includes "The Invitation" and "Corsica"; enlarged as *Poems: A New Edition, Corrected. To Which Is Added an Epistle to William Wilberforce, Esq.* (London: Printed for Joseph Johnson, 1792; Boston: Wells & Lilly, 1820);

Miscellaneous Pieces in Prose, by Anna Aikin and John Aikin (London: Printed for Joseph Johnson, 1773);

Lessons for Children from Two to Three Years Old (N.p., 1775?; reprinted, London: Printed for J. Johnson, 1778);

Lessons for Children of Three Years Old (London: Printed for J. Johnson, 1778);

Hymns in Prose for Children, by Barbauld and Hannah More (London: Joseph Johnson, 1781; Norwich, Conn.: Printed by John Trumbull, 1786);

Early Lessons for Children (London: Joseph Johnson, 1781);

Lessons for Children, from Three to Four Years Old (London: Joseph Johnson, 1784);

Lessons for Children, from Four to Five Years Old (London: Joseph Johnson, 1788; Philadelphia: Printed by B. F. Bache, 1788);

Lessons for Children of Four Years Old, part 2 (London: Joseph Johnson, 1788; Philadelphia: Printed by B. F. Bache, 1788);

An Address to the Opposers of the Repeal of the Corporation and Test Acts (London: Joseph Johnson, 1790);

Epistle to Mr. Wilberforce on the Rejection of the Bill for Abolishing the Slave Trade (London: Joseph Johnson, 1791);

Letter to John Bull (London: Joseph Johnson, 1792);

Anna Laetitia Barbauld (Engraving by I. Holloway, 1785 from a 1775 medallion by Josiah Wedgwood, in Betsy Aikin-Sneath Rodgers, Georgian Chronicle: Mrs. Barbauld & Her Family, *1958; Widener Library, Harvard University)*

Remarks on Mr. Gilbert Wakefield's Enquiry into the Expediency and Propriety of Public or Social Worship (London: Joseph Johnson, 1792);

Civic Sermons to the People, nos. 1 & 2 (London: Printed for Joseph Johnson, 1792);

Evenings at Home; or, The Juvenile Budget Opened: Consisting of a Variety of Miscellaneous Pieces for the Instruction and Amusement of Young Persons, 6 volumes (London: Joseph Johnson, 1792–1795; Philadelphia: Printed by T. Dobson, 1797);

Sins of the Government, Sins of the Nation; or, A Discourse for the Fast, Appointed on April 19, 1793 (London: Joseph Johnson, 1793);

Lessons for Children, Part II. Being the First for Children of Three Years Old (London: Printed for J. Johnson, 1794);

Lessons for Children, Part III. Being the Second for Children of Three Years Old (London: J. Johnson, 1795);

Essay on the Odes of Collins (London: Printed for T. Cadell Jr. and W. Davies, 1797);

Gothic Stories (Manchester: G. Nicholson, 1797);

Pastoral Lessons, and Parental Conversations. Intended as a Companion to E. [Or Rather A. L.] Barbauld's Hymns in Prose (London: Darton & Harvey, 1797);

Lessons for Children, 4 parts (London: Joseph Johnson, 1797–1798); reprinted as *Mrs. Barbauld's Lessons, Admirably Adapted to the Capacities of Children* (New York: Printed by D. Bliss, 1806);

Pastoral Lessons, and Parental Conversations: Intended as a Companion, to . . . Hymns in Prose (London: Printed by Darton & Harvey, 1803; Philadelphia: Printed by B. Johnson, 1803);

Eighteen Hundred and Eleven (London: Joseph Johnson, 1812; Boston: Bradford & Read; Philadelphia: Anthony Finley, 1812).

Collections: *Works*, edited by Lucy Aikin (London: Longman, Hurst, Rees, Orme, Brown & Green, 1825; New York: G. & C. Carvill, 1826);

A Legacy for Young Ladies, Consisting of Miscellaneous Pieces, in Prose and Verse, edited by Lucy Aikin (London: Printed for Longman, Hurst, Rees, Orme & Green, 1826; Boston: Reed, 1826);

Tales, Poems, and Essays by Anna Laetitia Barbauld, with a Biographical Sketch by Grace A. Oliver (Boston: Roberts, 1884);

Poems of Anna Barbauld, edited by William McCarthy and Elizabeth Kraft (Athens: University of Georgia Press, 1993);

The Works of Anna Laetitia Barbauld; with a Memoir, by Lucy Aikin, introduction by Caroline Franklin (London: Routledge/Thoemmes Press, 1996).

OTHER: *Essays on Song-Writing: With a Collection of Such English Songs as Are Most Eminent for Poetical Merit*, written and collected by Barbauld and John Aikin (London: Printed for J. Johnson, 1772);

Devotional Pieces, Compiled from the Psalms and the Book of Job (London: Joseph Johnson, 1775);

The Poetical Works of Mr. William Collins, preface by Barbauld (London: Printed for T. Cadell Jr. & W. Davies, 1797);

The Correspondence of Samuel Richardson . . . Selected from the Original Manuscripts, Bequeathed by Him to His Family, to Which Are Prefixed, a Biographical Account of That Author, and Observations on His Writings, 6 volumes, edited by Barbauld (London: Richard Phillips, 1804);

Selections from the Spectator, Tatler, Guardian, and Freeholder, 3 volumes, edited by Barbauld (London: Printed for J. Johnson by R. Taylor, 1804);

Mark Akenside, *The Pleasures of Imagination*, with a critical essay by Barbauld (London, 1806);

Akenside, *The Poetical Works of Mark Akenside*, edited by Barbauld (London: W. Suttaby, 1807);

The British Novelists: With an Essay and Prefaces, Biographical and Critical, 50 volumes; edited by Barbauld (London: Rivington, 1810);

The Female Speaker; or, Miscellaneous Pieces in Prose and Verse, Selected From the Best Writers, and Adapted to the Uses of Young Women, edited by Barbauld (London: Printed for J. Johnson, 1811; Boston: Wells & Lilly, 1824).

Anna Laetitia Barbauld was an historian, poet, editor, essayist, and educator who made strides for women's involvement in the literary community, politics, and history of her time. In spite of being a woman writer during a time when the literary climate was still hostile to female authors, Barbauld wrote prolifically. Her career gradually became increasingly political. By the turn of the century she had added to the tradition of women's political writing.

Anna Laetitia Aikin was born 20 June 1743 in Leicestershire, England, the only daughter of prominent classicist and Nonconformist minister John Aikin. Her father, who at that time was a teacher at Kibworth, Leicestershire, was the child's primary educator. Some sources claim that she was already literate by age three and early in her childhood was reading the best literature that England had to offer. Undoubtedly, the early demonstration of her academic ability was what persuaded her father, who typically did not approve of advanced education for women, to allow her to continue her unusually broad studies in French, Italian, Greek, and Latin.

When Anna was fifteen years old, her family moved to Warrington, where John Aikin took a teaching position at the Warrington Academy, which had recently been established to provide a university education for Dissenters, who were unwelcome at Oxford and Cambridge. At this time Anna entered a new phase of her education, as she became closely acquainted with some of Britain's leading intellectuals—including Joseph Priestley, William Enfield, and Gilbert Wakefield; they became both her friends and her teachers. After spending fifteen years in this intellectual environment (until she was thirty), Anna had a head start on the difficult task of forging a public identity. The dissenting intellectuals of the academy served as her first audience when she began circulating her poems. The politically charged atmosphere of the academy also fostered the

Warrington Academy, 1757, where Barbauld taught (after an engraving by H. J. Bellars, in Betsy Aikin-Sneath Rodgers, Georgian Chronicle: Mrs. Barbauld & Her Family, *1958; Widener Library, Harvard University)*

debates that likely influenced Anna's future political involvement.

In 1773 Anna's brother, John Aikin, a physician who shared his sister's literary interests, encouraged Anna to publish the poetry for which she had been so widely praised by her intimate academic audience. As a result, her first volume of poetry, *Poems,* appeared in publication that year. Later, lines from both "The Invitation" from this early book and her poem "Summer Evening Meditation" appeared in the first edition of *Bartlett's Familiar Quotations* (1851), making her one of only four women to be quoted in the publication.

The poem "Corsica," also published in Anna Aikin's first volume, showed her interest in historical subjects. It outlined the history of the island as it escaped the poverty and oppression experienced under the French regime and developed into an independent state. Through such poems, Aikin expressed the political views that she had developed within the dissenting intellectual arena at Warrington; by lamenting the fallen heroes of the island she was able to discuss her concepts of liberty and the freedom of the mind in more-general terms. This mode of expression allowed her to convey the political views of a dissenting intellectual that would not have been well received by society without a literary cloak. Her ingenuity won her the praises of contem-

porary author and poet Lady Mary Wortley Montagu. Aikin's first volume achieved such acclaim that it went through four editions in the first year.

Also in 1773 Aikin joined forces with her brother for the publication of *Miscellaneous Pieces in Prose.* The joint publication went through several reprints in the first year, but attributing every work to either Aikin or her brother is difficult, because they did not sign all of their pieces. In any case, the work was a success and included some of Anna Aikin's most renowned essays, such as "Inconsistency in Our Expectations" and "On Romances."

The following year she married Rochemont Barbauld, who was a student at Warrington Academy when the two first met. He was the son of a Huguenot refugee family, and his father sent the young man to Warrington in hopes of his receiving the best education in England. At Warrington, however, young Barbauld also converted to Nonconformity before beginning his own career as an educator. Soon after their marriage, the minister and his new wife moved to Palgrave, Suffolk, where he established a school for boys. Despite Rochemont's growing mental instability, Anna's active role in the school ensured that it was successful until they permanently left Suffolk in 1785.

In addition to her new responsibilities as a wife and teacher, Anna Barbauld continued writing prolifically. By 1775 the Barbaulds had adopted one of Anna's nephews, a step that led to her writing such works as *Lessons for Children, from Two to Three Years Old* (1775?) and others that explored ways to educate small children.

Also in 1775, Barbauld wrote *Devotional Pieces, Compiled from the Psalms and the Book of Job,* and, while it was received respectfully, it never earned as much acclaim as some of her later works, such as *Hymns in Prose for Children* (1781). *Hymns in Prose for Children* quickly became her most widely read work, as it was translated into French, German, and Italian and earned her the most widespread attention of any of her publications. In the text she used "measured prose" rather than a more elementary writing style, because she proclaimed that poetry should not be entirely diminished in order to suit younger learning capacities. The result was a work that was designed to imprint religious views on children as early as possible by connecting them to the natural world. Undoubtedly, Barbauld had drawn from her Enlightenment background and combined it with a subdued version of her dissenting religious views to create a publication that was so popular that it went through several editions and was translated into several European languages. Through *Devotional Pieces* and *Hymns in Prose for Children,* Barbauld documented the broader eighteenth-century social desire to instill religious values into children at an early age, regardless of religious sect.

In 1781 Barbauld also published *Early Lessons for Children,* which went through several editions and was eventually translated into French. With each publication, Barbauld's literary reputation grew and, along with it, the reputation of the academy that she oversaw. Soon, her home became a sort of salon for dissenting intellectuals and mirrored the atmosphere that she had left behind at Warrington. Within this realm, she further developed her own political, educational, and religious views, which encouraged future publication.

By 1785 the Barbaulds' establishment at Palgrave could not be maintained; Rochemont's declining mental health forced the couple to leave the school and travel to the Continent. In 1786 they returned to England and moved to Hampstead, where Rochemont again tried his hand as a congregational minister. Anna returned to her role as an educator and began teaching a small group of female students, most of them day students, while others boarded at the Barbaulds' home. Again, Anna Barbauld reached out to the intellectual community within her proximity and, at this time, forged friendships with prominent local literary figures from whom she could draw her own inspiration, including Joanna Baillie, Hannah More, and Fanny Burney.

Because of her role as a teacher, Barbauld had great insight into the minds of children, which was further illustrated in *Lessons for Children, from Four to Five Years Old* and *Lessons for Children of Four Years Old,* part 2 (1788). Barbauld had long noted the absence of age-appropriate books that taught concepts beyond the typical moralizing issues. Consequently, she turned to a more empirical world of observation to inspire young minds.

Barbauld's involvement in the Hampstead literary community also inspired her to turn her own writings toward more-contemporary social issues. Because of her dissenting background, she sympathized with various groups who were excluded from the civic realm and even wrote essays against the inherent injustices in slavery. As a result, in 1790 she published *An Address to the Opposers of the Repeal of the Corporation and Test Acts,* in which she denounced the denial of governmental participation for non-Anglicans. Continuing her crusade against social injustices, the following year she wrote *Epistle to Mr. Wilberforce on the Rejection of the Bill for Abolishing the Slave Trade* (1791). Barbauld had returned to her old medium of verse, but her focus was a harsh attack on those who had rejected a bill that proposed to end the slave trade. As an active Dissenter, her voice for liberty was vehement. In fact, she later became an ardent supporter for the French Revolution, which she viewed as an important movement toward civil liberties.

As Barbauld denounced the slave trade and civil prohibitions imposed upon non-Anglicans, she documented some of the most controversial issues of her time. She also illustrated the views of leading dissenting intellectuals who comprised a smaller but vocal portion of the English literary community. Perhaps more importantly, she recorded the reconciliation of religious views and Enlightenment reasoning that continued to shape her nation for many decades.

Barbauld continued to write social commentary in 1792 with her publication *Letter to John Bull,* which negated the idea that to criticize England or its constitution was to be disloyal to the nation. Many religious and political conservatives maintained that those who did not uphold the views of the Anglican Church were disloyal, because it was the Church of England, but Barbauld and her fellow dissenters saw their views as an enlightened form of free speech. While advocating this sort of free speech, she also chronicled the debates surrounding the English constitution and individual rights. Undoubtedly, the polemical voice in her historical essays prefigured the kind of feminine social consciousness that became so prevalent in later Victorian novels.

Also in 1792, Barbauld joined forces with her brother, John Aikin, a second time to publish the initial six volumes of *Evenings at Home; or, The Juvenile Budget Opened: Consisting of a Variety of Miscellaneous Pieces for the Instruction and*

Amusement of Young Persons, not completed until 1795. While Barbauld may have written some fifteen papers for the work, most scholars agree that the vast majority of the publication should be attributed to her brother. Regardless, the series added to her growing reputation, as she and Aikin addressed issues surrounding the education of older children, such as the need for a more rigorous form of teaching for them.

The same year, Barbauld published *Remarks on Mr. Gilbert Wakefield's Enquiry into the Expediency and Propriety of Public or Social Worship* (1792), in which she again wrote of civil liberties. She maintained that all individuals should have the freedom to worship as they chose, but she was careful not to state her dissenting views too strongly, as she knew it would damage her growing reputation. Nonetheless, through this work Barbauld again documented the contemporary debates surrounding the issue of religious freedoms. She recorded both the arguments launched in attack of Dissenters and the dissenting view while maintaining a relatively unbiased view of her own. Her use of objectivity and writing in more-general ideas allowed her to promote her views, protected her from the backlash of her audience, and provided a less-biased historical account of contemporary debates.

Barbauld's career had to be put on hold for awhile, as Rochemont's mental health began to take another turn for the worse. By 1802, his condition worsened to the point that he had to give up his position as minister, and the couple moved to Stoke Newington near Anna's brother. Two years later, Anna edited *Selections from the Spectator, Tatler, Guardian, and Freeholder* (1804). She also edited *The Correspondence of Samuel Richardson . . . Selected from the Original Manuscripts, Bequeathed by Him to His Family, to Which Are Prefixed, a Biographical Account of That Author, and Observations on His Writings* (1804), which appeared as a six-volume series.

Meanwhile, Rochemont's mental health continued its downward spiral, and by 1808 his physical health was beginning to fail as well. In 1808 Rochemont, who had become completely mentally disabled, died in London. Soon after his death, Anna was able to return to her career and began her work as editor of *The British Novelists: With an Essay and Prefaces, Biographical and Critical* (1810). Her contributions to the extensive publication included an essay titled "Origin and Progress of Novel Writing" and introductory biographies for each author included in the collection.

The next year, Barbauld edited *The Female Speaker* (1811), a compilation of works by some of England's most notable poets and prose authors. The work was intended to be employed for the education of young women, and its use quickly spread among teachers who hoped to provide young girls with proper literary backgrounds. Despite the widespread acclaim for *The Female Speaker,* the work also

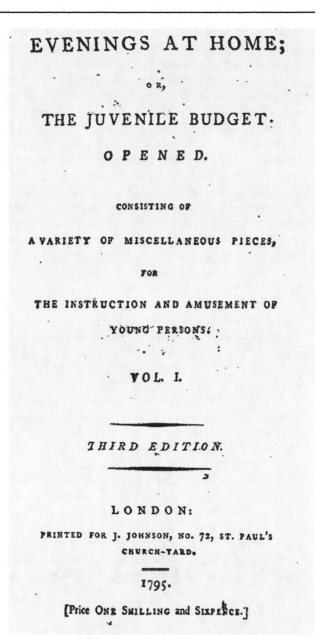

EVENINGS AT HOME;

OR,

THE JUVENILE BUDGET.

OPENED.

CONSISTING OF

A VARIETY OF MISCELLANEOUS PIECES,

FOR

THE INSTRUCTION AND AMUSEMENT OF

YOUNG PERSONS;

VOL. I.

THIRD EDITION.

LONDON:

PRINTED FOR J. JOHNSON, NO. 72, ST. PAUL'S
CHURCH-YARD.

1795.

[Price ONE SHILLING and SIXPENCE.]

Title page for one of Barbauld's popular works for family entertainment (Eighteenth-Century Collections Online, Gale Group)

earned Barbauld great notoriety, because in the text she openly criticized Samuel Taylor Coleridge's poem *The Rime of the Ancient Mariner* (1797–1799), which she said lacked a moralizing theme. Thus, Barbauld was remaining true to her enlightened philosophical background but failed to appreciate a work that ventured away from the voice of reason into a more romantic and artistic realm.

Although Barbauld's education was quite exceptional for a woman of her time, she did not advocate such an extensive education for other young women. In *The Female Speaker,* she expressed her view that young girls should be prepared with a more practical education than she had received, which would better ready them for their roles as wives and mothers. While she saw the study of the literary ideas she presented in *The Female Speaker* and other works as useful for refining young ladies, she did not deem it a necessary part of education for all females. In fact, when Elizabeth Montagu proposed that Barbauld establish a school for young girls, Barbauld declined the invitation, because she claimed that girls were better off being educated at the hands of their fathers and other family members. Thus, her views on the education of women were surprisingly conventional considering her own educational background, her public and intellectual career, and many of her more-progressive views. She saw her situation in life as an exception to the broader feminine world. As she recorded her views in *The Female Speaker,* she also documented the extent to which her reading public held to such beliefs, since the text was so widely praised and accepted by her contemporaries.

In 1812, with her publication of the long poem *Eighteen Hundred and Eleven,* Barbauld first outraged the public. For nearly forty years, Barbauld had managed to avoid staunch public criticism, but the many negative reviews she received for the poem essentially ended her publishing career. In *Eighteen Hundred and Eleven* she no longer cloaked her dissenting views and criticisms of the British government but openly attacked Britain for its continued involvement in the war with France while ignoring the deplorable economic and social conditions at home. Not only was the poem denounced as unpatriotic, but it also received a great deal of hostility because of the waning national morale. Robert Southey's review in *The Quarterly Review* was particularly harsh, as it not only criticized her views but also attacked her as a woman. The public response to her work records the widespread hostilities against Dissenters and the plight of women who sought to voice unpopular opinions, even when they viewed the traditional roles of wife and mother to be more appropriate for most women. While some reviews were much harsher than others, the resounding opinion implicitly defined the line that women writers were not allowed to venture past.

Undoubtedly, *Eighteen Hundred and Eleven* was one of Barbauld's most significant historical works, as it documented the declining economic and social conditions of Britain in 1812. In addition, the public's reaction to Barbauld's summation was indicative of the patriotic sentiment of the nation even in the midst of the Napoleonic Wars. It also illustrates that even women who established lucrative and well-respected writing careers remained subject to criticisms that their male counterparts did not have to fear when they voiced the same opinions.

Although Barbauld's public career ended with *Eighteen Hundred and Eleven,* she continued to be actively involved with a like-minded group of intellectuals, which included Montagu, More, and Priestley. She also continued to write letters and other minor pieces that her niece, Lucy Aikin, compiled after her aunt's death into a two-volume publication simply titled *Works* (1825). Barbauld died in Stoke-Newington 9 March 1825.

Despite the reception of her final publication, Anna Laetitia Barbauld's publishing career was successful for its time. She challenged a long-standing system, however indirectly, in the broader literary realm. Her writings also document many aspects of contemporary culture, such as the debates over slavery and individual freedoms. Barbauld contributed to recording the history of her nation and paving the way for future women polemicists and authors.

Thomas Birch

(23 November 1705 – 19 January 1766)

Mercy Cannon

Stephen F. Austin State University

BOOKS: *A General Dictionary, Historical and Critical: In Which a New and Accurate Translation of That of the Celebrated Mr. Bayle, with the Corrections and Observations Printed in the Late Edition at Paris, Is Included; and Interspersed with Several Thousand Lives Never Before Published. The Whole Containing the History of the Most Illustrious Persons of All Ages and Nations Particularly Those of Great Britain and Ireland, Distinguished by Their Rank, Actions, Learning and Other Accomplishments. With Reflections on Such Passages of Bayle, as Seem to Favor Scepticism and the Manichee System,* 10 volumes, by Birch, J. P. Bernard, John Lockman, and George Sale (London: G. Strahan, etc., 1734–1741; London: Printed by J. Bettenham, 1734–1741);

The Life of Mr. William Chillingworth (London: Printed for D. Midwinter, etc., 1742);

The Heads and Characters of Illustrious Persons of Great Britain, 2 volumes, engravings by Jacobus Houbraken and George Vertue, biographies by Birch (London: J. & P. Knapton, 1743, 1751);

The Life of the Honourable Robert Boyle (London: A. Millar, 1744); also published in *The Works of the Honourable Robert Boyle. In Five Volumes. To Which Is Prefixed the Life of the Author,* 5 volumes, edited by Birch (London: Printed for A. Millar, 1744; revised, 6 volumes, London: Printed for J. & F. Rivington, etc., 1772);

An Inquiry into the Share, Which King Charles I. Had in the Transactions of the Earl of Glamorgan, afterwards Marquis of Worcester, for Bringing over a Body of Irish Rebels to Assist That King, in the Years 1645 and 1646 (London: A. Millar, 1747; revised to include an appendix, including several letters of the King to the Earl of Glamorgan from the originals in the Harleian library of manuscripts, London: A. Millar, 1756); republished as *Charles the First Pourtrayed; or, A Relation of Authentic Facts,* 2 volumes (London: J. Richardson; P. Davey & B. Law, 1758);

An Historical View of the Negotiations Between the Courts of England, France, and Brussels, from the Year 1592 to

Thomas Birch (portrait by John Faber Jr., after James Wills, 1741; National Portrait Gallery, London)

1617: Extracted Chiefly from the Ms. State-papers of Sir Thomas Edmondes . . . and of Anthony Bacon, 8 volumes (London: Printed for A. Millar, 1749);

The Wisdom and Goodness of God Proved from the Frame and Constitution of Man. A Sermon, Etc. (London: A. Millar, 1749);

The Life of the Most Reverend Dr. John Tillotson, Lord Archbishop of Canterbury. Compiled Chiefly from His Original Papers and Letters (London: J. & R. Tonson, and others, 1752); also published in *The Works of the*

Most Reverend Dr. John Tillotson, Lord Archbishop of Canterbury, 3 volumes, compiled, edited, and with a biographical essay, by Birch (London: Printed for J. & R. Tonson, and others, 1752);

The Life of Mons. Du Fresnoy, in Charles-Alphonse, *De arte graphica; or, The Art of Painting*, translated by James Wills (London: Printed for R. Francklin, 1754);

Memoirs of the Reign of Queen Elizabeth from the Year 1581 till Her Death. In Which the Secret Intrigues of Her Court, and the Conduct of Her Favourite Robert, Earl of Essex Are Particularly Illustrated. From the Original Papers of Anthony Bacon, Esquire, and Other Manuscripts Never Before Published, 2 volumes (London: Printed for A. Millar, 1754; New York: AMS, 1970);

Authentic Memoirs of the Life of Richard Mead, M.D., 8 volumes, by Birch and Matthew Maty (London: Printed for J. Whitson & B. White, 1755);

An Account of the Life of John Ward, Professor of Rhetoric in Gresham College, etc. (London: Printed for P. Vaillant, 1756);

The Life of Henry, Prince of Wales, Eldest Son of King James I. Compiled Chiefly from His Own Papers (London: A. Millar, 1760; Dublin: G. Faulkner, 1760).

OTHER: John Macky, *Memoirs of the Secret Services of J. Macky . . . Including, Also, the True Secret History of the . . . English and Scots Nobility, . . . and Other Persons of Distinction, from the Revolution*, edited by A. R., with marginal notes by Dean Swift, and transcribed by Birch (London, 1733);

John Greaves, *Miscellaneous Works of Mr. John Greaves . . . to the Whole Is Prefix'd an Historical and Critical Account of the Life and Writings of the Author*, 2 volumes, edited, with an introduction, by Birch (London: Printed by J. Hughs for J. Brindley & C. Corbett, 1737);

John Milton, *A Complete Collection of the Historical, Political, and Miscellaneous Works of John Milton Correctly Printed from the Original Editions, with an Historical and Critical Account of the Life and Writings of the Author (By T. Birch), Containing Several Original Papers of His, Never Before Published*, 2 volumes, life of Milton and criticism, and edited by Birch (London: A. Millar, 1738); republished as *The Works of John Milton, Historical, Political, and Miscellaneous. Now More Correctly Printed from the Originals, than in Any Former Edition, and Many Passages Restored, Which Have Been Hitherto Omitted. To Which Is Prefixed, an Account of His Life and Writings (by Birch)*, edited by Birch and R. Barron? (London: A. Millar, 1753);

Athenian Letters: or, The Epistolary Correspondence of an Agent of the King of Persia, Residing at Athens during the Peloponnesian War. Containing the History of the Times, in Despatches to the Ministers of State at the Persian

Court. Besides Letters on Various Subjects Between Him and His Friends, 4 volumes, by Birch, Philip Yorke, second Earl of Hardwicke, Charles Yorke, and others, and edited by Birch (London: James Bettenham, 1741–1743; reprinted for the public, London, 1781); revised as *Athenian Letters; or, The Epistolary Correspondence of an Agent of the King of Persia, Residing at Athens During the Peloponnesian War. Containing the History of the Times, in Despatches to the Ministers of State at the Persian Court. Besides Letters on Various Subjects Between Him and His Friends. A New Edition: To Which Is Prefixed a Geographical Index . . . Illustrated with Engravings, and a Map, Etc.*, 2 volumes (London: T. Cadell & W. Davies, 1810);

William Chillingworth, *The Works of William Chillingworth of the University of Oxford: Containing His Book, Intitled, The Religion of Protestants, a Safe Way to Salvation: Together with His Nine Sermons Preached Before the King . . . His Letter to Mr. Lewgar . . . His Nine Additional Discourses. And an Answer to Some Passages in Rushworth's Dialogues, Concerning Traditions*, edited, with an introductory biography, by Birch (London: Printed for D. Midwinter, etc., 1742; Philadelphia: R. Davis, 1840);

John Thurloe, *A Collection of the State Papers of John Thurloe, Esq. Secretary to the Council of State and the Two Protectors Oliver and Richard Cromwell: To Which Is Prefixed the Life of Mr. Thurloe, with a Complete Index to Each Volume by T. Birch*, 7 volumes, edited, with a biographical essay, by Birch (London: Printed for the executor of F. Gyles, 1742);

Ralph Cudworth, *The True Intellectual System of the Universe . . . with a Discourse Concerning the True Notion of the Lord's Supper; and Two Sermons, on I John II. 3, 4. and I Cor. XV. 57 . . . The Second Edition; in Which Are Now First Added References to the Several Quotations in the Intellectual System; and an Account of the Life and Writings of the Author*, 2 volumes, edited by Birch and Ralph Cudworth the Younger (London: J. Walthoe, etc., 1743); revised and expanded as *The True Intellectual System of the Universe: Wherein All the Reason and Philosophy of Atheism Is Confuted, and its Impossibility Demonstrated. A New Ed.; With References to the Several Quotations in The Intellectual System; and an Account of the Life and Writings of the Author*, 4 volumes (London: R. Priestly, 1820); reprinted as *The True Intellectual System of the Universe: Wherein All the Reason and Philosophy of Atheism Is Confuted, and Its Impossibility Demonstrated. A Treatise on Immutable Morality; with a Discourse Concerning the True Notion of the Lord's Supper: and Two Sermons on 1. John 2: 3, 4, and 1. Cor. 15: 27*, 2 volumes (Andover, Md.: Gould & Newman, 1837–1847);

Robert Boyle, *The Works of the Honourable Robert Boyle. In Five Volumes. To Which Is Prefixed the Life of the Author,* 5 volumes, edited by Birch (London: Printed for A. Millar, 1744; revised, 6 volumes, London: Printed for J. & F. Rivington [etc.], 1772);

Catharine Cockburn, *The Works of Mrs. Catharine Cockburn, Theological, Moral, Dramatic, and Poetical. Several of Them Now First Printed. Rev. and Published, with an Account of the Life of the Author,* 2 volumes, edited by Birch (London: Printed for J. & P. Knapton, 1751);

Walter Ralegh, *The Works of Sir Walter Ralegh, Kt. Political, Commercial, and Philosophical; Together with His Letters and Poems . . . To Which Is Prefix'd, a New Account of His Life by Tho. Birch,* 2 volumes, edited by Birch (London: Printed for R. Dodsley, 1751); revised and expanded as *The Works of Sir Walter Ralegh, Kt: Now First Collected: To Which Are Prefixed the Lives of the Author,* 8 volumes, lives written by, and edited by William Oldys and Birch (Oxford: Oxford University Press, 1829; reprinted, New York: Burt Franklin, 1829);

Edmund Spenser, *The Faerie Queene . . . with an Exact Collation of the Two Original Editions . . . to Which Are Now Added a New Life of the Author (By T. Birch) and Also a Glossary. Adorn'd with Thirty-two Copper-Plates, from the Original Drawings of the Late W. Kent,* 3 volumes, edited by Birch (London: J. Brindley, 1751);

John Tillotson, *The Works of the Most Reverend Dr. John Tillotson, Lord Archbishop of Canterbury,* 3 volumes, compiled, edited, and with a biographical essay, by Birch (London: Printed for J. & R. Tonson, & others, 1752);

Royal Society, *The History of the Royal Society of London for Improving of Natural Knowledge,* 4 volumes, compiled and edited by Birch (London: Printed for A. Millar, 1756–1757);

A Collection of the Yearly Bills of Mortality [within the London District] from 1657 to 1758, Inclusive, edited by Birch (London: Printed for A. Millar, 1759);

Colonel Robert Hammond, *Letters Between Col. R. H., Governor of the Isle of Wight, and the Committee of Lords and Commons at Derby House, General Fairfax, Lieut. General Cromwell, Commissary General Ireton, Etc., Relating to King Charles I., While He Was Confined in Carisbrooke-Castle in That Island, Now First Published [By T. Birch]. To Which Is Prefixed a Letter from John Ashburnham Esq. To a Friend, Concerning His Deportment Towards the King in His Attendance on His Majesty at Hampton-court, and in the Isle of Wight,* compiled and edited by Birch (London: Printed for Robert Horsfield, 1764);

Francis Bacon, *The Works of Francis Bacon, Baron of Verulam,* 5 volumes, edited by Robert Stephens and John Locker, and published after their deaths by Thomas Birch; edited throughout by John Gambold, the Latin volumes revised by William Bowyer (London: A. Millar, 1765);

Charles I, King of England, *The Court and Times of Charles the First; Illustrated by Authentic and Confidential Letters, from Various Public and Private Collections; Including Memoirs of the Mission in England of the Capuchin Friars . . . by Father Cyprien De Gamache,* 2 volumes, compiled by Birch, edited, with an introduction and notes, by Robert Folkestone Williams (London: Henry Colburn 1848);

James I, King of England, *The Court and Times of James the First; Illustrated by Authentic and Confidential Letters, from Various Public and Private Collections,* 2 volumes, compiled by T. Birch and edited, with an introduction and notes, by Folkestone Williams (London: Henry Colburn, 1848).

Although Thomas Birch occupies a relatively minor place in the field of historical scholarship, his accomplishments are nonetheless significant. Working with an astonishing amount of primary material, Birch published dozens of biographies, histories, and letters. Unlike more celebrated historians, Birch did not analyze or judge his subjects but attempted to render faithfully their historical records. This conservative approach to history is both his greatest strength and his greatest weakness. Instead of offering inventive historiography, Birch compiled a store of well-documented sourcebooks for contemporary and future historians. By recording, synthesizing, and preserving this material, however, he contributed to British culture a legacy of original sources.

On 23 November 1705 Thomas Birch was born in Clerkenwell, at the northern edge of London. His parents, Joseph and Rebecca Birch, were devout Quakers of modest means. As the son of a coffee-mill maker, Thomas received an education appropriate to the merchant class: day school from age nine to twelve, boarding school for two years, then back to Clerkenwell for two more years of schooling. Instead of pursuing his father's trade, however, Thomas followed his academic interests, tutoring in three schools for four years. The Commonplace Book that he kept during that final year (1725–1726) reveals a young man who thought deeply about philosophical problems, mathematical principles, and scientific discovery. Birch's "Notes for an Autobiography," written in his declining years, also points to his early interests in theology, history, poetry, current events, and the theater. Most significant, his work as an usher introduced him to the family who profoundly influenced his life, the Hardwickes. Scholars suggest that Lord Hardwicke, who later became Lord Chancellor, employed Birch as a tutor for his sons and continued to patronize Birch for much of his career. This old-fashioned patronage arrangement clearly enabled Birch to pursue his historical interests, and it continued with Lord Hardwicke's eldest son, Philip Yorke.

In 1728 Birch married Hannah Cox, the daughter of a curate, who gave birth to their son Joseph in July 1729. Two weeks later both Hannah and Joseph died of fever. Although his comfortable income and genial disposition made him an eligible bachelor, Birch never married again. He continued to reside in Clerkenwell until his father's death in 1730. Electing to pursue a career in the Anglican Church, Birch went through the process of ordination from 1730 to 1731. Although this decision came as some surprise to Birch's friends, who assumed he would follow his parents' Quaker faith, Birch's "Notes" shows that he had an abiding interest in theological controversies and liberal humanism. It is generally accepted that the Hardwicke family's influence helped Birch achieve both the vicarage of Ulting in Essex in 1732 and his appointment to help write *A General Dictionary, Historical and Critical: In Which a New and Accurate Translation of That of the Celebrated Mr. Bayle, with the Corrections and Observations Printed in the Late Edition at Paris, Is Included* (1734–1741). The church may have been Birch's livelihood, but his activities as a churchman were overshadowed by his passionate involvement in historical scholarship, including his first and most lasting achievement, *A General Dictionary*.

This work was first designed to update the 1710 translation of Pierre Bayle's *Dictionnaire historique et critique* (1697–1706), an impressive volume featuring some 2,110 biographies. Birch was invited by John Lockman to submit a sample biography to publisher Nicholas Prevost, who accepted Birch as an editor for the project. This ten-volume dictionary followed a strict timetable of publication that stretched over nine years and supplied Birch with a dependable supplement to his church income. Along with co-editors Lockman, J. P. Barnard, and George Sale, Birch added 889 biographies to Bayle's work, at least 618 of which were written by Birch himself. Lockman and Barnard translated much of Bayle's work, and Sale took responsibility for the oriental history section. Utilizing unpublished manuscripts, letters, wills, Royal Society records, information from family members and close friends, and prior biographical accounts, *A General Dictionary* set the standard for historical scholarship. The dictionary followed a format that was later repeated in *A Biographia Britannica* (1747)—a concise narrative of the subject's life followed by bibliographical references to that narrative, critical remarks that presented detailed examples and disputed

accounts, and bibliographical references to the critical remarks. Birch meticulously researched and recorded the subjects' lives and works, correcting previous inaccuracies and supplying new information.

Although *A General Dictionary* was a collective effort, Birch became the sustaining force of the project. On several occasions, to judge from the correspondence among the editors, he rescued the project from near collapse, and he produced the bulk of the articles. Birch supplied biographies for such important Englishmen as Geoffrey Chaucer, John Milton, William Shakespeare, and Isaac Newton. In fact, some of his biographies were the first detailed treatments of the subjects: Christopher Wren, John Locke, John Dryden, and Ben Jonson are but a few examples. Birch's achievement was so significant that, in his article "Thomas Birch and the 'General Dictionary,'" James Marshall Osborn states, "It may safely be said that no individual has contributed more to the materials of British biography than Thomas Birch." Clearly, Birch brought indefatigable energy and dedication to a project that he considered the most important of his life. It brought him financial rewards, social distinction, and personal satisfaction.

Birch chose to dedicate the first volume of the dictionary to the Royal Society of London and presented the first two volumes to the society himself. This action—coupled with the patronage and nominations of botanist John Martyn, physician Richard Middleton, and astronomer Edmund Halley—resulted in Birch's admission to the Royal Society in 1735, for which he later served as secretary (1752–1765) and unofficial historian. Cultivating the acquaintance of astronomers and mathematicians also enabled Birch to gather more information on several of the scientific men whose lives he recorded in *A General Dictionary*. His association with the Royal Society must have been especially gratifying to Birch, who never received a university education but who energetically pursued scholarly and academic work. Through the society, Birch developed lasting friendships with many of the leading scientists, physicians, and scholars of the eighteenth century. His involvement in erudite circles also gave him the opportunity to serve as treasurer to the short-lived Society for the Encouragement of Learning (1736–1738), which provided authors with financial assistance so they might publish.

Birch's efforts on *A General Dictionary* also resulted in much longer biographical projects. While working on the entry for John Greaves, Professor of Geometry at Gresham College, Birch gathered enough material to publish a two-volume collection, *Miscellaneous Works of Mr. John Greaves* (1737), which he introduced with a short biography. This publication was Birch's first encounter with publisher Andrew Millar, who helped

A GENERAL
DICTIONARY,
Historical and Critical.

A

AARON, High-Priest of the Jews, and brother of Moses. As we have a copious account of him in the Pentateuch, in Moreri's Dictionary, and that of Mr. Simon, to give a large article of him here would be superfluous. I therefore shall only observe, that his weakness in complying with the superstitious desires of the Israelites, with regard to the golden Calf, has given rise to a multitude of Fictions [A]. One Moncæius published, about the beginning of the seventeenth Century, an Apology for Aaron (a), which the Inquisition of Rome condemn'd, as Cornelius à Lapide the Jesuit had foretold the author (b). 'Tis supposed in this Apology, that Aaron intended to exhibit the same image which Moses represented some time after, I mean a Cherubim; and that the Israelites worshipped it, contrary to the Intentions of Aaron. A Doctor of the Sorbonne, Canon of Amiens (c), completely refuted these Suppositions in 1609. According to some authors, the only reason of Aaron's criminal Indulgence on this occasion, was, the fear he was under of being fell'd by the people; and that he hoped to elude their request, by requiring the women to contribute their ear-rings, imagining they would chuse to continue without a visible Deity, rather than give up any of their personal Ornaments; but found however, that such Minds as are intoxicated with superstition and idolatry (d), will sacrifice every thing to their darling enthusiasm. The Scriptures don't any way favour the opinion of those, who assert that the Golden Calf was only of gilded Wood [B]

We

(a) 'Tis entitled, *Aaron purgatus.* It was reprinted at Francfort anno 1675, in 8vo. The Leipsic edition of 1689, in 12°, mentioned in Tome 17, of the *Bibliotheque Universelle,* is exactly the same with that of Francfort, except that the booksellers publish'd it with a new title.

(b) Cornel. à Lapide Commentar. in Exod. xxxii. 4. pag. 605.

(c) His name is *Visrius,* and his book is entitled, *Destructio Pseudo-Cherubi Moncæi.*

(d) Idem Cornel. à Lapide. ibid.

[A] *Has given rise to a multitude of Fictions.*] I. Rabbi Solomon (1) imagined, that the calf which the Israelites worshiped was a living animal; and that Aaron seeing it walk and eat like other calves, erected an altar in its honour, something like which is related in the Alcoran (2). II. Several Rabbis to justify Aaron, relate, that he himself did not make the golden calf, but only threw the gold into the fire, purely to free himself from the importunities of the people; and that certain Magicians who mixed with the Israelites at their leaving Egypt, cast this metal into the form of a calf. As the Scripture declares expresly, that the calf was first cast, and afterwards improved by the graving-tool, two things may be inferred; either that a mold was made in the form of the animal abovementioned, and the melted gold poured into it; or that the metal was cast in an unshapen mass, and afterwards wrought into the figure of a calf by the Sculptor's hand. III. Many writers think, that Aaron did not make a whole calf, but the head only. IV. It is related (3) *That the ashes of the golden calf which Moses caus'd to be burnt and mixed with the water, that was drunk by the Israelites, stuck to the beards of such as had fallen down before it, by which they appeared with gilt beards, as a peculiar mark to distinguish those who had worshipped the calf.* This idle story is interwoven with the 32d chapter of Exodus, in a French Bible printed at Paris, in 1538, by Anthony Bonnemere; who says thus in his preface: *This French Bible was first printed in 1495, at the request of his most Christian Majesty, Charles VIIIth; and afterwards reprinted with emendations.* It declares further: *That the French translator has added nothing but the genuine truth, according to the express terms of the Latin Bible; nor omitted any thing but what was improper to be translated.* So that we are to look upon this fiction of the gilded beards as matter of fact, and another of the same stamp, inserted in the chapter

(1) Cornel. à Lapide in Exod. pag. 605.

(2) *Ascendi Taurum fudit corporeum, emittentem mugitum;* i. e. Ascendi cast a corporeal bull that bellow'd. *Annot xxx Latini Codicis, ex Arabici,* apud Seldenum de Diis Syris, Synt. 1. Cap. IV. pag. 54.

(3) See Jeremiah de Pours' *Divine Melodie,* pag. 229.

above-mentioned, viz. that *upon Hur's refusing to make Gods for the Israelites, they spit upon him with so much fury and violence, that they quite suffocated him.* The book (4) whence these particulars are extracted, was written by a Walloon Minister, who does not fail to exclaim against the audaciousness of those, who thus added or suppress'd as they pleased. A double crime this! an obreptitious and surreptitious version, interspers'd with childish traditions! at the same time that the preface promises nothing *but the genuine truth; and declares, that this translation was not calculated for Clerks, but for the Laity, and for unlearned Monks and Hermits.* These assertions aggravate the infidelity of the translator; for persons of erudition may guard against the snare, which the ignorant cannot. [The Bible abovementioned was translated by Guiars des Moulins, Canon of Aire in Artois, in the year 1224, with several glosses or insertions in the text, taken out of Petrus Comestor's *Historia Scholastica.* John de Reby, Confessor to King Charles VIII, and afterwards Bishop of Angers, revised and corrected it by order of that Prince, and got it printed at Paris by Ant. Verard about the year 1487, and not 1495, as Jer. de Pours affirms. To a subsequent edition, printed by the said Verard, was prefixed the Preface cited by de Pours. That Bible has been reprinted several times, with the said Preface, before Bonnemere's edition of 1538. Le Long *Bibliotheca Sacra.* Crit. Rem.] To conclude, the story of the golden beards is not the only fiction the Rabbis have palm'd upon the world. They tell us, that the water, impregnated with the particles of the golden calf, which Moses forced them to swallow, had very near the same effect as the waters of jealousy; for it made tumours and ulcers to break out on the guilty, but did not hurt the innocent (5).

[B] *That the Golden Calf was only of gilded Wood.*] 'Tis said expresly in the Scriptures (6) that it was a molten

(4) 'Tis entitled, *La Divine Melodie du Saint Psalmiste, by Jeremie de Pours,* and printed at Middleburgh, anno 1644, in 4°.

(5) See Salian, vol. 2. p. 165. Bocharti Hierozoic. part 1. lib. 2. cap. 34.

(6) Exod. xxxii. 4.

A

First page for Birch's 1734 biographical dictionary, which added 889 biographies to Pierre Bayle's earlier work on which it was based (Thomas Cooper Library, Rare Books and Special Collections, University of South Carolina) establish Birch's reputation as a serious scholar and who remained one of Birch's most ardent supporters. One year later, with the assistance of Millar, Birch edited two volumes of Milton's poetry and prose from information supplied by Jonathan Richardson, Halley, and Sir Thomas Clark. Indeed, Birch's distinguished reputation led many families who inherited musty manuscripts to request his help in compiling, editing, and publishing these documents. Fletcher Gyles, for example, commissioned Birch to publish original manuscripts of John Thurloe, whose role in the English Revolution earned him the title "Cromwell's spy." Supplementing those documents with additional contributions, Birch produced the seven-volume *A Collection of the State Papers of John Thurloe* (1742), which brought him considerable financial remuneration. He also published his *The Works of William Chillingworth* in 1742, and the following year added a biography of Ralph Cudworth to Cudworth's *The True Intellectual System of the Universe.*

The Hardwicke family, whose patronage enabled Birch to obtain several church appointments, remained an important part of Birch's life. Philip Yorke, Lord Hardwicke's eldest son and the second Earl of Hardwicke, employed Birch around 1740 as his literary agent and private secretary, an arrangement that lasted until Yorke's death in 1765. One of Birch's more unusual duties, starting in 1741, was to supply Yorke with a weekly newsletter from London while Yorke resided at his country home at Wrest Park. Thus, every Friday during the summer season, for twenty-four years, Birch recorded any events, news, or gossip that came to his attention. This remarkable correspondence was interrupted only two times, once in 1747 when Birch suffered from eye strain and then in 1756, when Yorke remained in London for the summer. Yorke also assigned Birch the task of revising *Athenian Letters; or, The Epistolary Correspondence of an Agent of the King of Persia, Residing at Athens during the Peloponnesian War,* a fictional work written by Yorke and a large group of his friends. Privately published in 1741 and 1743, *Athenian Letters* did not reach the public until 1781, after the deaths of both Yorke and Birch, when it was well received.

A collaboration with Henry Miles yielded Birch's next publication, *The Works of the Honourable Robert Boyle* (1744). Although the two had begun this work in 1738 when Birch first met with Miles, Birch's efforts on the dictionary and the Thurloe papers prevented him from devoting much time to the project until 1742. Birch seems to have performed the function of editor in this collaboration. Critics, however, have suggested that Birch's efforts on this project were minimal and reflected his typical method of compilation and transcription with little analysis or interpretation. Marie Boas Hall, in "Henry Miles, F.R.S. (1698–1763) and

Thomas Birch, F.R.S. (1705–1766)," explains that Birch relied heavily on others' editorial work: "From the manuscript material available it is abundantly clear that the lion's share of credit for the 1744 edition of Boyle's *Works* belongs to Miles, not Birch." This tendency on Birch's part was perhaps what led to Samuel Johnson's critical remark, recorded in Sir John Hawkins's *Life of Samuel Johnson:* "a pen is to Tom a torpedo, the touch of it benumbs his hand and his brain: Tom can talk; but he is no writer." This criticism may be justified; nonetheless, Birch's transcriptions provided Johnson with the definitive source for his third biography, *Life of Admiral Blake* (1740). In fact, Birch's *General Dictionary* entry on Blake was the only source Johnson consulted, a fact attesting to his early confidence in Birch's scholarship.

Although the twenty-five-year association of Johnson and Birch began with some warmth in 1738, their correspondence and Johnson's later reviews of Birch's work lack any hint of genuine friendship. The strained relations between Johnson and Birch seem to have resulted from a romantic incident that took place in late 1738 and early 1739. Both men became friends with Elizabeth Carter, a young woman of exceptional intelligence who was later part of the Bluestocking Circle. Birch encouraged and promoted Carter's poetry and scholarly work, especially her 1739 translation of Francesco Algarotti's Italian work on Newton, *Sir Isaac Newton's Philosophy Explain'd.* Birch's patronage of Carter, however, had distinctly amorous overtones, as his letters to her reveal, and Johnson's continued presence during their meetings was apparently unwelcome. Carter seems to have ended the budding romance after she and Birch took a brief journey through the English countryside together. While Birch did not keep any letters from Carter that indicate an overt rejection, her polite responses to his increasingly tender letters demonstrate that she had no interest in his courtship. Critics conjecture that although Johnson had no romantic intentions toward Carter, Birch may have perceived him as an interloper in this ultimately failed courtship; consequently, the relationship between Johnson and Birch remained, at best, coolly polite.

The 1740s and 1750s were decades of considerable productivity for Birch. Starting in 1741 and continuing until 1756, he compiled and revised *The Heads and Characters of Illustrious Persons of Great Britain* (1743, 1751). Conceived as an accompaniment to *A General Dictionary,* the two volumes of this project included superb engravings by Jacobus Houbraken and George Vertue, which they created from oil paintings owned by Englishmen. Birch wrote the corresponding biographies. With eighty "heads" in the first volume and twenty-six in the second, these books were large and striking—and the families represented in them were suitably impressed: approximately 560 British families and institutions subscribed to receive this work. Also during this period, Birch compiled the works of Catharine Cockburn and the life and works of Archbishop Tillotson. Birch's most exciting scholarly task, however, came from an unanticipated source. In the summer of 1750, Thomas Herring, Archbishop of Canterbury, dropped by Birch's study with the first of sixteen volumes of the Anthony Bacon Charters and requested Birch's assistance in transcribing and editing them. These disordered and deteriorated volumes required all Birch's energies, preventing him from working on any other project or even visiting his patron, Yorke. Seventeen months later, Birch had completed work on the Charters. Anthony Bacon, the brother of Francis Bacon, was an ideal subject for Birch's historical work, and the Charters provided a wealth of information that enabled Birch to write *Memoirs of the Reign of Queen Elizabeth* (1754), on which he spent ten hours a day for two months. The Charters also enabled him to write *An Historical View of the Negotiations Between the Courts of England, France, and Brussels, from the Year 1592 to 1617* (1749) and to supplement *The Works of Francis Bacon, Baron of Verulam* (1765).

Birch performed a signal service to the Royal Society when he wrote the four-volume *The History of the Royal Society of London for Improving of Natural Knowledge* (1756–1757). Before this work, Thomas Sprat's 1667 history was the only account of the Royal Society's activities. Because Sprat concentrated on a more general justification of the society, Birch's *History of the Royal Society* offered a more thorough account of the society's work since its inception in 1660. Birch provided new information through detailed descriptions of meetings, papers presented, and written correspondence, giving readers access to the society's daily workings. Recognized as both an exacting recorder and an enthusiastic, faithful member of the society, Birch was elected its secretary in 1752. In this capacity he was given free rein over all archival material, minutes, Register-Books, Letter-Books, and other documents, which he used to present a thorough chronicle. Deeming such minute detail unnecessary and plodding, Johnson's review of *The History of the Royal Society* was less than enthusiastic. As with his other histories and biographies, Birch's *History of the Royal Society* showed his skill in compilation and editing rather than in interpretation and analysis. Although he intended to write the history of the society through 1750, Birch concluded the volumes at 1687. His diary gives no accounting for this change in plans; however, scholars speculate that Birch became overwhelmed by his duties with the newly established British Museum and that he considered the history suf-

ficiently close to the present time. Nevertheless, this work remains part of Birch's most enduring legacy to the Royal Society.

Through his membership and connections in the Royal Society, Birch received the opportunity to assist in founding the British Museum. In 1753 Sir Hans Sloane, former president of the Royal Society, left his sizable collections to a group of executors who, assisted by an Act of Parliament, established the British Museum. Birch was an elected trustee and, in that capacity, oversaw manuscript storage and transfers. Serving on the Standing Committee of Trustees, Birch helped plan building improvements, hire staff, edit documents, and manage bequests. His primary interest, however, remained the library of the British Museum, situated in Montagu House, where he spent considerable time and completed his final projects.

The years 1759 to 1766 marked a period of declining health, in which Birch published few significant works. These include *A Collection of the Yearly Bills of Mortality [within the London District] from 1657 to 1758, Inclusive* (1759); *The Life of Henry, Prince of Wales* (1760); and *Letters between Col. R. H., Governor of the Isle of Wight, and the Committee of Lords and Commons at Derby House, General Fairfax, Lieut. General Cromwell, Commissary General Ireton, Etc., Relating to King Charles I* (1764). Although he suffered from colds, influenza, rheumatism, and coughs in these last years, Birch spent at least a few days a week at the library of the British Museum to continue his transcriptions. He also continued to participate in the Royal Society until resigning from his post as secretary in 1765, just two months before his death. On 19 January 1766 Birch was thrown from his horse and died a few hours later in a fit of apoplexy. He willed his extensive library, historical documents, and personal papers to the British Library, along with £500 that would supplement the under librarians' stipends. Matthew Maty, a friend of Birch and later the principal librarian of the British Museum, catalogued the vast number of documents Birch left for future historians.

Thomas Birch was, by all accounts, a charming and affable person. While he may not have been known for originality and brilliance, neither was he known for malice or arrogance. Indeed, Birch's ability to sustain friendships produced his various church posts and scholarly opportunities, from his early usherships to his election to the board of trustees for the British Museum. Birch ultimately won his place in the history of scholarship through tireless devotion and meticulous attention to the original sources and manuscripts that enable scholars to reconstruct the past. In 1738, while they were still sociable, Samuel Johnson wrote an epigram to Birch in *The Gentleman's Magazine*:

TRUTH, in joyful witness of Thomas Birch
Author of the lives of brave, wise men
PRAYS, that when he's struck by the Spear of Death
There may arise another Birch to write of him

Birch spent years compiling and writing lives of others, and providing source material for many more biographies. That he should be acknowledged in kind seems fitting. Through his copious volumes of original manuscripts and documents, Thomas Birch has made significant and lasting contributions to historical scholarship.

References:

S. Austin Allibone, volume 1, *A Critical Dictionary of English Literature and British and American Authors, Living and Deceased, from the Earliest Accounts to the Latter Half of the Nineteenth Century,* 3 volumes (Philadelphia: Lippincott, 1902);

O. M. Brack Jr., "Johnson's 'Life of Admiral Blake' and the Development of a Biographical Technique," *Modern Philology,* 85, no. 4 (1988): 523–531;

A. E. Gunther, *An Introduction to the Life of the Rev. Thomas Birch D.D., F.R.S. 1706–1755* (Suffolk: Halesworth, 1984);

Gunther, "The Royal Society and the Foundation of the British Museum, 1753–1781," *Notes and Records of the Royal Society of London,* 33 (March 1979): 207–216;

Marie Boas Hall, "Henry Miles, F. R. S. (1698–1763) and Thomas Birch, F. R. S. (1705–1766)," *Notes and Records of the Royal Society of London,* 18 (June 1963): 39–44;

Sir John Hawkins, *The Life of Samuel Johnson, LL.D,* second edition (London: Printed for J. Buckland, J. Rivington, and others, 1787);

James Marshall Osborn, "Thomas Birch and the 'General Dictionary' (1734–1741)," *Modern Philology,* 36, no. 1 (1938): 25–46;

Edward Ruhe, "Birch, Johnson, and Elizabeth Carter: An Episode of 1738–1739," *PMLA,* 73, no. 5 (1958): 491–500.

Papers:

Thomas Birch's papers are held in the Birch Collection of the British Library, *British Library Catalogue of 1756–1782* (B.L. 1977); additional manuscripts are 4101–4478.

William Blackstone

(10 July 1723 – 14 February 1780)

Seán Patrick Donlan
University of Limerick

BOOKS: *An Essay on Collateral Consanguinity, It's Limits, Extent, and Duration: More Particularly as It Is Regarded by the Statutes of All Souls College in the University of Oxford* (London: Printed by W. Owen, 1750); republished in *Law Tracts,* 2 volumes (Oxford: Clarendon Press, 1762);

An Analysis of the Laws of England (Oxford: Clarendon Press, 1756); revised and republished as *An Analysis of the Laws of England to Which Is Prefixed an Introductory Discourse on the Study of the Law* (Oxford: Clarendon Press, 1758);

To the Rev Dr Randolph, Vice-Chancellor of the University of Oxford (Oxford, 1757);

Considerations on the Question Whether Tenants by Copy or According to the Custom of the Manor Though Not at the Will of the Lord Are Freeholders Qualified to Vote in Elections for Knights of the Shire (London: Printed for R. Baldwin, 1758);

A Discourse on the Study of the Law, Being an Introductory Lecture, Read in the Public Schools, October 25, 1758 (Oxford: Clarendon Press, 1758);

The Great Charter and Charter of the Forest, With Other Authentic Instruments: to Which Is Prefixed an Introductory Discourse, Containing the History of the Charters (Oxford: Clarendon Press, 1759); republished in *Law Tracts,* 2 volumes (Oxford: Clarendon Press, 1762);

A Treatise on the Law of Descents in Fee-Simple (Oxford: Clarendon Press, 1759);

Reflections on the Opinions of Messrs. Pratt, Morton, and Wilbraham, Relating to Lord Leitchfield's Disqualifications (Oxford, 1759);

A Case for the Opinion of Counsel on the Right of the University to Make New Statutes (London, 1759);

Law Tracts (Oxford: Clarendon Press, 1762; republished as *Tracts, Chiefly Relating to the Antiquities and Laws of England,* third edition (Oxford: Clarendon Press, 1771);

Commentaries on the Laws of England, 4 volumes (Oxford: Clarendon Press, 1765–1769; New York: Oceana, 1966);

William Blackstone, 1774 (portrait by Thomas Gainsborough; Tate Collection, Tate Britain, London)

A Reply to Dr Priestley's Remarks on the Fourth Volume of the Commentaries of the Laws of England (London: Printed for Charles Bathurst, 1769); later included in *An Interesting Appendix to Sir William Blackstone's Commentaries, &c.* (Philadelphia: Printed by Robert Bell, 1773) and *Palladium of Conscience* (Philadelphia, 1774);

A Letter to the Author of the Question Stated, as another Member of Parliament (London: Printed for Charles Bathurst, 1769);

Reports of Several Cases Determined in the Several Courts of Westminster Hall from 1746 to 1779, 2 volumes (London: Printed at His Majesty's Law Printers, for W. Strahan, T. Cadell and D. Prince, 1781).

William Blackstone—jurist, member of Parliament, and judge—was born on 10 July 1723 in Cheapside, London, to Charles Blackstone and Mary Bigg Blackstone. He was the youngest of three children, his older brothers both becoming churchmen in the Church of England. His father, a London silk merchant, died before his birth. His mother, of a landowning Wiltshire family, died when William was only twelve. He was subsequently raised by his uncle, Thomas Bigg, a London surgeon. Through his family connections, Blackstone was nominated to Charterhouse School by former Prime Minister Sir Robert Walpole. The death of Blackstone's parents entitled him to a free education there, and he was a favorite student of the Reverend James Hotchkis. Blackstone continued his education at Pembroke College of the University of Oxford (30 November 1738). He was a good classical scholar, something of a poet, and well read in English literature. Blackstone was elected a fellow of All Souls College, Oxford, in 1743. While he completed an unpublished treatise on architecture in the same period, he moved to the law faculty in 1740.

At Oxford, Blackstone studied Civil law, that based on the law of ancient Rome and still of considerable importance on the European continent. Although it was of limited relevance to a legal career in England, it was the only education in law then available in the English universities. The following year Blackstone entered the Middle Temple, one of London's "Inns of Court" in which English, Welsh, and Irish lawyers were then trained in the Common law, the legal system unique to England. He was, with many others of the day, deeply critical of the illiberal nature of English legal education. Training for future lawyers had long centered on the Inns of Court (the Inner Temple, Middle Temple, Gray's Inn, and Lincoln's Inn) and lesser Inns of Chancery. By the eighteenth century, the performance of legal exercises and requirements of residence at the Inns had become mere formalities, frequently excused for a small fee. Students were, in effect, required to educate themselves by self-directed reading or attendance in lawyers' chambers and the courts. Even the study of the Civil law at Oxford and Cambridge was in decline.

Blackstone bypassed the degree of Bachelor of Arts, perhaps for financial reasons. He received his Bachelor of Civil Law at Oxford in 1745, was called to the Bar the following year, and began to practice law. On the resignation of his uncle Seymour Richmond, Blackstone was also made Recorder (judge) of the borough of Wallingford, Berkshire (1749–1770). He was not successful in legal practice and returned to Oxford in 1753. There he continued a long association with All Souls College. He was junior and subsequently senior bursar of the college, as well as steward of the manors. He supervised the completion of the Codrington Library, took part in debates on the fate of the Bodleian Library and adjacent Radcliffe Camera, and assisted in the acquisition of the Pomfret Marbles. Blackstone also began writing for various purposes, including pieces on the accounts and privileges of the college. Perhaps most notably, he did much to reform the inefficient administration of Oxford's Clarendon Press. He was also made assessor in the university's Chancellor's Court (1753–1759).

During the mid eighteenth century a fundamental shift in British political alignments took place and, consequently, one in the language of public debates. These changes were particularly relevant to Blackstone's political activities and legal writings. They were, however, ultimately rooted in the political divisions of the previous century. The development of European historiography had been closely linked to legal scholarship on the Continent. But this legal humanism had little influence in England. The Common law was deeply historical; connected to the past through the cumulative development of precedent in legal judgments, English history was limited. As a result, English writers on law often lacked historical perspective. In an age obsessed with the origins of political obligation, ancient English history was of great importance to modern political debates. Sir Edward Coke, jurist and lord chief justice of England, common lawyers generally, and seventeenth-century Whigs were central to the political and legal arguments of both the seventeenth and eighteenth centuries.

"Whiggish" histories emphasized English exceptionalism and the virtues of its "ancient constitution" or structures of government. The more crude of these histories combined many propositions: the existence of perennial principles and immemorial institutions linking the present with the past, the relative insularity of English law, the role of Anglo-Saxon lawgivers in the introduction of shires and juries, and the antiquity of a Parliament, especially the House of Commons. They denied a Norman "conquest," which, according to contemporary legalism, would have validated both Norman changes to English law and subsequent monarchical privileges. They identified Norman tyranny, the so-called "Norman yoke," as the source of many of the ills of later English governments. The historians and laymen taking this approach also idealized the Magna Carta, or "Great Charter," the compact made between King John and his English barons in 1215. They often viewed it as a reaffirmation of the ancient liberties of the Saxon nation generally, rather than the liberties of the barons themselves. With the *Carta de foresta,* or "Charter of the Forest," the Magna Carta was perhaps the most important document in English legal and political history and mythology.

Connected to these arguments in the seventeenth century was the contemporaneous dominance of Common law over other more European-influenced English courts. While numerous, such courts—including the Equity, Admiralty, and Ecclesiastical courts—continued to be important, though they were increasingly subordinated to the principles and procedures of Common law. This subordination occurred, in no small part, through the efforts of Sir Edward Coke against English "civilians," or civil lawyers. In the seventeenth century, the Common law became synonymous with English law. These arguments were simultaneously employed against King James's claims to expansive royal powers, and consequently became entwined with broader constitutional critiques. Later, after long years of regicide, interregnum, and restoration, such Whiggish views became enshrined in English thought with the political structures erected in the Glorious Revolution of 1688. The ancient constitution, or that version created in the seventeenth century, thus established a model by which eighteenth-century claims about the separation of political powers was judged.

With many others, Blackstone's thought was deeply colored by the belief in England's ancient constitution. Other eighteenth-century political developments were also crucial. Political parties in the modern sense did not exist, and relationships between statesmen were fluid. Whiggish accounts of English history were initially associated with political Whigs. When in opposition in the early century, these Whigs had combined this history with "commonwealth" language, charging the government with acting on factional interests rather than political virtue and thereby corrupting the equilibrium of the ancient constitution. But with a long period of Whig political dominance under Harold Walpole, their political rivals, the Tories, adopted a similar critique against the Whig establishment. Especially in the work of Henry St. John, Lord Bolingbroke, such language of opposition became linked to the ancient constitution and the Common law. Political Tories thus maintained a view of history and of politics that reflected the Whiggish beliefs of the previous century.

From these complex sources, Blackstone's own historical and political beliefs were formed. He identified with the history of the seventeenth-century Common lawyers and Whigs, but his politics were those of mid-eighteenth-century Tories. In 1750 he received his Doctor of Civil Law degree, in part to qualify for a vote in the Oxford elections. He was involved in the election

of the chancellor of the university in 1758–1759 and the debates over the Laudian Statutes, which governed Oxford. Blackstone's political activities were not, however, merely academic. In the election for Oxford's parliamentary seat in 1754, he lobbied aggressively for Tory landowner Sir Roger Newdigate. Newdigate successfully defeated Robert Harney, the chosen candidate of then prime minister Henry Pelham. Blackstone remained a loyal, if politically undistinguished, Tory throughout his life.

Blackstone's legal pedagogy and scholarship, rather than his politics, secured his reputation. In England there had been discussion for centuries of providing university education in the Common law. But only in the eighteenth century was university education established in any meaningful sense in national law, as opposed to the Civil law and Canon law, in England or, for that matter, in France, Spain, or America. Blackstone's Oxford professorship of English law was made possible by the bequest of jurist Charles Viner, whose will had, as early as 1752, stipulated its establishment. In addition to *A General Abridgement of Law and Equity* (1742–1753), a massive work of legal reference, Viner left Oxford his law library and an estate of about £12,000. It was the largest benefaction received by the university in the eighteenth century.

Blackstone had applied for the Oxford Chair of Civil Law in the early 1750s. He lost to the less competent, but more politically acceptable, Robert Jenner. Blackstone quit his legal practice and initiated popular, but unofficial, lectures at Oxford on the Common law. He may have taken this course of action at the suggestion of William Murray, Lord Mansfield, one of the greatest Common-law judges of the century. Borrowing from Continental and Common-law sources, Blackstone in 1756 published *An Analysis of the Laws of England.* In it he laid out a skeletal scheme for legal education. He subsequently secured the Oxford chair after a long struggle and began the first formal university lectures on the Common law in October 1758, following the pattern of his earlier lectures. He argued that the English were, in comparison with the political elite of the Continent, deficient in an understanding of their own laws and constitution. Moreover, as he later wrote in *Commentaries,* the universities, rather than the Inns, were the proper place in which to study and teach the "rational science" of law.

Blackstone sought to provide a more liberal education in the law than that previously provided, balancing an understanding of legal principles with the practical education of the Inns. In *A Discourse on the Study of the Law* (1758), which later made up the first chapter of his *Commentaries on the Laws of England* (1765–1769), Blackstone wrote:

> If practice is the whole he [the law student] is taught, practice must also be the whole he will ever know: if he be uninstructed in the elements and first principles upon which the rule of practice is founded, the least variation from established precedents will totally distract and bewilder him; *ita lex scripta est* [thus the law was written] is the utmost his knowledge will arrive at; he must never aspire to form, and seldom expect to comprehend, any arguments drawn *a priori,* from the spirit of the laws and the natural foundation of justice.

In providing a general overview of the law, Blackstone sought to educate not only students but also the English landed classes and those who might become legislators. Citing Cicero, he argued that undeniably a "competent knowledge" of one's law was "the proper accomplishment of every gentleman and scholar; an highly useful, I had almost said essential, part of liberal and polite education." In the same period he published, as a result of a Bodleian benefaction, critical editions of the two charters in *The Great Charter and Charter of the Forest* (1759).

The Oxford effort at reform of English legal education was not entirely isolated. Trinity College, Dublin, inaugurated a similar professorship just a few years later. In 1762 the Inns themselves attempted to standardize the conditions required for a call to the Bar and to induce gentlemen to become barristers, including waivers of two years on the required terms for students of Oxford and Cambridge. But few of these attempts were successful. At Oxford, too, lesser men followed Blackstone, and the experiment in university-level legal education was rarely repeated in the following century. Not until the twentieth century did a university education become the typical route to a legal career in Britain and Ireland.

A more lasting legacy than Blackstone's lectures was his *Commentaries on the Laws of England*. Based on his informal and formal lectures at Oxford, *Commentaries on the Laws of England* was published, he suggested, to end the circulation of pirated and inaccurate lecture notes. The lectures were updated in some areas, most notably in light of the well-known judicial decisions of Lord Mansfield. The four volumes of the work comprise approximately two thousand pages. The first volume concerned English legal and political structures generally—in effect, the constitutional law of England. The second book dealt with property law; the third, with civil procedures and remedies; and the fourth, with criminal law and procedure.

The *Commentaries on the Laws of England* reflected a general European trend toward writing elementary textbooks treating national laws as a comprehensive system. Throughout eighteenth-century Europe, the development of university-level instruction in national law was combined with the creation of student texts written in the vernacular rather than Latin. These were "institutional," considerably influenced by the structures of Roman law, especially Emperor Justinian's *Institutes* (533), a student text simplifying the more elaborate *Digest* (533). Blackstone similarly drew on both European and English sources, including Sir Matthew Hale's seventeenth-century *Analysis of the Civil Part of the Law* (published posthumously, 1713). The arrangement of Blackstone's *Commentaries on the Laws of England* was especially important in making the Common law appear rational and systematic. Given the complexity and singularity of English law, both medieval and modern, this was no small achievement.

In addition to legal and historical observations in the works of Coke, Hale's Whiggish *History of the Common law of England* (published posthumously, 1713) was a significant influence on Blackstone. Indeed, much of the *Commentaries on the Laws of England* is dedicated to historical explanations of the origins of the Common law and of the constitutional structures of England. Blackstone married a Whiggish emphasis on the primitive virtues of the early Anglo-Saxons with a belief in the progressive return, following the Norman invasion, to the principles and liberties of the ancient constitution. He saw the period after the Norman invasion as "a gradual restoration of the ancient constitution, whereof our Saxon forefathers had been unjustly deprived, partly by the policy, and partly by the force, of the Normans." English history was, in significant measure, a legal history.

After an introductory lecture on legal study, in effect his earlier *Discourse on the Study of the Law,* Blackstone began the first book of the *Commentaries on the Laws of England* with a discussion of the "law of nature." Such a beginning was largely commonplace, but it helped to locate the law within a long tradition of moral and legal philosophy and to suggest the Common law's adherence to the requirements of natural law. In presenting this introduction, he relied heavily on the standard sources of the day, including the works of John Locke and Continental jurists Hugo Grotius, Samuel von Pufendorf, and Jean Burlamaqui. Blackstone was, however, critical of the more radical potential of these theories. For example, on the idea of a "social contract," he wrote, "Not that we believe, with some theoretical writers, that there ever was a time when there was no such thing as society, either natural or civil; but that, from the impulse of reason, and through a sense of their wants and weaknesses, individuals met together in a large plain, entered into an original contract, and chose the tallest man present to be their governor. . . ." In the English political context, Blackstone was careful to interpret natural law without the revolutionary implications of Locke.

But Blackstone has been judged a poor philosopher by most commentators. His discussion of natural law sits uneasily with his explanation of the powers of the British Parliament and the history of the Common-law courts. Appearing to disregard all he had said of the law of nature, Blackstone assigned an unlimited power of lawmaking to Parliament. If "the parliament will positively enact a thing to be done which is unreasonable," he wrote, "I know of no power that can control it: and the examples usually alleged in support of this sense of the rule do none of them prove, that where the main object of a statute is unreasonable the judges are at liberty to reject it; for that were to set the judicial power above that of the legislature, which would be subversive of all government." While this point may be read as practical, rather than philosophical, it is not unproblematic. Blackstone's account of parliamentary supremacy left language pregnant for future developments, especially in the next century, in which legislation (and its theoretical counterpart "legal positivism") became increasingly important in English law. But he devoted little attention to statute law, reflecting his view of its marginality in comparison to the judgments of the courts. He was, in fact, often hostile to legislation, seeing the legislature as largely responsible for the few failures of the Common law.

Like the belief in the ancient constitution, of which it was a central element, the Common law was mythologized by Blackstone and many of his contemporaries. In addition to his problematic account of natural law and legislation, Blackstone defended the traditional image of the Common law as the common custom of England. The Common law evolved on the basis of innumerable judgments, the case law, or jurisprudence made by the courts. In this way, it was often seen as rising up from among the English peoples to be confirmed by the courts. Statutes were seen simply to work remedially within the limits of the Common law. But insofar as this account was ever true, the eighteenth-century Common law was the antithesis of social practice. It was a judicial, rather than a popular, custom. In *Commentaries on the Laws of England,* Blackstone wrote that Common-law judges were "the depository of the laws; the living oracles, who must decide in all cases of doubt, and who are bound by an oath to decide according to the law of the land." Readers were, in effect, able to choose the emphasis—natural law, legislation, or case law—that suited them.

Following a scheme devised in the previous century by Hale, the second book of the *Commentaries on the Laws of England* deals with the laws of property. The importance of land, or "real property," linked to aristoc-

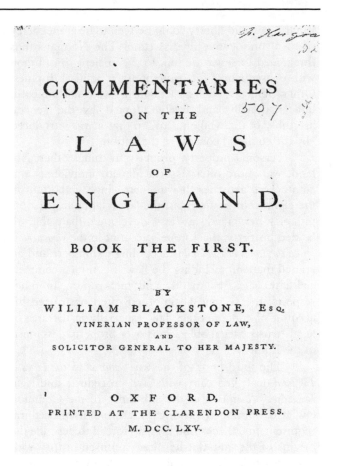

COMMENTARIES
ON THE
L A W S
OF
E N G L A N D.

BOOK THE FIRST.

BY
WILLIAM BLACKSTONE, Esq.
VINERIAN PROFESSOR OF LAW,
AND
SOLICITOR GENERAL TO HER MAJESTY.

OXFORD,
PRINTED AT THE CLARENDON PRESS.
M. DCC. LXV.

Title page for the first volume of Blackstone's monumental work on British Common law (Eighteenth-Century Collections Online, Gale Group)

racy and consequently to governance, remained central to the political structures of eighteenth-century England and Europe. While Blackstone engages in some speculation about the origins of property, he views these as largely irrelevant to contemporary law. Original, natural rights to property had long since been altered and were meaningless in eighteenth-century civil (or civilized) society. Feudal in origin, the rights to landed property were communitarian, rather than individualistic. As a result, such property resided not in individuals but in families, through generations. In addition, English "estates" were not the absolute ownership of land, but an interest in it for a period of time.

The discussion of property in the *Commentaries on the Laws of England* was also important to Blackstone's account of English history. Like many Whiggish historians, he blamed William "the conqueror" and the Normans for the corruption of English liberty. He denied, however, that William actually "gained England by right of conquest." Blackstone had to deny that idea because a "conquest" legally implied that all previous laws had been invalidated by the will of the conqueror.

English law and liberty could be seen to be at the mercy of royal prerogative or discretion. The Normans thus threatened to sever the link to the ancient constitution with consequences for contemporary political disputes. Other elements, such as feudalism, were not imposed, but "nationally and freely adopted by the general assembly of the whole realm" so that it was introduced "by the common consent of the nation."

Personal property, property in things other than land, was more often associated with individuals and commercial activities. It was increasingly important in the eighteenth century, but the law relating to personal property remained far less developed than that of landed property. Blackstone's account in the *Commentaries on the Laws of England* is accordingly thin here and on related matters, including the law of contract, commercial law, sales, bailments, and bankruptcy. In other respects, the scheme he imposed often obstructed his account of contemporary law, especially in the area of legal "trusts," legal obligations over property developed in the Equity courts.

The third book of the *Commentaries on the Laws of England* deals generally with civil procedures and legal remedies. As much of the substance of the Common law had developed historically around its procedural requirements, Blackstone is again forced to describe the origins of the law. But he often confused history with antiquarianism and frequently antedated English institutions. The modern structure of the English courts was, he argued, built on an ancient design instituted by King Alfred (871–901) and subsequently perfected by King Edward I (1272–1307). Perhaps Blackstone's most famous image was his analogy between the inheritance of the Common law development and "an old Gothic castle, erected in the days of chivalry, but fitted up for a modern inhabitant. The moated ramparts, the embattled towers, and the trophied halls are magnificent and venerable, but useless. The interior apartments, now converted into rooms of convenience, are chearful and commodious, though their approaches may be winding and difficult." Given the piecemeal development of English Common law and Blackstone's earlier interest in architecture, the metaphor is particularly interesting. In other parts of the book, including a discussion of the jurisdiction of the Ecclesiastical courts, he engaged in the anti-Catholic asides that are strewn throughout the *Commentaries on the Laws of England*.

The third book of Blackstone's *Commentaries on the Laws of England* also includes his praise of the trial by jury. The English jury trial involved laymen, rather than a judge or a body of judges as was common throughout Europe, in elements of decision-making in the courts. In *L'esprit des lois* (The Spirit of the Laws, 1748), one of the major works of European thought in the eighteenth century, Charles-Louis de Secondat, Baron de Montesquieu, had praised the English constitution. Blackstone was deeply influenced by the work, and he cites it repeatedly. But the Frenchman suggested that the liberty of England, as had the liberties of the ancient world, would ultimately perish. Related to contemporary debates over legislative changes in the powers of the jury, Blackstone took exception to Montesquieu's remarks. Blackstone suggests that the ancients had never known the English jury.

In the same book, Blackstone deals with the relationship of the Common-law and Equity courts. The Equity courts were originally created to alleviate the rigor of the Common law. They were substantively and procedurally similar to continental Civil law courts. In the *Commentaries on the Laws of England* Blackstone confusingly uses the term "equity" both in its specific meaning connected to the Equity courts and in the wider sense of justice. Perhaps under the influence of Lord Mansfield's judicial decisions, his explanation of Equity law diverges from that initially given in the Oxford lectures. Blackstone seems to agree with Mansfield's attempts to join the principles of both Common law and Equity courts. Indeed, their views are largely consistent in many areas of law, including the "law merchant," a body of law related to the usages and customs of merchants throughout Europe and traditionally administered in special courts. Mansfield sought, often successfully, to incorporate the principles of the law merchant into the Common law. His views agree, too, with Blackstone's in the areas of contract and quasi-contract, in which contractual obligations are imposed in the absence of real contracts.

The fourth book of the *Commentaries on the Laws of England* largely deals with criminal law and procedure. Blackstone's general complacency is less pronounced than elsewhere in the work. His comments were written in the context of widespread European criticism of the abuses of criminal or penal law. He is aware, for example, of Italian reformist Cesare Beccaria, whose *Dei delitti e delle pene* (1764) had just been translated into English in 1767 as *On Crimes and Punishments*. Blackstone recognized the particularly violent sentences of English law, however often mitigated in practice, and suggested modest reforms.

He ends the *Commentaries on the Laws of England* with a brief, and entirely uncritical, description of the "Rise, Progress and Gradual Improvements of the Laws of England." This progress was often a restoration of ancient liberties. The jury, for example, "this admirable criterion of truth, and most important guardian both of public and private liberty, we owe to our Saxon ancestors." He attributes to Alfred the centralization, and Edward I the elaboration, of the Common-law courts.

While the arrival of the Danes or Vikings set things back, with their expulsion, English law returned to the path of progress. Blackstone credits King Edgar (circa 943–975) for both establishing an English navy and initiating a digest or collection of laws subsequently completed by Edward the Confessor (1003–1066). The arrival of the Normans was more problematic than that of the Vikings; the results of the Normans' actions took centuries to correct. "From so complete and well concerted a scheme of servility," Blackstone wrote, "it has been the work of generations for our ancestors, to redeem themselves and their posterity into that state of liberty, which we now enjoy."

The Magna Carta and the Charter of the Forest were critical elements of this return to the ancient constitution. More surprisingly, Blackstone claims that the constitution reached its zenith in the reign of King Charles II (1630–1685). As Blackstone saw them, the seventeenth-century Restoration and the Habeus Corpus Act of 1679 removed the final vestiges of Norman oppression and secured English liberty. Blackstone ends by writing that

> Of a constitution, so wisely contrived, so strongly raised, and so highly furnished, it is hard to speak with that praise, which is justly and severely its due: . . . the thorough and attentive contemplation of it will furnish its best panegyric. It has been the endeavor of these commentaries, however the execution may have succeeded, to examine its solid foundations, to mark out its extensive plan, to explain the use and distribution of its parts, and from the harmonious concurrence of those several parts to demonstrate the elegant proportion of the whole.

Far from being a strictly legal treatise, Blackstone's *Commentaries on the Laws of England* was the culmination of Whiggish English histories.

The *Commentaries on the Laws of England* went through eight English editions during Blackstone's lifetime. It is the most significant work of Anglo-American legal scholarship in the eighteenth century, perhaps the most important book ever written on the Common law. Whatever its failings, Blackstone put the law into a comprehensive and reasonably organized form. If he was generally complacent and conservative, this ordering of the law made possible future reforms. It also permitted the Common law to withstand the codification movement of the nineteenth century, involving the systematic ordering and often modernizing revision of the law.

Blackstone's *Commentaries on the Laws of England* was especially influential in America, both before and especially after independence from Britain. Men as diverse as Alexander Hamilton, James Wilson, Thomas Jefferson, James Marshall, James Kent, and Joseph Story acknowledged, sometimes grudgingly, debts of different sorts to Blackstone. The comparative brevity and depth of the work was especially useful considering the absence of an American "Inn" and scarce law libraries. The new American nation also often looked to Civil law sources, and without the *Commentaries on the Laws of England* the United States might have received or adopted Continental law, rather than retaining Common law.

But Blackstone's life involved much more than the Oxford professorship and the *Commentaries on the Laws of England*. In 1761 he had married Sara Clitherow, eldest surviving daughter of the late James and Philippa Clitherow of Boston House, Brentford, Middlesex. His marriage brought many connections and much wealth. The same year he was elected a member of the Society of Antiquaries in recognition of his work on the Magna Carta. He also became King's Counsel. With the cajoling of William Petty Fitzmaurice, then Lord Shelburne, and the financial assistance of John Stuart, Lord Bute, Blackstone entered the House of Commons for Hindon in Wiltshire (1761–1768) to provide Tory support for the Bute administration. He was also offered, but declined, the chief justiceship of the Common Pleas of Ireland. He was shortly afterwards appointed a Bencher of Middle Temple and the Solicitor General to the Queen (1763), the title he used in the *Commentaries on the Laws of England*. He refused, however, the more political office of Solicitor General to the King. While Blackstone spent less and less time at Oxford, he held the principalship of New Inn Hall (1761–1766) and did not resign from his professorship until 1766.

On the basis of his assistance to Willoughby Bertie, earl of Abingdon, Blackstone was returned to Parliament as a member for Westbury in Wiltshire (1768–1770). As in the courts, however, he was not a success in Parliament. While the *Commentaries on the Laws of England* brought him fame and widespread praise, his political opinions often made him unpopular. He opposed, for example, the claims of the American colonists. He also actively sought the expulsion of John Wilkes in contradiction, as his opponents quickly pointed out, to the grounds laid out in the first edition of the *Commentaries on the Laws of England*. Blackstone declined again the position of Solicitor General to the King, but accepted a judgeship in the Court of Common Pleas (9 February 1770). He moved up temporarily to the King's Bench to accommodate another judge, Justice Yates. With Yates's death, Blackstone requested and received an appointment again with the Court of Common Pleas (22 June 1770). His judicial career was no more distinguished than his legal practice or parliamentary work, and his judicial decisions frequently generated new trials. His most famous judicial accomplishment was the reversal of Lord Mansfield's judgment in *Perrin v Blake* (1770), on a question of the law of real property.

While Blackstone's account of English history was seldom challenged, the *Commentaries on the Laws of England* did not go uncriticized. Dissenting ministers Joseph Priestley and Philip Furneaux challenged Blackstone's support of legal restraints on religious nonconformity. Blackstone responded with a pamphlet, but softened his remarks in future editions. He also made other changes in comments on slavery, the classification of colonies, and parliamentary privilege in the editions published before his death. Blackstone was also criticized by Irish writers who insisted that he had overstated the power of the British Parliament in respect to Ireland. He was criticized most notably, however, by philosopher-political theorist Jeremy Bentham. Bentham had attended Blackstone's lectures in the 1760s before the publication of the *Commentaries on the Laws of England*. In his *Fragment on Government* (1776), he attacked Blackstone's abilities as a philosopher and was particularly critical of Blackstone's conservatism and complacency. Though often unfair and pedantic, Bentham's remarks were highly influential in later assessment of Blackstone's achievement. More than any other, Bentham's pupil, John Austin, continued these criticisms into the nineteenth century.

William Blackstone spent the last twenty years of his life with his family at Priory Place (later Castle Priory) in Wallingford, Berkshire. He fathered nine children and was survived by seven of them, four sons and three daughters. His second son, James, later became the fourth Vinerian Professor of Common law at Oxford. Already by the 1770s, the senior Blackstone's health was failing, and he suffered bouts of gout and anxiety. After days of unconsciousness, he died of dropsy on 14 February 1780 at Wallingford, Berkshire, and is buried in the parish church there.

As a law lecturer at Oxford and as the author of *The Commentaries on the Laws of England*, Blackstone remains important to jurists and political scientists. His status as an historian, even judged by the standards of his time, is less secure.

References:

Harold J. Berman and Charles J. Reid, "The Transformation of English Legal Science: from Hale to Blackstone," *Emory Law Journal*, 45 (1996): 493–521;

Daniel J. Boorstin, *The Mysterious Science of the Law: An Essay on Blackstone's Commentaries Showing How Blackstone, Employing Eighteenth-Century Ideas of Science, Religion, History, Aesthetics, and Philosophy, Made of the Law at Once a Conservative and a Mysterious Science* (Chicago: University of Chicago Press, 1941);

J. W. Cairns, "Blackstone, the Ancient Constitution and the Feudal Law," *The Historical Journal*, 28 (1985): 711–717;

Cairns, "Blackstone: An English Institutist: Legal Literature and the Rise of the Nation State," *Oxford Journal of Legal Studies*, 4 (1984): 318–360;

I. G. Doolittle, "Sir William Blackstone and his Commentaries on the Laws of England (1765–1769): A Biographical Approach," *Oxford Journal of Legal Studies*, 3 (1983): 99–112;

Doolittle, *William Blackstone: A Biography* (Haslemere: I. Doolittle, 2001);

[D. Douglas], *The Biographical History of Sir William Blackstone* (London: Douglas, 1782);

Catherine Spicer Eller, *The Sir William Blackstone Collection in the Yale Law Library: A Bibliographical Catalogue* (New Haven: Yale University Press, 1938);

John Finnis, "Blackstone's Theoretical Intentions," *Natural Law Forum*, 12 (1967): 163–183;

M. D. Gordon, "The Vinerian Chair: An Atlantic Perspective," in *The Life of the Law: Proceedings of the Tenth British Legal History Conference–Oxford 1991*, edited by Peter Birks (London: The Hambledon Press, 1993), pp. 195–209;

Harold Greville Hanbury, *The Vinerian Chair and Legal Education* (Oxford: Basil Blackwell, 1958);

W. S. Holdsworh, "Some Aspects of Blackstone and His Commentaries," *Cambridge Law Journal*, 4 (1932): 261;

Gareth H. Jones, "William Blackstone," in *Biographical Dictionary of the Common Law*, edited by A. W. B. Simpson (London: Butterworths, 1984), pp. 57–61;

Jones, ed., *The Sovereignty of the Law: Selections from Blackstone's Commentaries on the Laws of England* (Toronto: University of Toronto Press, 1973);

Duncan Kennedy, "The Structure of Blackstone's Commentaries," *Buffalo Law Review*, 28 (1979): 205;

David Lemmings, "Blackstone and Law Reform by Education: Preparation for the Bar and Lawyerly Culture in Eighteenth-Century England," *Law & History Review*, 16 (1998): 211–255;

David Lieberman, "Blackstone's Science of Legislation," *Journal of British Studies*, 27 (1988): 117–149;

Lieberman, *The Province of Legislation Determined: Legal Theory in Eighteenth-Century Britain* (Cambridge: Cambridge University Press, 1989);

Michael Lobban, "Blackstone and the Science of Law," *Historical Journal*, 30 (1987): 311–335;

D. A. Lockmiller, *Sir William Blackstone* (Gloucester, Mass.: Peter Smith, 1938);

G. P. Macdonnell, "Blackstone, Sir William (1723–1780), Legal Writer and Judge," in *Dictionary of National Biography,* edited by Leslie Stephen (London: Smith, Elder, 1886), V: 133–140;

S. F. C. Milsom, "The Nature of Blackstone's Achievement," *Oxford Journal of Legal Studies,* 1 (1981): 1–12;

I. G. Phillip, *William Blackstone and the Reform of the Oxford University Press in the Eighteenth Century* (Oxford: Oxford University Press, 1957);

Gerard Postema, *Bentham and the Common Law Tradition* (Oxford: Clarendon Press, 1986);

Wilfred Prest, "Blackstone as Architect: Constructing the Commentaries," *Yale Journal of Law & Humanities,* 15 (2003): 103–133;

Lucy Sutherland, "William Blackstone and the Legal Chairs at Oxford," in *Evidence in Literary Scholarship: Essays in Memory of James Marshall Osborn,* edited by René Wellek and Alvaro Ribeiro (Oxford: Oxford University Press, 1979), pp. 229–240;

Lewis Christopher Warden, *The Life of Blackstone* (Charlottesville, Va.: Michie, 1938);

Julian S. Waterman, "Mansfield and Blackstone's Commentaries," *University of Chicago Law Review,* 1 (1933–1934): 549–571;

Alan Watson, "The Structure of Blackstone's Commentaries," *Yale Law Journal,* 97 (1988): 795.

Papers:

William Blackstone's papers are scattered. An annotated edition detailing their location can be found at the University of Adelaide. A bibliography of manuscripts and other original sources can be found in Doolittle (2001).

Henry St. John, first Viscount Bolingbroke

(16 September 1678 – 12 December 1751)

Robert W. Haynes
Texas A&M International University

See also the Bolingbroke entry in *DLB 101: British Prose Writers, 1660–1800, First Series.*

BOOKS: *A Letter to the Examiner* (London, 1710);

Considerations on the Secret History of the White Staff (London: Printed for A. Moore, 1714?);

The Representation of the Right Honourable the Lord Viscount Bolingbroke (London: Printed for J. Morphew, 1715);

The Occasional Writer, nos. 1–3 (London: Printed for A. Moore, 1727);

The Craftsman Extraordinary: Containing an Answer to the Defense of the Enquiry into the Reasons of the Conduct of Great Britain (London: Printed for R. Francklin, 1729);

Observations on the Publick Affairs of Great-Britain: With Some Toughts [sic] *on the Treaty Concluded and Signed (On What Terms God Knows) at Seville in Spain, Between His Catholick Majesty and the King of Great-Britain* (London: Printed for the author, 1729);

The Case of Dunkirk Faithfully Stated and Impartially Considered (London: Printed for A. Moore, 1730);

A Letter to Caleb D'Anvers, Esq.; Concerning the State of Affairs in Europe (London: Printed for R. Francklin, 1730);

A Final Answer to the Remarks on the Craftsman's Vindication (London: Printed for R. Francklin, 1731);

The Freeholder's Political Catechism (London: Printed for James Roberts, 1733; Dublin: Printed for T. Moore, 1733);

A Dissertation upon Parties: In Several Letters to Caleb D'Anvers, Esq.; Dedicated to the Right Honourable Sir Robert Walpole (London: Printed by H. Haines at R. Francklin's, 1735);

Letters to a Young Nobleman on the Study and Use of History (London: Privately printed, 1738); republished as *Letters of the Study and Use of History,* 2 volumes (London: Printed for A. Millar, 1752); corrected edition published as *Letters on the Study and Use of History. [To Which Are Added, Two Other Letters, and*

Henry St. John, first Viscount Bolingbroke (portrait by Charles Jervas; Government Art Collection, United Kingdom <http://www.gac.culture.gov.uk>)

Reflections upon Exile], 2 volumes (London: Printed for A. Millar, 1752);

Some Observations on the Occasional Writer: Numb. IV; Wherein the Folly and Treachery of That Writer Is Expos'd, and Set in a True Light (London: Printed for James Roberts, 1738);

The Idea of a Patriot King (London: Printed for T. C., 1740);

Remarks on the History of England: From the Minutes of Humphrey Oldcastle, Esq. (London: Printed for R. Francklin, 1743);

The Philosophical Works of the Late Right Honorable Henry St. John, Lord Viscount Bolingbroke, 5 volumes (London, 1745);

A Collection of Political Tracts (Edinburgh, 1747);

A Familiar Epistle to the Most Impudent Man Living (London: Printed for J. Millan, 1749);

Letters; On the Spirit of Patriotism: On the Idea of a Patriot King: and On the State of Parties, at the Accession of King George the First (London: Printed for A. Millar, 1749; Philadelphia: Printed & sold by B. Franklin & D. Hall, 1749);

Memoirs of the Life and Ministerial Conduct, with Some Free Remarks on the Political Writings, of the Late Lord Bolingbroke (London, 1752);

Reflections Concerning Innate Moral Principles (London: Printed for S. Bladon, 1752);

A Letter to Sir William Windham. II. Some Reflections on the Present State of the Nation. III. A Letter to Mr. Pope (London: Printed for A. Millar, 1753).

Editions and Collections: *The Philosophical Works of the Late Right Honorable Henry St. John, Lord Viscount Bolingbroke,* 5 volumes, edited by David Mallet (London: Printed for David Mallet, 1754);

The Misscellaneous [sic] *Works of the Right Honourable Henry St. John, Lord Viscount Bolingbroke,* 4 volumes (Edinburgh: Printed for A. Donaldson, 1768);

The Works of Lord Bolingbroke, 4 volumes (London: Henry G. Bohn, 1844; reprinted, London: Frank Cass, 1967);

Bolingbroke's Defense of the Treaty of Utrecht, edited by G. M. Trevelyan (Cambridge: Cambridge University Press, 1932);

Historical Writings, edited by Isaac Kramnick (Chicago: University of Chicago Press, 1972);

Contributions to the Craftsman, edited by Simon Varey (Oxford: Clarendon Press, 1982);

Bolingbroke: Political Writings, edited by David Armitage (Cambridge: Cambridge University Press, 1997).

The eloquent and erudite Henry St. John, first Viscount Bolingbroke played the game of politics with a tremendous vigor and imagination that won him the admiration of such notable writers as Jonathan Swift and Alexander Pope, but his opportunism and reported lack of principle ultimately led to his relegation to the role of historian, political journalist, and critic. At one critical point in the course of his turbulent public career, he went so far as to flee England for France, where he invited accusations of treasonable conduct by associating himself with the Pretender, James Edward Stuart, the exiled son of King James II.

After the disintegration of this inauspicious relationship, Bolingbroke eventually won permission to return to England, where, excluded from Parliament, he increasingly devoted his energies to writing political and philosophical works while serving as a central figure of a group of philosophers and literary men. His historical writings often reflect efforts to influence specific contemporary political decisions, though his growing recognition of the unlikelihood of his return to power led to efforts to establish a record of his own perspectives on history itself.

Born in Wiltshire to aristocratic parents Henry St. John and Mary Rich, young Henry was raised mainly by his conservative grandparents. He attended a school that has not been identified, and thereafter led an uninhibited youthful existence. John Churton Collins suggests that St. John was emulating his cousin, rakehell poet John Wilmot, Earl of Rochester. In any case, the young man eagerly embraced a life of hedonism and freethinking. Gifted with a powerful memory and remarkable eloquence, he developed his abilities further in travel upon the Continent, where he acquired an excellent command of French. Upon his return he was persuaded to continue his family's tradition of political engagement, and he successfully sought a seat in the House of Commons. He found Parliament congenial to his rhetorical and organizational skills and soon was in the thick of political events, distinguishing himself early as a man of ability and promise.

The British political environment in the early eighteenth century was substantially defined by issues that derived from the Glorious Revolution of 1688, when the last Stuart king, the Catholic James II, went into exile and was replaced by the Protestant William III. The Whig and Tory parties retained in some fashion the essential vestiges of their old inclinations as, respectively, Roundheads and Cavaliers, but there were also great differences: for example, the Tory party included a contingent of pro-Stuart politicians, the so-called Jacobites, as well as a majority professing loyalty to the reigning sovereign. In 1700 St. John married Frances Winchcombe, an heiress, and in 1701 he took his seat in Parliament as a Tory.

The leader of the Tory party was Robert Harley, and St. John rapidly developed an effective working relationship with him. St. John was energetic and soon achieved distinction in the party, assuming key roles in specific legislative projects and employing his persuasive talents in the give-and-take of political maneuvering. By 1704, after the death of King William (1702) and the coronation of Queen Anne, St. John had become Harley's secretary at war, a post he held until 1708. In this position, he was responsible for providing support for the British forces engaged on the Continent, and he consequently established a friendship with English general John Churchill, the first Duke of Marlborough.

In 1708 Harley and St. John resigned their administrative posts. St. John lost his parliamentary seat in the election of that year as well and was not returned to the House of Commons for two years. He returned in 1710 as Harley's secretary of state. The once-cordial relationship between Harley and St. John was giving way to suspicion and animosity, however, and a competitive if subdued hostility arose between the two Tory leaders. They continued to work together, nonetheless, as the Tories established a party journal, *The Examiner,* in which St. John published some pieces. This year also marked the beginning of St. John's friendship with Swift. The most significant of St. John's early publications was *A Letter to The Examiner,* which appeared in 1710. In this letter explaining the purpose of the new Tory publication he outlined some of his party's objectives and pointed out that the continued involvement of England in the continental war was not in the national interest. St. John's involvement with *The Examiner* was his first effort in political journalism in a period when the possibilities of such journalism were just being discovered. He wrote other articles for *The Examiner* before the burden of producing the journal was shifted to Swift in late 1710.

Upon resuming his career in political office, St. John supported efforts to end the War of the Spanish Succession, which had been declared in 1702 shortly after the death of William III. St. John's fluency in French served him well in the course of the negotiations, and the British government eventually succeeded in achieving peace by approving the Treaty of Utrecht in 1713.

In 1712 St. John had been created Viscount Bolingbroke, an honor he considered insufficient, as he had hoped to become an earl. His associate Harley had been temporarily incapacitated in an attempted assassination in 1711, thus giving St. John a seeming opportunity to eclipse his former friend; but Harley, who was made earl of Oxford soon after the attack, not only recovered but also acquired enough general sympathy to neutralize any advantage Bolingbroke might otherwise have enjoyed. Oxford did make note of Bolingbroke's opportunism, and the relations between the two men became even more strained. After the war came to an end, Bolingbroke felt himself to be strong enough to challenge Oxford for the Tory leadership, and he began an effort to discredit and supersede Oxford. Bolingbroke was eventually successful in bringing about this coup, but royal politics prevented him from profiting from his momentary victory.

Queen Anne, who had no surviving children, was in declining health, and each of the two claimants to the throne posed special problems. The Pretender, James Edward Stuart, son of James II, remained an uncom-

promising Catholic who enjoyed the patronage of the French king. Despite the presence of a substantial Jacobite minority in Parliament, the Pretender's claim to divine right was never likely to generate broad enthusiasm in post-1688 England, and his father's incompetence had not been forgotten.

The other possible successor, the aging Sophia of Hanover, granddaughter of James I, was actually never so much in consideration as was her son George Louis. George spoke no English and had little to recommend him except his status, according to the Act of Settlement (1701), as heir to his mother's claim to the English throne. Since Sophia died some two months before Queen Anne's death on 1 August 1714, George's claim was unimpeded, but his succession to the throne posed some immediate dangers to those in government, including Bolingbroke, who had been communicating surreptitiously with James Edward, the Pretender to the throne.

Bolingbroke made a public effort to establish good relations with the new king, but he was soon given to understand that George I had no sympathy for him. As the Whigs consolidated themselves in a new administration, their resentment of Bolingbroke and their suspicion of his connection to the Pretender led to the opening of an investigation of his activities. When the Whigs began seizing the papers of former Tory officials, Bolingbroke fled the country, going to France, where he was shortly in touch with James Edward. The Pretender welcomed the new expatriate at first, appointing him Secretary of State, but James Edward's court consisted of a disorganized and often quarrelsome crew, and Bolingbroke's efforts to advise the aspiring sovereign were largely unsuccessful. Though Bolingbroke opposed the plan, the Pretender insisted upon landing in Scotland in an attempt to seize the throne, and, when the invasion fell apart, James Edward removed his new advisor from office. By this time, Bolingbroke had learned that his talents were wasted in the service of such a man, and he began devoting himself to the arduous task of recovering his rights and his reputation in England, a task made more difficult by the charges of treason lodged against him by the Whigs, and particularly by their new leader, Robert Walpole, who assumed for Bolingbroke the role of archenemy. This flight from England and the subsequent public association with James Edward caused Bolingbroke a great deal of trouble almost immediately, and the conclusions drawn by many from this conduct left negative impressions that in some cases were ineradicable.

Bolingbroke's writings on history date from the period following his flight to France in 1715. His departure from England had allowed his opponents to deprive him of both his property and his political rights, but his passion for involvement kept him engaged in British politics, if at first from a distance, and he soon brought his rhetorical talents into play through the medium of writing. His first substantial written commentary on his predicament was *Reflections upon Exile,* which was written in France in 1716, though not published until much later (1752). In this work, he represents himself as philosophically reconciled to his new status. In the following year, he wrote *A Letter to Sir William Windham* (published posthumously in 1753), which was addressed to one of the chief Tory statesmen. These works were calculated to assert the intellectual integrity of their author and to defend his motives. In *A Letter to Sir William Windham* he describes his actions both before and after his flight. In this letter, which Bolingbroke describes as "a monument of my justification to posterity," he narrates his engagement in the negotiations leading to the Treaty of Utrecht, his battle against the earl of Oxford for the Tory leadership, the intense anxieties about the succession, the death of Queen Anne, the establishment of the new Whig regime, and his own escape and subsequent short-lived association with the Pretender. Bolingbroke's letter was intended not only for Sir William Wyndham, an old friend and a Tory leader, but also for other important Tories. Though the letter was not printed, it was soon read in Wyndham's circle of associates.

At about this time, Bolingbroke commenced an affair with the widowed Marquise de Villette. After his wife's death in 1718, he married the Marquise in the next year. He bought property near Orléans and resided there while continuing efforts to win a pardon so that he could return to England. His estate at La Source became something of a focus of intellectual activity during his years there, as his visitors included many gifted thinkers and writers, including Voltaire. Bolingbroke himself led a scholarly life, and Voltaire enjoyed his wit and erudition.

In 1723 Bolingbroke was able to persuade one of the King's mistresses to secure a pardon for him, and he made plans to return to England. His confiscated English estates were restored in 1725, in which year he returned to his native land, settling at Dawley, where, as in France, he gathered about him a congenial group of writers and intellectuals. Pope lived nearby, and Swift visited at times.

Though Walpole had grudgingly agreed to Bolingbroke's pardon and to the return of his property, the Whig leader was steadfastly opposed to Bolingbroke's being allowed to return to Parliament. Bolingbroke, who had made friendly but unsuccessful overtures to Walpole and the Whigs while he was seeking his pardon, took Walpole's insistence on his exclusion as a personal affront and began a series of attacks on the prime minister that continued for the next ten years.

These attacks were grounded on a philosophical perspective that Bolingbroke hoped would draw adherents from both of the major parties. This point of view focused upon the negative effects of mere factionalism and emphasized the shared interest of Whigs and Tories in maintaining the British tradition of individual freedom while resisting the effects of governmental economic innovations and the institutionalism of corruption. Late in 1726 Bolingbroke and Whig William Pulteney founded a journal called *The Craftsman* in order to promulgate their antifactional sentiments. Early in its publication history, *The Craftsman* established a wide readership and did much to rehabilitate Bolingbroke's reputation. In fact, Bolingbroke appeared in 1727 to be on the verge of persuading George I to reinstate him in politics, but the old king died unexpectedly, and once again Bolingbroke's hopes were frustrated by a royal death. This journal continued to publish many of Bolingbroke's writings against the Walpole government up until Bolingbroke returned to France in 1735.

One way in which the writers of *The Craftsman* employed history was as a source of parallels by which the administrative techniques of the Whigs in power could be proved similar to those of disreputable governments in the past or by which, conversely, the opponents of Walpole's regime could be compared favorably to virtuous politicians of the past. Another method was the adoption of an interpretation of British history that maintained that the people of England had an ancient prescriptive tradition of rights that extended long before the formal institution of the House of Commons. This tradition was associated with the landed gentry upon whom Bolingbroke's Tories and the dissident Whigs placed their political hopes. Walpole and his partisans, of course, argued vehemently that no such tradition had ever existed and that the English had only achieved their freedom with the Glorious Revolution and the rejection of divine-right monarchy. Neither side was able to make an overwhelming case for moral superiority, as Bolingbroke's explanation of his stint as standardbearer for the Pretender seemed inadequate to many, while the flagrant corruption of Walpole's government remained at least a minor national embarrassment. When in 1733 Walpole's government attempted to impose new taxes on wine and tobacco, the resulting excise crisis brought about by widespread resistance to the new taxes forced Walpole to revoke the proposed taxes, and the negative reaction to the government's conduct weakened his position somewhat. Bolingbroke, encouraged by these events, began publication in *The Craftsman* of *A Dissertation upon Parties* (published separately in 1735). *A Dissertation upon Parties* appeared in

LETTERS

ON THE

STUDY and USE

OF

HISTORY.

By the late RIGHT HONORABLE

HENRY ST. JOHN,

LORD VISCOUNT BOLINGBROKE.

A NEW EDITION Corrected.

LONDON,
Printed for A. MILLAR.

MDCCLII.

Title page for Bolingbroke's 1752 edition of his 1738 work addressed to a young nobleman, regarding the accuracy of the Old Testament and the rarity of anyone's studying history for the right reason (Cambridge University Library; Eighteenth Century Collections Online, Gale Group)

installments until December 1734, setting forth in detail Bolingbroke's thesis that contemporary party spirit was generally misguided and destructive. As in *Remarks on the History of England* (1743), he derived his conclusions from a reading of history, and he led his readers once again through English history, returning inevitably to his thesis that decent landowners think alike and should beware of factional impulses or provocations ("the sallies and transports of party"–Letter VIII). Also as in *Remarks on the History of England,* the rhetorical purpose of each of the individual installments required that each essay or letter be sufficiently self-contained for coherence and sufficiently focused to achieve the establishment of a main point. While this relative self-containment made the articles manageable for coffee-

house reading or for reading aloud, these pieces do when read sequentially reiterate fundamental themes, and to Bolingbroke's credit as author, his almost conversational discourse rarely if ever falls into unconsidered repetition.

Walpole, however, recovered from his misstep, and the next elections confirmed his political authority beyond doubt. At this point Bolingbroke, having spent some ten years battling Walpole, in 1735 decided to return to France, where at Argeville, near Fontainebleau, he composed *Letters to a Young Nobleman on the Study and Use of History* (1738; published in 1752 as *Letters on the Study and Use of History*). This work constitutes a significantly different kind of writing than the periodical productions of Bolingbroke's decade in England, because his audience is different, and because he is no longer focusing upon attacking Walpole's government. He is addressing this work privately to a fellow nobleman, Henry Hyde, Lord Cornbury, and thus he has no hesitation in attacking the historical accuracy of the Old Testament, and he is equally candid with respect to other topics regarding which a political journalist might be less forthcoming, including the rarity among those who study history of those who study it for the right reason. In 1736 he sent four final letters to be published in *The Craftsman,* but, despite occasional visits to England, Bolingbroke remained in France most of the time until his final return to England in 1744. He resumed his life of literary and philosophical activity in France, and he continued to write. He composed the *Letter on the Spirit of Patriotism* in 1736. It argues for the importance of diligent and vigorous participation in government by those who are possessed of virtuous minds and love of country. He defends the importance of maintaining an opposition based on the national interest rather than upon party interest. In this letter on patriotism, Bolingbroke concedes that his efforts in politics are largely behind him, and he expresses faith in the new generation of British politicians who are taking up the challenge of opposing the Whig government.

Although he did not abandon hope of a return to the political arena in England, he did realize that he was more likely to leave a lasting legacy by means of his writings than by legislative achievements, and he completed *The Idea of a Patriot King* and possibly *The State of Parties at the Accession of King George the First* in 1739 (published in 1740 and 1749). By 1738, he had become so hopeful of the prospects of a growing party associated with Frederick, the Prince of Wales, who had quarreled with the King, that he wrote *The Idea of a Patriot King* in an effort to connect his own views to what seemed a promising opposition movement. *The Idea of a Patriot King* essentially continues the promulgation of Bolingbroke's views with the modification that the restoration of the ancient constitution will be led by an enlightened monarch whose rational devotion to his state will free it from corruption and from the dangers of economic innovations. Already in his sixties, Bolingbroke clearly hoped that his political writings would justify his career.

Bolingbroke's father died in 1742, the year of Walpole's fall from power. Two years later, Bolingbroke returned to live on his father's estate at Battersea. In that same year, Pope, one of Bolingbroke's most devout admirers, died.

Bolingbroke recognized the rhetorical value of history, for in 1730 he had begun publishing in *The Craftsman* a series of articles constituting *Remarks on the History of England* (published separately in 1743), which argued that the nation's history had been characterized by a struggle to preserve the traditional constitution against usurpation by ambitious monarchs and their ministers. England, argued Bolingbroke in the person of "Humphrey Oldcastle," enjoyed proper government only when a mutual respect existed between monarch and Parliament. The reign of Queen Elizabeth was represented as such a regime, while that of Henry VIII, or that of Walpole, showed the negative consequences of usurpation. "Oldcastle" also argues against factionalism, suggesting that both Whigs and Tories have essential interests and perspectives in common. These issues of *The Craftsman* aroused the outrage of the government, which retaliated by arresting the publisher of the journal.

In order to demonstrate the superiority of the English constitution, which he carefully distinguishes from the English government, Bolingbroke adds to his account of English history a summary of the histories of Rome, of France, and of Spain. From this comparative analysis, he argues that England alone developed a political mechanism adequate for the correction of tyranny, though he also points out that the perfection of the English system is still a task in hand, despite what he ironically calls "the present wise, virtuous and triumphant administration" (Letter IX).

Another important theme of Bolingbroke's contributions to *The Craftsman* is his intense suspicion of economic developments which subordinate the traditionally fundamental role of the landed gentry to banking and investment interests which seemed to Bolingbroke to threaten the old connections between property ownership and social responsibility. He associated the new ideas of credit and speculative investment or stockjobbing with the ruling Whigs' corruption and unreliability. His discussions of stockjobbing tend to be presented with more vehemence and possibly less logic than his arguments based on history, in presenting which he is careful to maintain a tone of rational urbanity that combines wit and erudition. In all likelihood, Bolingbroke was relatively uncomfortable analyzing economics but felt an obligation to register objections, which he believed would find agreement among his audience.

Though he hoped that Frederick, the rebellious Prince of Wales, would adopt his political agenda, the aging Bolingbroke lived instead to see Frederick precede him in death in 1751. Bolingbroke's own death on December 12 of that year appears to have been the result of cancer.

Although little definite information is available about the formal education of Henry St. John, Viscount Bolingbroke, his writings and his comfortable associations with leading intellectuals of both England and France demonstrate that his eloquence and erudition were remarkable. His excellent memory was able to draw on his training in the Latin classics, and the Romans' predilections for history and satire were congenial to him. While he does not appear to have been a proficient Greek scholar, he does allude with familiarity to Plato and Homer, among other Greek authors. Yet, his main classical sources are Latin—particularly Cicero, Seneca, Livy, and Tacitus—and, of other historians, aside from Machiavelli, he tends to favor English sources.

Aside from what can be ascertained from evidence of his intellectual training, some significant indications of his mental abilities were the impressions he made upon such persons as Harley, Voltaire, Swift, and Pope—all among the most distinguished individuals of their day. Though Harley and Marlborough later regretted admiring Bolingbroke, both the political leader and the general recognized his abilities and potential as extraordinary. Though some contemporaries deplored Bolingbroke's libertinism, the memory of Charles II was not so distant as completely to have lost its power to sanction hedonism, and though Bolingbroke's rakish reputation may have been Queen Anne's reason for not granting him in 1712 the earldom he desired, his sexual adventures seem not to have hurt him a great deal otherwise. Voltaire, whom Bolingbroke had met in France in 1719, regarded him highly, at least in the early years of their acquaintance, and Swift and Pope, particularly the latter, were happy to become his friends.

Although Leslie Stephen remarks in his article on Bolingbroke in the *Dictionary of National Biography* that "Bolingbroke seems always to have been singularly shy of publishing anything under his own name," H. T. Dickinson has concluded that Bolingbroke's "great ambition was to justify his own conduct by a detailed history of his own times, but he was continually frustrated in his efforts to procure the necessary documentary evidence." His efforts to employ history to support his own rhetorical enterprises extended throughout his lifetime in politics, and one measure of his achievement is that his historical arguments forced his opponents to ground their arguments in history as well.

Letters:

The Letters and Correspondence, Public and Private, of Henry St. John, Viscount Bolingbroke during the Time He was Secretary of State to Queen Anne, 4 volumes, edited by Gilbert Parke (London: Printed for G. G. & J. Robinson, 1798);

"Letters of Henry St. John to James Brydges," edited by Godfrey Davies and Marion Tinling, *Huntington Library Bulletin,* 8 (October 1935): 153–170;

"Letters from Bolingbroke to James Grahme," edited by H. T. Dickinson, *Transactions Cumberland and Westmoreland Antiquarian and Archaeological Society,* new series, 48 (1988).

Bibliography:

Giles Barber, "Some Uncollected Authors XLI: Henry Saint John, Viscount Bolingbroke, 1678–1751," *Book Collector,* 14 (Winter 1965): 528–537.

Biographies:

Walter Sichel, *Bolingbroke and His Times,* 2 volumes (London: James Nisbet, 1901, 1902);

H. T. Dickinson, *Bolingbroke* (London: Constable, 1970).

References:

Rex A. Barrell, *Bolingbroke and France* (Lanham, Md.: University Press of America, 1988);

J. H. Burns, "Bolingbroke and the Concept of Constitutional Government," *Political Studies,* 10 (1962): 264–276;

John Churton Collins, *Bolingbroke; A Historical Study and Voltaire in England* (New York: Harper, 1886);

Bernard Cottret, ed., *Bolingbroke's Political Writings: The Conservative Enlightenment* (New York: Palgrave Macmillan, 1997);

Bertrand A. Goldgar, *Walpole and the Wits: The Relation of Politics to Literature, 1722–1742* (Lincoln: University of Nebraska Press, 1976);

J. H. Grainger, "The Deviations of Lord Bolingbroke," *The Australian Journal of Politics and History,* 15, (1969): 41–59;

Brean S. Hammond, *Pope and Bolingbroke: A Study of Friendship and Influence* (Columbia: University of Missouri Press, 1984);

Jeffrey Hart, *Viscount Bolingbroke: Tory Humanist* (London: Routledge & Kegan Paul, 1965);

Philip Hicks, "Bolingbroke, Clarendon, and the Role of Classical Historian," *Eighteenth-Century Studies,* 20 (Summer 1987): 445–471;

Henry Hyde, "David Mallett and Lord Bolingbroke," *ANQ,* 18 (Winter 2005): 24–28;

Sydney W. Jackman, *Man of Mercury: An Appreciation of the Mind of Henry St. John, Viscount Bolingbroke* (London: Pall Mall Press, 1965);

D. G. James, *The Life of Reason: Hobbes, Locke, Bolingbroke* (London: Longmans, Green, 1949);

Isaac Kramnick, "Augustan Politics and English Historiography: The Debate on the English Past, 1730–35," *History and Theory* (February 1967): 33–56;

Kramnick, "An Augustan Reply to Locke: Bolingbroke on Natural Law and the Origin of Government," *Political Science Quarterly,* 82 (December 1967): 571–594;

Kramnick, *Bolingbroke and His Circle: The Politics of Nostalgia in the Age of Walpole* (Cambridge, Mass.: Harvard University Press, 1968);

Harvey C. Mansfield, *Statesmanship and Party Government: A Study of Burke and Bolingbroke* (Chicago: University of Chicago Press, 1965);

Derek McKay, "Bolingbroke, Oxford and the Defense of the Utrecht Settlement in Southern Europe," *English Historical Review,* 86 (1971): 264–284;

Walter McIntosh Merrill, *From Statesman to Philosopher: A Study in Bolingbroke's Deism* (New York: Philosophical Library, 1949);

George H. Nadel, "New Light on Bolingbroke's Letters on History," *Journal of the History of Ideas,* 23 (October–December 1962): 550–557;

Folke Nibelius, *Lord Bolingbroke (1678–1751) and History: A Comparative Study of Bolingbroke's Politico-Historical Works and a Selection of Contemporary Texts as to Themes and Vocabulary* (Stockholm: Almqvist & Wiksell International, 2003);

Alexander Pettit, *Illusory Consensus: Bolingbroke and the Polemical Response to Walpole, 1730–1737* (Newark: University of Delaware Press, 1997);

Pat Rogers, "Swift and Bolingbroke on Faction," *Journal of British Studies,* 9 (May 1970): 71–101;

Frank T. Smallwood, "Bolingbroke vs. Alexander Pope: The Publication of the *Patriot King,*" *Papers of the Bibliographical Society of America,* 65 (1971): 225–241;

Simon Varey, *Henry St. John, Viscount Bolingbroke* (Boston: Twayne, 1984);

D. J. Womersley, "Lord Bolingbroke and Eighteenth-Century Historiography," *The Eighteenth Century: Theory and Interpretation,* 28 (Fall 1987): 217–234.

Papers:

The manuscripts of Henry St. John, Viscount Bolingbroke, are held throughout Great Britain, Europe, and the United States. Some important collections are in the British Library, the Public Record Office, and the New York Public Library. H. T. Dickinson includes a list of manuscript sources in his biography of Bolingbroke.

Edmund Burke

(1 January 1729 – 9 July 1797)

Seán Patrick Donlan
University of Limerick

See also the Burke entries in *DLB 104: British Prose Writers, 1660–1800, Second Series* and *DLB 252: British Philosophers, 1500–1799.*

BOOKS: *A Vindication of Natural Society; or, A View of the Miseries and Evils Arising to Mankind from Every Species of Artificial Society. In a Letter to Lord ****. By a Late Noble Writer* (London: Printed for M. Cooper, 1756; revised edition, with a new preface, London: Printed for Robert & James Dodsley, 1757);

A Philosophical Enquiry into the Origin of Our Ideas of the Sublime and Beautiful (London: Printed for Robert & James Dodsley, 1757); revised and enlarged as *A Philosophical Enquiry into the Origin of Our Ideas of the Sublime and Beautiful: With an Introductory Discourse Concerning Taste, and Several Other Additions* (London: Printed for Robert & James Dodsley, 1759; Philadelphia: Printed for S. F. Bradford by J. Watts, 1806);

An Account of the European Settlements in America: In Six Parts. I. A Short History of the Discovery of That Part of the World. II. The Manners and Customs of the Original Inhabitants. III. Of the Spanish Settlements. IV. Of the Portuguese. V. Of the French, Dutch, and Danish. VI. Of the English, attributed to Burke and William Burke, 2 volumes (London: Printed for Robert & James Dodsley, 1757; the 1777 edition reprinted in 1 volume, New York: Arno Press, 1972);

Annual Register (London: Printed for R. & J. Dodsley in Pall-Mall, 1758–1764?);

Observations on a Late State of the Nation (London: Printed for James Dodsley, 1769);

Thoughts on the Cause of the Present Discontents (London: Printed for James Dodsley, 1770);

Mr. Edmund Burke's Speeches at His Arrival at Bristol: And at the Conclusion of the Poll (London: Printed for John Wilkie, 1774);

Speech of Edmund Burke, Esq., on American Taxation, April 19, 1774 (London: Printed for James Dodsley, 1775; New York: Printed by James Rivington, 1775);

Edmund Burke (portrait by Sir Joshua Reynolds, The National Portrait Gallery, London)

The Speech of Edmund Burke, Esq. on Moving His Resolutions for Conciliation with the Colonies, March 22, 1775 (London: Printed for James Dodsley, 1775; New York: Printed by James Rivington, 1775);

The Political Tracts and Speeches of Edmund Burke, Esq. Member of Parliament for the City of Bristol (Dublin: Printed for William Whitestone, 1777);

A Letter from Edmund Burke, Esq.; One of the Representatives in Parliament for the City of Bristol, to John Farr, and John Harris, Esqrs. Sheriffs of That City, on the Affairs of America (Bristol: Printed by William Pine, 1777);

Two Letters from Mr. Burke to Gentlemen in the City of Bristol, on the Bills Depending in Parliament Relative to the

Trade of Ireland (London: Printed for James Dodsley, 1778);

Speech of Edmund Burke, Esq. Member of Parliament for the City of Bristol, On Presenting to the House of Commons (On the 11th of February, 1780) A Plan for the Better Security of the Independence of Parliament, and the Oeconomical Reformation of the Civil and Other Establishments (London: Printed by William Bowyer for James Dodsley, 1780);

A Letter from a Gentleman in the English House of Commons, in Vindication of His Conduct, with Regard to the Affairs of Ireland, Addressed to a Member of the Irish Parliament (London: Printed for John Bew, 1780); republished as *A Letter from Edmund Burke, Esq.; in Vindication of His Conduct with Regard to the Affairs of Ireland. Addressed to Thomas Burgh, Esq. Member of Parliament for Athy* (Dublin: Printed by Patrick Byrne, 1780); republished as *A Letter from Edmund Burke, Esq. in Vindication of His Conduct with Regard to the Affairs of Ireland, Addressed to Thomas Burgh, Esq. Member of the Irish Parliament* (London: Printed for John Bew, 1780);

A Speech of Edmund Burke, Esq. at the Guildhall, in Bristol, Previous to the Late Election in That City, upon Certain Points Relative to His Parliamentary Conduct (London: Printed for James Dodsley, 1780);

Ninth Report from the Select Committee, Appointed to Take into Consideration the State of the Administration of Justice in the Provinces of Bengal, Bahar, and Orissa (London: Printed by William Strahan for the House of Commons, 1783);

Eleventh Report from the Select Committee, Appointed to Take into Consideration the State of the Administration of Justice in the Provinces of Bengal, Bahar, and Orissa (London: Printed by William Strahan for the House of Commons, 1783);

A Letter from a Distinguished English Commoner, to a Peer of Ireland on the Penal Laws against Irish Catholics; Previous to the Late Repeal of a Part Thereof, in the Session of the Irish Parliament, Held A.D. 1782 (Dublin: Printed for Matthew Doyle, 1783);

Mr. Burke's Speech, on the 1st December 1783, upon the Question for the Speaker's Leaving the Chair, in Order for the House to Resolve Itself into a Committee on Mr. Fox's East India Bill (London: Printed for James Dodsley, 1784);

A Representation to His Majesty, Moved in the House of Commons, by the Right Honourable Edmund Burke, and Seconded by the Right Honourable William Windham, on Monday, June 14, 1784, and Negatived. With a Preface and Notes (London: Printed for John Debrett, 1784);

Mr. Burke's Speech on the Motion Made for Papers Relative to the Directions for Charging the Nabob of Arcot's Private Debts to Europeans, on the Revenues of the Carnatic, February 28th, 1785. With an Appendix, Containing Several Documents (London: Printed for James Dodsley, 1785);

Articles of Charge of High Crimes and Misdemeanors, against Warren Hastings, Esquire, Late Governor General of Bengal, five parts, by Burke and others (London: Printed for the House of Commons, 1786);

The Committee, to Whom It Was Referred to Prepare Articles of Impeachment against Warren Hastings, Esquire, Late Governor General of Bengal, Have, Pursuant to the Order of the House, Prepared Several Articles Accordingly: Which Articles Are as Followeth; Viz. Articles of Impeachment of High Crimes and Misdemeanors against Warren Hastings, Esquire, Late Governor General of Bengal, three parts, by Burke and others (London: Printed for the House of Commons, 1787);

A Letter to Phillip Francis, Esq. From the Right Hon. Edmund Burke, Chairman, . . . Members of the Committee for managing the Impeachment of Mr. Hastings. With Remarks (London: Printed for John Murray & John Stockdale, 1788);

Substance of the Speech of the Right Honourable Edmund Burke, in the Debate on the Army Estimates in the House of Commons, on Tuesday, the 9th Day of February, 1790, Comprehending a Discussion of the Present Situation of Affairs in France (London: Printed for John Debrett, 1790);

Reflections on the Revolution in France, and on the Proceedings in Certain Societies in London Relative to that Event. In a Letter Intended to Have Been Sent to a Gentleman in Paris (London: Printed by Henry Hughes for James Dodsley, 1790; revised, 1790; New York: Printed by Hugh Gaine, 1791);

Lettre de M. Burke à un membre de l'Assemblée nationale de France (Paris: L'Assemblée nationale, Chez Artaud, 1791); English version published as *A Letter from Mr. Burke to a Member of the National Assembly; in Answer to Some Objections to His Book on French Affairs* (London: Printed for James Dodsley, 1791; New York: Printed by Hugh Gaine, 1791);

Two Letters from the Right Honourable Mr. Burke, on the French Revolution: One to the Translator of His Reflections on the Revolution in France: the Other to Captain W----, On the Same Subject (London: Printed for H. D. Symonds, 1791);

An Appeal from the New to the Old Whigs, in Consequence of Some Late Discussions in Parliament, Relative to the Reflections on the French Revolution (London: Printed for James Dodsley, 1791; revised, 1791; revised and enlarged, 1791; New York: Printed by Childs & Swaine and sold by Berry & Rogers, New York; the principal booksellers in Philadelphia; Thomas

& Andrews, Boston; and W. P. Young, Charleston, S.C., 1791);

Lettre de M. Burke à M. l'Archevêque d'Aix; Et Réponse de M. l'Archevêque d'Aix, à M. Burke (N.p., 1791);

Lettre de M. Burke, sur les affaires de France et des Pays-Bas; adressée à M. le vicomte de Rivarol. Traduite de l'Anglais (Paris: Denné, 1791);

A Letter from the Right Hon. Edmund Burke . . . to Sir Hercules Langrishe, Bart. M.P. on the Subject of Roman Catholics of Ireland, and the Propriety of Admitting Them to the Elective Franchise, Consistently with the Principles of the Constitution as Established at the Revolution (Dublin: Printed by Patrick Byrne, 1792; revised, London: Printed for John Debrett, 1792);

Mr. Burke's Speech, in Westminster-Hall, on the 18th and 19th of February, 1788, with Explanatory Notes. This Speech Contains What Mr. Burke, in His Letter to the Chairman of the East India Company, Calls "Those Strong Facts Which the Managers for the Commons Have Opened as Offences, and Which Go Seriously to Affect Mr. Shore's Administration, As Acting Chief of the Revenue Board." With a Preface, Containing Mr. Burke's Letter to the Chairman on Sir John Shore's Appointment to the Government of Bengal, and Remarks upon That Letter (London: Printed for John Debrett, 1792);

Report from the Committee of the House of Commons, Appointed to Inspect the Lords Journals, in Relation to Their Proceeding on the Trial of Warren Hastings, Esquire (London: Printed for the House of Commons, 1794);

Substance of the Speech of the Right Honourable Edmund Burke, in the House of Commons, On Friday the 23rd Day of May, 1794, in Answer to Certain Observations on the Report of the Committee of Managers, Representing That Report to Have Been a Libel on the Judges (London: Printed for John Debrett, 1794);

A Letter from the Right Honourable Edmund Burke to a Noble Lord, on the Attacks Made upon Him and His Pension, in the House of Lords, by the Duke of Bedford and the Earl of Lauderdale, Early in the Present Sessions of Parliament (London: Printed for John Owen & Francis & Charles Rivington, 1796; revised, 1796; revised again, 1796; New York: Printed for T. Allen & A. Drummand, 1796);

Thoughts on the Prospect of a Regicide Peace, in a Series of Letters [unauthorized edition] (London: Printed for John Owen, 1796); revised as *Two Letters Addressed to a Member of the Present Parliament, on the Proposals for Peace with the Regicide Directory of France* [authorized edition] (London: Printed for F. & C. Rivington, 1796; revised, 1796; Philadelphia: Printed for William Cobbett by Bioren & Madan, 1797);

A Letter from the Rt. Honourable Edmund Burke to His Grace the Duke of Portland on the Conduct of the Minority in Parliament. Containing Fifty-Four Articles of Impeachment against the Rt. Hon. C. J. Fox. From the Original Copy in the Possession of the Noble Duke [unauthorized edition] (London: Printed for the editor and sold by John Owen, 1797; Philadelphia: Printed for James Humphreys, 1797); revised and enlarged as *Two Letters on the Conduct of Our Domestick Parties, With Regard to French Politicks; Including, "Observations on the Conduct of the Minority, in the Session of M.DCC.XCIII." By the Late Right Hon. Edmund Burke* [authorized edition] (London: Printed for Francis & Charles Rivington and sold also by John Hatchard, 1797);

Three Memorials on French Affairs Written in the Years 1791, 1792, and 1793 by the Late Right Hon. Edmund Burke, edited by Walker King and French Laurence (London: Printed for Francis & Charles Rivington and sold also by John Hatchard, 1797);

A Third Letter to a Member of the Present Parliament, on the Proposals for Peace with the Regicide Directory of France. By the Late Right Hon. Edmund Burke, edited by King and Laurence (London: Printed for Francis & Charles Rivington and sold also by John Hatchard, 1797);

Thoughts and Details on Scarcity, Originally Presented to the Right Hon. William Pitt, in the Month of November, 1795. By the Late Right Hon. Edmund Burke, edited, with a preface, by King and Laurence (London: Printed for Francis & Charles Rivington & John Hatchard, 1800);

The Works of the Right Honourable Edmund Burke, 16 volumes, edited by King and Laurence (volume 1, London: Printed by T. Gillet for Francis, Charles & John Rivington and sold also by John Hatchard, 1803; volume 2, London: Printed by Bye & Law for Francis, Charles & John Rivington and sold also by John Hatchard, 1803; volumes 3–8, London: Printed by T. Gillet for Francis, Charles & John Rivington and sold also by John Hatchard, 1803; volumes 9–10, London: Printed by Luke Hansard & Sons for Francis, Charles & John Rivington and sold also by John Hatchard, 1812; volumes 11–12, London: Printed by Luke Hansard & Sons for Francis, Charles & John Rivington and sold also by John Hatchard, 1813; volumes 13–14, London: Printed by Luke Hansard & Sons for Francis, Charles & John Rivington, 1822; volumes 15–16, London: Charles & John Rivington, 1827; revised edition, 12 volumes, Boston: Little, Brown, 1865–1867);

The Catholic Claims, Discussed; in a Letter from the Late Right Hon. Edmund Burke, to the Hon. William Smith, L.L.D. F.R.S. & M.R.I.A. Then a Member of the Irish Parliament; Now Third Baron of the Court of Exchequer in Ireland (Dublin: Printed by Graisberry & Campbell for John Archer, 1807; London: Printed by T. Curson Hansard and sold by Francis, Charles & John Rivington & John Hatchard, 1807);

The Writings and Speeches of Edmund Burke, Beaconsfield Edition, 12 volumes (Boston: Little, Brown, 1901);

A Note-Book of Edmund Burke: Poems, Characters, Essays and Other Sketches in the Hands of Edmund and William Burke, Now Printed for the First Time in Their Entirety, edited by H. V. F. Somerset (Cambridge: Cambridge University Press, 1957).

Editions and Collections: *Burke's Speeches: On American Taxation; On Conciliation with America & Letter to the Sheriffs of Bristol,* edited, with an introduction and notes, by F. G. Selby (London: Macmillan, 1908; London: Macmillan / New York: St. Martin's Press, 1954);

Edmund Burke: Selected Prose, edited, with an introduction, by Philip Magnus (London: Falcon, 1948);

Burke's Politics: Selected Writings and Speeches of Edmund Burke on Reform, Revolution and War, edited by Ross J. S. Hoffman & Paul Levack (New York: Knopf, 1949);

A Philosophical Enquiry into the Origin of Our Ideas of the Sublime and Beautiful, edited, with an introduction and notes, by James T. Boulton (London: Routledge & Kegan Paul, 1958; Notre Dame, Ind.: University of Notre Dame Press, 1968; revised edition, Oxford: Blackwell, 1987);

Reflections on the Revolution in France and on the Proceedings of Certain Societies in London Relative to That Event, edited by William B. Todd (New York: Rinehart, 1959);

The Philosophy of Edmund Burke: A Selection from His Speeches and Writings, edited, with an introduction, by Louis I. Bredvold and Ralph G. Ross (Ann Arbor: University of Michigan Press, 1960);

Selected Writings of Edmund Burke, edited by W. J. Bate (New York: Modern Library, 1960);

An Appeal from the New to the Old Whigs, edited, with an introduction, by John M. Robson (Indianapolis: Bobbs-Merrill, 1962);

Selected Writings and Speeches: Edmund Burke, edited by Peter J. Stanlis (Garden City, N.Y.: Anchor, 1963);

On the American Revolution: Selected Speeches and Letters, edited by Elliott Robert Barkan (New York: Harper & Row, 1966; republished, with new preface, Gloucester, Mass.: Smith, 1972);

Reflections on the Revolution in France: And on the Proceedings in Certain Societies in London Relative to That Event, edited, with an introduction, by Conor Cruise O'Brien (London & New York: Penguin, 1968);

The Writings and Speeches of Edmund Burke, edited by Paul Langford and others (Oxford: Clarendon Press / New York: Oxford University Press, 1981–)—includes volume 1, *The Early Writings* (1997), edited by T. O. McLoughlin and James T. Boulton; volume 2, *Party, Parliament, and the American Crisis, 1766–1774* (1981), edited by Langford; volume 3, *Party, Parliament, and the American War, 1774–1780* (1996), edited by W. M. Elofson and John A. Woods; volume 5, *India, Madras and Bengal, 1774–1785* (1981), edited by P. J. Marshall; volume 6, *India, the Launching of the Hastings Impeachment, 1786–1788* (1991), edited by Marshall; volume 7, *India, the Hastings Trial, 1789–1794* (2000), edited by Marshall; volume 8, *The French Revolution, 1790–1794* (1990), edited by L. G. Mitchell; and volume 9, part 1, *The Revolutionary War, 1794–1797,* and part 2, *Ireland* (1991), edited by R. B. McDowell;

A Vindication of Natural Society; or, A View of the Miseries and Evils Arising to Mankind from Every Species of Artificial Society: In a Letter to Lord **** by a Late Noble Writer, edited, with an introduction, by Frank N. Pagano (Indianapolis: Liberty Classics, 1982);

The Political Philosophy of Edmund Burke, compiled by Iain Hampsher-Monk (London: Longman, 1987);

Reflections on the Revolution in France, edited, with an introduction and notes, by J. G. A. Pocock (Indianapolis: Hackett, 1987);

A Philosophical Enquiry into the Origin of Our Ideas of the Sublime and Beautiful, edited, with an introduction, by Adam Phillips (Oxford & New York: Oxford University Press, 1990);

Reflections on the Revolution in France, edited, with an introduction, by L. G. Mitchell (Oxford & New York: Oxford University Press, 1993);

The Writings and Speeches of Edmund Burke, 9 volumes, edited by Paul Langford (Oxford: Oxford University Press, 1997);

A Philosophical Enquiry into the Origin of Our Ideas of the Sublime and Beautiful, and Other Pre-Revolutionary Writings, edited by David Womersley (London & New York: Penguin, 1998);

The Portable Edmund Burke, edited by Isaac Kramnick (London: Penguin, 1999; New York: Penguin, 1999);

Reflections on the Revolution in France, edited by J. C. D. Clark (Stanford, Cal.: Stanford University Press, 2001).

The "historical sense" of Edmund Burke, statesman and writer, is frequently acknowledged and even exaggerated. His historical writings, however, often remain overlooked. These works, largely anonymous or unpublished, predate his political career and confirm that Burke was neither a romantic nor a reactionary, but at the center of eighteenth-century "philosophical" histories. In addition, he was a friend and correspondent of the leading historians of his day and, in print and in politics, displayed an extensive understanding of European, British, and Irish history.

Burke was born in Dublin on 1 January 1729 to a mixed Protestant/Catholic marriage. His father, Richard Burke, was a lawyer and may have converted to the established church to pursue a career otherwise prohibited to Catholics by the Irish penal laws. His mother, Mary Burke (née Nagle), remained a Catholic. Edmund ("Ned") and his brothers were raised in their father's church, while, as was the custom, his sister was raised in their mother's faith. After attending schools in rural counties Cork and Kildare, Burke studied at the University of Dublin. At Trinity College, history was—along with math, logic, and poetry—one of his "furors." In addition to studying the classical historians of the college curriculum, he spent many hours in the library "endeavouring," he wrote Richard Shackleton (12 July 1747), "to get a little into the accounts of this our poor country." Burke organized the Trinity "Club," the first debating society in Britain or Ireland and the predecessor of the "Historical Society" (founded by Burke in 1747). After receiving his degree and briefly editing *The Reformer,* a Dublin journal, he departed for a legal education in London. Against his father's wishes, Burke eventually left his studies in pursuit of a literary career.

Burke's marriage on 12 March 1757 to Jane Mary Nugent, daughter of an Irish Catholic doctor, and the birth of two sons, Richard (who died in 1794) and Christopher (who died in infancy) brought acute and lifelong financial difficulties. He struggled to meet these obligations with extraordinary productivity in the late 1750s and early 1760s. His first publication was *A Vindication of Natural Society; or, A View of the Miseries and Evils Arising to Mankind from Every Species of Artificial Society. In a Letter to Lord ****. By a Late Noble Writer* (1756). Showing familiarity with Thomas Hobbes, Niccolo Machiavelli, and Francesco Guicciardini, Burke parodied the deism and historical writings of Henry St. John, Lord Bolingbroke. He sought, he later added, "to shew that . . . the same Engines which were employed for the Destruction of Religion, might be employed with equal Success for the Subversion of Government." His next publication was the still more successful *A Philosophical Enquiry into the Origin of Our Ideas of the Sublime and Beautiful* (1757). Praised by both David Hume and Immanuel Kant, the work presented a theory of aesthetics "founded on experiment and not assumed" in line with contemporary science.

Burke appears, too, to have collaborated in writing or revising *An Account of the European Settlements in America* (1757) with his friend William Burke (no relation). In this work, concerning at once history and ethnography, the Burkes discuss a variety of topics: the conquest of Mexico and Peru; Amerindian society and customs; religious toleration and intolerance in the British colonies; trade, manufacturing, and politics; and the various European settlements. Before the "spirit of discovery" initiated by Columbus, they said, the "manners of Europe were wholly barbarous" in terms of statecraft, politeness, and commerce. A digest of existing sources, they drew on many works of travel literature, most notably perhaps Joseph François Lafitau's *Moeurs des sauvages ameriquains, comparées aux moeurs des premiers temps* (1724; translated as *Customs of the American Indians Compared with the Customs of Primitive Times,* 1974–1977). Indeed, the Burkes cite the Jesuit a decade earlier than Adam Ferguson's better-known use of his work. *An Account of the European Settlements in America* was successful, going through several editions and being translated into Italian, French, and German. William Robertson, later a friend of Burke's, acknowledged borrowing from it for his own *History of America* (1776).

Comparative works such as the *Account of the European Settlements in America* allowed Europeans to speculate on their own, more-primitive, origins and even on human nature itself. Read together, Burke's published and unpublished works of this period suggest a complex vision of the natural and historical foundation for individual and social progress, a vindication of modern society. The empiricism of *A Philosophical Enquiry into the Origin of Our Ideas of the Sublime and Beautiful* offered an intersubjective and dynamic image of human association. *An Account of the European Settlements in America* suggested that this empiricism provided considerable latitude for divergent cultures, the "strange turns of the human mind, fashioned to any thing by custom." This balance of the natural and "artificial" may be at the root of Burke's broadly progressive vision of the history of Europe's civil society. Unlike many of his contemporaries, who celebrated the nobility or authenticity of primitive societies, Burke saw them as evidence of the possible stasis or even "corruption" of human nature.

Much of Burke's later more familiar thought can be seen in his most important historical works, the "Essay towards an Abridgement of the English History" (written 1757–1762?) and the brief "Fragment: An Essay towards an History of the Laws of England" (written circa 1757), both published posthumously in volume six of *The Works of the Right Honourable Edmund Burke* (1803). The state of British history was generally seen as poor, and Burke, with several successful publications, must have found the idea of an English history appealing. He signed a contract in early 1757 agreeing to present by Christmas the following year a work spanning the period from the Romans up to Queen Anne (1665–1714). It was, in fact, two years before the first sheets of "An Abridgement of the English History" were received. While a first impression was printed in 1760, and some people–Charles Burney, for instance–appear to have had copies of the work, it was never completed. Complete only through the Magna Carta, perhaps just over a quarter of the intended size, it is divided into three sections neatly enveloping the conquests of Britain by the Romans, the Anglo-Saxons, and the Normans. The existing elements of the abridgment show a dense synthesis, a balance of narrative and analysis, with occasional, brief character sketches. This fragment is in the style of contemporary "philosophical" histories, focusing not on bare facts and events, but on recurring (or enduring) principles of human history and nature and the progress of society in Europe.

In "Essay towards an Abridgement of the *English History*" and in the fragment on English law, Burke singled out for criticism the belief in English exceptionalism and insularity and the idea of a constitution that was eternal rather than ancient. Aware "that nothing has been a larger theme of panegyrick with all our writers on politicks and history, than the Anglo-Saxon Government," Burke saw the liberty of the ancient Britons as closer to that of the Native Americans than to modern Europe. Not surprisingly for the author of *A Vindication of Natural Society,* this view was a problem to be overcome rather than an ideal to pursue. Indeed, against much popular and political opinion, Burke acknowledged the civilizing effect of the Norman conquest on the "rude and barbarous" Saxons through "communication" with the Continent. British civilization was the result of a European inheritance. He emphasized, for example, that English law was

> a very mixed and heterogeneous mass, in some respects on our own; in more borrowed from the policy of foreign nations, and compounded, altered, and variously modified, according to the various necessities which the manners, the religion, and the commerce of the people have at different times imposed.

Burke problematizes all of the points dear to the more vulgar contemporary histories: perennial principles and immemorial institutions linking the present with the past; the role of Saxon "lawgivers" and the antiquity of shires, juries, and the Commons; the insularity of English law and the denial of a Norman "conquest"; and the Magna Carta as a reaffirmation of ancient liberties.

Burke was equally skeptical in the "Essay towards an Abridgement . . . " about current histories that saw modern progress as having occurred only with the Reformation, the Renaissance, or England's Glorious Revolution. And, with Charles de Secondat, Baron de Montesquieu, and Voltaire, Burke's focus was not simply on kings or constitutions but on the "changes, which have happened in the manners, opinions, and sciences of men . . . [and are] as worthy of regard as the fortune of wars, and the revolutions of kingdoms." These "manners," at once the mores and social practices of a people, influenced the character and content of their laws and government. With the dichotomy between nature and art, this distinction between manners and laws recurs throughout Burke's writings. But even Montesquieu, "the greatest genius, which has enlightened this age," was not above criticism. Of Voltaire, Burke wrote, at the time of his legal studies, in his notebook, not published until 1957 as *A Note-Book of Edmund Burke: Poems, Characters, Essays and Other Sketches in the Hands of Edmund and William Burke, Now Printed for the First Time in Their Entirety,* that he

> doubt[ed] of nothing himself, and expects his readers should accept of his assertion for Authority;–but– When Historians give us clearer and more perfect Account of things than could be expected from their means of Information, instead of believing them in those parts, we are apt to suspect they tell us no truth in any points.

In general, the abridgment of *English History* shows Burke seeking to "more fully enter into" the past and not to judge it "by ideas taken from present manners and opinions." He is more sensitive to historical sources and change than was Montesquieu and more aware of the complexity and continuity of the ancient and modern worlds than was Voltaire.

The abridgment also includes little of the anti-clericalism common to Montesquieu, Voltaire, Hume, and Edward Gibbon. In different measures, their histories emphasized the ignorance and "superstition" of the ancients, including its Christianity, suggesting that European enlightenment was a recent acquisition. Burke suggests, instead, slow, precarious progress through centuries. This development was safeguarded and nurtured, in significant ways, by the clergy. The Burkes had already noted the positive role of the Catholic clergy in America. In the abridgment, Burke writes that the "first openings of *civility* have been every where made by religion." But he thought this belief to be true even in pre-Christian times and goes to surprising lengths to commend the Druids. Indeed, the image of a corporate Druidic priesthood he presents is the reverse of that offered earlier in the century by countryman John Toland. Burke praises, too, those early Christians who built on pagan foundations, displaying in the process a "perfect understanding of human nature."

Once established, the clergy acted as trustees of learning and science, linking the ancient and wider European worlds, while Christianity gradually tamed ancient martial virtues. Burke emphasized the role, both pious and political, of the institutional church and papacy in European progress. Thirty years before the revolution in France, he noted that

> In abbeys the law was studied; abbeys were the palladiums of the publick liberty by the custody of the royal charters and most of the records. Thus, necessary to the great by their knowledge; venerable to the poor by their hospitality; dreadful to all by the power of excommunication; the character of the clergy was exalted above every thing in the State; and it could no more be otherwise in those days, than it is possible it should be so in ours.

Burke even mentions "school divinity" favorably for "enlarging the mind. The science may be false, or frivolous"; he wrote, "the improvement will be real." Even an event such as the Crusades could have positive consequences in encouraging European unity and communication.

In 1758 Burke began editing the *Annual Register* (1758–1764?), a yearly encyclopedic collection of articles on the arts with state papers, reports on the sciences, and extracts from leading writers of the period. Burke appears to have been responsible for many book reviews—of works by William Blackstone, Hume, Leland, McPherson, Robertson, and Adam Smith—and wrote the detailed "historical" accounts of current events. Without eschewing judgment, he "carefully adhered to that neutrality, which, however blameable in an advocate, is necessary in an historian, and without which he will not represent an image of things, but of his own passions" (*Annual Register*, 1763). By the end of the decade, Burke had also become acquainted with many leading thinkers and artists of the day. Gaining admission to Samuel Johnson's circle, he found himself alongside James Boswell and fellow countryman Oliver Goldsmith. He also began friendships with Hume and Smith, the first of many links to members of the Scottish Enlightenment. Indeed, Burkean history and jurisprudence is closer to the philosophical and conjectural histories of his Scottish associates than to that of English attorneys practicing common law.

If Burke and Hume impressed one another immediately, no significant relationship resulted. This failure may owe less to philosophical differences than to Hume's views on Irish history. Burke shared Hume's skepticism toward England's "ancient constitution" but saw the Scot uncritically repeating the more offensive and prejudicial portrayals of Ireland. In his *History of England,* Hume applauded British "civilization" of the native and Catholic Irish, whom he considered long barbarous and ignorant. His depiction of the Irish rebellion of 1641 as a Catholic massacre of Protestants drew on the most biased histories, and he credulously exaggerated the dead from several thousand to several hundred thousand. Shortly after their first meeting, the two men quarreled about the rebellion. Coming as it did at the eclipse of Gaelic Ireland, and involving confiscation and settlement, the events of 1641 confirmed a shift from colonial to confessional divisions. Portrayed as a series of Catholic atrocities, it set the tone for Protestant alarm and triumphalism in the eighteenth century. Burke sought, with Tobias Smollet and Irish historians Charles O'Conor of Belanagare and John Curry, to persuade Hume to reconsider his account of the English settlements in Ireland. Despite these efforts, Hume made only minor adjustments in future editions.

Burke began his first political employment (1759–1764) as private secretary to then Chief Secretary for Ireland William Hamilton and may have befriended O'Conor and Curry while working in Dublin. Both were founding members of the Catholic Association (1756)—later the Catholic Committee—whose attempts to secure reform of the Irish penal laws Burke supported. Burke even prepared an "Address and Petition to the King" (1764) on behalf of Irish Catholics. In 1779 he returned a gift of £300 from the Catholic Committee for his assistance in securing some relaxation of the laws. Given many gaps in the historical record and the unreliability of earlier bardic histories, Burke was more cautious than many Irish Catholic historians. He granted, however, Ireland's native and Catholic cultures a status often denied them by British and Irish Protestant historians. Indeed, his description of the Saxons in the abridgment of English history as "rude and barbarous" echoes a centuries-old trope common in English writing about the Irish.

In his *Dissertations on the Antient History of Ireland* (1753), O'Conor emphasized early Irish civility, noting that this civilization was undermined by the assaults of the Scandinavian ancestors of the Anglo-Normans. The second edition of the *Dissertations* (1766) notes Burke's "encouragement" and was sent to him in England. The abridgment of *English History* suggests that Burke did not, however, always agree with O'Conor, who often curiously transposed English constitutional and commercial models to the Irish past. More historian than antiquary, Burke said little about the pre-Christian era. But he claimed "the contemplative life" of Irish Christianity "and the situation of Ireland, removed from the horrour of those devastations, which shook the rest of Europe, made it a refuge for learning, almost extinguished every where else." Burke would have found little fault in O'Conor's argument that earlier Irish manners could be appropriate for the times. For Burke, this assertion was part of a wider analysis in which such manners were an element of universal, or at least European, progress. He made use of this analysis to critique Whig and Tory accounts of English history.

Burke may have begun writing an Irish history in the years before entering Parliament (circa 1759–1765). His discussion of Ireland in the abridgment of English history is brief but concerns conquest. English conquest and civilization myths were paralleled in Irish Protestant circles, often maintaining that the country had not been conquered but had acquiesced to the Anglo-Normans. This argument, and the Catholic character of much of "Old English" constitutional history claimed by the post-Reformation "New English" settlers, was deeply problematic. For Burke, conquest came about from the same type of native "faction and discontent" that had brought about Saxon and Norman influence in England. He relates that Henry II had long had designs on Ireland. After the brutal murder of Thomas Becket, archbishop of Canterbury, by the king's allies, the English king hoped to recover the good graces of Pope Adrian IV by conquering Ireland (1172) to reform the Irish Church and collect Peterspence (penny tax collected by English kings). Involved in one of many domestic disputes, Dermot McMurrough (Diarmuid Mac Muireadhaigh), king of Leinster, requested Henry's assistance, and, with the country divided, continuing English influence was assured.

Burke argued that a conquest had occurred, adding that Irish resistance continued for more than four centuries. But papal involvement in the conquest, by granting England authority to invade, created problems for eighteenth-century Catholics and Protestants alike. Many in the Church of England presented an image of an enlightened, pre-Norman and non-Roman Christianity, to which they could claim to have returned. Burke himself wrote in "Essay towards an Abridgement of English History" that early Irish Catholicism was "not very remote from the present Protestant persuasion." Ferdinando Warner, an English ecclesiastical historian Burke had met and the first volume of whose Irish history had received a largely favorable review in the *Annual Register,* argued along similar lines. Catholic historians often thought it better simply to avoid the issue. Burke was among the few Irish writers to point out that Adrian IV, the Pope who had given Henry authority, was himself English. The implications of such an observation were significant and "down to the Reformation," Burke noted ironically in the "Abridgement of English History," "the Kings of England founded their title wholly on this grant." The Roman Catholicism of Ireland was, he believed, the result of the forceful imposition of Protestantism.

Burke's failure to complete the abridgment has often been ascribed to the dominance of Hume's history. Its cancellation is as likely to have been the result of the incessant demands of Hamilton or of the *Annual Register*. In addition, having completed the work only up to the Magna Carta, Burke had already disturbed many popular legal and political myths. The prospect of continuing must have looked uninviting, particularly as he approached Irish affairs. Indeed, during the 1760s the Irish Whiteboy disturbances—so-called because those people involved wore white shirts over their clothing to distinguish one another—erupted. The response of the Dublin government to these uprisings—the result of general changes in agriculture—was harsh and sectarian, and members of Burke's extended family were implicated. He subsequently began an account of the events but discontinued that work as well, perhaps because Curry had taken up a similar project. More generally, not to see parallels between England and Ireland in Burke's discussions of conquest is difficult. The invasions of England had brought attendant benefits in joining it to Europe. In Ireland, the advantages were less clear.

Shortly before Burke entered Parliament, the poems of Macpherson, presented as the work of a third-century poet, Ossian, revised recurring debates between Irish and Scottish historians. While the primitivism of the works fit the universal stages of progress from rudeness to refinement suggested by Scottish historians and philosophers, they contradicted the Irish defense of civility before English conquest and commerce. Burke's response to Ossian was complex. He was clearly impressed by the work and at first may have believed it to be genuine. Under criticism, including that of Burke's friends Johnson and O'Conor, it became increasingly clear that the work was at least partially forged. Whatever the truth about ancient Ireland or Scotland, Burke was far more skeptical than were his Scottish associates—Hume, Smith, Robertson, and John Millar—of discrete stages of progress and their prioritization of commerce over

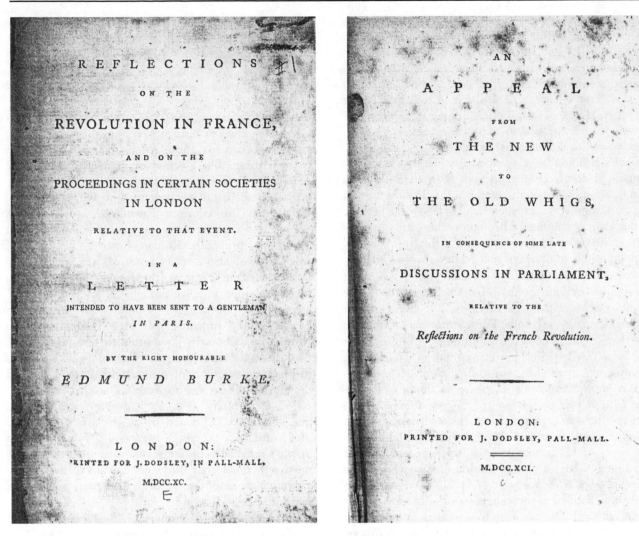

Title pages for two books by Burke expressing his opposition to what he regarded as mob rule of the French Revolution
(Special Collections, Thomas Cooper Library, University of South Carolina)

manners. In his defense of modern civil society, manners were more important than either laws or commerce.

Given that Irish Catholics and dissenters often had no civil or legal status, Burke's focus on manners is not surprising. His "Tracts on the Popery Laws" (circa 1759–1765?) was a vigorous critique of the penal laws restricting in various ways religious practice, education, and property ownership. Never published in his lifetime, several versions of the work circulated in the following decades among members of the English and Irish administrations. It was published posthumously in the *Works* (1792–1827). While he brought to his analysis considerable intellectual, legal, and rhetorical abilities, Burke's arguments closely reflected the thought of the Catholic Committee. In addition to appeals to reason, natural law, and history, he paid particular attention to the fragmentation and insecu-

rity of Catholic property holding and sought to show how the laws undermined the general interest of Ireland. But the work ends with a call for "an interior history of Ireland, the genuine voice of its records and monuments. . . . For they even now show to those who have been at the pains to examine them, and they may show one day to all the world, that these rebellions were not produced by toleration, but by persecution—that they arose not from just and mild government, but from unparalleled oppression." Burke spent considerable energy trying to ensure an "interior" history (the "genuine" Irish version) was told, but it did not meet his satisfaction. Reform of the penal laws met with somewhat more, though slow and sporadic, success.

Given these experiences, Burke may have seen London, rather than Dublin, as the best site for effecting Irish reform. Within two years of leaving Hamilton, he was working as personal secretary for Charles Watson Wentworth, Lord Rockingham, an important Whig leader and prime minister at Westminster. Shortly afterward, in 1766, Burke entered the British Parliament himself. "In truth," he wrote on 11 December 1783 to Charles O'Hara, friend and member of the Irish House of Commons, "I never was so myself." Though he continued to publish an impressive number of political tracts, for which he is best known, Burke's position largely ended his literary career. He remained deeply concerned with Irish affairs, though he became increasingly cautious as Ireland moved toward legislative independence (1782) during the American Revolution. Throughout his parliamentary career, he collected many artifacts of the Irish past and helped others to preserve such materials.

O'Conor repeatedly credited Burke with the suggestion that ancient Irish texts be translated before they were lost to later generations. The man best able to make such translations, Francis Stoughton Sullivan, first professor of feudal and common law at Trinity College (1761–1766), however, died in 1776 before completing much of the work. Burke may have known Sullivan, and Sullivan's *An Historical Treatise on the Feudal Law, and the Constitution and Laws of England* (1772) covers the same period as Burke's abridgment and fragment on law. Burke also remained an authority in the eyes of his contemporaries. He appears to have arranged to have a revised edition of Curry's *Historical Memoirs of the Rebellion of 1641* (1758) reviewed favorably by Smollet in the English *Critical Review*. Curry deferred to Burke, allowing him to alter or insert anything. Burke may also have influenced English travel writer and agriculturalist Arthur Young, whose *A Tour in Ireland* (1780) included another critique of penal legislation, and he corresponded with Irish antiquarians Sylvester O'Halloran and Chevalier Thomas O'Gorman.

Along with O'Conor, Burke strongly encouraged Leland to write an impartial, "interior" history of Ireland unburdened by confessional prejudice. Advising him to focus on the period after the invasion of Ireland, Burke made available several valuable manuscripts, originally from the collection of Welsh scholar Edward Lhwyd, then in the hands of Sir John Sebright, Member of Parliament for Bath. These same texts later provided the foundation for the Gaelic collection at Trinity College. Leland's *History of Ireland* (1773) represented but a small step toward impartiality. He described the rebellion of 1641 in terms only slightly milder than had Hume, laying again the ultimate responsibility for the rebellion on Catholic "superstition." The year before, when Burke was still hopeful about Leland's history, he insisted that the rebellion "was not only (as our silly things called Historys call it), not utterly *unprovoked* but . . . no History, that I have ever read furnishes an Instance of any that was so *provoked*." Not surprisingly, Burke, explicitly thanked in Leland's work, was—with O'Conor and Curry—disappointed by it.

In Parliament, Burke's writings and speeches provide extensive comments on English legal and constitutional history. These remain consistent with his early writings, but given their political purpose, are more difficult to interpret. Burke stressed modern liberties obtained, not ancient freedom reclaimed, especially with the Glorious Revolution of 1688. His predilection for precedent was always balanced by an appeal to principle. Roman history, like that of England, was also a ready resource. In his ultimately failed, fourteen-year impeachment of Warren Hastings for his actions as governor-general of India, Burke consciously modeled himself on Cicero's prosecution of Verres, the proconsul of Sicily. Drawing on the work of his associate, jurist-orientalist William Jones, Burke also became deeply involved in the study of the history and manners of India. Indians were, he told the House of Lords in a speech on Charles Fox's *India Bill* (1 December 1783), a "people for ages civilized and cultivated—cultivated by all the arts of polished life, whilst we were yet in the woods." When reading Burke's reflections on the revolutions in England, one must remember that Burke was aware of the significant limitations of the British constitution in America and India, as well as in Ireland.

In addition to Hume and the Irish historians, Burke also knew George William Lyttleton, Lord Lyttleton, and Gibbon, both historians and statesmen. Burke was, however, probably closer, personally and philosophically, to Robertson than to any other historian. Among other things in common, the two shared a sense of progress strengthened by the travel literature of the day. Burke wrote to Robertson that mankind possessed "at this time very great advantages towards the knowledge of human Nature. . . . We need no longer go to History to trace it in all its stages and periods . . . now the Great Map of Mankind is unrolld at once; and there is no state or Gradation of barbarism, and no mode of refinement which we have not at the same instant under our View" (9 June 1777). Robertson's works, written for the most part after Burke's aborted history, may usefully be compared to it, especially the preliminary volume of his *History of the Reign of the Emperor Charles V* (1769), an abridged "philosophical" history of European manners. Burke later wrote dramatist Arthur Murphy, who dedicated his translation of Tacitus to Burke (1793), on his view of contemporary historical writing. He noted a "feigned manner of *falsetto* . . . ," a strained, unnatural style; "no one modern historian, Robertson only excepted, is perfectly free" (8 December 1793).

As late as the 1780s, Burke was dragged into yet another Irish historiographical controversy. He had discussed Thomas Campbell's plan for an Irish history with Campbell. As he had with Leland, Burke lent papers and advised Campbell to begin with the Anglo-Norman invasion. Instead, Campbell entered the recurring debates on Irish origins against O'Conor, O'Halloran, and Charles Vallancey. Vallancey was an eccentric Englishman who had gone to Ireland as an army officer and had become an important stimulus to Irish history and the collection of antiquities. On the basis of specious linguistic analysis, Vallancey's defense of ancient Irish civility linked Ireland to the Phoenicians. Campbell was one of a new generation of Protestant historians who consciously sought to align themselves with Enlightenment writing. They suggested that Ireland was originally populated by Scandinavian barbarians and reasserted the claim that civility had come only with the Norman conquest. Burke found himself enlisted as an ally by both sides. The public debate left him disgusted, and when his son Richard was later made agent for the Irish Catholic Committee (1793), the elder Burke insisted Richard collect his manuscripts from Campbell.

Without appreciating Burke's rhetoric and earlier writings, the meaning of his *Reflections on the Revolution in France, and on the Proceedings in Certain Societies in London Relative to That Event* (1790) may easily be distorted. In it he wrote that "Sir Edward Coke, that great oracle of our law, and indeed all the great men who follow him, to Blackstone, are industrious to prove the pedigree of our liberties . . . ," but "if the lawyers mistake the particulars, it proves my position still the more strongly; because it demonstrates the powerful prepossession towards antiquity. . . ." The abridgment and his fragment on law clearly indicate that Burke believed both Coke and Blackstone had mistaken the particulars. Even in employing the vocabulary of the "ancient constitution," the appearance of continuity, not the constancy of English law, is important. His appeal to history is not a defense of Saxon liberty, but the slow, hard-won progress of centuries. This forward movement was to be, according to *Reflections on the Revolution in France,* "guided not by the superstition of antiquarians, but by the spirit of philosophical analogy."

With many of his enlightened contemporaries, Burke also employed *chivalry* as a term of art signifying the complex European union of manners. He defended his present, not the past. In echoes of the abridgment of English history, he wrote, "Nothing is more certain, than that our manners, our civilization, and all the good things which are connected with manners, and with civilization, have, in this European world of ours, depended for ages upon two principles: and were indeed the result of both combined: I mean the spirit of a gentleman, and the spirit of religion." Burke's view of the movement of history was progressive, but precarious. He had often used the civic humanist, or republican, rhetoric of "corruption" and "decay." His antirevolutionary writings show him making greater use of the language of neo-Roman "cyclical" theories of history, associated with Machiavelli, that suggest the rise and decline of societies. Burke saw in the attempts of the revolutionaries in France a threat to the advancement of centuries and the possibility of a regression to barbarism.

Given the possibility of an early civilization, whether pagan or Christian, destroyed by barbarism, Irish history might also have served as a meaningful model. In his public and private letters of the 1790s, Burke's attentions turned again to Ireland. He continued to press for Catholic relief as well as publishing material sympathetic to Catholic emancipation and returned to the subject of Irish history. In his *Letter from the Right Hon. Edmund Burke . . . to Sir Hercules Langrishe* (1792), he stressed the long-standing hostility of the British as well as the English in Ireland toward the native Irish, and the confiscations, feigned conspiracies, and judicial chicanery of the English during Ireland's long seventeenth century. These actions served

> for the purpose of the total extirpation of the interest of the natives in their own soil—until this species of subtile ravage, being carried to the last excess of oppression and insolence . . . kindled at length the flames of that rebellion which broke out in 1641. By the issue of that war, by the turn by which the Earl of Clarendon gave to things at the restoration, and by the total reduction of the kingdom of Ireland in 1691, the ruin of the native Irish, and in a great measure too, of the first races of the English, was completely accomplished.

All of these events preceded the penal statutes Burke had criticized three decades earlier. He had always seen the English revolution of 1688, rather than any Saxon golden age, as a watershed in British constitutional history. But, in Ireland, against the Catholic majority, "It was, to say the truth, not a revolution, but a conquest: which is not to say a great deal in its favour."

Edmund Burke died 9 July 1797, the year before another failed Irish rebellion. His long engagement with history—European, British, and Irish—left him deeply conscious of the difficulties of interpreting the past. He was no less aware of the complexity and fragility of progress. This sensibility had special significance in a revolutionary age that often seemed to deny the importance of its own history.

Letters:

The Correspondence of Edmund Burke, 10 volumes, edited by Thomas Copeland and others (Cambridge: Cambridge University Press / Chicago: University of Chicago Press, 1958–1978);

Selected Letters of Edmund Burke, edited, with an introduction, by Harvey C. Mansfield Jr. (Chicago: University of Chicago Press, 1984).

References:

Jeremy Black, "Edmund Burke: History, Politics, and Polemic," *History Today,* 37 (1987): 42–47;

Donald C. Bryant, *Edmund Burke and His Literary Friends* (St. Louis: Washington University Press, 1939);

Ann De Valera, "Antiquarian and Historical Investigations in Ireland in the Eighteenth Century," M.A. thesis, University College, Dublin, 1978;

Seán Patrick Donlan, "'Beneficence Acting by a Rule': Edmund Burke on Law, History, and Manners," *Irish Jurist,* new series, 36 (2001): 227–264;

Donlan, "'The Genuine Voice of Its Records and Monuments'?" Edmund Burke's 'interior history' of Ireland," in his *Edmund Burke's Irish Identities* (Dublin: Irish Academic Press, 2006);

Donlan, "'Language Is the Eye of Society': Edmund Burke on the Origins of the Polite and the Civil," *Eighteenth-Century Ireland/Iris an dá chultúr,* 18 (2003): 80–97;

Donlan, "'Little Better than Cannibals': Property and Progress in Sir John Davies and Edmund Burke," *Northern Ireland Legal Quarterly,* 54 (2003): 1–24;

Michael Fuchs, *Edmund Burke, Ireland, and the Fashioning of Self* (Oxford: Voltaire Foundation, 1996);

C. I. Gandy, "Burke and the Whig Historians, dissertation, University of Tennessee, 1973;

Rodney W. Kilcap, "Burke's Historicism," *Journal of Modern History,* 49, no. 2 (1977): 394–410;

F. P. Lock, *Edmund Burke: Volume I, 1730–1784* (Oxford: Clarendon Press, 1998);

Walter D. Love, "Charles O'Conor of Belanagare and Thomas Leland's 'philosophical' history of Ireland," *Irish Historical Studies,* 13 (1962): 1–25;

Love, "Edmund Burke and an Irish Historiographical Controversy," *History and Theory,* 2 (1962–1963): 180–198;

Love, "Edmund Burke, Charles Vallancey and the Sebright Manuscripts," *Hermathena,* 95 (1961): 21–35;

Love, "Edmund Burke's Historical Thought," dissertation, University of California, 1956;

Thomas H. D. Mahoney, "Edmund Burke as a Historian," abstracted by C. P. Ives, with commentary by Peter J. Stanlis, in *Burke Newsletter,* 2–3 (1961–1962): 85–91;

T. O. McLoughlin, *Contesting Ireland: Irish Voices against England in the Eighteenth Century* (Dublin: Four Courts, 1999);

McLoughlin, "Edmund Burke's Abridgement of English History," *Eighteenth-Century Ireland/Iris an dá chultúr,* 5 (1990): 45;

Clare O'Halloran, "Golden Ages and Barbarous Nations: Antiquarian Debate on the Celtic Past in Ireland and Scotland in the Eighteenth Century," dissertation, University of Cambridge, 1991;

J. G. A. Pocock, *The Ancient Constitution and the Feudal Law: A Study of English Historical Thought in the Seventeenth Century* (Cambridge: Cambridge University Press, 1986)–includes a retrospect;

Pocock, *The Parliamentary History of England from the Earliest Period to the Year 1803,* 30 volumes (London: T. C. Hansard, 1816);

Pocock, *Barbarism and Religion,* 2 volumes (Cambridge: Cambridge University Press, 1999);

Pocock, "Burke and the Ancient Constitution–a Problem in the History of Ideas," *Historical Journal,* 3 (1960): 125; reprinted in Pocock, *Politics, Language, and Time: Essays on Political Thought and History* (New York: Atheneum, 1973);

Pocock, *Virtue, Commerce, and History: Essays in Political Thought and History, Chiefly in the Eighteenth Century* (Cambridge: Cambridge University Press, 1985);

John Charles Weston Jr., "Edmund Burke as Historian," dissertation, University of North Carolina, 1956;

Weston, "Edmund Burke's Irish History: A Hypothesis," *PMLA,* 77 (1962): 397–403;

Weston, "Edmund Burke's View of History," *Review of Politics,* 23 (1961): 203–229.

Papers:

Edmund Burke's papers are located principally in the Fitzwilliam Mss. Collection (formerly known as Wentworth Woodhouse Mss.) in Sheffield Central City Library; in the Fitzwilliam Mss. Collection (formerly known as the Milton Mss.) in the Northhamptonshire Record Office, Lamport Hall; and in the British Library, London.

Charles Burney
(26 April 1726 – 12 April 1814)

Michael Griffin
University of Limerick

BOOKS: *An Essay towards a History of the Principal Comets That Have Appeared since the Year 1742* (London: Printed for T. Becket and P. A. de Hondt, 1769);

The Present State of Music in France and Italy: or, The Journal of a Tour through Those Countries, Undertaken to Collect Materials for a General History of Music (London: Printed for T. Becket, 1771; New York: Broude, 1969);

The Present State of Music in Germany, the Netherlands, and the United Provinces; or, The Journal of a Tour through Those Countries, Undertaken to Collect Materials for a General History of Music, 2 volumes (London: Printed for T. Becket; J. Robson; and G. Robinson, 1773; New York: Broude, 1969);

A General History of Music, From the Earliest Ages to the Present Period, volume 1 (London: Printed for the Author, 1776);

Account of the Infant Musician (London?: J. Nichols, 1779?);

A General History of Music. From the Earliest Ages to the Present Period, volume 2 (London: Printed for the author, 1782);

An Account of the Musical Performances in Westminster-Abbey, and the Pantheon, May 26th, 27th, 29th; and June the 3rd, and 5th, 1784. In Commemoration of Handel (London: Printed for the Benefit of the Musical Fund, 1785);

A General History of Music, from the Earliest Ages to the Present Period, volumes 3 and 4 (London: Printed for the Author, 1789);

Verses on the Arrival in England of the Great Musician Haydn (London?: T. Payne, 1791);

Memoirs of the Life and Writings of the Abate Metastasio, 3 volumes (London: Printed for G. G. and J. Robinson, 1796).

OTHER: Articles on music and musical biographies in *The Cyclopedia; or, Universal Dictionary of Arts, Sciences, and Literature,* edited by Abraham Rees (London: Printed for Longman, Hurst, Rees, Orme and Brown, 1802–1819).

TRANSLATIONS: Jean-Jacques Rousseau, *The Cunning-Man, a Musical Entertainment, in Two Acts* (London: Printed for T. Becket and P. A. de Hondt, 1766);

Charles Burney, circa 1781 (portrait by Sir Joshua Reynolds; National Portrait Gallery, London)

Gottlieb Conrad Pfeffel, *An Account of Mademoiselle Theresa Paradis, of Vienna, the Celebrated Blind Performer on the Piano Forte . . . by Her Blind Friend M. Pfeffel, London Magazine* (1785);

Franz Josef Haydn, *Hymn for the Emperor* (London: Broderip & Wilkinson, 1789).

SELECTED PERIODICAL PUBLICATIONS— UNCOLLECTED:
POETRY

"Advice to the Herald" (poem), *The Morning Herald,* 12 March 1782;

"Again the Day Returns of Holy Rest" (hymn), *Gentleman's Magazine,* 63 (December 1803): 1140.

NONFICTION

Review of Francis Maxwell, "An Essay upon Tune," *Critical Review*, 54 (August 1782): 117–125;

Review of Joseph Cooper Walker, "Historical Memoirs of the Irish Bards," *Monthly Review*, 57 (December 1787): 425–439.

Charles Burney was perhaps the first genuinely encyclopedic practitioner of musical history in England. His extensive European travel and musical talents qualified him to compile and compose a general history of music, as well as musicological accounts of European nations and several musical biographies. His great achievement was his *General History of Music*, published in four volumes between 1776 and 1789.

Burney's family background was somewhat irregular. He was the grandson and son of two James Macburneys. The "Mac" that prefixed his grandfather's and, for a time, his father's family name, was a mystery: "I never could find," he remarked, "at what period any of my ancestors lived in Scotland or in Ireland." His father, who settled on the name James Burney, was disinherited for eloping with a young actress named Rebecca Ellis of the Goodman's Fields Theatre. Within a year of Rebecca's death in 1720, James Burney married heiress Anne Cooper, with whom he had five children. On 26 April 1726, in Shrewsbury, twins–Charles and Susanna–were born to the couple. Charles was James Burney's last son; Charles's twin sister, Susanna, died early.

James Burney became a portrait painter, and the family moved to Chester, where young Charles was educated at the free school on a prestigious King's scholarship, for which he was nominated by Prebendary Prescott, a prominent local music lover. In 1741 he returned to Shrewsbury and began musical training under his half brother (another James Burney), the eldest child of his father's first marriage, who was the organist at St. Mary's of Shrewsbury. Charles also studied under Edmund Baker, organist of Chester Cathedral.

In 1744 Charles was introduced to celebrated composer and musician Thomas Arne, then traveling through Chester on his return from Ireland. Arne offered to complete Burney's musical training. Charles's father acceded, and Charles went to London with Arne in 1744. Actress Susannah Cibber was Arne's sister; in her house, Burney met with several of the literary and theatrical luminaries of the day, among them actor David Garrick and poets James Thomson and Christopher "Kit" Smart. Burney composed some of the music to Thomson's masque *Alfred* (revised by David Mallet in 1751). The first work to which Burney put his name was *Six Sonatas for Two Violins, with a Bass for the Violoncello or Harpsichord* ([1748]), dedicated to Robert Darcy, fourth Earl of Holdernesse, at whose house Burney befriended poet William Mason.

Burney remained with Arne for three trying years. In 1746 famed harpsichord-maker Jacob Kirkman introduced Burney to Fulke Greville. Greville was so impressed with Burney's playing and conversation that he paid Arne to release Burney from his apprenticeship so that he could travel with Greville. With Greville, Burney improved his profile as a teacher of music and as a socialite. Greville granted Burney consent to marry Esther Sleepe in 1749. That year Burney was appointed organist of St. Dionis Backchurch and was elected a member of the Royal Society of Musicians. He also conducted the "New Concerts" held at the King's Arms in Cornhill. He wrote the music for the burletta *Robin Hood*, with libretto by Moses Mendez, which was performed at Drury Lane in December 1750. Rather more successfully, he composed for the pantomime *Queen Mab*, also staged that month.

Burney's reputation was increasing, only to be curtailed at a crucial juncture by health problems. After a severe and mysterious illness that lasted thirteen weeks, Burney was compelled to leave London for Lynn Regis in Norfolk, where for nine years he occupied a lucrative, though to him limited and obscure, position as organist at St. Margaret's church. During this period, by way of correspondence and other research, he began tentatively to collect material for a projected history of music.

In 1760, with his health fully restored, he returned to live in London's Poland Street. His contentment on that return did not last, however: on 27 September 1762 his wife, Esther, died. Her death left Burney in a state of profound and temporarily debilitating grief. After Esther's death, Burney took his two daughters, Esther and Susanna, to Paris to continue their education.

Upon Burney's return to London, Garrick suggested that Burney adapt the opera *Le Devin du Village* by Jean-Jacques Rousseau–then better known as a composer and a critic than as a philosopher. Burney's *The Cunning-Man* was produced at Drury Lane in November 1766 and was performed fourteen times that season.

On 6 October 1767 Burney secretly married the widow of Stephen Allen, an old friend from Lynn Regis. Allen had left £40,000 to his wife, and this sum was a tremendous relief to Burney, who had been struggling to support his family since his theatrical career had subsided and the death of an elderly patron had deprived him of a substantial stipend.

The year 1769 was key in Burney's intellectual career. He received his doctorate in music from the University of Oxford. He indulged his long-standing astronomical interests, publishing in October *An Essay towards a History of the Principal Comets That Have Appeared since the Year 1742.* Upon recovery from a spell of rheumatic fever, Burney resolved to collect for his projected musical history in earnest; at this point, he committed himself to writing his career-defining *A General History of Music.*

He complained to William Mason in a letter of May 1770 that previous books and essays on music were disappointing and mutually derivative, even in error. On that basis, he resolved to travel to Europe in the summer of 1770 in order to collect as much primary material as possible. He left England on 5 June, equipped with letters of introduction to eminent scholars and musicians on the Continent.

Over the following three years he traveled to France, the Low Countries (The Netherlands, Belgium, and Luxembourg), Switzerland, Germany, and Italy, perhaps the nation whose music he most admired. In contrast, he sought in France only examples that confirmed his prejudices. Though generally Francophobic, he thought highly of the musical writings of Jean le Rond d'Alembert, and particularly of Rousseau. His account of these tours appeared in two installments. In 1771 he published *The Present State of Music in France and Italy;* two years later *The Present State of Music in Germany, the Netherlands, and the United Provinces* appeared, in two volumes.

In 1776 the first volume of Burney's *A General History of Music, From the Earliest Ages to the Present Period* appeared. Burney's preface justified the contents of the volume by lamenting the dearth of musical histories that had come down from the ancients. The first volume studied the musical theory of the ancient Egyptians, Hebrews, Romans, and—most substantially—the Greeks. He claimed that he had taken care to avoid jargon and pedantry. As an historian, he claimed that his methodology must move beyond oppositions of theory and narrative, for "a history is neither a body of laws, nor a novel. I have blended together theory and practice, facts and explanations, incidents, causes, consequences, conjectures, and confessions of ignorance, just as the subject produced them." His history of music, accordingly, aims to collect "the most interesting circumstances relative to practice and professors." He traces the involvement of music in matters of religion and war and its historical role in private and public amusements, always careful, he claimed, to gather as much reliable factual material as possible: "I have never had recourse to conjecture, when facts were to be found. In the historical and biographical parts, I have asserted nothing without vouchers."

The volume was well subscribed and positively, though calmly, praised by the periodical press, with the *Critical Review* proclaiming that the evidence of the first volume indicated that further volumes would finish out a well-conceived plan. The second volume, which traces the development of music from its introduction into the early medieval church, through the innovations of counterpoint, the timetable, and printing, was published in 1782. It was positively received in the monthly journals, echoing reviews of the first volume in the general sentiment that the author's knowledge and experience augered well for further installments.

Accordingly, volumes three and four concluded the series in 1789. The third volume, introduced by a liberal "Essay on Musical Criticism," studied the progress of national styles—English, Italian, German, French, Spanish, and Dutch—through the sixteenth and seventeenth centuries. "An Essay on the Euphony or Sweetness of Languages and their Fitness for Music" introduces the substantial consideration in the fourth volume of the most recent formal Italian innovations—in opera, comic opera, oratorio, and chamber music. A series of chapters on eighteenth-century musical developments in Germany, France, and England precedes a general, though brief, conclusion, in which Burney hopes that the second half of the *History of Music,* with its rigorous account of "the simplicity and harmonic merit" of seventeenth- and eighteenth-century music, might make amends for the "conjecture and speculation" on "barbarous Music" in the first.

Essays in the *Monthly Review* regarding the final two volumes, written by Burney's erstwhile collaborator Thomas Twining (who assisted Burney with much of the material on ancient Greek music), were predictably glowing, proclaiming that Burney had succeeded in supplying the want of a comprehensive musical history, a task insufficiently attempted in the *General History of the Science and Practice of Music*—a similar, contemporaneous study by John Hawkins, published in five volumes in 1776.

Through the 1770s and 1780s, following on the successes of his *History of Music,* Burney found himself in the thick of the literary groups of the day. He had been friendly with Samuel Johnson, and hence with many of the members of Johnson's Literary Club, for some time. Burney had collected six subscribers for Johnson's *Dictionary* in 1755. This friendship, though strong, was probably tempered on Johnson's side by a lack of interest in music. Though Johnson did not understand Burney's field, he recognized Burney's social and intellectual brilliance. Having been a friend to several of its members for many years beforehand, Burney was formally elected a member of the celebrated club in 1784. Burney was particularly friendly with Irish philosopher and politician Edmund Burke, who later helped

A

GENERAL HISTORY

OF

M U S I C,

FROM THE

EARLIEST AGES to the PRESENT PERIOD.

To which is prefixed,

A DISSERTATION

ON THE

MUSIC OF THE ANCIENTS.

BY

CHARLES BURNEY, Muf. D. F. R. S.

VOLUME THE FIRST.

LONDON,

Printed for the AUTHOR: And fold by T. BECKET, Strand; J. ROBSON,
New Bond-Street; and G. ROBINSON, Paternofter-Row.

MDCCLXXVI.

*Title page for the first volume of Burney's four-volume masterwork
(Eighteenth Century Collections Online, Gale Group)*

him to obtain the position of organist at Chelsea Hospital.

The year 1784 was also the centenary of George Friedric Handel's birth. Burney assisted with the preparations for the musical celebrations on that occasion and published an account of them the following January, along with a biography of the composer. In 1786 Burney applied for the position of Master of the Royal Music, vacated upon the death of John Stanley. Though Burney did obtain a desultory interview with George III and was thought by most observers in the musical establishment to be the best man for the post, he was unsuccessful in attaining it. His candidacy was undermined, some think, by the machinations of James Cecil, first marquess of Salisbury, the Lord Chamberlain. The post was given to William Parsons. Burney's daughter Fanny stressed that Burney felt no ill will or resentment to Parsons upon his appointment. Her biography, however, may have deliberately concealed Burney's genuine indignation.

After the *General History of Music* had been completed in 1789, Burney wrote for Ralph Griffith's *Monthly Review* on a regular basis, contributing reviews of musical treatises and books of travel, poetry, and biography. This writing was for Burney a useful way to supplement his income, but it was also a means of giving his own books publicity. He achieved that goal by pointing out plagiarisms of his research and comparative weaknesses in the works of other authors. He also began harshly criticizing books by supposed friends, such as William Mason and Irish antiquarian and historian of music Joseph Cooper Walker. Walker had corresponded politely with Burney for many years in the course of gathering materials for his *Historical Memoirs of the Irish Bards* (1786), but in his 1787 review of that work, Burney lambasted Walker with strong intonations against the credulousness of Irish antiquarianism. In so doing, he proclaimed, anonymously, "Dr. Burney's" own "great diligence," and "classical authority."

By 1793 Burney began to suffer from fevers and rheumatism, illnesses that necessitated trips to Bath's curative waters. But these illnesses did not prevent him from completing and publishing *Memoirs of the Life and Writings of the Abate Metastasio,* a three-volume biography of the renowned Pietro Trapassi, the Italian poet whose dramas were put to music by composers such as Handel, Franz Joseph Haydn, and Wolfgang Amadeus Mozart. Burney had recorded his 1772 meetings with Metastasio in Vienna in the account of his German tour. Though his *General History of Music* had discussed Metastasio's collaborations with composers, he had not allocated any substantial study to the poet himself, a lack which his biography sought to redress.

With this task completed, Burney began to gather his thoughts for a projected dictionary of music. His daughter Fanny claimed that he had, at one point, intended to translate Rousseau's 1767 *Dictionnaire de Musique* but had resolved, in spite of a competing project by Samuel Arnold, to work on an original. Burney's intentions were interrupted by the death of his second wife in 1796. Fanny sought to distract him from his grief by urging him to continue work on a long—and long dormant—poem on the ambitious subject of historical astronomy; however, this work was left unfinished and was eventually destroyed by Burney himself.

He was for a while distracted by Frances Crewe's suggestion that he edit, along with his daughter, an anti-Jacobin, promonarchical periodical. Indeed, much of Burney's correspondence is imbued with an unwavering belief in the rectitude of the English constitutional arrangement. For one who considered music and culture in their various national contexts, his traditionalist aesthetics were informed by his political beliefs. Even his biography of Mestastasio has been considered a reactionary paean to a cultural Golden Age, untainted by democratic disorders. He complained throughout the 1790s of the spreading French malaise, of the decline of traditional values. Music, as he had long seen it, was an "innocent luxury" best maintained in tranquil societies; it was a natural emanation of social and cultural health, a simple matter of taste that did not require any abstract theories, either to bring it forth or to make sense of it.

In the second year of the new century Burney suffered another serious blow, this time in the death of his daughter Susanna. In spite of–but perhaps because of– this bereavement, Burney resolved to stay busy. Between 1801 and 1805 he wrote lucrative musical biographies for Abraham Rees's *Cyclopedia*. In 1806 he was granted a state pension. The same year he suffered a minor paralytic stroke in his left hand, which prompted him, upon recovery, to resurrect and recommence memoirs that he had begun in 1782. Gradually withdrawing from society from this point on, he worked on his autobiography right up to his death on 12 April 1814. His memoirs were eventually deemed by his daughter to be too dense and monotonously detailed, though in reality she was censoring her father's frank accounts of his own parents' dissipation and neglect. He was interred in the Chelsea Hospital burial ground; a monument, inscribed by Fanny, was erected in Westminster Abbey.

"I knew that a history of Music was wanted by my countrymen," wrote Burney in the preface to his best-known work; "though I was utterly ignorant that any one else had undertaken to supply it." Though John Hawkins was Burney's closest rival in a national sense, the depth and breadth of the *General History of Music,* along with Burney's public profile, ensured his preeminence and the long success of his work.

Bibliographies:
B. C. Nangle, *Monthly Review: Indexes of Contributors and Articles, Second Series, 1790–1815* (Oxford: Clarendon Press, 1955)–includes Burney's contributions to the *Monthly Review;*

Roger Lonsdale, "Bibliography," in *Dr. Charles Burney: A Literary Biography* (Oxford: Oxford University Press, 1965), pp. 495–501.

Biographies:
Fanny Burney [as Madame d'Arblay], *Memoirs of Doctor Burney, Arranged from his own Manuscripts, from Family Papers, and from Personal Recollections,* 3 volumes (London: Edward Moxon, 1832);
Percy Alfred Scholes, *The Great Dr. Burney, His Life, His Travels, His Works, His Family and His Friends,* 2 volumes (London & New York: Oxford University Press, 1948);
Roger Lonsdale, *Dr. Charles Burney: A Literary Biography* (Oxford: Oxford University Press, 1965);
Kerry S. Grant, *Dr. Burney as Critic and Historian of Music* (Ann Arbor: University of Michigan Press, 1983);
Memoirs of Dr. Charles Burney, 1726–1769 (Lincoln & London: University of Nebraska Press, 1988).

References:
Miriam Benkovitz, "Dr. Burney's Memoirs," *Review of English Studies,* 10 (1959): 257–268;
John Wilson Croker, "Madame d'Arblay's Memoirs of Dr. Burney," *Quarterly Review,* 49 (1833): 97–125;
F. G. Edwards, "Dr. Charles Burney (1726–1814). A Biographical Sketch," *Musical Times,* 45 (1904): 435–439, 513–515, 575–580;
Roger Lonsdale, "Dr. Burney and the *Monthly Review,*" *Review of English Studies,* 14 (1963): 346–358; 15 (1964): 27–37.

Papers:
Collections of Charles Burney's manuscripts and correspondence are in Yale University's Beinecke Library (including the James M. Osborn Collection); the New York Public Library (the Berg Collection); the British Museum (including the Barrett Collection); the Bodleian Library, Oxford; the John Rylands Library, Manchester; the Folger Library, Washington, D.C.; and the Pierpont Morgan Library, New York.

Thomas Carte

(Baptized 23 April 1686 – 2 April 1754)

Michael R. Hutcheson
Landmark College

BOOKS: *The Irish Massacre Set in a Clear Light. Wherein Mr. Baxter's Account of It in the History of His Own Life, and the Abridgement Thereof by Dr. Calamy, Are Thoroughly Consider'd, and the Royal Martyr Fully Vindicated* (London: Printed for George Strahan, 1714; revised, 1715);

An History of the Life of James Duke of Ormonde, From His Birth in 1610, to His Death in 1688, 3 volumes (London: Printed by J. Bettenham, for J. J. and P. Knapton . . . G. Strahan, and others, 1735–1736);

A Collection of Original Letters and Papers, Concerning the Affairs of England, from the year 1641 to 1660 Found among the Duke of Ormonde's Papers, 2 volumes (London: A. Millar, 1739);

The History of the Revolutions of Portugal, from the Foundation of that Kingdom to the year MDCLXVII, anonymous (London: Printed for John Osborn, 1740);

The Blatant-Beast. A Poem (London: Printed for J. Robinson, 1742);

A Full Answer to A Letter from a By-Stander, as R.H., 2 volumes (London: Printed for J. Robinson, 1742);

A Full and Clear Vindication of the Full Answer to A Letter from a By-Stander, as the Author of the *Full Answer* (London: Printed for J. Robinson, 1743);

An Account of the Numbers of Men Able to Bear Arms in the Provinces and Towns of France (London: Printed for M. Cooper, 1744);

A Collection of the Several Papers Published by Mr. Thomas Carte, in Relation to His History of England (London: Printed for M. Cooper, 1744);

The Case Fairly Stated: In a Letter from a Member of Parliament in the Country Interest, to One of his Constituents, anonymous (London: Printed for M. Cooper, 1745);

A General History of England, 4 volumes (London: Printed for the author and sold by J. Hodges, 1747–1755).

TRANSLATION: Jacques Auguste de Thou, *History of Thuanus,* 7 volumes (London: Samuel Buckley, 1733).

OTHER: Preface to *Catalogue des rolles Gascons, Norman et Francois, conservés dans les archives de la Tour de Londres,* 2 volumes (London [i.e. Paris]: Jacques Barois, 1743).

Thomas Carte was a supporter of the Stuart monarchy who advanced his Jacobite political beliefs through a series of historical works published in the early eighteenth century. He wrote most extensively about the history of England and English interests in Ireland, although a period of continental exile led Carte also to produce works related to French and Portuguese history. While Carte has not earned a place among the leading historians of his time, he is notable for the documentary evidence he compiled to support his historical interpretations. Hampered by a repetitious writing style and extreme political partisanship, his works are often more valuable for their extensive quotations from primary sources than for their narration or analysis.

Carte was born in Clifton upon Dunsmore, in Warwickshire, England, presumably in early 1686. While some works list his birth in November of that year, parish records show baptism occurring on 23 April. His father, the Reverend Samuel Carte, was vicar in the town and a man of conservative theology who in several published sermons upheld the doctrine of the Trinity against Unitarian reformers. In 1691 Samuel Carte became head of the free school in Coventry, where Thomas received his early education before going to Rugby. Samuel Carte was also an antiquarian who published a chronology of bishoprics in 1714 and collected important material on the history of Leicester. Little is known about Thomas's mother, Anne, although church records indicate that she may have given birth to as many as thirteen children.

After three years at Rugby School, Thomas Carte enrolled at University College, Oxford, in 1698 during an era when matriculating at age twelve was not unusual. He took his B.A. degree at Brasenose College in 1702 and then went to Cambridge, receiving an M.A. degree from King's College in 1706. Carte followed his father into church service; he became a reader at Bath Abbey Church and was ordained a priest in 1710. A sermon he preached at Bath in January 1714 prompted Carte to produce his first historical work.

Marking the anniversary of Charles I's execution, Carte delivered a sermon that, in part, vindicated King Charles I from blame for the Irish uprising of 1641. While the date when Carte became a Jacobite is difficult to determine, his sermon and his refusal to take the Oath of Allegiance about this same time indicate that he was fully committed to the Stuart cause by 1714. A local dissenting minister, Henry Chandler, took exception to Carte's views, and in response Carte wrote *The Irish Massacre Set in a Clear Light* (1714). Supporters of Parliament had claimed since 1642 that Charles I conspired with Randal MacDonnell, first Marquess and second Earl of Antrim, and Sir Phelim O'Neill to encourage Irish Catholics to rise against the English forces, thereby unleashing the "atrocities" against Protestants in 1641 reported in the lurid English pamphlet literature of the English Civil War era. For many supporters of Parliament, the vastly exaggerated reports of 150,000 to 200,000 deaths provided an important justification for opposing the Stuarts in 1642 and 1688, for justifying Cromwell's massacre of the defenders of Drogheda in 1649, and for executing Charles I. Written as a letter to his accuser, Carte's first argument in *The Irish Massacre Set in a Clear Light* is based on deductive reasoning and published histories, such as the pro Royalist *History of the Rebellion and Civil Wars in England* (1702–1704) by Edward Hyde, Earl of Clarendon. The charge against the king, Carte says, "is wanting both in external and intrinsick Evidence . . . is inconsistent with the King's Character and Conduct on many Accounts, and . . . [has] been in the most unexceptionable manner refuted by Sir Phelim Oneal [that is, O'Neill]." Responding to a second letter from the still unconvinced Chandler, Carte's second edition of *The Irish Massacre* (1715) turns to documentary evidence, including specific references to the transcript of O'Neill's trial, sworn depositions, the correspondence between the king and the duke of Ormonde, and other primary sources.

Carte's thirty-three-page response to the dissenter's second letter provides a foretaste of his historical style: amassing documentary sources in order to overwhelm any counterargument, adopting a high moral tone, and ignoring any evidence that demonstrated the king's shortsightedness or poor political judgment. This debate was not merely historical for Carte: he recognized that disproving the conspiracy charge against Charles I not only would help redeem the king's reputation but also would bolster the current Jacobite cause gathering momentum in Scotland and Ireland in the days before the Rising of 1715.

Almost two decades passed before Carte's next historical work appeared. Initially, this hiatus occurred because Carte was in hiding after the Jacobite rising failed. More instrumental in the long run was Carte's association with Francis Atterbury, Bishop of Rochester. Atterbury, too, had become an increasingly devoted Jacobite since about 1713, and Carte appears to have been Atterbury's secretary for a time. The relationship was close enough that Atterbury secured a living for Thomas Carte's brother, John. In 1722, Atterbury was indicted for high treason. *The London Gazette* of 15 August includes a notice offering a reward of £1,000 for Carte's arrest as well, accompanied by a physical description of questionable accuracy. Carte fled to France under the name of Philips, along with Atterbury. According to Oxford historian and fellow Jacobite Thomas Hearne, in volume sixty-seven of *Remarks and Collections of Thomas Hearne*, Carte played only a peripheral role in Atterbury's circle in France because he was "a very great talker, and so imprudent . . . as not to distinguish friend from foe."

Excluded from inner Jacobite circles while in France, Carte continued his historical inquiries. The most successful product of this period was his translation of Jacques Auguste de Thou's insider history of the French court in the sixteenth century, *History of Thuanus* (1733). This work appears to have appealed to Carte because of its criticism of the Roman Catholic Church and its royalist sympathy. In fact, Carte may have embellished the translation to emphasize these qualities. In the miscellany in the final volume, Carte misdates one letter of French king Henry IV and extensively edits another to create the impressions that the king was persecuted by the Jesuits and that de Thou was a proto-Enlightenment rationalist. Nevertheless, the so-called Buckley-Carte edition of de Thou's history remained the standard scholarly edition for more than two centuries.

Carte was allowed to return to England in 1728, mainly because of a sympathetic London publisher's intercession with Queen Caroline. Chastened by exile but retaining his Jacobite convictions, Carte embarked on one of the two major works of his career, *An History of the Life of James Duke of Ormonde, From His Birth in 1610, to His Death in 1688* (1735–1736). Carte's subject was a member of the powerful Anglo-Irish Butler family, a commander of the king's forces in Ireland during the English Civil War and later three times lord lieutenant of Ireland. A paragon of the virtues in which Carte believed, Ormonde was a staunch Protestant in a pre-

A
GENERAL
HISTORY
OF
ENGLAND.

VOLUME I.

Containing an Account of the firſt Inhabitants of the Country,
and the Tranſactions in it, from the earlieſt Times
to the Death of King JOHN, A. D. MCCXVI.

By *THOMAS CARTE*, an ENGLISHMAN.

LONDON,
Printed for the AUTHOR, at his Houſe in Dean's Yard, Weſtminſter.
AND SOLD BY
J. HODGES, at the Looking-glaſs facing St. Magnus' Church, London Bridge.
MDCCXLVII.

Title page for Thomas Carte's history of England, which emphasizes
socio-economic development more than previous seventeenth-century
histories had, though it is primarily about reigns
(Eighteenth-Century Collections Online,
Gale Group)

dominantly Catholic family who proved his loyalty to the Stuarts by provisioning armies for the beleaguered Charles I.

Placing the first duke of Ormonde in his historical context allowed Carte to construct a thorough defense of the Stuart monarchy. From the ascent of King James I to the throne in 1603, Carte argued, the Stuarts had been dedicated to the welfare of the four kingdoms. Thus, the Stuart "plantation" of Ulster is presented not as an expropriation of land but as a reform assuring the native Irish status as subjects rather than as aliens. Similarly, the patent self-interest of the new English and Scottish planters who dominated the first Irish parliament in 1613 is, in Carte's analysis, the "publick approbation" of Stuart policy "by the representatives of the whole Nation." The lawsuits, dissent, and rebellion caused by the plantation, especially after it was extended into the province of Leinster, were not caused by Stuart policy but by unscrupulous planters and Crown commissioners on the one hand, and "swarms" of Jesuits and European-educated Catholic priests on the other. Likewise, the growing religious tension in seventeenth-century Ireland was not a result of reviving the Act of Supremacy and the Act of Uniformity but of "the alienating of the minds of the people from their lawful Prince, who by the favour of his extraction from the old kings of Ireland, might probably have ruled in their hearts." Through such assertions, Carte portrays the Stuarts as blameless in issues of landholding, parliamentary prerogative, and religious dissent before he reaches the battleground of the Civil War.

Focusing on Ormonde, a staunch Royalist who twice brokered temporary peace agreements in Ireland during the 1640s, also allows Carte to paint the parliamentary opposition as the source of all immoderation in the war. Shortly after Cromwell landed his army in Ireland, Ormonde despaired of any negotiated peace and went into exile in Europe in 1650, leaving his wife to manage the family's remaining lands. The duke's loyalty to the Stuarts in exile was finally rewarded when he returned to Ireland as lord lieutenant following the Restoration of 1660.

In compiling this biography, Carte had the support of the second duke, also a Jacobite, who opened the family archives, which in turn opened the purses of aristocratic subscribers. With the Jacobite cause, as always, foremost in his mind, Carte saw the opportunity to rewrite the history of the English Civil War and its aftermath from a proroyal perspective. In doing so, Carte was retreading the ground of Lord Clarendon's *History of the Rebellion and the Civil Wars in England* (1702–1704), but where Clarendon relied on his role in the events to inform his narrative, Carte provided source material. Especially valuable to future historians was the Ormonde correspondence, many examples of which were included in an appendix. Carte added to this documentary cache in 1739 with *A Collection of Original Letters and Papers, Concerning the Affairs of England, from the year 1641 to 1660 Found among the Duke of Ormonde's Papers.*

In 1740 Carte's father, Reverend Samuel Carte, died, leaving the bulk of his estate to Thomas. Included was his father's collection of papers on the history of Leicester. In this same year, Thomas Carte published his *History of the Revolutions of Portugal,* a distinctly British and somewhat one-dimensional view based on the letters of the British ambassador, Sir Robert Southwell, to the duke of Ormonde. Although not a major work, it once again illustrates Carte's faith in the letters of participants as an unimpeachable historical source.

From 1742 to 1747 Carte published only minor works and documentary collections. *The Blatant-Beast* (1742) is a versified political satire on Alexander Pope that includes nothing of its target's wit or versifying ability. Also in this period, Carte entered the perennial eighteenth-century pamphlet war over a standing army in *A Full Answer to A Letter from a By-Stander* (1742) and *A Full and Clear Vindication of the Full Answer to A Letter from a By-Stander* (1743). Carte's argument against a full-time professional army is based partly on his revulsion toward the power of Cromwell a century earlier, partly on his assessment of France's then-current politics and power, and partly on his historical analysis of English royal prerogatives and taxation since the time of William the Conqueror. Not surprisingly, Carte devoted the most space to exonerating the Stuarts from allegations that they had greatly expanded taxation and then squandered the proceeds, especially after the Restoration of 1660. In his exploration of traditional royal prerogatives (and to preliminary work on his forthcoming survey of English history), Carte assembled the *Catalogue des rolles Gascons, Norman et Francois* (1743), a calendar of documents detailing grants of office and land in those areas under English rule in the thirteenth century. Recognizing that war with France was increasingly likely, Carte compiled *An Account of the Numbers of Men Able to Bear Arms in the Provinces and Towns of France* (1744). A final piece of pamphleteering was *The Case Fairly Stated* (1745), in which Carte adopted the fictitious persona of a member of Parliament to criticize parliamentary politics in the wake of Sir Robert Walpole's resignation in 1742. Carte's distaste for Walpole and his faction was certainly intensified when, in 1739, Walpole tricked the politically earnest but naive Carte into revealing his advice to the Stuart Pretender, then living in France.

These pamphlets were created in the shadow of Carte's final major work, the four-volume *A General History of England* (1747–1755). As he did with his biography of the duke of Ormonde, in 1736 Carte published a prospectus for potential subscribers and a more substantial appeal two years later. His efforts produced the patronage not only of Jacobite sympathizers among the aristocracy but also the support of five Oxford colleges and "City" organizations such as the Goldsmiths' company and the London Court of Common Council. The latter sponsorship prompted Walpole to observe ruefully, according to Philip Hicks in *Neoclassical History and English Culture:* "The good City of London, who, from long dictating to the government, are now come to preside over taste and letters, have given one Carte, a Jacobite parson, fifty pounds a year for seven years, to write the history of England; and four aldermen and six Common council men are to inspect his materials and

the progress of the work. Surveyors of common sewers turned supervisors of literature!" Some of Carte's preliminary sketches and documents were gathered in *A Collection of the Several Papers Published by Mr. Thomas Carte, in Relation to His History of England* (1744), and the first volume of *A General History of England* was published three years later.

Carte's *A General History of England* is primarily a chronicle of royal administrations, but with more attention to socio-economic development than was common in early-seventeenth-century historical writing. Throughout the work Carte follows Restoration historian Robert Brady in attacking the Whig interpretation of the "ancient constitution" and upholding royal prerogative as the central feature of English history. The decline of this august tradition came with the replacement of "the old heroic race of nobility," as Carte says in volume four of his history, by "moneyed" men. Carte holds the Tudors, particularly founder Henry VII, primarily responsible for this ruinous development. Not surprisingly, given Carte's politics and previous works, the supporters of Parliament in the English Civil War come in for the greatest share of blame for the current debased condition of England. The executed Charles I is canonized as a saint and martyr, and his execution, Carte states, also in volume four, brought divine retribution on England. The "want of virtue, and publick spirit, the irreligion, immorality, and corruption" of contemporary England may be traced to "the execrable murther of K. Charles, and the subversion of the constitution at that time."

When volumes of *A General History of England* began to appear, the work immediately alienated many of its subscribers. The narrative was densely packed with documentation and exegeses, causing (according to Hicks) John Boyle, the fifth Earl of Orrery, to lament, "how shall I wade through Tom Carte's first volume? I believe it must stand like a wooden book, unmolested but well ornamented in my library." Even more troublesome for Carte's fortunes was a footnote in the first volume that claimed that the Stuart Pretender had successfully performed the ceremony of "touching for the king's evil"—healing scrofula by touch—in France. The controversy created by this claim and the manifest Jacobite partisanship cost Carte the support of many patrons: the initial printing for the first volume was 3,000 copies, for the later volumes only 750.

While Carte's *History of England* was notable for its wealth of documentation and socio-economic analysis, it was immediately superseded by David Hume's *History of England* (1754–1762), more gracefully written, more in tune with the developing late-eighteenth-century taste for philosophical history, and less overtly partisan, although still strongly anti-Whig and pro-Stuart. Hume referred to Carte, according to Hicks, as "a late author of great industry and learning, but full of prejudices, and of no penetration," but nevertheless, Hume did incorporate a great deal of Carte's documentation.

Carte did not live to see the final fruits of his labors. The fourth volume of his *General History of England,* truncated at the pre-Restoration 1650s, was published posthumously. Carte had suffered throughout his adult life with acute rheumatism; the letters of both Thomas Hearne and Jonathan Swift refer to attacks of rheumatism delaying Carte's work. It was diabetes, however, that caused Carte's death on 2 April 1754. He died at Caldecott House, near Abingdon, Berkshire, and was buried nine days later in the churchyard at Yattenden, near Newbury. His wife of seven years, Sarah Brett, received his entire estate, including the documents Carte had not yet bequeathed to the Bodleian Library at Oxford. His wife remarried, and after her death, her widower sold the remaining papers to the Bodleian. Along with the documentary evidence he included in his published works, Carte's most lasting legacy may be this archive, important especially on matters related to the Stuarts and the English Civil War. All historians of seventeenth-century English government are indebted to the trove of documentary material known ever since as the Carte Manuscripts.

Thomas Carte was among those who advanced British historiography in the late seventeenth and early eighteenth centuries by assiduously compiling manuscripts and collating facts. While this effort earned him only half-hearted admiration as "laborious" and "of great industry" by such contemporaries as Tobias Smollett and Hume, respectively, he garnered the respect of later historians such as Leopold von Ranke, who, in his *A History of England* (1875), called Carte "One of the most diligent compilers of the earlier English history" and considered his biography of the duke of Ormonde as "of immense importance for the period of which it treats."

References:

Eveline Cruickshanks and Howard Erskine-Hill, *The Atterbury Plot* (Basingstoke, U.K.: Palgrave Macmillan, 2004);

Thomas Hearne, *Remarks and Collections of Thomas Hearne,* 11 volumes, edited by C. E. Doble, D. W. Rannie, and H. E. Salter (Oxford: Printed for the Oxford Historical Society at the Clarendon Press, 1885–1921);

Philip Hicks, *Neoclassical History and English Culture: From Clarendon to Hume* (New York: St. Martin's Press, 1996);

William Lamont, "Richard Baxter, 'Popery' and the Origins of the English Civil War," *History,* 87 (2002): 336–352;

Laird Okie, *Augustan Historical Writing: Histories of England in the English Enlightenment* (Lanham, Md.: University Press of America, 1991);

Michael Perceval-Maxwell, *The Outbreak of the Irish Rebellion of 1641* (Montreal: McGill-Queens University Press, 1994);

J. G. A. Pocock, *The Ancient Constitution and the Feudal Law: A Study of English Historical Thought in the Seventeenth Century* (Cambridge: Cambridge University Press, 1957);

C. W. Russell and J. P. Prendergast, *The Carte Manuscripts in the Bodleian Library, Oxford* (London: H. M. Stationery Office, 1871);

Alfred Soman, "The London Edition of de Thou's History: A Critique of Some Well-Documented Legends," *Renaissance Quarterly,* 24 (1971): 1–12;

Leopold von Ranke, *A History of England, Principally in the Seventeenth Century* (Oxford: Clarendon Press, 1875).

Papers:

Many original documents collected by Thomas Carte are held by the Bodleian Library, University of Oxford.

Jeremy Collier

(23 September 1650 – 26 April 1726)

Tania Boster
University of Pittsburgh

SELECTED BOOKS: *The Office of a Chaplain Enquir'd Into, and Vindicated from Servility and Contempt* (Cambridge: Printed by John Hayes for Henry Dickinson, 1688);

The Desertion Discuss'd. In a Letter to a Country Gentleman (London, 1689);

Vindiciae juris regii; or, Remarques upon a Paper, Entituled, an Enquiry into the Measures of Submission to the Supream Authority (London, 1689);

A Caution Against Inconsistency: or, The Connexion Between Praying and Swearing; in Relation to the Civil Powers ([London, 1690]);

A Perswasive to Consideration, Tender'd to the Royalists, Particularly Those of the Church of England (London, 1693);

A Defence of the Absolution Given to Sr. William Perkins, at the Place of Execution, April the 3rd. With a Farther Vindication Thereof, Occasioned by a Paper Entituled a Declaration of the Sense of the Arch-bishops and Bishops, etc. (London, 1696);

A Short View of the Immorality and Profaneness of the English Stage, Together with the Sense of Antiquity upon this Argument (London: Printed for S. Keble, R. Sare, and H. Hindmarsh, 1698);

A Defence of the Short View of the Profaneness and Immorality of the English Stage, etc. Being a Reply to Mr. Congreve's Amendments, etc. And to the Vindication of the Author of the Relapse (London: S. Keble; R. Sare; and H. Hindmarsh, 1699);

A Second Defence of the Short View of the Prophaneness and Immorality of the English Stage, &c: Being a Reply to a Book, Entituled, The Ancient and Modern Stages Surveyed, &c (London: Printed for S. Keble, R. Sare, and G. Strahan, 1700);

Mr. Collier's Dissuasive from the Play-House: In a Letter to a Person of Quality, Occasion'd by the Late Calamity of the Tempest (London: Printed for Richard Sare, 1703);

An Ecclesiastical History of Great Britain, Chiefly England: From the First Planting of Christianity, to the End of the Reign of King Charles the Second. With a Brief Account of the Affairs of Religion in Ireland, etc., 2 volumes

Jeremy Collier (portrait by William Faithorne Jr., after Edmond Lilly [Lilley]; National Portrait Gallery, London)

(London: Samuel Keble & Benjamin Tooke, 1708, 1714);

An Answer to Some Exceptions in Bishop Burnet's Third Part of the History of the Reformation etc. Against Mr. Collier's Ecclesiastical History. Together with a Reply to Some Remarks in Bishop Nicholson's English Historical Library (London: Printed for Richard Sare, John Nicholson, Benjamin Took, Daniel Midwinter, and George Strahan, 1715);

Some Considerations on Doctor Kennet's Second and Third Letters. Wherein His Misrepresentations of Mr. Collier's Ecclesiast. History Are Lay'd Open; and His Calumnies Disprov'd (London: Printed and sold by John Morphew, 1717).

TRANSLATIONS: Marcus Aurelius, Emperor of Rome, *The Emperor Marcus Antonius: His Conversation with Himself,* translated by Collier (London, 1701);

Marcus Tullius Cicero, *Tully's Five Books De Finibus: or, Concerning the Last Object of Desire and Aversion . . . Done into English by S. P. Gent.,* revised, with a recommendatory preface, by Collier (London: Printed for Jacob Tonson and Robert Gibson, 1702);

Jacques Bernard, *An Appendix to the Three English Volumes in Folio of Morery's Great Historical, Geographical, Genealogical and Poetical Dictionary . . . This Appendix Being Collected . . . Chiefly from the French Supplement . . . Printed in Holland in the Year 1716 by Jer. Collier,* translated by Collier (London: Printed by George James, 1721).

OTHER: Louis Moréri, *The Great Historical, Geographical, Genealogical and Poetical Dictionary . . . Collected from the Best Historians . . . ,* second edition, revised and enlarged by Jean Le Clerc, 2 volumes, corrected, revised, and enlarged to the year 1688 by Collier (London: Printed for Henry Rhodes; Thomas Newborough; the assigns of L. Meredith; and Elizabeth Harris, 1701).

The "abdication" of King James II in the Glorious Revolution (1688–1689) was a triumph for those who feared that their Catholic king was a tyrant. But for many non-Catholic English men and women, especially High Church Anglicans, this event provoked a profound crisis of conscience. Believing that because kings ruled by divine right and hereditary succession the subjects' allegiance was due absolutely and unconditionally to James II, the nonjurors, as these clergymen were called, refused to take the oath to King William III and Queen Mary II. Eight Anglican bishops and four hundred priests resisted in this fashion, a defiance that cost them their livings, their offices, and, in some cases, even their affiliation with the Church of England. Among them was Jeremy Collier, a priest who defended his refusal to take the oath by appealing, in a series of pamphlets, to historical precedent and the laws of reason and nature. Collier is best known for his part in a pamphlet war concerning the immorality of the English stage. Collier's nonjuring stance, which caused considerable commotion, was a defining feature of most of his writing. His literary career may be divided into four main

categories: theological tracts, nonjuror pamphlets, attacks on the depravity of English theater, and historical works of reference. Characteristic of much of his writing is the use of historical evidence and legal argument to buttress controversial assertions regarding church and state authority and allegiance.

Jeremiah (Jeremy) Collier was born 23 September 1650, in Stow-cum-Quy outside Cambridge. His father, Jeremy Collier the elder, earned an M.A. degree at Trinity College, Cambridge, in 1643, where he was also ordained. His mother was Elizabeth Smith, and he had two brothers and a sister. The elder Collier made his living teaching grammar school and was a member of the Hartlib Circle. Jeremy the younger attended Caius College, Cambridge, as a sizar, or poor scholar. Granted his B.A. degree in 1673, he went on to earn his M.A., was ordained a deacon in 1676, and then a priest in 1677. He served as a private chaplain to the Countess Dawager of Dorset for a brief time (1678–1679) and then spent six years officiating as rector of a small parish at Ampton. Resigning from a benefice at Ampton in 1685, he moved to London, purportedly taking a lectureship at Gray's Inn, where he would have studied the common law.

In 1685 Collier launched persistent written protests claiming William and Mary's seizure of power in 1688–1689 an act of conquest and usurpation. Gilbert Burnet's *Enquiry into the State of Affairs and in Particular, Whether We Owe Allegiance to the King in These Circumstances? And Whether We Are Bound to Treat with Him and Call Him Back Again or Not?* (December 1688) defended the acceptance of William and Mary on the basis that James II had abdicated the throne. In *The Desertion Discuss'd. In a Letter to a Country Gentleman,* Collier also questions the validity of a constitutional body summoned by William, which first met in January 1689, to determine the course of the nation and officially proffer the crown to the new king and queen. After all, centuries of law proved that parliament could not technically meet unless called by the monarch. Furthermore, Collier argues, James had not abdicated the throne; he had been forced to flee for his safety. But this act, according to Collier, did not detract from his authority as king:

> In order to the confuting this Notion, I shall prove in the First place, That his Majesty, before his withdrawing, had sufficient Grounds to make him apprehensive of Danger, and therefore It cannot be called an *Abdication.* Secondly, That the leaving any Representatives behind him was impracticable at this Juncture. Thirdly, That we have no Grounds, either from the Laws of the Realm, or those of Nature, to pronounce the Throne void, upon such a Retreat of a King.

After recounting the events leading up to James's flight, Collier then appeals to medieval English history to make his case. Arguing that since the Norman Conquest of 1066, Edward II and Richard II represented the only two instances of royal abdication, he insists that both "were unjustly Deposed by their Subjects." This tactic—appealing to historical, legal precedent for legitimacy—Collier uses again and again in subsequent pamphlets, written to tar the revolution settlement and embolden the nonjurors' cause.

The Desertion Discuss'd so acutely threatened the new order that Collier was imprisoned at Newgate for several months before being released without trial. Continuing to practice as a nonjuring priest outside the established Church of England, by 1692 he had been without salary or church stipend for four years and was living in London. He persisted in publishing pamphlets, which the government considered inflammatory, and was arrested again in that year, accused of conspiring with another nonjuror to restore the Stuarts to the throne.

By 1696 Collier had associated himself with yet another serious controversy—the Jacobite plot to aid a French invasion. The plot failed, and the plotters were sentenced to death. Collier and two other Anglican priests visited Sir John Friend and Sir William Perkins, two of the condemned men, in Newgate prison, prayed for them, and even went with them to Tyburn, the site of execution. The standard practice of a priest delivering rites to those fated to die raised hackles in official circles and was all the more controversial because the priests allegedly granted absolution without first hearing the convicted men's confessions. That Collier would pay a price in such a dangerous and uncertain atmosphere, with the legitimacy of the Glorious Revolution and the life of the king at stake, should have come as no surprise.

Criticized by many, including the Archbishop of Canterbury, for condoning assassination, and charged with committing high misdemeanors, Collier defended his actions in a pamphlet dated 9 April 1696, *A Defence of the Absolution Given to Sr. William Perkins*. Collier wrote,

'Tis very hard a Man must be Persecuted for Performing the Obligations of his Office, and the Duties of common Friendship, and Humanity. As for any Methods of Murder, I dislike them no less than those who rail loudest; and nothing but a Mercenary Malice could suggest the contrary. But if the Functions of the Priesthood, and the Assistances of Religion, and the Reading the Publick Liturgy are grown a Crime, I am not concerned at the Imputation.

To those who believe that persons convicted of capital offences are irreconcilably damned, Collier brandishes his priestly authority, claiming that he would not be in compliance with the duties of his office in "the Ancient, and English Church" if he ignored Perkins's request for absolution. Collier also reports that following the execution, his

quarters were entered by six to eight people who broke into a trunk, seizing "some Papers of Value, tho' perfectly Inoffensive, and Foreign to their Purpose." Even if Collier believed that the absolution of attempted crown assassins was not an exceptional or politically charged act, the authorities evidently did, including those of the established church. Collier was outlawed for refusing to respond to his indictment for absolving a traitor.

Beginning in 1698, Collier transferred his efforts from nonjuror tracts to voicing his condemnation at the corruption of the English stage, thus occasioning another pamphlet war. Most historians and literary scholars focus on this aspect of his career. The significance of Collier's critical publications, according to John T. Harwood, "is his assertion that drama has a moral purpose." Theater should impart moral lessons, promoting virtue and discouraging vice, a function that, in Collier's eyes, was not being fulfilled by the most highly regarded and enjoyed playwrights of his day, including John Dryden, Thomas D'Urfey, William Congreve, Sir John Vanbrugh, and William Wycherley. The intention and effect of these plays, Collier argues in *Mr. Collier's Dissuasive from the Play-House: In a Letter to a Person of Quality, Occasion'd by the Late Calamity of the Tempest* (1703), is no less than to make England a den of iniquity: "They are Proof against Reason and Punishment, against Fines and Arguments, and come over again with their old Smut and Profaneness. One would think by their desperate Pushing, they were resolv'd to exterminate Religion, and subdue the Conscience of the Kingdom. . . . They have without Doubt pitched upon the most likely Expedient to make Vice absolute, and Atheism universal." The Church, the institution that could correct this morally hazardous state of affairs, is under attack in these plays as well, most distressingly in lampoons of the clergy, a point with which Collier takes particular issue.

Still outlawed and not legally even allowed to be in London, Collier in attacking the stage reportedly managed to inspire William III to grant him a royal pardon. Collier continued to engage in the debate for several years, and his final pamphlet on the subject, *A Farther Vindication of the Short View of the Profaneness and Immorality of the English Stage. In which the Objections of a late Book entitled A Defence of Plays, are Considered,* was published in 1708. The influence of Collier's criticism, however, lasted well beyond his death. As explained by David Self, who has studied the two-centuries-long consideration of Collier's significance by literary historians, "It has been suggested variously that he saw himself as a dramatic critic, as a priest, or as a propagandist on behalf of James II. Others have dismissed him as a blatant controversialist who enjoyed a good row and was simply courting notoriety in the hope of gaining fame and money." To his contemporaries, historians, and literary scholars Collier became and has remained the exemplar of reactionary theatrical criticism.

In the midst of the stage controversy, Collier translated, revised, enlarged, and published volumes one and

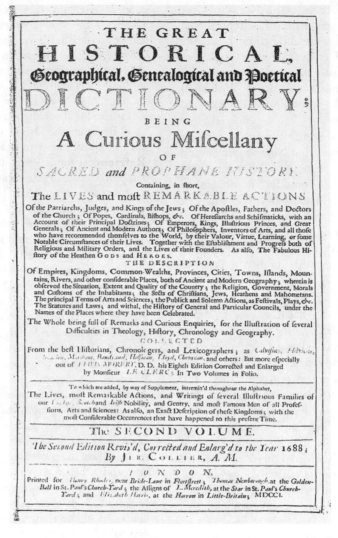

Title page for volume two of Collier's 1701 augmented translation of Louis Moreri's 1674 La Grande Dictionaire Historique
(Eighteenth-Century Collections Online, Gale Group)

two of *The Great Historical, Geographical, Genealogical and Poetical Dictionary* in 1701 and 1705 respectively, with an appendix that followed in 1721. The text is based on Louis Moréri's 1674 historical dictionary, *La Grande Dictionaire Historique,* which had been banned in Louis XIV's France and had passed through several editions and translations before Collier compiled his own. However, Collier clearly states in the preface to volume one that he has put a great deal of his own work, insight, and interpretation into this version and that it was not researched and written by committee but solely by himself in an effort to maintain a consistent style: "There are considerable Additions in History both Ecclesiastical and Secular; in Geography, Mythology, Painting, &c. Particularly I found it necessary to melt down some part of the English History and throw it into a new Form. . . . To speak clearly, I have made a great many Alterations upon

several Subjects, but I hope not without good Reason and Authority."

The dictionary is astonishing, according to its title page, in its range of subject matter, including biblical and church history, and descriptions of "Empires, Kingdoms, Common-Wealths, Provinces, Cities, Towns, Islands, Mountains, Rivers, and other considerable Places, both of Ancient and Modern Geography; wherein is observed the Situation, Extent and Quality of the Country; the Religion, Government, Morals and Customs of the Inhabitants; the Sects of Christians, Jews, Heathens and Mahometans. The principal Terms of Arts and Sciences; the Publick and Solemn Actions, as Festivals, Plays, &c. The Statutes and Laws; and withal, the History of General and Particular Councils, under the Names of the Places where they have been Celebrated." Collier includes his own as well as other historians' interpretations of theological controversies throughout history among the entries. He even includes a lengthy discussion of the history of dictionaries through time, dating back to the classical era, with strong emphasis on and praise extended to the work of early-modern humanists, such as Erasmus of Rotterdam. Collier did not underestimate the importance of his undertaking, saying also in the preface: "As for the Usefulness of this Work, 'tis a Collection of almost Universal Knowledge, and may be call'd rather a Library than a Book."

In 1708 and 1714 Collier published volumes one and two, respectively, of *An Ecclesiastical History of Great Britain,* the commanding work on the subject for the next century. His opinion regarding, for example, the necessity of the independence of the church from the state authority is clearly anti-erastian, consistent with nonjuror ecclesiastical theory, according to historian Mark Goldie. The history is, however, celebrated for its high-caliber historical scholarship and standards, such as the use of primary source materials and references to works cited. However, the work was not without its critics. Collier scholar Sister Rose Anthony notes that Burnet reacted to *An Ecclesiastical History of Great Britain* by accusing Collier of "a constant inclination to favour the popish doctrine." By 1717 Collier was under heavy attack from within the ranks of the nonjurors for his Catholic tendencies, such as his support in a series of pamphlets of the Four Usages: ancient liturgical practices, such as saying prayers for the dead, which were considered a Romish practice. In 1713, the year prior to the publication of volume two, Collier was consecrated bishop of the Nonjuroring Anglican Church, which was not sanctioned by the Church of England. As primus of the sect after 1715, he attempted to ally the schismatic Anglican Church with the Eastern Orthodox Church. He continued to pursue this design between the years 1718 through 1725, but was never brought to fruition. Collier died on 26 April 1726, at age seventy-six.

Jeremy Collier lived through a critical period of transition in English history and played an active role in both resisting the Revolution Settlement and in trying to influence the ways in which people would remember the events of his time. Evoking historical precedent, whether ecclesiastical or secular, was not unusual in an age when religion and politics were still thoroughly entangled.

References:

Sister Rose Anthony, S.C., *The Jeremy Collier Stage Controversy, 1698–1726* (New York: Benjamin Blom, 1937);

Jane Garrett, *The Triumphs of Providence: The Assassination Plot, 1696* (Cambridge: Cambridge University Press, 1980);

Mark Goldie, "The Nonjurors, Episcopacy, and the Origins of the Convocation Controversy," in *Ideology and Conspiracy: Aspects of Jacobitism, 1689–1759,* edited by Eveline Cruickshanks (Edinburgh: John Donald, 1982);

John T. Harwood, *Critics, Values, and Restoration Comedy* (Carbondale: Southern Illinois University Press, 1982);

David Self, *The Single Source of All Filth: A Consideration of the Opinions of Revd Jeremy Collier, M.A. on the English Stage, Together with the Views of His Defendants, Critics and the Dramatists* (Malvern: J. Garnet Miller, 2000).

Papers:

Collier's papers do not survive, but his correspondence with the nonjuror Thomas Brett is held at the Bodleian Library.

Anthony Collins

(21 June 1676 – 13 December 1729)

Jeffrey R. Wigelsworth
Dalhousie University

See also the Collins entry in *DLB 252: British Philosophers, 1500–1799.*

BOOKS: *A Letter to the Learned Mr. Henry Dodwell; Containing Some Remarks on a (Pretended) Demonstration of the Immateriality and Natural Immortality of the Soul, in Mr. Clark's Answer to His Late Epistolary Discourse,* anonymous (London: Printed for Anne Baldwin, 1707 [i.e., 1706]);

A Reply to Mr. Clark's Defence of His Letter to Mr. Dodwell. With a postscript Relating to Mr. Milles's Answer to Mr. Dodwell's Epistolary Discourse, anonymous (London, 1707);

An Essay concerning the Use of Reason in Propositions, the Evidence whereof Depends on Human Testimony, anonymous (London, 1707);

Reflections on Mr. Clark's Second Defence of His Letter to Mr. Dodwell, anonymous (London: Printed for John Darby, 1707);

An Answer to Mr. Clarke's Third Defence of His Letter to Mr. Dodwell; A Discourse of Free-Thinking, anonymous (London: Printed for Anne Baldwin, 1708);

Priestcraft in Perfection; or, A Detection of the Fraud of Inserting and Continuing this Clause (The Church Hath the Power to Decree Rites and Ceremonys, and Authority in Controversys of Faith) in the Twentieth Article of the Articles of the Church of England, anonymous (London: Printed for Benjamin Bragg, 1710);

A Vindication of the Divine Attributes. In some Remarks on His Grace the Archbishop of Dublin's Sermon, Intituled, Divine Predestination and Foreknowledge Consistent with the Freedom of Man's Will, anonymous (London: Printed for Anne Baldwin, 1710);

Reflections on a Late Pamphlet Intituled Priestcraft in Perfection, anonymous (London: Printed for John Baker, 1710);

A Discourse of Free-Thinking, Occasion'd by the Rise and Growth of a Sect Call'd Free-Thinkers, anonymous (London, 1713);

A Philosophical Inquiry Concerning Human Liberty (London, 1717);

Anthony Collins (from <http://www.filosofico.net/collins.htm>)

A Discourse of the Grounds and Reasons of the Christian Religion. In Two Parts: The First Containing some Considerations on the Quotations made from the Old in the New Testament, and Particularly on the Prophecies Cited from the Former and Said to Be Fulfill'd in the Latter. The Second Containing an Examination of the Scheme Advanc'd by Mr. Whiston in His Essay towards Restoring the True Text of the Old Testament, and for Vindicating the Citations thence Made in the New Testament. To which Is Prefix'd an Apology for Free Debate and Liberty of Writing, anonymous (London, 1724 [i.e. 1723]);

An Historical Essay, on the Thirty-Nine Articles of the Church of England, anonymous (London: Printed for Richard Francklin, 1724);

The Scheme of Literal Prophecy Considered; In a View of the Controversy, Occasion'd by a Late Book, Intitled, A Discourse of the Grounds and Reasons of the Christian Religion, anonymous (London: Printed by Thomas Johnson for the Booksellers of London & Westminster, 1726);

A Letter to the Author of the Discourse of the Grounds and Reasons of the Christian Religion, In Answer to Mr. Green's Letters, &c., anonymous (London: Printed for A. Moore, 1726);

A Letter to the Reverend Dr. Rogers: On Occasion of His Eight Sermons, concerning the Necessity of the Divine Revelation, and the Preface Prefix'd to Them, anonymous (London, 1727);

A Discourse on Liberty and Necessity: Wherein the Process of Ideas, from Their First Entrance into the Soul, until Their Production of Action, Is Delineated. With Some Remarks upon the Late Reverend Dr. Clarke's Reasoning on This Point . . . , as A.C., Esq. [that is, Collins] (London: J. Shuckburgh, 1729);

A Discourse concerning Ridicule and Irony in Writing: In a Letter to the Reverend Nathanael Marshall, anonymous (London: Printed for John Brotherton, 1729).

Editions and Collections: *A Discourse of Free-Thinking: Faksimile-Neudruck der Erstausgabe London 1713 mit deutschem Paralleltext,* edited and translated by Günter Galwick, preface by Julius Ebbinghaus (Stuttgart-Bad Canstatt: Fredrich Fromann, 1965);

A Discourse Concerning Ridicule and Irony in Writing (1729), introduction by Edward Bloom and Lillian D. Bloom, Augustan Reprint Society Publication, no. 142 (Los Angeles: William Andrews Clark Memorial Library, 1970);

Determinism and Freewill: Anthony Collins' A Philosophical Inquiry concerning Human Liberty: With a Discussion of the Opinions of Hobbes, Locke, Pierre Bayle, William King and Leibniz, edited by James O'Higgins, S. J. (The Hague: Martinus Nijhoff, 1976);

A Discourse of the Grounds and Reasons of the Christian Religion (New York: Garland, 1976);

A Reply to Mr. Clark's Defence of His Letter to Mr. Dodwell; Reflections on Mr. Clark's Second Defence of His Letter to Mr. Dodwell; An Answer to Mr. Clarke's Third Defence of His Letter to Mr. Dodwell, in *The Works of Samuel Clarke,* volume 3 (New York: Garland, 1978);

An Answer to Mr. Clarke's Third Defence of His Letter to Mr. Dodwell; A Discourse of Free-Thinking, in *Atheism in Britain,* volume 1, edited by David Berman (Bristol: Thoemmes Press, 1996).

OTHER: *The Independent Whig; or, A Defence of Primitive Christianity, and of Our Ecclesiastical Establishment, against the Exorbitant Claims and Encroachments of Fanatical and Disaffected Clergymen,* edited by John Trenchard and Thomas Gordon (London), 20 January 1720 to 11 January 1721–includes editorials by Collins;

Marcus Tullius Cicero, *M. Tullius Cicero Of the Nature of the Gods; In Three Books. With Critical, Philosophical, and Explanatory Notes* (London: Printed for Richard Francklin, 1741).

Anthony Collins was a self-described freethinker who challenged the authority of established religion. He argued that people should believe only things about which they can form clear ideas. Collins was the wealthiest and most socially advantaged of the deists, philosophers who rejected divine providence and revealed religion. Alternatively, they proposed a religion of nature comprising a moral code of conduct rather than an institutionalized church. Beginning in the late seventeenth century and lasting until the middle of the eighteenth, this group of thinkers was the focal point of many theological controversies in Britain. While Collins composed no well-known work of history, as did his fellow Britons David Hume and Edward Gibbon, his writings are laced with historical inquiry. He epitomizes the classical Enlightenment view of the past as a story of authoritarian restriction on thought and a celebration of the present age as one in which reason would triumph, with confidence in natural philosophy (science) as a sign of human progress.

Collins was born outside of London on 21 June 1676 into a family with a legal tradition. His namesake grandfather was a Bencher (highest rank of membership of an Inn of Court) and Treasurer of the Middle Temple (one of four inns entitled to call its members to the bar to practice law), and his father, Henry Collins, was called to the bar in 1667 but never practiced law. Collins's early schooling took place at Eton; in 1693 he then advanced to King's College, Cambridge. From there he moved on to the Middle Temple in 1694. Like his father, Collins never worked as a lawyer. In 1698 he married Martha Child, daughter of Sir Francis Child, Lord Mayor of London and member of Parliament. That year Collins came to control some of his father's land, an estate producing £1800 per year. The couple's first child, Henry, died in infancy. In 1701 their second son, Anthony, was born. Before Martha died in April of 1703, she and Collins also had two daughters, Elizabeth and Martha. After his wife's death, Collins spent much time in the Essex countryside. He moved there permanently in 1715 and lived as a country gentleman, holding the post of Justice of the Peace until his death. He also entertained England's elite; Richard Dighton, Collins's former servant, recalled in a letter (14 March 1731) that Collins "was visited several times by Queen Anne [and] Noblemen and Ladies of Qualities who took delight in walking in his fine gardens. . . ." Collins loved the Republic of Letters (the increased letter-writing between philosophers and other thinkers during the Enlightenment) and collecting books; his library is estimated to have been the third largest in England, containing approximately one hundred thousand volumes in various genres.

While in Essex, Collins befriended philosopher John Locke. The correspondence between the two men reveals their exceedingly close relationship. In one letter (29 October 1703) Locke claimed that "if I were now setting out in the world I should think it my great happyness to have such a companion as you who had a true relish of truth, would in earnest seeke it with me, from whom I might receive it undisguised, and to whom communicate what I thought true freely." The influence of Locke on Collins's intellectual development cannot be overstated. Locke claimed no one understood his *Essay concerning Human Understanding* (1690) better than Collins; moreover, he encouraged Collins's search for truth—whatever one believed to be reasonable even if it contradicted received wisdom—in all intellectual endeavors. Collins also embraced Locke's argument that knowledge comes from personal experiences and not from innate ideas or established tradition.

Around 1704 Collins began a friendship and correspondence with Matthew Tindal, deist and Fellow of All Souls College, Oxford. Tindal's *Christianity as Old as the Creation* (1730) has been called the deists' Bible; he also composed tracts against such ideas as the authority of priests, passive resistance to monarchs, and established religion. Also in 1704, another deist, John Toland, whose *Christianity not Mysterious* (1696) is seen as initiating the entire deist controversy, was one of Collins's associates. Toland visited Collins at his estate, where the library contained many of Toland's manuscripts and books.

Collins entered the literary and theological scene of his age in 1706 after Henry Dodwell suggested in print that the soul was a naturally mortal substance that achieves immortality by the will of God alone. Samuel Clarke, a Newtonian and Anglican theologian, admonished Dodwell that he was presenting an argument that led to atheism. In *A Letter to the Learned Mr. Henry Dodwell; Containing Some Remarks on a (Pretended) Demonstration of the Immateriality and Natural Immortality of the Soul, in Mr. Clark's Answer to His Late Epistolary Discourse* (1706), Collins defended Dodwell's right to advance any conception of the soul he thought fit. Collins also suggested

that the soul may be material; at least one could not be certain it was not. Addressing Clarke, Collins wrote, "There is nothing more unreasonable than to imagine there is any dangerous Consequence in allowing Men fairly to examine the Grounds of received Opinions. . . . For till Men have something besides Reason for their Direction, it is their Duty to follow that Light wherever it leads them." Clarke and Collins produced several pamphlets in the controversy that followed. In *An Answer to Mr. Clarke's Third Defence of His Letter to Mr. Dodwell; A Discourse of Free-Thinking* (1708), Collins strengthened the above position by arguing that no person, not even his deceased friend Locke, could force him to abandon his own reason in the search for truth: "I look on it to be contrary to the Duty of a rational Agent to pay any manner of Deference in matters of Opinion or Speculation to any Man, or Number of Men whatsoever." This axiom pervades all of Collins's writings and underlies his historical inquiry. Confrontations with Isaac Newton's disciples continued throughout Collins's life. He and William Whiston had a dozen personal meetings in coffeehouses and challenged one another in print during the 1720s.

Collins's assault on established religion continued in *Priestcraft in Perfection; or, A Detection of the Fraud of Inserting and Continuing this Clause (The Church Hath the Power to Decree Rites and Ceremonys, and Authority in Controversys of Faith) in the Twentieth Article of the Articles of the Church of England* and *Reflections on a Late Pamphlet Intituled Priestcraft in Perfection* (both 1710), in which he argued that the twentieth article of the Thirty-Nine Articles of the Anglican Church was false. Specifically, Collins denied that the Church had any right to hold elaborate ceremonies and control the form of one's devotion to God. Collins labeled the addition of these scripturally unfounded elements by clergy as "priestcraft." Like Toland and Tindal, Collins argued that one's conscience ought to be the deciding factor when choosing membership in any church. He returned to these issues in 1724 with *An Historical Essay, on the Thirty-Nine Articles of the Church of England*.

Collins produced his best-known book in 1713: *A Discourse of Free-Thinking, Occasion'd by the Rise and Growth of a Sect Call'd Free-Thinkers*. The book includes Collins's explicit statement that people ought to seek truth—that is, to think freely—in all matters, especially those of religion. He defines "Free-Thinking" as "The Use of the Understanding, in endeavouring to find out the Meaning of any Proposition whatsoever, in considering the nature of the Evidence for or against it, and in judging of it in according to the seeming Force or Weakness of the Evidence." If one used this faculty, the corrupt nature of current Christianity, which Collins saw as benefiting priests and not the laity, would be apparent.

However, Collins acknowledged that not all ages were conducive to freethinking. Only in his time were people able to think for themselves, whereas before, the priests crushed independent thoughts: "Thus before the Restoration of Learning, which men were subject to the Imposition of Priests, a prodigious Ignorance prevail'd."; priests were responsible for the stagnation of learning, which Collins believed subsumed most of the world until the present time. Therefore, many absurd notions prevailed among Christians, such as the power of the clergy to save or punish souls and the worship of images and saintly relics. Collins argued that true historic religion was free from all those notions. In support of his view Collins suggests that many of the greatest minds in history were freethinkers, as he himself was, noting in particular Marcus Tullius Cicero, Socrates, Plato, Aristotle, and Epicurus. They had been able to rise above the restriction of thought in their ages and promote what they viewed as the truth. These men were models to be emulated in the present age. Collins characterizes Francis Bacon, someone closer to his day, as "a great Free-Thinker" who outlined an admirable rejection of tradition and restoration of learning.

Like other Enlightenment historians who saw progress in natural philosophy as a precursor to progress in the human condition, Collins took solace in the advancements made in the Scientific Revolution (the overthrow of Aristotelian studies of nature). He noted that progress in thinking had greatly increased knowledge in astronomy and had led to the acknowledgment of a spherical Earth that orbits the sun. In the same way that the true nature of the universe became known in the period from Copernicus to Newton, Collins believed that the true nature of religion, too, would be known—that is, people would realize that religion, under the auspices of natural religion, ought to consist of moral duties to one another and respect for the opinions of others. As an historical example of what had been gained in natural philosophy by freethinking, Collins turns to the case of Galileo, who in the previous age "was imprison'd for asserting the Motion of the Earth," a notion Collins says all people now believe. The acceptance as true of things once thought heretical occurs when people have the right to think freely and do not allow their thoughts to be conditioned by some authority.

In *A Philosophical Inquiry Concerning Human Liberty* (1717) Collins questions why scholars and theologians wrote about the being of God when they claimed to have imperfect knowledge about their subject. He argues that one should compose a text only when one has clear and distinct ideas about his topic. In the past, clear ideas about God, religion, or nature were thought unavailable, and therefore people were forced to write

in a cloud of ignorance. Only in the current climate of freethinking did Collins believe one could write about such previously obscure things as the being of God. As he did in *A Discourse of Free-Thinking*, Collins states that intellectual giants from the past supported him and provided examples of his argument that progress comes when freethinking flourishes. He noted the work of the natural philosophers from the previous generation, such as Pierre Gassendi, René Descartes, Ralph Cudworth, and his English contemporary Newton, who had broken out of established Aristotelian modes of thought and created a true picture of the universe. True pictures of God, argued Collins, could not be far behind these intellectual triumphs.

In 1721 Collins wrote to his longtime friend Pierre Des Maizeaux, French Huguenot and future biographer of Toland and Pierre Bayle, that he was planning a translation of Cicero's dialogues, especially *De Natura Deorum* (On the Nature of the Gods), which he believed would be of great aid to, and promote good sense in, the present age. Just as Cicero analyzed Roman religion in his book, Collins hoped to use Cicero's example to encourage the same tendencies in eighteenth-century England and thereby have people discover what he already knew: Christianity was a shadow of its former historical self. Moreover, Cicero embodied one of the earliest examples of a free-thinker. Collins's *M. Tullius Cicero Of the Nature of the gods; In Three Books. With Critical, Philosophical, and Explanatory Notes* appeared posthumously in 1741. Collins's interest in antiquity is continued in subsequent works, which are more obviously historically focused.

The year 1723 became tragic for Collins when his only surviving son fell ill. The extant letters from Collins to Des Maizeaux reveal Collins's despair as his son's health deteriorated. Finally, on 19 December, Anthony Collins (junior) lost the battle with his illness. The following year, Collins married Elizabeth Wrottesley, the daughter of Sir Walter Wrottesley, with whom he had no children.

Also in 1723 Collins published *A Discourse of the Grounds and Reasons of the Christian Religion*. Collins argues that the Bible alone, independent of the accumulated trappings of priests and institutionalization, is the true source of Christianity. He claims that the Old Testament ought to be the "true canon of Scripture" as it had been at the beginning of Christianity. However, the ancient Christianity to which Collins refers was not the same as its present incarnation. Collins believes that Jews and Christians originally worshiped under the same Scripture and had few differences between them; in a sense both were members of the same religion. One could trace historically the current adversarial condition between the two faiths. Collins here follows the precedent set by Toland, who argued in *Nazarenus* (1718) that Judaism, Christianity, and Islam were originally the same religion.

Collins used history to demonstrate that true religion was simple, free from mysteries, and knowable by reason. He revealed the historic process of corruption: "Religion itself was deem'd a mysterious thing among the Pagans, and not to be publickly and plainly declar'd." Pagan priests introduced "allegories, or parables, or Hierogliphicks" to keep religion out of the reach of common people and to increase their dependence on priests as interpreters. The introduction of allegory came to Christianity during the Patristic era (the first through the eighth centuries, when Church Fathers defended the Gospel against misunderstandings and rival beliefs): "Many of the primitive fathers, and apologists for christianity, who for the most part wholly address themselves to Pagans, reason allegorically." Thus, to attract converts among the pagans, Church Fathers and priests altered the simple Christian religion to make it more like the familiar religion of pagans, thereby making Christianity subservient to priests, who constructed a mysterious religion, the tenets of which only they could decipher. Thus, priestcraft and corrupt religion were born. Collins argues that modern religious writers continue this affinity for allegory and priestcraft rather than natural religion.

The Scheme of Literal Prophecy Considered; In a View of the Controversy, Occasion'd by a Late Book, Intitled, A Discourse of the Grounds and Reasons of the Christian Religion (1726) was a sequel to *A Discourse of the Grounds and Reasons of the Christian Religion*. In *The Scheme of Literal Prophecy Considered,* Collins questioned the validity of fulfilled prophecy as an historical source of revealed religion. By the early eighteenth century, the argument from design was losing its ability to serve as the chief weapon of orthodox apologists. The problem was that their targets—usually the deists—agreed with them that God created the world and that the proof is evident in nature. Deists continued, however, to doubt the truth of revealed Christianity. For many Protestant thinkers, such as Whiston, with whom Collins clashed in this book, a fulfilled prophecy proved the truth of Christianity as a revealed religion by demonstrating divine providence and the prediction of the New Testament in the Old Testament. Collins denied predictive prophecy by insisting that prophecy applied only to the time in which it was first proclaimed. He suggested that one should reduce prophecy to nothing rather than to accept interpretations of its fulfillment far removed from the time of its original decree. He claimed no proof exists that prophecies were written before the time in which they are said to have been fulfilled. By calling into question the dates of origin for prophecies, Collins queries the

divine status afforded the Bible and Providence. He mocks Whiston, who claimed to have produced more than three hundred literal prophecies from Scripture, but Collins states that if Whiston had produced only one unquestionable literally fulfilled prophecy, it would be sufficient to convince skeptics such as himself. Prophecy, argued Collins, must conform to the same rigors of proof as factual statements of natural philosophy. Accounts of allegorically fulfilled prophecy are to be dismissed as are the histories of Christianity based upon them.

Collins's final book, *A Discourse Concerning Ridicule and Irony in Writing: In a Letter to the Reverend Nathanael Marshall* (1729), was an historical study of ridicule chiefly found in writings on religion. Collins saw England as a special case in which literature that ridiculed its subject formed part of the national discourse. The book was a challenge to the suggestion by some authorities that imprisonment was appropriate for those who laughed at and made fun of English laws. Collins reminded his adversaries of the use made by ridicule in attacks on Catholicism and popery in past ages. Moreover, he noted that Anglicans mocked Puritans and Dissenters. He concludes that in challenges to orthodoxy reversal is fair and that no one complains about the rhetorical strategy except its victims. The return of the monarchy to England in 1660, Collins asserts, brought with it legislative limits on dissent as well as ridicule. He hopes the eighteenth century will be more tolerant of those who follow their reason and seek what they believe true in matters of religion and challenge with farce and satire what seems unreasonable. On 13 December 1729 Collins died, after a long and painful ordeal with kidney stones. News of his death, according to Des Maizeaux, came "to the grief of all his Family but especially those who had been Eye Witness to most of his Actions near 30 years."

Anthony Collins believed the contemporary state of religion was a priestly construction and that the process of corruption could be revealed through an examination of history. He argued that the Christian religion was not an historical constant but an institution that had changed from its original inception. His writings show an affinity to other deists, such as Toland and Tindal. Moreover, his belief in a similar progress in humanity as seen in natural philosophy places him next to such Enlightenment historians as Voltaire. Collins also used history as a way to legitimize his program of freethinking. Through his claimed affiliation with historical writers, Collins was able to position his work, and that of other deists, as part of a long tradition of like-minded scholars who remained uncorrupted in their ages and hence give his arguments a long pedigree. His influence on English historiography was felt for decades after his death. When, in 1779, Henry Edward Davis criticized what he saw as Edward Gibbon's tendency to "prejudice, if not subvert Christianity" in *The History of the Decline and Fall of the Roman Empire* (1776–1788), he did so with the accusation that Gibbon was following the example found in Collins's writings on history.

Letters:

Pierre Des Maizeaux, ed., *A Collection of Several Pieces of Mr. John Locke, Never Before Printed, or Not Extant in His Works* (London: Printed by James Bettenham for Richard Francklin, 1720)—volumes 7 (1982) and 8 (1989) include what survives of Collins's correspondence with Locke;

E. S. De Beer, ed., *Correspondence of John Locke,* 8 volumes (Oxford: Clarendon Press, 1976–1989).

Biography:

James O'Higgins, S. J., *Anthony Collins: The Man and His Works* (The Hague: Martinus Nijhoff, 1970).

References:

David Berman, "Anthony Collins: Aspects of His Thought and Writings," *Hermathena,* 119 (1975): 49–70;

Berman, "Anthony Collins and the Question of Atheism in the Early Part of the Eighteenth Century," *Proceedings of the Royal Irish Academy,* 75C (1975): 85–102;

Berman, "Anthony Collins' Essays in the Independent Whig," *Journal of the History of Philosophy,* 13 (1975): 463–469;

Paul Russell, "Hume's Treatise and the Clarke-Collins Controversy," *Hume Studies,* 21 (1995): 95–115;

Stephen Snobelen, "The Argument over Prophecy: An Eighteenth-Century Debate between William Whiston and Anthony Collins," *Lumen,* 15 (1996): 195–213.

Papers:

Collections of Anthony Collins's letters are at the British Library, London; the Bodleian Library, Oxford University; and the Universiteitsbibliotheek, Leiden University. A single letter to Sir William Simpson is at the Department of Special Collections, Kenneth Spencer Research Library, University of Kansas, Lawrence. John Locke's letters to Collins are dispersed in several collections, the largest group being at the Harry Ransom Humanities Research Center, University of Texas at Austin. The manuscript catalogue Collins maintained of his library is at King's College, Cambridge. Documents relating to his civic role are in the Essex Record Office, Chelmsford. The marriage settlement that governed his marriage and property is in the Greater London Record Office.

Arthur Collins

(1681? – 16 March 1762)

Walter H. Keithley
Arizona State University

BOOKS: *The Peerage of England; or, An Historical and Genealogical Account of the Present Nobility* (London: Printed by G. J. for Abel Roper and Arthur Collins, 1709; second edition, greatly augmented and corrected, 1710); volume 2, *The Peerage of England; or, A Genealogical and Historical Account of all the Flourishing Families of This Kingdom* (London: Printed by E. J. for Abel Roper and A. C. 1714); third edition, corrected and augmented (London: Printed by E. J. and sold by Arthur Collins and J. Morphew, 1715); fourth edition, republished as *The Peerage of England; or, An Historical and Genealogical Account of the Present Nobility. Containing the Descent, Creations, and Most Remarkable Actions . . . To Which Is Added a General Index of the Several Families of Great Britain and Ireland* (London: Printed and sold by W. Taylor, 1717); fourth edition, corrected and continued to the present time (London: Printed for H. Woodfall, J. Beecroft, W. Strahan, Irvington W. Sandby, and others, 1768);

Proposals for Printing, a Genealogical History of All of the Baronets of England, Now Existing, from the First Erection of That Honor to the Present Time. Containing, the Descent, Creations, Memoirs, and Most Remarkable Actions of Them . . . with Their Arms Engrav'd (London, 1711);

The Baronetage of England: Being an Historian and Genealogical Account of Baronets, from Their First Institutions to the Reign of King James I, 2 volumes (London: Printed for W. Taylor; R. Gosling; and I. Osborn, 1720);

The English Baronage; or, An Historical Account of the Lives and Most Valuable Actions of Our Nobility; with Their Descents, Marriages, and Issue, volume 1 (London: Printed for Robert Gosling, 1727)–no more volumes printed;

The Life of That Great Statesman William Cecil, Lord Burghley . . . Publish'd from the Original Manuscript Wrote Soon after His Lordship's Death. . . . to Which Is Added, His Character by the Learned Camden, . . . With Memoirs of the Family of Cecil, Faithfully Collected (London:

Printed for Robert Gosling and Thomas Wotton, 1732);

Proceedings, Precedents, and Arguments, on Claims and Controversies, Concerning Baronies by Writ, and Other Honours. With the Arguments of Sir Francis Bacon, . . . and Others. Published from the Collections of Robert Glover, . . . and Others (London: Printed for the author, 1734);

The History of John of Gaunt, King of Castile and Leon, Duke of Lancaster, and Father of Henry IV, King of England (London: Printed for Thomas Osborne, 1740);

The Life and Glorious Actions of Edward Prince of Wales (Commonly Call'd the Black Prince) Eldest Son of King Edward the Third: Containing, Remarkable Occurences of Those Times . . . Also the History of His Royal Brother John of Gaunt . . . Collected from Records, Manuscripts, and Historians (London: Printed for Thomas Osborne, 1740);

Memoirs of the Antient and Noble Family of Sackville. Collected from Old Records, Wills, . . . and Other Authorities. Humbly Inscrib'd to His Grace Lionel, Duke of Dorset (London, 1741);

Letters and Memorials of State, in the Reigns of Queen Mary, . . . Part of the Reign of King Charles the Second, and Oliver's Usurpation. Written and Collected by Sir Henry Sidney, . . . Sir Phillip Sidney, and His Brother Sir Robert Sidney, . . . Robert, the Second Earl of Leicester, . . . Phillip Lord Viscount Lisle, . . . Whereunto Is Added, Genealogical and Historical Observations, 2 volumes (London: Printed for T. Osborne, 1746);

An History of the Ancient and Illustrious Family of the Percys, Barons Percy, and the Earls of Northumberland. Collected from Records, Authentick Manuscripts (London, 1750);

A Supplement to the Four Volumes of The Peerage of England, 2 volumes (London: Printed for W. Innys, J. and P. Knapton, and others, 1750);

Historical Collections of the Noble Families of Cavendishe, Holles, Vere, Harley, and Ogle, with the Lives of the Most Remarkable Persons . . . Containing Curious Private Memoirs . . . And Prints of the Principal Persons . . . Collected from Records, Manuscripts, . . . and Other

Undoubted Authorities (London: Printed for Edward
   Withers, 1752);
Historical Collections of the Noble Family of Windsor, . . . Con-
   taining Their Births, Marriages, and Issues: . . . and
   Valuable Memoirs, . . . Collected from Records, Old Wills
   (London: Printed for the author, 1754);
A History of the Noble Family of Carteret, Existing Before the
   Reign of William the Conqueror. . . . Collected from
   Records, Authentick Manuscripts (London, 1756).

In *Literary Ancedotes* (1778) John Nichols reprints a
letter written by Arthur Collins, a bookseller and gene-
alogist, to Thomas Pelham-Holles, Duke of Newcastle,
in which Collins complains about the disproportionate
allocation of government resources to other scholars.
As a testimony to unfair treatment, Collins writes, he is
leaving "in manuscript an account of my family, my life,
and the cruel usage I have undeservedly undergone."
Though there is no evidence that this manuscript exists
(or that it ever existed), the anecdote is an ideal segue
into the life of a man of whom there is relatively little
extant information and who, despite spending his
career chronicling the lives of English nobility, never
seemed to enjoy the advantages of any type of privilege
himself.

The surviving biographical information on the
life of Collins is extremely limited—a fact that has, in
large measure, accounted for the uncertainty of his
birth date, variously given as 1681 or 1682. He was the
son of William Collins, a gentleman usher to Queen
Catherine of Braganza (queen consort of King Charles
II of England and daughter of King John IV of Portugal), and his wife, Elizabeth Blyth, daughter of Thomas
Blyth. Likely, the family was Roman Catholic, though
no birth or marriage documents to support this belief
still exist among the records of the Portuguese Embassy
Chapel in London. In his youth, Collins likely received
a liberal education and might have squandered a large
fortune. He was first recorded as a bookseller at "the
Black Boy, opposite St. Dunstan's Church in Fleet
Street," in partnership with Abel Roper, who is listed
among the publishers of William Dugdale's *The Baron-*
age of England (1675).

Judging by written records spanning his career as
a publisher, Collins likely lived in Enfield during his
professional career, and, toward the end of his life, in
Holloway. Collins married in 1708, but the identity of
his wife is unknown. The name of one of their sons,
Major General Anthony Tooker Collins, however,
might give a hint to the identity of his mother. Another
son was a lieutenant in the Royal Navy, serving in two
campaigns in the Netherlands and fighting in the battles
of Fontenoy, Falkirk, and Culloden.

In 1709 Collins anonymously published the first
edition of *The Peerage of England,* although he and Roper
are identified as the publishers on the title page. An
octavo volume of 470 pages, the first edition of *The Peer-*
age of England supplied meager accounts of noble families and conferred peerages after the publication of
Dugdale's *Baronage,* intended, in the words of Collins in
the preface, "for the great Improvement of . . . young
Nobility and Gentry" as a "Pattern of their great Ancestors before them." In the preface to the second edition,
1710, Collins's comments on the success of *The Peerage*
of England, and the 1712 edition, he inserted crude
woodcuts of armorial bearings, intended for the instruction of young gentlemen in the terms of heraldry. Collins excused the quality of these woodcuts to the
sympathy of his audience, hoping that they would
understand the impracticality of publishing them. Collins gave up his business in Fleet Street in 1716, with the
expectation of a situation in the customhouse. In 1720
he published his *Baronetage of England,* with a dedication
to John Anstis, Garter King of Arms. Consisting of
well-developed biographies, *The Baronetage of England*
was written, according to Collins's preface, to provide
emulative models for its readership, for, as Collins
argues, "It is sufficient to say, that Experience teaches
us, that nothing makes a deeper Impression on the
Mind (which is naturally inclin'd to Knowledge) than
the Observation of the Behaviour and Success of other
Men." Also in the preface, however, Collins articulates
what would be one of a continual series of impediments
to his projects. Stressing the great amount of effort that
he had placed into the documentation of his work, he
laments the many discouragements to its completion by
families who would not let him view their pedigrees:

> When I first set about this Work, I flatter'd myself with
> Hopes, that each Family would have oblig'd me with a
> Sight of their Pedigrees, and such other Evidences, as
> might have brought to Light the Actions of many Per-
> sons of Worth and Note, to whom they were related,
> whereby it would have been greatly facilitated; but, in
> this I found myself disappointed; for after a great
> Expense in Trouble and Attendance, and gathering
> materials, I met with such Discouragements that had it
> not been out of Esteem and Respect for several Gentle-
> men of known worth and excellent Accomplishments, I
> should have wholly laid aside the Publishing of these
> Collections.

These difficulties were not to cease with *The Baronetage*
of England, however. In March 1723, Collins wrote to
Robert Walpole, the prime minister, claiming extreme
poverty and requiring provisions from the government.
Collins additionally explained that he did not intend to
publish any more editions of *The Baronetage of England*

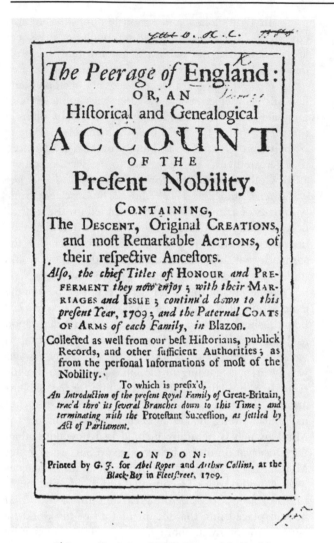

Title page for Arthur Collins's history of the English nobility (British Library)

but was instead preparing an enlarged peerage. A single-volume installment was published in 1727 as *The English Baronage*, which was fronted by a dedication to Robert Walpole and included an account of Walpole's family and the elevation to the peerage of Walpole's eldest son. In his preface, Collins commented on the tremendous expense he had incurred in gathering this large collection of materials, and he explained that he would publish the peerage in order of family precedence.

Collins admitted to having a Dugdale manuscript with many additions by Gregory King to which he added notes from his own research. Benefiting greatly from King's work, Collins in 1734 published *Proceedings, Precedents, and Arguments, on Claims and Controversies, Concerning Baronies by Writ, and Other Honours. With the Arguments of Sir Francis Bacon, . . . and Others*. In 1735 he published the first edition of his *Peerage of England* with engravings of the arms, crests, and supporters of the

then-existing peers. In the second edition of 1741, he added references to his authorities and dedicated the four volumes to Charles Manners, Duke of Rutland; Anthony, Earl of Shaftesbury; John, Lord Viscount Lymington; and Sir Robert Walpole—a move that brought him some much-needed financial relief. Thomas Wotton edited a fifth volume, published as *The English Baronetage* (1741) but more widely known as *Wotton's Baronetage*, in which one volume was dedicated to a different benefactor, Anthony Ashley-Cooper, fourth Earl of Shaftesbury. Though Wotton acknowledged the assistance of Collins, Wotton also admitted his obligations to the works of Peter Le Neve, which he purchased in 1731.

In his preface to the 1741 second edition of *The Peerage of England*, Collins complained that he had spent his fortune on research that he would not be able to publish without help. He further contrasted the assistance that he had received with the favor shown to Elias Ashmole and Dugdale. In a letter composed in 1752, he wrote to the Duke of Newcastle, complaining that he had engaged on a new edition of *The Peerage of England*, but did not have the money to pay a transcriber. In a subsequent letter to Newcastle, Collins became blunter, blaming his poverty on the cost of printing his account of Newcastle's mother's family, and directly asking for financial assistance. Ultimately, he received a pension of £400 a year from the king, which allowed him to complete the third of the large edition of *The Peerage of England* (1756), a volume that was dedicated to King George II and the Earls of Shaftesbury, Holdernesse, and Northumberland and Baron Abergavenny. Three posthumous editions of *The Peerage of England* were published, a remarkable fact because it demonstrates the transcendent value and adaptability of Collins's work. During the eighteenth century, peerages of different countries were widely considered to be separate entities, a belief discernible in Collins's work published during his lifetime. At the start of the nineteenth century, however, this perception shifted when the classification of peerages was widely reenvisioned to match rank to wealth, power, and general consequence. As a result, the three separate peerages of Scotland, Ireland, and England were more closely associated into one authentic British peerage. This shift in perspective was first reflected in the work of John Debrett, *Peerage of England, Scotland, and Ireland* (1802); of John Stockdale, *The Present Peerage of the United Kingdom* (1808); and the final edition of Collins's *The Peerage of England* (1812), which was edited by Sir Samuel Egerton Brydges and became the standard before the appearance of G. E. Cockayne's *The Complete Peerage of England, Scotland, Ireland, Great Britain, and the United Kingdom, Extant, Extinct, or Dormant* (1998).

In addition to his major works, *The Peerage of England* and *The Baronetage of England*, Collins worked on several smaller biographical and geneaological projects that were dedicated to individual historical figures and writers. These include *The Life of That Great Statesman William Cecil, Lord Burghley* . . . (1732), *The History of John of Gaunt* (1740), *The Life and Glorious Actions of Edward Prince of Wales* (1740), *Memoirs of the Antient and Noble Family of Sackville* (1741), *Letters and Memorials of State, in the Reigns of Queen Mary* (1746), *An History of the Ancient and Illustrious Family of the Percys* (1750), *Historical Collections of the Noble Families of Cavendishe, Holles, Vere, Harley, and Ogle, with the Lives of the Most Remarkable Persons* (1752), *Historical Collections of the Noble Family of Windsor* (1754); and *A History of the Noble Family of Carteret* (1756).

In all, Collins was considered a competent, if not particularly original, scholar. In his edition of *The English Baronetage* Wotton acknowledged Collins's skill. Carlyle, in his rectorial address to the students of Edinburgh University, acknowledged "a great deal of help out of poor Collins" when writing his life of Oliver Cromwell, and, according to the *Dictionary of National Biography,* he pronounced Collins's *Peerage of England* to be "a very poor peerage as a work of genius, but an excellent book for diligence and fidelity." In his preface to *The Peerage of England,* Brydges described the exceptional and indefatigable industry of Collins and his general accuracy, which rivaled Dugdale's.

If Arthur Collins had intended to be a philosopher, such comments might appear to be a case of damning him with faint praise. In light of Collins's perspectives on his own career, however, the comments seem highly appropriate. Usually referring to himself as a printer or bookseller, Collins took on the mantle of "author" only with great reluctance. In his own words in *Historical Collections of the Noble Families of Cavendishe, Holles, Vere, Harley, and Ogle,* his only purpose was to "preserve the memory of famous men," and he even went so far as to remark, in the preface to the first edition of *The Peerage of England,* "I have avoided all partial Characters and Reflexions, where-ever I have found them shew'd up and down in History, or other Publick Volumes I have follow'd; for, next to being void of Errors, I shall account myself as happy to have given no Offence."

Collins died on 16 March 1762 in Holloway and was buried at Battersea Church. He was survived by his son, Major General Arthur Tooker Collins, author of *The Account of the English Settlement in New South Wales* (1804), who died 4 January 1793, leaving a son, David Collins, who was a judge advocate in New South Wales, where he died on 24 March 1810.

Reference:

David Cannadine, *Aspects of Aristocracy* (New Haven: Yale University Press, 1994).

Papers:

The British Library holds Arthur Collins's historical notes and papers, including genealogical accounts of the Earl of Essex, and his letters to the Duke of Newcastle; the Bodleian Library at Oxford holds genealogical and heraldric papers; the Center for Kentish Studies holds his letters to William Perry; the Essex Records Office holds his letters to William Holman; and the Northumberland Record Office holds his correspondence with Sir William Swinburne and Edward Swinburne.

Daniel Defoe
(1660 – 26 April 1731)

Mark G. Spencer
Brock University

See also the Defoe entries in *DLB 39: British Novelists, 1660–1800; DLB 95: Eighteenth-Century British Poets, First Series;* and *DLB 101: British Prose Writers, 1660–1800, First Series.*

BOOKS: *A Letter to a Dissenter from His Friend at The Hague* (The Hague [i.e., London]: Printed by Hans Verdraeght [pseud.], [1688]);

Reflections upon the Late Great Revolution (London: Printed for Richard Chiswell, 1689);

A New Discovery of an Old Intreague: A Satyr . . . Calculated to the Nativity of the Rapparee Plott and the Modesty of the Jacobite Clergy (London, 1691);

Some Reflections on a Pamphlet lately Publish'd, Entituled An Argument Shewing that a Standing Army is Inconsistent with a Free Government, and Absolutely Destructive to the Constitution of the English Monarchy (London: Printed for E. Whitlock, 1697);

An Essay upon Projects (London: Printed by R.R. for Tho. Cockerill, 1697);

An Argument Shewing, that a Standing Army, with Consent of Parliament, Is not Inconsistent with a Free Government (London: Printed for E. Whitlock, 1698);

A Brief Reply to the History of Standing Armies in England. With some Account of the Authors (London, 1698);

The Poor Man's Plea . . . for a Reformation of Manners and Suppressing Immorality in the Nation (London, 1698);

The True-Born Englishman: A Satyr (London, 1700);

The History of the Kentish Petition (London, 1701);

[Legion's Memorial] (London, 1701);

The Original Power of the Collective Body of the People of England, Examined and Asserted (London, 1701);

The Present State of Jacobitism Considered (London, 1701);

The Succession to the Crown of England, Considered (London, 1701);

An Enquiry into Occasional Conformity (London, 1702);

The Shortest Way with the Dissenters; or, Proposals for the Establishment of the Church (London, 1702); republished as *The Shortest Way with the Dissenters. [Taken from Dr. Sach[evere]ll's Sermon, and Others]* (London: Printed & sold by the Booksellers, 1703);

Daniel Defoe (frontispiece for The History of the Union of Great Britain, *1709; courtesy of Special Collections, Thomas Cooper Library, University of South Carolina)*

A Brief Explanation of a late Pamphlet, Entituled, The Shortest Way with the Dissenters (London, 1703);

A Hymn to the Pillory (London, 1703);

The Opinion of a Known Dissenter on the Bill for Preventing Occasional Conformity (London, 1703);

Peace without Union. By Way of Reply, to Sir H--- M---'s [i.e. Sir Humphrey Mackworth's] Peace at Home (London, 1703);

An Essay on the Regulation of the Press (London, 1704);

A Review of the State of the English Nation, continued as *The Review of the Affairs of France,* continued as *Review of the State of the British Nation,* continued as *The Review,* 9 volumes (19 February 1704–11 June 1713) [exact title frequently changed];

A Serious Inquiry into This Grand Question; Whether a Law to Prevent the Occasional Conformity of Dissenters, Would not Be Inconsistent with the Act of Toleration (London, 1704);

The Storm; or, A Collection of the Most Remarkable Casualties and Disasters, Which Happen'd in the Late Dreadful Tempest, Both by Sea and Land (London: Printed for G. Sawbridge, 1704);

The Dyet of Poland: A Satyr (London?: Printed at Dantzick, 1705);

The Double Welcome. A Poem To the Duke of Marlbro' (London: Printed & sold by B. Bragg, 1705);

The Consolidator (London: Printed & sold by Benj. Bragg, 1705);

An Essay at Removing National Prejudices against a Union with Scotland (London, 1706);

Jure Divino: A Satyr in Twelve Books (London, 1706);

Caledonia: A Poem in Honour of Scotland, and the Scots Nation (Edinburgh: Printed by the Heirs and Successors of Andrew Anderson, 1706; London: Printed by J. Mathews & sold by John Morphew, 1707);

The History of the Union of Great Britain (Edinburgh: Printed by the Heirs and Successors of Andrew Anderson, 1709);

A Brief History of the Poor Palatine Refugees (London: Printed & sold by J. Baker, 1709);

The History of the Union of Great Britain (Edinburgh: Printed by the Heirs and Successors of Andrew Anderson, 1709);

A Speech without Doors (London: Printed for A. Baldwin, 1710);

Instructions from Rome (London: Printed & sold by J. Baker, 1710);

An Essay upon Publick Credit (London: Printed & sold by the Booksellers, 1710);

Reasons Why This Nation Ought to Put a Speedy End to This Expensive War (London: Printed for J. Baker, 1711);

Reasons Why a Party among Us, and also among the Confederates, Are Obstinately Bent against a Treaty of Peace (London: Printed for John Baker, 1711);

An Essay at a Plain Exposition of that Difficult Phrase a Good Peace (London: Printed for J. Baker, 1711);

An Essay on the History of Parties, and Persecution in Britain (London: Printed for J. Baker, 1711);

No Queen; or, No General (London: Printed & sold by the Booksellers of London & Westminster, 1712);

The Conduct of Parties in England (London, 1712);

Peace, or Poverty (London: Printed & sold by John Morphew, 1712);

The Present State of the Parties in Great Britain (London: Sold by J. Baker, 1712);

An Enquiry into the Danger and Consequences of a War with the Dutch (London: Printed for J. Baker, 1712);

And What if the Pretender Should Come? (London: Sold by J. Baker, 1713);

An Essay on the Treaty of Commerce with France (London: Printed for J. Baker, 1713);

Mercator, 26 May 1713–20 July 1714;

A General History of Trade, and Especially Consider'd as it Respects the British Commerce, 4 parts (London: Printed for J. Baker, 1713);

Memoirs of Count Tariff (London: Printed for John Morphew, 1713);

Reasons Against the Succession of the House of Hanover, with an Inquiry How Far the Abdication of King James, Supposing it to Be Legal, Ought to Affect the Person of the Pretender. . . (London, 1713);

Memoirs of John, Duke of Melfort (London: Printed for J. Moor, 1714);

The Secret History of the White Staff: Being an Account of Affairs under the Conduct of Some Late Ministers (London: Printed for J. Baker, 1714–1715);

Advice to the People of Great Britain (London: Printed for J. Baker, 1714);

Hanover or Rome (London: Printed for J. Roberts, 1715);

The Fears of the Pretender Turn'd into the Fears of Debauchery (London: Printed by S. Keimer, 1715);

An Appeal to Honour and Justice (London: Printed for J. Baker, 1715);

The Family Instructor, in Three Parts (London: J. Button/ Newcastle upon Tyne: Matthews, 1715);

An Account of the Conduct of Robert Earl of Oxford (London, 1715);

An Account of the Proceedings against the Rebels (London: Printed for J. Baker & Tho. Warner, 1716);

A True Account of the Proceedings at Perth (London: Printed for J. Baker, 1716);

Fair Payment No Spunge; or, Some Considerations on the Unreasonableness of Refusing to Receive Back Money Lent on Publick Securities (London: Sold by J. Brotherton & W. Meddows, and J. Roberts, 1717);

The Question Fairly Stated, Whether Now Is Not the Time to Do Justice to the Friends of the Government as Well as to its Enemies? (London: Printed for J. Roberts, J. Harrison & A. Dodd, 1717);

Memoirs of the Church of Scotland (London: Printed for Eman. Matthews and T. Warner, 1717);

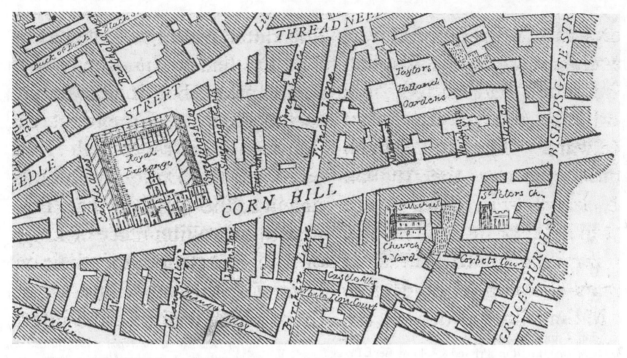

1750 map of Cornhill Ward, where Defoe had business interests (from <http://www.londonancestor.com/maps/map-cornhill.htm>)

Considerations on the Present State of Affairs in Great Britain (London: Printed for J. Roberts, 1718);

Memoirs of the Life and Eminent Conduct of that Learned and Reverend Divine Daniel Williams, D.D. (London: Printed for E. Curll, 1718);

Memoirs of Publick Transactions in the Life and Ministry of his Grace the D. of Shrewsbury (London: Printed for Tho. Warner, 1718);

The Family Instructor. In Two Parts (London: Matthews, 1718);

A Continuation of Letters Written by a Turkish Spy at Paris (London: Printed for W. Taylor, 1718);

The Memoirs of Majr. Alexander Ramkins (London: Printed for R. King & W. Boreham, 1719);

The Life and Strange Suprizing Adventures of Robinson Crusoe (London: Printed for W. Taylor, 1719);

The Anatomy of Exchange-Alley; or, A System of Stock-Jobbing (London: Printed for E. Smith, 1719);

The Farther Adventures of Robinson Crusoe (London: Printed for W. Taylor, 1719);

A Brief State of the Question, between the Printed and Painted Callicoes and the Woollen and Silk Manufacture (London: Printed for W. Boreham, 1719);

The Life and Strange Suprising Adventures of Robinson Crusoe, of York, Mariner (London: Printed for W. Taylor, 1719);

Manufacturer, 30 October 1719–17 February 1720;

The King of Pirates: Being an Account of the Famous Enterprises of Captain Avery (London: Printed for A. Bettes-

worth, C. King, J. Brotherton & W. Meadows, W. Chetwood, and sold by W. Boreham, 1720);

The Life, Adventures and Pyracies of the Famous Captain Singleton (London: Printed for J. Brotherton, J. Graves, A. Dodd & T. Warner, 1720);

Memoirs of a Cavalier; or, A Military Journal of the Wars in Germany, and the Wars in England; from the Year 1632, to the Year 1648 (London: Printed for A. Bell, J. Osborn, W. Taylor, and T. Warner, 1720);

The South-Sea Scheme Examin'd (London: Printed for J. Roberts, 1720);

The Fortunes and Misfortunes of the Famous Moll Flanders (London: Printed for & sold by W. Chetwood & T. Edling, 1721);

Due Preparations for the Plague, as Well for Soul as Body (London: Printed for E. Matthews and J. Batley, 1722);

Religious Courtship (London: Printed for E. Matthews & A. Bettesworth, J. Brotherton & W. Meadows, 1722);

A Journal of the Plague Year (London: Printed for E. Nutt, J. Roberts, A. Dodd & J. Graves, 1722);

The History and Remarkable Life of the Truly Honourable Col. Jacque (London: Printed & sold by J. Brotherton, T. Payne, W. Mears, A. Dodd, W. Chetwood, J. Graves, S. Chapman & J. Stagg, 1723);

The Fortunate Mistress; or, A History of the Life and Vast Variety of Fortunes of Mademoiselle de Beleau . . . Being the Person known by the Name of the Lady Roxana, in the Time of King Charles II (London: Printed for T.

Warner, W. Meadows, W. Pepper, S. Harding & T. Edlin, 1724);

The Great Law of Subordination Consider'd (London: Sold by S. Harding, W. Lewis, T. Worrall, A. Bettesworth, W. Meadows & T. Edlin, 1724);

A Tour thro' the Whole Island of Great Britain, Divided into Circuits or Journies, 3 volumes (London: Sold by G. Strahan, W. Mears, and others, 1724, 1725, 1727);

The Royal Progress (London: Printed by John Darby & sold by J. Roberts, J. Brotherton & A. Dodd, 1724);

A Narrative of All the Robberies, Escapes &c. of John Sheppard (London: Printed & sold by John Applebee, 1724);

The History of the Remarkable Life of John Sheppard (London: Printed & sold by John Applebee, J. Isted & the Booksellers of London and Westminster, 1724);

Every-body's Business, Is No-body's Business; or, Private Abuses, Publick Grievances (London: Sold by T. Warner, A. Dodd & E. Nutt, 1725);

A General History of Discoveries and Improvements, in Useful Arts, Particularly in the Great Branches of Commerce, Navigation, and Plantation, in all Parts of the Known World (London: Printed for J. Roberts, 1725–1726);

The Complete English Tradesman, 2 volumes (London: Printed for Charles Rivington, 1726; with supplement, 1727);

A Brief Historical Account of the Lives of the Six Notorious Street-Robbers, Executed at Kingston (London: Printed for A. Moore, 1726);

An Essay upon Literature; or, An Enquiry into the Antiquity and Original of Letters (London: Printed for Tho. Bowles, John Clark, and John Bowles, 1726);

Mere Nature Delineated; or, A Body without a Soul. Being Observations upon the Young Forester Lately Brought to Town from Germany (London: Printed for T. Warner, 1726);

The Political History of the Devil, as Well Ancient as Modern (London: Printed for T. Warner, 1726);

Some Considerations upon Street-Walkers (London: Printed for A. Moore, 1726);

A System of Magick; or, A History of the Black Art. Being an Historical Account of Mankind's Most Early Dealing with the Devil; and How the Acquaintance on Both Sides First Began (London: Printed by J. Roberts, 1727);

The Protestant Monastery; or, A Complaint against the Brutality of the Present Age (London: Printed for W. Meadows, 1727);

Conjugal Lewdness; or, Matrimonial Whoredom (London: Printed for T. Warner, 1727);

A Brief Deduction of the Original, Progress, and Immense Greatness of the British Woollen Manufacture . . . (London: Printed by J. Roberts and A. Dodd, 1727);

An Essay on the History and Reality of Apparitions (London: Printed by J. Roberts, 1727);

A New Family Instructor; In Familiar Discourses between a Father and his Children (London: Printed for T. Warner, 1727);

Parochial Tyranny (London: Printed & sold by J. Roberts, 1727);

Augusta Triumphans; or, The Way to Make London the Most Flourishing City in the Universe (London: Printed for J. Roberts & sold by E. Nutt, A. Dodd, N. Blandford & A. Stagg, 1728);

A Plan of the English Commerce (London: Printed for Charles Rivington, 1728);

Atlas Maritimus & Commercialis; or, A General View of the World, So Far as It Relates to Trade and Navigation (London: Printed for James & John Knapton; William & John Innys; John Darby; Arthur Bettesworth, John Osborn & Thomas Longman; John Senex; Edward Symon; Andrew Johnston; and the Executors of William Taylor, 1728);

Second Thoughts are Best (London: Printed for W. Meadows & sold by J. Roberts, 1729);

An Humble Proposal to the People of England, for the Encrease of Their Trade, and Encouragement of Their Manufactures (London: Printed for Charles Rivington, 1729);

The Advantages of Peace and Commerce (London: Printed for J. Brotherton & Tho. Cox, and sold by A. Dodd, 1729);

An Effectual Scheme for the Immediate Preventing of Street Robberies (London: Printed for J. Wilford, 1731);

The Compleat English Gentleman, edited by Karl D. Bülbring (London: David Nutt, 1890).

Editions and Collections: *The Works of Daniel De Foe,* edited by William W. Hazlitt (the Younger), 3 volumes (London: Clements, 1840–1843);

The Works of Daniel Defoe, 16 volumes, edited by G. H. Maynadier (New York: Sproul, 1903–1904);

The Works of Daniel Defoe, 44 volumes, edited by W. R. Owens and P. N. Furbank (London: Pickering & Chatto, 2000–   ).

Daniel Defoe was known to his contemporaries as a prodigious writer who employed a variety of genres to produce many pages on many topics. They saw him, perhaps foremost, as a journalist and pamphleteer, but also as a travel writer, political and religious thinker, social critic, poet, and sometimes historian. To modern scholars, however, Defoe the novelist has attracted the most readers and commentary, largely through innovative works of fiction such as *The*

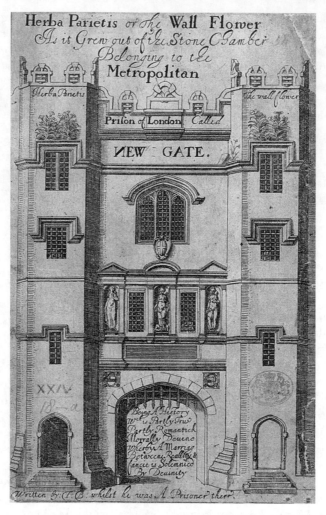

Title page for Thomas Bayly, Herba parietis; or, The Wallflower *showing Newgate Prison, where Defoe was incarcerated for a short time (<http://www.collectbritain.co.uk/personalisation/object.cfm>)*

Life and Strange Suprizing Adventures of Robinson Crusoe, of York (1719), *The Fortunes and Misfortunes of the Famous Moll Flanders* (1721), *A Journal of the Plague Year* (1722), and *The Fortunate Mistress; or, A History of the Life and Vast Variety of Fortunes of Mademoiselle de Beleau. . . . Being the Person known by the Name of the Lady Roxana, in the Time of King Charles II* [now commonly known as *Roxanna*] (1724). Neither his contemporaries nor the critics of the late twentieth and the twenty-first centuries have directed much serious attention to Defoe as an historian. Yet, compelling reasons suggest Defoe's historical writings deserve more attention.

Defoe wrote a considerable amount of history. His most notable historical works are his *History of the Union of Great Britain* (1709) and *Memoirs of the Church of Scotland* (1717). Both of these books continue to be essential sources for historians of their subjects. But other dimensions of Defoe's historical writings warrant

study, too. To understand Defoe's life as a writer in general, one needs to know something more of Defoe as historian in particular. Defoe often took an historical approach to the subjects on which he wrote, even when he was not writing history proper. That was the case, for instance, in economic writings such as *A General History of Trade, and Especially Consider'd as it Respects the British Commerce* (1713), in poems such as *The Dyet of Poland* (1705), and in instructional books such as *Due Preparations for the Plague, as Well for Soul as Body* (1722). The case in many of the novels was similar, as commentators have long appreciated. *Robinson Crusoe,* for instance, was loosely based on the life of Alexander Selkirk, a real-life castaway. In this and other novels Defoe constantly blended fact and fiction so seamlessly that the debate goes on to this day about where to draw divisions. Wherever one looks in the Defoe canon, one comes upon historical examples and allusions. Defoe systematically portrayed issues in an historical framework and consistently attempted to put historical knowledge to useful ends. He did so intending to reach a wide reading audience. For these reasons Defoe is of interest for the light he can cast on British historiography of the late seventeenth and early eighteenth centuries.

Assessing Defoe as an historian is made more difficult because of the uncertainty of identifying what writings constitute the Defoe corpus. Defoe often wrote anonymously. Possibly, even probably, Defoe wrote minor historical pamphlets and pieces published in periodicals that have not been attributed to him by modern scholars. Equally problematic for assessing Defoe as historian is the trend whereby works have been attributed to him that he may not have written.

Defoe was born Daniel Foe, possibly in the parish of St. Giles Cripplegate, certainly in or near London, probably in the autumn of 1660. Defoe's father, James Foe, was a tallow chandler and trained butcher. Not much is known about Defoe's mother, whose name was Alice; neither is much known about Defoe's earliest years. What is known is that the Foes were Presbyterians, that they were members of Samuel Annesley's "Nonconformist" congregation, and that Daniel first attended school at Dorking in Surry, where he began to study circa 1672 under the "dissenting" Reverend James Fisher. Defoe's dissenting background surfaced in historical writings throughout his life, especially informing his *Memoirs of the Church of Scotland*.

From 1674 until approximately 1679 Defoe was a student of the Reverend Charles Morton, whose Dissenting Academy was at Newington Green. Morton's school was well known and stood out for its instruction in English, rather than Greek or Latin, and for giving attention to history and science, subjects that were often ignored in other schools in favor of the Classics. Persecuted in the early 1680s, Morton later immigrated to New England, where he was on friendly terms with Increase Mather, who arranged for Morton to be appointed Harvard University's first vice president in 1697. No one knows if it was Morton who sparked Defoe's early interest in history, but by the time Defoe was a young man he reported that he had read "all the Histories of Europe, that are Extant in our Language, and some in other Languages." That Defoe's first extant historical writings can be dated close to his years with Morton is probably no coincidence.

In 1682 Defoe compiled his "Historical Collections or Memoires of Passages & Stories Collected from Severall Authors," a piece unknown to twentieth-century scholars until its discovery by Maximillian E. Novak. "Historical Collections" is a curious piece that was not published during Defoe's lifetime, but it shows Defoe's early interest in historical topics and characters,

such as Gustavus Adolphus, king of Sweden (1611–1632), [?] Adolphus later figured prominently in *Memoirs of a Cavalier; or, A Military Journal of the Wars in Germany, and the Wars in England; from the Year 1632 . . . to the Year 1648* (1720), Defoe's fictional account of the Thirty Years' War, which many of his contemporaries read as genuine history. "Historical Collections" evidences Defoe's early reading of a variety of historical works, ancient and modern, including the Venerable Bede's *Historia ecclesiastica gentis Anglorum [History of the English Church and People]* (completed 731; translated 1955), Thomas Fuller's *Worthies of England* (1662), Richard Knolles's *Generall History of the Turkes* (1603), Plutarch's *Lives,* and writings by Eusebius. "Historical Collections" was written for Defoe's future wife, Mary Tuffley, whom he married in 1684.

In the 1680s, with the backing of his new wife's substantial dowry of £3,700, Defoe pursued various mercantile enterprises, including hosiery and wine sales in London. He also brokered trade between several provincial towns; between England and European countries such as France, Portugal, and Spain, to which he traveled; and he even traveled to New World cities, such as Boston and New York. In 1684 his business activities were centered on Freeman's Yard, Cornhill.

In the summer of 1685 Defoe fought, as did other of Morton's students, with the duke of Monmouth in a failed rebellion against King James II of England. For these actions Defoe was pardoned in 1687. Born in the year of the Restoration, when Charles II was restored to the throne of England, Defoe was raised in turbulent times. Significant changes were going on around him, especially in London in the years of rebuilding that followed the Great Fire of 1666. That environment and also his reading led Defoe to think in historical terms about political, religious, and economic circumstances and their relationship.

Defoe's financial circumstances may also have had an impact upon his writing. His early mercantile pursuits gradually became bogged down in heavy debts and legal actions of various sorts. Schemes to collect musk from the urine of civet cats and to reap treasures from diving-bell operations were not successful. By 1692 he had accumulated debts totaling approximately £17,000, enough to bring about bankruptcy and Defoe's imprisonment at the Fleet Prison.

In 1694 Defoe made something of a fresh start, establishing a brick and pantile factory at West Tilbury, Essex. He won some government contracts and also secured various minor government employments, including a post as collector of duty on "Glasswares, Stone and Earthen Bottles." Defoe's fortunes appeared on the rise in the 1690s, and during these years he began to publish prolifically. His first significant published

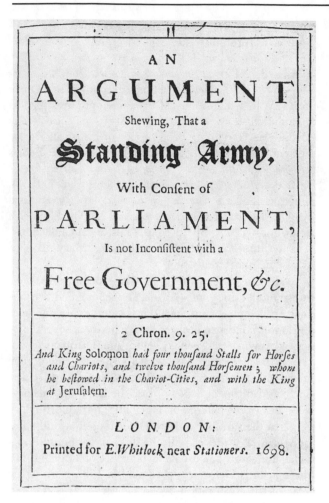

AN

ARGUMENT

Shewing, That a

𝕾𝖙𝖆𝖓𝖉𝖎𝖓𝖌 𝕬𝖗𝖒𝖞,

With Confent of

PARLIAMENT,

Is not Inconfiftent with a

Free Government, &c.

2 Chron. 9. 25.

And King Solomon had four thoufand Stalls for Horfes and Chariots, and twelve thoufand Horfemen ; whom he beftowed in the Chariot-Cities, and with the King at Jerufalem.

LONDON:

Printed for *E. Whitlock* near *Stationers.* 1698.

Title page for a pamphlet by Defoe (Microforms Collection, Thomas Cooper Library, University of South Carolina)

poem, *A New Discovery of an Old Intreague: A Satyr . . . Calculated to the Nativity of the Rapparee Plott and the Modesty of the Jacobite Clergy* (1691), is representative of the political tone of much of Defoe's early poetry. Other early publications, such as *An Essay upon Projects* (1697), with its introductory essay on the "History of Projects," illustrate the historical tendency of Defoe's writing from the beginning.

Defoe's pamphlets from this early period are filled with historical allusions and arguments. When he considered the question of the relationship between standing armies and the protection of liberties, for instance, the historical record formed a key part of his position. Arguing against John Trenchard and Walter Moyle's *An Argument Shewing that a Standing Army Is Inconsistent with a Free Government* (1697), Defoe maintained in *Some Reflections on a Pamphlet lately Publish'd, Entituled An Argument Shewing that a Standing Army is Inconsistent with a Free Government, and Absolutely Destructive to the Constitution of the*

English Monarchy (1697) that England's history showed, to all who cared to look, that a standing army was not inconsistent with free government. Defoe built upon that theme in subsequent pamphlets, such as *An Argument Shewing, that a Standing Army, with Consent of Parliament, Is not Inconsistent with a Free Government* (1698), in which he argued that the commercial nature of England necessitated more than a militia, and *A Brief Reply to the History of Standing Armies in England* (1698), in which Defoe argued that Queen Elizabeth had maintained a standing army with no ill effects to English liberty. On the issue of standing armies, Defoe the pamphleteer aimed to clarify current controversies by establishing more clearly the historical contexts from which they sprang. This method became a common formula for Defoe.

Other of Defoe's earliest works had historical orientations and show Defoe's interest in politics. Many of these were supportive of William III, whom Defoe frequently praised in print, especially in his verse-satire *The True-Born Englishman* (1700). A literary success, *The True-Born Englishman* went through many editions in Defoe's lifetime and was included in compilations such as *Poems on Affairs of State* (1703) and *A Collection of the Best English Poetry* (1717). Other publications of these years include *The History of the Kentish Petition* (1701), *The Present State of Jacobitism Considered* (1701), and *The Original Power of the Collective Body of the People of England, Examined and Asserted* (1701)—all of which illustrate Defoe's immersion in the historical and political issues of the day.

What received even more attention from his contemporaries was Defoe's ironic *The Shortest Way with the Dissenters; or, Proposals for the Establishment of the Church* (1702), a pamphlet that pretended to argue for the extirpation of Dissenters. Written in response to the Occasional Conformity Bill introduced on the accession of Queen Anne in 1702, Defoe's satire was at first read literally by many people—High Anglican Tories and Dissenters included. That mistake, when recognized as such, heightened the animosity many "High Flying" Tories of the Church of England felt toward the author of *The Shortest Way with the Dissenters,* an author they now aimed to identify and prosecute. When Defoe's authorship was discovered, he was charged with writing a seditious pamphlet, and an advertisement was printed offering a reward for his capture. Apprehended and eventually pleading his guilt, Defoe was fined, sentenced to three days in the pillory at the Royal Exchange in Cornhill, and imprisoned in Newgate Prison, from where he continued to write.

Upon his release from Newgate in 1703, largely owing to the intervention of Robert Harley, then Secretary of State for the Northern Department, Defoe found his brickworks in ruin. He altered his surname from

Foe to Defoe during this year as he increasingly turned to writing for his livelihood. Some of this writing developed more fully themes on which Defoe had already published, such as *Peace without Union* (1703), which argued against Sir Humphrey Mackworth's historical defense of single-religion states and test acts. Defoe's piece caused a stir and was answered in *Peace and Union* (1704) and *Reflections upon a Passage in a Pamphlet, Entituled Peace without Union* (1704). In 1704 Defoe had published *An Essay on the Regulation of the Press.* In this and other writings, Defoe was reaching out to a broader reading audience, the middling sort to whom he belonged, many of whom had begun to think of him as something of a popular hero. Perhaps Harley recognized Defoe's growing appeal with the public when he hired him as an agent for an annual salary of £200.

In 1704 Defoe also produced *The Storm; or, A Collection of the Most Remarkable Casualties and Disasters, Which Happen'd in the Late Dreadful Tempest, Both by Sea and Land,* a curious book that aimed to capitalize on the fierce hurricane that had struck England in late November 1703. Defoe argued that the recent storm was a warning from God, but he interpreted it in the context of an historical survey of storms that had visited Britain since ancient times. Defoe in this work showed he was skeptical of many past historical accounts and argued that ancient myths were often little more than fictions thrust on the unsuspecting. In his skepticism is the hint of the suspicious temperament that informed his later writings and that was important to a developing Enlightenment historiography. Similarly, Defoe considered the advent of print to be a useful step forward in establishing and disseminating true historical accounts. As he put it, "Printing of books is talking to the whole world," a sentiment that would appeal to those who considered themselves to constitute a "Republic of Letters" (Defoe's preface to *The Storm*).

On 19 February 1704 the first number of Defoe's *A Review of the State of the English Nation* was published. Defoe wrote and published this important journal, usually as a triweekly, through 11 June 1713, by which time it filled nine volumes. The periodical, under its various names, was long-lived, especially when measured against the standard lives of eighteenth-century periodicals. Had he written nothing else, on its own this periodical represents a significant quantity of writing with an historical tendency. Indeed, Defoe himself described his periodical as "history writing by inches." The "Work of Writing a Peny Paper," he wrote in issue number 9, "is only writing a History sheet by sheet." In its inaugural issue, Defoe maintained that "As these Papers may be Collected into Volumes, they will Compose a Compleat History of *France,* the Antient Part of which shall be a faithful Abridgment of former

Authors, and the Modern Affairs stated, as Impartially and as Methodical as the length of this Paper will permit." Defoe explained:

> We shall particularly have a Regard to the Rise and Fall of the Protestant Religion in the Dominions of *France;* and the Reader, if the Author live, and is permitted to pursue the Design, shall find this Paper a Useful Index, to turn him to the best Historians of the Church in all Ages.

> Here he shall find the mighty Struggle the Protestant Churches met with in that Kingdom for near 200 Years; the Strong Convulsions of their Expiring Circumstances; the True History of the vast Expence and mighty Endeavours of this Nation to support them. . . .

> All along we shall prosecute, with as much Care as possible, the Genuine History of what happens in the Matters of State and War, now carried on in *Europe.* . . .

Defoe promises that "the Matter of our Account will be real History, and just Observation" and vouches for "the Merit of an Impartial and Exact Historical Pen." Examination of the contents of his periodical shows that mixed with advertisements for books, Defoe's "Advice from the Scandalous Club," verse, and "Miscellanea" were many essays on the history of France, trade, foreign affairs, and relations between England and Scotland, all couched in terms designed to reach and influence a popular audience.

Defoe's involvement in the 1707 Treaty of Union between Scotland and England shows the merging of his historical, political, and literary interests. In the fall of 1706 he traveled north to Edinburgh, where he remained until the winter of 1707. On Harley's orders, he was enlisted to collect information about Scotland to be sent, by letters, to England. (Defoe wrote using the names "Alexander Goldsmith" and "Claude Guilot.") Defoe was also to promote the cause of union in Scotland. In the spring of 1706 he published, in Edinburgh, the first two parts of what became his six-part *An Essay at Removing National Prejudices against a Union with Scotland.* There Defoe built on material he had first worked up for an earlier number of *The Review,* that for December 1705. Also in 1706 he wrote and published a poem about Scotland, *Caledonia,* which emphasized historical aspects of Anglo-Scottish cooperation. At this time, too, he began to publish in Scotland a separate edition of *The Review* called *The Edinburgh Courant.* All of this activity was in the background as Defoe composed *The History of the Union of Great Britain.*

This volume was first advertised in *The Review* of 29 March 1707. Defoe aimed in this and subsequent advertisements, such as his separately printed "Propos-

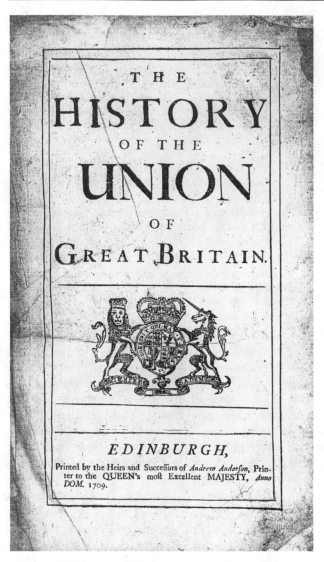

Title page for Defoe's account of the 1707 Treaty of Union between England and Scotland, which he promoted (Special Collections, Thomas Cooper Library, University of South Carolina)

als for Printing the History of the Union," to attract subscribers for the *History of the Union,* a large folio adorned with a frontispiece portrait of the author. An Edinburgh printer, Agnes Anderson, who had continued the business of her deceased husband, Andrew Anderson, published the book in late 1709. Notices appeared in Defoe's *Review* and also in *The Edinburgh Courant.*

One of Defoe's guiding themes was to set the Union of 1707 in its historical context. As he put it, "IN order to come to a clear Understanding in the whole Frame of this wonderful Transaction, THE UNION, 'tis necessary to let the Reader into the very Original of it, and Enquire where the first Springs are to be found, from whence this mighty Transaction has been

Form'd." The first edition of the *History of the Union* was dedicated to both the Queen and the Duke of Queensberry. Its text was divided into six parts. In part 1, "A General History of Unions in Britain," Defoe sketches the long-standing animosity between England and Scotland. He surveys past attempts at union, giving most attention to the efforts of Edward I in the thirteenth century but also discussing James I's Union of the Crowns and efforts under Charles II. A central concern was to show "That never any rational Prospect of Uniting these Kingdoms appeared in the World, but both the Nations unanimously agreed, that Union was for the mutual Advantage of both, and that it never was Opposed by either Nation, *as a Nation,* but only as Private Interests, Strength of Parties, Court Intrigues, and the Enemies of both the Nations have prevailed, to prevent their Happiness." Defoe assesses, in that context, the "Union of the Crowns" as "*a kind of Union*" that falls far short of a true "Union of the Kingdoms."

In part 2, "Of Affairs in Both Kingdoms, introductory of a Treaty of Union," Defoe outlines some of the events that had heightened, in the years immediately preceding the Union, a divisive attitude between England and Scotland. He catalogues government legislation such as the Act of Security in Scotland but also events such as the Affairs of *Glenco,* the Seizing of the ship *Worcester,* and the execution of Captain Green. In parts 1 and 2 Defoe used the works of several historians, including Robert Brady, George Buchanan, Thomas Craig, James Tyrrell, and John Spottiswoode. These parts are also indicative of Defoe's thoughts on providential history. He concludes, for instance, that "GOD's Providence Unravelled all these Schemes of Destruction, which mad Men had drawn for the Ruine of their Native Country."

In part 3, "Of the Last Treaty, Properly Called the Union," Defoe explicitly points to the historical lesson he wishes his readers to learn: "all the Miscarriages of former Treatises have been as Warnings to furnish the Experience of these Times to make them wary, and instruct them how to avoid the Rocks that others Split on." Large sections of part 3 consist of transcriptions of official documents, such as commission minutes and the "Articles of Union," but these are regularly interspersed with Defoe's "Observations." In his enthusiasm for reproducing primary sources, Defoe's historical work was similar to that of many of his contemporaries. As he explained in the preface, his intention was to include even more primary documents, but these had to be omitted as the book was "swelling beyond my Expectation."

In part 4, "Of the Carrying on of the Treaty in Scotland," and part 5, "An Abstract of the Proceedings on the Treaty of Union Within the Parliament of Scotland," Defoe provides a detailed, often firsthand, account of the actual debates in Scotland. He aimed to provide the view from Edinburgh, relaying the debates that the Union had occasioned in the Scottish parliament during the winter of 1706–1707. *History of the Union* ends with an appendix that reprinted many documents.

Initial reactions to Defoe's *History of the Union* were mixed. Some contemporaries and near contemporaries, such as George Chalmers, praised his account for its accuracy and completeness. Eighteenth-century historians referred to Defoe's text in their own historical narratives, such as Thomas Somerville's reference in *The History of Political Transactions, and of Parties* (1792) and Sir John Clerk of Penicuik's in *History of the Union of Scotland and England* (1799). Others, especially Scots nationalists, saw his history as a biased attempt to drum up support for the Unionists. In the nineteenth and early twentieth centuries, Defoe's *History of the Union* was referred to in works by Thomas Frognall Dibdin, John Hill Burton, Robert Chambers, William Law Mathieson, and Andrew Lang. On the other hand, modern historians, such as William Ferguson and P. W. J. Riley, have tended to side with Defoe's contemporary critics, pointing to factual errors, inconsistencies, and important omissions.

Certainly, by modern standards Defoe's *History of the Union* is a long way away from being a definitive account. As others have shown, for instance, in some cases Defoe missed the influence of important figures–Andrew Fletcher, for example. Clearly, too, in parts 1 through 3 Defoe largely gathered his historical survey from published secondary sources. Even in these parts, though, he is employing what for him was a standard formula: Defoe scoured existing historical accounts, fleshing out the historical context to set the stage for his own distinctive discussion of more recent historical affairs. His most novel contributions in the *History of the Union* are to be found in parts 4 and 5, sections that are still of use to historians to this day.

Defoe's second most important historical book, *Memoirs of the Church of Scotland*, also belongs to the period of his stay in Scotland. Although *Memoirs of the Church of Scotland* was not published until 1717, Defoe wrote in the appendix that it was composed "soon after the Union between *England* and *Scotland* was finish'd and ratify'd." *Memoirs of the Church of Scotland* was divided into four parts ("Part I. Of the Church in her Infant State"; "Part II. Of the Church in her Growing State"; "Part III. Of the Church in her Persecuted State"; and "Part IV. Of the Church in her Present State") and concluded with an appendix, "Of the State of the Church since the Union."

Written as a memoir, Defoe's account of the Church of Scotland was not a true history as the eighteenth century understood the term. As he said in his preface, his account "is it self but a Preface, or Introduction to some larger and fuller History." The guiding theme of the *Memoirs of the Church of Scotland* is Defoe's aim to set straight the historical record by turning a sympathetic ear toward the Covenanters. The Church of Scotland, he maintained:

> has been represented to the World in so many monstrous Shapes, drest up in so many *Devil's Coats,* and *Fool's Coats,* charg'd with so many Heresies, errors, Schisms, and Antichristianisms by the Mob of this slandering Generation, that when a Man comes to view her in her original Reformation, her subsequent settlement, her many Revolutions, Convulsions, and Catastrophe's in her subjected, persecuted State, and now in her glorious Restoration and Establishment, nothing can be more wonderful in humane Affairs, than to see how Mankind has been imposed upon about her.

For Defoe, understanding the true history of the Church of Scotland meant seeing the Scots as precursors of those who brought about the Glorious Revolution of 1688–1689. Arguing in terms he often employed, Defoe contended that "to give a true and concise Scheme" of the Church of Scotland "it will be needful to go back to its original Constitution" so to "hand down a right Understanding of its Circumstances to the present Time." He maintained that "the Reason of these Memoirs is to set the Matter of the past and present State of the Church of Scotland in a true Light, cleared from those Mists and Darkness which the partial Glosses of some late Patrons of Tyranny have spread over her History. . . ."

In parts 1 and 2, Defoe relied heavily on the works of other historians, in much the same way as he had in his *History of the Union*. On many points he follows Buchanan's *Rerum Scoticarum Historia* (1582), arguing that "tho' other Historians are more particular than he, yet the Enemies of the Reformation are not without Objections against the Reputation of their Writings, whereas Buchanan's Reputation, as an Historian, is unquestioned. . . . He is also concise, and more pertinent than some of them. . . ." Standard historical works Defoe referred to include David Calderwood's *True History of the Church of Scotland* (1678), John Knox's *Historie of the Reformation of Religion within the Realme of Scotland* (enlarged edition, 1644), and Spottiswoode's *The History of the Church of Scotland* (1655). In Part 3, covering the period from the Restoration of 1660 through to the Glorious Revolution of 1688, Defoe was more original. As N. H. Keeble has shown, in this part he relied on "both his own first-hand knowledge and the testimony of those who were involved in the events of those years."

MEMOIRS

OF THE

CHURCH

OF

SCOTLAND,

In FOUR PERIODS.

I. The Church in her Infant-State, from the Reformation to the Queen *Mary*'s Abdication.

II. The Church in its growing State, from the Abdication to the Restoration.

III. The Church in its persecuted State, from the Restoration to the Revolution.

IV. The Church in its present State, from the Revolution to the Union.

WITH AN

APPENDIX, of some Transactions since the UNION.

LONDON,

Printed for *Eman. Matthews* at the *Bible,* and *T. Warner* at the *Black-Boy,* both in *Pater-Noster-Row,* 1717.

Title page for the first edition of Defoe's history of the Scottish Presbyterians (Special Collections, Thomas Cooper Library, University of South Carolina)

In the years between his writing the *Memoirs of the Church of Scotland* and its publication, Defoe was busy with other publications. Among those with historical themes was *The Present State of the Parties in Great Britain* (1712), a sort of history of the political parties in England and Scotland during the early years of the eighteenth century. For his publication of *Reasons Against the Succession of the House of Hanover, with an Inquiry How Far the Abdication of King James, Supposing it to Be Legal, Ought to Affect the Person of the Pretender* . . . (1713) and other political pamphlets, Defoe was first imprisoned and then pardoned in 1713.

With the death of Queen Anne on 26 July 1714 and the loss of Harley as a benefactor, Defoe turned increasingly to writing for his income. Best remembered

are the novels, many of which were cast as "histories." But during these years Defoe also produced instructional books, political histories such as *The Secret History of the White Staff: Being an Account of Affairs under the Conduct of Some Late Ministers* (1714–1715), Defoe's defense of Harley, and many pages for the periodicals of the day, such as Nathaniel Mist's *Weekly Journal, The Whitehall Evening Post,* and the *Mercurius Politicus,* which Defoe edited for a time.

Historical elements are also evident in *Memoirs of a Cavalier, Due Preparations for the Plague,* and *A Tour thro' the Whole Island of Great Britain, Divided into Circuits or Journies* (1724, 1725, 1727). Defoe remarked in *A Tour thro' the Whole Island of Great Britain* that he had made himself "Master of the History, and ancient State of England" and "resolv'd in the next Place, to make my self Master of its Present State also." In this work Defoe also frequently comments upon antiquities and scenes of historical importance.

One of Defoe's most interesting later historical pieces was *A General History of Discoveries and Improvements, in Useful Arts, Particularly in the Great Branches of Commerce, Navigation, and Plantation, in all Parts of the Known World* (1725–1726). In this work Defoe aimed to give a brief account of the various "Discoveries" and "Improvements" of mankind. In the preface to this work, Defoe remarked that "THE Connection of past things with present, the State of the antient World, with the State of things Modern, in order to describe the growth of things from what they were to what they now are; makes it absolutely necessary to begin our Accounts at the beginning of those things which we give an account of; how else would we call our Work a History, much less a Compleat History?" That is what Defoe had in mind when he said that "Looking into Antiquity, is a Dry, Empty, and Barren Contemplation, any farther than as it is brought down to our present Understanding, and to bear a steady Analogy of its parts, with the Things that are before us."

In 1726 and 1727 Defoe published at least six works interesting for their historical dimensions. *An Essay upon Literature; or, An Enquiry into the Antiquity and Original of Letters* (1726) gave a conjectural history of the art of writing. *The Political History of the Devil, as Well Ancient as Modern* (1726) was one of Defoe's extended attempts to rid popular culture of what he took to be its false beliefs about Satan. Another was his *An Essay on the History and Reality of Apparitions* (1727). Defoe's skeptical attitude was similarly put to use in *Mere Nature Delineated; or, A Body without a Soul. Being Observations upon the Young Forester Lately Brought to Town from Germany* (1726), a book in which Defoe aimed to cast doubt on details of the story of the "wild boy" who apparently had been abandoned in the woods of Germany. In *A System of*

Magick; or, A History of the Black Art. Being an Historical Account of Mankind's Most Early Dealing with the Devil; and How the Acquaintance on Both Sides First Began (1727), Defoe traced the history of magic, intending to poke fun at the charlatans of his own day. In *A Brief Deduction of the Original, Progress, and Immense Greatness of the British Woollen Manufacture . . .* (1727), Defoe traced the early rise and success of the British woolen trade, from the time of Henry VII, in order to highlight what might be done to improve the trade. Defoe died on 26 April 1731 at his residence on Rope Maker's Alley. He is buried in Bunhill Fields.

Defoe's historical writings were never greatly removed from his economic, political, or religious agendas. History for Defoe was often the place to grind ideological axes. As was the case with most of his contemporaries, Defoe's historical perspective was also one in which Providence played a guiding role. As he said in *The Review,* "Providence often directs the times and connections of those otherwise natural causes to concur in such a manner, as may point out to us his meaning, and guide us to understand it." Much of Defoe's historical writing was also derivative, although he often provided a twist of his own. For the most part, Defoe's historical writing was of more significance to Defoe's early readers than it is to modern historians. Yet, in his rejection of fable and myth, and in his attempt to direct evidence toward improving ends, Defoe witnessed to a distinctly eighteenth-century conception of the past, which was to gain currency with British historians in the later eighteenth century.

Letters:

George Healey, ed., *The Letters of Daniel Defoe* (Oxford: Clarendon Press, 1955);

Paula R. Backscheider, "John Russell to Daniel Defoe: Fifteen Unpublished Letters," *Philosophical Quarterly,* 61 (Spring 1982): 161–177;

Backscheider, "Robert Harley to Daniel Defoe: A New Letter," *Modern Language Review,* 83 (October 1988): 817–819.

Bibliographies:

John Robert Moore, *A Checklist of the Writings of Daniel Defoe* (Bloomington: Indiana University Press, 1960);

John A. Stoler, *Daniel Defoe: An Annotated Bibliography of Modern Criticism, 1900–1980* (New York: Garland, 1984);

Spiro Peterson, *Daniel Defoe: A Reference Guide, 1731–1924* (Boston: G. K. Hall, 1987);

P. N. Furbank and W. R. Owens, *Defoe De-attributions, A Critique of J. R. Moore's Checklist* (London: Hambledon Press, 1994);

Defoe's monument in Bunhill Fields burial ground, London (from <http:viewfinder.english-heritage.org.UKgalley/700/cc9/cc97-00669.org>)

Furbank and Owens, *A Critical Bibliography of Daniel Defoe* (London: Pickering & Chatto, 1998).

Biographies:

George Chalmers, *The Life of Daniel De Foe* (London: John Stockdale, 1785; revised and enlarged edition, 1790);

Paula R. Backscheider, *Daniel Defoe: His Life* (Baltimore & London: Johns Hopkins University Press, 1989);

Maximillian E. Novak, *Daniel Defoe, Master of Fictions: His Life and Ideas* (New York: Oxford University Press, 2001).

References:

Paula R. Backscheider, "Cross-Purposes: Defoe's *History of the Union,*" *CLIO,* 11 (1982): 165–186;

Backscheider, "The Histories," in her *Daniel Defoe: Ambition & Innovation* (Lexington: The University of Kentucky Press, 1986), pp. 70–119;

Marialuisa Bignami, "Daniel Defoe's Military Autobiographies: History and Fictional Character," in Marialuisa Bignami, ed., *Wrestling with Defoe: Approaches from a Workshop on Defoe's Prose* (Milan: Università degli Studi de Milano, Facoltà di Lettere e Filosofia, 1997), pp. 91–108;

Laurence Dickey, "Power, Commerce, and Natural Law in Daniel Defoe's Political Writings, 1698–1707," in *A Union for Empire: Political Thought and the British Union of 1707,* edited by John Robertson (Cambridge: Cambridge University Press, 1995), pp. 63–96;

J. A. Downe, "Defoe, Imperialism, and the Travel Books Reconsidered," in *Critical Essays on Daniel Defoe,* edited by Roger D. Lund (New York: G. K. Hall, 1997), pp. 78–96;

P. N. Furbank and W. R. Owens, *The Canonisation of Daniel Defoe* (New Haven & London: Yale University Press, 1988);

Chester N. Greenough, "Defoe in Boston," *Publications of the Colonial Society of Massachusetts,* 28 (1935): 461–493;

Helmut Heidenreich, ed., *The Libraries of Daniel Defoe and Phillips Farewell* (Berlin: Privately printed, 1970);

N. H. Keeble, "Introduction," in *Memoirs of the Church of Scotland,* volume 6 in *Writings on Travel, Discovery and History by Daniel Defoe,* edited by W. R. Owens and P. N. Furbank (London: Pickering & Chatto, 2002), pp. 1–17;

D. P. Leinster-Mackay, *The Educational World of Daniel Defoe* (Victoria, B.C.: University of Victoria, 1981);

John McVeagh, "Introduction," in *A Tour thro' the Whole Island of Great Britain,* volume 1 in *Writings on Travel, Discovery and History by Daniel Defoe,* edited by Owens and Furbank (London: Pickering & Chatto, 2001), pp. 15–43;

J. H. P. Pafford, "Defoe's *Proposals* for Printing the *History of the Union,*" *The Library,* fifth series, 11 (1956): 202–206;

Katherine R. Penovich, "From 'Revolution Principles' to Union: Daniel Defoe's Intervention in the Scottish Debate," in *A Union for Empire: Political Thought and the British Union of 1707,* edited by Robertson, (Cambridge: Cambridge University Press, 1995), pp. 228–242;

Paul H. Scott, "Defoe in Edinburgh," in *Defoe in Edinburgh and Other Papers* (East Linton, U.K.: Tuckwell Press, 1995), pp. 3–17;

Arthur Secord, ed., *Defoe's Review, Reproduced from the Original Editions,* 22 volumes (New York: Published by the Facsimile Text Society for Columbia University Press, 1933);

Ilse Vickers, *Defoe and the New Sciences* (Cambridge: Cambridge University Press, 1996).

Papers:

Manuscripts of *The Compleat English Gentleman* and *Of Royal Education* are in the British Library; the "Meditations" are at the Huntington Library, San Marino, California; and the *Historical Collections* and "Humanum est Errare" are at the William Andrews Clark Library, Los Angeles. Most of the letters written by Daniel Defoe are in the British Library, although others are in the Public Record Office, the National Archives of Scotland, and the National Library of Scotland.

Laurence Echard
(1670? – 1730)

Charles W. A. Prior
University of Hull

BOOKS: *A Most Compleat Compendium of Geography, General and Special* (London: Printed for Tho. Salusbury, 1691; revised, London: Printed for J. Salusbury, 1697);

An Exact Description of Ireland (London: Printed for Tho. Salusbury, 1691);

Flanders; or, The Spanish Netherlands, Most Accurately Described (London: Printed for Tho. Salusbury, 1691);

The Gazetteer's, or, Newsman's Interpreter: Being a Geographical Index of All the Considerable Cities &c. in Europe (London: Printed for Tho. Salusbury, 1692; revised and enlarged, London: Printed for John Nicholson and Samuel Ballard, 1702);

The Roman History from the Building of the City, to the Perfect Settlement of the Empire by Augustus Caesar (London: Printed for M. Gillyflower, Jacob Tonson, H. Bonwick, and R. Parker, 1695; revised, 1697; revised, 1699; revised, 1702);

The Hainousness of Injustice Done under the Pretence of Equity: A Sermon (London: Printed for M. Wotton, 1698);

The Roman History from the Settlement of the Empire by Augustus Caesar, to the Removal of the Imperial Seat by Constantine the Great (London: Printed by T. H. for M. Gillyflower, J. Tonson, H. Bonwick, and R. Parker, 1698; corrected, 1702);

A General Ecclesiastical History, from the Nativity of Our Blessed Saviour to the First Establishment of Christianity under Constantine the Great (London: Printed by W. Bowyer for Jacob Tonson, 1702);

The History of England. From the First Entrance of Julius Caesar and the Romans, to the Conclusion of the Reign of King James the Second, and the Establishment of King William . . . upon the Throne, in the Year 1688, 3 volumes (London: Printed for Jacob Tonson, 1707–1718);

An Appendix to the Three Volumes of Mr. Archdeacon Echard's History of England. Consisting of Several Explanations and Amendments, as Well as New and Curious Additions to That History (London: Printed for Jacob Tonson, 1720);

Laurence Echard (copperplate engraving by George Vertue from a portrait by Sir Godfrey Kneller; reproduced by permission of McMaster University Library)

The History of the Revolution and the Establishment of England in the Year 1688. Introduced by a Necessary Review of the Reigns of King Charles and King James the Second (Dublin: Printed by and for J. Hyde and E. Dobson, for R. Gunne and R. Owen / London: Printed for Jacob Tonson, 1725);

Peace and Unity Recommended, a Sermon (London: Printed for J. Roberts, 1726).

TRANSLATIONS: Titus Maccius Plautus, *Plautus's Comedies. Amphitryon, Epidicus, and Rudens, Made English: With Critical Remarks upon Each Play* (London: Printed for Abel Swalle and T. Child, 1694);

Terence, *Terence's Comedies: Made English. With His Life; and Some Remarks at the End* (London: Printed for Abel Swalle and T. Child, 1694).

OTHER: *An Abridgement of Sir Walter Raleigh's History of the World,* edited by Echard (London: Printed for Mat. Gillyflower, 1698);

The Roman History from the Removal of the Imperial Seat by Constantine the Great, to the Total Failure of the Western Empire in Augustulus, volume 3, edited by Echard (London: Printed for Jacob Tonson, 1704);

The Roman History: From the Total Failure of the Western Empire . . . to the Restitution of the Same by Charles the Great, volume 4, edited by Echard (London: Printed for Jacob Tonson, 1704);

The Roman History: From the Restitution of the Empire by Charles the Great, to the Taking of Constantinople by the Turks, volume 5 and last, by the author of the third and fourth, edited by Echard (London: Printed for Jacob Tonson, 1705);

The Classical Geographical Dictionary, edited by Echard (London: Printed for J. Tonson, 1715);

John Tillotson, *Maxims and Discourses Moral and Divine: Taken from the Works of Arch-bishop Tillotson,* edited by Echard (London/Dublin, 1719).

Laurence Echard wrote one of the first complete histories of England at a time when the writing of history was charged with political significance. His *History of England* was among many such works published in the early eighteenth century, when English society was gripped by political, religious, international, and dynastic conflict. Echard's history also appeared in the context of unprecedented freedom of the press; after the lapse of the Licensing Act in 1695, many pamphlets, sermons, broadsides, poems, and longer works were published and gave birth to a coffeehouse culture in which affairs of state were broadly discussed. Frequent themes in these debates concerned the fortunes of the House of Stuart, the stability of the Church of England, and relations among the "three kingdoms" of England, Scotland, and Ireland. The point of departure for all of these matters was the history of England since the Reformation, and especially that of the turbulent seventeenth century. Yet, while his contemporaries tended to

write history in the service of either the Tory or Whig Parties, Echard urged the virtues of mixed government and the Protestant interest.

Echard's date of birth is not known for certain: circa 1670 is the date most frequently mentioned. The lack of a precise date is not unusual, since many people in early modern England were uncertain about their dates of birth, and hence their ages. Dates of death are better known because of the accuracy of parishional record keeping and Exchequer records for probate and wills. Echard was taught at home by his father, a practice more common for young girls than boys, who would normally have been sent to a local grammar school. That he was not enrolled at such an institution suggests that the Echards lacked sufficient funds, or the help of a wealthy patron. This opinion is perhaps confirmed by the fact that Echard entered Christ's College, Cambridge, in 1688 as a sizar, not as a scholarship boy. In those cases in which intellectual promise was accompanied by poverty, Cambridge colleges admitted undergraduates, granting them allowances to enable them to study. Like "servitors" at Oxford, sizars were expected to perform tasks normally undertaken by college servants—whether cleaning, waiting on senior members of the college, working in the kitchens, or serving in the college hall.

Echard was made a scholar of Christ's College in 1689, a designation that signaled the end of his probationary status and the beginning of his full membership in the college. He was awarded his B.A. degree in 1691 or 1692, and his M.A. degree in 1695. On 2 May 1696 he was ordained as a priest and given the living of Welton-le-Wold in the diocese of Lincoln. Echard held this benefice, worth between £48 and £55 per annum, until 1722. Clerical livings were much sought after, and ministers frequently held more than one benefice. Hence, in 1709, Echard was also appointed as vicar of South Elkington (worth £25 per annum), a post that he held until 1721. In addition to these livings, he was presented to important posts in his diocese: prebendary of Louth in Lincoln Cathedral, 1697–1730; chaplain to the Bishop of Lincoln; and archdeacon of Stowe, 1712–1730. This sparse biographical information suggests not only that Echard had a modest income, but also that he had the patronage of William Wake, Bishop of Lincoln from 1705 to 1716 and archbishop of Canterbury from 1716 to 1737. Echard was also recognized by his peers; he was elected as a Fellow of the Society of Antiquaries in February 1718. He sat for renowned portraitist Sir Godfrey Kneller, principal painter to William III and Queen Anne. An engraving by Kneller adorns the frontispiece of the 1720 edition of Echard's *History of England,* and the portrait on which it was based hangs in Christ's College. Little is known of Echard's personal life. He was married at Louth on 14 August 1697 to Jane Potter, who was buried there on 11 August 1704. On 14 April 1707 he married Justine Wolley. There is no record of children, and Echard left no letters or other papers.

Echard's time at Cambridge was apparently marked by much activity. Nothing is known of his course of study, but his subsequent ordination suggests that theology was among his areas of interest. The Faculty of Theology at Cambridge was noted for its humanist curriculum, and so Echard can be expected to have taken Latin, Greek, perhaps Hebrew, as well as ancient ecclesiastical history, patristic studies, and classical philosophy. Rhetoric and logic, central to the Renaissance course of study, were still taught as the arts central to literature, poetry, and philosophical debate. These skills were displayed in the writings Echard produced after 1695, but his early career reflected other concerns.

Briefly, these interests had to do with the political events that gripped England between 1688 and 1690. Since the Restoration of the monarchy after the period of the Civil Wars and the commonwealth and protectorate of Oliver Cromwell (1642–1659), the English were concerned about a return of "arbitrary government" and the erosion of the Protestant Church of England. The fortunes of the House of Stuart were shaped by these questions, and some constitutional crises were created over the question of whether the holder of the Crown was committed to the Church. Charles II (reigned 1660–1685) seemed to waver in his commitment to English Protestantism; penal laws were relaxed, and some people were concerned that the policy of legal strictures against Catholics would be swept away. The king's brother—James, Duke of York—was known to be a Catholic, and the issue came to a head when Charles fell ill in 1679. The "Exclusion Crisis" produced attempts on the part of the House of Commons to bar James from the throne in the event of his brother's death. A law, established in the reign of Elizabeth I, said that no Catholic could rule England. The bill was defeated, and Charles recovered. Yet, his death in 1685 reignited the debate, which came to a head when James II produced an heir with his second wife, Mary of Modena. Rumors spread that the boy had been baptized according to Catholic rite, and the resulting conflict ended with the arrival, in November 1688, of William of Orange, Stadholder of the United Provinces. Some people in England maintained that James had been deposed, while others believed that he had willingly abdicated the throne. Whatever the argument, the reign of the House of Stuart, which had begun with James I (1603–1625) was now at an end, and the definition of the English monarchy had been altered. This question shaped perceptions of the monarchy for the next 150 years and served as the context for much of Echard's writing.

In 1691 Echard published his first work, *A Most Compleat Compendium of Geography*. The second edition of Edmund Bohun's *Geographical Dictionary* was published in the same year, and geographical writings were generally abundant. Echard dedicated his work to John Covell, Master of Christ's College from 1688. Covell had been a chaplain at Constantinople and had traveled extensively in Asia; these accounts are now held in the manuscripts collections of the British Library. Echard praised Covell's worldliness in the preface and expressed his hope that the "science" of geography would come to a place of greater prominence in the university. The text itself described the known regions of the world, their inhabitants, climates, and relative distance and orientation to one another. An appendix set forth various rules for the science of geography; in it Echard mentioned that Isaac Newton, himself a former sizar, and then Lucasian Professor of Mathematics at Trinity College, "approved of the method." Echard described this plan as consisting of the geographical boundaries of states; the nature of their government, religion, language, and commodities and physical features; and finally "Patriarchs, Arch-bishops, Bishops, and Universities."

Echard's compendium may therefore have been intended as a handbook for statesmen and the science of geography, a branch of knowledge useful to a burgeoning internationalist agenda promulgated by William III. Indeed, not only was the king obliged to carry on the English agenda in Europe, but he also retained his Dutch title and the military obligations that came with it. Soon, these interests coincided: in 1690 a combined navy of English and Dutch ships was defeated by the French at Beachy Head, an event that was the impetus for a reorganization of the Royal Navy. The Revolution settlement with Ireland had taken place against the backdrop of the siege of Londonderry and the Battle of the Boyne (1 July 1690), in which the Protestant army led by William III defeated the Catholic forces of James II. Hence, the Revolution of 1688 can be seen partly as a solution to dynastic and religious issues and partly as the opening of a new phase of religious and political struggles.

Echard's next two publications reflected these concerns. First, Ireland was a lingering problem, and Ireland itself was the subject of many popular misconceptions. Perhaps such misunderstandings explain Echard's decision to publish *An Exact Description of Ireland* in 1691. No evidence exists that he actually visited the country; rather, the work was based on "the latest surveys" and "new maps." Clearly, Echard was eager to further the science of geography by example, but the work had an additional element. In the preface, for example, Echard noted that Ireland "is at present a Place of Considerable Action"; this fact served to justify the work itself, the subject of which was of such "concern to the nation." Like the compendium, this new work furnished a close description of the land, climate, regional variations, and inhabitants, all of which made reference to a detailed map. The work was prefaced by a brief history of Ireland; the narrative emphasized the theme of conquest, and the treatment was clinical, rather than sympathetic. Also, in 1691 Echard published *Flanders; or, The Spanish Netherlands,* about another region of great importance to English political and military interests, and one about which the English knew little. The plan for the work followed that of the compendium of geography and the description of Ireland and was written for "all such as are Curious and Inquisitive after the Affairs of these Times."

Echard's most successful early work was *The Gazetteer's, or, Newsman's Interpreter,* first published in 1692 and still popular in its sixteenth edition in 1751. Conceived along the same lines as his early geographical works, it was intended to be used as a kind of pocket reference and came in the form of a portable duodecimo. At 228 pages, it was longer than the geographical works and was arranged like a modern dictionary. Alphabetical entries appeared in double columns on pages headed by a letter key, and each entry was indexed to a series of maps. In entries that concerned obscure towns or principalities, Echard sought to orient his reader by giving the direction and distance of principal cities—for example, Paris, Rome, Geneva, Copenhagen, and Madrid. The work suggests that Echard possessed the skills needed for larger works; he could clearly organize and present a large amount of information, marshal an abundant library of reference material, and explain complex topics. For example, a passage in the preface gave instructions for those "that do not know what Longitude and Latitude is."

The publication of *The Gazetteer's, or, Newsman's Interpreter* marked a turning point in Echard's career as a writer. Having taken his M.A. in 1695, he embarked on a career in the Church of England. A divine of Echard's evident bookishness might be expected to contribute a work to the thriving enterprise of religious controversy, wherein beneficed members of the clerical establishment took aim at the doctrinal propositions advanced by "nonconformists"—that is, those who refused to subscribe to the established Church of England. He chose to devote his time to the second principal genre of religious writing, the sermon. In 1698 Echard published a sermon preached at the Lincoln assizes in August of the same year. Assizes were a medieval form of judicial procedure, in which judges visited towns in order to hear felony cases that carried a maximum punishment of death. This process had long been an effective way of asserting the power of the central government in the localities, and sermons were a frequent aspect of the procedure. That Echard was invited to preach such a sermon, particularly that he was invited to publish it, suggests that he was well known and admired by the local justice of the peace. The sermon, *The Hainousness of Injustice Done under the Pretence of Equity* (1698), extolled the link, made in Prov. 11:1, between justice and equity, while the text itself employed biblical and classical examples of just magistrates. Echard concluded that although the virtues of earthly judges might falter, all were accountable before God, whose judgment was final.

In addition to writing works of his own, Echard was a busy translator and editor. In 1694 both his annotated edition of the comedies of the Roman Plautus, whose plays were popular fare on the seventeenth-century stage, and an edition of the comedies of the Roman poet Terence, prepared by "severall hands," including Echard's, were published. In later years he reprised his interest in geography in *The Classical Geographical Dictionary* (1715) and published as well a collection of the sayings of John Tillotson, the nonconformist preacher who in 1691 rose to become archbishop of Canterbury. Perhaps Echard's most ambitious bibliographical effort was his 1698 abridgment of Sir Walter Ralegh's *History of the World* (1614). In the preface, Echard noted that his aim in publishing the work was to improve upon previous abridgments, particularly that of Alexander Ross, chaplain to Charles I. The chronology chosen by Echard was organized around religious and classical themes; in five books he traced a general history of pre-Roman regions, especially Asia Minor and the lands and peoples described in the Old Testament. Hence, the "world" being described was that whose history was set forth in Scripture and that culminated in the rise of the Roman Empire. For Protestants, its narrative confirmed the existence of an ancient and pure church, established by Christ and handed to the apostles, and subsequently eclipsed by the rise of Rome and its doctrinal and papal "corruption."

The Roman Empire and its history served as the impetus for Echard's massive *The Roman History,* the first volume of which appeared in 1695. It was dedicated to John Sommers, Lord Chancellor, a powerful figure at the court of William III and a patron of literary men such as Joseph Addison, Richard Steele, and Jonathan Swift. Echard's dedication put forth the case that wisdom and "industry" were crucial for those who sought to involve themselves in public affairs and that success in this sphere was predicated upon a sound understanding of the "customs, laws, and magistrates" of Rome. The work was divided into three books, which covered the period from the settlement of Rome by the Etruscans (600 B.C.) to the end of the reign of Augustus (A.D. 14). The narrative focused on the qualities of leaders and the evolution of Rome from an uncivilized "barbarian" state to a society governed by the ancient virtues that so fascinated Echard and his contemporaries. In fact, Echard's history fit within what may be called the neoclassical tradition, in which historical narratives served to illustrate the nature of timeless qualities that defined just leaders and virtuous polities. Seventeenth-century authors, among them Thomas Hobbes and Edward Hyde, first Earl of Clarendon, took Niccolò Machiavelli's *Discourses* (1531) on the histories of Titus Livy as a model of this kind of history. In addition, for English writers of the late seventeenth century, the history of Rome furnished a parallel for the history of England; for political journalists, too, the Roman story teemed with examples of both liberty and corruption, progress and power. In this vein Echard chronicled the development of Rome from "small beginnings," its often violent rise and "progress," and its "revolutions" in power and prestige. For the educated reader who had firsthand knowledge of the English civil wars, the restoration of the monarchy in 1660, and the subsequent conflicts with the French and the Dutch, the parallel was probably suggestive. So, too, was the moral that Echard sought to draw out: by the end of the reign of Augustus, Roman "reason" and "prudence" had created a "polite and sociable" society, feared by its enemies and stable within; yet, this nation was not ruled by tyranny in the manner of the Tarquins, for in Rome the "arts and sciences" flourished, complementing power with reason. England also wished to see itself this way: polite, commercial, yet feared by its enemies.

The first volume of *The Roman History* went through three revisions between 1695 and 1697, and in 1698 Echard added a second volume. It took up the story of the empire from the death of Augustus and continued it to the reign of Constantine, when the empire was made Christian and when its capital was shifted from Rome to Byzantium (renamed Constantinople). Echard's narrative emphasized the fateful nature of this decision, for the so-called Empire of the West was sacked by invading tribes during the fifth century. Hence, the reign of Constantine represented the advent of the destruction of the empire. Yet, whereas the first volume of *The Roman History* had celebrated the classical virtues of wisdom and prudence, the second volume sought to convey a moral that was intelligible to Christian readers: the fall of the empire had come about as the result of a punishment "drawn down from Heaven." Echard depicted Constantine as having forsaken the

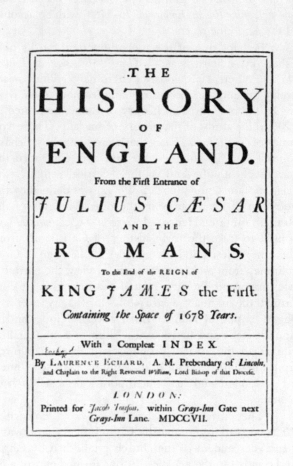

Title page for volume one of Echard's history of England based on religion and dynastic politics (Eighteenth Century Collections Online, Gale Group)

traditions and heritage of Roman virtue, whose exemplar was Augustus, and at the same time having embraced "tyranny"; this abandonment of wisdom and prudence created hatred among his subjects and moved his trusted advisers to rebel against him. Echard placed a great deal of symbolic importance on Constantine's decision to abandon Rome and found a new capital; in so doing, Echard implied, a life-giving nerve of tradition was severed, and the Roman Empire was doomed. A further theme that underscored the volume was Providence—the belief that God was active in the affairs of people, punishing evil and rewarding virtue—and the theme was one that Echard found even in examples from the pre-Christian empire. For example, Marcus Aurelius exemplified the best of "heathen" rulers, whom Echard commended to the attention of Christian princes who wished to preserve peace and stability. Significantly, Edward Gibbon—who read and admired

Echard's history—began his epic *The History of the Decline and Fall of the Roman Empire* (1776–1788) with an account of the Antonine rulers.

Perhaps one of the more important works published by Echard was *A General Ecclesiastical History* (1702). Whereas previously Echard devoted his considerable grasp of ancient history and learning to the writing of the pre-Christian history of Rome, he turned in 1700 to the study of the history of his faith. Those volumes of *The Roman History* that were written by Echard himself (that is, volumes one and two) concluded the narrative with the end of the "classical" empire; the reign of Constantine (circa 274–337) was defined by the adoption of Christianity as the official religion of the Roman Empire. Hence, *A General Ecclesiastical History* sought to trace the early history of Christianity from the time of Jesus and the apostles to the reign of Constantine. From an historical point of view, the narrative was important for two related reasons. First, it confirmed the ultimate victory of Christianity over the pagan empire of Rome, which governed Judea in the time of Jesus and had executed him in a manner that confirmed the ancient prophecies. Yet, what followed from the Christianizing of the empire was also of interest to Echard and his contemporaries—the Church of Rome.

The purpose of Echard's *A General Ecclesiastical History* was to argue that the Church of England was a "true" descendent of the church established by Christ and handed to the apostles. It thus formed part of a literature that can be traced back to the English Reformation in 1559, when the Church of England was effectively created by Parliamentary statute, and the jurisdiction of the papacy over English Christians was ended once and for all. What dominated the literature of religious controversy from 1559 onward was a debate between defenders of the English Church and their Catholic and Protestant critics. The former maintained that since Christ had handed the early Church to Peter (the first pope), then the succession of the popes served as a sign that the Roman Church was ancient and apostolic. Protestant Reformers, having attacked the Roman Church since the time of the continental Reformation, urged the governors of the English Church to pursue further reform of its doctrine and governance. What complicated these debates was that the Church of England was established by law and governed by the Crown: it was a "state" church, included as part of the English constitution. Therefore, scholars from the Elizabethan theologian Richard Hooker to Echard himself were occupied with the task of demonstrating that the controversial aspects of the English Church were, in reality, part of the ancient Christian worship restored to use in 1559.

Echard dedicated his history to Queen Anne (reigned 1702–1714), the last of the Stuarts to occupy the English throne. The House of Stuart itself had a checkered history as defenders of the faith, and this history prompted the passage of the Act of Settlement in 1701. This act provided that, after the death of Anne, the Crown of England would be settled on the Electress Sophia of Hanover—a Protestant. This order of succession was justified by contemporaries as a measure necessary to protect the English Church from the further negligence of Stuart monarchs, tainted by suspicions of Catholicism. That Echard did not share this view is an indicator of his position in the complex political issues of the time. In the dedication to the queen, he extolled her as "the great protector and nursing mother of the noblest branch of that church here treated of and described." By this statement Echard meant to argue that the English Church represented, in a way the Catholic and Protestant churches of the Continent did not, the perfection of the ancient church founded by Christ. Thus, Echard sought to trace the antiquity of episcopacy, ceremonies, and liturgy that were central to the early-eighteenth-century English Church.

Religion and dynastic politics became the central theme in Echard's remaining work and defined the narrative set forth in his monumental *History of England,* the work for which he is best known, and the one that has received the bulk of the scholarly attention paid to him. Yet, scholars have disagreed about the political vision Echard sought to promote in the work: did he blame Charles I and James II for the constitutional crises that defined their reigns, or did these upheavals stem from a weak and ill-defined constitutional arrangement? Presumably, a decisive response to such questions could be found in Echard's *History of England,* the first volume of which appeared in 1707. The writing of history in England was driven, in part, by the Civil Wars, and for the educated classes, the composition of "historical" works served to advertise where one stood on the question of the dynastic claims of the House of Stuart.

The first volume of the history covered the period from ancient Britain to the death of James VI (of Scotland) and I (of England). It was dedicated to James Butler, the second Duke of Ormond, who was a staunch supporter of William of Orange. In the general introduction, Echard observed that the completion of the work had been delayed one year, but he was not specific as to the nature of the interruption; poverty and lack of leisure may have been what held up the writing. However, what seems more likely is that the size of the work itself caused the delay. *The History of England* departed from Echard's previous work in its scope, and particularly in the vast number of sources on which the narrative was based: Roman; Saxon; the chronicles compiled by English monks and Raphael Holinshed; histories such as those by Polydore Vergil (commissioned by Henry VII to write a history of England); and the works of seventeenth-century authors such as Richard Baker; Edward Hyde, the first Earl of Clarendon; John Hayward; Gilbert Burnet; John Speed; Robert Brady; and James Tyrrell. In all, Echard consulted nearly three hundred separate authors in composing *The History of England*. A cleric with Echard's income could not afford to own copies of these works: most were large folios and would have been prohibitively expensive. Echard may have worked in the library of his diocese, but more likely he journeyed to either Oxford or Cambridge in order to consult works held in the university libraries. A second aspect of *The History of England* that suggested a departure from Echard's previous writings was that it included reflections on the writing of history and on historical method. The procedure Echard used was shaped partly by the times, for the constitutional upheavals of the seventeenth century meant that to advocate a particular version of English history was also to declare one's position on contemporary politics. For a cleric such as Echard, dependent on the continuing patronage of powerful men, these questions had to be handled with some delicacy. Hence, his strategy in *The History of England* was to announce his own impartiality and to suggest that the historian "should be of the same side as truth."

When Echard took up the writing of the history, the dominant historiographical question concerned the nature and location of sovereignty in England. Two main positions on this question were in turn defined by particular interpretations of the history of English law and institutions. One side held that the English Parliament could be traced to the Saxon period, while the other maintained that the legislature was the product of feudal practice introduced to England during the Norman Conquest (1066–1154). The Saxon interpretation emphasized the presence of "commoners" in the legislature, a fact that in turn implied election and legislative freedom from the whims of the nobility; the Norman interpretation was promoted by those who wished to argue that, in relation to the Commons, the Crown and nobility occupied a superior constitutional role.

Neither interpretation is strongly evident in Echard's history. Instead, the first volume was concerned with the themes of conflict and religion. The ancient Britons were depicted as numerous and powerful, but lacking religion; Echard traced their development to the point at which Christianity was introduced into Britain, and here he recapitulated the theme of *A General Ecclesiastical History*. Early British Christianity was portrayed as a pure ancient strand of the faith established by Christ. As had been the case in *The Roman History*, Echard emphasized the theme of Providence and suggested that rulers who embraced tyranny felt the wrath of God; this perspective informed Echard's discussion of Richard III, less a tragic figure than an impious one. In fact, the strand underpinning the narrative from Roman Britain to the Battle of Bosworth (1485) was the tendency for the British to war with each other and their neighbors, and to be punished by God for departing from just and orderly modes of governance. The age of the Tudors was also the age of the Reformation, and Echard emphasized the degree to which the English Reformation was an act of state, intended to restore the pure and ancient form of British Christianity that existed prior to the rise of the Roman Church. Reforming monarchs such as Henry VIII, Edward VI, Elizabeth I, and James I were shown to be both "godly" and "virtuous"; Mary, who reversed the reforms of Edward VI and returned England to the Catholic fold, suffered the fate deserved of one who betrayed the true faith. Summing up the reign of James I, Echard observed that, despite the reestablishment of Protestantism under Elizabeth I (1559), a debate still raged concerning the nature of the visible Church of England and its place in the realm.

The second volume of *The History of England* was devoted to the period from 1625 to 1660, taking in the reign of Charles I, the Civil Wars, the King's execution in 1649, the establishment and fall of the Commonwealth and Protectorate of Oliver Cromwell, and the restoration of the monarchy of Charles II. This period in English history was the most dynamic, and its central aspects are still debated by historians. For them, as for Echard and his contemporaries, the point of contention was what caused the English to go to war and who was at fault for the conflict. Most people blamed Charles himself for ruling without Parliament between 1629 and 1641, for imposing illegal taxes, and for undermining the Protestant orthodoxy of the English Church. Echard blamed the conflict on the House of Commons and various other "factions" that attempted to seize power for themselves; moreover, he suggested that the "seeds of the following discontents" were planted in the reign of Charles's father, James I. Chief among these was the question of whether the Church of England could assert its power in Scotland. The attempt to impose the Book of Common Prayer in 1637 led to the drafting of the National Covenant, in which the Scots pledged to "defend" their church against foreign rulers; the difficulty was that Charles was also king of Scotland and hence "governor" of the Scottish Church as well as that in England. The Bishop's Wars (1638–1640) were fought between English and Scottish armies over the question of the king's ecclesiastical jurisdiction in both kingdoms. Echard condemned the Scots for trying to seize power that belonged to the king alone and defended Charles's ecclesiastical sovereignty. Echard also cast the English Parliament in a negative light and devoted hundreds of pages to the 1640s, when the conflict between the Parliament and the king spilled onto the battlefield and culminated in the execution of William Laud, Archbishop of Canterbury (1645), and finally of Charles I himself. Significantly, Echard portrayed Charles as "the royal martyr," a pious king who suffered as the result of the treachery and tyranny of others. By "others" Echard meant Parliament and Oliver Cromwell, the general-turned-ruler of a kingless England. Echard portrayed the eleven years of the commonwealth as the rule of "usurpers" and "tyrants," and their ultimate defeat as brought about by the "merciful" hand of God.

The final volume of *The History of England* covered in the years 1660 to 1690–the reigns of Charles II and James II, and the first two years of that of William III. The theme of conflict and religion are again large. The restoration of the monarchy and the Church of England in 1660 reignited some of the conflicts from the first part of the century. Many people feared that Charles I's sympathy to Catholicism meant that steps had to be taken against Catholics in England, and this dread raised once again the question of the monarch's own faith. Charles II worked to demonstrate his commitment to the Church of England, but a lack of funds forced him to enter into the secret Treaty of Dover (1670) with France, a Catholic country. In exchange for a subsidy granted by Louis XIV, Charles agreed to convert to Catholicism. The Anglo-Dutch Wars (1665–1667, 1672–1674) placed further strain on the Crown's finances. Conflict between the king and Parliament soon developed, and Echard traced these events in detail. A great deal of attention was paid to the attempt to exclude James, Duke of York, from the throne, and to the "popish plot," whereby the King would be assassinated, London burned, and James placed on the throne with the support of a secret Catholic army. Upon Charles's death in 1685, James II gained the throne, only to be deposed in 1688 by the Protestant William of Orange. Echard looked on this vast tapestry and drew a simple lesson: the religion of England, established in Protestantism by Elizabeth, was the chief pillar of the constitution, and the king who threatened the faith he was charged to defend would inevitably suffer the fate of all "impious rulers" of the sort that Echard had chronicled in his *Roman History*. Similarly, an ancient British pattern of mixed government held that rule was to be shared between king, lords, and Commons; should one "estate" trespass on the sovereignty of the others, then the constitution would be compromised.

In 1720 Echard published a folio pamphlet as an "appendix" to *The History of England*. In it he took the opportunity to list further sources and confirmed that his remote living at Louth prevented him the necessary access to "libraries and learned men." He also renewed his attack on figures associated with the "republican" party that executed the king and sought to rule in his place: the poet John Milton's antiroyalist writings were refuted, and Echard suggested that Oliver Cromwell gained power as the result of a bargain with Satan. The most evident theme in the work was the role of Providence in history, and Echard argued at length that the student of history soon found evidence of "many noble instances of the Divine Providence." Certainly, this interest lay at the core of both *The Roman History* and *The History of England,* but Echard's adherence to Providence in history put him seriously out of step with his contemporaries.

A further work by Echard, published in 1725, returned to the theme of conflict and religion and sought to identify the causes of the constitutional crisis that culminated in the deposition of James II in 1688. *The History of the Revolution* ranged the Tudor and Stuart periods for evidence of religious conflict, the struggle between Parliament and Crown, and the internecine conflicts of the three kingdoms. The aim of the work seems to have been to impose some measure of unity on the analysis presented in volumes two and three of *The History of England* and to situate the story told there within the broader reaches of English history. Since the time of Henry VIII, Echard noted, a series of "conspiracies" against the religion of the realm had arisen, and this fact served to animate English, and ultimately British, history in the period. Whereas the case against Charles I was complex, Echard described James II as having "deserted" the throne, and condemned the "nation" to "dereliction." In short, Echard assessed English kings not according to the classical virtues celebrated in *The Roman History,* but according to the demands of governing an ancient realm possessed of its own sovereign and national Church.

Echard's final published work was a sermon, *Peace and Unity Recommended* (1726). It was a political sermon, as well as a meditation on the nature of conflict in the seventeenth century. For a writer who lived in the age of Sir Robert Walpole, Echard's attention was overwhelmingly directed to the political questions of a nearly vanished age; the sermon may be interpreted as a kind of eulogy. In the party contests that defined the period after 1714 Echard found a political process in which "pride" and "interest" supplanted more important "graces and virtues, as make men happy and delightful to each other." To look into government by party, he continued, was to discover a "mean and depreciating account of human nature." Instead, he urged his readers to consider the "established constitution" and the "Founders and Preservers of it"; the theme in this work was the Protestant religion, the public spirit, and the courage of those who were willing to sacrifice the monarchy in order to preserve the stability of the English Church and constitution. He therefore celebrated 1688 as the "restoration" of the ancient "British constitution," an arrangement that protected the power of the Crown and the liberties of the people—mixed government in which power was channeled through the "estates" of king, lords, and Commons ruling jointly, and in order to protect the "Protestant interest."

Thus far, scholarly attempts to describe Echard's political sensibilities have been confined to the narrow interpretation of party, and this analysis has led to conflicting views of his place in early-eighteenth-century ideas. Echard the Whig historian is depicted as looking with approval on examples from the seventeenth century, in which the Crown and its prerogatives were made to give way to popular liberty. The Tory interpretation emphasizes Echard's obvious sympathy for the plight of Charles I and his condemnation of Cromwell's seizure of power. A third view emphasizes the point that Echard's position was more complex. The reader of *The History of England* is struck by its evenhandedness, which is borne out by his use of seventeenth-century writers who were recognized spokesmen for the royalist and republican sides. Yet, he was not necessarily either uncommitted or a quietist. As his extensive discussion of the fate of Charles I suggests, Echard sought to point his readers toward a concept of "tradition" that animated English history. Kings had been killed and deposed before, he argued, but in 1649 the House of Commons had risen against the king, and hence one "estate" of the constitution had waged war on another. For Echard, this conflict represented a fundamental breakdown of an ancient mode of governance that he traced to post-Roman Britain and that succeeding generations had perfected. After the English Reformation, the concept of the Protestant interest was incorporated into a pattern of rule by king, lords, and Commons. The conflicts of the seventeenth century represented instances in which either the House of Commons or the king sought to rule independently of the other estates and in a manner that compromised the Church of England. This theme was what Echard sought to bring out in works published after the appearance of *The History of England*.

Scholars commonly regard Lawrence Echard to be significant because he wrote the first complete history of England. Yet, his career as a writer also sheds light on the intellectual culture of early-eighteenth-century England. He was an amateur historian, writing works for his own pleasure and, as his prefaces frequently point out, for the interest and edification of students and others concerned with public affairs. His learning and quality of mind were considerable, but they were not harnessed to the engine of progress and the rise of commercial society. Instead, Echard was a man of the seventeenth century who sought to draw useful lessons from its turbulent history. Like Edmund Burke at the end of the eighteenth century, Echard sought to defend the virtues of tradition, custom, heritage, the institutions of mixed government, and the stability of the Church of England.

Biography:

Richard W. Goulding, *Laurence Echard, M.A., F.S.A.* (London: Society of Antiquaries, 1927).

References:

Philip Hicks, *Neoclassical History and English Culture: From Clarendon to Hume* (London: MacMillan, 1996);

Isaac Kramnick, "Augustan Politics and English Historiography: The Debate on the English Past, 1730–1735," *History and Theory*, 6, no. 1 (1967): 33–54;

Royce MacGillivray, *Restoration Historians and the English Civil War* (The Hague: Nijhoff, 1974);

J. G. A. Pocock, *The Ancient Constitution and the Feudal Law: A Study of English Historical Thought in the Seventeenth Century. A Reissue with a Retrospect* (Cambridge: Cambridge University Press, 1957);

Pocock, *Barbarism and Religion,* 3 volumes (Cambridge: Cambridge University Press, 1999–2003);

Roger Schmidt, "Roger North's *Examen:* A Crisis in Historiography," *Eighteenth-Century Studies*, 26, no. 1 (1992): 57–75;

Deborah Stephan, "Laurence Echard–Whig Historian," *Historical Journal*, 32, no. 4 (1989): 843–866;

Blair Worden, *Roundhead Reputations: The English Civil Wars and the Passions of Posterity* (London: Allen Lane, 2001).

Adam Ferguson

(20 June 1723 – 22 February 1816)

Troy Bickham
Texas A&M University

SELECTED BOOKS: *An Essay on the History of Civil Society* (London: A. Millar & T. Cadell / Edinburgh: A. Kincaid & J. Bell, 1767; Boston: Hastings, Etheridge & Bliss, 1809);

Institutes of Moral Philosophy: For the Use of Students in the College of Edinburgh (Edinburgh: Printed for A. Kincaid & J. Bell, 1768; revised and enlarged 1773; revised again, 1785; New York: Garland, 1978);

Remarks on a Pamphlet Lately Published by Dr. Price, Intitled Observations on the Nature of Civil Liberty, the Principles of Government, and the Justice and Policy of the War with America, &c. in a Letter from a Gentleman in the Country to a Member of Parliament (London: Printed for T. Cadell, 1776);

History of the Progress and Termination of the Roman Republic, 3 volumes (London: Printed for W. Strahan; T. Cadell in the Strand; and W. Creech, in Edinburgh / Edinburgh: Kincaid & Bell / Dublin: Printed for Messrs. Price, Whitestone, Colles, Moncrieffe, Jenkin (and 8 others), 1783; revised and enlarged, 1793; Philadelphia: T. Wardle, 1841);

Principles of Moral Political Science, a Retrospect of Lectures Delivered at the College of Edinburgh, 2 volumes (Edinburgh: Printed for A. Strahan & T. Cadell, London; and W. Creech, Edinburgh, 1792; revised, 5 volumes, Edinburgh: Bell & Bradfute and G. G. & J. Robinson, London, 1799; New York: AMS Press, 1973).

Edition: *An Essay on the History of Civil Society,* edited by Fania Oz-Salzberger (Cambridge & New York: Cambridge University Press, 1995).

Adam Ferguson was a philosopher and historian who rose from modest origins to the highest echelons of Europe's intellectual elite. He made a lasting mark on human understanding of social development. Many consider him the founding father of sociology.

Ferguson was born 20 June 1723 at the manse at Logierait, Perthshire, Scotland, the son of Adam Fergu-

Adam Ferguson (portrait by Sir Joshua Reynolds
<http://www.burnsscotland.com>)

son, a clergyman, and his wife, Mary Gordon, daughter of an Aberdeenshire farmer. The Fergusons were a respectable, but relatively poor, family who relied heavily upon the favor of the aristocracy and gentry. Adam senior had been born in modest circumstances on 4 August 1672, only a few miles away from Logierait at the parish of Moulin. He had attended the University of St. Andrews, where he prepared for the ministry in the Church of Scotland. After working as a minister and tutor at various places, he secured a comfortable position as Logierait's minister—a place granted him by the Duke of Athole, who was the brother of one of the senior Ferguson's school friends.

Ferguson was the last of his parents' many children. Growing up in Logierait was not without advantages, but young Adam quickly caught the attention of his elders as an intellectually gifted child, so he was sent to James Martin's grammar school in Perth. At the age of fifteen he won a competitive examination for a scholarship to attend St. Andrews, perhaps the least acclaimed university in Scotland at the time, to study for a master of arts degree. Scotland's universities rewarded diligence and attendance over talent and ingenuity, so his studies probably were part of a standard curriculum that included moral philosophy, natural philosophy, Latin, metaphysics, and mathematics—all taught by relatively undistinguished clergymen. After four years Ferguson received his M.A. in 1742, by which time his reputation as a scholar of the first rank was already emerging. He then followed in his father's footsteps and enrolled in St. Andrews' Divinity Hall to prepare to enter the clergy.

Shortly after enrolling in St. Andrews' Divinity Hall, Ferguson moved to Edinburgh to continue his training at the university there. His reasoning for the change is unclear, but he certainly benefited from it. In Edinburgh he socialized and intermingled with the present and future intellectual elite of Scotland and formed important associations with such men as Hugh Blair, William Robertson, Alexander Carlyle, and Henry Home, Lord Kames. Together they formed the Speculative Society, and in this social context Ferguson blossomed.

Despite his apparent enjoyment of his Edinburgh company, Ferguson left after completing only two of the usual six years of study to become the chaplain of the Forty-second (Black Watch) Highland Regiment. The Fergusons' longtime patrons, the Atholes, had placed one of their own, Lord John Murray, in the regiment as colonel, and so Murray's mother, the Duchess Dowager of Athole, arranged to have Ferguson appointed deputy-chaplain of the regiment. He seized the opportunity to join the prestigious and much-used regiment and with them campaigned in Flanders during the War of Austrian Succession, later serving in Brittany and Ireland. His regiment did not serve in the campaign to repress the failed 1745–1746 Jacobite uprising, which attempted to reinstate the deposed House of Stuart as the rulers of Britain. Ferguson, like his father, was a vehement anti-Jacobite, however, and he preached a sermon against the uprising, which the Duchess Dowager of Athole had published in Gaelic. In July 1745 the General Assembly of the Church of Scotland granted him special dispensation for ordination in lieu of his services.

In 1754 Ferguson resigned his commission when the regiment was deployed for service in North America as part of the military buildup in preparation for the Seven Years War (French and Indian Wars). That same year he ended his career as a clergyman. The reasons for his decision are not clear, although he may have been bitter over the Duke of Athole's decision not to appoint him as his father's successor at Logierait. Equally probable is that after living in two university cities and traveling throughout Europe with the Black Watch, Ferguson did not want to settle into the comfortable but dull life of a rural clergyman.

After resigning his commission, Ferguson returned to Edinburgh to renew pursuit of his intellectual interests. The next few years were difficult for Ferguson as he pursued an academic career with limited success. He held various small posts and worked as a tutor, but none of these activities paid sufficiently. His brief stint as tutor to the sons of John Stuart, third Earl of Bute—later, prime minister and mentor to George III—opened new opportunities, as did his developing friendship with David Hume, who aided him in securing the University of Edinburgh position of keeper of the Advocates' Library and clerk to the faculty. In 1758 Hume helped to find an academic appointment for Ferguson. The plan was to lure Adam Smith to the University of Edinburgh with an offer of the Regius Chair of Public Law and the Law of Nature and Nations and to acquire for Ferguson the position in moral philosophy at the University of Glasgow that Smith would vacate. The scheme failed, but the touting that Ferguson's friends had done on his behalf paid off the following year when he was made professor of natural philosophy at the University of Edinburgh. Although totally unsuited to the field, Ferguson took his duties seriously, using the opportunity to mingle with physical and moral scientists and to promote his ambition to hold a post in mental and moral philosophy. Such efforts benefited him in more ways than one. Five years later he was elected to the coveted Professorship in Moral Philosophy and Pneumatics at Edinburgh, a position he held until his retirement in 1785. In 1766 he married Katherine Burnet, a niece of his colleague and friend Joseph Black, a noted chemist.

Ferguson flourished in Edinburgh as a teacher and writer. As the unofficial capital of the Scottish Enlightenment, Edinburgh drew the greatest minds from around the Western world to its lecture halls and coffeehouses, where informal discussions acted as inspirations and sounding boards for the creation of the modern social sciences and substantial advancements in the medical, biological, and physical sciences. By the 1760s Ferguson's friends of the Select Club were no longer poor students but were emerging as Scotland's intellectual, political, and spiritual leaders.

Ferguson assumed a mentoring role, forming the new Poker Club in 1762 when the Select Club disbanded. He was a founder of the Royal Society of Edinburgh, which served as the hub of Scotland's scientific community. He also mentored many of the throngs of students who attended his lectures, including John MacPherson, future governor-general of Bengal. Ferguson even facilitated the only meeting between Scottish literary giants of the age–Sir Walter Scott, then a young family friend, and Robert Burns–who met in Ferguson's home.

Ferguson's academic literary career met with great success. In 1767 he published what is his best-known work, *An Essay on the History of Civil Society,* which subsequently won the hard-earned praise of a diversity of noted philosophers, including Johann Gottfried Herder, John Stuart Mill, and Karl Marx. *An Essay on the History of Civil Society* was the culmination of at least a decade of careful consideration. Earlier unpublished drafts had received high praise from Adam Smith and William Robertson, and their opinions proved well founded when the work was published. With the exception of David Hume, who objected to its style more than to its conclusions, *An Essay on the History of Civil Society* met with admiration virtually everywhere it appeared. An article in the *Critical Review* (March 1767) represented the majority opinion: "This is one of the few modern compositions which unites preciseness of reasoning and depth of judgement, to an uncommon elegance of diction." In this rare instance, the arch rival of the *Critical Review,* the *Monthly Review,* concurred, proclaiming in May 1767 that Ferguson "has shewn a manly and original turn of thought thro' the whole of his performance." Even the *Scots Magazine* agreed, noting in the opening lines of its review from March 1767 that "The subject is interesting to mankind, and Dr Ferguson has treated it in a manner suitable to its dignity." Soon the work was translated into German and French and appeared on bookshelves throughout the Western world.

At its core, Ferguson's *Essay on the History of Civil Society* addresses the concerns and queries of a European culture whose cosmology was being poked and prodded by rapid advancements in science, encounters with new societies, and social changes brought on by the emergence of a powerful mercantile middle class. Nowhere were these changes more evident than in Scotland, which, as England's junior partner since 1707, had experienced the effects of these changes at every level. Scotland's poor poured into the North American colonial frontiers and the ranks of the British armed forces that patrolled the four corners of the earth; the profits of imperial trade built the emerging cities of Glasgow and Aberdeen and funded the mer-

chants and professionals that governed them; and Scotland's elite went out to govern British imperial possessions from Calcutta to Charlestown. As the eighteenth century progressed, Britons from weavers to tobacco merchants were acutely aware that events on the other end of the world could have profound effects on their lives. They stayed informed and discussed relevant issues in the prolific and relatively free press. Although literacy rates are impossible to determine, anecdotal evidence suggests that the reading public included men and women and ranged from the aristocracy to the upper tiers of the working ranks. The questions many were asking as they read the vibrant accounts of Japanese warlords, Indian Brahmins, Chinese gardeners, Tahitian queens, Egyptian cities, and Cherokee warriors pertained to why there was so much social difference in the societies of a human race that was assumed to have the same origins. Ferguson's *Essay on the History of Civil Society* addressed this audience and these questions.

In his *Essay on the History of Civil Society* Ferguson both shaped and popularized conjectural history and a stadial theory of society. In its most basic form, this approach assumes that human societies move through stages–in most cases four–which begin with the hunter-gatherer stage and conclude with modern urban-based commercial societies. Although certainly not the first to make use of the conjectural and stadial framework, Ferguson was arguably the best at it, and he certainly propelled it into the mainstream of eighteenth-century Western thought. Unlike his predecessors, Ferguson engaged directly with known societies and drew illustrative examples from the same contemporary accounts of Chinese, American Indian, and Indian cultures that his audience were reading in the press. For example, when he described the first stage of human society as living in illiterate kin-based groups that relied on a mixture of hunting, gathering, and limited agriculture, he enveloped his arguments with known descriptions of the Iroquois. Such illustrations made his work both more accessible and more authoritative to readers.

This approach also was a remarkable shift in the works of the Scots philosophers, since it was an overt attempt to use other cultures to understand their own origins. In the classical accounts of Caesar, Polybus, Thucydides, and Tacitus, Ferguson found enough evidence to conclude that the ancient inhabitants of Scotland lived in a social state similar to that of the American Indians of the eastern woodlands. He argued vehemently that such similarities offered a means through which the so-called polished nations could peer into their own past. "The inhabitants of Britain, at the time of the first Roman invasions, resembled, in many things, the present natives of North America," he declared. "It is in their [the American Indians'] present condition, that we are to behold, as in a mirrour, the features of our own progenitors," he continued, "and from thence we are to draw our conclusions with respect to the influence and situations, in which, we have reason to believe, our fathers were placed." Such comparisons struck a chord with the Scots and other European peoples who were in the tumultuous throes of transformation from traditional societies based on subsistence agriculture into urban-based commercial societies. Scots such as Ferguson, who had lived in both the tribal, clan-dominated Highlands and the polished urban center of Edinburgh, were acutely aware of Scotland's own "barbaric" past and the social chasms that separated societies in flux.

Ferguson's explanation of human societal evolution focuses on the idea of property as a social phenomenon. Declaring that private "property is a matter of progress," Ferguson argued that regard for property was a reflection of a society's social stage. Societies in the first stage had little use for private property because most things were held in common, and an abundance of resources provoked limited competition. During the pastoral and agricultural stages, extensive development of private property reflected individuals' desires to control food production. In the final stage, technological advances in food production allowed a portion of the society to engage in trade, which in turn extended that society's concept of property to include luxuries.

Just as Ferguson was under no illusion that the first stage was an Eden inhabited by noble savages, he was unwilling to endorse the flawless superiority of the fourth stage that polished nations inhabited. The boasted refinements of the polished stage, he asserted, were not divested of danger: "They open a door, perhaps, to disaster, as wide and accessible as any of those they have shut," he warned. His primary concern was that the pursuit of refinement and luxuries would ultimately weaken the nation from within. He feared that the benefits of applying the division of labor in manufacturing would be applied to the government and defense of a society at its peril. "By having separated the arts of the clothier and the tanner, we are better supplied with shoes and cloth," he explained, but the same principle does not transfer with equal benefit to governance:

> But to separate the arts which form the citizen and the statesman, the arts of policy and war, is an attempt to dismember the human character, and to destroy those very arts which we mean to improve. By this separation, we in effect deprive a free people of what is neces-

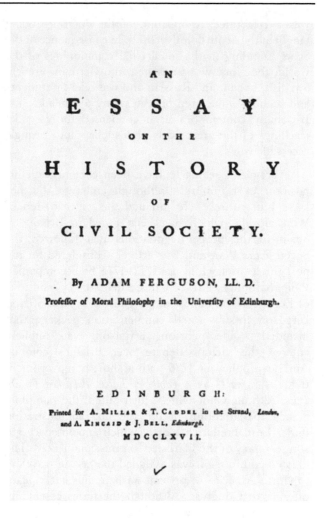

A N

ESSAY

ON THE

HISTORY

OF

CIVIL SOCIETY.

By ADAM FERGUSON, LL. D.

Professor of Moral Philosophy in the University of Edinburgh.

EDINBURGH:

Printed for A. MILLAR & T. CADDEL in the Strand, London, and A. KINCAID & J. BELL, Edinburgh.

MDCCLXVII.

✔

Title page for Ferguson's work that suggests that all civilizations go through the same stages of development (Eighteenth-Century Collections Online, Gale Group)

sary for their safety; or we prepare a defence against invasion from abroad, which gives a prospect of usurpation, and threatens the establishment of military governments at home.

The worst enemies of polished nations, therefore, were their own citizens, whose abdication of responsibility for protecting their freedoms to others would ultimately lead to the destruction of those freedoms. The activity he advocated was military service in the tradition of the citizen armies of the ancient Roman Republic. Military service as an expression of political participation, he claimed, would offset the effeminizing influences of luxury and politeness.

In 1768 Ferguson published *Institutes of Moral Philosophy,* an expanded summary of his Edinburgh lecture notes. The work itself had little original material, but it was a celebrated compilation of the doctrines being taught at the Scottish universities. In consequence of the Scots' standing in the intellectual communities of the world, the work was translated into German, French, Swedish, Italian, and Russian and was read by students and scholars alike from St. Petersburg to Philadelphia. For many contemporaries it condensed the essential teachings of the great Scots philosophers into a single accessible work.

Ferguson seems to have been content with his position in Edinburgh, although ambition did not leave him entirely. He pursued the governorship of West Florida, which had been ceded to Britain by Spain in the peace negotiations that followed the Seven Years War, and was actively considered for the post for a brief while. In 1773–1774 he accompanied Philip Stanhope, Earl of Chesterfield, on a grand tour of Europe at the behest of his guardians, who offered Ferguson a substantial compensation package that included a life pension. Ferguson even publicly entered the vicious debate over Britain's colonial American policy in 1776 with a short progovernment treatise, *Remarks on a Pamphlet Lately Published by Dr. Price*. Although not widely distributed, the pamphlet gained the attention of the reigning administration under Lord Frederick North, which appointed Ferguson secretary of the Carlisle Commission in 1778. The ill-fated commission was assigned the task of traveling to North America to present Parliament's latest peace offering to Congress. Although the terms essentially gave in to all of Congress's demands with the exception of total independence—Parliament feared the turn that the war would take if France and Spain entered it—Congress, now more confident than ever, refused to meet with the commissioners. George Washington refused even to allow Ferguson through his lines under a flag of truce. Ferguson's return to Edinburgh that autumn marked the end of his public forays into politics.

In 1783 Ferguson published the *History of the Progress and Termination of the Roman Republic*. This multivolume work covered the period from the First Punic War to the end of Augustus's reign and further enhanced Ferguson's reputation as an historian. Although translated into German and French, the work received only moderate praise, and the breadth of its readership relied more upon the grand reputation of its author than upon its own merits. It relied heavily on classical sources and borrowed extensively from the evidence and interpretation of Charles-Louis de Secondat, Baron de Montesquieu. Nevertheless, this work sustained Ferguson's reputation from the early nineteenth century to the mid twentieth century,

more than any other written during the years of the Scottish Enlightenment.

In 1785 Ferguson retired from his Edinburgh professorship for reasons of ill health—he had suffered a debilitating stroke in 1780—leaving the post vacant for his favored successor and student, Dugald Stewart. In 1792 Adam Ferguson published a substantial reworking of the *Institutes* as *Principles of Moral Political Science, a Retrospect of Lectures Delivered at the College of Edinburgh*. This publication was his final major one, and the reception of this edition of his lectures—no further editions were published in his lifetime, and the work was translated only into French—reflects the waning influence of Ferguson and that of the Scottish Enlightenment by that time. The following year he visited the European continent one last time, traveling primarily to Germany and Italy. Upon his return to Scotland, he published a revised edition of his history of the Roman Republic in 1793. That same year he became the first Scot in two decades to be elected to membership in the Berlin Royal Academy of Science and Arts. Two years later his wife died, and Ferguson left Edinburgh. After spending a year in the decaying castle of Neidpath on the Tweed, he moved to the village of Hallyards, where he remained until his sight began to fail. He was then was taken in 1808 into the care of friends in St. Andrews, where he died on 22 February 1816 at the age of ninety-two.

Despite a space of more than two centuries since the peak of his career, Ferguson's thought continues to resonate in the social science disciplines he helped to father. Although many of his conclusions have largely been disregarded today, his key questions of how and why human societies develop and are so diverse are as relevant in the twenty-first century as they were in the eighteenth.

Letters:

The Correspondence of Adam Ferguson, edited by Vincenzo Merolle, 2 volumes (London: Pickering, 1995).

References:

David Allan, *Virtue, Learning and the Scottish Enlightenment* (Edinburgh: Edinburgh University Press, 1993);

David Daiches, "The Scottish Enlightenment," *A Hotbed of Genius, The Scottish Enlightenment, 1730–1790,* edited by Daiches (Edinburgh: Saltire Society, 1986);

Ernest Gellner, "Adam Ferguson and the Surprising Robustness of Civil Society," in *Liberalism in Modern Times: Essays in Honour of Jose G. Merquior,* edited by Gellner and Cesar Cansino (London: Central European University Press, 1996), pp. 119–131;

H. M. Hopfl, "From Savage to Scotsman: Conjectural History in the Scottish Enlightenment," *Journal of British Studies,* no. 17 (1978): 19–40;

David Kettler, *The Social and Political Thought of Adam Ferguson* (Columbus: Ohio State University Press, 1965);

W. C. Lehmann, *Adam Ferguson and the Beginnings of Modern Sociology* (New York: Columbia University Press, 1930);

Donald G. MacRae, "Adam Ferguson," in *The Founding Fathers of Social Science,* edited by Timothy Raison (London: Penguin, 1969), pp. 17–26;

Ronald Meek, *Social Science and the Ignoble Savage* (Cambridge: Cambridge University Press, 1979);

Fania Oz-Salzberger, *Translating the Enlightenment: Scottish Civic Discourse in Eighteenth-Century Germany* (Oxford: Clarendon Press, 1995);

Nicholas Phillipson, "Towards a Definition of the Scottish Enlightenment," *City and Society in the 18th Century,* edited by P. Fritz and D. Williams (Toronto: Hakkert, 1973), pp. 125–147;

Richard Sher, *Church and University in the Scottish Enlightenment: The Moderate Literati of Edinburgh* (Princeton, N.J.: Princeton University Press, 1985).

Papers:
The University of Edinburgh is the primary depository of Adam Ferguson's papers and correspondence; the National Library of Scotland also holds some of his correspondence.

Andrew Fletcher

(1653 – 15 September 1716)

Ralph Stewart
Acadia University

PAMPHLETS: *A Discourse Concerning Militia's and Standing Armies, with Relation to the Past and Present Governments of Europe, and of England in Particular* (London, 1697);

A Discourse of Government with Relation to Militia's (Edinburgh, 1698; London, 1699);

Two Discourses concerning the Affairs of Scotland (Edinburgh, 1698);

Discorso delle cose di Spagna scritto nel mese di Luglio [A Discourse on the Affairs of Spain] (Naples [Edinburgh], 1698);

A Speech upon the State of the Nation; In April 1701 (London, 1701?);

Speeches by a Member of the Parliament Which began at Edinburgh the 6th of May, 1703 (Edinburgh, 1703);

An Account of a Conversation concerning a Right Regulation of Governments for the Common Good of Mankind. In a Letter to the Marquiss of Montrose, the Earls of Rothes, Roxburg and Haddington, from London the First of December, 1703 (Edinburgh & London, 1703).

Collections: *The Political Works of Andrew Fletcher, Esq.* (London: A. Bettesworth, C. Hitch & J. Clarke, 1732);

The Political Works of Andrew Fletcher, Esq; of Saltoun (Glasgow: G. Hamilton & J. Balfour, 1749)–includes translation of *Discorso*, and two descriptions of Fletcher by contemporaries;

The Political Works of Andrew Fletcher (London: H. D. Symonds, 1797)–includes a short biography;

Andrew Fletcher of Saltoun: Selected Political Writings and Speeches, edited by David Daiches (Edinburgh: Scottish Academic Press, 1979);

Andrew Fletcher: Political Works, edited by John Robertson (Cambridge: Cambridge University Press, 1997).

Andrew Fletcher of Saltoun is best known in Scotland as a patriotic member of the last Scottish Parliament, who bitterly but unsuccessfully opposed its absorption into the English Parliament in 1707, an event that marked the end of Scottish independence. In his speeches and pamphlets, Fletcher used his wide knowledge of modern and ancient history to analyze the political situation in Scotland and other countries: his ideas were influential in his own time and are still discussed. He was born in 1653 at the family estate of Saltoun, fifteen miles east of Edinburgh, to Sir Robert Fletcher and Katherine Bruce. (Scottish women did not change their names after marriage.) His father died in 1665, soon after appointing Gilbert Burnet as local minister and arranging for him to tutor Andrew, an arrangement that lasted two years. Fletcher and Burnet were not friendly in later life, but their careers had much in common. Both opposed the government, went into exile, and then joined invasions of England. They later returned to power–Fletcher to the Scottish Parliament and Burnet (as Bishop of Salisbury) to the English House of Lords–where, in the stormy debates that culminated in the Union of Parliaments, both harangued their peers on the wrongs to Scotland. Yet, Burnet was relatively conservative and later described Fletcher, justly, as "of great parts [abilities] and many virtues, but a most violent republican and extravagantly passionate."

Fletcher later spent a year at St. Andrews University and then, at fifteen set off on a tour abroad that lasted ten years. He stayed mainly in London and Paris and, in this period established the pattern of his life, except that the Netherlands replaced Paris as his main European residence. Despite his patriotism, his only long continuous periods in Scotland were from 1678 to 1682, and again from 1701 to 1708. He never married. In 1678 he returned to his estate and became a member of the Scottish Convention of Estates, an informal parliament, and then of the regular parliament. Fletcher was anticlerical, but he sympathized with the quasirepublican views of the more extreme Scottish Presbyterians. He voted against supplying money for troops to subdue the Presbyterians and against the "Succession" and "Test" Acts that demanded explicit oaths in favor of the existing government and the government-backed Church of England (Anglican Church). Such views got him into trouble, and he was twice charged with hindering the operations of the government. He went to England in May 1682 and the next year to the Netherlands. In May 1685, after the death of British king Charles II, Fletcher sailed for England with James, Duke of Monmouth (Charles II's illegitimate son), in an attempt to have Monmouth crowned king instead of James, the late king's brother. Unfortunately, Fletcher contributed to the failure of the expedition. He was to have acted as a cavalry officer and had appropriated a horse brought in by one of Monmouth's right-hand men, Thomas Dare. In an altercation, Fletcher killed Dare. Fletcher was hastily sent away on a ship bound for Spain, where he seems to have been imprisoned but escaped. Meantime, he was attainted (his civil rights taken away) as a traitor in Scotland and stripped of his estates. In 1688 Fletcher and his old tutor, Burnet, joined William of Orange's successful invasion. (King James II, in an attempt to mollify his people, had issued a general pardon the previous month, but excepted both Fletcher and Burnet.) Fletcher went on to Scotland, where eighteen months later his conviction for treason was annulled and his estate restored. He thought, however, that the new government was slow in moving. According to G. W. T. Omond, Fletcher is reported to have said to the Duke of Hamilton: "Tell the King that Fletcher of Saltoun has a better right to his estate than his Majesty has to the Crown." For the next ten years, Fletcher moved between Scotland and London, in contact with many major political figures, such as Hamilton.

Though he initially approved the choice of William of Orange as king, Fletcher soon came to believe that, like other rulers, William aimed to enlarge his powers at the expense of the people's liberties. The need to prevent rulers from becoming tyrants is the underlying concern in Fletcher's pamphlets, all of which appeared between 1697 and 1704. Although frequently polemical, they are also scholarly, for Fletcher was fluent in French, Italian (at least as a written language), Latin, and Greek, and well read in these languages. His essay *A Discourse of Government with Relation to Militia's* (1698), an expanded version of one published the previous year, is wider-ranging and more historical than the title suggests. From the fall of the Roman Empire to the end of the Middle Ages (in approximately 1500), he says, the European norm was a feudal system in which kings' powers were limited because they had to depend on their barons' armies, raised from the ordinary people on a part-time basis—that is, "militias." In the fifteenth century, inventions such as printing and the compass needle (which made possible much wider exploration) led to greater sophistication and expense. Barons began to accept money rents from their tenants, instead of service as soldiers, to pay for the luxuries they now coveted. Kings had a good pretext to raise "mercenary" armies, which were full-time, worked for pay, and were often made up of foreign troops, but were responsible only to the kings. With these armies, they could work toward establishing absolute power. Fletcher argues that British kings should have a hard time justifying having a "mercenary" and permanent ("standing") army since the island of Britain offered a natural defense, and the Scots were not a serious threat to the English. In the seventeenth century, however, Charles I and James II had nearly succeeded in setting up such armies, and William of Orange was now master of one. The solution was to revive the militia. Fletcher again looked to history to discuss both modern states (such as Holland, Switzerland, and Venice) and ancient ones (such as Sparta, Carthage, and Rome), arguing that, in the long run, states depending on militias flourish and those depending on standing or "mercenary" armies decay. He then moved on to a fairly detailed proposal for establishing camps, Spartan ones, to train the militia.

In the summer of 1698, Fletcher wrote two essays (or "discourses") on Scotland and emerged as a vehement supporter of Scottish independence—the stance he became known for. His reading of the current situation is, again, based on historical analysis. Like other European peoples, the Scots have lost their arms and civil rights, he says; and their situation is especially bad as they have, since the Union of Crowns in 1603, been exploited by the English. Currently, the English are working against the colony at Darien, near Panama, on which the Scots have staked most of the liquid capital of their country. (Fletcher himself committed £1000, a craftsman's salary for perhaps twenty-five years.) Meantime, he claims, there is a "serious dearth" of food. Fletcher believed that the only possible remedy was to hold back taxes from the London government and use the money to strengthen a native militia. The second discourse on Scotland was written soon afterward, but by that time the "dearth" had become a famine. Fletcher's wider historical explanation of the problem is that the Christian and Moslem religions were originally to blame for freeing slaves and thus creating large numbers of untended poor. His solution is to reintroduce slavery, or at least serfdom, in Scotland. He foresaw some limitations on a master's powers: killing and torture would be unacceptable. Obviously, there is a striking contrast between the proposals in the first discourse, which is aimed at maintaining Scottish independence and freedom, and in the second, which is to make many Scots into serfs. But Fletcher is reacting to the appalling situation around him; "fellow citizens," he says, are dying of hunger as he speaks. He believes that a qualified serfdom is better than starvation, though he admits that many of the poor—notably Highlanders—would prefer starvation. (He also makes rather complicated proposals for improving food production, allowing tenants enough capital to develop their farms.) Whatever one thinks of Fletcher's proposed solution, his grim analysis of Scotland's political and economic state, as untenable and needing drastic change, was accepted by both sides in the union debate that soon followed.

About this time, Fletcher wrote a discourse in Italian on "the Affairs of Spain," warning about the dangers of one country's dominating the world. (The reasons for writing in Italian remain doubtful, but John Robertson presents an explanation in "Andrew Fletcher and the Treaty of Union, in Scotland and England, 1286–1815," 1987) Spain had been extremely powerful because, Fletcher suggests, it had had a dominating geographical position since the discovery of the Americas. He explains its decline in the sixteenth century as caused by overly harsh and arbitrary rule, and consequent depopulation. At home, the Jews and then the Moors were expelled: abroad, native Americans were killed in enormous numbers. Spain has temporarily conquered the Low Countries (now Holland and Belgium), but these locations are hard to administer because they are separated by the powerful kingdom of France and also because Spain's savage rule has made the Dutch desperate in their resistance. However, these are mistakes that can be retrieved, and Spain could rise again and, indeed, become the superpower. *A Speech upon the State of the Nation; In April 1701* (1701?) is, despite its title, mainly a study of foreign affairs and a continuation of the previous discourse (nor, apparently, was it delivered as a speech). Fletcher is warning that France may inherit and incorporate Spain and become even more powerful. William of Orange may be able to combine Britain and the Low Countries into another empire, but that will be no real solution, since it will entail loss of liberty at home.

A month later Fletcher was a member of the new Scottish Parliament, and his vehement speeches addressed more immediate concerns. At this time he was described by John Macky as a "low, thin man, of a brown complexion; full of fire; with a stern, sour look." The speeches he gave in 1703 (the only ones published) insist that the Scottish Parliament must reassert Scottish independence. The immediate context is the problem of succession. Anne, who had succeeded William in 1702, had no surviving children, and the next in line would normally be the Stuarts, James II and his progeny. This succession was unacceptable to the majority in either country, and the English Parliament declared that the succession fell on the German House of Hanover (descended from a daughter of James I, James II's grandfather). The English Parliament assumed that the Scottish Parliament would follow suit. But this English position gave the Scots an opportunity: they could threaten to offer the crown of Scotland to the Stuarts or to someone else—the dukes of Hamilton had a claim. This move might possibly lead to independence and was at least a card to play for achieving better terms in a union with England. Admittedly, there was an element of bluff, as James II was probably as unpopular in Scotland as in England, and the Scots had no other convincing candidate to propose. Fletcher, however, seized the opportunity and proposed an "Act for the security of the kingdom," stating that when Anne died, power in Scotland would devolve on the Scottish Parliament, which would alone decide on her successor. If it were the same sovereign as England chose, then that sovereign would accept twelve "limitations," which would give the Scottish Parliament great powers and make it largely independent of the King and the London government. The main act passed in the Scottish Parliament, as did a diluted version of the limitations. The Crown finally accepted it the next year, but as a prelude to negotiating union. In March 1705 the English Parliament asked the Queen to name "Commissioners" to negotiate a union. They also passed several anti-Scottish measures and declared the Scots aliens from the end of the year—unless they accepted the same successor to Anne as England had. Negotiations had effectively begun.

Meantime, in 1703 Fletcher's last publication appeared, *An Account of a Conversation concerning a Right Regulation of Governments for the Common Good of Mankind*, detailing a conversation between Fletcher and three Unionists, one Scottish (George Mackenzie, first Earl of Cromarty) and two English (Sir Edward Seymour and Sir Christopher Musgrave), in which Fletcher makes the case for greater Scottish independence, arguing that Scotland had been impoverished by the Union of Crowns in 1603. English indifference is illustrated by Seymour's comment that Scotland is like "a beggar with a louse to her portion." Cromarty's apparently sincere argument that Scotland will prosper in an incorporating union, as part of greater Britain, is countered by the examples of Wales and Ireland, which even the relatively liberal Musgrave views as conquered nations without rights. The possibility of England's invading Scotland is raised, but Fletcher argues from historical precedent that Scotland is hard to conquer and harder to hold in subjection. He then moves to a much wider forum, looking back to an initial discussion about the great corruption that arises in large cities and the tendency of such cities to bleed the outlying parts of the country. Fletcher has a startling solution: the world should be divided into blocks of land about the size of the current larger nations, but each would be split into about a dozen, fairly autonomous, city provinces. The disadvantages of large cities would thus be avoided, and–Fletcher claims–the subsequent balance of power would prevent one country from totally dominating another. The model is based on the city-states of ancient Greece. To illustrate, Fletcher names twelve cities within the British-Irish block that might serve as centers. The Scottish ones are Stirling and Inverness, and the most northerly English one is York–one hundred miles south of the Scottish border. Seymour has some reason to object that Fletcher wants to reorganize the world to make Scotland independent of England.

The Scottish Parliament met again in the summers of 1704 and 1705, principally to debate the succession and the issue of union with England. Fletcher frequently clashed with his opponents and was close to dueling with at least four men, including James Hamilton, fourth Duke of Hamilton. According to one account in Omond's book, a duel with John Ker, fifth Earl of Roxburgh (once Fletcher's ally), was halted with only seconds to spare by the arrival of the Horse-Guards. Meantime, many pamphlets were published for and against the prospective Union. The terminology of the debate is confusing in that both sides claimed to be in favor of some kind of union: the true pro-Unionists wanted an "incorporating union" in which the Scottish Parliament, and probably the country, would be submerged in England. Anti-Unionists such as Fletcher often claimed, rather disingenuously, to be in favor of a "federal" union, in which Scotland would retain her own parliament: but this union could be defined in such a way that Scotland was virtually independent.

Fletcher's party lost, betrayed by the Duke of Hamilton, who had been officially head of the anti-Union party. On the evening of 1 September 1705, with many members absent, he suddenly moved that the Queen should nominate the Scottish negotiators, and his motion passed. It meant that the London government could now appoint men prepared to pass their version of Union and that was approximately what happened. The next fall, the Scottish Parliament met again, and Fletcher fought a strong rearguard action to prevent the Treaty from being accepted, but by that time union was almost inevitable. England had, however, made major concessions to achieve it. With only about a fortieth of England's wealth–then considered more relevant than population–Scotland got close to a tenth of the British members of Parliament. Scotland also won full rights of trade with England and the English colonies and retained the Scottish church, law, and educational system (though the House of Lords later chipped away at the former two). Although the

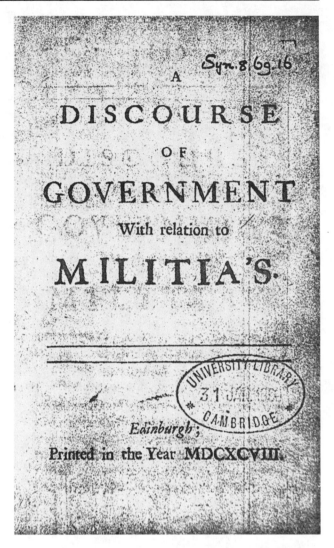

Title page for Andrew Fletcher's essay in which he argues that the power of kings was limited by their dependency on barons' armies (Thomas Cooper Library, Microforms Collection, University of South Carolina)

expected benefits in trade were a long time in coming, Scotland was left in a much better position than either Wales or Ireland. Fletcher, who had strengthened Scotland's bargaining position with his intransigence, can take some credit for this success.

In the spring of 1708 Fletcher was imprisoned on a spurious charge of plotting with the Jacobites to overthrow the king, but he was released after some weeks. The last part of his life was spent in Saltoun, Holland, and–mostly–London, where he mixed with influential people but seems to have taken no active part in politics. He moved to Paris in 1715, from where he complained in a letter to his brother in a letter of 27 October that "all things are excessively dear and bad." One of his major concerns was buying books. He went to London in August with his nephew, was too ill to travel farther, and died there on 15 September 1716. His last letter to his brother (who automatically inherited Saltoun) is an informal will. He asks that £200 be paid to relieve Jacobite prisoners: two of their cousins had been "out" in the Jacobite rebellion that ended in defeat after the Battle of Sherrifmuir in November 1715. Fletcher's nephew wrote that his uncle's last words were "Lord have mercy on my poor Countrey that is so barbarously oppressed." He is remembered as a Scottish patriot, whom even enemies described as honest and brave; and as a notable scholar and theorist, who applied his historical insights to his own time. Most of the topics he dealt with are relevant to the present—for example, how small countries may be independent, the right to bear arms, absolute power, degrees of freedom, over-powerful internal armies, and the danger from one country's dominating the world. His historical overviews and suggested solutions are still worth examining.

Letters:

Letters of Andrew Fletcher of Saltoun and His Family, 1715–1716, edited by I. J. Murray, in *Miscellany of the Scottish Historical Society,* fourth series, 27, no. 2 (1965): 145–173.

Bibliography:

Robert Andrew Scott Macfie, *A Bibliography of Andrew Fletcher of Saltoun, 1653–1716* [with portraits and facsimiles] (Edinburgh: Privately printed, 1901).

Biographies:

G. W. T. Omond, *Fletcher of Saltoun* (New York: Scribners, 1897);

William Cook Mackenzie, *Andrew Fletcher of Saltoun. His Life and Times* (Edinburgh: Porpoise Press, 1935);

P. H. Scott, *Andrew Fletcher and the Treaty of Union* (Edinburgh: John Donald, 1992);

Kenneth Fraser, *Andrew Fletcher: The Patriot* (Stirling: Scots Independent Newspapers, 2004).

References:

Gilbert Burnet, *Bishop Burnet's History of His Own Time,* 6 volumes, edited by M. J. Routh, second edition (London: Oxford University Press, 1833): III, p. 20;

David Daiches, *Scotland and the Union* (London: Murray, 1977);

John Macky, *Memoirs of the Secret Service of John Macky* (London, 1733), p. 223;

P. W. J. Riley, *King William and the Scottish Politicians* (Edinburgh: John Donald, 1979);

John Robertson, "Andrew Fletcher's Vision of Union," in *Scotland and England 1286–1815,* edited by Roger A. Mason (Edinburgh: John Donald, 1987), pp. 203–225.

Papers:

Andrew Fletcher's papers are among the *Saltoun Papers* in the National Library of Scotland, Edinburgh.

Edward Gibbon

(27 April or 8 May 1737 – 16 January 1794)

Anthony W. Lee
Kentucky Wesleyan College

See also the entry on Gibbon in *DLB 104: British Prose Writers, 1660–1800, Second Series.*

BOOKS: *Essai sur l'étude de la littérature* (London: Becket & De Hondt, 1761); translated by Gibbon as *An Essay on the Study of Literature* (London: Printed for T. Becket & P. A. De Hondt, 1764; New York, Garland, 1970);

Mémoires littéraires de la Grande Bretagne pour l'an 1767, by Gibbon and Georges Deyverdun (London: Becket & De Hondt, 1767);

Mémoires littéraires de la Grande Bretagne pour l'an 1768, by Gibbon and Deyverdun (London: Becket & De Hondt, 1768);

Critical Observations on the Sixth Book of the Aeneid (London: Printed for P. Elmsley, 1770);

The History of the Decline and Fall of the Roman Empire (6 volumes, London: W. Strahan & T. Cadell, volume 1, 1776; revised, 1777; volumes 2 and 3, 1781; volumes 4–6, 1788; 8 volumes, Philadelphia: Published by William Y. Birch & Abraham Small, Printed by Robert Carr, 1804–1805);

A Vindication of Some Passages in the Fifteenth and Sixteenth Chapters of the Decline and Fall of the Roman Empire (London: Printed for W. Strahan & T. Cadell, 1779); reprinted in *History of Christianity Comprising All That Relates to the Progress of the Christian Religion in The History of the Decline and Fall of the Roman Empire; and, A Vindication of Some Passages in the 15th and 16th Chapters,* edited by Peter Eckler (New York: Peter Eckler, 1891);

Mémoire Justificatif pour Servir de Réponse à l'Exposé de la Cour de France (London: N.p., 1779);

Miscellaneous Works of Edward Gibbon, Esquire, with Memoirs of His Life and Writings, Composed by Himself, edited by John Baker Holroyd, Lord Sheffield (2 volumes, London: A. Strahan & T. Cadell, jun., and W. Davies, 1796; 5 volumes, augmented and revised, London: John Murray, 1814; New York: F. DeFau, 1907);

Edward Gibbon (frontispiece for David Morrice Low, Edward Gibbon, 1737–1794, *1937; Thomas Cooper Library, University of South Carolina)*

The Autobiographies of Edward Gibbon, edited by John Murray (London: John Murray, 1896; New York: F. De Fau, 1907);

The Memoirs of the Life of Edward Gibbon, edited by G. B. Hill (London: Methuen, 1900; New York: Putnam, 1900);

Gibbon's Journal to January 28th, 1763: My Journal, I, II, and III and Ephemerides, edited by David M. Low (London: Chatto & Windus, 1929; New York: Norton, 1929);

Le Journal de Gibbon à Lausanne, edited by G. A. Bonnard (Lausanne: F. Rouge & Cie, 1945);

Gibbon's Journey from Geneva to Rome: His Journal from 20ᵗʰ April to October 1764, edited by Bonnard. (London & New York: Thomas Nelson, 1961).

Editions and Collections: *The History of the Decline and Fall of the Roman Empire,* 7 volumes, edited by J. B. Bury (London: Methuen / New York: Macmillan, 1896–1900);

The History of the Decline and Fall of the Roman Empire, edited and abridged, D. M. Low (London: Chatto & Windus, 1960);

Memoirs of My Life, edited by Georges A. Bonnard (London: Nelson, 1966);

The English Essays of Edward Gibbon, edited by Patricia B. Craddock (Oxford: Clarendon Press, 1972);

Autobiography, edited by Betty Radice (New York: Penguin, 1991).

In Lausanne, Switzerland, between eleven and midnight on the night of 27 June 1787, Edward Gibbon wrote: "It was among the ruins of the Capitol [in Rome] that I first conceived the idea of a work which has amused and exercised near twenty years of my life, and which, however inadequate to my own wishes, I finally deliver to the curiosity and candour of the public." Gibbon wrote these words in the "final conclusion" to his monumental historical masterpiece, *The History of the Decline and Fall of the Roman Empire* (1776–1788). Even in a century known for producing lengthy books (including one of the longest significant novels in English, Samuel Richardson's *Clarissa* [1747–1748], and James Boswell's immense *Life of Samuel Johnson LL.D.* [1791]), the size of Gibbon's magnum opus was an unusual achievement. It was published over a period of twelve years in six folio volumes of more than three thousand pages. It comprises 71 chapters, approximately 1,500,000 words, and nearly 8,000 footnotes. It covers a time span of close to 1,500 years and the geographical regions of Europe, Africa, Asia, and the Middle East. It traces the history of Rome from its "Golden Age" under the Antonines through its demise and eventual collapse, to the revival of interest in classical Roman civilization in the early Renaissance. By any measure, it is an heroic endeavor that brought its author enduring fame. Students still read *The History of the Decline and Fall of the Roman Empire* as a reliable history of the Roman Empire, as a document of late-eighteenth-century thought and culture, and as a literary artifact of the highest order—according to Roy Porter, "the greatest prose epic in the English tongue."

Edward Gibbon was born on 8 May 1737 in Putney to Edward Gibbon II and Judith Porten. Gibbon's grandfather, the first Edward Gibbon, made a fortune in the early part of the century as a financial speculator; he rose to become one of the directors of the South Sea Company. He bequeathed a substantial estate, which enabled his son and then his grandson to establish themselves comfortably as leisured gentleman. (The second Edward Gibbon's financial imprudence, however, later created problems for both himself and his son). Gibbon's mother, Judith Porten Gibbon, infatuated with her husband, spent little time with her son, and he felt emotionally isolated from her until her death when he was ten.

Because of frequent childhood illnesses, Gibbon often missed school; the illnesses and the encouraging influence of his aunt, Catherine Porten, led him to spend much of his time in solitary reading. This pursuit formed a lasting habit for Gibbon. Later in life, as he reports in his *Memoirs of My Life* (1966), "while so many of my acquaintance were married, or in parliament, or advancing with a rapid step in the various roads of honours and fortune, I stood alone, immoveable and insignificant." His voracious reading and scholarly independence also contributed significantly to *The History of the Decline and Fall of the Roman Empire*. It was based upon an exhaustive reading of many primary sources (Gibbon's personal library contained between six and seven thousand books) and was undertaken and completed without any academic or institutional support. Reading the Latin poets and the continuation of Laurence Echard's Roman history (three additional volumes written by an unknown person) incited an early interest in what became his great life project.

When he was about fourteen, Gibbon's health unexpectedly improved, and his father arranged for him to enter Magdalen College, Oxford, on 3 April 1752. Gibbon, according to his memoirs, was scandalized by the intellectual laxity he found at the University: "As a gentleman commoner I was admitted to the society of the fellows, and fondly expecting that some questions of literature would be the amusing and instructive topics of their discourse. Their conversation stagnated in a round of college business, Tory politics, personal stories and private scandal." Gibbon found the intellectual integrity of the professors to be little better than the students', and he grew disillusioned by academic higher education. However, the lack of intellectual and spiritual guidance available at Oxford allowed Gibbon to continue his intensive solitary reading. In addition to history, he began reading theology, especially Catholic writings, and became a Catholic convert in 1753. Being a Catholic in eighteenth-century England entailed serious legal disadvantages, such as inability to hold public office. Gibbon's father quickly moved to curb this religious enthusiasm by sending his son to Lausanne, Switzerland, where he was instructed by Calvinist minister Daniel Pavillard. In 1755 he returned to the Protestant faith, but his intellectual inquiries into theology probably led him to become a religious skeptic—a perspective that later colored his unflattering appraisal of Christianity in *The History of the Decline and Fall of the Roman Empire*. Additionally, Gibbon's personal experiments in religion taught him intellectual moderation and contributed to the deep mistrust of emotional fanaticism that he later exhibited in his history. Gibbon also learned from Pavillard disciplined study habits that enabled him to augment his knowledge of Latin literature, Greek, geography, and history. His immersion in the French language and his study of Blaise Pascal's *Les provinciales* (1656–1657; translated as *Provincial Letters*, 1657), influenced the development of his mature style, especially his technique of irony.

In 1757 Gibbon met a young Swiss woman, Suzanne Curchod. Her physical beauty and intellectual distinction strongly attracted him, and he declared his love for her. His father disapproved of the match, however, and ordered him to abandon the affair and to return home to England. Dutifully, Gibbon consented; in *Memoirs of My Life* he said, "I sighed as a lover: I obeyed as a son." Despite the rift between them, Gibbon remained a lifelong friend of Suzanne, who eventually married French minister of finance Jacques Necker and gave birth to Anne-Louise-Germaine Necker, who married and became Baronne de Staël-Holstein, better known as writer Madame de Stael.

After returning to England, Gibbon divided his time between living in London and the family estate at Buriton, Hampshire. Lacking a fixed occupation, he engaged in both socializing and intense reading. He continued to study classical literature, rereading *The Iliad* and *The Odyssey* in Greek, but he also read modern history, including David Hume's *History of England* (1754–1762) and Voltaire's *Siècle de Louis XIV* (1751; translated as *The Age of Lewis XIV*, 1752). He served as a captain in the Hampshire militia from 1759 to 1762, an experience to which he later attributed an increased knowledge of military life that, as he wrote in his *Memoirs of My Life*, "has not been useless to the historian of the Roman Empire." After completing his militia duties, he published, in French, *Essai sur l'étude de la litérature* (1761), which he translated in 1764 as *An Essay on the Study of Literature,* a fifty-five-chapter disquisition seeking to demonstrate that the study of the classics of ancient Greece and Rome offers the best education for the mind. This book garnered him a modest literary reputation in both England and France.

From 1763 to 1765 he undertook the Grand Tour of the European continent—visiting France and Italy, and revisiting Lausanne. While in Paris he became acquainted with many of the writers and intellectuals of the French Enlightenment, including Claude Adrien Helvétius; Paul Henri-Dietrich, baron d' Holbach; Jean

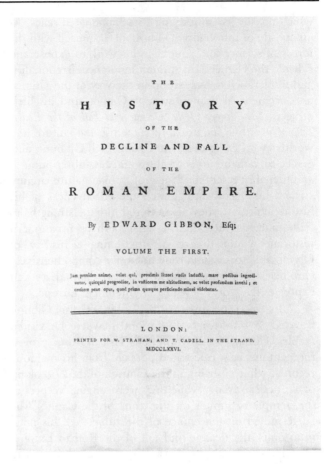

Title page for volume 1 of the 1776 edition for Gibbon's monumental history (from Sotheby's The Collection of the Garden Ltd., Magnificent Books and Manuscripts, *no. 157, 1989; Bruccoli Clark Layman Archives)*

Le Rond d'Alembert; and Denis Diderot. (Gibbon had previously met Voltaire while living in Switzerland.)

Gibbon's experience in Paris is significant, for it underscores his extensive connections with Enlightenment thought, connections noted by modern British historian Hugh Trevor-Roper in his 1963 introduction to an edition of *The History of the Decline and Fall of the Roman Empire*. Gibbon's Continental excursions indicate his cosmopolitan perspective; he was equally at home in Switzerland, France, and London. His close ties with the philosophes of late-eighteenth-century France were based upon a shared worldview. Gibbon extolled a public, communal focus rather than a private, esoteric one and wrote with the intention of the moral improvement of society. He saw himself as a practical historian, as well as a philosophical one, thus subscribing to Enlightenment faith in human progress. He vigorously opposed what he viewed as the lingering remnants of superstition and intolerance and, like Voltaire, mounted a vigorous critique against an institutional Christianity, which he saw as embodying these antiquated relics. As an apostle of rationality, Gibbon allied himself with the forces of science and sought in his work to expose and ridicule the elements of human ignorance, irrationality, and intolerance, which stood in the way of the rational improvement of human society. Gibbon and his life's project, *The History of the Decline and Fall of the Roman Empire,* are thus inextricably rooted in the culture and worldview of Enlightenment optimism. If Gibbon's allegiance to Enlightenment values and his subscription to an untenably essentialist view of human nature circumscribed his vision and limited the effectiveness of his historical project, they also offered him the strengths to undertake and accomplish what perhaps no modern historian would dream of attempting—a history of Olympian proportions that not only comprehensively chronicles the Roman world but also summarizes and expresses the worldview of Enlightenment Europe.

In 1764, accompanied by William Guise, Gibbon traveled in Italy for twelve months, where he visited Naples, Florence, and Rome. His visit to Rome proved momentous, as a celebrated passage from his memoirs records: while "musing in the Church of the Zoccolanti or Franciscan friars, while they were singing Vespers in the Temple of Jupiter on the ruins of the Capitol," he "determined on the choice of the subject" of his magnum opus, the decline and fall of the Roman Empire. He fell in love with the city and spent many hours visiting and studying its spectacles and ruins.

After returning to England, Gibbon began preparing to write his history of the Roman Empire. He was not too busy, however, to engage in other literary projects. In the years 1767 and 1768, he and his close Swiss friend Georges Deyverdun wrote *Mémoires littéraires de la Grande Bretagne pour l'an 1767* (Literary Review of Great Britain for the Year 1767) and *Mémoires littéraires de la Grande Bretagne pour l'an 1768* (Literary Review of Great Britain for the Year 1768). These annual literary digests of works published in England were intended to be read by foreigners on the Continent interested, according to Patricia B. Craddock in *Young Edward Gibbon: Gentleman of Letters,* in "the best books of every kind which come out during each period." Few read the first volume, however, and even fewer read the second, and the two friends discontinued their efforts. On 3 February 1770 Gibbon anonymously published his *Critical Observations on the Sixth Book of the Aeneid,* an attack upon the allegorical interpretation of Virgil by celebrated critic William Warburton. Several reviewers and serious critics applauded Gibbon's effort.

Gibbon's enjoyment of his success was curtailed, however, by the death of his father later in the year. Since Deyverdun departed for the Continent in this year, Gibbon relied heavily upon the advice and emo-

tional support of his other lifelong friend, John Baker Holroyd (who later, as Lord Sheffield, became Gibbon's literary executor). Gibbon decided to sell his family estate at Buriton and live in London. Settling in a house in Bentinck Street, Cavendish Square, he spent 1771 and 1772 reviewing his materials, and, finally, in 1773 he began actual composition of *The History of the Decline and Fall of the Roman Empire.*

While composing this work, Gibbon maintained an active public and social life. In 1774 he was elected a Member of Parliament for Liskeard, in Cornwall, a seat he held until 1780. The Liskeard seat was a pocket borough, and Gibbon was elected without actually visiting Cornwall. Although he served as a Member of Parliament during the tumultuous years of the American Revolution, Gibbon was not an active politician; he did not give a single speech during his tenure. While he theoretically opposed the way the government handled the rebellious colonies, he refrained from open criticism. During this time he also began mixing in London literary circles, gaining admittance to the prestigious Literary Club and becoming close friends with such luminaries as Joshua Reynolds and David Garrick. He was also presented at Court.

After several years of study, preparation, and composition, at age thirty-nine Gibbon finally published the first installment of *The History of the Decline and Fall of the Roman Empire* on 17 February 1776. Critics hailed it as a masterpiece of literature and a monumental contribution to historical writing. Horace Walpole called it "a truly classic work," and contemporary historians Hume and William Robertson bestowed high praise upon it. Public opinion concurred with critical judgment: the first impression sold out within fifteen days. Gibbon himself remarked that it was "very well received by men of letters, men of the world and even by fine feathered Ladies." Gibbon became a celebrity overnight and acquired a European-wide reputation as a scholar and man of letters. He spent the next twelve years completing the task of writing the remaining volumes.

While continuing to work on the remaining volumes of his history, Gibbon continued his social and political activities. In 1777 he traveled to France where, while staying with his old friends the Neckers, he met Benjamin Franklin and was lionized by the intellectual elite of the Parisian salons. Back in London, he faced financial worries. The annuity secured from his grandfather's inheritance proved insufficient to maintain the gentleman's lifestyle to which he had become accustomed, and he succeeded in securing a lucrative post as one of the Lords of Trade in 1779. In 1780 Gibbon witnessed the Gordon Riots, anti-Catholic demonstrations that quickly escalated into random mob violence. This experience shook Gibbon's faith in the rational progress and improvement of humankind. In 1781 volumes two and three of his history were published. While these received high praise, and four thousand editions were printed, the public reception proved cooler than his previous triumph in 1776. According to Richard N. Parkinson, the Duke of Gloucester, upon receiving his presentation copy of the work, is reported to have remarked humorously: "Another damned thick, square book. Always scribble, scribble, scribble! Eh! Mr Gibbon."

In 1782 Gibbon lost his additional income when the Lords of Trade was abolished. Realizing that he could not afford to continue living in London on his income, in 1783 he moved back to Lausanne, where he set up a household in a spacious Swiss villa, La Grotte, with his old friend Deyverdun. Here he completed his history, publishing volumes four, five, and six on 8 May 1788, the same day he celebrated his fifty-first birthday. In his *Memoirs of My Life* he describes his feelings upon finally completing *The History of the Decline and Fall of the Roman Empire:*

> After laying down my pen, I took several turns in a *berceau* or covered walk of Acacias which commands a prospect of the country the lake and the mountains [sic]. The air was temperate, the sky was serene; the silver orb of the moon was reflected from the waters, and all Nature was silent. I will not dissemble the first emotions of joy on the recovery of my freedom and perhaps the establishment of my fame. But my pride was soon humbled, and a somber melancholy was spread over my mind by the idea that I had taken my everlasting leave of an old and agreeable companion, and that, whatsoever might be the future date of my history, the life of the historian must be short and precarious.

Gibbon's completed history possesses an organic unity, moving in a circular motion from the apogee of Roman civilization, the descent of this civilization into barbarism, and its recovery and resurrection by the Renaissance humanists. Gibbon begins his work with a survey of the Roman Empire at the peak of its development and geographical extent. Chapters 1–3 examine the geographical, political, cultural, military, and constitutional aspects of Roman life under the Antonines (the period between 138 and 180 A.D.). Chapters 4–8 trace the decline from the superior height the Empire attained under Marcus Aurelius by tracing the inglorious and vicious reigns of the emperors from Commodus, Aurelius's son, through Philip (180–249). Chapters 9–10 examine external enemies to the Empire, Persia and Germany. Chapters 11–14 resume the chronological survey of the emperors, from Trajan Decius to Constantine the Great (249–333), including the division of

Gibbon's second book-plate (frontispiece for J. A. W. Bennett, Essays on Gibbon, *1980; Thomas Cooper Library, University of South Carolina)*

the Empire into Eastern and Western partitions. Chapters 15–16 examine the rise of Christianity and its contribution to the decline of the Empire. Chapters 17–21, which begin volume two, closely examine the Empire under Constantine and his sons (307–360), while chapters 23–24 examine the reign of Julian the Apostate (360–363), who sought to reverse the Christian policies of Constantine. Chapters 25–27 examine the events of the reigns of the emperors Jovian through Theodosius (363–395). Chapter 28 analyzes the final triumph of Christianity over paganism. Chapters 29–31 examine the beginning of the Gothic invasions. Chapters 32–33 examine the reigns of the emperors Arcadius and Theodosius II in the East (395–450) and Honorius through Valentian III in the West (395–455). Chapters 34–35 discuss the career of Attila the Hun and his invasion of Gaul and Italy. Chapter 36 details the sack of Rome by the Vandals and the extinction of the Empire in the West.

Chapters 37–38 analyze the development of Christian monasticism and the conversion of the barbarians to Christianity. Chapters 39–40 examine the reigns of the Eastern emperors from Zeno through Justinian I (474–565). Chapters 41–45 examine the military and political events in the West from the collapse of Rome through the pontificate of Gregory I (476–604). Chapter 46 discusses events in Persia (570–628), while chapter 47 examines theological controversies in the early Christian Church. Chapter 48 surveys the Greek emperors in the Eastern Empire (641–1185). Chapter 49 examines the rise of Charlemagne (774–814), while chapters 50–52 examine the Arabian world, the career of Mohammed, and the founding of Islam (569–609). Chapters 53–54 discuss events in the Eastern Empire in the tenth century, while chapters 55–56 focus on events in western Europe. Chapters 57–58 examine the Turkish Empire and the beginning of the Crusades. Chapters 59–63 trace the fortunes of Empire in the East and developments in western Europe from the eleventh through the fourteenth centuries. Chapter 64 discusses the career of Genghis Khan (1206–1227), while chapter 65 examines the career of Tamerlane (1361–1405). Chapters 61–63 trace events in both the East and West up to the conquest of Constantinople by the Turks (1453), the event officially marking the extinction of the Roman Empire in the East. Gibbon concludes his history by tracing the rise of the Renaissance, symbolized by the coronation of Petrarch (1341) in chapters 69–70, and surveys the prospect of the ruins of the Empire in the city of Rome from a modern vantage in chapter 71.

In assessing Rome's decline, Gibbon identifies many causes. The most important of these include the excessive and mercenary influence of the Praetorian Guard in state affairs (especially the election of the emperor), the loss of industry and military discipline because of peaceful prosperity, the proliferation of luxury, the admittance of barbarians into the army to serve as mercenaries, the external pressures exerted by barbarian tribes, and the development and growth of Christianity within the Empire. In chapters 15 and 16 Gibbon focuses upon this last cause, identifying five principal ways in which Christianity helped erode the Empire:

1. The inflexible . . . the intolerant zeal of the Christians . . .
2. The doctrine of a future life . . .
3. The miraculous powers ascribed to the primitive church . . .
4. The pure and austere morals of the Christians . . .
5. The union and discipline of the Christian republic . . .

This analysis immediately became the most controversial part of Gibbon's history, leading to vehement attacks from many critics, who found his treatment of Christianity harsh and unfair. In *The Life of Samuel Johnson, LL.D.* (1791) Boswell, a fellow member of the Literary Club who disliked Gibbon, remarked to Samuel Johnson (who concurred with his judgment) that *The History of the Decline and Fall of the Roman Empire* was "written in a very mellifluous style, but, under the pretext of another subject, contained much artful infidelity. . . . [Gibbon] should have warned us of our danger, before we entered his garden of flowery eloquence, by advertising, 'Spring-guns and men-traps set here.'" According to Parkinson, Gibbon wrote so profusely in this part of the history that he found himself required to undertake "three successive revisals from a large volume to their present size."

Gibbon's adverse treatment of Christianity is rooted in several factors. It was part of a larger distaste for emotional zeal and religious intolerance that marks his attitude. Such a view was typical of the Enlightenment period in general and eighteenth-century England in particular, which viewed with retrospective horror the violent excesses and civil warfare perpetrated in the name of religion in seventeenth-century France and England. Gibbon's personal experience in shifting from the Anglican communion to Catholicism and being proselytized back to the Protestant fold by the Calvinist Pavillard significantly colored his mistrust of religious extremism. In addition, Gibbon was devoted to the values of the classical world, and his inquiry into Roman history demonstrated the inimical perspective that the early Christians maintained toward the classics, as this quotation from chapter 15 reveals:

> The condemnation of the wisest and most virtuous of the Pagans, on account of their ignorance or disbelief of the divine truth, seems to offend the reason and the humanity of the present age. But the primitive church, whose faith was of a much firmer consistence, delivered over, without hesitation, to eternal torture the far greater part of the human species. A charitable hope might perhaps be indulged in favour of Socrates, or some other sage of antiquity, who had consulted the light of reason before that of the Gospel had arisen. But it was unanimously affirmed that those who, since the birth or the death of Christ, had obstinately persisted in the worship of the daemons, neither deserved nor could expect a pardon from the irritated justice of the Deity.

Gibbon's discussion of the success of the early church in spreading throughout the world discloses a subtle series of criticisms. He finds the zeal with which early Christians spread their message excessive and repugnant; he views with cynical doubt both their pretensions of the soul's immortality and their testimony of miracles; and he views with skepticism their reputation for austere morality, finding instead evidence of pride and greed. He also questions the statistical veracity of the high number of martyrs claimed by the early church.

Immediately after the publication of both volume one (1776) and volumes two and three (1781), Gibbon's urbane Enlightenment rationality provoked many religious pamphlets protesting his criticism of the Christian religion. In his *Memoirs of My Life* Gibbon expresses surprise "that the majority of English readers were so fondly attached even to the name and shadow of Christianity." This remark seems to corroborate the skeptical attitude toward Christianity that outraged so many of his readers. In the nineteenth century, Thomas Bowdler published an expurgated version of *The History of the Decline and Fall of the Roman Empire,* suppressing the "indecent" elements in the history. Catholic reviewer John Miley labeled Gibbon's work "incomparably the most pernicious work that ever issued from the press."

By the late nineteenth and early twentieth centuries, some historians began offering more balanced assessments. The view that Gibbon wrote the entire *The History of the Decline and Fall of the Roman Empire* as an assault upon traditional Christianity began to be replaced by the view that his treatment of Christianity was simply one part of a larger historical perspective. Historians began to realize that he was not necessarily singling Christianity out for special derision: his larger target was fanaticism and intolerance, as his unflattering treatment of religious extremism among other religions, such as Islam and Zoroastrianism, reveals. More recent readers, led by such studies as Giuseppe Giarrizzo's 1954 book *Edward Gibbon e la cultura europea* (Edward Gibbon and European Culture), have turned from either judging or condemning Gibbon to analyzing the validity and correctness of his assessment. Craddock, in her *Edward Gibbon, Luminous Historian: 1772–1794,* acknowledges the salutary influence of Gibbon's approach: "But in the course of the century, most readers came to realize that the *Decline and Fall* was not *just* an attack on the Christian church. Virtually all professional historians saw Gibbon's secularization of Christian history either as something to be taken for granted or a positive contribution to historiographical practice."

The general strengths of *The History of the Decline and Fall of the Roman Empire* and its broad historical value are manifold. For many it is the finest historical work of the eighteenth century and the greatest history written in the English tongue. It affords unparalleled access to the events and personalities of European history from the time of Christ to the revival of learning. It is intricately detailed and exhaustively researched. Gibbon's scholarly accuracy is meticulous and based upon an immense collection of documentary evidence. His amalgamation of the details into a cohesive narrative is a remarkable achievement. Gibbon sketches portraits of a

Sketches of Gibbon by Lavinia, Countess Spencer, 1785 (from Patricia B. Craddock, Edward Gibbon, Luminous Historian, 1772–1794, *1989; Thomas Cooper Library, University of South Carolina)*

vast array of historical figures, from Nero to Muhammed, from Attila the Hun to Petrarch. He analyzes historical figures with psychological depth and offers incisive moral assessments.

A principal strength of the work lies in its style, especially in use of Gibbon's use of parallelism. *The History of the Decline and Fall of the Roman Empire* is controlled by an intricate structure of balance and antithesis. Examples of this technique abound at all levels of the work: sentence, paragraph, chapter, and volume. For example, in volume one, Gibbon begins by sketching an idealized portrait of the serenity and cultural splendor Roman civilization achieved under the Antonine dynasty (chapters 1–3). This section is immediately balanced by four chapters canvassing the chaos and degradation the Empire suffered at the hands of Commodus, Caracalla, Severus, and their successors (chapters 4–7). In volume two Gibbon organizes his material around two characters, Constantine the Great and Julian the

Apostate. In chapters 27–31 Gibbon examines the reign of Constantine, his conversion of the Empire to Christianity, and the consequences of this conversion upon Roman life. In chapters 32–34 Gibbon sketches the reign of Julian, who sought to return the Empire to the pagan religion. The tension between these two opposing religious movements offers Gibbon the opportunity to extend the criticism of Christianity that he began in chapters 15 and 16 of volume one, and to heroicize, in the figure of Julian, the classical ideals that Gibbon himself admired. In volume three, Gibbon again structures his narrative antithetically by dividing the volume into two halves, assigning the first six chapters (chapters 27–32) to Theodosius and affairs in the Eastern Empire, and the last six chapters (chapters 33–38) to the Western Empire. Within this general division he achieves a more intricate parallelism, using the rhetorical figure of the chiasmus, which pairs chapters inversely. This pairing allows the first half of the volume to mirror precisely, in reverse order, the second half of the volume. Chapters 27 and 38 are each devoted to the reigns of political rulers Theodosius and Clovis; chapters 28 and 37 each examine religious life; chapters 29 and 36 each examine a rupture to the Empire, the former its division, the latter its extinction with the sack of Rome in the West; chapters 30–31 and 34–35 are devoted to two barbarian generals, Alaric the Goth and Attila the Hun; and chapters 32 and 33 each discuss the condition of the Empire in the East and the West, respectively. This bracketing of antithetical units gives the history an invaluable texture of tightness and unity, and prevents it from degenerating into a confused medley of jarring facts, dates, and names.

As Parkinson has noted, within this static architecture a more mobile pattern of organization subsists: a narrative development of rising movement toward a climax. For example, volume one proceeds along a roughly chronological order, arriving at the last two chapters (15 and 16), which climactically offer an extended description and critique of Christianity and discuss its major contribution to the decline of the Roman Empire. Volume two develops a narrative motion that climaxes with the decisive crossing of the Danube by the Goths in chapter 26, foreshadowing the barbarian incursions soon to follow. Volume three offers a grand climax, not just of that individual volume, but of the first half of *The History of the Decline and Fall of the Roman Empire* (volumes 1–3), as chapters 36–38 chronicle the sack of Rome by the Vandals and the collapse of the Empire in the West. The climax of the entire book occurs in the penultimate chapter of the final volume (chapter 70) with the description of the character of Petrarch and his coronation as poet laureate. By focusing upon Petrarch, the symbolic father of

the Renaissance, Gibbon concludes *The History of the Decline and Fall of the Roman Empire* with a redemptive note: although Rome fell because of the forces of ignorance, greed, and barbarism, the ideals of classical civilization live on.

Complementing this upward movement is Gibbon's technique of situating his narrative point of view from an elevated prospect, a technique discussed by W. B. Carnochan's study, *Gibbon's Solitude: The Inward World of the Historian.* Using a perspective similar to an eighteenth-century prospect poem—taking some point of elevated vantage to offer moral, political, and philosophical observations upon life—Gibbon surveys life under the Roman Empire from a lofty vantage. This narrative posture contributes powerfully to the studied composure that marks the tonal center of *The History of the Decline and Fall of the Roman Empire* and mitigates the danger of Gibbon's becoming lost in the immense array of detail that his history marshals. Furthermore, the Olympian prospect contributes significantly to the moral, humanistic effort of examining historical life, specific human endeavors, and activities from a unified philosophical point of view. The great ideals that Gibbon upholds are human rationality and progress; yet, time and time again the agents of his history betray this promise of human potential through examples of greed, irrationality, pride, and moral squalor. In this respect, Gibbon's work is more than a chronologically ordered history: it is a didactic satire intended to expose the follies and errors of humankind and to proffer the hope of general moral improvement.

Gibbon's stately language is one of the great styles in the English language. Like the larger contours of *The History of the Decline and Fall of the Roman Empire,* Gibbon's style is formed upon the precise coherence of parallelism, balance, and antithesis. In addition to this ordering principle, Gibbon's style is characterized by his use of literary allusion, personification, litotes (understatement), and elevated diction. The key element in Gibbon's style, however, is his use of irony. Irony was a frequently used trope in the line of Augustan wit tracing back to John Dryden in the Restoration period, and through such early-eighteenth-century practitioners as Jonathan Swift, Alexander Pope, and John Gay. By Gibbon's day, irony as a dominant literary trope was on the wane: Gibbon, along with Johnson and novelist Laurence Sterne, number among its last major exponents. Gibbon frequently uses irony to contrast the rational ideals to which humans aspire with the imperfect and irrational reality of actual experience. This paragraph from chapter 16, in which Gibbon discusses the early Christian martyrs, exhibits all Gibbon's major stylistic techniques:

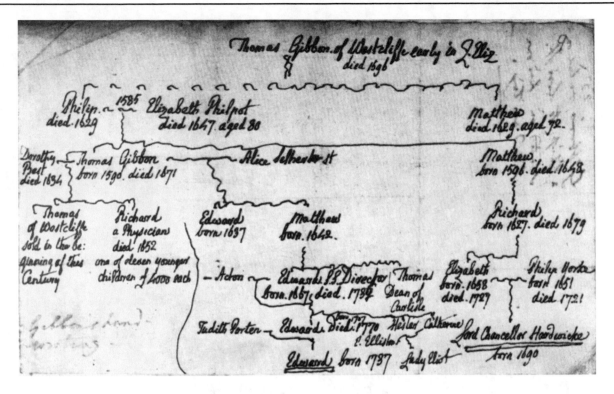

Gibbon's genealogy in his own hand (from Joseph Ward Swain, Edward Gibbon the Historian, *1966;
Thomas Cooper Library, University of South Carolina)*

Some of these were persons oppressed by poverty and debts, who blindly sought to terminate a miserable existence by a glorious death. Others were allured by the hope that a short confinement would expiate the sins of a whole life; and others, again, were actuated by the less honourable motive of deriving a plentiful subsistence, and perhaps a considerable profit, from the alms which the charity of the faithful bestowed on the prisoners. After the church had triumphed over all her enemies, the interest as well as the vanity of the captives prompted them to magnify the merit of their respective suffering. A convenient distance of time or place gave an ample scope to the progress of fiction; and the frequent instances which might be alleged of holy martyrs whose wounds had been instantly healed, whose strength had been renewed, and whose lost members had been restored, were extremely convenient for the purpose of removing every difficulty and silencing every objection. The most extravagant legends, as they conduced to the honour of the church, were applauded by the credulous multitude, countenanced by the power of the clergy, and attested by the suspicious evidence of ecclesiastical history.

Gibbon's irony consists of subtle understatement and delicately corrosive innuendo. As Hume assaults miracles in his *Philosophical Essays Concerning Human Understanding* (1748), Gibbon casts doubt upon the veracity of supernatural accounts through the skepticism of probability. Using a psychological analysis, he subverts the pious sincerity of the martyrs by ascribing to them the unholy motives of desperation and greed. His indirect method veils his true sentiments and hence shields him from the dangers of being charged with apostasy or atheism by his more pious contemporaries. Gibbon's ironic stance establishes him as a satirist in the Augustan tradition of Dryden, Pope, and Swift, and scholar Paul Fussell places Gibbon among this company in his influential study of the Augustan tradition, *The Rhetorical World of Augustan Humanism* (1965).

After completing his history, Gibbon turned to other projects, none of which was completed. The most important of these was an autobiography, begun in 1788. He crafted six different versions of this work, which was left unfinished at his death and was published posthumously in 1796 by his literary executor, Lord Sheffield. In his *Memoirs of My Life,* Gibbon offers an engagingly modest portrait of his personality and scholarly inclinations:

> I am endowed with a chearful [sic] temper, a moderate sensibility and a natural disposition to repose rather than to action: some mischievous appetites and habits have perhaps been corrected by philosophy or time. The love of study, a passion which derives fresh vigour from enjoyment, supplies each day, each hour, with a perpetual source of independent and rational pleasure. . . .

Manuscript page from Gibbon's memoirs, probably written in the last five years of his life (the British Museum; from David M. Low, Edward Gibbon, 1737–1794, *1937; Thomas Cooper Library, University of South Carolina)*

His *Memoirs of My Life,* in addition to offering valuable information about his life and background details on the composition of *The History of the Decline and Fall of the Roman Empire,* is among the earliest of modern autobiographies. Along with Jean-Jacques Rousseau's *Confessions* (published within the same decade, 1781–1788), and Boswell's unpublished journals, Gibbon's *Memoirs of My Life* can be said to anticipate the Romantic preoccupa-

tion with subjectivity that came to mark European culture in the early nineteenth century.

In September 1788 Deyverdun suffered a stroke; he died in July of the following year. Gibbon was strongly afflicted by the loss of his friend of thirty-three years. He was also disturbed by news of the disorder erupting in neighboring France, as the French Revolution began. He continued to live at Lausanne, where he presided over the local social scene with oracular authority. In 1790 he sought to begin a seventh volume of *The History of the Decline and Fall of the Roman Empire,* as well as a history of the House of Brunswick, but ill health prevented him from making serious progress in either work.

In 1793 Gibbon learned of the death of the wife of his one remaining intimate friend, Lord Sheffield. Gibbon returned to England to offer his solace. But in this year his own health problems worsened. Gibbon suffered periodic bouts with gout, and since his days in the militia, he had endured a painful swelling in one of his testicles, diagnosed as a hydrocele, but possibly a hernia. Gibbon underwent two operations in November to relieve this swelling; after undergoing a third in January, he died at Sheffield on 16 January 1794.

Gibbon's *The History of the Decline and Fall of the Roman Empire* established his international reputation as an historian and belletristic writer in his own lifetime, and this reputation continues long after his death. General assessments among historians and the reading public have proved diverse and illuminating. In the nineteenth century Gibbon's history acquired authoritative status and was used as a general textbook of ancient history. His chapter on Roman law (chapter 44) was used as a textbook for law students. John Henry Newman, while deploring Gibbon's apparently scandalous treatment of Christianity, grudgingly admitted, according to Porter, the authority of *The History of the Decline and Fall of the Roman Empire* in Church history: "It is melancholy to say it, but the chief, perhaps the only, English writer who has any claim to be considered an ecclesiastical historian, is the unbeliever Gibbon." Many statesmen—including William Gladstone, Winston Churchill, and German diplomat Friedrich von Gentz—pored painstakingly over the pages of *The History of the Decline and Fall of the Roman Empire,* finding within its pages fundamentally complete liberal arts education incorporating philosophy, economics, law, and human psychology as well as history.

French historian Francois Guizot, who edited a French edition of *The History of the Decline and Fall of the Roman Empire,* summarized the nineteenth-century consensus by praising both Gibbon's exhaustive erudition and his philosophic marshaling of his facts. German historiographers Leopold von Ranke and Barthold Niebuhr greatly esteemed Gibbon's achievement. Twentieth-century historian Trevor-Roper called Gibbon "the greatest of the historians of the Enlightenment, the only one of them who is still read not only as a stylist but as a historian." J. B. Bury, who meticulously prepared the standard critical edition of *The History of the Decline and Fall of the Roman Empire* (7 volumes, 1896–1900),

remarked, "in the main things he is still our master, above and beyond 'date.'"

Not everyone has viewed the book so positively, however. In 1967 English historian Geoffrey Elton proclaimed, "hardly anyone reads him any longer." As Porter notes in his 1988 study, *Gibbon: Making History,* Gibbon's work suffers from several weaknesses and limitations. As an historical document, it has, in many respects, been rendered obsolete, and Gibbon's interpretation of his materials has come into question. For example, his negative appraisal of the "Barbarians" overlooks their positive contributions to the vigor of the Roman Empire, and his unfavorable assessment of Byzantine civilization has proven to be inadequate and distorted. In addition to his interpretations, Gibbon's methodology has aroused criticism. A major limitation in his approach lies in its one-sided reliance upon print sources, especially literary sources. Gibbon ignored such elements of historical evidence as manuscripts, archives, coins, medals, inscriptions, and monastic and civil records. In a sense, then, he simply synthesized what had already been known. Additionally, his attitude toward the sources he did use was uncritical. In this respect, Gibbon may be reproached with the charge of being unscientific. He is too much, in this view, an amateur dabbler lacking methodological discipline and rigor.

Furthermore, Gibbon may be said to lack true historical sense; as Porter explains, "Gibbon's prejudices fatally flawed his historical understanding." The eighteenth century, while strongly interested in history, tended to appropriate history for contemporary moral purposes. Based upon what might be described as a uniformitarian view of human nature, which posits that humans are essentially the same in all times and places, and that cultural differences are dispensable vestments, *The History of the Decline and Fall of the Roman Empire* fails to recognize truly, let alone discover, the essential difference of the ancient world from modern times. In this light, Gibbon's historical portraits must be seen more as expressions of eighteenth-century notions of human nature and psychology than as true historical figures. In other words, blinded by the cultural biases of his own age, Gibbon fails to penetrate his subject completely.

Apart from its literary merit and its value as a history, *The History of the Decline and Fall of the Roman Empire* finally must be reckoned important as a document of its times. J. G. A. Pocock's study *Barbarism and Religion* meticulously and complexly situates Gibbon in his historical context. As Parkinson notes in his 1973 study, *Edward Gibbon,* placing Gibbon within the intellectual and cultural milieu of eighteenth-century England establishes him as a representative example of the Enlightenment period. The coherent, orderly nature of

Gibbon's burial place, the Sheffield vault in the north transept of the Parish Church at Fletching, Sussex (from Gibbon's Miscellaneous
Works, *1814; reproduced in Joseph Ward Swain,* Edward Gibbon the Historian,
1966; Thomas Cooper Library, University of South Carolina)

Gibbon's style and the structure of *The History of the Decline and Fall of the Roman Empire* reveal his allegiance to the eighteenth-century ideals of decorum, politeness, and rationality. If *The History of the Decline and Fall of the Roman Empire* chronicles violence and anarchy, its modulated tone and elevated perspective envelop these ruptures within a balanced structure reflecting the eighteenth-century ideals of reason and order.

If Gibbon's allegiance to Enlightenment values and his subscription to an untenably essentialist view of human nature circumscribe his vision and limit the effectiveness of his historical project, they also offer him the strengths to undertake and accomplish what perhaps no modern historian would dream of attempting. *The History of the Decline and Fall of the Roman Empire* is one of the monuments of world historiography, taking its place among such classics as Thucydides's *History of the Peloponnesian War* (fifth century B.C.), Tacitus's *Annals* (first or second century), Francesco Guicciardini's *History of Italy* (sixteenth century), Jules Michelet's *History of France* (1833–1867), and Ranke's *History of the World* (1881–1888). Sophisticated, artful, and complex, *The*

History of the Decline and Fall of the Roman Empire has attracted and antagonized readers from Gibbon's day to the present. It was used as a history textbook in the nineteenth century, and knowledge of it has long been esteemed as the mark of an educated mind. Despite its apparent weaknesses as an historical document, the work continues to command formidable respect. As a literary artifact, *The History of the Decline and Fall of the Roman Empire* testifies to the culture of the Enlightenment and eighteenth-century Britain and one of the glories of eighteenth-century literary culture.

Letters:

J. E. Norton, ed. *The Letters of Edward Gibbon,* 3 volumes (London: Cassell, 1956).

Bibliographies:

Jane E. Norton, *Bibliography of the Works of Edward Gibbon* (New York: Burt Franklin, 1940);

Geoffrey Keynes, *The Library of Edward Gibbon: A Catalogue of His Books* (London: Bibliographic Society, 1950);

Patricia B. Craddock and Margaret Craddock Huff, *Edward Gibbon: A Reference Guide* (Boston: G. K. Hall, 1987).

Biographies:

David M. Low, *Edward Gibbon, 1737–1794* (London: Chatto & Windus, 1937);

G. M. Young, *Gibbon* (London: Rupert Hart-Davis, 1948);

Joseph Ward Swain, *Edward Gibbon the Historian* (New York: St. Martin's Press, 1966);

Gavin De Beer, *Gibbon and His World* (London: Thames & Hudson, 1968);

Patricia B. Craddock, *Young Edward Gibbon: Gentleman of Letters* (Baltimore: Johns Hopkins University Press, 1982);

J. W. Burrow, *Gibbon* (Oxford: Oxford University Press, 1985);

Craddock, *Edward Gibbon: Luminous Historian, 1772–1794* (Baltimore: Johns Hopkins University Press, 1989).

References:

Harold L. Bond, *The Literary Art of Edward Gibbon* (Oxford: Clarendon Press, 1960);

G. W. Bowerstock, John Clive, and Stephen R. Graubard, eds., *Edward Gibbon and The Decline and Fall of the Roman Empire* (Cambridge, Mass.: Harvard University Press, 1977);

Leo Braudy, *Narrative Form in History and Fiction* (Princeton, N.J.: Princeton University Press, 1971);

Martine Watson Brownley, "Appearance and Reality in Gibbon's History," *Journal of the History of Ideas*, 38 (1977): 651–666;

Brownley, "Gibbon's Artistic and Historical Scope in *The Decline and Fall*," *Journal of the History of Ideas*, 42 (1981): 629–642;

Brownley, "Gibbon's *Memoirs*: The Legacy of the Historian," *Studies on Voltaire and the Eighteenth Century*, 201 (1982): 209–220;

Brownley, "The Theatrical World of the 'Decline and Fall,'" *Papers on Language and Literature*, 15 (1979): 263–277;

W. B. Carnochan, *Gibbon's Solitude: The Inward World of the Historian* (Stanford: Stanford University Press, 1987);

A. O. J. Cockshut and Stephen Constantine, *Edward Gibbon* (New York: Columbia University Press, 1998);

Peter Cosgrove, *Impartial Stranger: History and Intertextuality in Gibbon's Decline and Fall of the Roman Empire* (Newark: University of Delaware Press, 1999);

Patricia B. Craddock, "Edward Gibbon (1737–1794)," in *Medieval Scholarship: Bibliographical Studies on the*

Formation of a Discipline (New York: Garland, 1995), pp. 47–61;

Craddock, "Historical Discovery and Literary Invention in Gibbon's *Decline and Fall*," *Modern Philology*, 85 (1988): 569–587;

Craddock, "'Immortal Affectation': Responses to Gibbon's Style," in *The Age of Johnson*, edited by Paul J. Korshin (New York: AMS Press, 1987), pp. 327–346;

H. T. Dickinson, "The Politics of Edward Gibbon," *Literature and History*, 8 (1978): 175–196;

Oliver Elton, *Gibbon and Rome* (New York: Sheed & Ward, 1958);

Per Fuglum, *Edward Gibbon, His View of Life and Conception of History* (Oxford: Blackwell, 1953);

James Garrison, "Gibbon and 'the treacherous language of panegyrics,'" *Eighteenth Century Studies* (Fall 1977): 40–62;

Garrison, "Lively and Laborious: Characterization in Gibbon's Metahistory," *Modern Philology* (November 1978): 163–178;

Peter Gay, *Style in History* (New York: Basic Books, 1974);

Lionel Gossman, *The Empire Unpossess'd* (Cambridge: Cambridge University Press, 1981);

G. J. Gruman, "Balance and Excess as Gibbon's Explanation of the Decline and Fall," *History and Theory*, 1 (1960): 75–85;

David P. Jordan, *Gibbon and His Roman Empire* (Champagne-Urbana: University of Illinois Press, 1971);

A. Lentin, "Edward Gibbon and the Golden Age of the Antonines," *History Today* (July 1981): 33–37;

Shelby McCloy, *Gibbon's Antagonism to Christianity* (Chapel Hill: University of North Carolina Press, 1933);

Rosamond McKitterick and Roland Quinault, eds., *Edward Gibbon and Empire* (Cambridge: Cambridge University Press, 1997);

Frank Palmieri, "History as Monument: Gibbon's *Decline and Fall*," *Studies in Eighteenth-Century Culture*, 19 (1989): 225–245;

Catherine N. Parke, "Edward Gibbon by Edward Gibbon," *Modern Language Quarterly*, 50 (1989): 23–37;

Richard N. Parkinson, *Edward Gibbon* (New York: Twayne, 1973);

J. G. A. Pocock, *Barbarism and Religion*, 2 volumes (Cambridge: Cambridge University Press, 1999);

Pocock, "Gibbon's *Decline and Fall* and the World View of the Eighteenth-Century Enlightenment," *Eighteenth-Century Studies*, 8 (1982): 287–303;

Pocock, "Superstition and Enthusiasm in Gibbon's History of Religion," *Eighteenth-Century Life*, 10 (1977): 83–94;

Roy Porter, *Edward Gibbon: Making History* (London: Weidenfeld & Nicolson, 1988);

Hugh Trevor-Roper, "Gibbon and the Publication of *The Decline and Fall of the Roman Empire, 1776–1976*," *Journal of Law and Economics,* 19 (October 1977): 489–505;

Trevor-Roper, "The Historical Philosophy of the Enlightenment," *Studies on Voltaire and the Eighteenth Century,* 27 (1963): 1667–1687;

Trevor-Roper, "Introduction," *The Decline and Fall of the Roman Empire and Other Selected Writings* (New York: Twayne, 1963);

Paul Turnbull, "The Supposed Infidelity of Edward Gibbon," *The Historical Journal,* 5 (1982): 23–51;

Lynn T. White, ed., *The Transformations of the Roman World, Gibbon's Problem after Two Centuries* (Berkeley: University of California Press, 1966);

David Womersley, *Gibbon and the 'Watchmen of the Holy City': The Historian and his Reputation, 1776–1815* (Oxford: Clarendon Press, 2002);

Womersley, *The Transformation of The Decline and Fall of the Roman Empire* (Cambridge: Cambridge University Press, 1988);

Womersley, ed. *Edward Gibbon: Bicentenary Essays* (Oxford: Voltaire Foundation, 1997).

Papers:

The most important collection of Edward Gibbon's papers is that in the British Library, formerly the property of Lord Sheffield. Another extensive collection, formerly the property of the Sévery family, is in the Archives Cantonales Vaudoises in Lausanne. Smaller but important are holdings in the Pierpont Morgan Library, New York City, and the Magdalen College Library, Oxford. An important collection of Lord Sheffield's papers, including the correspondence concerned with the publication of the *Miscellaneous Works,* and an interleaved copy of the first edition, used in preparing the second, is at the Beinecke Library of Yale University. Other papers of Lord Sheffield are in the East Sussex Record Office. Many books once in Gibbon's library, a few with marginal annotations by the historian, are in the King's College Library, Cambridge University.

William Godwin

(3 March 1756 – 7 April 1836)

Rowland Weston
University of Waikato

See also the Godwin entries in *DLB 39: British Novelists, 1660–1800; DLB 104: British Prose Writers, 1660–1800, Second Series; DLB 142: Eighteenth-Century British Literary Biographers; DLB 158: British Reform Writers, 1789–1832; DLB 163: British Children's Writers, 1800–1880;* and *DLB 262: British Philosophers, 1800–2000.*

BOOKS: *The History of the Life of William Pitt, Earl of Chatham,* anonymous (London: G. Kearsley, 1783);

A Defence of the Rockingham Party, in Their Late Coalition with the Right Honorable Frederic Lord North, anonymous (London: J. Stockdale, 1783); reprinted in *Four Early Pamphlets, 1783–1784,* edited by Burton R. Pollin (Gainesville, Fla.: Scholars' Facsimiles and Reprints, 1966);

An Account of the Seminary That Will Be Opened on Monday the Fourth Day of August, at Epsom in Surrey, for the Instruction of Twelve Pupils in the Greek, Latin, French, and English Languages, anonymous (London: T. Cadell, 1783); reprinted in *Four Early Pamphlets, 1783–1784;*

Sketches of History, in Six Sermons, some copies anonymous (London: T. Cadell, 1784); as Godwin (Alexandria, Va., 1801);

The Herald of Literature: or, A Review of the Most Considerable Publications That Will Be Made in the Course of the Ensuing Winter: With Extracts, anonymous (London: J. Murray, 1784); facsimile in *Four Early Pamphlets, 1783–1784;*

Instructions to a Statesman. Humbly Inscribed to the Right Honourable George Earl Temple, anonymous (London: J. Murray, J. Debrett & J. Sewell, 1784); facsimile in *Four Early Pamphlets, 1783–1784;*

Damon and Delia: A Tale, anonymous (London: T. Hookham, 1784);

Italian Letters; or, The History of the Count de St. Julian, 2 volumes, anonymous (London: G. Robinson, 1784; Lincoln: University of Nebraska Press, 1965);

William Godwin (engraving by P. Roberts; National Portrait Gallery, London);

Imogen: A Pastoral Romance. From the Ancient British, 2 volumes, anonymous (London: W. Lane, 1784; New York: New York Public Library, 1963);

The History of the Internal Affairs of the United Provinces, from the Year 1780, to the Commencement of Hostilities in June 1787, anonymous (London: G. G. J. & J. Robinson, 1787);

The English Peerage; or, A View of the Ancient and Present State of the English Nobility, 3 volumes, anonymous (London: G. G. & J. Robinson, 1790);

An Enquiry concerning Political Justice, and Its Influence on General Virtue and Happiness, 2 volumes (London: G. G. J. & J. Robinson, 1793); revised as *Enquiry concerning Political Justice, and its Influence on Morals and Happiness,* 2 volumes (London: G. G. & J. Robinson, 1796; revised, 1798; 2 volumes, Philadelphia: Bioren & Madan, 1796);

Things As They Are; or, The Adventures of Caleb Williams (3 volumes, London: B. Crosby, 1794; 2 volumes, Baltimore: H. & P. Rice, 1795; revised edition, 3 volumes, London: G. G. & J. Robinson, 1796; revised again, 3 volumes, 1797); revised as *Caleb Williams* (1 volume, London: H. Colburn & R. Bentley, 1831, 2 volumes; New York: Harper, 1831);

Cursory Strictures on the Charge Delivered by Lord Chief Justice Eyre to the Grand Jury, October 2, 1794, anonymous (London: D. I. Eaton, 1794); reprinted in *Uncollected Writings (1785–1832),* edited by Jack W. Marken and Pollin (Gainesville, Fla.: Scholars' Facsimiles and Reprints, 1968);

A Reply to an Answer to Cursory Strictures, Supposed to Be Wrote by Judge Buller. By the Author of Cursory Strictures, anonymous (London: D. I. Eaton, 1794);

Considerations on Lord Grenville's and Mr. Pitt's Bills, concerning Treasonable and Seditious Practices, and Unlawful Assemblies. By a Lover of Order, anonymous (London: J. Johnson, 1795); reprinted in *Uncollected Writings (1785–1832);*

The Enquirer. Reflections on Education, Manners, and Literature. In a Series of Essays (London: G. G. & J. Robinson, 1797; Philadelphia: Robert Campbell, 1797; revised edition, Edinburgh: John Anderson / London: W. Simkin & R. Marshal, 1823);

Memoirs of the Author of A Vindication of the Rights of Woman (London: J. Johnson/G. G. & J. Robinson, 1798; revised edition, London: J. Johnson, 1798); republished as *Memoirs of Mary Wollstonecraft Godwin, Author of "A Vindication of the Rights of Woman"* (Philadelphia: James Carey, 1799);

St. Leon: A Tale of the Sixteenth Century (4 volumes, London: G. G. & J. Robinson, 1799; 2 volumes, Alexandria, Va.: J. & J. D. Westcott, 1801; revised, 1 volume, London: H. Colburn & R. Bentley, 1831);

Antonio: A Tragedy in Five Acts (London: G. G. & J. Robinson, 1800; New York: D. Longworth, 1806);

Thoughts. Occasioned by the Perusal of Dr Parr's Spital Sermon, Preached at Christ Church, April 15, 1800: Being a Reply to the Attacks of Dr Parr, Mr Mackintosh, the Author of an Essay on Population, and Others (London: G. G. & J. Robinson, 1801); reprinted in *Uncollected Writings (1785–1832);*

Bible Stories. Memorable Acts of the Ancient Patriarchs, Judges, and Kings: Extracted from Their Original Historians. For the Use of Children, 2 volumes, as William Scholfield (London: R. Phillips, 1802; Albany, N.Y.: Charles R. & George Webster, 1803); republished as *Sacred Histories; or, Insulated Bible Stories,* 2 volumes (London: R. Phillips, 1806);

Life of Geoffrey Chaucer: The Early English Poet: Including Memoirs of his Near Friend and Kinsman, John of Gaunt, Duke of Lancaster: With Sketches of the Manners, Opinions, Arts and Literature of England in the Fourteenth Century, 2 volumes (London: R. Phillips, 1803);

Fleetwood; or, The New Man of Feeling (3 volumes, London: R. Phillips, 1805; 2 volumes, New York: I. Riley, 1805; Alexandria, Va.: Cotton & Stewart, 1805; revised edition, 1 volume, London: R. Bentley, 1832);

Fables, Ancient and Modern. Adapted for the Use of Children, 2 volumes, as Edward Baldwin (London: T. Hodgkins, 1805; New York: Increase Cooke, 1807);

The Looking Glass: A True History of the Early Years of an Artist. Calculated to Awaken the Emulation of Young Persons of Both Sexes, in the Pursuit of Every Laudable Attainment: Particularly in the Cultivation of the Fine Arts, as Theophilus Marcliffe (London: T. Hodgkins, 1805);

The Life of Lady Jane Grey, and of Lord Guildford Dudley, Her Husband, as Theophilus Marcliffe (London: T. Hodgkins, 1806);

The History of England. For the Use of Schools and Young Persons, as Edward Baldwin (London: T. Hodgkins, 1806);

The Pantheon; or, Ancient History of the Gods of Greece and Rome. Intended to Facilitate the Understanding of the Classical Authors, and of the Poets in General, as Edward Baldwin (London: T. Hodgkins, 1806); edited by Burton Feldman (New York: Garland, 1984);

Faulkener, A Tragedy by Godwin, Daniel Defoe, Charles Lamb, and others (London: R. Phillips, 1807);

Essay on Sepulchres; or, A Proposal for Erecting Some Memorial of the Illustrious Dead in All Ages on the Spot Where Their Remains Have Been Interred (London: W. Miller, 1809; New York: M. & W. Ward, 1809);

The History of Rome: From the Building of the City to the Ruin of the Republic, as Edward Baldwin (London: M. J. Godwin, 1809);

Outlines of English History, Chiefly Abstracted from the History of England, For the Use of Children from Four to Eight Years of Age, as Edward Baldwin (London: Printed for M. J. Godwin, 1810);

Lives of Edward and John Philips. Nephews and Pupils of Milton. Including Various Particulars of the Literary and Political History of their Times (London: Longman, Hurst, Rees, Orme & Brown, 1815);

Letters of Verax, to the Editor of the Morning Chronicle, on the Question of a War to be Commenced for the Purpose of Putting an End to the Possession of Supreme Power in France by Napoleon Bonaparte (London: R. & A. Taylor, 1815); reprinted in *Uncollected Writings (1785–1832)*;

Mandeville. A Tale of the Seventeenth Century in England (3 volumes, Edinburgh: A. Constable / London: Longman, Hurst, Rees, Orme & Brown, 1817; 2 volumes, New York: W. B. Gilley / Philadelphia: M. Thomas, 1818);

Letter of Advice to a Young American: On the Course of Studies It Might Be Most Advantageous for Him to Pursue (London: M. J. Godwin, 1818); reprinted in *Uncollected Writings (1785–1832)*;

Of Population. An Enquiry concerning the Power of Increase in the Numbers of Mankind, Being an Answer to Mr. Malthus's Essay on That Subject (London: Longman, Hurst, Rees, Orme & Brown, 1820; New York: Augustus M. Kelley, 1964);

The History of Greece: From the Earliest Records of That Country to the Time in Which it Was Reduced into a Roman Province, as Edward Baldwin (London: M. J. Godwin, 1821);

History of the Commonwealth of England. From Its Commencement, to the Restoration of Charles the Second, 4 volumes (London: H. Colburn, 1824–1828);

Cloudesley: A Tale (3 volumes, London: H. Colburn & R. Bentley, 1830; 2 volumes, New York: Harper / Albany, N.Y.: O. Steele/Little & Cummings, 1830);

Thoughts on Man, His Nature, Productions and Discoveries. Interspersed with Some Particulars Respecting the Author (London: Effingham Wilson, 1831; New York: Augustus M. Kelley, 1969);

Deloraine (3 volumes, London: R. Bentley, 1833; 2 volumes, Philadelphia: Carey, Lea & Blanchard, 1833);

Lives of the Necromancers; or, An Account of the Most Eminent Persons in Successive Ages, Who Have Claimed for Themselves, or to Whom Has Been Imputed by Others, the Exercise of Magical Powers (London: F. J. Mason, 1834; New York: Harper, 1835);

Essays, Never before Published, by the Late William Godwin, edited by C. Kegan Paul (London: H. S. King, 1873);

The Elopement of Percy Bysshe Shelley and Mary Wollstonecraft Godwin, as Narrated by William Godwin, edited by H. Buxton Forman (London: Bibliophile Society, 1911; Boston, Mass.: Privately printed, 1912).

Editions and Collections: *Memoirs of Mary Wollstonecraft,* edited by W. Clark Durant (London: Constable, 1927; New York: Greenberg, 1927);

Memoirs of Mary Wollstonecraft, with a preface by John Middleton Murray (London: Constable, 1928; New York: R. R. Smith, 1930);

Enquiry concerning Political Justice, and Its Influence on Morals and Happiness, facsimile of the third edition corrected, edited with variant readings of the first and second editions, and with a critical introduction and notes by F. E. L. Priestly, 3 volumes (Toronto: University of Toronto Press, 1946);

Four Early Pamphlets (1783–1784), edited by Pollin (Gainesville, Fla.: Scholars' Facsimiles and Reprints, 1966);

Uncollected Writings (1785–1832), edited by Jack W. Marken and Barton R. Pollin (Gainesville, Fla.: Scholars' Facsimiles and Reprints, 1968);

Caleb Williams, edited by David McCracken (Oxford: Oxford University Press, 1970; revised, 1982);

Enquiry concerning Political Justice and Its Influence on Modern Morals and Happiness, edited by Isaac Kramnick (London: Penguin, 1976);

Things As They Are; or, The Adventures of Caleb Williams, edited by Maurice Hindle (London: Penguin, 1988);

The Collected Novels and Memoirs of William Godwin, 8 volumes, edited by Mark Philp, Pamela Clemit, and Hindle (London: Pickering & Chatto, 1992);

The Political and Philosophical Writings of William Godwin, 7 volumes, edited by Philp, Clemit, and Martin Fitzpatrick (London: Pickering & Chatto, 1993);

St. Leon: A Tale of the Sixteenth Century, edited by Clemit (Oxford: Oxford University Press, 1994);

Fleetwood; or, The New Man of Feeling, edited by Gary Handwerk and A. A. Markley (Peterborough, Ont. & Orchard Park, N. Y.: Broadview, 2001);

Memoirs of the Author of A Vindication of the Rights of Woman, edited by Clemit and Gina Luria Walker (Peterborough, Ont.: Broadview, 2001);

History of the Commonwealth of England: From the Commencement, to the Restoration of Charles the Second (Bristol: Thoemmes, 2003).

OTHER: Simon Fraser Lovat, *Memoirs of the Life of Simon Lord Lovat,* translated by Godwin (London: G. Nichol, 1797);

Mary Wollstonecraft, *Posthumous Works of the Author of A Vindication of the Rights of Woman,* 4 volumes, edited by Godwin (London: J. Johnson, 1798);

Outlines of English Grammar, Partly Abridged from Hazlitt's New and Improved Grammar of the English Tongue, edited by Godwin as Edward Baldwin (London: M. J. Godwin, 1810);

William Frederick Mylius and Godwin, as Edward
Baldwin, *Mylius's School Dictionary of the English Lan-
guage. To Which Is Prefixed A New Guide to the English
Tongue* (London: M. J. Godwin, 1819);

Mary Shelley, *Valperga; or, The Life and Adventures of
Castruccio, Prince of Lucca,* revised by Godwin (London: G. & B. W. Whittaker, 1823);

Preface, *Transfusion; or, The Orphans of Unwalden, by the late
William Godwin Jun.,* 3 volumes (London: J.
Macrone, 1835; New York: Wallis & Newell,
1836);

"The Moral Effects of Aristocracy," in William Hazlitt,
The Spirit of Monarchy (London: Wakelin, 1835).

Over a long and productive literary career, William Godwin wrote novels, biographies, works of philosophy, pedagogy, political commentary, and
children's literature. He also wrote significant histories
of fourteenth- and seventeenth-century England: *Life of
Geoffrey Chaucer: The Early English Poet: Including Memoirs of
his Near Friend and Kinsman, John of Gaunt, Duke of Lancaster: With Sketches of the Manners, Opinions, Arts and Literature of England in the Fourteenth Century* (1803) and *History
of the Commonwealth of England. From Its Commencement, to
the Restoration of Charles the Second* (1824–1828). Yet, modern scholars have focused most attention on two works
that first appeared in the midst of the intense moral and
political debate created by the French Revolution. *An
Enquiry concerning Political Justice, and Its Influence on General
Virtue and Happiness* (1793) is often regarded as the first
systematic anarchist text in the Western tradition. The
novel *Things As They Are; or, The Adventures of Caleb Williams* not only caused a sensation when it first appeared
in 1794, but also has subsequently been regarded as a
pioneer in the genres of the detective novel and the psychological thriller. Yet, almost all Godwin's vast and
varied literary output reveals an intense fascination for
the past and an ongoing concern with the nature and
function of historical writing. His fiction often employs
historical settings in order to provide striking and
unusual illustrations of contemporary political and
ideological issues, and to explore the historical origins
of contemporary problems. His educational writings, as
well as his books for children, are underpinned by the
conviction that history provides the best source of
moral instruction. His mammoth works of fourteenth-
and seventeenth-century English history, above all, make
Godwin a notable, albeit underrated, eighteenth-century
British historian.

Born on 3 March 1756 in Wisbech, Cambridgeshire, Godwin was the seventh of thirteen children. Both his father and his paternal grandfather were
Nonconformist, or Dissenting, ministers. Theological
descendants of sixteenth- and seventeenth-century Puri-

tans, Dissenters, along with Roman Catholics, were
marginalized by mainstream English life in the eighteenth century. Unable to take degrees at the two
English universities or to attain civil service posts and
commissions in the military, English Dissenters were
effectively second-class citizens who nonetheless maintained proud and conscious links to their Puritan forebears.

Because of disputes with his congregation—a not
uncommon phenomenon in Dissenting life—Godwin's
father moved the family twice in William's infancy, first
to Debenham in Suffolk and then to Guestwick in Norfolk. Godwin's earliest reading included typical Nonconformist fare such as John Bunyan's *Pilgrim's Progress*
(1678, 1684) and James Janeway's *A Token for Children:
Being an Exact Account of the Conversion, Holy and Exemplary
Lives and Joyful Deaths of Several Young Children* (1671–
1672). By the age of eight he was well versed in the
Christian Scriptures. His temper of mind was serious in
the extreme and gravitated readily to his father's Cal-
vinism. Godwin fixed on the idea of becoming a minister and took every opportunity to practice his calling on
available family and friends. In 1764 he attended school
in nearby Hindolveston, and in 1767 he was sent to
Norwich, where for three years he was the sole pupil of
Nonconformist minister Samuel Newton. Newton subscribed to a theological refinement of mainstream Cal-
vinism—Sandemanianism. This sect emphasized the
sovereignty and holiness of God and the wretchedness
of humanity, the importance of open debate in the pursuit of truth and consensus, and the subservience of the
emotions to the intellect. A brutal, bigoted, and despotic
man, Newton nonetheless exercised an enormous influence on Godwin, and the tenets of Sandemanianism
became an essential part of Godwin's belief system.
Godwin later reflected that his sober and serious adult
character was essentially fixed by this hyper-Calvinist
upbringing. He also noted the formative effect on his
character of the praise for his intellectual abilities he
received as a child (although not, significantly, from his
parents). To these influences he added a third—his reading of Charles Rollin's *Ancient History* (1730–1738) as a
twelve-year-old. He recalled how he would secretly
avail himself of Newton's library in order to indulge
this passion. It awakened in him a love of republican
Greece and Rome, which persisted his entire life. Upon
finishing his time with Newton, in 1772 Godwin
returned to his old school in Hindolveston as an usher,
or assistant teacher.

A young man of obvious ability, Godwin was des-
tined to attend one of the academies that had been
established to provide higher education for Dissenters.
In 1773, after being rejected by Homerton Dissenting
Academy, which feared his Sandemanianism, Godwin

was accepted by Hoxton College in London, where he remained until 1778. Hoxton was one of the best of the Dissenting academies and more recognizably modern in its curriculum than the established universities. The teaching staff included Abraham Rees, a renowned encyclopedist, and biographer Andrew Kippis, who, typically for Dissenters of a modernistic or rationalistic turn, advanced a conception of history as a process of gradual enlightenment. As well as tackling a formidable curriculum, which included philosophy, theology, Classics, mathematics, Hebrew, and history, Godwin imposed upon himself a strenuous regime of extracurricular reading in philosophy and theology. By the time of his graduation from Hoxton in May 1788, Godwin had the outlook of a "Rational Dissenter." Rational Dissent—as embodied by men such as Rees, Kippis, and scientist, theologian, philosopher, and historian Joseph Priestley—maintained its historical connections to old Dissent, but was more sympathetic to the philosophical and scientific developments of the Enlightenment, and was especially given to the pursuit of political reform, religious toleration, and the safeguarding of individual conscience.

Godwin's first ministerial post was at Ware in Hertfordshire, where he met Joseph Fawcett, another Dissenting minister, who was devoted to American theologian Jonathan Edwards and Anglo-Irish politician and philosopher Edmund Burke. After a disagreement with his congregation, Godwin left Ware and spent four months in London in late 1779. There he closely followed parliamentary debates on the American Revolution and became a staunch supporter of Burke and Charles James Fox, and of secessionist Americans. In 1780 Godwin moved to a job as minister at Stowmarket in Suffolk, where he made the acquaintance of a tradesman, Frederick Norman. Norman was greatly interested in French philosophy and introduced Godwin to it. Reading on this subject profoundly affected Godwin's faith. In particular, Paul Henri Thiry, baron d'Holbach's *Système de la Nature* (1770) encouraged him into a brief flirtation with Deism before he relapsed into Socinianism—a sect affirming belief in God but denying the divinity of Christ. At this time Godwin was also influenced by the writings of satirist Jonathan Swift. Godwin later noted that reading Swift's works and that of the Roman historians sealed his conversion to republicanism, thus putting a final end to the conservative political convictions he had formed under the tutorship of Newton. In April 1782 Godwin once again left his living after a dispute with his congregation and returned to London, where he commenced a brief and unsuccessful career as a full-time author. During this time he commenced work on a biography of William Pitt the Elder, former prime minister (1756–1761). This

Title page for Godwin's biography of the British prime minister (from Eighteenth-Century Collections Online, Gale Group)

work appeared anonymously on 20 January 1783, by which time Godwin was again working in the ministry, this time at Beaconsfield in Buckinghamshire. *The History of the Life of William Pitt, Earl of Chatham* (1783) went through four editions. Godwin sent a complimentary and, it appears, unacknowledged copy to Burke.

Again, Godwin's unorthodoxy caused concern among his congregation, and in June 1783 he quit the ministry for good, returning to London, where he took up journalistic work and hackwork. His initial employment in London consisted of piecework for *The English Review* at two guineas a sheet—a guaranteed annual income of, at best, twenty-four guineas. At this time Godwin also quickly wrote three generally unremarkable novels and published *An Account of the Seminary That Will Be Opened on Monday the Fourth Day of August, at Epsom in Surrey, for the Instruction of Twelve Pupils in the Greek, Latin, French, and English Languages* (1783). The project itself was never realized, but the essay is of significance because it details Godwin's abiding conviction that moral knowledge ought to be the objective of all education and that it is best attained through the study of history conceived primarily as a "science of character and biography." The essay especially advocates introducing students to the "noble freedom of mind" that was characteristic of the republicans of ancient Greece and Rome, and that has, Godwin insists, "scarcely any parallel among ourselves." As was typical of Britons of his time and political sympathies, Godwin contrasts the stoical, civic virtue of republican Greece and Rome with the moral laxity and self-interest of contemporary British society.

In *The Herald of Literature: or, A Review of the Most Considerable Publications That Will Be Made in the Course of the Ensuing Winter: With Extracts,* published on 17 November 1784, Godwin "reviewed" nonexistent later volumes of William Robertson's *The History of America* (1777) and Edward Gibbon's *The History of the Decline and Fall of the Roman Empire* (1776–1788). So plausibly did Godwin create sizable excerpts for quotation that many of his contemporaries (as well as later scholars) were duped. In his *Sketches of History, in Six Sermons* (1784) Godwin published several of his sermons in which biblical events and personalities—deprived of their specifically spiritual resonance—are used to draw generally uncontentious moral lessons.

None of these works met with success, and times were financially difficult for Godwin. From July 1784, at the suggestion of his former tutor Kippis, Godwin became "historical" writer for the liberal periodical *The New Annual Register.* He was paid an annual salary of sixty guineas. The position required·that he keep abreast of contemporary political issues and events and, where necessary, explain their historical background. Such regular employment marked a definite improvement in Godwin's pecuniary situation, and he was no longer required to make his daily visit to the pawnbroker in order to pay for food. Between 1783 and 1785 he also reviewed books for *The English Review.* Godwin's income was further, albeit briefly, supplemented when he was invited to contribute to the *Political Herald,* a journal established in 1785 by leading men among the Whig opposition.

In 1786 Godwin made the important acquaintance of autodidact former-shoemaker, now journalist, translator, novelist, and dramatist Thomas Holcroft. The two later became firm friends. In 1787 Godwin published anonymously his *History of the Internal Affairs of the United Provinces, from the Year 1780, to the Commencement of Hostilities in June 1787.* More a political than an historical work, it was drawn in large part from Godwin's recent articles on Dutch history in *The New Annual Regis-*

ter. In this survey of the contention between the stadtholder and the Dutch states, Godwin defends the aristocratic and democratic alliance against the stadtholder, William V. The work appeared in September 1787 and was, in the main, well reviewed.

After a full year's work, Godwin anonymously published *The English Peerage; or, A View of the Ancient and Present State of the English Nobility* (1790). Doubtless with an eye to its limited potential readership, he insists that the best in English history could be seen encapsulated in the English nobility. Before he had completed this work, however, the aristocracy of Europe was shaken by revolution in France. For Britons of liberal, reformist, or democratic leanings, the French Revolution was an event of thrilling moment, evidencing the progressive march of human history toward a new era of justice, freedom, and enlightenment. This enthusiasm was well summed up in *A Discourse on the Love of Our Country,* Dissenting minister Richard Price's address on 4 November 1789 to the London Revolution Society. The Revolution Society had been established to commemorate the Glorious Revolution of 1688, an event to which most Britons attributed their renowned liberties and distinctively balanced constitution. Price spoke for many in the polity, especially those of a liberal, Dissenting background, when he claimed that events in France were part of a progressive historical process with its antecedents in the Glorious and the American Revolutions.

One who was outraged by Price's equation of the French Revolution with both the Glorious Revolution and the more recent American Revolution was Burke. Consequently, on 1 November 1790 Burke published a scathing critique of Price's revolutionary sentiments in *Reflections on the Revolution in France.* In its turn, Burke's book provoked a flood of rejoinders, notably Mary Wollstonecraft's *A Vindication of the Rights of Men* (1790) and Thomas Paine's *Rights of Man* (1791). Godwin and Wollstonecraft met on 13 November 1791 at the home of publisher Joseph Johnson, where a dinner had been organized in Paine's honor. Keen to converse with Paine, Godwin found Wollstonecraft annoying and intrusive. She was similarly unimpressed. In January of 1792 Wollstonecraft's extension of the libertarian doctrines of her earlier work to the female sex appeared in her pioneering feminist tract *A Vindication of the Rights of Woman* (1792).

In the midst of this heated discussion of political fundamentals, Godwin approached publisher George Robinson for an advance, in order to devote himself full-time to writing the definitive treatment of the topic. Robinson agreed to pay Godwin's expenses and a fee of one thousand guineas. Godwin gave up his work for *The New Annual Register* and on 4 September 1791 began writing a treatise on political philosophy conceived, partially at least, in answer to Burke. During this time he was heavily influenced by Holcroft, and he also met novelist Elizabeth Inchbald, philologist John Horne Tooke, and Scottish writer Sir James Mackintosh, author of the anti-Burke polemic *Vindicae Gallicae* (1791).

An Enquiry concerning Political Justice, and Its Influence on General Virtue and Happiness was published on 14 February 1793, with subsequent, substantially revised editions appearing in 1796 and 1798. The work was not just a biting critique of existing aristocratic and monarchic governments; ultimately, it condemned all forms of government for their inescapable tendency to override and undermine individual private judgment. Indeed, as both Mark Philp and George Crowder argue, this emphasis on the inviolability of private judgment is the key, cohering tenet of *An Enquiry concerning Political Justice* and betrays Godwin's ongoing indebtedness to the culture of Rational Dissent. For Godwin, the right of private judgment is not only essential to personal integrity but is also a precondition for social utility, since truly just outcomes can only occur when individuals judge each particular moral case on its merits. Correct moral action, then, depends upon rational calculations of utility arrived at independently of the dictates of existing moral, legal, or religious codes or the promptings of habit and instinct. Godwin memorably illustrates his point in the Fénelon Fire Case. He argues that if one has the opportunity to save either a member of one's family or the great author and social critic Archbishop Fénelon from a burning house, then reason dictates that one saves the archbishop, for his survival would, in all likelihood, confer greater benefits on humanity. This repudiation of familial instincts and emotions or "domestic affections" as inimical to personal independence contributed most to Godwin's subsequent reputation as an unfeeling arch rationalist.

In *An Enquiry concerning Political Justice,* Godwin maintains that the greatest danger to private judgment comes through government. One reason is that subjects are often coerced by force or the threat of force into acting against the dictates of their own judgment or conscience. Also, governments condition and modify the personalities of their subjects in myriad imperceptible, but pervasive, ways. Drawing on the psychological and political theories of John Locke and Charles-Louis de Secondat, Baron de Montesquieu, Godwin insists that all government is both constituted by and productive of particular intellectual qualities in its subject peoples. "Government," he constantly asserts, "is founded in opinion." Yet, this reciprocal relationship is not an entirely closed or static system. For changes in ideas can occur independently of the prevailing political institution, and these will inevitably cause related changes in

government. While Godwin remains convinced that the disappearance of all government represents the appropriate end of political evolution, he favors democracy as an interim measure en route to this anarchist end, for democracy helps inculcate and extend the independent habits of mind ideally possessed by all individuals.

As a distillation, extension, and popularization of late Enlightenment preoccupations, *An Enquiry concerning Political Justice* assumed an extreme version of extant Rationalist views of history evident—implicitly or explicitly—in the writings of historians such as Giambattista Vico, Voltaire, David Hume, Robertson, and Gibbon. Godwin claims in *An Enquiry concerning Political Justice* that the ancient republics of Greece and Rome represent a political and intellectual high point from which subsequent cultures have descended. Godwin—and many of his Rationalist forebears and contemporaries—thought that this ensuing "dark age" had been perpetuated, if not caused, by the medieval Catholic Church. Moreover, like most Rationalists, Godwin asserts that the fifteenth-century revival of letters or Renaissance marked the advent of a new, progressive era of intellectual and political liberty, which promised not only to reclaim, but eventually to surpass, the achievements of Greece and Rome.

An Enquiry concerning Political Justice caused a sensation when it appeared: three thousand copies of the first edition were quickly sold. As Godwin's fellow Dissenter, essayist William Hazlitt—whom Godwin met in 1794—later reflected in *The Spirit of the Age: or, Contemporary Portraits,* "No work in our time gave such a blow to the philosophical mind of the country as the celebrated *An Enquiry concerning Political Justice.* Tom Paine was considered for the time as a Tom Fool to him, Paley an old woman, Edmund Burke a flashy sophist. Truth, moral truth, it was supposed, had here taken up its abode; and these were the oracles of thought." Paine's *Rights of Man* had been banned by an increasingly paranoid and repressive government in May 1792; and scholars such as Peter H. Marshall and William St. Clair remark that Godwin's much larger work might have received the same treatment had the authorities not been convinced that its high cost would keep it out of the hands of those most likely to be influenced by its radical message. Although many readers would not have condoned the more radical sentiments of the work, *An Enquiry concerning Political Justice* was well reviewed in the main. Only the conservative periodical *The British Critic* condemned it outright. The work certainly attracted the attention of both conservatives and the young and radically inclined, including poets Robert Southey, William Wordsworth, and Samuel Taylor Coleridge.

In the immediate aftermath of the publication of the first edition of *An Enquiry concerning Political Justice,*

Godwin's reputation was at its height. To the astonishment of the reading public, Godwin then produced an equally feted novel, *Things As They Are; or, The Adventures of Caleb Williams*. A tale of oppression, injustice, and the capacity of political structures to infiltrate and modify the personalities of all subjects, the novel was a deliberate attempt to deliver the arguments of *An Enquiry concerning Political Justice* in a more accessible form. By this time Britain was at war with France. With mounting fear of pro-French subversion in Britain, government pressure rose to formally silence dissent. The mode arrived at was the charge of treason as laid by Lord Chief Justice Eyre, with treason defined as any intention to alter Parliament through nonconstitutional means. On 12 May 1794 twelve of the leaders of the radical "movement" in London were arrested; they were then to be tried for treason. The accused included Godwin's friends Holcroft, Horne Tooke, and journalist and political activist John Thelwall. Godwin's anonymous piece *Cursory Strictures on the Charge Delivered by Lord Chief Justice Eyre to the Grand Jury, October 2, 1794* (1794) was of great importance in securing their acquittal. This work was published in *The Morning Chronicle* and later released as a separate pamphlet. Godwin's work was instrumental not only in securing the acquittal of those on trial but also in staying the prosecution of potentially hundreds of others. Marshall, in *William Godwin,* claims the decision was a landmark in British judicial history, establishing that treason could not be constituted by what a person "said and wrote."

In January 1796 Godwin and Wollstonecraft met again, this time at the house of novelist, biographer, and historian Mary Hays. In complete contrast to their previous meeting, the two on this occasion felt an immediate, mutual attraction. A sexual relationship soon developed. Wollstonecraft became pregnant, and the two were married in March 1797. Godwin thus acquired a daughter, Fanny Imlay, Wollstonecraft's illegitimate child by American diplomat and businessman Gilbert Imlay. This period was the happiest of Godwin's life; scholars such as Mitzi Myers maintain that the relationship had a direct impact upon his philosophy—as evidenced in the revisions made to the second and third editions of *An Enquiry concerning Political Justice*. Other scholars, however, notably Mark Philp, insist that the change in Godwinian thought in the mid 1790s came more from a reading of the moral philosophy of Adam Smith and David Hume and the literature of sensibility. Certainly, Godwin made substantial revisions to the 1796 and 1798 editions of *An Enquiry concerning Political Justice*. In particular, he moved away from the extreme rationalism of the first edition and argued for feeling as a dominant and proper factor in human motivation.

Central to an understanding of the evolution of Godwin's historical thought is the manuscript essay "Of History & Romance," written in 1797 and first published as an appendix to the 1988 Penguin edition of *Things As They Are; or, The Adventures of Caleb Williams*. In this essay Godwin distinguishes two types of history. The first is "general history," the study of nations or large structural change; the second is "individual history," or the study of particular historical actors. Godwin claims that individual history is far more significant: it not only facilitates self-knowledge but also provides exemplary characters worthy of emulation. He insists that thus he is not concerned primarily with the veracity of such history but with its moral impact on the reader: "I ask not, as a principle point, whether it be true or false. My first enquiry is, Can I derive instruction from it? Is it a genuine praxis upon the nature of man? Is it pregnant with the most generous motives & the most fascinating examples? If so, I had rather be profoundly versed in this fable, than all the genuine histories that ever existed." Clearly, "romance" or fictitious history or fiction equally (indeed better) serve Godwin's predominantly moral objectives. As Jon Klancher argues, "Of History & Romance" (like the earlier historical parodies in *The Herald of Literature*) formed part of a deliberate attempt in late-eighteenth-century Britain to challenge the rigidity of existing literary genres with the ultimate aim of promoting broader social and intellectual change. Such testing of generic boundaries was encouraged, if not suggested, by Godwin's growing skepticism about the status of historical knowledge. In *The Enquirer. Reflections on Education, Manners, and Literature. In a Series of Essays* (1797), Godwin itemizes the inherent and inescapable defects. These include the impossibility of discerning motive; the complexity of human activity; subjectivity and overt bias among the sources; and the necessary guesses and constructions of the historian. He concludes that "History is in reality a tissue of fables."

On 30 August 1797 Mary Wollstonecraft gave birth to a daughter, Mary; ten days later Wollstonecraft was dead of puerperal fever. Godwin was devastated, but almost immediately he commenced work on his *Memoirs of the Author of A Vindication of the Rights of Woman* (1798). The memoirs did much to sully Godwin's reputation, as well as that of his dead wife. Contrary to the biographical conventions of the time, it is a work of remarkable frankness. It includes accounts of Wollstonecraft's father's violent behavior, her romantic liaisons, her suicide attempts, the illegitimate birth of her daughter Fanny, and a detailed account of her death. While publication of Wollstonecraft's memoirs provided a particular occasion of public disapprobation, the general mood of the British public had already turned against Godwinism, mostly as a consequence of the war with France and concerted government repression of radicals and liberals. For conservatives and reactionaries, Godwin was the emblem and leader of what was termed "The New Philosophy." The government-subsidized *Anti-Jacobin Review* was established in 1798 with the express purpose of detecting and trouncing unpatriotic, Francophilic ideas such as political democracy, economic and sexual equality, and religious freedom. Reaction spawned a subgenre of anti-Godwinian literature, including Thomas Robert Malthus's *An Essay on the Principle of Population* (1798). Despite Godwin's revisionism, the main focus of this criticism was the philosopher's early repudiation of domestic affections. Even former friends and supporters, such as Mackintosh and Coleridge, joined in the outcry against him.

Countering this reputation as an antagonist of feeling and domestic affections was a key objective of Godwin's next novel, *St. Leon: A Tale of the Sixteenth Century* (1799), in which he gives a fulsome and approving depiction of family life. The novel tells the story of a young French nobleman who acquires the secrets of immortality and exhaustless wealth. Despite his best intentions to use these gifts for the benefit of his family and society at large, St. Leon only manages to estrange his family and become a vilified and persecuted social outcast. The novel is also concerned, as was *Things As They Are; or, The Adventures of Caleb Williams*, with the issue of institutional oppression of the freethinking individual. Gary Kelly notes that in both *Things As They Are; or, The Adventures of Caleb Williams* and *St. Leon, A Tale of the Sixteenth Century* "Godwin is exploring in fiction the nature of 'Protestant history,'" and that he is connecting St. Leon's curious and investigative spirit—the essence of Caleb Williams's character—with that of the imminent Reformation and, indeed, with all epochs of historical progress. In doing so, Godwin makes conscious parallels between "old philosophy and new"—that is, between the philosophical activity of the early sixteenth century and that of the late eighteenth. The novel proved extremely popular. Unsurprisingly, given the depth to which Godwin's reputation had sunk, reviews from the conservative press at least were unfavorable, although *The Anti-Jacobin Review* (January–February 1800) approvingly noted Godwin's new appreciation of the domestic affections.

Although Coleridge had been among those former allies who joined in the reaction against Godwin, by 1799 the two men had become reconciled. From this time, Coleridge exercised a major influence on Godwin, most notably in eroding the philosopher's atheism. Hazlitt also became a regular visitor and confidant; and an enduring friendship with essayist, critic, and poet Charles Lamb dates from 1800. At this time

Godwin also developed symptoms of a fainting sickness—possibly narcolepsy—which intensified over the following years.

The death of Wollstonecraft had left Godwin emotionally bereft and with two young children to care for. With unseemly if understandable haste, Godwin proposed marriage to Harriet Lee in 1798 and Maria Reveley in 1799. Each declined his offer. In May 1801 Godwin met Mary Jane Clairmont, a widow who earned a precarious living as a writer of children's books and translator of French and who had two children of her own, Jane (or "Claire") and Charles. Godwin and Clairmont married in December 1801. In doubling the size of his family, Godwin found the need for money more pressing, especially when a fifth child was added to the family with the birth of William Godwin Jr. in 1803.

Possibly encouraged by the 1796 success of "The Iron Chest," a dramatic adaptation of *Things As They Are; or, The Adventures of Caleb Williams*, Godwin conceived a long-standing and ill-founded conviction that he could make money writing historical drama. In 1800 he wrote *Antonio: A Tragedy in Five Acts* (1800), set in fifteenth-century Spain, and the following year he wrote *Abbas*, a tragedy set in Safavid Persia. *Faulkener, A Tragedy* (1807)—loosely connected to the period of the English Civil Wars—was the most successful of Godwin's dramatic enterprises, finally appearing at Covent Garden in 1807 and running for three nights. It was Godwin's last attempt at drama. At this time he embarked upon a new literary genre, which proved more lucrative. No doubt influenced by his new wife's admittedly modest successes in the field, Godwin wrote his first book for children. *Bible Stories. Memorable Acts of the Ancient Patriarchs, Judges, and Kings: Extracted from their Original Historians. For the Use of Children* was published in 1802 under the pseudonym William Scholfield. It was reprinted throughout Godwin's lifetime. Godwin was proud of the work, and later in life he repeatedly drew attention to its preface, in which he outlined his view that a child's imaginative and sympathetic faculties were best cultivated by an exposure to historical incidents and exemplars.

Godwin was determined, however, that his historical writings reach a wider audience. When publisher Richard Phillips contracted him to write a biography of fourteenth-century poet Geoffrey Chaucer, Godwin took Coleridge's advice in a letter of 10 June 1803, that he "Make the Poet explain his age, and the Age explain the poet" and in October 1803 produced *Life of Geoffrey Chaucer*, an enormous work that—as many contemporary reviewers pointed out—tends to stress the age rather than the poet. For example, *The Annual Review*—which had formerly been relatively favorable to Godwin—was especially critical of his decision to focus less

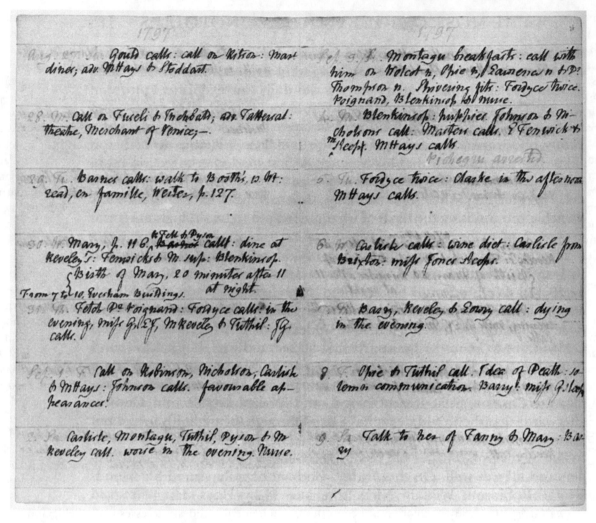

Page from Godwin's diary, 27 August–9 September 1797 (Bodleian Library, Oxford, owned by Lord Abinger; in Peter H. Marshall,
William Godwin, 1984; Thomas Cooper Library, University of South Carolina)

on Chaucer and more on the social, cultural, and intellectual history of the late Middle Ages. The review also took issue with the conjectural nature of many of Godwin's biographical and historical assertions. Godwin's former disciple Southey wrote this review under cover of anonymity, seasoning it with several unedifying personal comments about the author. While avoiding such personal asides, *The European Magazine and London Review* also commented negatively (April 1806) on the relative absence of the poet in the work, but was pleased with what it perceived as Godwin's long-overdue revisionism, later commenting that *Life of Geoffrey Chaucer* "will convey his name safe into the harbour of immortality, when, on account of the rottenness of the materials with which they were constructed, his Novels and *Political Justice* shall have perished in the Gulf of Oblivion."

Such commendatory appraisals occurred not least in response to a perception of Godwin's increasing con-

servatism—in his attitude toward morals and history. As *The Anti-Jacobin Review* (July 1804) maintained, "Mr. Godwin's notions, on the whole, appear to be greatly altered, and altered for the better." While the medieval Catholic Church—and medieval culture generally—tends to be accorded a negative role in Godwin's earlier Rationalist historiography, *Life of Geoffrey Chaucer* is far more sympathetic. Godwin argues, in fact, that medieval Christendom was not the instigator of the Dark Ages, but rather saved Western culture from a deeper descent into superstition and barbarism. Moreover, Godwin parts company with mainstream Enlightenment or Rationalist historiography in denying the centrality of the late-fifteenth- and early sixteenth-century Renaissance to the development of enlightened modernity. In contrast, Godwin locates the origins of crucial elements of the modern world in medieval Scholasticism and feudalism. In particular, he maintains that the strict hierarchy and mutual dependence characteristic of feudal social structure is analogous to those instinctive familial relations and emotions which he now believed to be integral to moral life. As a consequence, he defends feudalism as a form of social organization that had a profound civilizing effect on European life. Yet, despite this Burkean appreciation of medieval, feudal culture, Godwin remains a democrat and a progressivist. Valuable though medieval culture, religion, and social structure had been, Godwin insists that by the fourteenth century they were outliving their usefulness. From the intellectual revolution developed under Scholasticism and the growth of commerce and a new middle class, he said, came "the dawn of what almost solely deserves the name of freedom." *Life of Geoffrey Chaucer* is clearly not, however, solely an analysis of long-term changes in the structure of European life. The wealth of antiquarian detail in the study, as well as Godwin's historicist determination to understand the fourteenth century on its own terms, marks the work as, in part, a "Romantic" history. Furthermore, Godwin's detailed presentation of a range of life experiences and social practices as instances of broader cosmological and cultural truths categorizes the work, as Mark Salber Phillips observes, as an early kind of "microhistory."

Although *Life of Geoffrey Chaucer* sold well, Godwin's share in the profits was disappointingly small. Thus, after the relatively unsuccessful sales of his next novel, *Fleetwood; or, The New Man of Feeling* (1805), Godwin and his wife decided to carve out a slice of the increasingly lucrative market in children's writing. In 1805 they opened a bookshop in premises on Hanway Street. Among other products, the business provided an outlet for the writings of Godwin and his wife, as well as, in time, of those of some of their friends—most notably Hazlitt, and Charles and Mary Lamb. In order to ensure his reputation would not adversely affect sales, Godwin wrote under the pseudonyms Theophilus Marcliffe and Edward Baldwin. For the same reason, the shop was registered under the name of its manager, Thomas Hodgkins.

In 1805 Godwin entered into contract negotiations with Phillips to write a history of England to the Revolution of 1688. This work never appeared; he did, however, write a children's history, *The History of England. For the Use of Schools and Young Persons,* which he published in 1806 under the pseudonym Baldwin. In this text, pride of place is given to key incidents in liberal and radical history: the seventeenth-century English republic, the Cromwellian Protectorate, and the American and French Revolutions of the eighteenth century. Despite these libertarian foci, Godwin managed to submerge his radical tendencies well enough that most reviews were favorable. The work was popu-

lar and was in its eighth edition by the time of Godwin's death. An abridged version of this work, *Outlines of English History, Chiefly Abstracted from the History of England, For the Use of Children from Four to Eight Years of Age* was published in 1810 and also sold well.

The Pantheon; or, Ancient History of the Gods of Greece and Rome. Intended to Facilitate the Understanding of the Classical Authors, and of the Poets in General (1806) was predictably attacked by *The Anti-Jacobin Review,* as an "eulogium on idolatry" (February 1807). Even so, *The Pantheon* was a popular text that remained in circulation for many years and is known to have influenced the poetry of John Keats. Like *Life of Geoffrey Chaucer, The Pantheon* evidences both Rationalist and Romantic historiographical tendencies. On the one hand, Godwin sees much ancient mythology as a salutary lesson in the intellectual excesses to which an ignorant, unenlightened mind might be led. On the other hand, with greater sensitivity to historical context, Godwin praises in ancient mythology what he considers an appropriate (and morally invigorating) religiosity. He is especially fulsome in his praise of the sincerity and piety of Roman religion and finds in Greek religion a particular capacity to stimulate the imagination and, thus, the moral sense. This conviction that history had a pivotal role to play in the moral improvement of the young led to Godwin's writing *The Life of Lady Jane Grey, and of Lord Guildford Dudley, Her Husband* (1806). He insists that the story is of interest not least because the lives of his protagonists are embedded in the period of the Renaissance and Reformation, and, as he says in the preface, he hopes that his book might prove an incentive for readers to "search further into that grand magazine of instruction." In this work, as elsewhere in his oeuvre, Godwin says that repudiation of "superstition and idolatry" by Protestantism marks it as the purest religious expression of the Renaissance and as a necessary precondition for subsequent enlightenment. Generally, Godwin's children's books were favorably received and sold well. But the profitability of the business—The City Juvenile Library (under the name M. J. Godwin and Company)—was undermined by staff embezzlement. In 1807 both home and business moved to new premises at 41 Skinner Street. The business survived, but continued to suffer financial instability.

In 1809 Godwin published, under his own name and to generally favorable if somewhat perplexed reviews, *Essay on Sepulchres; or, A Proposal for Erecting Some Memorial of the Illustrious Dead in All Ages on the Spot Where Their Remains Have Been Interred.* Herein he proposes a scheme to mark the burial spots of the morally great in order to enable contemporaries to reflect most effectively upon and be inspired by their special qualities. *The Critical Review* (January 1810) called *Essay on Sepul-*

chres an "ingenious and feeling essay." It was not, however, the kind of work that could alleviate Godwin's financial problems. He thus returned to his writing for children, although the topic he chose was an especially congenial one. *The History of Rome: From the Building of the City to the Ruin of the Republic* (1809) proved to be yet another popular addition to Godwin's children's histories, was generally well reviewed, and by 1829 had run to a fifth edition. Godwin leaves the reader in no doubt as to the educational value of Roman history: " . . . it contains the finest examples of elevated sentiment and disinterested virtue, that are to be met with in the history of any country of the earth" (Don Locke, in *A Fantasy of Reason* [1980]). Godwin notes the extant spirit of criticism, which tended to query the veracity of some of the more outstanding examples of Roman virtue, but responds that, true or not, the reader will benefit morally from such tales.

In January 1812 Godwin received a letter from Percy Bysshe Shelley, an ardent, even fanatical, disciple of the doctrines of *An Enquiry concerning Political Justice.* The two men met later that year. Godwin now had not only another young and enthusiastic devotee, but a financial benefactor; for as the son of a wealthy country squire, Shelley could borrow against his expected inheritance. Yet, this new friendship exacted a huge personal cost from Godwin. In July 1814 Shelley left his wife, Harriet Westbrook, and eloped to the Continent with sixteen-year-old Mary Godwin. Moreover, Godwin's stepdaughter "Claire" Clairmont went with them to France and thence to Switzerland. The elopement was a source of great shock and shame to Godwin and his family. Especially affected was Fanny, who had her mother's susceptibility to depression and committed suicide by taking a laudanum overdose. The cycle of tragedy was completed a month later with the suicide of Shelley's wife, Harriet. Shelley and Mary promptly married. Godwin never reconciled with Shelley, although he continued to accept money from him—much to the disgust of Godwin's contemporaries and subsequent commentators.

Godwin rejoined the world of "adult" writing with *Letters of Verax, to the Editor of the Morning Chronicle* (1815), a defense of the deposed French emperor, Napoléon Bonaparte. In the same year, he produced *Lives of Edward and John Philips. Nephews and Pupils of Milton. Including Various Particulars of the Literary and Political History of their Times.* The work marks the commencement of a period of almost fifteen years in which Godwin's focus is predominantly on the seventeenth-century Puritan and republican moment in English history. This field of historical inquiry was still highly contentious, since polite society was generally unable to regard the religious and political revolutionaries of the

1640s and 1650s in anything other than pejorative terms. Indeed, Tillotama Rajan claims that such was the general antipathy to the republican moment in England that Godwin felt compelled to conceal his true interests and objectives within a work of apparently apolitical literary biography. Godwin's sympathies are not, however, hard to discern. As both nephews of Milton experienced the Puritan revolution and the Restoration of the Stuart monarchy, the work provides Godwin with ample opportunity to compare the moral, intellectual, and political character of these two periods in English history. Puritan republicanism is unequivocally presented as an outstanding moral and intellectual occurrence. "But the Restoration," says Godwin in *Lives of Edward and John Philips,* "was an event of unmitigated calamity. The character of the English nation at this time became retrograde; and though the expulsion of the Stuart family to a certain degree reduced the disease, yet it is probable that the nation has never recovered that tone of independence, strong thinking, and generosity, which the Restoration so powerfully operated to destroy."

In a letter to Mary Shelley of 30 March 1820, Godwin reveals that the period between the publication of *Fleetwood* in 1805 and the commencement of work in 1816 on his next novel, *Mandeville. A Tale of the Seventeenth Century in England* (1817), was one of unrelieved mental exhaustion. He also claimed, according to C. Kegan Paul in *William Godwin: His Friends and Contemporaries,* that since 1816 he had felt a new lease on intellectual life and "shall never leave off writing again." Possibly, recourse to his favorite historical period–the seventeenth century–had revived Godwin's intellectual energies; and as preparation for *Mandeville,* Godwin once again immersed himself in the history and personalities of the Civil Wars. As Marion Omar Farouk argues, Godwin's purpose in the novel was to display the way in which character is formed entirely from the social and intellectual conditions obtaining in a particular historical milieu. Godwin's alienated, bigoted, and ultimately insane protagonist, Charles Mandeville, is clearly the product of both a strictly Calvinist upbringing and the sectarian violence besetting this period of British and Irish history. Most reviews acknowledged Godwin's special ability in psychological examination, although predictably some critics objected to so lengthy and detailed a study of a less than laudable character.

Godwin reiterates his belief in the preeminent moral and educational value of historical writing in his *Letter of Advice to a Young American: On the Course of Studies it Might Be Most Advantageous for Him to Pursue* (1818). Characteristically, he emphasizes ancient Greece and Rome, but he also devotes some space to the study of "Modern History," in particular the Middle Ages and the period "between the accession of Elizabeth and the Restoration." He recommends Hume on English history in his *Letter of Advice to a Young American,* despite that writer's defect of "a worthless partiality" to the Stuart monarchs and an incapacity to appreciate the value and interest of the Middle Ages. Godwin advises his reader to take special care with the Stuart period, recommending a breadth of reading so as to overcome the partisanship the subject arouses. *Letter of Advice to a Young American* proved much more popular in North America than in Britain.

In 1809 Godwin had commenced a history of Greece but had shelved the project. He took it up again in 1821, finally producing, as Edward Baldwin, *The History of Greece: From the Earliest Records of That Country to the Time in Which it Was Reduced into a Roman Province* (1821). This text also proved popular, a new edition appearing as late as 1862. But if Godwin was enjoying a period of improved literary productivity and fulfillment, his financial difficulties were approaching a point of crisis. As a result of confusion over the lease, Godwin had been living rent-free at Skinner Street. In 1822 the matter was finally settled in the courts, and Godwin was evicted. The family moved to 195 The Strand. Following the death of her husband in the same year, Mary Shelley returned to England and settled with her father. By this time Godwin was at work on his four-volume history of the English republic. It was his largest undertaking, requiring seven years to complete. As John Morrow notes, Godwin's *History of the Commonwealth of England* stands apart from contemporary studies of the period both in its focus on the republican party and in its avoidance, to a large degree, of the simplistic, partisan spirit that informed other works on the period. Godwin's study is—if not an entire rehabilitation of the Puritan and Cromwellian ethos of the mid seventeenth century—an attempt to examine sympathetically the principles of, and possibilities afforded by, the republican government attempted then. Godwin's work is also remarkable for its wide-ranging and intensive use of primary sources. He closely studied surviving parliamentary papers, the memoirs of the protagonists, and the myriad political and religious pamphlets of the period.

Godwin's primary purpose in this history is to celebrate the Commonwealthsmen as exemplary moral and political leaders and their attempted polity as a visionary exercise or experiment in a form of government superior to anything envisioned by the seventeenth, or, for that matter, the nineteenth century. Given that Godwin's political thought owes much to his Dissenting background, it is perhaps unsurprising that he portrays British politics in the 1640s and 1650s as a debate over the true meaning and implications of the Reformation for both religious practice and political and social organization. Adherents of the Puritan party are depicted as motivated almost entirely by the principles of spiritual and intellectual independence and integrity. Anglicanism, in contrast—at least in the first three volumes—is portrayed as a faith held more from habit and political self-interest than from deep conviction. Furthermore, Godwin stresses the 1643 split in the Puritan party as fundamentally a religious issue. He argues that in contrast to the Presbyterians, who tended to favor a limited monarchy, the republican Independents alone were prepared to work out and pursue the logical consequences of the personal moral and intellectual independence that lay at the heart of the Reformation.

The work is also threaded through with another of Godwin's fundamental political maxims: that "Government is founded in opinion: and the sentiments and prejudices of a greater or smaller portion of its subjects form its basis." "In the second place," he adds in volume three, "opinion depends very much on prescription. So much as our forefathers believed, the creed, religious or political, which they have handed down to us, we are inclined to entertain." For this reason, Cromwell's coup and assumption of the quasi-monarchical title of Lord Protector was enabled by the ingrained monarchical sentiments and reflexes of the population. Thus, by the fourth volume, Godwin revises his initial assessment of the motivation of the royalists. He acknowledges that such motives as habit, tradition, custom, and loyalty have their own moral value and are essential to the continued functioning and reproduction of society. Ultimately, however, Godwin's sympathy is with the republican party, whose failed attempt at a more advanced polity continues to provide an inspiring example—an intellectual and moral resource productive of future innovation and progress. Predictably, most reviewers detected a republican, Cromwellian bias—although some were prepared to admit Godwin's attempt at evenhandedness. Even so, Godwin's focus on the motives and political conceptions of the republican party made his Commonwealth history generally unpalatable to nineteenth-century readers. Yet, as Morrow asserts, it is only in the latter half of the twentieth century that historians have managed to improve on this truly innovative aspect of Godwin's study.

During the writing of his Commonwealth history, Godwin's financial situation had reached its nadir. After years of struggle, in 1825 the firm of M. J. Godwin was finally declared bankrupt, and Godwin and his family moved to 44 Gower Place. But if Godwin's financial circumstances were worsening, the general political and intellectual climate of Britain was, from his perspective, improving. By the late 1820s, the liberalization of British life was well under way. In 1828 the official proscriptions against Dissenters—the Test and Corporation Acts—were repealed. In the following year, similar restrictions against Catholics were lifted; and in November 1830 the Whigs were back in power. By 1832 parliamentary reform had removed long-standing anomalies in the electoral system and extended the franchise. During this period Godwin published two novels—*Cloudesley* (1830) and *Deloraine* (1833)—as well as a collection of philosophical essays, *Thoughts on Man, His Nature, Productions and Discoveries. Interspersed with Some Particulars Respecting the Author* (1831). Godwin must also have been gratified by the republication—in Bentley's Standard Novels, a new series of "classic" novels—of his *Things As They Are; or, The Adventures of Caleb Williams* (1831), *St. Leon* (1831), and *Fleetwood* (1832). In 1833 the incumbent Whig government pensioned Godwin by awarding him the sinecure of Office Keeper and Yeoman Usher of the Receipt of the Exchequer. The position enabled Godwin to enjoy his final years with a measure of comfort and financial security. Yet, this time was not without its sadness. In 1832 Godwin lost his son, William Jr., aged twenty-nine, to cholera. His friends Thelwall and Coleridge died in 1834.

Always a man of the Enlightenment, concerned to weed out and debunk superstition and irrational dogmatism, Godwin explored, in his final works, notable instances of human credulity and irrationality in the history of Western civilization. Conceived not least as an opportunity to make money, *Lives of the Necromancers; or, An Account of the Most Eminent Persons in Successive Ages, Who Have Claimed for Themselves, or to Whom Has Been Imputed by Others, the Exercise of Magical Powers* (1834) is also an attempt to give a more rounded picture of human history. As Godwin notes in his preface, "The record of what actually is, and has happened in the series of human events, is perhaps the smallest part of human history. If we would know man in all his subtleties, we must deviate into the world of miracles and sorcery." Godwin insists, also in the preface, that the variety of supernatural and fantastical beliefs he summarizes is testament both to the bounty of the human imagination and—in the excesses of that necessary human faculty—to the "crimes and cruelties" to which it has led humanity over the ages. The work covers ancient Greece and Rome, West Asia, and medieval Europe before treating at length Europe in the sixteenth and seventeenth centuries.

Turning from such generally unsanctioned supernatural beliefs to those of the contemporary mainstream, Godwin spent his last days on a critique of Christianity, "Genius of Christianity Unveil'd." Godwin left the manuscript to Mary Shelley, convinced of its value—both intellectual and financial. Despite his evaluation, the work is an unexceptional and unoriginal summation of Enlightenment critiques such as those advanced by Gibbon, Hume, and the French materialists. Unpublished in Godwin's lifetime, "Genius of Christianity Unveil'd" was published posthumously by Kegan Paul in 1873 as *Essays, Never before Published, by the Late William Godwin.*

William Godwin died in London on 7 April 1836 from catarrhal fever and was buried in St. Pancras Churchyard in the same grave as Mary Wollstonecraft. The works that secured his reputation in the 1790s—*Political Justice* and *Caleb Williams*—remained the basis of his reputation throughout the nineteenth and twentieth centuries, although clearly, as Pamela Clemit remarks, nineteenth-century appraisals of Godwin acknowledged a greater range of his work than did most twentieth-century scholarship. From the last decades of the twentieth century, however, scholars have been reassessing the full range of Godwin's literary achievement. What is becoming increasingly clear is that Godwin made important and innovative contributions not only to political and moral philosophy and fiction but also to educational philosophy, biography, children's literature, and history.

Letters:

Shelley and His Circle, 1773–1822, 8 volumes, Carl H. Pforzheimer Library, volumes 1–4 edited by Kenneth Neill Cameron, volumes 5–8 edited by Donald H. Reiman (Cambridge, Mass.: Harvard University Press, 1961–1986);

Godwin & Mary: Letters of William Godwin and Mary Wollstonecraft, edited by Ralph M. Wardle (Lawrence: University of Kansas Press, 1966).

Bibliography:

Burton R. Pollin, *Godwin Criticism: A Synoptic Bibliography* (Toronto: University of Toronto Press, 1967).

Biographies:

Ford K. Brown, *The Life of William Godwin* (London: Dent, 1926);

George Woodcock, *William Godwin, A Biographical and Critical Study* (London: Porcupine Press, 1946);

Don Locke, *A Fantasy of Reason: The Life and Thought of William Godwin* (London: Routledge & Kegan Paul, 1980);

Peter H. Marshall, *William Godwin* (New Haven & London: Yale University Press, 1984);

William St. Clair, *The Godwins and the Shelleys: The Biography of a Family* (London & Boston: Faber & Faber, 1989).

References:

B. Sprague Allen, "The Reaction against William Godwin," *Modern Philology,* 16 (1918): 57–75;

Pamela Clemit, *The Godwinian Novel: The Rational Fictions of Godwin, Brockden Brown, Mary Shelley* (Oxford: Oxford University Press, 1993);

Clemit, ed., volume 1, in *Lives of the Great Romantics: Godwin, Wollstonecraft and Mary Shelley by Their Contemporaries,* 3 volumes (London: Pickering & Chatto, 1999);

George Crowder, *Classical Anarchism: The Political Thought of Godwin, Proudhon, Bakunin and Kropotkin* (Oxford: Clarendon Press, 1991);

Thomas Balfour Elder, "Godwin and 'The Great Springs of Human Passion,'" *Ariel,* 14 (January 1983): 15–31;

Marion Omar Farouk, "Mandeville: A Tale of the Seventeenth Century–Historical Novel or Psychological Study?" *Essays in Honour of William Gallacher* (Berlin: Humboldt University, 1966), pp. 111–117;

Martin Fitzpatrick, "William Godwin and the Rational Dissenters," *Price-Priestley Newsletter,* 3 (1979): 4–28;

Kenneth W. Graham, *William Godwin Reviewed: A Reception History, 1783–1834,* AMS Studies in the Nineteenth Century, no. 20 (New York: AMS Press, 2001);

Gary Handwerk, "History, Trauma, and the Limits of the Liberal Imagination: William Godwin's Historical Fiction," in *Romanticism, History, and the Possibilities of Genre: Re-forming Literature 1789–1837,* edited by Tillotama Rajan and Julia M. Wright (Cambridge: Cambridge University Press, 1998), pp. 64–85;

William Hazlitt, *The Spirit of the Age: or, Contemporary Portraits* (London: J. M. Dent, 1910), pp. 35–54;

Gary Kelly, *The English Jacobin Novel 1780–1805* (Oxford: Oxford University Press, 1976), pp. 179–269;

Jon Klancher, "Godwin and the Republican Romance: Genre, Politics and the Contingency in Cultural History," *Modern Language Quarterly,* 56 (June 1995): 145–165;

Jack W. Marken, "William Godwin's History of the United Provinces," *Philological Quarterly,* 45 (April 1966): 379–386;

D. H. Monro, *Godwin's Moral Philosophy: An Interpretation of William Godwin* (London: Oxford University Press, 1953);

John Morrow, Introduction to William Godwin, *History of the Commonwealth of England* (Bristol: Thoemmes Press, 2003), pp. v–xxxiv;

Morrow, "Republicanism and Public Virtue: William Godwin's *History of the Commonwealth of England,*" *Historical Journal,* 34 (1991): 645–664;

Mitzi Myers, "Godwin's Memoirs of Wollstonecraft: The Shaping of Self and Subject," *Studies in Romanticism,* 20 (Fall 1981): 299–316;

C. Kegan Paul, *William Godwin: His Friends and Contemporaries,* 2 volumes (London: Henry S. King, 1876);

Mark Salber Phillips, *Society and Sentiment: Genres of Historical Writing in Britain, 1740–1820* (Princeton: Princeton University Press, 2000);

Mark Philp, *Godwin's Political Justice* (London: Duckworth, 1986);

Tillotama Rajan, "Uncertain Futures: History and Genealogy in William Godwin's *The Lives of Edward and John Philips, Nephews and Pupils of Milton,*" *Milton Quarterly,* 32 (1998): 75–86;

William Stafford, "Dissenting Religion Translated into Politics: Godwin's Political Justice," *History of Political Thought,* 1 (1980): 279–299;

Rowland Weston, "Politics, Passion and the Puritan Temper: Godwin's Critique of Enlightened Modernity," *Studies in Romanticism,* 41 (Fall 2002): 445–470.

Papers:

The majority of William Godwin's letters, notes, and manuscripts, as well as his journal, form part of the Abinger Collection, which is held in the Department of Western Manuscripts at the Bodleian Library, Oxford University. Duke University also has a microfilm copy of Godwin's journal. Other papers and manuscripts–including *Life of Geoffrey Chaucer* and *History of the Commonwealth of England*–are held in the Forster Collection of the Victoria and Albert Museum, London. The Pforzheimer Library in New York holds the manuscript of *Fleetwood* and miscellaneous correspondence and material relating to *St. Leon.*

Oliver Goldsmith

(10 November 1728 – 4 April 1774)

Michael R. Hutcheson
Landmark College

See also the Goldsmith entries in *DLB 39: British Novelists, 1660–1800; DLB 89: Restoration and Eighteenth-Century Dramatists, Third Series; DLB 104: British Prose Writers, 1660–1800, Second Series; DLB 109: Eighteenth-Century British Poets, Second Series;* and *DLB 142: Eighteenth-Century British Literary Biographers.*

BOOKS: *An Enquiry into the Present State of Polite Learning in Europe,* anonymous (London: R. & J. Dodsley, 1759);

The Bee. Being Essays on the Most Interesting Subjects (London: Printed for J. Wilkie, 1759);

The Mystery Revealed: Containing a Series of Transactions and Authentic Testimonials Respecting the Supposed Cock-Lane Ghost (London: Printed for W. Bristow, 1762);

The Citizen of the World; or, Letters from a Chinese Philosopher, Residing in London, to His Friends in the East, anonymous, 2 volumes (London: J. Newbery, 1762);

The Life of Richard Nash, of Bath, Esq., anonymous (London: J. Newbery / Bath: W. Frederick, 1762);

A History of England, in a Series of Letters from a Nobleman to his Son, anonymous, 2 volumes (London: J. Newbery, 1764);

The Traveller; or, A Prospect of Society (London: J. Newbery, 1764);

Essays. By Mr. Goldsmith (London: Printed for W. Griffin, 1765);

The Vicar of Wakefield (London: F. Newbery, 1766);

The Good Natur'd Man (London: W. Griffin, 1768);

The Roman History, from the Foundation of the City of Rome, to the Destruction of the Western Empire, 2 volumes (London: Thomas Davies, 1769);

The Deserted Village (London: Printed for W. Griffin, 1770);

The Life of Henry St. John, Lord Viscount Bolingbroke, anonymous (London: Thomas Davies, 1770);

The Life of Thomas Parnell, D.D. (London: Printed for Thomas Davies, 1770);

Oliver Goldsmith (engraving by James Fittler taken from a painting by Sir Joshua Reynolds; frontispiece in Frank Frankfort Morre, The Life of Oliver Goldsmith, *1911; Thomas Cooper Library, University of South Carolina)*

The History of England, from the Earliest Times to the Death of George II, 4 volumes (London: Thomas Davies, 1771); 1 volume abridgment (1773);

She Stoops to Conquer (London: F. Newbery, 1773);

Grecian History from the Earliest State to the Death of Alexander the Great, 2 volumes (London: Printed for J. & F. Rivington, 1774);

Retaliation; A Poem (London: G. Kearsly, 1774);

An History of the Earth, and Animated Nature, 8 volumes (London: J. Nourse, 1774);

The Haunch of Venison: A Poetical Epistle to Lord Clare (London: Printed for J. Ridley & G. Kearsly, 1776);

A Survey of Experimental Philosophy, Considered in Its Present State of Improvement, 2 volumes (London: J. Newbery, 1776).

Edition and Collections: *Essays. By Mr. Goldsmith* (London: W. Griffin, 1765);

The Miscellaneous Works of Oliver Goldsmith with an Account of His Life and Writings, 4 volumes, edited by Washington Irving (Paris: Baudry's European Library, 1837);

Collected Works of Oliver Goldsmith, 5 volumes, edited by Arthur Friedman (Oxford: Clarendon Press, 1966).

Best known in the early twenty-first century as a writer of fiction and drama, particularly for his novel *The Vicar of Wakefield* (1766) and his play *She Stoops to Conquer* (1773), Oliver Goldsmith was in his day a popular writer of history as well. His historiographical contribution was to synthesize and popularize the work of other historians, often borrowing extensively from their words, lending his readable style to broad historical surveys. While for the most part the popularity of Goldsmith's histories did not extend into the twentieth century, they provided many late-eighteenth- and nineteenth-century English and American students with their first instruction in classical, English, and natural history.

Although some sources continue to list his birth date as unknown, sufficient evidence exists to indicate that Goldsmith was born on 10 November 1728 in the hamlet of Pallas, near Ballymahon in County Longford, Ireland. He was the fifth of eight children and the second son of Charles Goldsmith and the former Ann Jones. At the time of Oliver's birth his father was a Church of Ireland curate in Kilkenny West, but within two years was appointed rector, settling in Lissoy, County Westmeath. While novels should not be read as autobiography, the portrayal of the vicar of Wakefield in the novel of the same name owes more than a little to Oliver's father.

Goldsmith attended the village school in Lissoy, where the schoolmaster imparted a taste for folk ballads. After an interruption of his schooling because of a bout of smallpox, which left him permanently scarred, he went to school at Elphin, then at Athlone, and finally at Edgeworthstown, County Longford. The expense of educating Oliver's older brother and providing a wedding dowry for an older sister left the family unable to support Oliver's matriculation at Trinity College, Dublin, so he attended as a sizar, waiting on tables at the evening meal in return for his board. Although his career at Trinity was marked more by dressing and socializing beyond his financial means than by academic achievement, Goldsmith was awarded a B.A. degree in 1749. Certainly, his later attainments as author and playwright rather than his student record led Trinity in the 1860s to place a statue of Goldsmith at the College Green entrance, where it still stands across from that of his contemporary Edmund Burke.

After taking his baccalaureate degree, Goldsmith made several feints at establishing a career. He sabotaged whatever chance at ordination in the Church of Ireland that might have survived his raucous student reputation by reportedly appearing for his interview with the Bishop of Elphin in scarlet breeches. An uncle lent him money to study law at the Inner Temple in London, but Goldsmith made it no farther than a card game in Dublin. He finally enrolled in the medical school at Edinburgh in 1752, where he continued to indulge his taste for outlandish clothing and social bonhomie but did not complete his degree. Some literary critics see Goldsmith's two years in Edinburgh at the peak of the Scottish Enlightenment as an important source of his future themes and prose style. In the words of Declan Kiberd: "Already the thinkers of the Scottish Enlightenment were emphasizing the value of feeling over analysis: and from them Goldsmith learned the value of a natural style in speech and writing, free of false refinement yet purged of any vulgarity."

Claiming an interest in observing medical techniques on the Continent, Goldsmith borrowed funds for an excursion to Europe in 1755. In a decidedly low-budget version of the Grand Tour, Goldsmith traveled through the Netherlands, France, Switzerland, and Italy, later claiming to have met several Enlightenment thinkers such as Voltaire and Denis Diderot along the way. He returned to England penniless in 1756, and he never again returned to Ireland, not even for the funeral of his mother in 1770. In England, Goldsmith made a half-hearted and wholly underfunded attempt to set up a medical practice in Southwark, London, claiming that he had passed his medical examinations in Padua. When Goldsmith sat for the "hospital mate" examination at England's Royal College of Surgeons in 1758, however, he was found "not qualified." A brief stint as an administrator at a school in Peckham, Surrey, led to an acquaintance with the owner of *The Monthly Review,* initiating Goldsmith into the world of eighteenth-century writing for hire.

Goldsmith worked for *The Monthly Review* for six months in 1757, living in the house of the editor, Ralph Griffiths. The heavy workload, low pay, and repeated editing of his articles by Griffiths and his wife led Gold-

Remains of Goldsmith's parents' house at Lissoy, where he grew up (photograph by W. Swanston; in Frank Frankfort Moore, The Life of Oliver Goldsmith, *1911; Thomas Cooper Library, University of South Carolina)*

smith to resign. Goldsmith did contribute an additional four articles in December 1758, apparently to repay Griffiths for a suit he had lent Goldsmith for the medical examination, which Goldsmith then pawned along with some of Griffiths's books. The following year, Goldsmith began writing for the rival *Critical Review*. These early, anonymous reviews and criticism are unremarkable, but they did deepen Goldsmith's contacts with London publishers, who later hired him to compile his historical works. One early review is noteworthy for its statement of principles regarding historical writing. In a review of Tobias Smollett's *A Compleat History of England* (1757–1758), Goldsmith argues for the primacy of eyewitness testimony: "Strictly speaking, the eye-witness alone should take upon him to transmit facts to posterity; and as far as the Historians, the Copyists, the Annotators, who may follow him, if possessed of no new and genuine materials, instead of strengthening, they will only diminish the authority of their guide: for, in proportion as History removes from the first witnesses, it may recede also from truth. . . ." And truth, Goldsmith continues, is the historian's primary goal: "*Truth* should be the main object of the Historian's pursuit; *Elegance* is only its ornament. . . ." Smollett, according to Goldsmith, was guilty of valuing style over substance by omitting source references.

Also at this time, Goldsmith's first major work appeared: *An Enquiry into the Present State of Polite Learning in Europe* (1759). In it, Goldsmith generalizes about belles lettres and university education in the European states, often from limited personal and scholarly knowledge. The Germans are dismissed as a nation of critics; the Dutch as having a borrowed language and imported culture; and Spain, Sweden, and Denmark as among the nations "immersed in ignorance, or making but feeble efforts to rise." England and France, on the other hand, are treated in greater depth because they represent for Goldsmith the pinnacle of current literary accomplishment. Although Goldsmith is not uncritical–he denounces the overuse of blank verse and "solemnity of manner" in English poetry–and although some of Goldsmith's later works criticize and satirize English society, he never lost his admiration for English letters, wanting to see his name ranked among its leading practitioners.

The Bee. Being Essays on the Most Interesting Subjects (1759) is a collection of essays on contemporary topics Goldsmith had published in a financially unsuccessful periodical also named *The Bee*. This volume includes a few historical pieces, such as "The History of Hypasia" and "A Flemish Tradition." These short pieces are indicative of Goldsmith's later historical work in several ways. First, they see historical incidents as important mainly for their narrative interest. Second, these narrative accounts become the basis for moral instruction. Finally, also as in his later historical work, these essays largely violate his earlier stated principle by quoting extensively from other sources without attribution. Long sections of the article on Hypasia, for example, are taken from volume five of Diderot's *Encyclopedie*.

Goldsmith also borrowed the premise of *The Citizen of the World* (1762) from the contemporary vogue for fictitious "foreign observer" accounts of European society, the best known of which was Charles-Louis de Secondat, Baron de Montesquieu's *Persian Letters* (1721). Goldsmith's protagonist is a Chinese traveler who composes letters contrasting London with his homeland. The depiction of Chinese national character as "sensualist" prefigures some of the discussion of human "kinds" in Goldsmith's later work, *An History of the Earth, and Animated Nature* (1774). Although the sections on Chinese culture are a pastiche of French sources, one begins in this work to glimpse Goldsmith's mature prose style, conveying pointed social observations in an entertaining, readable manner. Some of the flavor of Goldsmith's social commentary is apparent in the fictional Chinese philosopher's comments on English women in letter 3: "the ladies here are horridly ugly; I can hardly stand the sight of them; they no way resemble the beauties of China; the Europeans have a quite different idea of beauty from us; when I reflect on the small-footed perfections of an Eastern beauty, how is it possible I should have eyes for a woman whose feet are ten inches long." Typically, Goldsmith's satire cuts against the foreigner making the observation. The publication of *The Citizen of the World* was not the literary event that Goldsmith had hoped, but it did bring him into a circle that by 1764 became the "Literary Club," which included Samuel Johnson and his best-known biographer, James Boswell, as well as painter Sir Joshua Reynolds and actor David Garrick.

Even more extensively based on literary "borrowing" were Goldsmith's biographical works, the first of which was *The Life of Richard Nash, of Bath, Esq.* (1762). Goldsmith wrote four biographies, all as the anonymous hireling of a publisher. In addition to *The Life of Richard Nash,* he wrote part of an unfinished work on Voltaire, published in serial form in the *Lady's Magazine* in 1761. Goldsmith also wrote a brief biographical account of Anglo-Irish vicar Thomas Parnell as a preface to a republication of Parnell's poems in 1770 and a more substantial work, *The Life of Henry St. John, Lord Viscount Bolingbroke* (1770). While Goldsmith used family papers and other primary sources in writing biographical works, he often resorted to including long sections from previous writers. Part of the reason for this practice was Goldsmith's tenuous financial position early in his career. He was living in poverty in London, trying to earn a living as a writer by churning out contract work as quickly as possible. For instance, regarding the Voltaire biography, Goldsmith told his brother in a let-

ter of January 1759 that he had "spent but four weeks on the whole performance for which I had receiv'd twenty pound." Such time and money pressures, and a relaxed attitude about scholarship evident from his university days, resulted in extensive plagiarism. About one-tenth of *The Life of Richard Nash* was taken from John Wood's earlier work, and *The Monthly Review* of February 1771 immediately recognized that Goldsmith's *The Life of Henry St. John, Lord Viscount Bolingbroke* was "patched up, by the mere aid of amplification" from an entry in the *Biographia Britannica*.

Goldsmith's historical writing may also have closely paraphrased his sources because of the writing method he adopted in composing *A History of England, in a Series of Letters from a Nobleman to his Son* (1764). In a 1793 essay in *The European Magazine, and London Review,* William Cooke relates that Goldsmith read a portion of a standard English history, such as that of David Hume, in the morning, marking passages and making notes. After spending the day "generally convivially" in walking and dining with friends, Goldsmith returned to his books and notes at bedtime and wrote a chapter before going to sleep. "This latter exercise," Cooke writes, "cost him very little trouble, he said: for having all his materials ready for him, he wrote it with as much facility as a common letter." This "facility" was likely a double-edged sword, assuring not only the readability of Goldsmith's histories but also their cavalier incorporation of unacknowledged source material.

In the two-volume *A History of England, in a Series of Letters from a Nobleman to his Son,* the son's implied responses show a growing awareness of Classical Greece and Rome, a realization that allows Goldsmith license for classical allusion. In letter 1, the fictional nobleman offers advice that echoes Goldsmith's earlier statement of principles regarding historical writing: "Above all things, I would advise you to consult the original historians in every relation. Abridgers, compilers, commentators, and critics, are in general only fit to fill the mind with unnecessary anecdotes, or lead its research astray." Despite these noble ideals, the history that follows is a broad narrative of political developments, largely drawn from Hume's six-volume *History of England* (1754–1762), but without Hume's defense of the Stuarts, critique of Christianity, or attention to detail. Goldsmith's is a generalized history, curiously devoid of facts.

Although Goldsmith's next two original works were literary, not historical, both include themes that inform some of his histories. *The Traveller; or, A Prospect of Society* (1764), written in couplets, is ostensibly based on Goldsmith's sojourn in Europe. In it he discusses national character as he had in the earlier *An Enquiry into the Present State of Polite Learning in Europe,* adding, how-

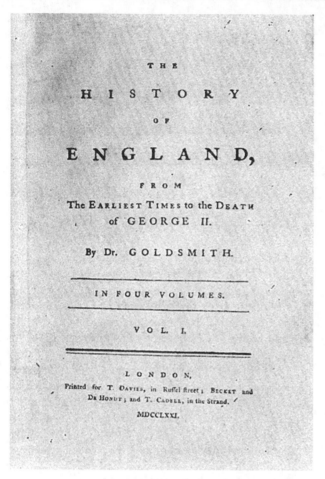

Title page for Goldsmith's history of England (from Temple Scott, Oliver Goldsmith Bibliographically and Biographically Considered, 1928; Thomas Cooper Library, University of South Carolina)

ever, an interest in the effect of climate on shaping that character. This idea, too, was explored by other eighteenth-century writers, notably by Montesquieu in his *L'Esprit des lois* (1748, translated as *The Spirit of the Laws*). Johnson, whose friendship Goldsmith was assiduously cultivating, told Boswell that "There has not been so fine a poem *[The Traveller]* since Pope's time" (from *The Life of Samuel Johnson, LL.D.* [1791]). The popular reception of this work created the opportunity to gather Goldsmith's early essays in *Essays. By Mr. Goldsmith* (1765), which in various editions was reprinted dozens of times over the next century. With the proceeds, Goldsmith attempted to restart his medical practice, but he did not get much farther than buying a new purple silk suit.

The other original literary work proved to be one of Goldsmith's most enduring. *The Vicar of Wakefield* was completed at least two years before its publication. Johnson, who esteemed Goldsmith's writing

as fully as he ridiculed his character, took it to his publisher, who paid Goldsmith £60 but delayed publication for two years. *The Traveller* was the more immediate success, and because of its reputation, the sales of the novel increased steadily. Among its themes, *The Vicar of Wakefield* voices Goldsmith's concern that the manners and mores of the city are overtaking those of the village, to the detriment of sturdy, charitable families such as the vicar's. The reversal of fortunes suffered by the Primrose family is, in Goldsmith's telling, emblematic of a weakness in the English social order. A conservative monarchist by temperament, Goldsmith worried that the rise of a commercial state was creating a new aristocracy that destroyed the "natural ties that bind the rich and poor" (chapter 19, *The Vicar of Wakefield*) in its insatiable desire for wealth. This notion became the central idea in Goldsmith's later poetic work *The Deserted Village* (1770), and traces of it can be found in his histories of Rome and England.

Expressly written "for the use of schools and colleges," Goldsmith's *The Roman History, from the Foundation of the City of Rome, to the Destruction of the Western Empire* (1769) was a publishing response to the marketplace. It is a serviceable and, as always, readable narrative of political administration and wars based on the primary Roman historians, but it includes no original research or interpretation. Despite his monarchism, Goldsmith expresses greater admiration for the Republic than for the Empire in his account of Rome. The reason seems to be his distaste for the wealth and leisure that arose from the spoils of empire, possibly because of the perceived parallel with Great Britain's recent experience. Although Edward Gibbon's *History of the Decline and Fall of the Roman Empire* (1776) raised the standard of scholarship on Classical Rome far above anything Goldsmith was capable of meeting, Goldsmith's *The Roman History* continued to be widely assigned to students throughout the eighteenth and nineteenth centuries.

It also earned the praise of Johnson. In a spirited exchange with Boswell, who argued for the superiority of Scottish historians Hume and William Robertson on matters Roman, Johnson countered, "Goldsmith tells you shortly all you want to know: Robertson detains you a great deal too long. No man will read Robertson's cumbrous detail a second time; but Goldsmith's plain narrative will please again and again" (Boswell, *The Life of Samuel Johnson, LL.D.*). Johnson's defense of Goldsmith serves as an important reminder that historical writing was often viewed in the eighteenth century as a form of belles lettres, to be distinguished by a pleasing style rather than by demanding scholarship. Further evidence for this attitude can be found in the decision by the Royal Academy of Arts in December of 1769 to name Goldsmith a Professor of Ancient History.

The following year, one of Goldsmith's best-known poetic works, *The Deserted Village,* was published. Echoing *The Vicar of Wakefield,* the poem returns to the decline of village life and the effects on the nation. Written at the same time as his *The Life of Henry St. John, Lord Viscount Bolingbroke, The Deserted Village* shares the political view of Bolingbroke's "Country" faction in its attack on Robert Walpole's administration of the 1720s. Auburn, the village of the poem, combines Goldsmith's memories of Lissoy with English hamlets of his time. The desertion of the village is depicted as both literal and symbolic. The young people have left to "seek a kinder shore" because "trade's unfeeling train / Usurp the land and dispossess the swain" (ll. 73, 63–64). Where once sturdy yeomen tilled the land, the wealthy now build estates and deer parks:

> . . . The man of wealth and pride,
> Takes up a space that many poor supplied;
> Space for his lake, his park's extended bounds,
> Space for his horses, equipage, and hounds;
> The robe that wraps his limbs in silken sloth,
> Has robbed the neighbouring fields of half their growth.
> (ll. 277–282)

Great Britain, in Goldsmith's analysis, is deserting its rural virtues in pursuit of Mammon, and the effects can be seen in the degraded environment—an echo of the association between environment and national culture Goldsmith first explored in *The Traveller.* The result of forsaking traditional village life will be catastrophic, Goldsmith warns:

> O luxury! Thou curst by heaven's decree,
> How ill exchang'd are things like these for thee!
> . . . .
> Kingdoms by thee, to sickly greatness grown,
> Boast of a florid vigour not their own.
> At every draught more large and large they grow,
> A bloated mass of rank unwieldy woe;
> Till sapped their strength, and every part unsound,
> Down, down they sink, and spread a ruin round. (ll. 387–388, 391–396)

Goldsmith's nostalgia for traditional village life was satirized, most notably by George Crabbe in his poem *The Village* (1783). However, the combination of eighteenth-century polemic and proto-Romantic sensibility in *The Deserted Village* immediately appealed to the public, and the book went through six print runs in less than six months.

Goldsmith offered a much more restrained critique of English society when he returned to the history of his adopted homeland in the four-volume *The History of England, from the Earliest Times to the Death of George II* (1771). As with his earlier historical works, this project was shaped by the marketplace, and Goldsmith's proven record in writing popular history earned him the impressive sum of £500. This history of England is essentially a slightly more detailed version of his two-volume work of 1764, without the epistolary framework. In fact, Goldsmith reproduced entire sections of the previous work in the pages of the new one. In his preface, Goldsmith also acknowledges the same sources that were the basis of his earlier English history—the surveys of Paul de Rapin-Thoyras, Thomas Carte, Smollett, and Hume. In addition, Goldsmith returns to some of his characteristic themes, such as the support of monarchy and the distrust of the new commercial oligarchy. As earlier expressed in his *A History of England, in a Series of Letters from a Nobleman to his Son,* and *The Vicar of Wakefield,* monarchy is depicted as a better guarantor of liberties, for "A king may easily be restrained from doing wrong, as he is but one man; but if a number of the great are permitted to divide all authority, who can punish them if they abuse it?" For these reasons, Goldsmith's later *The History of England* is largely indistinguishable from his earlier history of England.

Goldsmith's financial windfall from *The History of England* was followed by another success, the staging of his play *She Stoops to Conquer* at Covent Garden in March 1773. Despite being performed at the end of the season, the play was an immediate critical and popular triumph and was brought back for the fall season. Before the year was over, the play was being performed in Dublin, Paris, and New York, as well as many English cities. Goldsmith had finally attained what he had sought, a literary reputation and an income to support his appetite for expensive clothing and fine living. Goldsmith was also charitable to a fault, freely giving money away when he had little and becoming profligate when he had more.

Typically, he also had several other projects at various stages of completion in 1773. Published in 1774, his two-volume *Grecian History from the Earliest State to the Death of Alexander the Great* was a companion to his *Roman History.* Again, the focus is on placing political and military events in a general narrative, with perfunctory treatments of cultural matters such as literature. Goldsmith's historical consciousness, as expressed in *Grecian History* shares some common elements with beliefs of the early eighteenth century. First, biblical chronology and the primacy of the Judeo-Christian heritage is unquestioned. Goldsmith cites as the first event in Greek history the founding of Sicyon, "in the year of

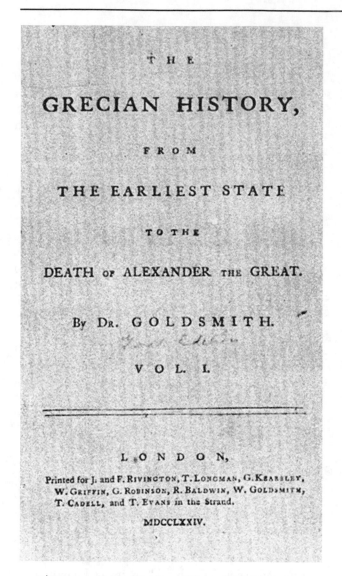

THE

GRECIAN HISTORY,

FROM

THE EARLIEST STATE

TO THE

DEATH OF ALEXANDER THE GREAT.

By DR. GOLDSMITH.

VOL. I.

LONDON,

Printed for J. and F. RIVINGTON, T. LONGMAN, G. KEARSLEY,
W. GRIFFIN, G. ROBINSON, R. BALDWIN, W. GOLDSMITH,
T. CADELL, and T. EVANS in the Strand.

MDCCLXXIV.

Title page for Goldsmith's history of Greece (from Temple Scott,
Oliver Goldsmith Bibliographically and Biographically
Considered, *1928; Thomas Cooper Library, Annex,*
University of South Carolina)

riches, a happy substitute for the want of these refinements they bestow." In the brief cultural excurses, the reader can also see Goldsmith's aesthetic principles. Chapter 10, for example, concludes with a brief estimation of Greek writers in which Aeschylus is criticized for having too harsh a style, lacking "musical arrangement," while Sophocles is appreciated for his eloquence and more-artful plots.

The other assignment on which Goldsmith was laboring was a multivolume natural history, published in 1774 in eight volumes as *An History of the Earth, and Animated Nature.* Goldsmith began with the idea of translating and updating Pliny the Elder's fanciful *Natural History* (completed 77). However, after reading the available volumes of the *Histoire naturelle, générale et particulière* (1749–1804) by Georges-Louis Leclerc, Comte de Buffon, Goldsmith decided to produce a more extensive work. One can see some of the preliminary ideas that made their way into his *An History of the Earth, and Animated Nature* in essays Goldsmith wrote for *The Royal Magazine* from June through September 1760 and in *The Citizen of the World* and *The Traveller.* In most of the detailed execution of *An History of the Earth, and Animated Nature,* however, Goldsmith borrowed extensively (although in this case, generally with attribution) from his source material, mainly Buffon's work. Given Goldsmith's lack of expertise in natural history, this borrowing is not surprising, and it did not prevent his work from becoming another commercial success.

An History of the Earth, and Animated Nature is a repository of popular eighteenth-century Western assumptions about the earth and its flora and fauna. In the first volume, Goldsmith sifts through various geological theories, assuming a need to reconcile them with the indisputable historicity of the Creation and the Flood. In the second volume he offers a distinction between plant and animal life based purely on function, and a limited function at that. Animals are defined as organisms that provide for their own protection, whereas vegetables do not. Added to this assertion is the conviction that humans occupy a central role in God's plan and Creation, evident in the fact that humans find both animals and vegetables equally appetizing.

Much of the natural description that fills the eight volumes of *An History of the Earth, and Animated Nature* is either commonplace or closely paraphrased from sources such as Buffon's history. Occasionally, Goldsmith's stylistic charms emerge, as in volume five when he describes the rooks visible from his window. But the element of the book that arguably had the greatest impact was Goldsmith's ranking of the "types" of human beings. Drawing on Swedish botanist Carl Linnaeus and Buffon, Goldsmith creates a hierarchy of six

the world" 1915, "before Jesus Christ" 2089. This dating matches the view, worked out most precisely by Church of Ireland Archbishop James Ussher, that the earth was created in 4004 B.C. In addition, Goldsmith echoes the popular biblical interpretation that the Greeks were founded by Javan, son of Japheth. Goldsmith's now-familiar theme of the dangers of commercial wealth finds expression in his account of Sparta under Lycurgus the Lawgiver. The leader's genius, Goldsmith states, was not only to divide the lands but also to drive down the value of gold and silver, substituting iron money. "Thus," he concludes in his Grecian history, "not only riches, but their attendant train of avarice, fraud, rapine and luxury, were banished from this simple state; and the people found in ignorance of types: (in ascending order) the Polar, the Tartar, the Southern Asiatic, the Negro, the [Native] American, and the European. The differences between them, Goldsmith says, are a result of "the varieties of climate, of nourishment, and custom." The inferiority of the Polar type–including the Laplanders, Esquimaux, and Greenlanders–is evidenced by their short stature, misshapen features, and barbarous customs. In the Tartar nations, including the Chinese and Japanese, "the women are as ugly as the men," and the majority "have no religion, no settled notions of morality, no decency of behavior." At the top of the scale, the Europeans are distinguished by their larger limbs, their beauty, and their superior powers of reasoning. Goldsmith even vows that Europeans resemble the original human, Adam, more closely than any other descendants. Within the general category of Europeans, the English are placed at the apex, for they are the whitest, and, as Goldsmith confidently states, "whiteness is the colour to which mankind naturally tends." While in retrospect such patent racism and chauvinism are easy to dismiss, Goldsmith helped to popularize a pseudoracial, quasicultural taxonomy of human beings that exerted a strong intellectual influence in the West. The influence of Goldsmith's schema was assured by the popularity of *An History of the Earth, and Animated Nature,* reprinted in more than twenty English and American editions in the century after its initial publication in 1774.

Goldsmith, however, did not live to witness this final success. In late March of 1774 he was overtaken by the chronic urological condition and low-grade fever that had affected him in the past few years. Ignoring the advice of an apothecary friend, Goldsmith prescribed himself fever powders. Unfortunately, this remedy contained antimony, which depresses cardiac function. To make matters worse, Goldsmith took too high a dosage of the powders, poisoning himself. During the morning of 4 April 1774, he suffered a fit of vomiting and convulsions as his body attempted to purge the poison. His heart could not withstand the exertion and stopped beating. The author was five months past his forty-fifth birthday. Reynolds, perhaps his closest friend, estimated Goldsmith's indebtedness at £2,000, to which Boswell responded, "Was ever poet so trusted before?" (*The Life of Samuel Johnson, LL.D.,* volume one).

At the time of his death, Goldsmith was working on another compilation, *A Survey of Experimental Philosophy, Considered in Its Present State of Improvement,* two volumes of which were published posthumously in 1776. His publisher had rejected an earlier draft of this work, and Goldsmith had tired of revising it, so the results are far from his most distinguished work. Moreover, like much of Goldsmith's nonfiction work since his earliest

essays, the contents were largely taken from the French *Encyclopedie.*

Johnson eulogized his friend in Latin for the inscription on Goldsmith's monument in Westminster Abbey. The epitaph reveals the appreciation of an earlier age, beginning "To the memory of Oliver Goldsmith, poet, naturalist and historian." The valuing of Goldsmith as an historian by Johnson and thousands of readers was based on a view of history writing as a form of belles lettres. Eighteenth-century English readers commonly distinguished between antiquarians, such as Thomas Hearne, who labored over manuscript sources, and the belletrists, such as Goldsmith, who embroidered history.

Among those of a later generation who recognized the limitations of Goldsmith's approach to history was Jane Austen. As a teenager she satirized Goldsmith's *The History of England* in her "The History of England from the reign of Henry the 4th to the death of Charles the 1st" (1791), which included the subtitle "by a partial, prejudiced, and ignorant Historian." Goldsmith's *History of Rome* was immediately superceded by the grand narrative of Gibbon's *History of the Decline and Fall of the Roman Empire* and its standards of documentation, although Goldsmith's text continued to be used as an introductory school text. Similarly, the popularity of Goldsmith's multivolume *An History of the Earth, and Animated Nature* continued well into the nineteenth century, but its quainter explanations of natural history and mixed schema of physical-cultural categorization could not withstand the minute observations and standards of evidence established by Charles Darwin. Despite their limitations, Goldsmith's histories are nevertheless valuable as a window into the popular historical sensibilities of the eighteenth century.

Letters:

The Collected Letters of Oliver Goldsmith, edited by Katherine C. Balderston (Cambridge: Cambridge University Press, 1928).

Biographies:

Thomas Percy, "Memoir of Goldsmith," in volume 1, *The Miscellaneous Works of Oliver Goldsmith, M.B.* (London: Printed for J. Johnson by H. Baldwin, 1801);

Ralph M. Wardle, *Oliver Goldsmith* (Lawrence: University of Kansas Press, 1957).

Bibliography:

Temple Scott, *Oliver Goldsmith Bibliographically and Biographically Considered* (New York: Bowling Green Press, 1928).

References:

James Boswell, *Boswell's London Journal 1762–1763* (New York: McGraw-Hill, 1950);

Boswell, *The Life of Samuel Johnson, L.L.D.* (London: Printed by Henry Baldwin for Charles Dilly, 1791);

Conrad Brunstrom, "'I Would Have All Men Kings. I Would Be a King Myself': Goldsmith's Republicanism and the History of Rome," paper presented at the Eighteenth-Century Ireland Society conference, Dublin, Ireland, May 2003;

Terry Eagleton, *Crazy John and the Bishop and Other Essays in Irish Culture* (Cork: Cork University Press, 1998);

Arthur Friedman, "Goldsmith's *Life of Bolingbroke* and the *Biographia Britannica*," *Modern Language Notes*, 50, no. 1 (January 1935): 25–29;

William Hawes, *An Account of the Late Dr. Goldsmith's Illness* (London: W. Brown, 1774);

Frederick W. Hilles, ed., *The Age of Johnson: Essays Presented to Chauncey Brewster Tinker* (New Haven: Yale University Press, 1949);

Elizabeth E. Kent, *Goldsmith and His Booksellers* (Clifton, N.J.: Augustus M. Kelley, 1973)–reprint of 1931 edition;

Declan Kiberd, *Irish Classics* (Cambridge, Mass.: Harvard University Press, 2001);

G. S. Rousseau, ed., *Goldsmith: The Critical Heritage* (London: Routledge & Kegan Paul, 1974);

A. Lytton Sells, *Oliver Goldsmith: His Life and Works* (London: Allen & Unwin, 1974);

Andrew Swarbrick, ed., *The Art of Oliver Goldsmith* (New York: Barnes & Noble, 1984);

Everett Zimmerman, *The Boundaries of Fiction: History and the Eighteenth-Century British Novel* (Ithaca, N.Y.: Cornell University Press, 1996).

Papers:

Few of Oliver Goldsmith's manuscripts survive; the largest collection is in the British Library (Add. MSS 42515-42517). The manuscript of *The Haunch of Venison: A Poetical Epistle to Lord Clare* is held by the New York Public Library. Margaret M. Smith supplies a full list of surviving autograph manuscripts in the eighteenth-century volume *The Index of English Literary Manuscripts*.

Thomas Gordon

(ca. 1692 – 28 July 1750)

H. T. Dickinson
University of Edinburgh

BOOKS: *A Modest Apology for Parson Alberoni,* anonymous (London: James Roberts, 1719 [1718]; Boston: 1724);

A Dedication to a Great Man concerning Dedications, anonymous (London: James Roberts, 1718);

An Apology for the Danger of the Church . . . Being a Second Part of the Apology for Parson Alberoni, anonymous (London: James Roberts, 1719);

Cardinal Alberoni's Letter to the Right Reverend Father in God for the Support of the Church, anonymous (London: James Roberts, 1719);

A Letter to the Lord Archbishop of Canterbury, anonymous (London: James Roberts, 1719);

The Character of an Independent Whig, anonymous, with John Trenchard (London: James Roberts, 1719);

Considerations Offered upon the Approaching Peace and upon the Importance of Gibraltar to the British Empire, anonymous, with Trenchard (London: James Roberts, 1720);

The Craftsmen: A Sermon or Paraphrase upon Several Verses of the 19th Chapter of the Acts of the Apostles (London: Printed for A. Moore, 1720; New York, 1753);

The Humourist, Being Essays upon Several Subjects, anonymous, with other authors (London: William Boreham, 1720);

A Learned Dissertation upon Old Women, Male and Female, Spiritual and Temporal in All Ages (London: James Roberts, 1720);

The Independent Whig, nos. 1–53, anonymous, with Trenchard and A. Collins (London: John Peele, 1721; enlarged edition, 3 volumes, London: John Peele, 1732–1735; Philadelphia: Bradford, 1740);

The Conspirators; or, The Case of Catiline, in two parts, anonymous (London: James Roberts, 1721);

Francis, Lord Bacon; or, The Case of Private and National Corruption and Bribery Impartially Consider'd, anonymous (London: James Roberts, 1721);

Three Political Letters to a Noble Lord Concerning Liberty and the Constitution, anonymous (London: James Roberts, 1721);

An Essay towards Preventing the Ruin of Great Britain, anonymous (London: James Roberts, 1721);

Cato's Letters, anonymous, with Trenchard (partial collection, London: James Roberts, 1721; first complete edition, 4 volumes, London: Wilkin, Walthoe, Woodward & Peele, 1724; third revised edition, 4 volumes, London: W. Wilkins, 1733; final corrected edition, 4 volumes, London: Walthoe, 1754–1755);

A Compleat History of the Late Septennial Parliament (London: John Peele, 1722);

An Examination of the Facts and Reasonings in the Lord Bishop of Chichester's Sermon Preached before the House of Lords on the 31st of January Last, anonymous (London: John Peele, 1732);

A Sermon Preached before the Learned Society of Lincoln's-Inn, anonymous (London: John Peele, 1733);

The Tryal of William Whiston, Clerk, for Defaming and Denying the Holy Trinity Before the Lord Chief Justice Reason (London: James Roberts, 1734);

An Appeal to the Unprejudiced, Concerning the Present Discontents Occasioned by the Late Convention with Spain (London: T. Cooper, 1739);

An Essay on Government, anonymous (London: James Roberts, 1747);

A Collection of Papers, All Written . . . During the Late Rebellion, anonymous (Dublin: J. Kilburn, 1748);

Essays against Popery, Slavery, and Arbitrary Power, anonymous, with others (Manchester: R. Whitworth, 1750).

Collections: *A Cordial for Low Spirits, Being a Collection of Valuable Tracts, by the Late Thomas Gordon, Esq.,* 2 volumes (London: R. Griffiths, 1751; expanded edition, London: Wilson & Fell, 1763);

A Collection of Tracts by the Late John Trenchard, Esq. and Thomas Gordon, Esq. (London: F. Cogan, 1751);

The English Libertarian Heritage: From the Writings of John Trenchard and Thomas Gordon in "The Independent Whig" and "Cato's Letters," edited by David L. Jacobson (Indianapolis: Bobbs-Merrill, 1965); new edition, with a foreword by Ronald Hamowy (San Francisco: Fox & Wilkes, 1994);

Cato's Letters or Essays on Liberty, Civil and Religious, and Other Important Subjects by John Trenchard and Thomas Gordon, 2 volumes, edited by Hamowy (Indianapolis: Liberty Fund, 1995).

TRANSLATIONS: Cornelius Tacitus, *The Works of Tacitus,* 2 volumes (London: T. Woodward & John Peele, 1728, 1731; revised edition, 1737);

Sallust, *The Works of Sallust,* 2 volumes (London: J. Woodward & John Peele / R. Ware, 1744).

Little is known about the private life of Thomas Gordon, since only a handful of letters and a few personal comments about him have survived. His reputation therefore rests almost exclusively upon his writings published over the last thirty years or so of his life. He published many of his works anonymously, but he achieved fame for two substantial series of essays that he wrote mainly in collaboration with John Trenchard. These became known by the titles given to their subsequent collected editions as *The Independent Whig* and *Cato's Letters.* These essays aroused considerable interest when they were published, and they were undoubtedly thorns in the sides of those in power. They are well known today because all historians interested in the political ideas of the Anglo-American world of the eighteenth century recognize the impact they had on radical Whigs in Britain in the 1720s and on American patriots in the age of the American Revolution. Gordon continued writing less influential political essays for the rest of his life, but he earned a wide reputation in the 1730s and 1740s as a translator and commentator on the works of Roman authors Cornelius Tacitus and Sallust.

Despite his subsequent fame, almost nothing is known about the early life of Gordon. Likely he was born in Kirkcudbright in Scotland, but his parentage and the date of his birth are unknown. A student with this name attended King's College, Aberdeen, in 1713, and a Thomas Gordon presented a law thesis in Latin, *Disputatio juridica,* to the University of Edinburgh in 1716. There is, however, no way of knowing whether these students were the same person or whether either was the Thomas Gordon who later gained fame as an essayist and translator. It is a common Scottish name. At some stage Thomas Gordon the essayist moved south, possibly to teach languages. He made his first public appearance as a writer in London in the late 1710s, though even in his years of fame little is known about his personal life.

Gordon's first publications were a series of light, ironic essays on manners, morals, and cultural topics that were later collected and published in *The Humourist*

in 1720. Gordon then became embroiled in the notorious Bangorian controversy when Benjamin Hoadly, Bishop of Bangor, in pamphlet and sermon, aroused the ire of many High Church clergymen with his claims that the church was clearly subordinate to the civil authorities with respect to the appointment of clergymen and that God did not favor a particular church establishment, but rather private judgment. Hoadly's comments provoked a host of hostile replies. Gordon joined the controversy, producing anonymously four pamphlets in support of the bishop. They are rather feeble contributions to this fierce war of words, but they do give an indication of Gordon's opposition to the privileges of the established Church of England, his hostility to the pretensions of the High Churchmen, and his general anticlericalism. They also had a profound effect on Gordon's subsequent career because they attracted the attention of Trenchard, a wealthy gentleman from Somerset, who had already built up a reputation as a radical Whig polemicist. In the late 1690s Trenchard had contributed to the debate on the merits of a standing (that is, a professional) army as opposed to a citizen militia, campaigning strongly for the latter as the best defense of a free government and the liberties of the people.

Trenchard appears to have met Gordon for the first time, either by accident or design, at the Grecian Coffee House in Devereux Court, London, in 1719. Trenchard was then in his late fifties, probably twenty or thirty years older than Gordon and certainly much wealthier and better connected. Within a short time, however, the two men had struck up a close relationship. Trenchard may have initially employed Gordon as an amanuensis or secretary, but they soon embarked on joint writing and publishing ventures that brought them many admirers, as well as some critics, from within the governing elite. Their first joint publication was *The Character of an Independent Whig* (1719), a pamphlet that repeated Trenchard's attack on standing armies and Gordon's anticlerical views, but which was marked in particular by a plea for greater religious toleration, especially for Protestant dissenters. This work was followed by another collaborative pamphlet, *Considerations Offered upon the Approaching Peace and upon the Importance of Gibraltar to the British Empire* (1720), which urged the government not to make a peace with Spain that involved handing back Gibraltar.

Then followed a series of almost weekly essays—known collectively as *The Independent Whig*—which appeared between 20 January 1720 and 4 January 1721. All appeared on the Wednesday of each week, except two, numbers 50 and 52, which were published on Saturday 24 and Saturday 31 December. These essays also appeared anonymously, though the identity of the two main authors (Trenchard and Gordon) were soon known and were identified in the collected edition by the letters "T" and "G." A third author, whose essays appeared above the letter "C," has been identified by David L. Jacobson as Anthony Collins and, more convincingly, by Ronald Hamowy as Arthur Collins. At first, Trenchard was the more prominent contributor to this series of fifty-three essays, but, in the end, Gordon had written twenty-two of them, Trenchard had contributed eighteen, the two had written three jointly, and "C" had written ten.

These highly influential essays dealt primarily with religious topics and with church-state relations in particular. Their authors were anti-Catholic, anticlerical, and opposed to the privileges of the Church of England. They stressed that religion was a private matter and that the form of worship adopted by men should be a voluntary act. The state had no right to examine the consciences of its citizens, but should allow them free will and free expression in religious matters. Reason was the only guide given to men in the state of nature, and men should be allowed to use it as their guide in civil society. Reason and freedom of expression would enable men to promote all arts and sciences, and to advance commerce and pursue personal happiness. Truth would prevail if men could enjoy freedom of conscience, free expression, and a free press. The authors of *The Independent Whig* were clearly anxious to extend a much greater degree of religious toleration than prevailed in England under the Toleration Act of 1689. Their concern, however, was with the position of Protestant dissenters. They did not campaign for toleration for Catholics, because they saw them as supporters of an authoritarian religion that would undermine the free constitution and personal liberties of the British people.

This series of essays appeared as a collected edition in book form as early as 1721. Other editions appeared regularly over the next thirty years, expanding into four volumes. The fifth edition in 1732 first added the initials "G," "T," "T & G," and "C." The sixth edition in 1735 added more than twenty new essays, all most likely written by Gordon. The original essays were partly serialized in New York as early as 1724, and a full edition appeared in Philadelphia in 1740. As late as 1817 an edition appeared in Connecticut. In 1767 most of the essays were translated into French and published in Paris by Paul-Henri Thiry, Baron d'Holbach, as *L'Esprit du Clergé, ou le Christianisme primitif vengé des enterprises et des excés de nos prêtres modernes.*

Even before the last of *The Independent Whig* essays had been published, Gordon and Trenchard had already embarked on an even more ambitious and influential series of essays written under the pseudonym "Cato." This name was chosen because Cato the Younger was an implacable opponent of Julius Caesar;

Title page for the first collection of a series of political essays by Thomas Gordon and his collaborator, John Trenchard (John Rylands University Library of Manchester; Eighteenth Century Collections Online, Gale Group)

an uncle of Marcus Brutus, the latter's principal assassin; and an unswerving supporter of liberty and republican principles. This series of essays, known later as *Cato's Letters,* was launched in *The London Journal* on 5 November 1720. This journal rapidly increased its readership largely as a result of the popularity of *Cato's Letters.* The essays started with a sustained assault on the parliamentary elite for allowing the South Sea Bubble to grow uncontrollably so that financial disaster destroyed the fortunes of many, and political corruption undermined the independence of Parliament and the liberties of the subject. This assault so alarmed Robert Walpole, the new prime minister, who was seeking desperately to restore financial stability and the political reputation of the government, that he sought to silence his critics by offering Elizée Dobrée, the proprietor of *The London Journal,* a substantial subsidy if he would cease publishing *Cato's Letters.* The offer was accepted, and the series published in *The London Journal* ended on 8 September 1722. A week later, on 15 September, essay number 94 was published in the newly founded, but less widely read, *British Journal.* The series continued until 27 July 1723, when essay number 138 appeared. Trenchard's health was now precarious, and he died on 17 December 1723. His death did not prevent Gordon from writing a further six essays, this time as "Criton" (though one is signed "T" in later editions), which appeared in *The British Journal* between 24 August and 7 December 1723. All *Cato's Letters* were written by Trenchard and/or Gordon. In the sixth edition, 76 of the original 138 essays are assigned to "G," 56 to "T," and 6 to "T" and "G." Gordon wrote at least 5 of the additional 6 essays.

The first complete edition of the initial 138 essays appeared in 1724, and the 6 additional letters were added to the third edition of 1733. Six editions had appeared in book form by 1754. *Cato's Letters* was widely known and much admired not only in Britain but also in the American colonies. Many copies crossed the Atlantic, and individual essays were reprinted in colonial newspapers in colonies from Massachusetts to South Carolina. During the American Revolution they were available in many libraries and booksellers' catalogues, and they influenced such leading and different patriots as Benjamin Franklin, John Adams, and Thomas Jefferson. Bernard Bailyn claimed in *The Ideological Origins of the American Revolution* (1967): "In America, where they were republished entire or in part again and again . . . and referred to repeatedly in the pamphlet literature, the writings of Trenchard and Gordon ranked with the treatises of Locke as the most authoritative statement of the nature of public liberty and above Locke as an exposition of the social sources of the threats it faced."

The essays in *Cato's Letters* cover a much wider range of topics than those in *The Independent Whig.* Only a minority discuss religious issues, while the vast majority debate political affairs. About 25 of the original 138 essays deal with questions of public morals and manners, 18 debate the importance of liberty and free speech, 15 consider the threat of tyranny and bad government, 13 deal with the South Sea Bubble and the issue of political corruption, and 10 seek to alert readers to the dangers posed by Papists, Jacobites, and High Churchmen. Written with vigor and clarity, they were

enormously popular with the critics of particular government policies and of Walpole's methods of political management and with those who wished to advance the cause of a free constitution and the liberties of the individual. When American colonists later believed that their free governments and personal liberties were under threat from George III's ministers, they found much food for thought and ideals to emulate in *Cato's Letters.*

All modern historians interested in the political ideas of the Anglo-American world of the eighteenth century now recognize the importance of *Cato's Letters* and their influence on the early opposition to Walpole's regime in Britain and the patriot cause in America. Where they disagree quite sharply, however, is over where they would locate *Cato's Letters* within the two different political discourses or paradigms that historians believe existed and competed for dominance in the eighteenth century. One discourse, the language of classical republicanism or civic humanism, stresses that a minority of citizens, those possessing sufficient landed property to make them economically independent of others, should develop their civic virtue and actively participate in the political life of their community. While landed men can be trusted to show a public-spirited interest in defending their liberty, merchants and financiers cannot. The latter can easily be corrupted into destroying a free constitution and undermining liberty. Classical republican writers often look back to the republics of ancient Greece and Rome for their models and also appeal to the ancient constitution of England as an historical example of a free form of government. The other paradigm, in contrast, is dominated by the natural-rights political philosophy of John Locke and his disciples. This political discourse stressed that all men were essentially equal in the state of nature; they possessed the inalienable natural rights to life, liberty, and property; and they created civil government by means of an original contract in order to protect these rights more effectively. The civil government thus created was based on consent, and magistrates held their authority on trust for the benefits of the people. If they betrayed this trust, the people could resist and use force in order to return to the state of nature and to erect a new form of government should they decide so to do.

J. G. A. Pocock, in *The Machiavellian Moment* and elsewhere in his many works, locates *Cato's Letters* within the classical republican paradigm. Some grounds exist for this decision. *Cato's Letters* did launch a bitter attack on the financial scandal associated with the South Sea Bubble, and they show a deep concern with the way in which leading politicians use corrupt methods to undermine the independence of Parliament and to threaten the liberties of the subject. They regard a standing army as another threat to a free government. In places, *Cato's Letters* favors a wide distribution of property and even an agrarian law, or something like it, which would prevent an unequal distribution of property, and they urge the landed freeholders to preserve free elections. They show no desire to bring the laboring poor within the political system. They also advance several favorable comments on the virtues of a mixed government and a balanced constitution, rather than in support of a wide franchise and a genuinely democratic form of government.

Although such elements as these of the classical republican discourse can be detected in *Cato's Letters,* some historians have challenged the thesis that these essays can be firmly and safely located within this political paradigm. Caroline Robbins, Isaac Kramnick, Marie P. McMahon, and Shelley Burtt have all argued that *Cato's Letters* not only promotes the civic virtue of the classical republicans but that it also advances the natural rights and individual liberties of Locke's philosophy. Hamowy and Michael Zuckert have gone much further. While they acknowledge that there are a few elements in *Cato's Letters* that can be located within the classical republican discourse, and they admit that Cato refers approvingly to Algernon Sidney more often than to Locke, they insist that the essential discourse of these essays must be located firmly within a liberal, Lockean paradigm. They stress how far these essays follow and endorse Locke's ideology, from a belief in natural rights through the creation of a free government by consent to a right of resisting tyranny. They even go beyond. They insist that *Cato's Letters* is primarily concerned with individual liberty and with freeing the citizen from state power, not with advocating that a public-spirited elite must actively participate in the political process. While they accept that *Cato's Letters* does reflect alarm about financial and political corruption, Hamowy and Zuckert maintain that it does not confer political authority on landed men alone and it shows no hostility at all to the worlds of commerce and public credit per se. Instead, it praises commerce and a well-run financial system as the means of enriching both the nation and private citizens within the nation. In opposition to Pocock, Zuckert states quite baldly: "The sponsors of the classical republican approach single out Cato for much of their attention, but mistakenly present him as an anti-Lockean. This is the opposite of the truth: Cato was a source from whom both the English and the Americans of the eighteenth century learned Lockean politics."

Gordon's substantial contributions to *The Independent Whig* and to *Cato's Letters* did not prevent him from writing other political essays that appeared as separate pamphlets. In 1721 alone, Gordon published four sepa-

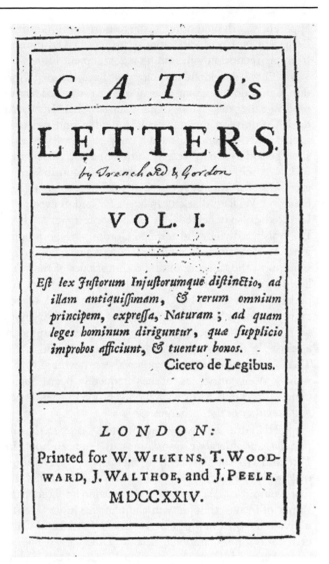

Title page for Gordon's second series of essays, written for The London Journal, *about liberty and republican ideals (British Library; Eighteenth-Century Collections Online, Gale Group)*

rate pamphlets, all dealing with the dangers posed by political corruption and the financial crisis of the South Sea Bubble and all urging the need to preserve political and religious liberty. It was *Cato's Letters* in *The London Journal,* however, that caused Walpole's government the most concern and that provoked a ministerial response. In June 1721 Gordon was questioned by a parliamentary committee investigating libels against the government. Gordon was never prosecuted, but two months later the offices of *The London Journal* were raided, its printing press smashed, and some members of its staff arrested. Benjamin Norton Defoe, a natural son of Daniel Defoe, was charged with seditious libel for an essay critical of the way the government handled the inquiry into the South Sea Bubble affair, an essay that apparently originated in a suggestion from Gordon. Benjamin Norton Defoe appears to have saved himself from prosecution by becoming a government informer.

These developments may well have alarmed Gordon. Other developments may also have persuaded him to moderate the political tone of his writings. When Trenchard died, Gordon lost the support of a wealthy and well-connected ally. At some later stage (suggestions vary from a short period to twenty years) Gordon married Trenchard's widow, Anne, who inherited her husband's fortune and a great deal of money from her wealthy coal-merchant father, Sir William Blackett. In later life Gordon lived well. In 1728 he also benefited from a handsome legacy left by a Dr. Walsh, a divine who admired Gordon's religious opinions. At some point in the later 1720s Walpole appointed Gordon to the sinecure of first commissioner of the wine licenses, a reward that helped further moderate Gordon's political tone. Possibly, Gordon was concerned to see Henry St. John, Viscount Bolingbroke, a former Tory minister and former Jacobite, leading the press campaign against Walpole's Whig administration from 1726. That Gordon abandoned political-essay writing or his radical Whig principles, as has frequently been maintained, is certainly an exaggeration. The evidence does not sustain either of these charges.

His fame as a writer now rested, however, on his popular and lucrative translations of Latin authors. In 1728 and 1731 he published by subscription a translation of *The Works of Tacitus* in two volumes. He dedicated the first volume to Walpole and the second to Frederick, Prince of Wales, though with compliments in prefaces to individual works in the latter volume to John, Lord Carteret, and John Campbell, second Duke of Argyll. A revised second edition appeared in 1737. In 1744 Gordon produced a translation in two volumes of *The Works of Sallust,* to which he added a translation of Cicero's "Four orations against Catiline." He dedicated the first volume to George II's son, the Duke of Cumberland, and the second volume to Evelyn, Duke of Kingston. Though not good translations by modern standards, since they were both too free and too affected in style, Gordon's translations remained the standard versions throughout the rest of the eighteenth century; both were translated into French, and Gordon's translation of Cornelius Tacitus was republished even in the late nineteenth century. These translations not only brought Gordon financial rewards but also allowed him to continue to propagate his still quite radical Whig views. He included in both works elaborate and detailed discourses on Roman politics. These discourses allowed him to advance his old views on the merits of a free constitution and a mixed form of government, on the advantages of liberty and free speech, and on the threats posed by standing armies and political corruption. He also discussed his traditional

concerns about the dangers of factions and parties, corruption and vice, and of granting the clergy too much power over civil affairs. Though less polemical and controversial, these discourses were in a similar vein to his earlier political writings. Like *Cato's Letters,* these translations were widely read in the American colonies.

Gordon continued to publish political pamphlets, though they were mainly aimed at his old French, Catholic, and Jacobite enemies and in support of the existing constitution and political order. In *A Sermon Preached before the Learned Society of Lincoln's-Inn* (1733) he sympathized with the resistance mounted in the American colonies to the expanding influence of the Church of England, comparing colonial resistance to the English opposition to ecclesiastical tyranny in the 1640s. In 1732 he published a pamphlet condemning a sermon preached before the House of Lords by Francis Hare, Bishop of Chichester. Although, as Alexander Pettit has argued in *Illusory Consensus,* the bishop may not have meant this work to appear to be a defense of arbitrary monarchy and the High Church position, Gordon interpreted it thus. In response, he repeated many of the points he had previously made in *The Independent Whig.* He again attacked the absolute and arbitrary power wielded by Charles I, supported by later Jacobites and advocated by the High Churchmen in all periods. In 1734 he again attacked the religious intolerance of High Churchmen in *The Tryal of William Whiston.* Five years later he was defending Walpole's vain attempts to negotiate a peaceful commercial settlement with Spain in *An Appeal to the Unprejudiced, Concerning the Present Discontents Occasioned by the Late Convention with Spain* (1739). In three pamphlets published between 1747 and 1750 Gordon again attacked his old adversaries—the French, the Catholics, and the Jacobites—and tried to rally his readers in defense of the Glorious Revolution and the Hanoverian Succession when they were threatened by the Jacobite rebellion of 1745–1746. Shortly after his death, many of his essays and short pamphlets were republished in *A Cordial for Low Spirits* (1751) and *A Collection of Tracts by the Late John Trenchard, Esq. and Thomas Gordon, Esq.* (1751). Gordon left unfinished and in manuscript form a substantial "History of England." Some 170,000 words long in 920 folio pages, with text on both sides, it starts at 1066 and ends abruptly in 1610. It is now in the British Library.

Little is known about Gordon's private life or his personal characteristics. When he died in 1750, his will clearly indicated that he must have had a first wife who may have died before 1719 and long before he married Trenchard's widow. There is no evidence about this spouse, but Gordon's will mentions three children by this marriage: Thomas, William, and Patty. Gordon had no children by his second wife, who long survived him and who was his sole executor. Gordon left little correspondence, and few contemporaries have commented upon him. Three of his surviving letters, published in an appendix to the *Eighth Report of the Royal Commission on Historical Manuscripts* (1881), show that he was on good terms with John, Duke of Argyll, and that he sometimes spent hours in private company with Walpole. William Cole described Gordon as "the author of many infidel books, . . . a man of no address and of a most ungain [*sic*] and awkward large person, with a monstrous belly and red face." Alexander Pope also referred to him dismissively as "Silenus" in Book V of *The Dunciad*.

Thomas Gordon's works on Tacitus and Sallust, well known in their day, are no longer read for the quality of his translations from the original Latin. Their sole value now is for the evidence they provide of Gordon's political views in the 1730s and 1740s. Most of Gordon's political works also have not stood the test of time, and they are little read today. On the other hand, the many essays he contributed, with Trenchard, to *The Independent Whig* and *Cato's Letters* are still widely read by those historians interested in understanding the radical Whig stance in the Anglo-American world of the eighteenth century. These essays reveal much about the criticisms of the political and religious establishment at Westminster launched with little effect by its radical opponents in Britain in the early 1720s and advanced more effectively some decades later by Whig patriots in the American colonies.

Biography:

J. M. Bulloch, *Thomas Gordon: The Independent Whig* (Aberdeen: Aberdeen University Press, 1918).

Bibliography:

A Bibliography of Thomas Gordon (ca. 1692–1750), edited by J. A. R. Séguin (Jersey City, N.J.: Ross Paxton, 1965).

References:

Bernard Bailyn, *The Ideological Origins of the American Revolution* (Cambridge, Mass.: Belknap Press of Harvard University Press, 1967);

Shelley Burtt, *Virtue Transformed: Political Argument in England, 1688–1740* (Cambridge: Cambridge University Press, 1992), pp. 64–86;

William Cole, "Extracts from William Cole's Account of Conyers Middleton," in *The Yale Edition of Horace Walpole's Correspondence,* edited by W. S. Lewis (New Haven, Conn.: Yale University Press, 1952), 15: 305–315;

Ronald Hamowy, "Cato's Letters, John Locke, and the Republican Paradigm," *History of Political Thought,* 11 (Summer 1990): 273–294;

David L. Jacobson, "Thomas Gordon's Works of Tacitus in Pre-Revolutionary America," *Bulletin of the New York Public Library,* 69 (1965): 58–64;

Isaac Kramnick, *Bolingbroke and His Circle: The Politics of Nostalgia in the Age of Walpole* (Cambridge, Mass.: Harvard University Press, 1968), pp. 243–252;

William Thomas Laprade, *Public Opinion and Politics in Eighteenth Century England: To the Fall of Walpole* (New York: Macmillan, 1936);

Marie P. McMahon, *The Radical Whigs, John Trenchard and Thomas Gordon: Libertarian Loyalists to the New House of Hanover* (Lanham, Md.: University Press of America, 1990);

Alexander Pettit, *Illusory Consensus: Bolingbroke and the Polemical Response to Walpole, 1730–1737* (Newark, N.J.: University of Delaware Press, 1997);

J. G. A. Pocock, *The Machiavellian Moment: Florentine Political Thought and the Atlantic Republican Tradition* (Princeton, N.J.: Princeton University Press, 1975), pp. 467–477;

Charles B. Realey, "*The London Journal* and Its Authors, 1720–1723," *Bulletin of the University of Kansas,* 36 (December 1935): 1–38;

Caroline Robbins, *The Eighteenth-Century Commonwealthman* (Cambridge, Mass.: Harvard University Press, 1959), pp. 115–125;

Michael Zuckert, *Natural Rights and the New Republicanism* (Princeton, N.J.: Princeton University Press, 1994), pp. 297–319.

Papers:

Thomas Gordon's uncompleted manuscript "History of England" is held by the British Library, London.

Richard Gough

(21 October 1735 – 20 February 1809)

Clare Callaghan
University of Maryland

BOOKS: *The History of Carausius; or, An Examination of What Has Been Advanced on That Subject by Genebrier and Stukeley,* anonymous (London: Printed for T. Becket and P. A. Hondt [sic], 1762);

Anecdotes of British Topography; or, An Historical Account of What Has Been Done for Illustrating the Topographical Antiquities of Great Britain and Ireland, anonymous (London: Printed by W. Richardson and S. Clark, 1768); corrected and enlarged as *British Topography; or, An Historical Account of What Has Been Done for Illustrating the Topographical Antiquities of Great Britain and Ireland,* 2 volumes (London: R. Payne, 1780);

Conjectures on an Antient Tomb in Salisburg Cathedral (London, 1773);

A Catalogue of the Coins of Canute, King of Denmark and England (London: Printed by W. Bowyer & John Nichols, 1777);

Observations on the Round Towers in Ireland and Scotland (London? 1779);

The History and Antiquities of Croyland-Abbey, in the County of Lincoln (London: John Nichols, 1783);

A Comparative View of Antient Monuments of India, Particularly Those in the Island of Salset near Bombay (London: G. G. J. and J. Robinson, 1785);

A Short Genealogical View of the Family of Oliver Cromwell (London: John Nichols, 1785);

A Mosaic Pavement in the Prior's Chapel at Ely: With a Brief Deduction of the Rise and Progress of Mosaic Work since the Introduction of Christianity. Read at the Society of Antiquaries Dec. 2, 1790 ([London, 1790]);

Observations on a Roman Horologium Found in Italy. Read at the Society of Antiquaries Dec. 16, 1790 (London, 1790);

A Roman Altar Inscribed to Belatucader: Illustrated by Mr. Gough. Read at the Society of Antiquaries March 25, 1790 ([London, 1790]);

An Account of a Rich Illuminated Missal. Executed for John Duke of Bedford, Regent of France under Henry VI. And Afterwards in the Possession of the Late Duchess of Portland (London: John Nichols, 1794);

Description of the Beauchamp Chapel, Adjoining to the Church of St. Mary at Warwick, and the Monuments of the Earls of Warwick (London, 1796);

Coins of the Seleucidae, Kings of Syria; from the Establishment of Their Reign under Seleucus Nicator; To the Determination of it under Antiochus Asiaticus. With Historical Memoirs of Each Reign (London: Printed by John Nichols for T. Payne, 1803);

The History and Antiquities of Pleshy, in the County of Essex (London, 1803);

A Catalogue of the Entire and Valuable Library (With the Exception of the Department of British Topography, Bequeathed to the Bodleian Library) of That Eminent Antiquary, Richard Gough, Esq., Deceased Which Shall Be Sold by Auction, by Leigh and Sotheby . . . on Thursday, April 5, 1810, and Nineteen Following Days, by Gough and Nichols (London: John Nichols, 1810).

OTHER: Thomas Martin, *The History of the Town of Thetford: In the Counties of Norfolk and Suffolk, from the Earliest Accounts to the Present Time,* edited by Gough (London: John Nichols, 1779);

A Collection of All the Wills, Now Known to Be Extant, of the Kings and Queens of England, Princes and Princesses of Wales, and Every Branch of the Blood Royal, from the Reign of William the Conqueror to that of Henry the Seventh, collected by Gough (London: John Nichols, 1780);

Joseph Ames and William Herbert, *Typographical Antiquities; or, An Historical Account of the Origin and Progress of Printing in Great Britain and Ireland: Containing Memoirs of Our Ancient Printers, and a Register of Books Printed by Them, from the Year MCCCCLXXI to the Year MDC,* 3 volumes, edited by Gough (London: Printed for the editors, 1785);

Sepulchral Monuments in Great Britain: Applied to Illustrate the History of Families, Manners, Habits and Arts, at the Different Periods from the Norman Conquest to the Seventeenth Century. With Introductory Observations, 2 volumes, edited by Gough (London: John Nichols, 1786, 1796);

John Topham, *Liber quotidianus contrarotulatoris garderobae anno regni regis Edwardi Primi vicesimo octavo ex codice ms. in bibliotheca sua asservato typis edidit Soc. Antiq. Londinensis,* edited by, and glossary by, Gough (London: John Nichols, 1787);

William Camden, *Britannia; or, A Chorographical Description of the Flourishing Kingdoms of England, Scotland, and Ireland, and the Islands Adjacent; from the Earliest Antiquity,* 3 volumes, translated and enlarged by Gough (London: Printed by John Nichols for T. Payne; G. G. J. and J. Robinson, 1789);

Jacob Schnebbelie, *The Antiquaries Museum: Illustrating the Antient Architecture, Painting, and Sculpture, of Great Britain: From the Time of the Saxons to the Reign of James I,* completed and edited by Gough and John Nichols (London: Printed by John Nichols for the author; and by G. G. and J. Robinson, 1791[–1800]);

John Hutchins, *The History and Antiquities of the County of Dorset: Compiled from the Best and Most Ancient Historians, Inquisitiones Post Mortem, and Other Valuable Records and Mss.,* 4 volumes, second edition, corrected, enlarged, and edited by Gough and Nichols (London: Printed by John Nichols, 1796–1815).

TRANSLATIONS: *The History of the Bible* (London: James Waugh, 1747);

Abbé Fleury, *The Customs of the Israelites* (London: James Waugh, 1750).

SELECTED PERIODICAL PUBLICATIONS–
UNCOLLECTED: "On the Disregard Paid to Ancient Monuments in the Reparation of Churches," *Gentleman's Magazine,* 34 (1764): 359–360;

"Inscription on an Ancient Dish, or Offertory Bason [sic]," *Gentleman's Magazine,* 53, no. 1 (1783): 187–188;

"Pronunciation among the Romans," *Gentleman's Magazine,* 54, no. 1 (1784): 269–270;

"Medals, Their Use, as Memorials of Notable Events," *Gentleman's Magazine,* 54, no. 2 (1784): 831–832;

"Antiquities Explained," *Gentleman's Magazine,* 55, no. 1 (1785): 193–194;

"Devil Cross. Roman Milliary Explained," *Gentleman's Magazine,* 57, no. 2 (1787): 659–660;

"A Remarkable Old Brief [repair of Salisbury Cathedral, 1423]," *Gentleman's Magazine,* 58, no. 1 (1788): 511–512;

"Edward the Confessor's Chapel at Islip," *Gentleman's Magazine,* 58, no. 2 (1788): 1149;

"Observations on Certain Stamps or Seals Used Antiently by the Oculists. Read Dec. 4, 1788," *Society of Antiquaries* (1789): 227–242;

"Review of Edward Gibbon's *The History of the Decline and Fall of the Roman Empire,* volume IV," *Gentleman's Magazine,* 59, no. 1 (1789): 152–156;

"Ancient and Present State of the Cathedral at Salisbury," *Gentleman's Magazine,* 59, no. 2 (1789): 873–875;

"Observations on Fonts in England," by Gough, Samuel Pegge, and Samuel Carte, in *Papers Read at the Society of Antiquaries* (November 1790–January 1791);

"Note on Bas Relief Illustrated in Previous *GM,*" *Gentleman's Magazine,* 60, no. 1 (1790): 116;

"Bust of Charles I," *Gentleman's Magazine,* 61, no. 1 (1791): 221;

"Inscriptions in Salisbury Cathedral; Sir John Cheney," *Gentleman's Magazine,* 62, 2 (1792): 1089–1090;

"Observations on a Greek Inscription at London," *Society of Antiquaries* (1792): 48–49;

"Remarks on County Histories," *Gentleman's Magazine,* 63, no. 1 (1793): 202–203;

"Bells at Christchurch," *Gentleman's Magazine,* 63, no. 2 (1793): 694;

"Church Notes from Chesterfield, Taken in 1789," *Gentleman's Magazine,* 64, no. 1 (1794): 15–17;

"Review: The Monuments and Painted Glass in One Hundred Churches, &c. &c.," *Gentleman's Magazine,* 64, no. 2 (1794): 742–743;

"Roman Road from Colchester to Carlisle Investigated," *Gentleman's Magazine,* 65, no. 1 (1795): 363–364;

"Topographical Description of Lydington and Its Hospital," *Gentleman's Magazine,* 66, no. 1 (1796): 457–458;

"Effigy of Lord Vere," *Gentleman's Magazine,* 67, no. 2 (1797): 1087;

"Flete Church.–Old English Sermon," *Gentleman's Magazine,* 68, no. 2 (1798): 925;

"Description of Great Shelford Church, Cambridgeshire," *Gentleman's Magazine,* 69, no. 1 (1799): 185–187;

"On an Antient Cusic Inscription," *Gentleman's Magazine,* 69, no. 1 (1799): 188–189;

"Various Descriptions of Pompey's Pillar Contrasted," *Gentleman's Magazine,* 70, no. 1 (1800): 325–329;

"Review: Report of the Commission of Arts to the First Consul Bonaparte, on the Antiquities of Upper Egypt," *Gentleman's Magazine,* 71, no. 1 (1801): 141–142;

"Anecdote of Cicero and MS of Livy," *Gentleman's Magazine,* 71, no. 2 (1801): 1170–1171;

"Pic Nic Explained," *Gentleman's Magazine,* 72, no. 1 (1802): 224–225;

"Mammoth [Bones Found in South Carolina and (as reported by Thomas Jefferson) in Virginia]," *Gentleman's Magazine,* 72, no. 1 (1802): 493–494;

"Spirit of Britons," *Gentleman's Magazine,* 73, no. 2 (1803): 932;

"Note on Bayeux Tapestry," *Gentleman's Magazine,* 74, no. 1 (1804): 103;

"Antient Sculpture," *Gentleman's Magazine,* 75, no. 1 (1805): 408;

"Note on an Epitaph at Chobham," *Gentleman's Magazine,* 76, no. 1 (1806): 404;

"Note on Inscribed Babylonian Bricks," *Gentleman's Magazine,* 76, no. 2 (1806): 896;

"Antient Seals, Celts, &c.," *Gentleman's Magazine,* 77, no. 1 (1807): 529;

"O[liver] Cromwell's Watch," *Gentleman's Magazine,* 78, no. 2 (1808): 1074;

"Biographical Memoirs of Richard Gough, Esq. [autobiographical fragment published posthumously]," *Gentleman's Magazine,* 79, no. 1 (1809): 491–493.

Richard Gough redefined the field of British antiquarian studies in the later eighteenth century. Before this time, antiquarian studies typically meant gentlemen examining Greek and Roman artifacts as part of their grand tours to the European continent. Gough argued that Britain possessed items worth studying—not simply the Roman relics in Britain but also native British items such as churches—and that these native items deserved as much attention. Gough worked tirelessly to provide authoritative references for Britain, from compiling maps to collaborating on local histories, and contributed greatly to the intellectual life of Britain through his writings.

Gough was born on 21 October 1735 in Winchester Street, London. His parents were Harry Gough, a merchant and member of Parliament, and Elizabeth, daughter of Morgan Hynde, a wealthy brewer. Of his three sisters, Judith, Anne, and Elizabeth, two died young. Both parents were religious Dissenters, and therefore their births were not recorded in a parish registry. Harry Gough was involved in trade with China and the Indies; he was a director of the East India Company from 1731 onward. With his wealth, he acquired extensive property throughout England, including an estate in Warwickshire known as Middlemore and another, Enfield, in Middlesex. In 1734 Harry Gough was elected to Parliament for Bramber, in Sussex.

Educated at home, Gough studied, among other subjects, Greek, poetry, and history. His first tutor, a Courlander named Barnewitz, taught Gough as well as the sons of some of their London neighbors, such as

Noah Titner and Edmund Boehm. Later, Roger Pickering, a Dissenting minister, took over Gough's education. In addition to his regular studies, Gough also produced many translations of French works, a few of which were privately printed by his mother.

After his father died in 1751, Gough was admitted as a fellow-commoner at Corpus Christi College at Cambridge University, with John Barnardiston as his tutor. A fellow-commoner takes classes but is not enrolled for work toward a degree. This status allowed Gough to study but avoid the religious requirements, such as taking communion, that conflicted with his Dissenting religious background. Later, though, Gough rejected his Presbyterian background and committed himself to the Anglican church. Gough's later contributions to *The Gentleman's Magazine* reflect this religious transition; mixed in with his contributions on antiquities are reviews of ministerial sermons and frequent critiques of Dissenters.

While at Cambridge, Gough involved himself in the antiquarian traditions of scholarship that faculty of Corpus Christi College had established. Also, Gough met many other people interested in antiquarianism, the start of his extensive network of like-minded collaborators. Gough left Cambridge in 1756 without a degree. Independently wealthy after the death of his father, Gough suffered no professional difficulties by not having a degree. Nor did he appear bitter over his college circumstances; in 1799 he presented a Roman altar to Trinity College, Cambridge.

After leaving Cambridge, he toured Peterborough, Stamford, and Croyland Abbey for their antiquities, following the route of a Corpus Christi predecessor, William Stukeley. In later life, Gough credited this trip with inspiring him to devote himself to antiquarian scholarship. Additionally, this trip served as a model for his later trips around England, Wales, and Scotland. Together, these trips furnished material and correspondents for Gough's writings—in particular, for his 1789 revision of William Camden's *Britannia.*

In 1762 Gough began publishing his antiquarian scholarship, with *The History of Carausius.* This first work focuses on medals dating to early emperor Marcus Aurelius Carausius, a usurper who ruled Britain as a distinct, non-Roman country from about 286 to 293 A.D. This history criticizes the conclusions of Stukeley, whose path Gough had followed in that post-Cambridge tour, as well as of Claude Genebrier, a French historian. Both men had developed elaborate theories about how Carausius had risen to seize control of Britain, seeking to position Carausius as an early noble British hero rather than a lucky rebel against the then-Roman emperor Maximilian.

Gough argues in *Carausius* that these conclusions are supported by neither geography nor other historical evidence. For example, Carausius cemented his control in a naval battle. Gough points out the reasons why the location Stukeley identified for it cannot be correct. Also, Stukeley claimed the battle was a second Actium, but against an even stronger Roman navy. To this assertion, Gough responds, "A cotemporary [sic] Panegyrist scruples not to affirm that Maximilian lost the Day by the Inexperience of his People in naval Matters; Carausius's being all thoroughly trained. Eumeius assigns two other Causes: a desperate Bravery in Favour of Carausius, and stormy Weather against Maximilian."

Likewise, Gough disputes the interpretations Stukeley assigns to the medals of Carausius's reign. Again, his arguments point out inconsistencies between the interpretations offered and other known facts, including calendar dates and the established practices of minting coins in Carausius's time. Through these criticisms, Gough demonstrates the breadth of his own knowledge of Roman Britain and his careful attention to contemporary scholarship. His other writings demonstrate these characteristics as well.

In 1764 Gough began his writings for the popular press, specifically for *The Gentleman's Magazine*. Published by his friend (and frequent publisher) John Nichols, *The Gentleman's Magazine* was a broadly targeted monthly journal on topics of cultivated interest, such as antiquities and poetry, plus news and political coverage; its issues included parliamentary activities, cost tables of commodities, marriages, deaths, and general news.

One of Gough's earliest contributions was titled "On the Disregard Paid to Antient Monuments in the Reparation of Churches." This 1764 article lays the foundation for Gough's arguments that church restorations are a public concern not limited to their parishioners. He mentions Westminster Abbey and speaks specifically of St. Saviour, a parish church built in the twelfth century and now being renovated for the third time in a century. He points out the architectural details lost over time, such as the details on statues, and he identifies the problems of waiting for "friends" to pay for specific renovations. He concludes with a call to the readership of the magazine:

> I would therefore by the channel of your useful Magazine, recommend it to the Society of antiquaries, to revive the beauty of this venerable piece [the parish's central tomb], since the parishioners will not do it, nor suffer it to remain in its present state. There is no time to be lost.

Gough became one of the leading contributors to *The Gentleman's Magazine*, providing more than two thousand letters, reviews, and articles under pseudonyms used by many other contributors as well. He typically identified himself as "R.G.," "D.H.," "Q.," "P.Q.," "H.D.," "H.H.," "Q.Q.," and even "***." He commented on inscriptions, major renovations of the day, responses to queries of others, church architecture, and dozens of other topics. Often, Gough provided sketches of the items in question—such as buildings, seals, and Oliver Cromwell's watch—and transcribed any markings. For each, he detailed as much as possible, identifying not only where items were found but also their markings, shapes, and approximate colors.

Often, Gough responded to articles written by others and inquired about forthcoming works. For example, he questioned conclusions others had developed about the antiquities they had found by pointing out conflicting evidence. Also, he frequently forwarded information from his correspondents in other places, including other counties, if not other countries.

In 1767 he was elected as a Fellow of the Society of Antiquaries. In 1768 Gough's first major work appeared, *Anecdotes of British Topography; or, An Historical Account of What Has Been Done for Illustrating the Topographical Antiquities of Great Britain and Ireland*. This work compiled all published and unpublished local history and topography for the region. It included diverse sources, such as charts, chronicles, and public records. The introduction describes the effort as follows: "These Anecdotes have informed and amused the collector:—if they only amuse the readers I shall not be absolutely condemned;—if they inform them, my passion for British antiquities becomes a zeal to serve the public."

Anecdotes of British Topography is remarkable for the detail within its scope, tracing all sources relating to British topography in the modern period. Gough begins by summarizing the Roman information on Britain, then the ecclesiastical and natural histories. Then, Gough dedicates a chapter to each county as well as London. For each topic, he traces the available information from the earliest to the most current, and his focus is on breadth, not historical merit. For example, in discussing London during the plague year, Gough mentions mortality bills, poetry, historical accounts of the plague, and even Daniel Defoe's *A Journal of the Plague Year* (1722). Of this work, he notes, "This is professed to be wrote by a sadler in White-chapel, but the real author was Daniel Defoe."

Gough does comment about the quality of the sources, at times recommending they be reexamined and compared against the original, or simply noting extensive damage and the reasons for it. However, he generally refrains from the point-by-point criticism he used in *The History of Carausius,* instead seeking to include sources. Although its scale meant it had many

THE

HISTORY

OF

CARAUSIUS,

OR, AN

EXAMINATION

Of what has been advanced on that Subject

BY

GENEBRIER and STUKELEY.

IN WHICH

The many Errors and Inaccuracies of both WRITERS are pointed
out and corrected.

WITH

An APPENDIX, containing Observations on their Method of explaining
Medals.

Magnis & piis tamen excidit ausis.   ACTA GOTTINGEN.

Si je ne me trompe c'est abuser des ses talens que de donner au public des explications si bizarres
& si etrangeres au sujet.   GENEB. *Hist. de Car.* p. 149.

LONDON:

Printed for T. BECKET and P. A. HONDT, at Tully's Head, in the Strand,

MDCCLXII.

*Title page for Richard Gough's first publication of antiquarian
scholarship, which focuses on medals dating to early Roman
emperor Marcus Aurelius Carausius (from Eighteenth
Century Collections Online, Gale Group)*

inaccuracies, *Anecdotes of British Topography* was popular
and netted Gough a profit of seven pounds. It was
republished in an expanded and corrected second, two-
volume edition in 1780, as *British Topography.*

Gough became the director of the Society of Antiquaries in 1771, a job he held until 1797. As director,
Gough oversaw the publication of its journal, *Archaeolog-
ica,* and actively assisted rising scholars with their publications. He encouraged rigorous scholarship among the
members and the papers they presented. He personally
preferred Roman antiquities in Britain but helped legitimize Saxon antiquities as an area of study. Overall, he
promoted the view that antiquities should be preserved
and restored as a matter of public service, not simply
fashion. In 1793 he was also selected to be a Fellow of
the Royal Society of London, but he left that society in
1795.

In 1774 Gough's mother died, and he inherited
the last of his father's estates, Enfield in Middlesex.
Also that year, Gough married Anne, a daughter of
Thomas Hall of Goldings, Hertfordshire. Although
their marriage was childless, it was happy. The couple
wintered in London in the house where Gough was
born, summered on various antiquities expeditions, and
spent the rest of the year at Enfield.

Gough became the leading reviewer for *The Gentleman's Magazine* in 1786. In this capacity, he reviewed
recent publications and authors, such as Edward Gibbon, for their scholarship, accuracy, and original contributions. Trite works were quickly dismissed, but
Gough detailed significant ones regardless of their relation to historical periods. For example, Gough extensively reviewed both a report to Napoléon Bonaparte
about the contents of the Egyptian tombs and a compilation of royal correspondence seized after revolutionaries took over Versailles.

Also while director of the Society of Antiquaries,
Gough published his two most significant works: *Sepulchral Monuments in Great Britain* (1786, 1796) and a revision of Camden's *Britannia. Sepulchral Monuments in Great
Britain* was supposed to be three volumes, providing a
British counterpoint to the French antiquary Bernard
de Montfauçon's *Monuments de la monarchie Françoise*
(1729). The first two volumes were completed, the first
in 1786 and the second in 1796. An introduction was
published in 1799. The interest in tombs evidenced by
this work was typical of contemporary antiquarians.
However, Gough differentiated his interest, and these
works, by his approach: he focused on the artistic form
of the monuments and then considered the monuments
as indicators of the social customs of the time. The illustrations were chiefly engravings done by James Basire,
whose assistant, William Blake, also helped with the
project.

First published in 1586, *Britannia* traced British
history from the pre-Roman era to the sixteenth century. In his preface, Camden explains that he has been
around the country and seen the sights or spoken with
those who have, establishing credibility for his comments. Camden also notes in "To the Reader" that he
has been "imploied for many yeares with a firme setled
study of the truth, and sincere antique faithfulnesse to
the glory of God and my country."

Gough admits similar motives in his preface to his
own edition. He also criticizes the prior editions
because they lack scholarly merit—instead of presenting
a new, updated edition, the booksellers were simply
replenishing their stocks. To ensure his edition had
merit, Gough employed his extensive network of
friends and correspondents to identify additional information, check proofs, and suggest revisions on the text.

His preface names many friends and many clergy who offered their libraries for reference and their time for research. For example, the new Lincolnshire material resulted from the minutes of the local antiquarian society, made available by the founder's grandson, Fairfax Johnson, as well as the papers of one Rev. Dr. Gordon, a local cleric.

Above all, the revised *Britannia,* plus the earlier *British Topography,* demonstrate Gough's contributions to the accurate, comprehensive topography of Britain that incorporates historical facts with historical artifacts. *British Topography* includes a systematic inventory of previous maps of Britain, including the manuscript maps frequently assembled by monks. The revised *Britannia* included county maps specially commissioned by John Cary. *Britannia* occupied Gough for sixteen years; he spent seven years retranslating the text and then an additional nine on the actual printing. Finally, *Britannia* was released in 1789, then reprinted, with corrections and additions to only the first volume, in 1806. A third volume was intended but never completed, because of Gough's declining health and the 1808 fire at the offices of his printer, Nichols.

Gough's position as director of the Society of Antiquities was his formally acknowledged role in public life. However, the conversations he began were influential beyond that. For example, a trend for renovating sixteenth- and seventeenth-century churches developed in the late eighteenth century. The work frequently destroyed the original aesthetic values of the edifices in the name of fashion. Gough firmly opposed James Wyatt's renovations at Lichfield and Salisbury Cathedrals; Gough resigned rather than accept Wyatt as a member of the Society of Antiquities. His opposition began a gradual but national conversation about renovation, restoration, and preservation.

Gough died on 20 February 1809, after an increasingly serious illness of several months. His wife, Anne, survived him. The sale of his library yielded £3,552; the sale of his miscellaneous antiquities provided £517. His collection of British topographical materials, including notes for future books, were left to the Bodleian Library at Oxford. *The Gentleman's Magazine* printed an autobiographical sketch that Gough had written shortly before he died. It summarizes Gough's

publications and also notes that he guarded the correspondence of his peers from "the impertinence of modern Editors."

Horace Walpole, a leading contemporary literary and cultural figure as well as an antiquarian himself, considered Gough boring and native antiquities barbaric. However, Gough's contributions are undeniable. He collaborated with correspondents around the nation to establish a well-rounded sense of local history, and he began the British conversation about native antiquities and preservation. Above all, though, Richard Gough was instrumental in redefining British antiquities, expanding the definition from the obvious Roman relics to the everyday objects of gravestones and parishes.

References:

William Camden, *Britannia,* translated by Philemon Holland (London: Printed by F. K., R. Y., and I. L. for George Latham, 1637)—a variant of the editions with "A. Heb.," <http://gateway.proquest.com>;

John Evans, *History of the Society of Antiquaries* (Oxford: Oxford University Press, 1956);

John M. Frew, "Richard Gough, James Wyatt, and Late 18th-Century Preservation," *Journal of the Society of Architectural Historians,* 38 (December 1979): 366–374, JSTOR <http://links.jstor.org>;

Emily Lorraine de Montluzin, *Attributions of Authorship in the Gentleman's Magazine, 1731–1868: An Electronic Union List* (Charlottesville: University of Virginia, 2001–2003), <http://etext.lib.virginia.edu/bsuva/gm2/GMintro.html>;

John Nichols, *Literary Anecdotes of the Eighteenth Century: Comprizing Biographical Memoirs of William Bowyer, Printer, F.S.A. and Many of His Learned Friends* (London: Nichols & Bentley, 1812), VI: Part 1;

Nichols, *Minor Lives: A Collection of Biographies by John Nichols,* edited by Edward L. Hart (Cambridge, Mass.: Harvard University Press, 1971);

Rosemary Sweet, "Antiquaries and Antiquities in Eighteenth-Century England," *Eighteenth-Century Studies,* 34, no. 2 (2001): 181–206, <http://muse.jhu.edu/>;

Gwyn Walters, "The Antiquary and the Map," *Word & Image,* 4 (April–June 1988): 529–544.

William Harris

(1720 – 4 February 1770)

Patrick Gill
Johannes Gutenberg University

BOOKS: *An Historical and Critical Account of Hugh Peters. After the Manner of Mr. Bayle,* anonymous (London: Printed for J. Noon & A. Millar, 1751);

An Historical and Critical Account of the Life and Writings of James the First, King of Great Britain. After the Manner of Mr. Bayle (London: Printed for James Waugh, 1753);

An Historical and Critical Account of the Life and Writings of Charles I, King of Great Britain. After the Manner of Mr. Bayle. Drawn from Original Writers and State-Papers (London: Printed for R. Griffiths; T. Field; and C. Henderson, 1758);

An Historical and Critical Account of Oliver Cromwell. To Which Is Added an Appendix of Original Papers (London: Printed for A. Millar, 1762);

An Historical and Critical Account of the Life of Charles the Second, King of Great Britain. After the Manner of Mr. Bayle. To Which Is Added an Appendix of Original Papers, Etc., 2 volumes (London: Printed for A. Millar, 1766).

Edition: *An Historical and Critical Account of the Lives and Writings of James I. and Charles I. and of the Lives of Oliver Cromwell and Charles II, After the Manner of Mr. Bayle, from Original Writers and State Papers. A New Edition, with a Life of the Author, Etc.* (London: Printed for F. C. and J. Rivington, T. Payne, etc., 1814).

SELECTED PERIODICAL PUBLICATION–UNCOLLECTED: "Observations on the Julia Strata; and on the Roman Stations, Forts and Camps, in the Counties of Monmouth, Brecknock, Carmarthen, and Glamorgan," *Archaeologia,* 2, no. 1 (1770).

A dissenting divine and minor historian of the mid eighteenth century, William Harris published a succession of biographies of English rulers from 1603 to 1685. Harris saw the insistence on ecclesiastical uniformity as the principal problem of this era and employed extensive footnotes to comment on contemporary issues and to argue in favor of religious toleration. His inclusion of historical accounts and documents in his work usually receives favorable comments from critics, but it cannot make up for his frankly partisan views. This lack of impartiality, together with the unimaginative style of Harris's writing and his over-enthusiastic use of footnotes, is probably responsible for his lowly standing among both his contemporaries and modern historians.

Born the son of a Nonconformist tradesman in Salisbury, Wiltshire, in 1720, William Harris was educated for the ministry by Henry Grove and his nephew, assistant, and eventual successor Thomas Amory at the Taunton Academy, a center of learning for dissenters in the west of England. Harris's education at this institution seems to have caused him little trouble, since his "early love of books and a thirst for knowledge, rendered application easy and profitable" ("Sketch of the Life of the Author," preface to *An Historical and Critical Account of the Lives and Writings of James I. and Charles I. and of the Lives of Oliver Cromwell and Charles II* [1814]).

At the age of eighteen, Harris was considered qualified to preach and began officiating for a congregation in Looe, Cornwall, from which he soon moved on to Wells, Somersetshire, where he was ordained on 15 April 1741. Shortly after his ordination Harris married Elizabeth Bovet, and they settled in her hometown of Honiton, Devonshire. Harris began tending to the small congregation of Luppitt near Honiton, a position he held until his death in 1770.

Apparently, no record exists giving the denomination Harris belonged to, and his works give little indication of any affiliation with a particular sect of Nonconformists. According to "Sketch of the Life of the Author," Harris's sermons are "said to have been plain and practical," but since none of them was published, no assessment of their literary or theological merit can be made. Harris "soon courted fame in a different pursuit," namely that of writing biographies, the first of which was published anonymously in 1751. The choice of independent divine Hugh Peters (1598–1660) as his subject may seem surprising, but it illustrates Harris's preoccupation with the history of the dissenters in England.

An Historical and Critical Account of Hugh Peters (1751) is subtitled *After the Manner of Mr. Bayle,* as are all but one of Harris's biographical accounts. This affinity with the French philosopher and critic Pierre Bayle is discernible in both the form and the content of Harris's books. Bayle suffered religious persecution himself and set out his views on philosophical as well as theological arguments in his *Dictionnaire historique et critique,* published in 1697, taking frequent recourse to lengthy commentary on the text. Harris shared not only Bayle's attitude toward religious toleration but also his conviction that documentation and personal comment can be part of historical writing. In his historical account of Peters, however, Harris overshoots the mark. As Donald A. Stauffer comments on Harris's writing in *The Art of Biography in Eighteenth-Century England:* "The ultimate in footnotes, reminiscent of Swift's fleas with other fleas to bite 'em, is to be found in William Harris's lives of the Stuarts, which consist principally of footnotes. Footnotes on footnotes are regular occurrences with him, and if the type had permitted him . . . he would have had a footnote on a footnote on a footnote."

In the case of Harris's *An Historical and Critical Account of Hugh Peters,* the account proper consists of a mere 731 words, an average of under twenty words per page. The majority of the book is taken up by the footnotes, in which Harris cites his sources and addresses what he feels to be shortcomings in church, law, and society in the time he investigates as well as in his own day. The admiration Harris expresses for Peters is thus undermined by the biographer's seeming much more engaged in his own train of thought than in any faithful rendering of his subject's life.

Following his account of Peters, Harris embarked on a series of biographies of English rulers, in which he clearly intends to trace their roles in the historical processes that led to the outbreak of the English Civil War, the Restoration, and, finally, the Glorious Revolution. The method he employs in these accounts is similar to that used in the biography of Peters except that Harris had little to commend and much to criticize about the Stuart kings. His series of regal biographies begins with *An Historical and Critical Account of the Life and Writings of James the First, King of Great Britain,* published under his name in 1753. He continues with *An Historical and Critical Account of the Life and Writings of Charles I, King of Great Britain,* published in 1758. Harris is highly critical of both these monarchs, who were notorious for their firm adherence to uniformity in ecclesiastical doctrine and ritual. In 1762 Harris published his next work, *An Historical and Critical Account of Oliver Cromwell,* in which—as

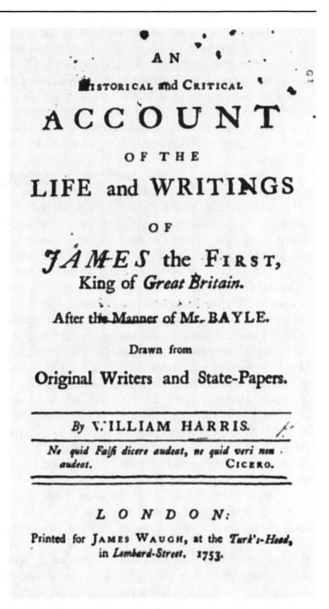

Title page for William Harris's biography of Britain's King James I, one of a series of royal biographies (Eighteenth-Century Collections Online, Gale Group)

before in his account of Peters—he offers a much more positive verdict than in the Stuart biographies.

In December 1765 the title of Doctor of Divinity was bestowed on Harris by the University of Glasgow. In *Literary Anecdotes of the Eighteenth Century* (1812) John Nichols sees Thomas Hollis, Harris's "munificent patron . . . who had presented him with many valuable books in reference to the subjects of his Histories," as the main influence behind this bestowal. Together with historian and biographer Thomas Birch, Hollis must be counted among the circle of scholars who, because his subjects and opinions were congenial to them, supported Harris in his work.

Harris's final book, *An Historical and Critical Account of the Life of Charles the Second, King of Great Britain* was published in 1766, four years after the account of Oliver Cromwell. Harris had planned to add an account of James II, thus taking in all the rulers from the Stuart accession to the Glorious Revolution, but this last work was never completed since Harris fell ill and died 4 February 1770. He was survived by his wife and left no children.

Even in his own lifetime, Harris was by no means universally respected as an historian. As is stated in "Sketch of the Life of the Author," his desire was "to rescue his [nonconformist] brethren from obloquy, and afford them a larger share in the merit of perpetuating the liberties" of Britain. Together with what Stauffer calls "a burning sense of injustice and an intense sensitivity on questions of national honour," Harris's zealous defense of English dissenters was only too obvious in his works and disqualified them from being considered reliable historical accounts. An increasing interest in the conservation of historical documents briefly secured Harris a place as a collector and compiler, but recommendations such as that made by S. Austin Allibone in *A Critical Dictionary of English Literature and British and American Authors Living and Deceased* (1859), to the effect that the "historical reader should not fail to procure [Harris's] vols.," no longer ring true, unless the "historical reader" is interested in Harris's own period rather than the periods of his subjects.

William Harris's relative obscurity is borne out by the bibliographical confusion his far from uncommon name seems to have caused. Thus, he is credited with having written more than he really did by some bibliographers and conflated into a single entity with other writers by other bibliographers. The *Bibliotheca Britannica,* for instance, credits Harris with the authorship of the *Essays upon Money and Coins,* a work usually attributed to Joseph Harris, who, as assay master of the mint, was incomparably better qualified to write such a treatise. S. Halkett and J. Laing's *Dictionary of Anonymous and Pseudonymous English Literature* (1882–1888), on the other hand, lists a "William Harris (1726–1767)" who is credited with both Harris's biographies and the works of one William Harris (1675?–1740), a Presbyterian divine and prolific writer on theological topics. Even Stauffer gives no indication in his book that the name William Harris refers to two separate authors.

References:

S. Austin Allibone, *A Critical Dictionary of English Literature and British and American Authors Living and Deceased: From the Earliest Accounts to the Middle of the Nineteenth Century,* volume 1 (Philadelphia: Childs & Peterson, 1859);

S. Halkett and J. Laing, *Dictionary of Anonymous and Pseudonymous English Literature,* 4 volumes (Edinburgh: W. Paterson, 1882–1888; Boston, Mass.: Lockwood, Brooks, 1882; enlarged edition by James Kennedy, W. A. Smith and A. F. Johnson, Edinburgh: Oliver & Boyd, 1926–[1962]);

"William Harris (1720–1770)," *The Dictionary of National Biography: From Earliest Times to 1900* (London: Oxford University Press, 1917);

John Nichols, *Literary Anecdotes of the Eighteenth Century: Comprizing Biographical Memoirs of William Bowyer, Printer, F.S.A, and Many of His Learned Friends,* volume 3 (London: Printed for the Author, 1812), p. 9;

Donald A. Stauffer, *The Art of Biography in Eighteenth-Century England* (Princeton: Princeton University Press, 1941);

Robert Watt, *Bibliotheca Britannica* (Edinburgh: Printed for A. Constable, 1824; reprinted, New York: Burt Franklin, 1965).

Sir John Hawkins

(30 March 1719 – 21 May 1789)

Walter H. Keithley
Arizona State University

See also the Hawkins entries in *DLB 104: British Prose Writers, 1660–1800, Second Series* and *DLB 142: Eighteenth-Century Literary Biographers.*

BOOKS: *Memoirs of the Life of Agostino Steffani* (London? 1740?);

Observations on the State of the Highways, and on the Laws for Amending and Keeping Them in Repair; with a Draught of a Bill for Comprehending and Reducing into One Act of Parliament the Most Essential Parts of All the Statutes in Force relating to the Highways, and for Making Provision for the More Easy and Effectual Repair of the Highways (London: Printed by His Majesty's law-printer for J. Worrall, 1763);

An Account of the Institution and Progress of Ancient Music. With a Comparative View of the Music of Past and Present Times. By a Member (London: Privately printed, 1770);

A Charge to the Grand Jury of the County of Middlesex. Delivered . . . on Monday the Eighth Day of January 1770 (London: Printed for J. Worrall & B. Tovey, 1770);

A General History of the Science and Practice of Music, 5 volumes (London: Printed for T. Payne, 1776);

Of the Office of Bidding Prayers, with an Ancient Form of Such Bidding; As Also, a Form of Cursing, Communicated by Sir John Hawkins (London? 1779);

A Charge to the Grand Jury of the County of Middlesex. Delivered . . . on Monday the Eleventh day of September, 1780 (London: Printed for Edward Brooke, 1780);

A Dissertation on the Armorial Ensigns of the County of Middlesex, and of the Abbey and City of Westminster (London, 1780);

Remarks on the Forty Second and Forty Third Psalms (London? 1781?);

The Life of Samuel Johnson, LL.D. (London: Printed for J. Buckland, J. Rivington, T. Payne, L. Davis, B. White, 1787; second edition, revised and corrected, 1787);

Political Miscellanies: Part the First, by Hawkins and Joseph Richardson (London: Printed for J. Ridgway, 1987).

Sir John Hawkins (frontispiece by James Roberts for Bertram Hylton Davis, A Proof of Eminence: The Life of Sir John Hawkins, *1973; Thomas Cooper Library, University of South Carolina)*

Edition: *The Life of Samuel Johnson, LL.D.*, edited, abridged, with an introduction, by Bertram H. Davis (New York: Macmillan, 1961; London: Cape, 1961).

OTHER: Izaak Walton and Charles Cotton, Esq., *The Complete Angler: or, Contemplative Man's Recreation,* edited by Hawkins, with a preface and a life of Walton by Hawkins, and with a life of Cotton by William Oldys (London: Printed for Thomas Hope, 1760); revised and enlarged with Hawkins's life of Cotton replacing Oldys's (London:

Printed for John, Francis & Charles Rivington, 1784);

Samuel Johnson, The Works of Samuel Johnson, LL.D. Together with His Life, and Notes on His Lives of the Poets by Sir John Hawkins, 11 volumes (London: Printed for J. Buckland, J. Rivington, T. Payne, 1787);

Dr. William Boyce, Cathedral Music, Being a Collection in Score of the Most Valuable and Useful Compositions for That Service, by the Several English Masters of the Last Two Hundred Years, prefix by Hawkins (London: Printed for John Ashley, 1788).

SELECTED PERIODICAL PUBLICATIONS–UNCOLLECTED: "Short Is the Day in Which Ill Acts Prevail, But Honesty's a Rock, Will Never Fail," *The Gentleman's Magazine,* 9 (1739): 117–118;

"Essay on Honesty," *The Gentleman's Magazine,* 9 (1739): 232–233;

"Of Honesty &c." *The Gentleman's Magazine,* 9 (1739): 359;

"Essay on Diligence," *The Gentleman's Magazine,* 10 (1740): 50–52;

"Aenigma," *The Gentleman's Magazine,* 10 (1740): 410;

"Concerning the Pretender's Behavior in Scotland," *The Gentleman's Magazine,* 16 (1746): 33.

Sir John Hawkins is known in the twenty-first century primarily for writing one of the first biographies of Samuel Johnson as well as an ambitious history of music. His treatment of Johnson has been recognized for the value of the original material it includes, and his history of music continues to be a helpful text for scholars interested in the music of antiquity. What is unfortunate, however, is that these works have come to serve as the sole representatives of the oeuvre of Hawkins, a problem compounded by their both having had to compete for the status of their relative merit with equally ambitious contemporary works, James Boswell's *The Life of Samuel Johnson LL.D.* (1791) and Charles Burney's *General History of Music* (1776–1789). On both accounts, Hawkins's work has been historically judged slightly inferior, for reasons not always relevant to the merit of his works, but often on the basis of his cantankerous personality. What most critics have failed to point out, however, is that Boswell never attempted to write an ambitious history of music, nor did Burney write an authoritative biography of the most significant literary figure of the English eighteenth century. Though Hawkins's work might be considered slightly inferior to that of the other two men, his intelligence was deep enough to write significant, well-regarded works on both topics and many other subjects as well. Over the course of his lifetime, Hawkins was an accomplished lawyer, public official, historian, and miscellaneous writer who contributed significantly to each field. Hence, while the reader might agree that Hawkins does not belong to the first rank of contemporary thinkers such as Johnson, Horace Walpole, or even Boswell, he does belong to the elite class of English intellectuals in the eighteenth century.

John Hawkins was born in London on 30 March 1719 to John Hawkins and Elizabeth Gwatkin Hawkins. Throughout his life, Hawkins claimed that he was the descendent of famous seaman John Hawkins, a claim that cannot be corroborated. Hawkins's father was a carpenter who ascended to the position of surveyor, a vocation that he intended for his son. In about 1736 the junior Hawkins studied under Edward Hoppus for this purpose but soon changed his mind and was articled to John Scott, an attorney at Bishopsgate. In this position Hawkins, a notoriously early riser, found time not only to study law but also to pursue his love of literature. These studies led to Hawkins's acquaintance with Edward Cave, a bookseller and editor of *The Gentleman's Magazine* in St. John's Gate. Hawkins's first published piece appeared in this venue; it was an essay on honesty titled "Short Is the Day in Which Ill Acts Prevail, But Honesty's a Rock, Will Never Fail" (1739); several other short prose and poetry pieces by Hawkins appeared in the magazine before 1748. More significantly, however, Cave provided Hawkins an opportunity to meet Johnson sometime during this period. Johnson had come to London from Lichfield with David Garrick in 1737 and had been out of work for almost a year before Cave employed him to write the "Reports on the Debates in the Senate of Lilliput" (1740–1744), a thinly disguised account of the proceedings of Parliament. When Cave provided the opportunity for the two to meet, a mutually beneficial relationship commenced that lasted until the death of Johnson in 1784.

At this point also Hawkins began to indulge his taste for music. In 1741 he became an original member of the Madrigal Society and the Academy of Ancient Music, where he was able to form acquaintances with the best of the contemporary amateur musicologists. In 1742 he wrote the words for five solo cantatas, which (along with another written by his friend Foster Webb) were set to music by John Stanley. Hawkins wrote more cantatas a few months later; all were warmly received at Vauxhall and Ranelagh. In the meantime, Hawkins had acquitted himself well under Scott and, upon receiving his emancipation, was commended to Peter Storer, a wealthy conveyancer who lived on the summit of Highgate Hill. Hawkins had met Storer through the popularity of his cantatas and became a frequent visitor to the Storer music room. Hawkins eventually became Storer's assistant and, finally, a recognized attorney, enjoying enough success to cease living with his father in 1746 and take a house in Clement's Lane, Lombard Street, with a Dr. Munckley.

St. John's Gate, London, location of The Gentleman's Magazine *and probable meeting place of Hawkins and Samuel Johnson*
(from Bertram Hylton Davis, A Proof of Eminence: The Life of Sir John Hawkins, *1973;*
Thomas Cooper Library, University of South Carolina)

Further testament to Hawkins's success as an attorney is evidenced by his marriage to Sidney Storer, a daughter of Peter Storer, on 24 March 1753, a union that brought Hawkins a fortune of £10,000. With his new wife, Hawkins went to live in a house in Austin Friars, to which he also removed his office. By all accounts, Sidney Hawkins was one of the few persons that held her husband's complete trust, and together they shared a happy and productive marriage. As their daughter Laetitia-Matilda later reflected, they shared a mutual love of music and the arts, and Sidney Hawkins was a good host to her husband's friends. Hawkins gave her unlimited permission to open all of his letters. In 1759, upon the death of Sidney Hawkins's brother, Peter Storer Jr., the couple inherited an additional fortune of £1,000 a year. Upon this designation, Hawkins transferred his business to his clerk Richard Clark and took a house at Twickenham (where he and his wife settled until 1771) and another at Hatton Street as a town residence.

In 1761, after settling in Twickenham, Hawkins became a Middlesex Magistrate. He was an active magistrate, at first refusing to accept fees for his services, but, upon finding that such a practice only encouraged litigation, he adopted the policy of accepting fees and giving them to the poor of the parish. In 1763 he published *Observations on the State of the Highways, and on the Laws for Amending and Keeping Them in Repair,* which successfully called for a new statute to improve the maintenance of highways. In 1764 Hawkins managed to oppose successfully a bill for the rebuilding of Newgate that would have put an undue portion of the cost upon the county of Middlesex. As a result of this action, he was elected chairman of the Middlesex Quarter Sessions on 19 September 1765, thereby becoming chief magistrate. In 1769 Hawkins again came to the defense of his neighbors when he successfully petitioned the city of London not to move the Fleet Prison to Ely House. He was handsomely rewarded for his work with a silver cup worth £30.

At the same time that he was enjoying considerable professional success, Hawkins was also pursuing his avocations with the same enthusiasm that he had previously done while working under Scott. His residence at Twickenham brought him into the frequent company of such literary and artistic notables as Walpole, Joshua Reynolds, and Garrick. In 1749 Hawkins had been invited by Johnson to join the Ivy Lane Club, a group consisting, in addition to Johnson and Hawkins, of Samuel Salter, a Cambridge divine; John Hawkesworth, a writer; John Ryland, Hawkesworth's brother-in-law; John Payne, a bookseller, who later sold some of Hawkins's books; John Dyer, a mathematician; and three physicians—William M'Ghie, Edmund Barker, and Richard

Letter from Hawkins to his publisher, John Nichols (Bertram Hylton Davis, A Proof of Eminence:
The Life of Sir John Hawkins, *1973; Thomas Cooper Library, University of South Carolina)*

Bathurst. The purpose of the Ivy Lane Club was to provide Johnson with an opportunity to discourse on contemporary social and literary topics. Hawkins, however, did not remain in the group for long. Citing his new marriage, Hawkins claimed that he could no longer bear to spend his evenings away from home and was not part of any of Johnson's club ventures until the formation of "The Club" (later, The Literary Club) in 1764.

Despite this lapse in club activity, however, Hawkins's reputation as a scholar was affirmed with his editing of Izaak Walton and Charles Cotton's *The Complete Angler: or, Contemplative Man's Recreation* in 1760, a reprint of the fifth edition of a work titled *The Universal Angler,* first published in 1676. Hawkins, himself an avid fly fisherman at Twickenham, expanded the notes of a previous editor, Moses Brown, and contributed more of his own. Additionally, he added a biography of Walton for his first edition, and one of Cotton for the fourth edition. Johnson himself approved of Hawkins's treatment of the text, commenting to George Horne, Bishop of Norwich, in 1774 that the work had fallen into good hands. At about this same time, Hawkins supplied notes for the University of Oxford's 1771 republication of Sir Thomas Hanmer's 1743–1744 edition of Shakespeare's works as well as for Johnson's edition of Shakespeare, which appeared in 1765. In 1764 Hawkins was invited to join Johnson's Literary Club. The original members of The Club, in addition to Hawkins and Johnson, included Reynolds, Edmund Burke, and Oliver Goldsmith. Never popular at The Ivy Lane Club, Hawkins's unsociable reputation was

cemented by his behavior at The Literary Club. Although Hawkins claims to have left The Club on his own volition, again citing that his domestic arrangements did not permit him to be out as late as the activities of The Club required, other members of the group reported much different stories. Boswell reports that one evening Hawkins attacked Burke so viciously that all members of the group voiced their displeasure, an account that was later corroborated by Laetitia-Matilda Hawkins. Whatever the case, Hawkins shortly quit the meetings of The Club, and when Johnson formed the Essex Head Club in 1784, Hawkins was not invited to participate. What did linger from the incident, however, was a bad reputation for Hawkins, in which his natural tendencies to coarseness and excessive pride were amplified and eventually codified in the appraisal of his work by future critics.

Despite this negative reputation, Hawkins, shortly after leaving The Club, demonstrated considerable bravery in the suppression of the election riots in Brentford in 1768 and the Moorfield riots in 1769. For his efforts in both situations, he was recommended to the king and was knighted on 23 October 1772. In 1771 Hawkins suffered the loss of his father. Shortly thereafter, he decided to leave Twickenham because his father had been fond of the residence. Hawkins settled in Hatton Street, but again moved, this time to Queen Square, Westminster, after three attempted burglaries on his home. In 1785 he was forced to move for a last time after a fire destroyed his house, along with his valuable collection of books and art. He took a residence in Broad Sanctuary, Westminster, where he resided until his death on 21 May 1789.

GUIDO ARETINUS A BENEDICTINE MONK, HAVING REFORMED THE
SCALE OF MUSIC AND INVENTED A NEW METHOD OF NOTATION,
COMMUNICATES HIS IMPROVEMENTS TO POPE JOHN XX,
WHO INVITES HIM TO ROME AND BECOMES HIS DISCIPLE.

*Frontispiece and title page for Hawkins's most ambitious work (Special Collections, Thomas Cooper Library,
University of South Carolina)*

In the final years of his life, long after he had left The Club, Hawkins wrote his two most significant works, *A General History of the Science and Practice of Music* (1776) and *A Life of Samuel Johnson, LL.D.* (1787). The genesis for *A General History of the Science and Practice of Music* probably came in 1760 when Walpole suggested that Hawkins take up the topic. In addition to his life-long interest in music, several other factors qualified Hawkins for the task. First, he had previously written at least two significant pieces on music, *Memoirs of the Life of Agostino Steffani* (1740?) and his defense of the Academy of Ancient Music, *An Account of the Institution and Progress of Ancient Music* (1770). Furthermore, Hawkins had the support of many amateur and professional musicians who either provided materials or contributed in other ways to his text. Stanley, William Gostling, and George Frideric Handel, for example, provided reliable input for Hawkins. Walpole, acting through the British ambassador to Italy, collected valuable Italian texts, which Hawkins was able to supplement further with the purchase of significant portions of the library of John Christopher Pepusch, the director of the Lincoln's Inn Fields Theater, and materials gathered in 1771 during a visit to the Oxford and Bodleian libraries. After fifteen years of painstaking research, Hawkins was finally able to publish his history. In it he sought, in accord with contemporary methods of historiography, to give the history of his subject from the earliest instances of antiquity down through the latest possible moment—in this case, the death of Handel. Though meticulous in its preparation, Hawkins was labeled as an aspiring antiquarian and not a historian of music, a charge that is somewhat verified by the relative strength of the "ancient" portions of his text. Most of the criticism that was leveled against Hawkins's work, however, was merely invective, aimed at his prose style, status as a knight, or his preexisting negative social reputation.

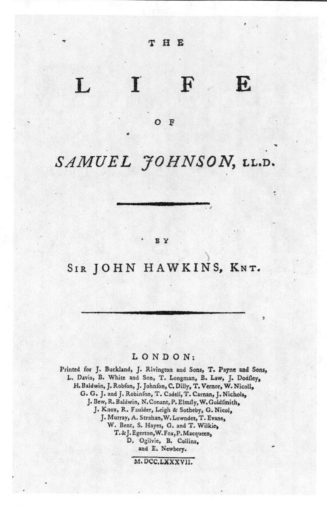

THE

LIFE

OF

SAMUEL JOHNSON, LL.D.

BY

SIR JOHN HAWKINS, KNT.

LONDON:

Printed for J. Buckland, J. Rivington and Sons, T. Payne and Sons,
L. Davis, B. White and Son, T. Longman, B. Law, J. Dodſley,
H. Baldwin, J. Robſon, J. Johnſon, C. Dilly, T. Vernor, W. Nicoll,
G. G. J. and J. Robinſon, T. Cadell, T. Carnan, J. Nichols,
J. Bew, R. Baldwin, N. Conant, P. Elmſly, W. Goldſmith,
J. Knox, R. Faulder, Leigh & Sotheby, G. Nicol,
J. Murray, A. Strahan, W. Lowndes, T. Evans,
W. Bent, S. Hayes, G. and T. Wilkie,
T. & J. Egerton, W. Fox, P. Macqueen,
D. Ogilvie, B. Collins,
and E. Newbery.

M. DCC. LXXXVII.

Title page for Hawkins's work written three years after Johnson's death (Strozier Library, Florida State University)

In addition to *A General History of the Science and Practice of Music,* which he considered to be his magnum opus, Hawkins is also remembered for his *The Life of Samuel Johnson, LL.D.* Johnson and Hawkins had been friends since at least 1748, and shortly before his death in 1784, Johnson had made Hawkins the executor of his estate. Upon Johnson's death, Hawkins was approached by several booksellers to write a biography of Johnson and to edit a collection of his works, a request that Hawkins happily took up, reflecting how fortunate it was to be asked to do a task that he had already planned to take on. When Hawkins's life of Johnson first appeared in 1787, it was almost universally criticized. Such criticism was probably appropriate for his edition of Johnson's works, which includes pieces that are clearly not by Johnson. The life, however, was widely criticized both on account of Hawkins's reputation and because it did not portray Johnson in a flattering light. Despite such criticism, however, Hawkins's *The Life of Samuel Johnson, LL.D.* adds many anecdotes and incidentals about

Johnson that could only be accumulated over forty years of friendship and are simply unavailable elsewhere. Additionally, more recent scholarship has persuasively demonstrated that the more "human" analysis Hawkins applies to Johnson's life was a rhetorical construction intended to defend his subject from charges of unorthodoxy. Such a viewpoint takes Johnson squarely out of the intellectual "John Bull" depiction by Boswell and places him more firmly in the cast that he created for himself in his autobiographical *Prayers and Meditations* (1785).

Personality flaws and all, John Hawkins was a man of considerable intellectual ability and achievement who deserves to be evaluated on the strong merit of his work. Though not traditionally regarded highly in critical circles, both his major and minor works should be recognized for their potentially valuable contributions to eighteenth-century English cultural studies in general, and the Johnsonian circle in particular.

References:

Gay Wilson Brack, "Sir John Hawkins, Biographer of Johnson: A Rhetorical Analysis," dissertation, Arizona State University, 1992;

Bertram H. Davis, *A Proof of Eminence: The Life of John Hawkins* (Bloomington: University of Indiana Press, 1973);

Austin Dobson, "Sir John Hawkins, Knight," in *Old Kensington Palace and Other Papers* (New York: Fredrick A. Stokes, 1910);

"Sir John Hawkins," *General Biographical Dictionary,* edited by John Gorton (London: H. G. Bohn, 1851);

Laetitia-Matilda Hawkins, *Anecdotes, Biographical Sketches and Memoirs* (London: Longman, 1822);

Hawkins, *Memoirs, Anecdotes and Opinions* (London: Longman, 1824);

C. A. Miller, *Sir John Hawkins: Dr Johnson's Friend-Attorney-Executor-Biographer: A Reorientation of the Knight, the Lady, and Boswell* (Washington, D.C.: Privately printed, 1951);

Percy Scholes, *The Life and Activities of Sir John Hawkins: Musician, Magistrate, and Friend of Johnson* (New York: Da Capa, 1978);

Sir Leslie Stephen, ed., "Sir John Hawkins," *DNB* (London: Oxford University Press, 1921–1922).

Papers:

Few of Sir John Hawkins's papers survive, and most of these concern his work in the Middlesex Quarter Sessions. The largest group is housed in the Greater London Records Office. Most of the rest are in the Public Records Office. The locations of individual letters and other documents are recorded in Bertram H. Davis's *A Proof of Eminence: The Life of John Hawkins.*

Thomas Hearne

(? July 1678 – 10 June 1735)

Michael R. Hutcheson
Landmark College

See also the Hearne entry in *DLB 213: Pre-Nineteenth-Century British Book Collectors and Bibliographers.*

BOOKS: *An Index of the Principal Passages in Sir Roger L'Estrange's Translation of Josephus into English,* compiled by Hearne (London, 1702);

The History and Antiquities of Glastonbury (Oxford: Sheldonian Theatre, 1722);

A Letter Containing an Account of Some Antiquities between Windsor and Oxford; with a List of the Several Pictures in the School Gallery Adjoining the Bodleyan Library (Oxford, 1725);

Liber Niger Scaccarii, 2 volumes (Oxford: Sheldonian Theatre, 1728);

Ectypa Varia ad Historiam Britannicam Illustrandum. (Oxford, 1737);

Catalogus Impressorum Librorum Bibliothecæ Bodleianæ in Academia Oxoniensi, by Hearne and Thomas Hyde (Oxford: Sheldonian Theatre, 1738);

The Life of Mr. Thomas Hearne, of St. Edmund's Hall, Oxford; from His Own MS. Copy, in the Bodleian Library (Oxford: Clarendon Press, 1772);

Reliquiae Hearniae: The Remains of Thomas Hearne, M.A., of Edmund Hall, 2 volumes, edited by Philip Bliss (Oxford: Printed for the editor by James Wright, [1857]); expanded edition, 3 volumes (London: J. R. Smith, 1869);

Remarks and Collections of Thomas Hearne, 11 volumes, edited by C. E. Doble, D. W. Rannie, and H. E. Salter, *Oxford Historical Society Publications,* 2, 7, 13, 34, 42, 43, 48, 50, 65, 67, 72 (Oxford: Clarendon Press, 1885–1921);

The Remains of Thomas Hearne [1-volume abridgment of *Reliquiae Hearniae*], edited by John [i.e., Philip] Bliss, revised by John Buchanan-Brown (London: Centaur Press, 1966; Carbondale: Southern Illinois University Press, 1967).

Collection: *The Works of Thomas Hearne,* 4 volumes (London: Printed for S. Bagster, 1810).

Thomas Hearne (from The Life of Mr. Thomas Hearne, of St. Edmund's Hall, Oxford; from His Own MS. Copy, in the Bodleian Library, *1772; Huntington Library; Eighteenth Century Collections Online, Gale Group)*

OTHER: Edward Hyde, Earl of Clarendon, *The History of the Rebellion and Civil Wars in England,* edited by Hearne, index by Hearne (Oxford: Sheldonian Theatre, 1702–1704);

Sir Thomas Bodley, *Reliquiae Bodleianae; or, Some Genuine Remains of Sir Thomas Bodley,* edited by Hearne (London: Printed for John Hartley, 1703);

Eutropius, *Eutropii Breviarum Historiae Romanae, cum Paenii Metaphrasi Graeca,* edited by Hearne (Oxford: Sheldonian Theatre, 1703);

Pliny the Younger, *C. Plinii Caecilli Secundi Epistolae et Panegyricus,* edited by Hearne (Oxford: Sheldonian Theatre, 1703);

Ductor Historicus; or, A Short System of Universal History, and an Introduction to the Study of It, 2 volumes–volume 1 by Abbé de Vallemont, volume 2 by Hearne? second edition, edited by Hearne (London: Printed for Tim. Childe, 1704–1705; 3rd edition, revised, 1714; 4th edition, revised again (London: Printed by H. Clark for J. Knapten & J. Wyatt, 1723);

Justinus, *M. Juniani Justini Historiiarum ex Trogo Pompeio Libri xliv,* edited by Hearne (Oxford: Sheldonian Theatre, 1705);

Livy, *T. Livii Patavini Historiarum ab Urbe Condita Libri Qui Supersunt,* 6 volumes, edited by Hearne (Oxford: Sheldonian Theatre, 1708);

Sir John Spelman, *The Life of Aelfred the Great by Sir John Spelman . . . with Considerable Additions, and Several Historical Remarks,* edited by Hearne (Oxford: Sheldonian Theatre, 1709);

John Leland, *The Itinerary of John Leland the Antiquary,* 9 volumes, edited by Hearne (Oxford: Sheldonian Theatre, 1710–1712);

Henry Dodwell, *Henrici Dodwelli de Parma Equestri Woodwardiana Dissertatio,* edited by Hearne (Oxford: Sheldonian Theatre, 1713);

Acta apostolorum Graeco-Latine, Litteris Majusculis, e Codice Laudiano, edited by Hearne (Oxford: Sheldonian Theatre, 1715);

John Leland, *Johannes Lelandi Antiquarii de Rebus Britannicis Collectanea. Ex Autographis Descripsit Ediditque T. Hearnius, Qui et Appendicem Subjecit, Totumque Opus . . . Notis et Indice Adornavit,* 6 volumes, edited by Hearne (Oxford: Sheldonian Theatre, 1715);

Alfred, of Beverley, *Aluredi Beverlacensis Annales, Sive Historia de Gestis Rerum Britanniae,* edited by Hearne (Oxford: Sheldonian Theatre, 1716);

Livy, *Titi Livii Foro-Juliensis Vita Henrici Quinti, Regis Angliae,* edited by Hearne (Oxford: Sheldonian Theatre, 1716);

William Roper, *Guiliemi Roperi Vita D. Thomae Mori Equitis Aurati, Lingua Anglicana Contexta,* edited by Hearne (Oxford?: Veneunt apud editorem, 1716);

John Rous, *Joannis Rosi Antiquarii Warwicensis Historium Regum Angliae,* edited by Hearne (Oxford: Sheldonian Theatre, 1716);

William Camden, *Guiliemi Camdeni Annales Rerum Anglicarum et Hibernicarum Regnante Elizabetha,* 3 volumes, edited by Hearne ([Oxford], 1717);

William of Newburgh, *Guiliemi Neubrigensis Historia Sive Chronica Rerum Anglicarum,* 3 volumes, edited by Hearne (Oxford: Sheldonian Theatre, 1719);

Thomas Sprott, *Thomae Sprotti Chronica,* edited by Hearne (Oxford: Sheldonian Theatre, 1719);

A Collection of Curious Discourses Written by Eminent Antiquaries upon Several Heads in Our English Antiquities, edited by Hearne (Oxford: Sheldonian Theatre, 1720);

Ernulf, Bishop of Rochester, *Textus Roffensis,* edited by Hearne (Oxford: Sheldonian Theatre, 1720);

Robert, of Avesbury, *Roberti de Avesbury Historia de Mirabilibus Gestis Edvardi III* (Oxford: Sheldonian Theatre, 1720);

John Fordun, *Johannis de Fordun Scotichronicon Genuinum,* 5 volumes, edited by Hearne (Oxford: Sheldonian Theatre, 1722);

Hemigus, *Hemingi Chartularium Ecclesiae Wigoriensis,* 2 volumes, edited by Hearne (Oxford: Sheldonian Theatre, 1723);

Robert, of Gloucester, *Robert of Gloucester's Chronicle,* 2 volumes (Oxford: Sheldonian Theatre, 1724);

Peter Langtoft, *Peter Langtoft's Chronicle, as Illustrated and Improv'd by Robert of Brunne,* 2 volumes, edited by Hearne (Oxford: Sheldonian Theatre, 1725);

Joannes, monk of Glastonbury, *Johannis Glastoniensis, Confratris & Monachi Chronica Sive Historia De Rebus Glastoniensibus,* 2 volumes, edited by Hearne (Oxford: Sheldonian Theatre, 1726);

Adam, of Domerham, *Adami de Domerham Historia de Rebus Gestis Glastoniensibus,* 2 volumes, edited by Hearne (Oxford: Sheldonian Theatre, 1727);

Thomas Elmham, *Thomae de Elmham Vita & Gesta Henrici Quinti,* Anglorum regis, edited by Hearne (Oxford: Sheldonian Theatre, 1727);

John de Trokelowe, *Johannis de Trokelowe annales Edvardi II: Henrici de Blaneforde Chronica, et Edvardi II Vita,* edited by Hearne (Oxford: Sheldonian Theatre, 1729);

Historia Vitae et Regni Ricardi II. Angliae Regis, a Monacho Quodam de Evesham Consignata, edited by Hearne (Oxford: Sheldonian Theatre, 1729);

Thomas Caius, *Thomae Caii Vindiciae Antiquitatis Academiae Oxoniensis contra Joannem Caium, Cantabrigiensem,* 2 volumes, edited by Hearne (Oxford: Sheldonian Theatre, 1730);

Walter de Hemingford, *Walteri Hemingford, Canonici de Gisseburne, Historia De Rebus Gestis Edvardi I, Edvardi II, et Edvardi III,* 2 volumes, edited by Hearne (Oxford: Sheldonian Theatre, 1731);

Thomas Otterbourne, *Duo Rerum Anglicarum Scriptores Veteris, Viz. Thomas Otterbourne et Johannes Whetmanstede,* 2 volumes, edited by Hearne (Oxford: Sheldonian Theatre, 1732);

Richard de Morin, *Chronicon sive Annales Prioratus de Dunstaple, Una cum Excerptis E Chartulario Ejusdem Prioratus,* 2 volumes, edited by Hearne (Oxford: Sheldonian Theatre, 1733);

Benedictus, Abbas Petroburgensis, De Vita & Gestis Henrici II et Ricardi I, 2 volumes, edited by Hearne (Oxford: Sheldonian Theatre, 1733–1735).

Thomas Hearne was an archivist and antiquarian "who studied and preserved antiquities," as his self-written epitaph states. In his role as archivist, first as assistant and then as second keeper of the Bodleian Library at Oxford University, Hearne catalogued important parts of the collection. As an antiquarian, Hearne annotated manuscripts and published them in critical editions that incorporated supporting materials. While these supplementary materials are of varying relevance, Hearne must be credited as a tireless researcher of manuscripts who kept scrupulous records of the sources for his editions. Hearne's extensive correspondence and diaries have also supplied historians with detailed accounts of life in early-eighteenth-century Oxford, particularly of the contentious relations between Jacobites and other members of the university community.

Hearne was born at Littleton Green in White Waltham, Berkshire. Although his birth date is not recorded, he was baptized on 11 July 1678. His father, George Hearne, had been parish clerk since 1670, and his mother, Edith Wise, was from nearby Shottesbrooke. His father, an amateur investigator of local antiquities, educated Thomas as best he could, but the family's financial need compelled the boy to become a day laborer. Thomas's scholarly abilities, however, brought him to the attention of Francis Cherry of Shottesbrooke, who became his patron and began his Latin instruction. Cherry financed Hearne's enrollment at the Free School of Bray in 1692, and in 1695 he took Hearne into his house, treating him as a son.

It proved significant for Hearne's life and career that Cherry and the headmaster at Bray were "nonjurists," members of a group who refused to take an oath of allegiance to the monarchs who succeeded the Stuart dynasty deposed in 1689. At Cherry's home, Hearne also met many other nonjurists and was especially impressed by Henry Dodwell, a theologian who based his nonjuring beliefs on extensive patristic scholarship. With such role models, Hearne, who probably had heard Jacobite sentiments at home, became a lifelong Jacobite in politics and nonjurist in conscience.

THE
LIFE
OF
ÆLFRED THE GREAT,
By Sir JOHN SPELMAN Kt.
FROM THE
Original Manuscript in the BODLEJAN *Library:*
WITH
CONSIDERABLE ADDITIONS,
And
SEVERAL HISTORICAL REMARKS,
By the Publisher
THOMAS HEARNE, M.A.

OXFORD,
Printed at the THEATER for *Maurice Atkins* at the *Golden-Ball* in St *Paul's* Church-Yard, Lond. MDCCIX.

Title page for Hearne's edition of an early English manuscript (British Library; Eighteenth Century Collections Online, Gale Group)

Francis Cherry sponsored Hearne's matriculation at Edmund Hall, Oxford, where Hearne took up residence in 1696, receiving a B.A. in 1699 and an M.A. in 1703. To enter Oxford, Hearne had to take an oath of allegiance, an act that he justified in two long letters written to his patron. These letters, found among Cherry's papers after his death, were published by Hearne's opponents in 1731 as "A Vindication of Those Who Take the Oath of Allegiance." The publisher of the autobiographical *The Life of Mr. Thomas Hearne, of St. Edmund's Hall, Oxford; from his own MS. Copy, in the Bodleian Library* (1772) found Hearne's account of this incident unsuitable, saying in the preface, "Sentiments were expressed with such a degree of Acrimony, as could not be pleasing to the Reader, it was therefore judged proper to omit that part. . . ." Hearne's acrimony about

THE

ITINERARY

OF

JOHN LELAND

THE

ANTIQUARY.

VOL. THE FIRST.

Publiſh'd from the Original MS. in the

BODLEIAN LIBRARY

By THOMAS HEARNE M. A.

To which is prefix'd

Mr. LELAND'S *New-Year's Gift*:

And at the end is ſubjoyn'd

A Diſcourſe concerning ſome Antiquities lately found in

YORK-SHIRE.

OXFORD,

Printed at the THEATER for the Publiſher.

MDCCX.

Title page for the first book in a nine-volume work edited by Hearne
(British Library; Eighteenth Century Collections
Online, Gale Group)

this publication, however, is displayed in his diaries from 1731 and after.

While at Oxford, Hearne earned income transcribing manuscripts for Cherry and Dodwell and for James Mill's edition of the New Testament (1707). He was also offered a position in Maryland that combined missionary work and overseeing the libraries of the colony, but Hearne declined in order to continue indexing and cataloguing bequests to the Bodleian Library. This devotion to the library earned him the attention of John Hudson, who, upon becoming librarian at the Bodleian in 1701, immediately named Hearne his assistant. Hearne continued his thorough indexing work, producing such works as *An Index of the Principal Passages in Sir Roger L'Estrange's Translation of Josephus into English* (1702),

the *Index to Lord Clarendon's History of the Rebellion* (1702–1704), and completing the catalogue of the Bodleian's coin holdings. During this period Hearne's first true work was published, *Reliquiae Bodleianae; or, Some Genuine Remains of Sir Thomas Bodley* (1703). It is emblematic of all of Hearne's published works: it is not a work of historical narrative or synthesis, but, as the title indicates, a miscellany including biographical information, letters, and drafts of the statutes creating the Oxford library that bears Sir Thomas Bodley's name.

During his first decade at the Bodleian, Hearne also produced his other early signature works: scholarly editions of classical historians such as Pliny the Younger (*C. Plinii Caecilli Secundi Epistolae et Panegyricus* [1703]), Eutropius (*Eutropii Breviarum Historiae Romanae, cum Paenii Metaphrasi Graeca* [1703]), Justinus (*M. Juniani Justini Historüarum ex Trogo Pompeio Libri xliv* [1705]), and Livy (*T. Livii Patavini Historiarum ab Urbe Condita Libri Qui Supersunt* [6 volumes, 1708]). These editions of about 120 printed copies, financed by John Hudson, were well received, especially the edition of Livy's work.

In this same period Hearne edited one volume and rewrote a volume of *Ductor Historicus; or, A Short System of Universal History, and an Introduction to the Study of It* (1704–1705). This French work by the Abbé de Vallemont was a history of the world from Creation through, curiously, the Pied Piper of Halberstadt in 1376. It was first printed in English in 1698, in an edition "Partly translated from the French . . . , but chiefly composed anew by W. J. M.A." [title page]. This "W. J." is often said to be Hearne, but the early publication date, Hearne's busyness with his studies and with making transcriptions for Cherry and Dodwell, and the lack of reference to the first edition in his autobiography make that attribution unlikely. It proved to be a popular work, however, and Hearne added passages and introductory material that expanded his second edition to two volumes. In this early work Hearne demonstrates an interest in the historical nature and basis of monarchy, a focus related to the political agenda of the Jacobites that both informed and brought reproach on his later works.

In his introduction to the second volume of *Ductor Historicus,* Hearne argues for another issue important to his work as an antiquarian, the study of inscriptions and coins: "Because Inscriptions and Coynes are slighted by some who are otherwise very much inclined to the Study of History, and esteemed to be of little Use in acquiring a compleat skill in it, I shall take this Opportunity to show in short, how Necessary an Insight therein is, for such at least, as design to be accurately acquainted with any Part of Ancient History." Cataloguing the coin collection in the Bodleian had clearly given Hearne an appreciation for the role of numismatics in understanding history. Additional revised editions of *Ductor Historicus* appeared in 1714 and 1723, testaments to the popularity of the work.

The second stage of Hearne's publishing career was inaugurated in 1709 with *The Life of Aelfred the Great by Sir John Spelman*. From this point on, Hearne's primary scholarly activity was preparing editions of manuscripts related to the early history of Britain. In addition to its monarchical subject, this particular manuscript interested Hearne for at least two other reasons. First, Alfred was mistakenly thought to be the founder of University College, and therefore of the university Hearne so loved. Second, Spelman's original work was dedicated to Charles II of the deposed Stuart monarchy, and therefore appealed to Hearne's Jacobitism. The original dedication of *The Life of Aelfred the Great,* and general anxiety over the role of nonjurors at Oxford, led the manager of the university press, Arthur Charlett, to oppose the publication of the work. Although *The Life of Aelfred the Great* was published, this incident provided a foretaste of the trouble that Hearne's nonjuring Jacobitism created for his career.

At this same time Hearne was preparing for publication the nine volumes of *The Itinerary of John Leland the Antiquary* (1710–1712). Henry VIII had appointed John Leland "antiquarius" and funded his travels throughout England to catalogue objects of antiquarian value, an important activity, given Henry's dissolution of the monasteries and the consequent threat to the treasures they held. As Joseph Levine states in his 1991 *The Battle of the Books: History and Literature in the Augustan Age:*

> Leland had been the first to see the value of canvassing all the original sources of English history, both written and archeological, and to take an inventory of them in a geographical fashion. He taught his successors the importance of literary documents and the monumental remains, especially the ancient manuscripts, coins, and inscriptions, for retrieving and understanding the past; and he saw the need to recover the lost languages of ancient Britain, Latin of course, but also Celtic and Anglo-Saxon.

Leland succumbed to insanity before he could complete his charge, and his manuscripts came to be housed in the Bodleian. In his edition of Leland's *Itinerary,* Hearne included a wide range of related materials, including some investigations of local antiquities by his father. A few years later Hearne compiled a miscellany of Leland-related studies titled *Johannes Lelandi Antiquarii de Rebus Britannicis Collectanea* (1715). In Leland, Hearne found a model for his own antiquarianism, as evidenced by the latter's edition of *The History and Antiquities of Glastonbury* (1722) and the publication of *A Letter Containing an Account of Some Antiquities Between Windsor and Oxford; with a List of the Several Pictures in the School Gallery Adjoining the Bodleyan Library* (1725).

Hearne's next publication again provoked University authorities. Dodwell, the nonjuring theologian who had encouraged and employed Hearne, died in 1711. Out of loyalty, Hearne prepared an edition of Dodwell's analysis of a Roman shield, titled *Henrici Dodwelli de Parma Equestri Woodwardiana Dissertatio* (1713). As Theodor Harmsen notes, Hearne in his introduction to the volume "turned what was originally an antiquarian work into a statement for the non-juring cause," a decision that resulted in the suppression of the book. The book was soon published, but this confrontation began the series of altercations that resulted in Hearne's being removed in 1716 from his position as second keeper of the Bodleian, the post to which he had been elevated in 1712. Hearne's Jacobitism undoubtedly played a role in this decision. In 1713 a visitor to the Anatomy School, of which Hearne was also keeper, complained that Hearne showed him an engraving of the Stuart "Pretender" as part of the school's collection. Although Hearne was too reclusive to be a political activist, his sympathies are clear: throughout his diaries he refers to James Edward Stuart as "James III" and faithfully notes the celebrations in Oxford on the would-be king's birthday. Adding to Hearne's political difficulties was his 1715 election as architypographus of the university press and superior beadle in civil law. These positions required the Oaths of Supremacy and Allegiance. Hearne swore the oaths but insisted in his diary that he had spoken, sotto voce, the name of King James III. Holding these two new offices meant sacrificing his position as second keeper of the Bodleian, which Hearne was in no haste to do. Some university officials were concerned about the power of Jacobites within the Oxford colleges, especially since the government was preparing in 1715 a university reform bill that would give the monarch the authority to nominate heads and fellows. When objection was lodged against Hearne's holding multiple offices, he resigned as architypographus. However, his opponents, including Vice Chancellor Bernard Gardiner, and now Hudson himself, were not mollified. The locks to the Bodleian, to which Hearne held the keys, were changed. Without access to the Bodleian Library, Hearne could not discharge his duties and was as a result relieved of his position as second keeper in 1716.

Hearne realized that the works he chose to publish also played a role: "They say I publish Antiquity on purpose to expose those that comply against Principle," he wrote in a 1716 letter. This charge was leveled against the two publications that Hearne was preparing during 1716. One was a reprint of Roper's life of Thomas More, *Guiliemi Roperi Vita D. Thomae Mori Equitis*

THE

LIFE

OF

Mr. THOMAS HEARNE,

OF ST. EDMUND'S HALL, OXFORD;

From his own MS. Copy, in the BODLEIAN LIBRARY.

ALSO

An accurate CATALOGUE of his WRITINGS and
PUBLICATIONS, from his own MS. Copy, which he
designed for the Press.

TO WHICH ARE ADDED,

Several PLATES of the ANTIQUITIES, &c.
mentioned in his Works.

NEVER BEFORE PRINTED.

OXFORD,

AT THE CLARENDON-PRESS. M DCC LXXII.
PRINTED FOR J. AND J. FLETCHER IN THE TURL;
AND J. POTE AT ETON.

*Title page for Hearne's autobiography (Huntington Library; Eighteenth
Century Collections Online, Gale Group)*

Aurati, Lingua Anglicana Contexta (1716), which praised
More and excoriated Henry VIII for his persecution of
a man of conscience. The second was an edition of William Camden's *Annales* of Elizabeth I's reign, *Guiliemi
Camdeni Annales Rerum Anglicarum et Hibernicarum Regnante
Elizabetha* (1717). Camden's work was originally commissioned by James I, who wanted a more sympathetic
historical portrait of his mother–Mary, Queen of
Scots–than was typical in Elizabethan accounts.
Hearne's edition includes the original text, published in
1615, along with Camden's manuscript notations.
While the subject matter itself was sufficient to bring
political opprobrium on Hearne, he worsened the situation by including texts by nonjurists in the supplementary material.

Although the British history texts Hearne chose
to publish supported his political sentiments, many of
these works transcend politics. Perhaps the most important to future historians were chronicles dating from the
twelfth through the fourteenth centuries. Two literary

examples, composed in metered Middle English, were
Robert of Gloucester's Chronicle (1724) and *Peter Langtoft's
Chronicle, as Illustrated and Improv'd by Robert of Brunne*
(1725). Oxford antiquarian Anthony Wood had published portions of *Robert of Gloucester's Chronicle* the preceding century, but Hearne published a more complete
edition, based on the three extant manuscripts of the
work. For both publications, Hearne once again supplied a variety of supplementary materials intended to
verify historical accuracy of the chronicles–some
twenty items in *Robert of Gloucester's Chronicle*, fifty in *Peter
Langtoft's Chronicle*. The latter included a pamphlet on a
nunnery near Little Gidding, a portion of the Pipe Rolls
concerning Glastonbury Abbey, a discourse concerning
roods and "King Henry the Eighth's enormities," and a
fanciful explanation of Stonehenge–typical of Hearne's
wide-ranging and sometimes indiscriminate scholarship. Many of Hearne's other published chronicles
detailed events during the reigns of English monarchs,
including Henry V (*Thomae de Elmham Vita & Gesta Henrici Quinti* [1727]), Edward II (*Johannis de Trokelowe annales
Edvardi II* [1729]), and the first three Edwards (*Walteri
Hemingford, Canonici de Gisseburne, Historia De Rebus Gestis
Edvardi I, Edvardi II, et Edvardi III* [1731]).

In addition to his accurate editions of important
late-medieval British texts, Hearne's other historical
contribution was as a diarist. The 145 volumes of diaries that Hearne left at his death were later collected
into *Remarks and Collections* (1885–1921). These diaries,
while not of the literary caliber of Samuel Pepys's, are
valuable for three reasons. First, they scrupulously
record the sources of Hearne's publications. Second,
they depict the complex world of historical writing and
publishing in the late seventeenth and early eighteenth
centuries, important for historiography, the history of
printing, and their vivid portrayal of the impact of capitalism on the production of knowledge. Finally, they are
a valuable glimpse into the extent and impact of Jacobitism in the daily life of Oxford during this period.

Hearne's reverence for manuscripts brought him
both acclaim and criticism. His faithfulness to the
arcane vocabulary and spelling of the manuscripts
made him the target of Alexander Pope, who satirized
Hearne as "Wormius" in Book III of *The Dunciad*
(1728): "To future ages may thy dulness last, / As thou
preserv'st the dulness of the past!" Near the end of his
life, Edward Gibbon provided a more sober but equally
critical assessment of Hearne in "An Address &c."
(1793). Asked to write a prospectus for a subscription
series of the early historians of England, Gibbon surveyed the available editions, saying "The last who has
dug deep in the mine was Thomas Hearne, a Clerk of
Oxford poor in fortune and indeed poor in understanding. His minute and obscure diligence: his voracious

and undistinguishing appetite, and the coarse vulgarity of taste and style have exposed him to the ridicule of idle wits." Despite the patrician disdain in this assessment, Gibbon admits, "Yet it cannot be denied that Thomas Hearne has gathered many gleanings of the harvest; and if his own prefaces are swelled with crude and extraneous matter, his editions will be always recommended by their accuracy and use."

In the two decades after his dismissal from the Bodleian in 1716, Hearne's friends secured him other employment offers, as the Camden Professor of History, keeper of the University Archives, head librarian of the Bodleian, and librarian of the Royal Society. Hearne rejected all of these rather than swear the required oath of allegiance to the House of Hanover. He was, nevertheless, allowed to retain his residence at Edmund Hall, Oxford, where he died on 10 June 1735.

Hearne can be seen as the last in a line of English antiquarians extending back to Leland, who attempted to discover, catalogue, and preserve antiquities related to England's past. Hearne rarely cast his work in the narrative/analytical mode of Gibbon and other "modern" historians of the eighteenth century, preferring to compile miscellanies. His chief contribution was as a meticulous editor of manuscripts, whose publications of medieval chroniclers were the best available in English at the time, and in some cases until the nineteenth century.

References:

Harry Carter, *A History of the Oxford University Press* (Oxford: Clarendon Press, 1975);

David C. Douglas, *English Scholars 1660–1730,* second revised edition (London: Eyre & Spottiswoode, 1951);

Edward Gibbon, *The English Essays of Edward Gibbon,* edited by Patricia B. Craddock (Oxford: Clarendon Press, 1972);

Stanley G. Gillam, "Thomas Hearne's Library," *Bodleian Library Record,* 12 (1985–1988): 52–64;

Theodor Harmsen, *Antiquarianism in the Augustan Age: Thomas Hearne 1678–1735* (Oxford: Peter Lang, 2000);

Joseph M. Levine, *The Battle of the Books: History and Literature in the Augustan Age* (Ithaca & London: Cornell University Press, 1991);

Levine, *Humanism and History: Origins of Modern English Historiography* (Ithaca: Cornell University Press, 1987);

Ian Philip, *The Bodleian Library in the Seventeenth and Eighteenth Centuries* (Oxford: Clarendon Press, 1983);

Philip, "The Genesis of Thomas Hearne's *Ductor Historicus,*" *Bodleian Library Record,* 7 (July 1966): 251–164;

Joan H. Pittock, "Thomas Hearne and the Narratives of Englishness, "*British Journal for Eighteenth-Century Studies,* 22 (1999): 1–14;

D. R. Woolf, *Reading History in Early Modern England* (Cambridge: Cambridge University Press, 2000).

Papers:

Thomas Hearne's papers, including manuscript catalogues of his book collection, are mainly located in the Bodleian Library, Oxford; Hearne's letters to Hans Sloane (1710–1732) are held by the British Library, London.

John Home

(22 September 1722 – 5 September 1808)

Michael Brown
University of Aberdeen

See also the entry on Home in *DLB 84: Restoration and Eighteenth-Century Dramatists, Second Series.*

BOOKS: *Douglas: A Tragedy* (Edinburgh: G. Hamilton, J. Balfour, W. Gray & W. Peter, 1756?; London: A. Millar, 1757; Dublin: G. Faulkner, 1757; Philadelphia: Printed by Enoch Story, 1790);

Agis: A Tragedy (London: A. Millar, 1758; London: Printed for M. Cooper, 1758; Edinburgh: Printed for G. Hamilton & J. Balfour, 1758; Dublin: G. & A. Ewing, 1758);

The Siege of Aquileia: A Tragedy (London: A. Millar, 1760; Edinburgh: A. Kincaid & J. Bell, 1760; Dublin: Printed for G. & A. Ewing / Dublin: Printed for W. Smith, 1760);

The Dramatic Works of John Home (London: A. Millar, 1760)—comprises *Douglas, Agis,* and *The Siege of Aquileia;*

The Fatal Discovery: A Tragedy (London: T. Becket & P. A. De Hondt, 1769; Dublin: Printed for W. & W. Smith, 1769);

Alonzo: A Tragedy (London: Printed for T. Becket, 1773; Dublin: W. Wilson, 1773; Belfast: Printed by J. Magee, 1773); republished as *Alonzo and Ormisinda* (Philadelphia: Printed by Robert Bell, 1777);

Alfred: A Tragedy (Dublin: Printed by Bryn for the Company of Booksellers, 1777; London: Printed for T. Becket, 1778; New York, 1954);

The History of the Rebellion in the Year 1745 (London: A. Strahan for T. Cadell Jun. & W. Davis, 1802); republished as *The History of the Rebellion in Scotland in 1745* (Edinburgh: Brown, 1822).

Editions and Collections: *The Dramatic Works of John Home Esq.,* 2 volumes (Edinburgh: Geo. Reid, 1798); republished as *The Plays of John Home,* edited, and with an introduction, by James S. Malek (New York: Garland, 1980);

The Works of John Home Esq., 3 volumes (Edinburgh: Archibald Constable, 1822; London: Hurst, Robinson, 1822).

John Home (from The Works of John Home, Esq., *1822; Thomas Cooper Library, University of South Carolina)*

PLAY PRODUCTIONS: *Douglas,* Edinburgh, Canongate Theater, 14 December 1756; London, Theatre Royal in Covent Garden, 14 March 1757;

Agis, London, Theatre Royal in Drury Lane, 21 February 1758;

The Siege of Aquileia, London, Theatre Royal in Drury Lane, 21 February 1760;

The Fatal Discovery, London, Theatre Royal in Drury Lane, 23 February 1769;

Alonzo, London, Theatre Royal in Drury Lane, 27 January 1773;

Alfred, London, Theatre Royal in Covent Garden, 21 January 1778.

John Home was a minister in the Church of Scotland and the private secretary of the first Scot to be prime minister of Britain: John Stuart, third Earl of Bute. A member of the Scottish Enlightenment, Home was also a dramatist of some note in the sentimental tradition. An early celebrant of the Scottish national contribution to Britain, his central historical work, *The History of the Rebellion in the Year 1745* (1802) recounts the military action of that year from the vantage point of a participant on the side of the government.

Born in Leith, Scotland, on 22 September 1722 to Alexander Home (pronounced Hume), a town clerk, and Christian Hay Home, John Home was educated in the grammar school there and at the University of Edinburgh, receiving an M.A. degree in 1742. He proceeded to study divinity and was licensed as a probationer in 1745. However, his career path was disrupted by the Jacobite Rebellion of that year. Home volunteered for the Hanoverian side, enlisting in the College Company of Volunteers, and although he slept through the Battle of Edinburgh, he served under Sir John Cope until the Battle of Prestonpans (2 October 1745). He subsequently became a lieutenant in the Glasgow Volunteers and was present at the Battle of Falkirk (17 January 1746). Imprisoned in Doune Castle after his capture at the battle, he escaped out of a window by tying together bedsheets.

On 11 February 1747 Home was called to the congregation of Athelstaneford, East Lothian. He associated with the emerging "Moderate party" within the church. Led by William Robertson, the Moderates blended a defense of church authority, based on the power of noble patrons to choose ministers, with an enlightened mixture of tolerance for other religious denominations and a language of polite sensibility that infused their sermons with Stoic philosophy rather than overt reiteration of Christian doctrine. They were opposed in the General Assembly by the more evangelical and scripturalist "Popular party," so known because its members believed the choice of minister should be vested in the congregation. The Moderates accepted the Patronage Act of 1712 that vested the choice in the local nobility.

As a minister, Home appears to have been a reasonable success. In an unusual preaching style, he delivered the first two-thirds of his sermons from a prepared script, while he delivered the final remarks impromptu. Later, when Home purchased a house near his by-then-abandoned parish, his old parishioners apparently helped him to renovate it, as a mark of respect.

From his earliest time at Athelstaneford, Home wrote verse. In the last months of 1747, he went to London to forward his play *Agis* (not performed or published until 1758), based upon the life of the Spartan king found in Plutarch's *Parallel Lives* (circa first or second century). It concerned the attempts by Lysander to defend the king against the corrupt magistrate Amphares. Although David Garrick of Drury Lane declined the play, Home was favored with the friendship of William Pitt. Upon his return to Edinburgh, Home found favor with Andrew Fletcher, Lord Milton, and Archibald Campbell, Duke of Argyll.

In 1755 Home returned to London with a manuscript titled "Gill Morrice." Again rejected, he retreated to Edinburgh, where, following rehearsals in the Griskin Club, the play was performed in an unlicensed theater in the Canongate on 14 December 1756 under the title *Douglas.* The plot involves a series of mistaken identities, most notably the unknown and dashing hero Norval, who has saved Scotland from the invading Danes and is discovered to be the long-lost son of Lady Randolph and Lord Douglas. Born after the death of his father, Douglas had been spirited away and raised as a shepherd boy. However, the play ends tragically, with the death of Douglas, who dies protecting his mother from the scheming and ambitious Glenalvon, and with the suicide of his grieving mother. Critic Gerald D. Parker argues that "in its form and vision, the play demonstrates with considerable clarity the major features of the pathetic and the neo-classical traditions that dominated early and mid-eighteenth-century tragedy."

The play prompted a strong negative reaction from many within the Church of Scotland, who frowned upon the use of phrases such as "oh desperate fate!" and "Oh God of Heaven!" and were horrified by the apparent validation of suicide. That it was written by a churchman and attended by other churchmen also prompted disquiet. Home's friend and fellow minister, Alexander Carlyle of Inveresk, provided the play with advertisements, publishing *A Full and True History of the Bloody Tragedy of Douglas.* A more generalized war pamphlet followed, debating the morality and merits of drama, while Adam Ferguson and others defended Home in *The Morality of Stage-Plays Seriously Considered* (1757). As quoted by Alasdair Cameron, the Presbytery of Edinburgh disagreed, ensuring that "An Admonition" was read from every pulpit in the city, reminding congregations that "the opinion which the Christian Church has always held of the stage and players, as prejudicial to the interests of religion and morality is well known; and the fatal influence which they have on the far greater part of mankind, particularly the younger sort, is too obvious to call into question." The matter went all the way to the General Assembly in May 1757, where the Moderates gained a notable victory by underlining the decision taken by the Synod of Lothian and Tweeddale to censor both parties to the dispute and instructing Carlyle to forgo attending theatrical performances in the future.

Success in England followed that in Scotland, with a nine-night run in Covent Garden under the direction of John Rich beginning 14 March 1757. According to Richard B. Sher, William Pitt had arranged for the staging to take place. Henry Grey Graham, however, says that Samuel Johnson scathingly remarked that it was "without ten good lines." Back in Scotland, Home was cited to appear before the presbytery of Haddington for his authorship of the work, but he deferred attending by removing to London in February 1757. Subsequently, on 7 June 1757, he resigned his ministry, but the play had guaranteed him an entrée into London society.

Home was taken up by Scottish politician Lord Bute, who made him his private secretary. While Home may have written a series of pro-Bute interventions in the press during the brief period in which Bute was prime minister, the relationship was apparently based on personal friendship and political affiliation as much as private interest on either side. While Home was targeted by anti-Bute writers, notably Charles Churchill and John Wilkes, the extent of his influence over Bute's decision making is impossible to gauge. Carlyle recalled how "Home was now entirely at the command of Lord Bute, whose nod made him break every engagement." Garrick had by now altered his opinion of Home's merit and staged a heavily revised *Agis* for eleven nights, starting on 21 February 1758. Again the play divided audiences, although this time the split was along party lines, with the patriotic and civic theme of the play, alongside the known links to Bute and the Prince of Wales, leading to its being read as a party political piece. According to Sher, Horace Walpole remarked of it that "the Prince of Wales went three times to see *Agis,* a new tragedy written by John Home, and so indifferent a one, that nobody else could bear to go to it twice." Twentieth-century criticism suggests that Garrick was correct in his first assessment of the quality of the play, with Sher describing the work as "pompous."

Home's next dramatic effort, *The Siege of Aquileia,* was staged in Drury Lane on 21 February 1760. Its theme was the tension between paternal affection and public virtue, in which the latter won out. The play fed into the militia controversy of that year, in which Scottish intellectuals agitated for the extension of the English militia structure north of the border. A year earlier, in 1759, Home and his friend and fellow militia campaigner Carlyle had met poet James Macpherson at the Bowling Green at Moffat. Home introduced Macpherson to Edinburgh society, ultimately leading to the publication of Macpherson's poetry, purportedly translated by him from the Gaelic of ancient poet-warrior Ossian. It in turn caused an extensive controversy.

In 1760 Home's three tragedies were published in a collected edition, dedicated to the Prince of Wales, who was Bute's patron and took the throne that year as George III. Home soon received from the monarch a pension of £300. In 1763 Home was also granted a sinecure worth another £300, as Conservator of the Privileges of Campvere–a town in Holland. This post entitled Home to attend the General Assembly of the Church of Scotland on an annual basis, which, alongside the fall of Bute from the premiership that year, prompted Home's resettlement in Scotland. The fall of Bute also led Home to ascribe his next play, *The Fatal Discovery,* produced by Garrick on 23 February 1769, to "a young Oxford student." Anti-Bute, anti-Scottish sentiment was then flourishing in London, and the initial public interest fell away when Home declared himself to be the author. Nonetheless, Carlyle declared it to be "to my taste, the second best of Home's tragedies."

In 1770 Home married Mary Home, daughter of his cousin William, the minister of Foggo. The marriage remained childless. According to Graham, when asked by David Hume what had prompted his decision to marry Mary, Home was said to have remarked, "Ah David, if I had not, who else would have taken her?" That year Home bought a property in Kilduff, East Lothian, near his old parish. His play *Alonzo* was staged in Drury Lane beginning on 27 January 1773 and running for eleven nights. His final play, *Alfred,* opened on 21 January 1778 but was considered a commercial and critical failure.

Later that year, Home moved to Edinburgh, having started his *The History of the Rebellion in the Year 1745.* He also joined the South Fencibles, causing a stir by attending the General Assembly in military uniform. His history was finally published in 1802, offering a closely wrought account of the Jacobite Rebellion. It had broken out when Prince Charles Edward Stuart, son of the exiled claimant to the throne of Scotland as James VIII and of England as James III, landed at Moidart on 25 July 1745. The clans slowly came out in his favor, and the standard was raised at Glenfinnan on 19 August. The rebel forces gained Edinburgh on 17 September, and on 21 September they won a key engagement against the Hanoverian troops at the Battle of Prestonpans. In a tactical miscalculation they remained in Scotland until 31 October, although once they moved south, they quickly captured Carlisle and, on 4 December, Derby. However, they gained few recruits within England, and on 6 December Charles decided to retreat to Scotland. The slow defeat of the rebellion culminated in the Battle of Culloden on 16 April 1746, when one thousand men were lost in a bitter and brutal engagement with the troops of the Duke of Cumberland. Charles sailed for France 20 September, leaving the Highlands to be ravaged by the Hanoverian forces. An estimated 120 prisoners were executed, and around 1,150 were banished.

Despite the savage aftermath of the rebellion, Home's narrative was strongly biased toward the Hanoverian government, with the Duke of Cumberland in particular being exonerated for his role in repressing the rebellion. However, the central purpose of the text, according to Sher, was to explain the failure of Lowland Scotland to defend itself against the Jacobite forces. Home identified the problem with the Union of Crowns in 1603, which, through hereditary succession, had brought the kingdoms of Scotland and England under the sole rule of James I (James VI of Scotland). The removal of the Scottish king to London had damaged Lowland society, eliminating the noble virtues of military valor and moral independence, a process that he also connected to the end of militia service:

> When James the sixth succeeded to the crown of England, at the death of Queen Elizabeth, the English and the Scots (that is the Lowlanders of Scotland) at once laid down their arms, which seemed to be an unnecessary burden, when their ancient enemies became their fellow subjects. The untasted pleasures of peace were delicious to both nations, and during the pacific reign of James, they enjoyed them in perfect security. The militia was totally neglected, and for a course of years, arms were so little regarded that when the civil war broke out in the reign of Charles I, few arms were to be found in the country, and nobody could use them without learning a new trade as recruits for the army do at present.

> Meanwhile, the Highlanders continued to be the same sort of people that they had been in former times: Clanship flourished, depredations and petty war never ceased: then it was, that the Highlanders became superior to the Lowlanders in arms.

The Lowland community was left to the mercy of the still martial Highlanders, who had become increasingly disaffected with British rule as the capacity of the Lowlanders to defend themselves decreased. This dis-

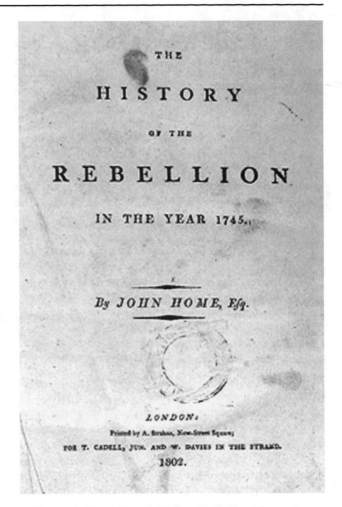

Title page for Home's history of the Scottish rebellion (Thomas Cooper Library, University of South Carolina)

content, according to Home's history, was coupled with the shifting international situation, which played into Highland hands:

> Notwithstanding the frequent rebellions during that long and eventful period, raised by a handful of men in a corner of the island, no efforts were taken to reconcile them to government; or to enable the other inhabitants of Britain to resist the Highlanders when they thought it proper to rebel . . . every rebellion was a war carried on by the Highlanders against the standing army; and a declaration of war with France or Spain, which required the service of the troops abroad, was a signal for a rebellion at home.

In this interpretation, Home not only exculpated the Lowlanders of guilt for their failings in that year, but he also promulgated the myth that the Highlanders were solely responsible for the devastation that the Rebellion generated. Paradoxically, he left open the possibility that, in the war-like virtues that had prompted the rebellion, the Highlanders might have a role to play in a greater British empire.

While Home had originally intended to publish the book after his death, he decided to alter and amend the text, making it feasible to publish while he was alive—a decision Henry Mackenzie described as "unfortunate," since he considered the work marred Home's literary reputation. The central value of the history, which was dedicated to the king, resides in offering the account of a participant, for "It is universally acknowledged that the most complete instruction and entertainment are to be found in histories written by those illustrious persons who have transmitted to posterity an account of the great actions which they themselves performed." Home thereupon placed himself self-consciously in the tradition of classical historians, of whom he mentioned Xenophon and Caesar in particular.

To aid this rhetorical decision, he appended a large collection of contemporary correspondence to his narrative, including lengthy extracts from the letters passing between John, the fourth Marquis of Tweeddale, the Secretary of State, and Andrew Fletcher, Lord Milton, the Justice Clerk. Home thereby supplied his readers with evidence of more than one rendition of crucial events. Alongside his own account of the escape of Charles Stuart to Islay, he supplied as an appendix a "Narrative of Flora Macdonald." He also offered two contradictory accounts of the crucial meeting at Derby, where the Jacobite forces decided to retreat into Scotland. Whether the decision was prompted by Lord George Murray, as Home believed, or was the collective decision of the Jacobite chieftains, as the account he presented in the appendix protested, he was able to assure his readers that "both accounts agree in one circumstance, which is that Charles was extremely averse to the retreat, and so much offended when it was resolved to return to Ashburn, that he behaved for some time as though he no longer thought himself commander of the army."

In general, Home's narrative concentrated on providing a close military history of the rebellion, rather than accounting for its diplomatic importance or philosophical significance. Maps were provided for the major battles, and Home supplied an extensive, and technical, rendering of troop movements and tactical decision making. He concluded each engagement by listing the fallen leaders, in a fashion also reminiscent of Classical authors. The effect was to highlight his stance as an eyewitness and an active participant and to supply readers with a dramatic, at times vivid, portrayal of the hardships of the conflict.

Home died on 5 September 1808 in Merchiston, just outside of Edinburgh, and his collected works were published, with a life of the author written by Henry Mackenzie attached as a preface in 1822. His friend and colleague Carlyle wrote of him that he

> was an admirable companion and most acceptable to all strangers who were not offended with the levities of a young clergyman, for he was very handsome and had a fine person, about five feet 10 ½ inches, and an agreeable catching address; he had not much wit, and still less humour, but he had so much sprightliness and vivacity; and such an expression of benevolence in his manner, and such an unceasing flattery of those he liked (and he never kept company with anyone else)—the kind commendations of a lover, not the adulation of a sycophant—that he was truly irresistible, and his entry to a company was like opening a window and letting the sun into a dark room.

Elsewhere, however, Carlyle was less flattering, writing of how Home chose to befriend those who thought well of his work and how "he was in no respect a man of business, though he now and then spoke with some energy and success in the General Assembly; but he had no turn for debate, which made me glad he was disappointed in his wish of obtaining a seat in the House of Commons." Mackenzie agreed: "His temperament was of that warm susceptible kind which is aught with the heroic and the tender and which is more fitted to delight in the world of sentiment than to succeed in the bustle of ordinary life." A more positive assessment is provided by Sher, who wrote that "Home may have been vain, foolish, or naïve, but he was not insincere or crudely opportunistic. In his own life, as well as in his plays, he consistently and enthusiastically espoused civic, patriotic values."

In the early twenty-first century, John Home is known primarily as a dramatist. *The History of the Rebellion in the Year 1745* was not a success. Graham remarks of it that "all were disappointed with the work; some were angry, but others kindly remembered that the author was old." Sher shares this assessment, writing of how "late in life Home lost the ability to deal intelligibly with recent events, and his last major literary effort was appropriately a history of the '45.'" However, the political implications of this work should not be underestimated: Home offered a cogent philosophical analysis of the causes of the rebellion and a strident defense of the British political establishment, a task particularly pertinent at a time of war with revolutionary France.

References:

Alasdair Cameron, "Theatre in Scotland," in *The History of Scottish Literature, Volume II 1660–1800,* edited by Andrew Hook (Aberdeen: Aberdeen University Press, 1987), pp. 191–208;

Alexander Carlyle, *Autobiography of Alexander Carlyle of Inveresk* (Edinburgh: T. N. Foulis, 1910);

Adam Ferguson, *The Morality of Stage-Plays Seriously Considered* (Edinburgh, 1757);

Henry Grey Graham, *Scottish Men of Letters in the Eighteenth Century* (London: Adam & Charles Black, 1901), pp. 60–77;

Henry Mackenzie, *An Account of the Life and Writings of John Home Esquire* (Edinburgh: Archibald Constable / London: Hurst, Robinson, 1822);

Gerald D. Parker, ed., *Douglas* (Edinburgh: Oliver & Boyd, 1972);

Richard B. Sher, *The Church and University in the Scottish Enlightenment: The Moderate Literati of Edinburgh* (Edinburgh: Edinburgh University Press, 1985);

Sher, "'The Favourite of the Favourite': John Home, Bute and the Politics of Patriotic Poetry," in *Lord Bute: Essays in Reinterpretation,* edited by Karl B. Schweizer (Leicester: Leicester University Press, 1988), pp. 181–211;

Sher, "Percy, Shaw and the Ferguson 'Cheat': National Prejudice in the Ossian Wars," in *Ossian Revisited,* edited by Howard Gaskill (Edinburgh: Edinburgh University Press, 1991), pp. 207–245.

Papers:
The Huntington Library in San Marino, California, holds correspondence of John Home; the National Library of Scotland holds Home's correspondence with Lord Milton and with Andrew Stuart as well as papers; and Edinburgh University Library holds both letters and literary manuscripts.

Nathaniel Hooke

(1685? – 19 July 1763)

Gareth Sampson
University of Manchester

and

Ian Macgregor-Morris
University of Nottingham

and

James Moore
University of London

BOOKS: *The Roman History from the Building of Rome to the Ruin of the Commonwealth,* 4 volumes (London: Printed by James Bettenham, 1738–1771);

An Account of the Conduct of the Dowager Duchess of Marlborough, from Her First Coming to Court to the Year 1710 (London: Printed by James Bettenham for George Hawkins, 1742; Dublin: Printed for William Smith & George Faulkner, 1742);

Observations on I. The Answer of M. L'abbé de Vertot to the Late Earl Stanhope's Inquiry, concerning the Senate of Ancient Rome: Dated December 1719. II. A Dissertation upon the Constitution of the Roman Senate, by a Gentleman: Published in 1743. III. A Treatise on the Roman Senate, by Dr. Conyers Middleton: Published in 1747. IV. An Essay on the Roman Senate, By Dr. Thomas Chapman: Published in 1750 (London: Printed by George Hawkins, 1758);

Six Letters to a Lady of Quality from the Manuscript of the Late Nathaniel Hooke, upon the Subject of Religious Peace and the True Foundations of It (London: Printed by A. Gordon, 1816).

TRANSLATIONS: Andrew Ramsay, *The Life of François de Salignac de la Motte Fenelon: Archbishop and Duke of Cambray* (London: Printed for Paul Vaillant and James Woodman, 1723);

The Travels of Cyrus, with a Discourse on Mythology (London: Printed by T. Woodward & J. Peele, 1730; Burlington, N.J.: Printed by Isaac Neale, 1793).

OTHER: Antonio de Solis y Ribadenyra, *The History of the Conquest of Mexico by the Spaniards,* translated by

Nathaniel Hooke (portrait by Bartholomew Dandrige; National Portrait Gallery, London)

Thomas Townsend, edited by Hooke (London: Printed by H. Herringman for T. Woodward, J. Hooke & J. Peele, 1730; 2 volumes, revised and corrected by Hooke, London: Printed for J. Osborn, 1738; New York: AMS Press, 1973);

Nathaniel Hooke (1664–1738), *Révolutions d'Eccosse et d'Irelande, en 1707, 1708 et 1709,* edited by Hooke (the yngr) (The Hague: Aillaud, 1758); translated as *The Secret History of Colonel Hooke's Negotiations in Scotland, in Favour of The Pretender, in 1707, Including the Original Letters and Papers Which Passed between the Scotch and Irish Lords and the Courts of Versailles and St. Germains,* edited by Hooke (London: Printed for Thomas Becket, 1760; Edinburgh: Printed by R. Fleming, 1760).

Nathaniel Hooke was the leading eighteenth-century British historian on the Roman Republic. He lived a controversial literary life as a biographer of the Duchess of Marlborough and as part of a literary circle that included Alexander Pope, Richard Glover, Sir John Fielding, and Jonathan Swift. He was also a prominent Roman Catholic and possibly a Jacobite agent. The complexity of his life reflects the fractured nature of English politics in the eighteenth century.

Hooke was born into the Irish branch of the Anglo-Norman Hooke family, descended from Sir Florence de la Hougue, a Norman knight who came to Ireland in the reign of Henry II. The family supported the Parliamentary cause in the Civil War, and his mother, Elizabeth Lambert, was the daughter of Parliamentary general John Lambert. His father, John Hooke, became a sergeant at arms and the Chief Justice of Caernarvon in Wales. A staunch Protestant, he also wrote a pamphlet titled *Catholicism without Popery* (1699), a case for a unified church free from Rome. John Hooke died in 1712. Nathaniel Hooke was born in England circa 1685, the eldest son of John and Elizabeth Hooke. He had at least one brother, William.

Nathaniel Hooke's uncle, also called Nathaniel Hooke, was a Jacobite spy who was at various times the Duke of Monmouth's chaplain, liaison between the exiled court of Charles II and Louis XIV, and personal agent of Louis XIV charged with planning a Jacobite revolt in England and Scotland. He became a naturalized French citizen and a lieutenant-general in the French army and was made a baron of Ireland by Louis XIV. This elder Nathaniel Hooke died in 1738.

Little is known of the younger Nathaniel Hooke's early life, except for an apocryphal story claiming that he attended the Catholic school at Twyford in England with Pope, although no evidence backs this assertion, nor does Hooke's early religion support the claim. At one point, Hooke registered to study law at Lincoln's Inn, but he returned to Ireland without completing his studies. In Ireland he married Mary Gore, an English Protestant, of Manorhamilton. The union produced two sons, both born in Dublin—Thomas in 1712 and Luke Joseph in 1714—and at least one daughter, Jane Mary. An Elizabeth Hooke who was left a legacy by

Hooke's close friend Martha Blount may also have been his daughter.

The education of Hooke's two sons raises an interesting issue. The eldest son, Thomas, was raised as a Protestant, while Luke Joseph was sent to France in the 1720s to be raised a Catholic by his uncle. The latter decision prompts the key question as to when Hooke became a Roman Catholic. Likely, it was within a few years of the birth of his first son. This conversion may explain why Lady Gore, his sister-in-law, raised his first son, while his second was raised in France by Hooke's uncle. An alternative explanation is that his penury resulting from his losses in the South Sea Bubble meant that he could no longer support them.

By 1717 Hooke was working as private secretary to his uncle in Paris and operating as his uncle's agent in London. The exact nature of these activities is not clear, but they led to lifelong accusations that Hooke was a Jacobite spy. His literary activities commenced with a translation of the life of François de Salignac de la Motte Fénelon written by Sir Andrew Ramsay, another leading Jacobite exile. Letters reveal that Hooke and Fénelon met in Paris, and Hooke's brand of Catholicism, which was often said to have a mystical quality, closely resembled Fénelon's. This time may mark the point of Hooke's conversion to Catholicism. This translation also reveals another of Hooke's qualities, namely his contacts within the British nobility. In a letter (dated 17 October 1722) to Stuart sympathizer Robert Harley, first Earl of Oxford and Mortimer, Hooke asks the peer for employment, confessing to having "been seized by the late distemper" that was the South Sea Bubble. The peer appears to have looked kindly upon Hooke, and the translation of the life of Fénelon was thus dedicated to Lord Oxford.

Hooke's connection to Ramsay and mysticism continued, and Swift's correspondence reveals that Hooke may still have been in Paris in the late 1720s. In 1730, apparently in the space of only twenty days, he translated Ramsay's *Les voyages de Cyrus, avec un discours sur la mythologie* (1727) as *The Travels of Cyrus, with a Discourse on Mythology.* Also in 1724 Hooke edited Thomas Townsend's *The History of the Conquest of Mexico by the Spaniards,* a translation of Antonio de Solis y Ribadenyra's *Historia de la conquista de Mexico* (1684).

Hooke's literary direction changed during the 1730s, away from translations and toward the field of Roman history. It also is the first period in which solid evidence appears of his friendship with Pope, in a letter of 1731. During the 1730s Hooke embarked on the creation of the first substantial Roman history in English. This project was parallel to and drew substantially upon the *Histoire Romaine* (1731) of the Jesuit scholar François Catrou. Catrou had started his work in Paris in the late 1720s, and in all likelihood the two men met or corresponded.

While translations of Catrou were in preparation, such as those by Richard Bundy and John Ozell, Hooke aimed for his work to be the first original work in English on the Roman Republic. Not only did he draw on the contemporary work of Catrou, but he also used the great historical works of Charles Rollin and Louis de Beaufort. Hooke even made reference to earlier generations of historical writers, including notable figures such as Sir Isaac Newton and Sir Walter Ralegh. Hooke's history was written in a highly readable but critical manner, with sources ancient and modern coming under close scrutiny, supported by extensive footnotes.

The work was originally conceived as two volumes, covering the history of Rome during the years 753–122 B.C., from the foundation of the city to the death of Gaius Gracchus. As early as 1731 Hooke sought subscriptions to fund the work, aided by the efforts of Pope and Ralph Allen; however, these efforts met with limited success. Swift appeared to be unaware of Hooke's project in 1731, and by 1736, Hooke required the financial support of Allen to maintain progress on his history. Advertisements appeared through the 1730s, but the first volume of *The Roman History from the Building of Rome to the Ruin of the Commonwealth* did not appear until 1738. Volume one focuses on the foundation of Rome to the start of the First Punic War (753–264 B.C.) and is dedicated to Pope. It is prefaced with a dissertation on Newton's *Chronology of the Seven Kings of Rome*. The second volume was advertised as being published in 1739 but did not appear until 1745.

In 1739–1740 Hooke received a collection of correspondence that had belonged to his uncle Nathaniel Hooke, who had died the previous year. The papers were sent by the late Nathaniel's son, James Hooke, an officer in the French army. The correspondence originally comprised all of his uncle's papers detailing his various efforts for the Jacobite cause from 1689 to at least 1723; however, the French government confiscated the majority of them on grounds of security, and only the papers for the years 1705–1707 arrived in England. These papers included secret correspondence between the elder Hooke and many British aristocrats and included documents that revealed their secret associations with leaders of the Jacobite cause. Prominent among these are letters between Hooke and the first duke of Marlborough, John Churchill, implying that the two men were in contact with an eye to Marlborough's defection.

During this time, Hooke was closely associated with Patrick Hume, Earl of Marchmont, and Philip Dormer Stanhope, Earl of Chesterfield, and through these men he gained a commission from Sarah, the dowager duchess of Marlborough (widow of John Churchill, Duke of Marlborough), to write her autobiography. The book, *An Account of the Conduct of the Dowager Duchess of Marlborough* (1742), was a vindication of her early career in the Court of Queen Anne. In her eighties she had become increasingly preoccupied with securing the reputation of both herself and her late husband. For his work, Hooke was paid the substantial sum of £5,000, which ended his penury and secured his financial position for life. Whether this sum was solely as a reward for his literary talents or was designed to ensure the suppression of his uncle's letters, which could have been compromising to the Churchill family's reputation, is open to speculation. Hooke and his daughter spent almost a year in the duchess's residence while compiling the autobiography, prompting Pope to claim that Hooke was her prisoner. The relationship between Hooke and the duchess appears to have been a fraught but close one. During this time, she engaged Hooke to negotiate with Pope concerning the suppression of one of Pope's characters in return for the sum of £3,000. On her death, Hooke was granted a legacy of £500 per year from the duchess's estate to write a biography of her late husband. The book was never written, however, and whether Hooke ever drew on this legacy is not known. A well-known story suggests that Hooke attempted to convert the duchess to Catholicism as he "found her without religion" (letter from Pope to Allen [8 December 1742]). This tale is echoed by the story claiming that in 1744, when Pope was on his deathbed, Hooke procured a Catholic priest for him to perform a deathbed conversion.

The book on Sarah, Duchess of Marlborough, appeared in March 1742, taking the form of an autobiography written in the first person. Hooke's name does not appear on the volume, but clearly extensive editing of the duchess's dictated notes must have taken place. This volume appears to have contributed significantly to Hooke's literary reputation, however, and it provoked a flurry of responses, both supportive and hostile, to the duchess's account.

The delayed second volume of *The Roman History* was eventually published in 1745. It covered the period from the First Punic War to the death of Gaius Gracchus (264–122 B.C.). It was dedicated to Hugh, Earl of Marchmont, and was prefaced by a dissertation on Beaufort's theories regarding the credibility of the history of the first five hundred years of Rome. Beaufort raised doubts about the validity of using later Roman sources for the earlier period between 753 and 264 B.C., arguing that they were unreliable. Hooke, however, refutes this argument in "A Dissertation on the Credibility of the History of the First 500 Years of Rome" (in volume two of *The Roman History*), claiming that "falsehood is mingled with truth, but that there are means by which they may be distinguished." This approach is reflected throughout his history, highlighting his sophisticated critical method and interpretative skill.

The second volume also includes an important appendix titled "The Capitoline Marbles, or Consular Calendar." It provides details of the office holders of the Republic that were discovered on a monument excavated from the Capitol in Rome in 1545; it is identical to the list in the appendices to Catrou's *Histoire Romaine*, but it includes much information in addition to that on the Capitoline Marbles. This additional information was taken from the work of sixteenth-century Dutch scholar Stephanus Pighius.

The publication of this volume concluded Hooke's original project, although revised editions of these two volumes were published in 1751 and 1757. His views on the early years of the Republic underwent some modification, and minor changes were made to the second and third editions of the first volume.

Having completed these works, Hooke turned his attention to a more-specialized topic in the field of Roman history and in 1758 published his *Observations on I. The Answer of M. L'abbé de Vertot to the Late Earl Stanhope's Inquiry, concerning the Senate of Ancient Rome: Dated December 1719. II. A Dissertation upon the Constitution of the Roman Senate, by a Gentleman: Published in 1743. III. A Treatise on the Roman Senate, by Dr. Conyers Middleton: Published in 1747. IV. An Essay on the Roman Senate, By Dr. Thomas Chapman: Published in 1750* (1758). This book, dedicated to Arthur Onslow, speaker of the House of Commons, was a critical review of four previously published treatises on this subject by eminent scholars, including Abbé de Vertot (1719), Conyers Middleton (1747), and Thomas Chapman (1750). This work shows Hooke at the zenith of his scholarly development, displaying a sophisticated critique of contemporary academic debates. He particularly attacked the positions of Chapman and Middleton, who at the time were regarded as representing the established view, for their uncritical acceptance of the ancient writer Dionysius of Halicarnassus.

In 1758 the controversial letters of Hooke's uncle Nathaniel Hooke were published in French in The Hague under the title *Révolutions d'Eccosse et d'Irelande, en 1707, 1708 et 1709* (1758). The letters were then in the possession of the younger Hooke, and according to William D. Macray, who edited the 1870 edition, Hooke edited this first publication himself. The letters appeared in English as *The Secret History of Colonel Hooke's Negotiations in Scotland, in Favour of The Pretender . . . Written by Himself* in 1760. Although the translator of this edition is unknown, the publication was likely also edited by the younger Hooke.

THE
ROMAN HISTORY,

FROM THE

Building of *Rome* to the Ruin of the *Commonwealth*.

Illustrated with Maps and other Plates.

VOL. I.

By N. HOOKE, Esq;

LONDON:
Printed by *James Bettenham*,
And Sold by A. BETTESWORTH and C. HITCH in *Paternoster-Row*, and G. HAWKINS at *Milton's* Head between the two *Temple-Gates* in *Fleetstreet*.
M.DCC.XXXVIII.

Title page for Hooke's history of Rome, the first one in English of any importance (British Library; Eighteenth-Century Collections Online, Gale Group)

In the years leading up to his death, Hooke made preparations for an extension of *The Roman History,* building upon the success of his two previous volumes. Before the third volume could be published, however, he died on 19 July 1763, after several years of ill health. Hooke was buried in the village of Hedsor in Berkshire, where he had resided in his final years. A commemorative tombstone was erected in 1801 by his friend Frederic Irby (Lord Boston), hailing Hooke as a great Roman historian.

The third volume of his Roman history was published posthumously in 1764, with a preface stating that the volume was printed under his inspection before his "final illness." Unlike the previous volumes, there was no dedication or introductory critical dissertation, merely a continuation of the history of the Republic from the death of Gaius Gracchus (122 B.C.) to the outbreak of the Second Civil War between Caesar and Pompey in 50 B.C.

A fourth volume was published in 1771, detailing the period from the Second Civil War to the collapse of the Republic (49–28 B.C.). Although published under Hooke's name, the volume is believed to have been compiled by Gilbert Stuart, a noted historian and reviewer, over the period 1768–1771. There is, however, no indication in the volume as to who was responsible for assembling this work. The volume is of a similar style and nature to Hooke's, but no one knows what level of access the compiler had to Hooke's own notes. The fourth volume proved to be the most controversial volume in the series; in particular, Hooke's view of Caesar was widely criticized; however, how much the narrative within the volume is genuinely representative of Hooke's views is unclear. The appendix includes a continuation of information from the Capitoline Marbles, covering the period of the last two volumes, again drawing on Catrou and Pighius.

The entire *Roman History* series proved to be an enduring success and was republished many times. Since 1830, however, it has not been republished in any form.

In 1816 a pamphlet appeared titled *Six Letters to a Lady of Quality from the Manuscript of the Late Nathaniel Hooke, upon the Subject of Religious Peace and the True Foundations of It*. Hooke had given the letters to the widow of Dr. George Berkeley, Bishop of Cloyne, who then passed them on to the Reverend Sir Adam Gordon, who published them. They are in essence a religious treatise discussing aspects of the personal conduct of a noblewoman, and they illustrate important aspects of Hooke's religious convictions. The identity of the particular noblewoman and date of composition are uncertain, although the letters appear to relate to the period in which Hooke was involved with the duchess of Marlborough, and they may have been aimed at her critics.

Hooke's theological and literary endeavors were followed by those of his two sons. Thomas, raised as a Protestant, attended St. Mary's Hall at the University of Oxford and was author of a translation of Tasso's *Jerusalem* published in 1736. He went on to become a rector of Birkby and vicar of Leek, Yorkshire, serving until his death in 1791. Luke Joseph, who was raised as a Catholic, was educated in France and graduated from the Sorbonne in 1736, where he became professor of theology and later of Hebrew, librarian of the Mazarin Library, and a prolific writer of religious tracts. He also translated his father's *Roman History* into French (published 1770–1784) and is believed to have republished *Révolutions d'Eccosse et d'Irelande* in 1775. Excommunicated but later pardoned by the Pope, during the revolution he refused to take an oath of allegiance to the civil constitution of the clergy. He died in 1796.

Hooke's lasting reputation was as a Roman historian, as evidenced by the many reprints of his *Roman History*. This work remained the definitive history of the period until the mid nineteenth century. His work was admired by Samuel Taylor Coleridge and Samuel Johnson, and as late as 1855, Eugene Lawrence described his work as "still the best account of the Romans we have in the language." Hooke's scholarship formed the basis of the work of later Roman histories, including those of Oliver Goldsmith and Adam Ferguson, although their works were widely regarded as inferior. Hooke's reputation suffered at the hands of the university-based historians of the mid to late nineteenth century. Renowned German historian Barthold Georg Niebuhr dismissed Hooke's work but confessed to not having read it, an attitude that still prevails; however, Hooke's *Roman History* is both analytical and insightful, while his *Observations* is a forensic study focused on a specialized area of constitutional history. Both remain valuable to the modern scholar of the Roman Republic.

References:

Philip Ayres, *Classical Culture and the Idea of Rome in Eighteenth Century England* (Cambridge & New York: Cambridge University Press, 1997);

Henry Fielding, *A Full Vindication of the Duchess Dowager of Marlborough* (London: Printed for J. Roberts, 1742);

Joseph Gillow, *A Literary and Biographical History; or, Bibliographical Dictionary of English Catholics from the Breach with Rome, in 1534, to the Present Time*, volume 3 (London: Burns & Oates, 1885);

Nathaniel Hooke (1664–1738), *The Secret History of Colonel Hoocke's negociations in Scotland in 1707: Being the Original Letters and Papers which passed between the Scotch and Irish Lords and the Courts of Versailles and St. Germains* (Edinburgh, 1755);

Eugene Lawrence, *Lives of the British Historians*, volume 11 (New York: Scribner, 1855);

William D. Macray, *The Correspondence of Colonel N. Hooke, Agent from the Court of France to the Scottish Jacobites 1703–1707*, 2 volumes (London: J. B. Nichols, 1870, 1871);

Thomas O'Connor, *An Irish Theologian in Enlightenment France: Luke Joseph Hooke 1714–96* (Dublin: Four Courts Press, 1995);

Alexander Pope, *The Correspondence of Alexander Pope*, volumes 3–5 (Oxford: Clarendon Press, 1956);

G. Rose, *A Selection of Papers from the Earls of Marchmont 1685–1750, in the Possession of the Right Hon. Sir George Henry Rose*, volume 2 (London: J. Murray, 1831);

Horace Walpole, *Horace Walpole's Correspondence with Thomas Gray, Richard West and Thomas Ashton*, volumes 13, 17, 20, and 46, edited by W. S. Lewis, George L. Lam, and Charles H. Bennett (London: Oxford University Press, 1948).

David Hume

(26 April 1711 – 25 August 1776)

Carey M. Roberts
Arkansas Tech University

See also Hume entries in *DLB 104: British Prose Writers, 1660–1800, Second Series* and *DLB 252: British Philosophers, 1500–1799.*

BOOKS: *A Treatise of Human Nature: Being an Attempt to Introduce the Experimental Method of Reasoning into Moral Subjects,* 3 volumes (volumes 1 and 2, London: Printed for John Noon, 1739; volume 3, London: Printed for Thomas Longman, 1740; reprinted, 2 volumes, London & New York: Longmans, Green, 1874);

An Abstract of a Book Lately Published; Entituled, A Treatise of Human Nature, &C. Wherein the Chief Argument of That Book Is Farther Illustrated and Explained, anonymous (London: C. Borbet [sic], 1740);

Essays Moral and Political, 2 volumes (volume 1, Edinburgh: Printed for A. Kincaid, 1741; revised, 1742; volume 2, Edinburgh: Printed for A. Kincaid, 1742); volumes 1 and 2 republished with *Three Essays, Moral and Political* (1748) as *Essays, Moral and Political,* third edition, corrected, with additions, 1 volume (London: Printed for A. Millar and for A. Kincaid, Edinburgh, 1748);

A Letter from a Gentleman to His Friend in Edinburgh: Containing Some Observations on a Specimen of the Principles Concerning Religion and Morality Said to be Maintain'd in a Book Lately Publish'd Intitled, A Treatise of Human Nature, etc. (Edinburgh, 1745);

Philosophical Essays Concerning Human Understanding (London: Printed for A. Millar, 1748; revised edition, London: Printed for M. Cooper, 1751); republished as *An Enquiry Concerning Human Understanding* in *Essays and Treatises on Several Subjects* (London: Printed for A. Millar and for A. Kincaid & A. Donaldson, Edinburgh, 1758);

Three Essays, Moral and Political: Never before Published (London: A. Millar; Edinburgh: A. Kincaid, 1748);

A True Account of the Behaviour and Conduct of Archibald Stewart, Esq.; Late Lord Provost of Edinburgh (London: Printed for M. Cooper, 1748);

David Hume *(portrait by Allan Ramsay; frontispiece for Ernest Campbell Mossner,* The Life of David Hume, *1954; Thomas Cooper Library, University of South Carolina)*

An Enquiry Concerning the Principles of Morals (London: Printed for A. Millar, 1751);

Political Discourses (Edinburgh: Printed by R. Fleming for A. Kincaid & A. Donaldson, 1752);

Essays and Treatises on Several Subjects (4 volumes, London: Printed for A. Millar and for A. Kincaid & A. Donaldson, Edinburgh, 1753; revised, 1753–1756; revised again, 1 volume, 1758; revised again, 4 volumes, 1760; revised again, 2 volumes, 1764; revised again, London: Printed for A. Millar and for A. Kincaid, J. Bell & A. Donaldson, Edinburgh, and sold by T. Cadell, 1768; revised again, 4 volumes, London: Printed for T. Cadell and A. Kincaid & A. Donaldson, Edinburgh, 1770; revised posthumous edition, 2 volumes, with author's last corrections, London: Printed for T. Cadell in the Strand, and A. Donaldson & W. Creech at Edinburgh, 1777);

The History of Great Britain. Vol. I Containing the Reigns of James I and Charles I (Edinburgh: Printed by Hamilton, Balfour & Neill, 1754; revised edition, London: Printed for A. Millar, 1759);

Four Dissertations: I. The Natural History of Religion. II. Of the Passions. III. Of Tragedy. IV. Of the Standard of Taste (London: Printed for A. Millar, 1757);

The History of Great Britain, Vol. II Containing the Commonwealth, and the Reigns of Charles II and James II (London: Printed for A. Millar, 1757);

The History of England under the House of Tudor, 2 volumes (London: Printed for A. Millar, 1759);

The History of England, From the Invasion of Julius Caesar to the Accession of Henry VII, 2 volumes (London: Printed for A. Millar, 1759);

The History of England, from the Invasion of Julius Caesar to the Revolution in 1688 (6 volumes, London: Printed for A. Millar, 1762; revised, 8 volumes, 1763; posthumous edition with author's last revisions, London: Printed for T. Cadell, 1778; reprinted, 4 volumes, Philadelphia: E. Littell, 1828); republished as *The History of England, from the Invasion of Julius Cæsar to the Abdication of James the Second, 1688,* 6 volumes (New York: Harper, 1850);

The Life of David Hume, Esq.: Written by Himself (London: Printed for W. Strahan & T. Cadell, 1777; Philadelphia: Printed by Robert Bell, 1778);

Dialogues Concerning Natural Religion (London: Printed for Robinson, 1779); reprinted, Henry D. Aiken, ed. (New York: Hafner, 1948).

Editions: *The Philosophical Works of David Hume,* edited by T. H. Green and T. H. Grose, 4 volumes (London: Longmans, Green, 1874–1875);

The Natural History of Religion, edited by H. E. Root (Stanford: Stanford University Press, 1957);

The History of England, from the Invasion of Julius Caesar to the Revolution in 1688, abridged, edited, and with an introduction by Rodney W. Kilcup (Chicago: University of Chicago Press, 1975);

The History of England, from the Invasion of Julius Caesar to the Abdication of James the Second, 1688 (1788 edition), 6 volumes (Indianapolis: Liberty Classics, 1983);

Essays, Moral, Political, and Literary, edited by Eugene F. Miller (Indianapolis: Liberty Classics, 1985).

While modern scholars view David Hume as one of the foremost philosophers of the eighteenth century, his contemporaries thought of him as an historian. In many ways, Hume might be considered the foremost historian of his generation. He was the first to consider the history of religion from an analytical rather than a theological perspective. Unlike others during the Enlightenment, he conceived of human societies as sharing some important features, but he believed historical traditions played a greater role in human development than did natural reason alone. Hume was the first to explain the pivotal part played by economic concerns in the overall development of a society, and thus he could be considered the father of economic history. Above all, as a philosopher Hume took seriously the study of history and grounded his philosophical reflections in a naturalistic and historical understanding of human life and thought.

Hume's monumental work, *The History of England* (1759–1763), remains his most published and best-known work. As for all his historical work, Hume's writings should be understood through four parallel aspects of his thought and career. The first involves his philosophy of human nature, the cornerstone of his life-long accomplishments. The second emanates from Hume's religious skepticism, a position grossly misunderstood by Hume's antagonists and later observers and one that should not be confused with an antipathy to all things religious. The third factor relates to the ideological parameter of eighteenth-century British politics, specifically the Whig intellectual faction powerful in London political circles and one with which Hume initially sympathized but later came to despise. Finally, political economy—a new science of the eighteenth century that Hume helped pioneer—offered an important component to how Hume treated historical change and events.

Hume was born in Edinburgh, Scotland, on 26 April 1711, to John and Katherine Home, whose name David anglicized early in his career. John Home supervised the family estate, Ninewells, situated in Berwickshire in eastern Scotland. He was not considered wealthy even though the family managed to live comfortably. David Hume intermittently spent the larger portion of his life there and always considered Scotland his home and first love.

In the year Hume was born, Scotland stood at the threshold of a momentous change. The Act of Union between England and Scotland had recently solidified Scotland's precarious relationship with the English Parliament. In addition to settling centuries of disputes with their northern neighbors, the English now enjoyed relative calm after nearly a century of political unrest. The last of England's North American colonies were being settled, and the mounting debt of the country soon led to the critical and nearly catastrophic South Sea Bubble of 1720. Learned men spent their time reading the philosophical works of John Locke and the reprinted political tracts of Algernon Sidney. Sir Isaac Newton continued to correct and publish his scientific treatises, eagerly awaited by a discriminating public. Yet, the rational world of the seventeenth century was giving way. A year after Hume's birth, Jean-Jacques Rousseau was born in Switzerland. A few years later, while Hume was still a child, his adulthood friend Adam Smith, was born; his birth was followed the next year by that of Immanuel Kant. In life and in thought, Hume stood between two poles: the rationalism of Locke and Newton and the subjectivity of Rousseau and Kant. It was the time of the Scottish Enlightenment, a time shaped by Hume's love for philosophy and history.

Hume's older brother inherited the family property after the untimely death of their father when Hume was still an infant. Hume's mother dedicated herself to raising the children, and though Hume reminisced fondly of his mother, she apparently had little time to encourage his latent genius. In 1723 he entered the University of Edinburgh, the center of Newtonian philosophy outside of Cambridge. His mother and brother expected Hume to enter the legal profession, but at Edinburgh he immersed himself in classical literature, philosophy, and Newtonian natural history. After graduation an unsuccessful stint in Bristol as a businessman convinced Hume that a career in letters would be more promising than one in business. After being stricken by a nervous disorder in 1729, he found solace in La Flèche, France. Hume felt a lifelong affinity for France, celebrating its pace of life and often wishing to settle there permanently. Also while in France, Hume, then only eighteen, considered writing a philosophical treatise, which became *A Treatise of Human Nature: Being an Attempt to Introduce the Experimental Method of Reasoning into Moral Subjects* (1739–1740).

France offered Hume many things that a young intellectual desired. It gave him distance and independence from his family. It enabled him to live frugally but still enjoy some aspects of fine living. It offered him invaluable exposure to the writings of French intellectuals, such as René Descartes, Pierre Bayle, and Nicholas Malebranche. France also provided Hume an intellectual refuge from English philosophers, who might have dominated his philosophical reflections had he remained in Scotland or England at this critical point. Hume was always resentful of the English and their control over his native Scotland—always aware that the English elite would frown upon his native customs and habits, even his Scottish brogue.

Hume completed the first volume of *A Treatise of Human Nature* in 1734, after which he returned to England in search of a publisher. The first two books of *A Treatise of Human Nature* appeared in print in 1739, and the final, third book was published the next year. Late in life Hume lamented the speed with which he had completed the treatise and attempted to revise some of its misleading prose and recanted some of his positions. He summarized its reception by noting that when it appeared, it ". . . fell dead-born from the press." Unlike contemporary critics, who Hume believed did not understand the work, he attributed its failure to his own ambitious attempt at securing a better basis for understanding human nature than the religious philosophy common in his day. His critics—the sympathetic ones—labeled Hume a skeptic, thereby rejecting his claims for a universal science of human nature out of hand. Harsher critics called Hume a heretic who sought to destroy all religious sensibility. Hume never satisfied his religious attackers and often gave them more evidence to use against him.

The focus of *A Treatise of Human Nature,* however, is best understood in light of Hume's naturalism, not his supposed skepticism. This interpretation gained ascendancy with Hume scholars by the twentieth century and is a more fitting one for the way Hume wished his works to be read.

Hume's philosophical foundations, evolving as they did over the course of his life, can be traced to several principles laid down in *A Treatise on Human Nature;* thus, any attempt at understanding his significance as an historian must begin with it. Hume's position is normally situated within the Scottish Common Sense School, even though many members of that school, such as Thomas Reid, criticized Hume's position. Nonetheless, Hume's understanding of common sense, since it was rooted first in his appreciation for what he called "common life," is the starting point for all his philosophical inquiries. Real philosophy, he noted in *A Treatise on Human Nature,* is that which most nearly approximates the reasoning of common people, not of intellectuals so divorced from society that they lose their capacity for common-sense reasoning.

The rationalistic philosophers popular in Great Britain during Hume's life were of this type. The Cambridge Platonists, particularly Henry More, argued that human consciousness was divided into two universal categories: reason and passion. Ethical behavior rested on how well a person chose to act reasonably at the expense of his passions. The name of the group belies how old this idea was, and Hume recognized the need to challenge a tradition of philosophical inquiry dating back to the ancients as well as a contemporary intellectual movement with which he disagreed. Hume denied that people acted according to pure reason and refuted the idea that reason and passion were in constant combat. He also attacked the notion that a person could

Hume's bookplate, from a copy of Sallust that had belonged to his brother John (from Ernest Campbell Mossner, The Life of David Hume, *1954; Thomas Cooper Library, University of South Carolina)*

reflect upon reasonable subjects from a standpoint independent of those subjects. Proponents of such a view insisted that philosophical reflection necessitated such independence of thought. Those scholars within the rationalistic tradition emphasized the power of pure mathematics to serve as a model for reasonable action. The truthfulness of a belief, for example, depended upon the mathematical progression of its postulates from axioms. These axioms were self-evident and needed no proof of their own. Following the manner of Isaac Newton, Hume insisted that philosophy could not be founded upon self-evident truths, but upon only those things that could be proved through experimentation. Furthermore, he believed that history could not be explained from deducible first principles. Whereas Newton applied experimentation to the natural sciences, Hume was among the first to apply experimenta-

tion to moral philosophy or the study of human nature. In doing so, Hume ranks among the first proponents of what was later called social sciences. Human beings as well as the communities their relationships produce can be studied using the scientific method.

But the first step in creating this new science required Hume to offer a different basis upon which human reasoning could be founded. If there were no universal, self-evident, and deducible principles guiding human reason, and if there was no distinction between reason and passion, then from where did knowledge come?

Hume's answer to this question went far beyond anything that the rationalists were willing to accept. Leaving behind the encumbrances and terse style of *A Treatise on Human Nature,* Hume published *Essays Moral and Political* in two volumes, one in 1741 and the other in 1742. The origin of human reason, according to Hume, was custom, or as he later wrote in *An Enquiry Concerning Human Understanding,* "a species of natural instincts, which no reasoning or process of the thought and understanding is able either to produce or to prevent." Hume's contemporaries warned that his contentions were overly radical because he effectively claimed that the origin of philosophy lay in something nonphilosophical. Hume denied the accusation and insisted that the source of human belief could be found only in nonrational sources, which for him was what human nature was all about.

Hume finally gained a scholarly reputation after publication and positive reception of his *Essays Moral and Political,* which were combined with *Three Essays* and republished in 1748. Thanks to his newfound popularity, Hume sought a chairmanship in philosophy at Edinburgh between 1744 and 1745, but he faced severe public scrutiny over his alleged atheism. Hume denied the attack, but he left no question that his faith was uncertain at best. His religious views did little to enhance his candidacy, nor did the divisive political climate at the university. With *A Letter from a Gentleman to His Friend in Edinburgh* (1745) Hume defended himself to no avail from charges that his philosophy undermined religious principles. After losing to an inconsequential academic, Hume accepted an offer in 1745 to be the tutor of the marquess of Annandale. His hopes were soon thwarted, however, by the young marquess's impending insanity.

The time spent as a tutor proved productive for Hume, who used his time to write several important essays. Some were published in 1748 under the title *Philosophical Essays Concerning Human Understanding.* Others of more historical importance appeared in subsequent collections. They included an early draft of the medieval history of England and "Of the Protestant

Succession," his view of the Jacobite Rebellion. Hume propounded a theme to which he returned in *The History of England:* both sides possessed legitimate legal claims regarding which family should reign in England. Complicating matters even more was that, according to Hume, those who defended the Hanoverian claim were as guilty as those supporting the Stuarts in resorting to violence.

Shortly after leaving the marquess in 1746, Hume served as secretary to his cousin General James St. Clair in a military campaign against France. The expedition was expected to launch a campaign against Canada, but most of the fighting occurred on the coast of Brittany and Quiberon. The English lost, and Hume blamed ministerial incompetence for not adequately supplying the troops. During the campaign, Hume spent his time as St. Clair's judge advocate. Doubtless, his service quickened Hume's experience with law and military affairs, both of which served his historical understanding well, and the remuneration for his services supplied him with the means of living the life of a gentleman.

The following year, Hume returned to the family estate at Ninewells, only to accept another offer from General St. Clair a few months later. St. Clair requested that Hume accompany him to Vienna, Austria, and Turin, Italy, where St. Clair would serve as a military diplomat. St. Clair believed the young historian would be of great assistance. While to assess how well Hume lived up to St. Clair's expectations is difficult, Hume greatly enjoyed his European tour and benefited from it both intellectually and monetarily. According to L. M. Angus-Butterworth, Hume's physique, however, suffered from the trip, and in exaggeration, he wrote his relatives that he had become the "master of near a thousand pounds." Hume returned to Scotland in 1749 to live with his sister in Edinburgh. If his physique suffered from his European tour, his literary productivity flourished because of it.

Over the course of two years he produced *An Enquiry Concerning the Principles of Morals* (1751), a revised version of the third volume of his *A Treatise of Human Nature,* and many essays published in 1752 under the title *Political Discourses.* Hume sporadically published many essays on political and economic topics over the course of his life, though few were as important as those produced in the early 1750s and collected in various revised editions of *Essays and Treatises on Several Subjects.* Of all these, Hume's economic writings were the most far-reaching and were rivaled at that time only by those of his close friend Smith. Like Smith, Hume analyzed many phenomena, such as rudimentary operations of the law of supply and demand, monetary policies, and international trade. Hume and Smith exchanged ideas about virtually every aspect of what was then consid-

ered moral philosophy and is now called political economy.

Hume's many essays on political and economic topics exhibited an impressive understanding of what Frederick Bastiat described as "what is seen and what is unseen." He perceived the unintended consequences of political action and recognized an underlying order to economic life. Several of the essays—including "Of Commerce," "Of Money," "Of Interest," and "Of Public Credit"—challenged many assumptions prevalent in his day. Contrary to the commercial elite of England, who long depended upon special economic privileges, thanks to their political connection with Parliamentarians, Hume insisted that free trade benefited everyone, rich and poor alike. He denied that massive emissions of public credit could long promote economic prosperity and criticized those who championed state regulation.

Above all, Hume challenged the assumptions of mercantilists, who believed bullion constituted inherent wealth, thus requiring competing nation-states to accumulate large surpluses of money by fostering favorable balances of trade. Hume insisted that money, or more accurately money substitutes, holds no value in and of itself but is only a medium of exchange. Or as he explained in "On Money," "It is none of the wheels of trade: It is the oil which renders the motion of the wheels more smooth and easy." From his analysis of monetary history, Hume concluded that the quantity of money makes little or no difference in terms of the actual wealth of a country. All things being equal, if the supply of money increased, its purchasing power would decrease, and prices would rise accordingly. He admitted that in the short term, some increase in money might be beneficial to some industries. In his essay "Of Interest," he explained the origins of interest rates as resulting from the demand for borrowing, the amount of wealth supplying the borrowed funds, and the health of the commercial activity of an area. Most of his economic writings concerned international trade, about which he relied heavily upon his understanding of ancient and modern history to challenge mercantilist ideas. He refused to believe trade between nations necessitated winners and losers, claiming instead that trade benefits all people involved in the exchange and raises their standard of living. Altogether, Hume's economic ideas were rooted in theory, but he continually used historical examples to support his conclusions. Technically then, he was not an economic historian, but his theoretical framework set the stage for Smith's work on international trade as well as similar work by David Ricardo.

One other important aspect to Hume's economic treatises deserves attention in light of his understanding of history. Hume rejected the accepted wisdom of his day that revered the ancient world and posited that era as exemplary for its public virtue and simple living. Contemporaries, especially Hume's acquaintance Rousseau, idolized the ancient republics and presumed their societies to be more virtuous than the present ones. They then reasoned that since ancient societies were more virtuous, they also must have been more populous. Not only did Hume offer cogent reasons undermining this position, but he also stressed the merits of his own time over those of the past. In terms of manners, habits, customs, quality of life, and population, Hume showed how the modern world was vastly superior to that of the ancients. He attributed all of these improvements to commercial development–to what is now called capitalism. What the modern world needed was not a return to the rustic living of the ancients, but further development of the economic exchange that did so much to improve human life. The key point is to understand that Hume did not believe in a golden age in the past, and since there was no golden age, there was no sense to interpreting history as a conflict between those upholding the virtues of the past versus corruption in the present.

After failing to secure another academic appointment, Hume entered his most promising years as an historian in 1752 when he took the appointment of Keeper of the Advocates Library at Edinburgh, the National Library of Scotland. During this period, with unlimited access to the sizable library, Hume wrote his monumental *History of England*. Equally important, Hume finalized essays for his *Political Discourses*.

Hume's writings during the period depended in large part on his access to the Advocates' Library. The large collection of English historical works, combined with the Scottish holdings, inspired Hume's historical imagination. Whatever sources were not available, agents purchased from abroad. His writing style also improved as he learned to take great care in his choice of words and took the time to go through countless drafts of his work. In doing so, Hume became a model stylist for British historians and signified a break from the convoluted prose of the Latin period to the clean, clearly expressed text of the modern period. He insisted that a great history must also be of great literary merit. The historian did not have at his disposal every possible subject, Hume believed, so a historian should focus on those things his contemporaries would find both interesting and useful. Rodney W. Kilcup, in his 1975 introduction to *The History of England*, quotes Hume as explaining to William Robertson, a Scottish historian who proposed to study Charles V, "tho' some Parts of the Story may be entertaining, there would be

many dry and barren, and the whole seems not to have any great Charms."

The proceeds Hume received from *The History of England* rivaled anything earned by a man of letters in Scotland at that time. His dreams of financial independence came true beyond anything he previously imagined. Happy with his success, Hume purchased an impressive residence but lived there only briefly before leaving Edinburgh.

During a period of diplomatic uncertainty, Hume returned to France in 1763 in service to the British embassy and found himself in the center of Paris's intellectual society. His fat form, Scottish brogue, and gentlemanly manners delighted many socialites, including the Countess Amalie de Boufflers, with whom he had an affair. In the Paris salons, he met with many French intellectuals, including Rousseau, Paul Henri Thiry, and Baron d'Holbach.

In 1766 Hume returned to London, where he served as the Undersecretary of Scottish Affairs, from which position he exerted considerable influence and patronage. Two years later he settled again in Edinburgh (on "St. David's" Street). He lived his last years happily by spending time with friends, finishing a few scholarly writings, and engaging in a few intellectual debates. He died in August 1776, just two months before his friend Smith published his *Wealth of Nations*.

Without question, Hume's most important contribution to the study of history during the eighteenth century was *The History of England*. The first volume appeared in 1754 and covered the reigns of Charles I and James I; then Hume published the second volume, focusing on the events surrounding the Glorious Revolution. He published the remaining four volumes in reverse order. Two volumes on the Tudor dynasty were published in 1759, and he also published two volumes on the history of the British Isles from Julius Caesar to Henry VII. As a testament to Hume's skill and influence, the volumes continuously remained in print well into the nineteenth century, making *The History of England* one of the most popular histories of all time.

Hume's all-encompassing history of England displeased Tory and Whig alike. His favoritism for the constitutional policies of James I and Charles I as well as his concern about the radicalism of Civil War Whigs undoubtedly made many enemies among the Whig elite of the mid eighteenth century. The other side was not neglected either, as Hume's condemnation of Charles II and James II elicited great displeasure from Tories. When he began his study, Hume wrote to John Clephane, "My views of *things* are more conformable to Whig principles; my representations of *persons* to Tory prejudices."

To be sure, Hume wished to overcome the epistemological problems to studying history, which had formed during the late Middle Ages. By then, history was the study of God's transcendent order in name only, since discussions of historical topics had become nothing more than theological quibbles. In reaction to sectarian history, Renaissance historians became obsessed with fortune and accident as the principal causation of historical change, a belief that did little to explain real historical development. Post-Reformation historians either carried the Renaissance approach further by following an extreme skepticism that questioned all empirical knowledge, or they suffered from an obsession to recover a sense of transcendent order. In other words, they attempted to bring God back into the picture. Because of the intimate connection between politics and religion in the seventeenth century, religious historians employed methods that championed their political cause. As Kilcup explains, few embraced a truly immanent view of history. Historians either simplistically attributed historical change to God and His choice of their political tradition over another, or they rejected any further meaning to historical change than mere accident.

Hume's understanding of human nature formed the foundation of his radical departure from philosophical currents of his day whether Lockean, Cartesian, or that of the French physiocrats. Hume's understanding of history was that it also must be explored on the foundation of naturalism. His ideas regarding political economy shed much light on how he approached the study of history. A third, equally important dimension to Hume's historical investigations relates to the historical interpretations he opposed—interpretations that proved integral to the political and ideological foundation of eighteenth-century English politics.

The leading school of historical thought in eighteenth-century Great Britain was that of the Whig historians, and their most cherished subject was the English Civil War. Most Whig historians took a republican approach to English history; they traced a linear progression of English liberty from ancient times to the present. The story of the development of liberty began, depending upon the author, either in Saxon England or shortly after the Norman Invasion. In both cases, Whigs attributed the beginning of English liberty to the establishment of popular government. Indeed, liberty for Whig historians was defined as popular rule, and thus their histories illustrated the development of popular rule over time. For the Whigs, liberty was a political device and resulted when a concerted body of people who happened to exercise political influence planned its creation. That is, liberty required deliberate action on the part of a population, and if it were to be enjoyed and

THE

HISTORY

OF

GREAT BRITAIN.

VOL. I.

CONTAINING

The Reigns of JAMES I. AND CHARLES I.

By DAVID HUME, Efq;

EDINBURGH:

Printed by HAMILTON, BALFOUR, and NEILL.

M,DCC,LIV.

Title page for the first edition for Hume's history meant to trace the development of government (Bruccoli Clark Layman Archives)

protected, the population must continue to embrace it. Integral to the Whig interpretation of English history was the connection between English liberty and ancient constitutional rights, which were guaranteed to all Englishmen. These rights, rooted as they were in English custom, depended upon how well the constitution was honored. Should a population fail to embrace their liberty and guard their rights, liberty might deteriorate and even vanish. A paranoid style thus characterized many Whig histories, the authors ranging from Algernon Sidney to Locke. For the Whigs, the story of the progression of liberty was a drama in which liberty was always placed at peril. Only the virtuous and those knowledgeable of the origin of liberty could successfully protect it.

Whig historians focused their attention not only on the English Civil War, but also more specifically on the alleged attacks by Charles I against ancient English liberties and popular rule. Charles, they argued, placed liberty in a precarious position by openly violating key aspects of the English constitution. Only armed conflict could prevent the minions of Charles from finally destroying the fragile liberty Englishmen inherited. Happily for the Whigs, the Civil War drove the Cavaliers from power and taught them a lesson—until Charles II and James II attempted to do the same thing. Ultimately, liberty once again prevailed with the triumph of Parliament during the Glorious Revolution and the ascension to the throne of William III and Mary.

The Whig theory of history, then, involved a philosophy about the nature of liberty, and all of history was written in accord with the philosophy. Those on the side of the Crown were usually treated as villains while those on the side of Parliament, jury trials, and English rights were hailed as heroes. History involved a story, but a story written solely to honor English political development. History was not really about human interaction and complexity but about a struggle for liberty. Virtually all of history could be explained as a clash between the forces of liberty and the forces of tyranny. In other words, the Whigs had their own form of dialectical history, but one that predated the better-known German version by more than one hundred years.

Hume aimed his attack against the Whig's philosophical foundations. For Hume, history was not about liberty so much as it was about the development of complex human relationships and the interaction of those relationships with certain environments. For the Whigs, history demanded a duty from those who understood it: they must protect liberty if not actually create it. For Hume, as with other thinkers in the Scottish Enlightenment, human society did not need to be self-consciously ordered to produce liberty. It could emerge spontaneously and parallel to communal development. History was not the study of forces, or inevitability, or even the evolution of underlying social structures. Nor did history have any inherent direction or theme. Above all, history was without the dialectic confrontation of the forces of good against the forces of evil so prevalent among Whig writings and in many ways symptomatic of nineteenth-century German dialectics. Above all, Hume possessed an understanding of history, not a philosophy of it.

The contest between Tory and Whig historical interpretations began with differing ideas about constitutional order and liberty. To make matters more confusing, each side gradually adopted elements from the other while abandoning certain tenets of their own positions. For example, seventeenth-century Whigs insisted that the unbroken ancient constitution of England produced institutions guaranteeing popular rule to all Englishmen. History progressed or regressed according to how well present English institutions upheld the principles of the constitution. Tories, on the other hand, emphasized right order, the monarch's paternal responsibility over Englishmen, and their responsibility to uphold the monarch's authority. However, during Hume's lifetime the political situation had changed. Quite secure in their political power, the Whigs adopted a new style of politics shaped by a language of rights and liberties. The constitution, while always honored, yielded its place in Whig history to "rights speak," whether the rights of Englishmen or natural rights. At the same time, Tories relinquished their dedication to the divine right of kings in favor of adopting the Whig theme of an ancient constitution—albeit as a means of commenting on Whig policies they opposed. Hume believed both sides were equally wrong because they applied metaphysical precepts to history, by which he meant they interpreted history through their own political ideology.

By emphasizing the constancy of human nature and the manner in which custom, habit, culture, geography, religion, and a host of other variables shaped human nature, Hume found his starting point for understanding history. He explained history in terms of change, but that change was strictly limited by the dictates of human nature. As Kilcup explains, "The uniformity of nature, human nature in particular, runs through the *History* like a golden thread, as the ready assumption in the background that serves to make human conduct understandable in private isolation or in massive social combination." While Hume's own biases affected his work, his accomplishments rest on his attempt to free himself and his study of history from these biases. His task, which he performed with consummate proficiency, involved producing the first modern, scientific history in which only objective observations—free from the prejudices of philosophy, ideology, and religion—could be valued.

The basic premise from which Hume started *The History of England* involved concern over the nature of legitimate government. For many Whigs as well as Hume's contemporaries on the Continent, the measure of good government rested either on how much liberty was promoted or how well the government conformed to its constitution. Hume sympathized with their assessments but could not bring himself to accept them from the standpoint of history. Liberty, he believed, was a natural product of any government as long as it conformed to the habits of a people. Instead of being the product of political decisions, liberty usually emerged out of social and economic custom. Writing of the state of liberty at the end of the Middle Ages, he claimed that "*personal* freedom became almost general in Europe—an advantage which paved the way for the increase of *political* or *civil* liberty, and which, even where it was not attended with this salutary effect, served . . . the community." The real test of the merit of a government was its legitimacy, or the extent to which a population supported its government officials. As Hume noted in his *Essays and Treatises on Several Subjects,* the form a government took mattered little, since all governing officials comprised a minority of the total population. Outnumbered and dependent upon the wealth of the popular body, governing officials were by definition always a minority, and as such, always required the consent of the majority. Force could only be taken so far to win a people's approval. Ultimately, the longevity of a regime or political institution depended upon how well it matched popular sentiment and habit. Public opinion was the only absolute, timeless standard by which to judge the efficacy of a government. Furthermore, what standard existed changed over time in accordance with the traditions of a society.

Hume's beliefs about legitimacy should not be confused with relativism. He never denied that moral absolutes existed, nor did he refrain from making moral judgments about his subjects. For that matter, Hume never denied the consistency of human nature, the cornerstone of his philosophy. However, he admitted that human nature could be shaped by education, culture, geography, religion, and tradition—shaped, not changed. At times he attributed much of the historical change he described to accident and force; he always had faith that underneath all the complexity of history, a universal form of human nature continued to operate. Kilcup summarizes Hume's position as setting "him free to appreciate the uniqueness of the historical moment."

Hume's *History of England* is based on three principles. First, it is a constitutional history focusing on the evolution of political institutions and the origins of English liberty. Second, its overriding concern is the impact of ideological, metaphysical, or religious absolutes relying on material interests. Commitment to such absolutes, Hume believed, represented the absence of reason and propelled a society toward extremism and civil war. Third, Hume believed that legitimacy and authority come naturally to a government that leaves alone or at least respects the customs and traditions of its people.

Beginning with medieval England, Hume traced the development of English liberty from a complex, if not muddled, constitution to a new plan of liberty consummated by the Glorious Revolution of 1688. Far from being the primordial ooze from which Whigs attributed the origin of liberty, Saxon liberty, as Hume saw it, originated in the absence of liberty. Hume's view of Norman England was little better except that competition between the nobility and the new feudal kings offered some hope that arbitrary power might be lim-

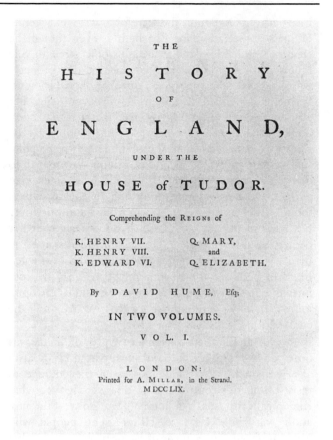

THE

HISTORY

OF

ENGLAND,

UNDER THE

HOUSE of TUDOR.

Comprehending the REIGNS of

K. HENRY VII.   Q. MARY,
K. HENRY VIII.   and
K. EDWARD VI.   Q. ELIZABETH.

By DAVID HUME, Esq;

IN TWO VOLUMES.

VOL. I.

LONDON:
Printed for A. MILLAR, in the Strand.
M DCC LIX.

Title page for the first edition of Hume's popular history, which had gone through more than 150 editions by the end of the nineteenth century (Bruccoli Clark Layman Archives)

ited. However, the limits on power that did exist occurred only because monarchs found working with the nobility easier than working against them—not because either side held to a preconceived notion of the rule of law. The single exception to this rule was the operation of the Church, which Hume thought offered some palliative to an otherwise tyrannical situation. Gradually, enough people appealed to the Magna Carta that it entered public parlance and came to be accepted as a political principle. Yet, few agreed as to what that principle actually meant in the late medieval period, and rarely did its popular appeal restrain self-interested politicians from grappling for power. To prove his point, Hume used the civil war of the fifteenth century to explain that the quest for power was the overruling desire of most English rulers.

Hume treated the ascension of the Tudor dynasty with great care, hoping to avoid falling into the same interpretive quandary as his contemporaries. He believed the Tudors were not without merits and faults, and he consistently sought to provide what he thought was their accurate portrayal. More specifically, he challenged many common assumptions about the reign of

Elizabeth I. One must be careful not to exaggerate Hume's appreciation for Elizabeth I, even though he claims she ruled England at the apex of its strength. She followed the customs of her day, insured that property was protected, and suppressed unruly political factions. Hume commended Elizabeth I for never using her absolute power arbitrarily or in a manner that questioned established customs and constitutional rights. Elizabeth managed to harmonize the interests of a political system in which religious groups threatened to interject absolute principles. By no means was her reign perfect. On the contrary, according to Kilcup, Hume thought she "possessed . . . uncontrolled authority over her Parliaments, and . . . extensive influence over her people. . . ." Nevertheless, Hume concluded that Elizabeth I was the most popular sovereign who ever ruled England because "the maxims of her reign were conformable to the principles of the times, and to the opinion generally entertained with regard to the constitution."

During Elizabeth's reign a new plan of liberty was born, thanks in part to the Puritans, whom Hume usually lamented. They alone possessed the courage to resist Elizabeth's control and, in doing so, ignited what Kilcup calls the "spark of liberty." The irony of the situation was quite clear to Hume. The people who brought about a new form of English liberty—one that celebrated limited government and popular rule, and thus one that championed a government dependent upon the customs of its society—were the ones most responsible for upsetting the political order by their own commitment to religious abstractions. Liberty developed spontaneously from the everyday operation of society, but the political system, which was needed to support its continuation, could not be sustained without proper claims of authority.

Unable to adjust to popular acceptance of English rights, the Stuarts found themselves in a precarious position. Their interpretation of their constitutional powers, Hume thought, was probably more accurate than that of the Puritans, but the Puritans had public opinion on their side. To make matters more difficult for the Stuarts, they could not return to the use of force common in medieval England, because a lack of funds and prospects for sufficient revenue precluded the creation of a large standing army. They also lacked Elizabeth's finesse and shrewdness.

Despite the contradictory constitutional positions of the Stuarts and the Puritans, Hume saw in both an accurate understanding of the political and constitutional customs at their disposal. The Stuarts defended the divine right of kings and the regal prerogatives enjoyed by their predecessors. The Puritans and friends of Parliament championed rights and liberties by then considered by the people to be traditional. Hume did his best to explain both positions. He admitted that the authority of the English king, in government and in law, was absolute, and that the constitution seemed to support this view. Likewise, he agreed with those who loved liberty and who looked to the practice of ages to defend the powers of assemblies and Parliament.

Hume believed both sides were correct in that they both settled for custom: the Stuarts for the customary powers of the monarchy, the opposition for the customary privileges of Parliament. Both appealed to centuries of tradition, and in the end, both appealed to religion. As Hume interpreted the situation, the problem rested on customs not universally embraced by the English people. Indeed, the customs were antithetical, causing each side to favor tenaciously abstract political thinking. As passions swelled, chances for compromise withered away, leaving only civil war as an alternative. Hume did not embrace inevitability, but even he could not fathom what Charles I might have done to alleviate the crisis.

The Civil War is described in redundant and sometimes confusing terms, though Hume's interpretation of its events comprises his most important and far-reaching historical contribution. At a time when most Europeans could be shocked by the thought of a people beheading their own monarch, his account of the Civil War provided a much needed and balanced account of its events. He deplored the assault on liberties favored by the Rump Parliament and found solace in the self-restraint imposed by the Long Parliament. Passions continued to flare to the point that Oliver Cromwell instituted, in Hume's view, the most despotic government in English history. As Donald W. Livingston explains, Hume attributed the execution of Charles and Cromwell's military despotism to "an intellectual and spiritual pathology mingled with ambition. . . . What the Puritans eventually sought was not reform but a total transformation of the social and political order in accord with a religious ideology."

Gradually, when the cause of liberty was used to justify despotism, English opinion retreated from its unlimited endorsement of liberty and began once more to cherish principles such as legitimacy, authority, and peace. The restoration of the Stuart monarchy served to delineate constitutional prerogatives while leaving the careful new balance between Parliament and the crown still precariously unstable. Hume granted that Charles II was no tyrant; neither were his Whig opponents saints. He criticized the techniques of the opposition, especially their embrace of the Popish Plot, and he attributed most of their measures to mere partisan faction rather than to a genuine embrace of liberty. The Whigs' factionalism alarmed the English public and forced them to side with the crown, almost to the point at which they were prepared to sacrifice their liberty to protect themselves from purported supporters of liberty. As with the opponents of Charles I, who jettisoned common sense for religious fanaticism and military rule, the Whigs seemed to teeter on the edge of a zeal irreconcilable with an orderly society.

Fortunately, wrote Hume, the cause of liberty survived Whig fanaticism, thanks to the death of Charles II and to the incompetence of James II. As Hume wrote, James "might have succeeded in surmounting at once their liberties and religion, had he conducted his schemes with common prudence and discretion." James's ineptitude in attacking religion did more than ignite religious passions; it united the country against the king who held the best chance of regaining lost prerogatives. Finally, the lines of demarcation between crown and Parliament, magistrate and people, were delineated by the Convention, and William of Orange pledged to uphold them in return for the throne.

Hume's history of England illustrates the almost accidental evolution of English liberty and how far it actually was from Whiggish insistence on the unbroken march of liberty. Only by understanding English liberty for what it was—with all its irregularities, accidental extensions, and the many times it was nearly lost—did Hume think it stood a chance of survival in his own day. In short, what the English needed was not an abstract understanding of their history but, Hume insisted, a natural history free from mindless speculation and religious dogma.

His use of the scientific method to understand the facts of history better and to free historical study from abstract reasoning can be seen in his other important works. His success as an historian depended entirely upon *The History of England,* but his contributions to the study of history in the eighteenth century and beyond should be seen in another as well. In many ways, Hume was one of the first true historians of religion, or someone who attempted to analyze religious thought and evolution from a scientific perspective.

Hume believed that two fundamental questions must be answered regarding religion. The first concerns the causes of religious belief, or why religious ideas take the forms they do. He pursued this subject in his *Dialogues Concerning Natural Religion,* published posthumously in 1779. More important for Hume was the second question—to explain the origin of religious belief and account for its development over time. His *Natural History of Religion,* published in 1757, served as his vehicle for providing the historical account. Hume's contemporaries and modern observers concur on one thing concerning Hume's own religious beliefs: he was certainly not orthodox in his views. Christians deplored his skepticism while later Deists recognized in Hume's writings serious challenges to their own ideas.

In terms of the evolution of religion, Hume claimed that human beings engaged in religious belief for reasons contrary to those offered by his contemporaries. He believed environmental circumstances could not account for religious belief. People believed, according to H. E. Root, as a response to their "perpetual suspense between life and health and sickness, plenty and want." Human beings reflected upon the unknown and the uncertainty of life to produce religious thought. Why, Hume asked, would anyone wish to determine the origins of those things most familiar to them? As he explained, "the more regular and uniform . . . nature appears, the more is he familiarized to it, and the less inclined to scrutinize and examine it."

Hume admired polytheism, which he believed predated monotheism by a considerable period. Not surprisingly, his attitude toward polytheism coincided with his assumption that polytheists are more tolerant than monotheists, less prone to abstract and theological thinking, and more likely to instill manly values and honor. He relegated religious belief to the "secondary" constituents of human nature because he believed it was not universally prevalent among all peoples. This view also supported his contention that since religious belief was not a part of the more mysterious primary aspects of human nature, religion could be studied empirically. One must only observe what religious people say they believe in order to determine what religious belief is. The effects of religious belief are equally as important as are its impact upon the morals of society—that is, how it shapes the moral climate and traditions of a culture. As with any custom, it changes over time.

Herein lies an important aspect of Hume's historical understanding. He saw little need in levying moral claims against or in favor of a particular kind of religious belief. A careful description of the effects of a religious belief should suffice. In short, Hume believed the facts could speak for themselves. Students of his analysis admit that his application of empiricism to religion outraged his contemporaries more than anything else. His detached, objective, even-handed approach was what upset them, not what he said. He summarily praised and attacked pagan and Christian alike. Modern readers are likely to see problems in this approach but for different reasons. While his purported objectivity fails to amaze, the uniformity of his treatments of various religious groups is rather dull. The complexity of history, so apparent in *The History of England,* is lost in his interpretation of religion.

Hume's historical understanding met a warm reception almost immediately in North America and in

*Hume (left) shaking hands with Jean-Jacques Rousseau (engraving by
T. Holloway, c. 1766; from Ernest Campbell Mossner,* The
Life of David Hume, *1954; Thomas Cooper Library,
University of South Carolina)*

for *Federalist* No. 10. In France, Hume's works were also
well received, as revealed by the work of Laurence L.
Bongie in the late twentieth century. Many Frenchmen
used Hume's account of the Puritan Revolution in
England as a starting point for understanding their own
Revolution. In a manner similar to the Puritans', the
Jacobins were motivated by an ideological zeal to trans-
form society.

Bongie's works, as well as those of such recent
scholars as Livingston, point to an unusual dimension
of Hume's influence and his historical understanding.
Hume despised the introduction of ideological thinking
into politics. He thought of it as a pathology that
robbed people of their ability to understand and work
with custom and habit. Far from trying to decipher
some hidden meaning, some great undercurrent of
human affairs that would be the key to unlocking all of
history, Hume relied on a keen observation of what
might be called the surface of history. People, he
believed, made history, and it could be revealed by
studying what people in the past thought they were
doing, not by attributing human action to irrational
forces beyond their control.

David Hume's historical writings, the most far-
reaching of any eighteenth-century British historian,
continued to exert considerable influence well into the
twentieth century. More than 150 editions of *The History
of England* were published by the late nineteenth century,
including a "republicanized" version abridged by John
Baxter, which Thomas Jefferson praised. Generations
of English schoolchildren, including Winston Churchill,
learned their history from a student edition of *The History of England,* and an edition or abridgement of *The
History of England* did not cease being in print until the
end of the twentieth century.

France. Hume greatly sympathized with the North
American colonists and refused to offer criticism of
their cause. In 1775 he wrote to his friend William
Mure of Caldwell, "I am an American in my principles,
and wish we would let them alone to govern or misgov-
ernment themselves as they think proper." Some people
think that as early as 1768 Hume supported the seces-
sion of the thirteen colonies from the British Empire, a
position far ahead of most North Americans. His
denunciation of the classical belief that republics could
exist only on a small scale—a position revived by
Charles-Louis de Secondat, Baron de Montesquieu—
influenced many American Revolutionary leaders,
especially James Madison, who relied heavily on Hume

Letters:

*Life and Correspondence of David Hume. From Papers
    Bequeathed by His Nephew to the Royal Society of Edin-
    burgh; and Other Original Sources by John Hill Burton,*
    2 volumes (Edinburgh: William Tate, 1846);

G. Birkbeck Hill, ed., *Letters of David Hume to William
    Strahan* (Oxford: Clarendon Press, 1888);

J. Y. T. Greig, ed., *The Letters of David Hume,* 2 volumes
    (Oxford: Clarendon Press, 1932);

Raymond Klibansky and Ernest C. Mossner, eds., *New
    Letters of David Hume* (Oxford: Clarendon Press,
    1954).

Bibliographies:

T. E. Jessop, *A Bibliography of David Hume and of Scottish
    Philosophy, from Francis Hutcheson to Lord Balford*
    (London: Brown, 1938);

William B. Todd, "David Hume, A Preliminary Bibliography," in *Hume and the Enlightenment: Essays Presented to Ernest Campbell Mossner,* edited by Todd (Edinburgh: Edinburgh University Press, 1974), pp. 189–205;

Roland Hall, *Fifty Years of Hume Scholarship: A Bibliographical Guide* (Edinburgh: Edinburgh University Press, 1978)–updates by Hall, in November issues of *Hume Studies* (1977–).

Biographies:

T. E. Ritchie, *Account of the Life and Writings of David Hume* (London, 1807);

John Hill Burton, *Life and Correspondence of David Hume,* 2 volumes (Edinburgh: William Tate, 1846);

J. Y. T. Greig, *David Hume* (London: Cape, 1931);

Ernest Campbell Mossner, *The Life of David Hume,* second edition, revised (Oxford: Clarendon Press, 1980).

References:

L. M. Angus-Butterworth, *Ten Master Historians* (Freeport: Books for Libraries Press, 1969);

Laurence L. Bongie, *David Hume: Prophet of the Counter-Revolution,* foreword by Donald W. Livingston, second edition (Indianapolis: Liberty Fund, 1998);

Nicholas Capaldi, *David Hume: The Newtonian Philosopher* (Boston: Twayne, 1975);

Capaldi, *Hume's Place in Moral Philosophy* (New York: Peter Lang, 1989);

Donald W. Livingston and James T. King, *Hume: A Reevaluation* (New York: Fordham University Press, 1976);

Livingston, *Hume's Philosophy of Common Life* (Chicago: University of Chicago Press, 1984);

Livingston, *Philosophical Melancholy and Delirium: Hume's Pathology of Philosophy* (Chicago: University of Chicago Press, 1998);

John Valdimir Price, *David Hume* (New York: Twayne, 1968);

Norman Kemp Smith, *The Philosophy of David Hume* (London: Macmillan, 1941);

John B. Stewart, *The Moral and Political Philosophy of David Hume* (New York: Columbia University Press, 1963);

John P. Wright, *The Sceptical Realism of David Hume* (Minneapolis: University of Minnesota Press, 1983).

Papers:

The most significant holding of David Hume's papers is the Hume Manuscripts at the National Library of Scotland. Other manuscripts, journals, and official papers are held at the Huntington Library; the British Library; the British Museum; the Pierpont Morgan Library; the Keynes Library, King's College, Cambridge University; the Public Record Office, London; the William Andrews Clark Memorial Library; the City Chambers, Edinburgh; and the New Register House, Edinburgh.

White Kennett

(10 August 1660 – 19 December 1728)

Annamarie E. Apple
University of Pittsburgh

BOOKS: *A Letter from a Student at Oxford . . . Concerning the Approaching Parliament, in Vindication of His Majesty, the Church of England, and University,* anonymous (London: Printed for John Seeres, 1681);

To Mr. E. L. on His Majesties Dissolving the Late Parliament at Oxford, 28 March 1681 (London? 1681);

A Dialogue between Two Friends Occasioned by the Late Revolution of Affairs, and the Oath of Allegiance (London: Printed for Richard Chiswell, 1689);

Parochial Antiquities Attempted in the History of Ambrosden, Burchester, and Other Adjacent Parts in the Counties of Oxford and Bucks (Oxford: Printed at the Theater, 1695);

The Righteous Taken Away from the Evil to Come: Applied to the Death of the Late Excellent Queen Mary in a Sermon Preached January the Twentieth 1694/5 (Oxford: Printed by Leonard Lichfield for George West, 1695);

Some Remarks on the Life, Death, and Burial of Mr. Henry Cornish, B. D., an Eminent Dissenting Teacher (London: Printed for John Nutt, 1699);

Ecclesiastical Synods and Parliamentary Convocations in the Church of England: Historically Stated, and Justly Vindicated from the Misrepresentations of Mr Atterbury (London: Printed for A. & J. Churchill, 1701);

An Occasional Letter on the Subject of English Convocation (London: Printed for A. & J. Churchill, 1701);

The Case of the Praemunientes Considered: In an Answer to the Letter Sent Lately to a Clergyman in the Country Concerning the Choice of Members, and Execution of the Parliament-Writ for the Ensuing Convocation (London: R. Sare, 1702);

The Present State of the Convocation (London: Printed for A. & J. Churchill, 1702);

The History of the Convocation of the Prelates and Clergy of the Province of Canterbury, Summon'd to Meet at the Cathedral Church of St. Paul, London, on February 6, 1700 (London: Printed for A. & J. Churchill, 1702);

A Letter from the Borders of Scotland, Concerning Somewhat of Agreement Between a Scotch General Assembly, and an

White Kennett *(portrait by John Faber, 1719; National Portrait Gallery, London, NPG D3475)*

English Provincial Convocation (London: A. Baldwin, 1702);

The Present State of Convocation in a Letter Giving the Full Relation of Proceedings in Several Late Sessions (London: Printed for A. & J. Churchill, 1702);

A Reconciling Letter, upon the Late Differences about Convocational Rights, and Proceedings as Manag'd by Those Who Have Maintain'd Liberties of the Lower Clergy (London: Printed for Richard Sare, 1702);

A Sermon Preached at Bow-Church, London, before the Societies for Reformation on Monday the 29th of December, 1701 (London: Printed for A. & J. Churchill, 1702);

The Glory of Children in Their Fathers: A Sermon Preached in the Cathedral Church of St. Paul London, before the Sons of the Clergy, December the 3d 1702, (London: Bonwicke, 1703);

The Case of Impropriations and of the Augmentation of Vicarages and Other Insufficient Cures, Stated by History and Law (London: Printed for A. & J. Churchill, 1704);

Christian Honesty Recommended at the Assizes Hold at Chelmsford, for the County of Essex. On the 23d of March, 1703/4: In a Sermon Preach'd (London: Printed by S. Holt for A. & J. Churchill, 1704);

The Christian Scholar: In Rules and Directions for Children and Youth Sent to English Schools (London: Printed for Richard Sare, 1704);

A Compassionate Enquiry into the Causes of the Civil War, in a Sermon Preached on January 31, 1703/4, the Day of Fast for the Martyrdom of King Charles the First (London: Printed by H. Hills, 1704);

Moderation Maintain'd, in Defence of a Compassionate Enquiry into the Causes of the Civil War . . . in a Sermon Preached the Thirty-First of January (London: D. Defoe, 1704);

A Sermon Preached on the Day of Thanksgiving for the Late . . . Victory Obtain'd over the French and Bavarians . . . by the Forces of Her Majesty and Her Allies (London: Printed for A. & J. Churchill, 1704);

Some Remarks, or Short Strictures, upon a Compassionate Enquiry into the Causes of the Civil War: In a Sermon by White Kennett (London: Printed for C. Brome, 1704);

The Happiness of This Church and Nation . . . A Sermon Preached before the Lord Mayor March 8, the Day of Her Majesty's Accession (London: Printed for A. & J. Churchill, 1705);

An Account of Proceedings in the Convocation Which Began Oct. 25, 1705 (London, 1706);

The Charity of Schools for Poor Children Recommended in a Sermon Preach'd May 16, 1706 (London: Printed by J. Downing & J. Churchill, 1706);

A Complete History of England with the Lives of All the Kings and Queens Thereof; from the Earliest Account of Time to the Death of His Late Majesty William III, 3 volumes, by Kennett, John Hughes, and John Strype (London: Printed for B. Aylmer, Reb. Bonwick, Sam. Smith, and Benj. Walford, etc., 1706);

The Duties of Rejoycing in a Day of Prosperity. Recommended in a Sermon Preached before the Queen at Her Royal Chapel in Windsor (London: Printed by H. Hills, 1706);

The Office and Good Work of a Bishop: A Sermon Preach'd in Lambeth Chappel at the Consecration of the Right Reverend Father in God, William, Lord Bishop of Lincoln on Sunday October 21, 1705 (London: Printed for A. & J. Churchill and R. Sare, 1706);

A Sermon Preached before the Honourable House of Commons January 30 1704/5 (London: Printed by D. Brown, 1706);

A Sermon Preach'd at the Funeral of the Right Noble William, Duke of Devonshire, in the Church of All-Hallows in Derby on Fryday [Sic] Septem. 5th, MDCCVII (London: Printed by H. Hills, 1707);

Charity and Restitution: A Spital Sermon on Luke. With an Application to the Vain Attempts of a Spanish Invasion, in the Year 1588 (London: Printed for J. Wyat, 1708);

The Excellent Daughter (London: Printed by J.T., 1708);

A Sermon Preach'd at the Funeral of the Right Noble William Duke of Devonshire, with Memoirs of the Family of Cavendish (London: Printed by H. Hills, 1708);

Glory to God and Gratitude to Benefactors: A Sermon Preached before the Queen, 22 November 1709, the Day of Publick Thanksgiving for the Signal and Glorious Victory at Blaregnies near Mons (London: Printed for John Churchill, 1709);

A True Answer to Dr. Sacheverell's Sermon before the Lord-Mayor, November 5, 1709. In a Letter to One of the Aldermen (London: Printed by A. Baldwin, 1709);

A Vindication of the Church and Clergy of England, from Some Late Reproaches Rudely and Unjustly Cast upon Them (London: Printed by J. Baker, 1709);

An Account of the Late Conversion of Mr. John Barville, Alias Barton, from Popery to the Reformed Church of England: With the Form of His Solemn Abjuration of the Romish Religion, by Kennett and John Barville (London: Printed for John Phillips, 1710);

A Visit to St. Saviour's Southwark, with Advice to Dr. Sacheverell's Preachers There (London: Printed, and to be sold by A. Baldwin in Warwicklane, 1710);

The Works of Charity. In a Spittal Sermon Preach'd before the Lord Mayor and Governors of the Several Hospitals of the City of London, on Tuesday in Easter-Week, 1710 (London: J. Chrchill [sic], 1710);

An Argument in Defence of Passive Obedience in Opposition to All Manner of Tenets Advanc'd by Several Pretended Fathers of the Church, and Other Eminent Writers on the Side of Resistance to the Supreme Powers (London: Printed for John Morphew, 1711);

The Christian Neighbour. A Sermon Preach'd in the Church of St. Lawrence-Jewry, Before the Right Honourable the Lord Mayor, the Aldermen, Sheriffs, and Commonalty of the City of London, upon the Election of a Mayor for the Year Ensuing, on the Feast of St. Michael, MDCCXI (London: Printed for J. Churchill, 1711);

A Sermon Preached before the Convocation Held by the Archbishop, Bishops, and the Clergy of the Province of Canterbury (London: Printed by J. Morphew, 1711);

A Sermon Preached before the Convocation . . . with Some Account of the Sermons and Speeches Made in Former Synods, during the First Century after the Reformation (London: Printed for J. Churchill, 1711);

Doing Good the Way to Eternal Life . . . A Spiritual Sermon (London: J.R., 1712);

The Lets and Impediments in Planting and Propagating the Gospel of Christ. A Sermon Preached Before the Society for the Propagation of the Gospel in Foreign Parts (London: Printed by J. Downing, 1712);

A Memorial to Protestants on the Fifth of November, Containing a More Full Discovery of Some Particulars Relating to the Happy Deliverance of King James I and the Three Estates of the Realm of England, from the Most Traiterous and Bloody Intended Massacre by Gun-powder, Anno 1605. In a Letter to a Peer of Great Britain (London: Printed for J. Churchill, 1712);

Bibliothecae Americanae Primordia. An Attempt towards Laying the Foundation of an American Library in Several Books, Papers and Writings Humbly Given to the Society for the Propagation of the Gospel in Foreign Parts (London: Printed for G. Churchill, 1713); republished as *The Primordia of Bishop White Kennett, the First English Bibliography on America* (Washington, D.C.: Pan American Union, 1959 [i.e., 1960]);

A Letter by W. K. to the Lord Bishop of Carlisle, concerning One of His Predecessors, Bishop Merks; On Occasion of a New Volume for the Pretender, Intituled, The Hereditary Right of the Crown of England Asserted (London: S. Buckley, 1713);

A Memorial to Protestants on the Fifth of November: Containing a More Full Discovery of Some Particulars Relating to the Happy Deliverance of King James I and . . . Three Estates of the Realm from . . . Massacre by Gunpowder, Anno 1605 (London: J. Churchill, 1713);

The Properties of Christian Charity: A Spital Sermon Preached on Easter Tuesday March 30, 1714 (London: Printed for J. Churchill, 1714);

A Short Account of the State of England, When King James Design'd to Call His Second Parliament (London: Printed by J. Smith, 1715);

The Wisdom of Looking Backward, Etc. (London: Printed for J. Roberts, 1715);

The Witch-Craft of the Present Rebellion (London: Printed for J. Churchill, 1715);

A Seasonable Discourse upon the Rise, Progress, Discovery and Utter Disappointment of the Gunpowder Treason and Rebellion Plotted by the Papists in 1605 . . . as Delivered in a Sermon Preached on 5 Nov 1715 Before the Lord Mayor, Aldermen and Citizens of this City (London: Printed for J. Churchill, 1715);

The Faithful Steward (London: Printed for J. Churchill, 1716);

A Second Letter to the Lord Bishop of Carlisle . . . upon the Subject of Bishop Merks; Wherin the Nomination, Election, Investiture, and Deprivation of English Prelates Are Shew'd to Have Been Originally Constituted and Govern'd by the Sovereign Power of Kings and Their Parliaments . . . against the Pretension of Our New Fanaticks (London: Printed by Sam. Buckley, 1716);

A Thanksgiving Sermon for the Blessing of God in Suppressing the Late Unnatural Rebellion, June 7, 1716 (London: Printed for J. Churchill, 1716);

A Third Letter to the Lord Bishop of Carlisle, Lord Almoner to His Majesty, upon the Subject of Bishop Merks (London: Printed by Sam. Buckley, 1717);

Dr. Snape Instructed in Some Matters . . . by a Member of the Convocation (London: Printed for James Knapton and Timothy Childe, 1718);

A Sermon Preached before the Lords on January 30, 1719 (London: Printed for W. Taylor, 1719);

Monitions and Advices Delivered to the Clergy of the Diocese of Peterborough . . . at the Primary Visitation (London: Printed by J. Wyat, 1720);

A Register and Chronicle, Ecclesiastical and Civil, Containing Matters of Fact . . . with . . . Notes and References towards Discovering and Connecting the True History of England from the Restauration of King Charles II. Vol. I Faithfully Taken from the Manuscript Collections of the Lord Bishop of Peterborough (London: Printed for R. Williamson, 1728);

The Providence of God in Protecting the Protestant Religion; and Securing the Protestant Succession: In a Discourse Delivered Nov 5, 1728 (London: Printed for R. Williamson, 1729);

An Historical Account of the Discipline and Jurisdiction of the Church of England (London: Printed for O. Payne, J. Whitaker, W. France, and L. Stokoe, 1730).

TRANSLATIONS: Desiderius Erasmus, *Witt against Wisdom; or, A Panegyric upon Folly* (Oxford: Printed by L. Lichfield for Anthony Stephens, 1683); republished as *In Praise of Folly* (Chicago: P. Covici, 1925);

Pliny, the Younger, *An Address of Thanks to a Good Prince: Presented in the Panegyrick of Pliny upon Trajan, the Best of Roman Emperors* (London: Printed by M. Flesher for Thomas Fickus, 1685).

OTHER: William Somner, *A Treatise of the Roman Ports and Forts in Kent,* edited by James Brome, with a biography of Somner by Kennett (Oxford: Printed at the Theatre, 1693); enlarged by Kennett as *A Treatise of Gavelkind, Both Name and Thing* (London: Printed for F. Gyles, 1726);

The Interpreter of Words and Terms, Used Either in Common or Statute Laws of this Realm, and in Tenures and Jocular

Customs: with an Appendix, Containing the Antient Names of Places in England . . . First Publish'd . . . in . . . 1607, and Continu'd by Tho. Manley . . . to the Year 1684, augmented by Kennett (London: Printed for W. Battersey, etc., 1701).

White Kennett, controversial historian, political polemicist, and ecclesiastical official, has been the subject of few scholarly works. The first biography written about Kennett was composed by William Newton in 1730. Newton, a protégé of Kennett, felt compelled to defend his late mentor because many Jacobite enemies continued to malign his name, even after his death. Newton's biography celebrated Kennett's life and the causes he held dear—namely history, politics, religion, and charity. Kennett was a prolific writer; however, the works that were ultimately published represent only a small sample of the volume of works he completed in his lifetime. Many of his unpublished works are preserved today at the British Museum in the Lansdowne collection. Historian G. V. Bennett produced the most recent biography of Kennett in 1957. Since this work, historians have given little attention to Kennett and his contributions to the preservation of history in late-seventeenth- and early-eighteenth-century England.

Kennett was born on 10 August 1660 to Basil and Mary Kennett in the parish of St. Mary in Dover. His parents named their first-born son after his maternal grandfather, Thomas White, in what some have interpreted as a calculated attempt by his father to curry favor with his prosperous father-in-law. At the time of Kennett's birth, Basil Kennett was a mere storekeeper who aspired to attaining a role in the Anglican Church. Kennett's father achieved his goal and received holy orders on 7 August 1668. White Kennett grew up intending to follow in his father's path and to seek a position of authority in the church hierarchy. His mother, the eldest daughter of Thomas White, was disappointed in her expectations of inheriting her father's wealth when her father remarried late in life; the Kennett family were disinherited in favor of the three children produced in White's second marriage.

Kennett received his early education in two local schools, Elham and Wye. He later attended Westminster School. In June of 1678, at the age of seventeen, he entered St. Edmund Hall in Oxford. Kennett was deeply affected by his education at the University of Oxford, which led the field in Anglo-Saxon studies at the time. While at Oxford, he was instructed by respected scholars such as Andrew Allam, Thomas Marshall, and Anthony Wood. Kennett even learned Anglo-Saxon and other northern languages from George Hicks, whom he later engaged in heated quarrels. During his undergraduate years Kennett studied with Wood, who encouraged his interest in antiquarian and historical studies. As a tutor at both Oxford and Queen's College and as vice principal of St. Edmund

Hall, Kennett also influenced younger students, including Edmund Gibson and Thomas Tanner, to pursue medieval studies.

Kennett's career as a published writer began early, as he was still an undergraduate when his first work, *A Letter from a Student at Oxford . . . Concerning the Approaching Parliament, in Vindication of His Majesty, the Church of England, and University,* was anonymously published in 1681. He wrote this work in hopes of influencing the Parliament that was summoned to Oxford on 21 March 1681. Kennett spouted loyalist theory and criticized the citizens of Oxford for not supporting their sovereign. Indeed, he went as far as accusing the House of Commons of trying to obstruct Charles II's rule, but declared that they had never had the power to act on their own. This letter enraged the Whig Party, who attempted to ascertain the identity of the writer so that they could inflict an appropriate punishment. Fortunately for Kennett, Charles II dissolved the Parliament suddenly, and Kennett's authorship remained undiscovered. Continuing to be controversial, Kennett published a short poem on 28 March 1681; *To Mr. E. L. on His Majesties Dissolving the Late Parliament at Oxford, 28 March 1681,* which criticized the members of Parliament. Indeed, Kennett startled even the staunchest royal supporters by writing that "our King's a God on Earth."

Also during this period, Kennett assisted Wood in the collection of epitaphs and notices of eminent Oxford men to form an historical account of the area. Kennett received his bachelor of arts degree on 2 May 1682. With this part of his education finished, in 1683 Kennett published a new edition of Erasmus's *Moriae Encomium,* which he titled *Witt against Wisdom; or, A Panegyric upon Folly.* This time Kennett's work was popular. In fact, by 1740 *Witt Against Wisdom* had been published no less than six times. He pursued his master's degree, which he received on 22 January 1684. After taking holy orders as his father had, Kennett became curate and assistant to Samuel Blackwell. In September 1685 Sir William Glynne presented Kennett to the vicarage of Ambrosden. In 1685 Kennett published *An Address of Thanks to a Good Prince: Presented in the Panegyrick of Pliny upon Trajan, the Best of Roman Emperors,* which expressed his loyalty to James II in lavish praise. His loyalty to the king, however, was soon transferred to William and Mary. For this complete change in allegiance, friends nicknamed him "Weathercock" Kennett. The enemies he had gained were much crueler in their assessment of his character for his switch in loyalty.

Although Kennett's first published works were political commentaries, Bennett writes that "White Kennett's early reputation among his contemporaries was that of a historian and antiquary." Indeed, Kennett considered himself to be an historian, and he spent a great deal of time writing biographies and other works of great historical value. In 1693 his first published historical work, a biogra-

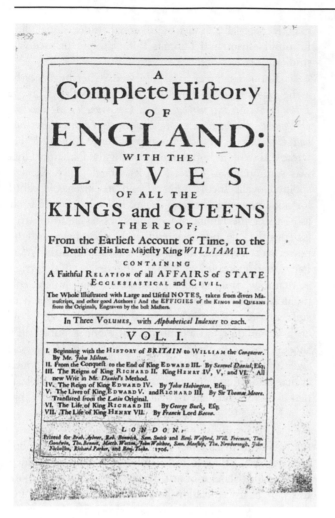

Title page for Kennett's 1706 work in which he attempted to include an impartial account of recent English history (Eighteenth-Century Collections Online, Gale Group)

phy of antiquarian William Somner, was included in James Brome's edition of Somner's work *A Treatise of the Roman Ports and Forts in Kent*. In this work, Kennett stresses to the reader the importance of historical study as he praises Somner for preserving the antiquities of Canterbury. This work was subsequently enlarged and republished in 1726 under the title *A Treatise of Gavelkind, Both Name and Thing*.

In 1695 Kennett published the fruit of his antiquarian studies in *Parochial Antiquities Attempted in the History of Ambrosden, Burchester, and other Adjacent Parts in the Counties of Oxford and Bucks*. This work focused on the history of this specific area and reprinted the Doomsday records. Many scholars, including William Nicolson, considered *Parochial Antiquities* a groundbreaking work and praised Kennett for his contribution to parish history. Bennett noted that contemporaries viewed this work as "new in its critical, thorough and learned examination of evidence, producing a

clear and sober book unmarred by polemical purpose." Kennett and other scholars, including Gibson and Tanner, were planning a new edition of William Camden's *Britannia* (1586), but this work was never realized.

Meanwhile, Kennett's previous outspoken dedication to James II crumbled when the king's views of ecclesiastical policy clashed with his own. In 1688 Kennett utilized his pulpit to warn against the dangers of popery that he believed were present at James's court. Moreover, Kennett adamantly refused to read in his church the "Declaration for Liberty of Conscience" passed down by the king that same year. For these reasons, Kennett became widely known as a staunch supporter of William and Mary's cause. He circulated a manuscript that was not published, providing compelling arguments for the swearing of the oaths of allegiance and supremacy to William and Mary. For his switch in loyalties, Kennett drew fire from many Jacobites. His work *A Dialogue between Two Friends* (a Jacobite and a Williamite), published in the year of the Glorious Revolution, 1689, clarified his position on this issue, using historical arguments to prove that William and Mary had a legitimate claim to the throne of England.

As for Kennett's personal life, he married three times and also assumed the care of his two younger brothers after his father's death in 1686. Kennett took special care of his brother Basil, who also became a well-published scholar. Kennett's first marriage, to Sarah Carver, daughter of Robert and Mary Carver of Bicester, took place on 6 June 1693. She died in childbirth on 2 March 1694 before the couple's first wedding anniversary. Kennett was griefstricken over her loss and experienced his own health crisis at this time. Nevertheless, he married for a second time 6 June 1695, to Sarah Smith. This second marriage produced a son, White Kennett (who died 6 May 1740), and a daughter, Sarah (who died 22 February 1756).

Kennett, realizing a dream and surpassing his father's educational achievements, received his doctorate of divinity from Oxford on 19 July 1700. This same year he was made rector of St. Botolph in Aldgate. In 1701 Kennett continued to ascend to higher ecclesiastical offices and became chaplain to Bishop Gardiner of Lincoln and archdeacon of Huntingdon. At this time, Kennett became embroiled in what became known as the Convocation controversy. This controversy involved the prorogation of the convocations of Canterbury and York by both Charles II and James II. Francis Atterbury ably argued for the High Church side that the convocation was the highest spiritual court in the land and was an essential part of Parliament. Therefore, Atterbury attested that the convocation should be held while Parliament was in session. William Wake responded for the Episcopal side by arguing for royal supremacy in *The Authority of Christian Princes over Their Ecclesiastical Synods Asserted* (1697). Atterbury anonymously answered back with *The Rights, Powers, and*

Privileges of an English Convocation (1701). This work attacked the weakest points of Wake's arguments, and the High Church side seemed about to win the day. Kennett, who had just moved to London, joined the debate. Despite the hopes of some church officials, including Sir Bartholomew Shower, that Kennett would support their cause, he surprised them by supporting Wake. In *Ecclesiastical Synods and Parliamentary Convocations in the Church of England: Historically Stated, and Justly Vindicated from the Misrepresentations of Mr Atterbury,* published on 10 February 1701 and officially dedicated to Archbishop Tenison, Kennett debated the historical position set forth by Atterbury. He used his scholarly background to refute Atterbury and provide a clear historical argument based on his study of early Saxon sources. He showed that the archbishop had the singular authority to summon convocations.

In addition, in June of 1701 Kennett was named one of the original members of the Society for the Propagation of the Gospel in Foreign Parts, an organization whose purpose was to emphasize missionary work in the North American colonies. More specifically, the group lobbied for a bishop to be placed in America. Kennett's second wife died in August of 1702. Kennett married his third wife, Dorcas Fuller, in 1703. No children were produced in this third marriage, but Kennett accepted responsibility for the care and upbringing of his wife's daughter, Dorcas, from her first marriage to Clopton Havers, a medical doctor.

In 1706 Kennett wrote *An Account of the Society for Propagating the Gospel in Foreign Parts,* on the history of the society; he also intended to elucidate its progress. In 1711 he revised the work, but it was only officially published posthumously in 1730, although not under his name. Kennett also collected more than three hundred items while researching the work. This collection of books, maps, and documents from the North American colonies, perhaps of greater historical value than *An Account of the Society for Propagating the Gospel in Foreign Parts,* was published as *Bibliothecae Americanae Primordia* in 1713. Kennett continued to add pertinent documents, and they were placed in a permanent collection in 1727.

In 1706 John Hughes asked Kennett to contribute to a complete history of England, a work that compiled a continuous account of English history. Kennett's anonymous effort for *A Complete History of England with the Lives of All the Kings and Queens Thereof; from the Earliest Account of Time to the Death of His Late Majesty King William III* covers the reigns of Charles I to William III and represents an attempt to set down an objective and impartial account of more recent history. He delves into what he believes were the causes of the English Civil War, including fear of popery, arbitrary government, "French interest," and Charles's personal responsibility. This work represented an alternate version of history from

Edward, Earl of Clarendon's *History of the Rebellion and Civil Wars in England, Begun in the Year 1641* (1702–1704), which portrayed King Charles as the victim of evil courtiers. Kennett's identity as the author of this work did not remain a secret, however, and his Jacobite enemies attacked him for it. On the other hand, his popularity at court soared, and, as a result, Queen Anne named him one of her personal chaplains.

Meanwhile, Kennett continued to attain higher ecclesiastical positions within the Anglican Church. He was named dean of Peterborough on 8 January 1708. He attained the position of prebendary of Farrendon-cum-Balderton at Lincoln. Several years later he was elected bishop on 25 October 1718 and installed at Lambeth on 9 November 1718. While diligently attending to his ecclesiastical duties, he also used his historical and antiquarian skills to enhance the library at Peterborough. His scholarly efforts ensured that the collection would become one of the foremost storehouses of information at that time.

In addition to his other works, throughout his life Kennett published a dozen of his most important sermons from the period between 1694 and 1728. Some examples include *Some Remarks on the Life, Death, and Burial of Mr. Henry Cornish, B.D., an Eminent Dissenting Teacher* (1699), *Ecclesiastical Synods and Parliamentary Convocations in the Church of England: Historically Stated, and Justly Vindicated from the Misrepresentation of Mr. Atterbury* (1701), and *A Memorial to Protestants on the Fifth of November, Containing a More Full Discovery of Some Particulars Relating to the Happy Deliverance of King James I and Three Estates of the Realm from . . . Massacre by Gun-powder, Anno 1605* (1713). One of his more provocative sermons was preached to his congregation on the fast day for Charles I. This sermon, *A Compassionate Enquiry into the Causes of the Civil War* (1704), instead of praising Charles I as a martyr as was expected on this particular day, pointed out what Kennett perceived to be the errors of Charles I's reign. In particular, he criticized the influence of the Catholic queen, Henrietta Maria, and the king's ministers. This controversial sermon produced angry reactions from Tories and nonjurors, thus prompting Kennett to publish two defenses of his words in the same year.

Kennett also published less-controversial sermons that aimed at spiritual guidance and the promotion of charity and good works. Indeed, he frequently emphasized the necessity of education. In a sermon preached on 16 May 1706, he recommended to wealthy patrons the establishment of charity schools in order that poor children receive a proper Christian education. In a 1704 sermon, *The Christian Scholar: In Rules and Directions for Children and Youth Sent to English Schools,* he again emphasized his belief in education and illustrated a plan for Christian course work.

In 1707 Kennett resigned from the rectory of St. Botolph, Aldgate, in favor of the smaller rectory of St. Mary Aldermary, London, in order to have more time to attend to his historical and antiquarian studies. In addition, he focused on promoting both his political and his ecclesiastical views. Notably, Kennett attacked the idea that lay baptism was invalid and published a sermon to refute Henry Sacheverell's public address to the lord mayor of London. Further creating controversy in 1710, Kennett refused to join many of his peers in their congratulations to the queen. For his stance, Kennett gained more enemies within the High Church party. Furthermore, he angered nonjurors and High Churchmen alike with his pamphlets, and especially his spital sermon delivered to the lord mayor on 30 March 1714. This sermon, *The Properties of Christian Charity,* argued that lay baptism was valid. Again, his loyalty appeared to change as he began to be critical of Queen Anne and issues concerning the succession. As a result of Kennett's outspoken support of the Hanoverian heirs, the queen began to withdraw her favor. A clear visual representation of his unpopular position in the eyes of High Churchmen was the Whitechapel altarpiece, in which the painter depicted Kennett (clearly identifiable with a black patch on his forehead from an early injury) as Judas Iscariot in a rendition of the Last Supper. The rector, Richard Welton, commissioned this inflammatory painting, which was hung in London, where it caused quite a stir and enticed many visitors to view the spectacle.

Kennett's last major work, *A Register and Chronicle, Ecclesiastical and Civil* (1728), digested in exact order of time, was one of his best-known works. His thorough and precise antiquarian work preserved information that might otherwise have been lost. Amazingly, the work only covers the years 1660–1662, but it consists of 938 large folio pages.

Kennett died on 19 December 1728 as a result of an unknown illness. He was buried with full pomp and dignity in Peterborough Cathedral. Kennett's contributions and the causes he believed in were many. At a crucial time in English historical studies, when methodology was undergoing change, he represented the new way of thinking by working closely with documents and basing his conclusions on the evidence presented. Although many critics accused him of "political Whiggism," Kennett always tried to pursue an objective view of history. He is remembered as an historian who advanced historical and antiquarian studies, as a polemicist who had a major impact on the Convocation Controversy and helped to establish the legitimacy of the Glorious Revolution, and as a concerned cleric who advanced social programs for the poor. White Kennett's lifetime of work not only preserved medieval history for posterity but also reflects the times in which he lived.

Biographies:

William Newton, *The Life of the Right Reverend White Kennett, Late Bishop of Peterborough* (London: Printed for S. Billingsley, 1730);

G. V. Bennett, *White Kennett (1660–1728), Bishop of Peterborough* (London: S.P.C.K., 1957).

References:

Charles Harding Firth, "The Development of the Study of the Seventeenth Century," *Transactions of the Royal Historical Society,* series 3, 7 (1913): 25–38;

Janelle Greenberg, *The Radical Face of the Ancient Constitution: St. Edward's "Laws" in Early Modern Political Thought* (Cambridge: Cambridge University Press, 2001);

Evarts B. Greene, "The Anglican Outlook on the American Colonies in the Early Eighteenth Century," *American Historical Review,* 20, no. 1 (1914): 64–85;

Martin Greig, "Heresy Hunt: Gilbert Burnet and the Convocation Controversy of 1701," *Historical Journal,* 37, no. 3 (1994): 569–592;

Clyve Jones, "Debates in the House of Lords on 'The Church in Danger,' 1705 and on Dr. Sacheverell's Impeachment, 1710," *Historical Journal,* 19 (September 1976);

J. G. A. Pocock, "Robert Brady, 1627–1700: A Cambridge Historian of the Restoration," *Cambridge Historical Review,* 10 (1951): 186–204;

Roger Schmidt, "Roger North's Examen: A Crisis in Historiography," *Eighteenth-Century Studies,* 26 (Autumn 1992): 57–75;

Deborah Stephan, "Laurence Echard–Whig Historian," *Historical Journal,* 32 (December 1989): 843–866;

Norman Sykes, "Archbishop Wake and the Whig Party, 1716–23," *Cambridge Historical Journal,* 8, no. 2 (1945): 93–112;

Sykes, "Episcopal Administration in England in the Eighteenth Century," *English Historical Review,* 47 (1932): 414–446;

Sykes, "Queen Anne and the Episcopate," *English Historical Review,* 50 (1935): 433–464.

Papers:

White Kennett's manuscripts and letters are located in the British Museum, the Bodleian Library, the Dean and Chapter Library at Peterborough, and Cambridge University Library.

Thomas Leland

(1722 – 22 August 1785)

Seán Patrick Donlan
University of Limerick

BOOKS: *History of the Life and Reign of Philip King of Macedon, the Father of Alexander,* 2 volumes (London: Printed by Thomas Harrison for W. Johnston, 1758);

Longsword, Earl of Salisbury: An Historical Romance (Dublin: Printed for G. Faulkner, 1762; London: Printed for W. Johnston, 1762; New York: New York University Press, 1957);

A Dissertation on the Principles of Human Eloquence; With Particular Regard to the Style and Composition of the New Testament; In Which the Observations on This Subject by the Lord Bishop of Gloucester, in His Discourse on the Doctrine of Grace, Are Distinctly Considered; Being the Substance of Several Lectures Read in the Oratory School of Trinity College, Dublin (London: Printed for W. Johnston, 1764);

An Answer to a Letter to the Reverend Doctor Thomas Leland. Containing, an Examination of the Criticism on a Late Dissertation on the Principles of Eloquence. In Which Is Particularly Shewn, That the Lord Bishop of Gloucester's Idea of an Inspired Language . . . Is Acknowledged to Be Indefensible by the Learned Vindicator (London: Printed for W. Johnston, 1765);

An Examination of the Argument Contained in a Late Introduction to the History of the Ancient Irish and Scots, anonymous (London: J. Johnson, 1772);

The History of Ireland from the Invasion of Henry II. With a Preliminary Discourse on the Antient State of That Kingdom, 3 volumes (Dublin: Printed by R. Marchbank for R. Moncriffe, 1773; London: J. Nourse; T. Longman & G. Robinson; and J. Johnson, 1773; Philadelphia & New York: Printed by Hugh Gaine, Robert Bell, and John Dunlap, 1774);

A Sermon, Preached Before the University of Dublin, on Friday the 13th of December, 1776, Being the Day Appointed by Authority for a General Fast and Humiliation (London: Printed for E. Johnston and N. Conant, 1777; Dublin: Printed by W. Hallhead, 1777);

The Love of Our Country: A Sermon, Preached in the Parish Church of Saint Anne's, Dublin, on Sunday, June 23

Thomas Leland (portrait by John Dean, after Sir Joshua Reynolds; National Portrait Gallery, London)

(London: Sold by Mr. Longman, London, and Mr. Wilson, Dublin, 1782);

Sermons on Various Subjects, 3 volumes (London: George Bonham, 1788).

TRANSLATIONS: Demosthenes, *All the Orations of Demosthenes, Pronounced to Excite the Athenians against Philip King of Macedon: Translated into English; Digested and Connected, So As to Form a Regular History of the Progress of the Macedonian Power* (London:

213

Printed for W. Johnston, 1756; second edition, corrected, 1757; New York: AMS Press, 1975; republished as volume one of augmented three-volume edition retitled as *Orations against Philip: Orations on Public Occasions, with the Oration of Dinarchus against Demosthenes: Orations of Aeschines and Demosthenes on the Crown* (London: Printed for W. Johnston, 1763–1770);

Histoire d'Irlande, depuis l'Invasion d'Henri II, avec un Discours preliminaire sur l'ancien état de ce Royaumme, 7 volumes (Maestricht: Dufout & Roux, 1779).

The Ireland of the 1760s and 1770s was a time of great political and intellectual possibility, not least in history and historiography. Protestant historians, often the descendants of colonization and settlement before and during seventeenth-century Ireland, began to draw from native Gaelic sources. They increasingly viewed the ancient history of Ireland, safely removed from more-contemporary controversies, as their own. Catholic historians, whose ancestors were both Gaelic and "Old English," were also beginning to engage in the wider British tradition and to protest their loyalty to the British state. Though the penal (or "Popery") laws were not yet without effect, a "patriotic" rapprochement of Ireland communities seemed possible. These hopes were embodied in the clergyman Thomas Leland. Encouraged to write a "philosophical history" unburdened by confessional prejudice, he wrote a *History of Ireland* (1773) that satisfied almost no one.

Leland was born in Dublin in 1722. He may have been related to John Leland, nonconformist minister and writer of *View of the Principal Deistical Writers That Have Appeared in England in the Last and Present Century* (1754–1756). He studied with Thomas Sheridan before entering the University of Dublin (Trinity College) as a pensioner (1737/1738). There he was elected a scholar (1741) and graduated with a B.A. (1742). He failed to receive a university fellowship in his first attempt (1745) but succeeded the following year by unanimous vote. In 1748 he entered holy orders in the established church and the same year wrote a discourse, "On the Helps and Impediments to the Acquisition of Knowledge in Religious and Moral Subjects." At the university, Oliver Goldsmith, perhaps Edmund Burke, and many other future Irish statesmen studied under him.

Leland translated and published, with the assistance of John Stokes, a Latin edition of the *Philippic Orations of Demosthenes* (1754), with critical notes. In 1756 he translated part of the work into English as *All the Orations of Demosthenes, Pronounced to Excite the Athenians against Philip King of Macedon;* in 1770 he republished it as part of a three-volume work titled *Orations against Philip: Orations on Public Occasions, with the Oration of Dinarchus against*

Demosthenes: Orations of Aeschines and Demosthenes on the Crown. The *Orations against Philip* raised Leland's status as a scholar and was reprinted into the next century. In 1758 he published his first historical work, *History of the Life and Reign of Philip King of Macedon, the Father of Alexander* (1758), drawing heavily on Greek sources. In it, he wrote many reflections on politics, and the work was later used by Oliver Goldsmith in his *Grecian History from the Earliest State to the Death of Alexander the Great* (1774). Leland received a D.D. from the university in 1757, and, having been approached with the idea of a Dublin school emphasizing reading, writing, and public speaking, he lent his support, becoming superintendent of the Hibernian Academy in 1759. He was subsequently appointed the University of Dublin's professor of oratory and history (1761–1762) and then of oratory (1762–1781).

Leland composed several other works in the 1760s. He wrote, though seems not to have acknowledged, *Longsword, Earl of Salisbury: An Historical Romance* (1762), perhaps the first historical romance in English. While his opinions were in the mainstream of the church, he engaged in theological debates on the role of rhetoric. William Warburton, bishop of Gloucester, in his *Doctrine of Grace* (1762), launched an attack on rhetoric. Part of a critique of methodism, then a movement within the established church, he suggested that eloquence was deceptive, often designed to pervert rational judgment. In defense of oratory, Leland published *A Dissertation on the Principles of Human Eloquence; With Particular Regard to the Style and Composition of the New Testament; In Which the Observations on This Subject by the Lord Bishop of Gloucester, in His Discourse on the Doctrine of Grace, Are Distinctly Considered; Being the Substance of Several Lectures Read in the Oratory School of Trinity College, Dublin* (1764). This work was subsequently answered anonymously by Richard Hurd, friend of the bishop and himself later bishop of Worcester. Leland replied in his *An Answer to a Letter to the Reverend Doctor Thomas Leland. Containing, an Examination of the Criticism on a Late Dissertation on the Principles of Eloquence. In Which Is Particularly Shewn, That the Lord Bishop of Gloucester's Idea of an Inspired Language . . . Is Acknowledged to Be Indefensible by the Learned Vindicator* (1765). Leland is generally thought to have gotten the better of the argument.

Leland was an increasingly important member of the intellectual community of Dublin. On his suggestion, the university bestowed an honorary doctorate of laws on Samuel Johnson (1765), an honor acknowledged in a letter collected in James Boswell's *The Life of Samuel Johnson, LL.D.* (1791). Through his friend George Faulkner, a well-known Irish printer, Leland was introduced to Charles O'Conor of Belanagare. The Catholic O'Conor was the last of the Irish Gaelic aristocracy, whose family had only been able to maintain lands through a cooperating Protestant family. He was at this time already an accomplished historian and writer, whose *Dissertations on the Antient History of Ireland* (1753) was one of the most important Irish publications of the century. Along with Burke, O'Conor strongly encouraged Leland to write a "philosophical" or impartial history of Ireland. Both Burke and O'Conor had been deeply critical of past "protestant" histories of Ireland, seeing them linked to the perpetuation of the penal laws. While slowly passing into desuetude, the laws were not without effect, as O'Conor later discovered when his brother temporarily converted and claimed the family estate.

Leland seemed an ideal choice for Ireland's "philosophical historian." O'Conor believed that Leland "would fill such a post with Dignity. He would thro' his Philosophical Knowledge render us wiser than we are, and no Nation ever wanted the true Knowledge of their proper Interests more than ours. History in such Hands would reform us much" (*Letters*, no. 161, 13 June 1767). Many people thought that Ireland, after years of acrimonious division, was ready for an historian of the caliber of David Hume and William Robertson, whose works on England and Scotland respectively were considerable advances in British historiography. Such an historian, able to portray the Irish past with accuracy and justice, might, it was hoped, also provide the basis on which a shared future could develop. "Would to God he could be brought to think of this Matter, this Duty I should say which he owes his country . . . ," O'Conor noted of Leland in the 13 June 1767 letter; "if we do not exhibit a Hume or a Robertson in our Island, it will be his fault."

Although not an Irish speaker, Leland made significant contributions to Gaelic scholarship and employed Irish scribe Muiris Ó Gormáin for research. Leland had already begun to preserve Gaelic manuscripts, presenting the University of Dublin with several texts purchased from the library of the late John Fergus (Seán mac Macraith Ó Fearghusa). O'Conor noted these efforts in the second edition of his *Dissertations on the Antient History of Ireland* (1766). Having taken up the challenge to write an Irish history, Leland received considerable assistance, not least that of James Caufield, Lord Charlemont, and George, Lord Macartney. Burke, too, made available several valuable manuscripts, originally from the collection of Welsh scholar Edward Lhwyd, then in the hands of Sir John Sebright, member of Parliament for Bath. These same texts later provided the foundation for the university's Gaelic collection. Leland requested O'Conor's assistance, though even he had difficulty with the antiquated "law Irish" the manuscripts included. An assistant librarian begin-

ning in 1752, Leland took on duties as university librarian in 1768. He arranged for O'Conor to have library access, a privilege otherwise denied him as a Catholic.

Not surprisingly, given his post as professor of oratory, Leland was a noted, energetic preacher. In the late 1760s he was appointed chaplain to George, Viscount Townsend, then lord lieutenant of Ireland (1768). The same year he became prebend of Rathmichael, in the cathedral church of St. Patrick's, Dublin, united with the vicarage of Bray, county Wicklow (1768–1773). The position provided little income, and he seemed to have expected a bishopric, but it permitted him to continue his university fellowship. Shortly thereafter (1769) he decided to take up the challenge of an Irish history. In "the glorious retirement of a Country Parson," he wrote Burke (22 March 1770), "I think little of the vices & follies of the present Irish race, but I have studied those of their progenitors with great care. And my History of the affairs of Ireland . . . is in great forwardness."

O'Conor hesitated, however, to tell some Catholic allies about Leland's work. His friend John Curry, Catholic physician and historian, was especially skeptical. Curry specialized in the Irish rebellion of 1641, on which he had already written two books. Among other events, the rebellion remained significant to eighteenth-century Ireland. Coming as it did at the eclipse of Gaelic Ireland, confiscation, and settlement, it confirmed a shift from colonial to confessional divisions. Portrayed as a series of Catholic atrocities, Protestant alarm and triumphalism set the tone for the next century. Curry noted that Leland had preached the annual sermon (1771) celebrating the victory of Protestant forces in 1641. Sermons on this occasion typically emphasized the barbarity and treason of Irish Catholics and the continuing necessity of the penal laws. While Leland suggested that Catholic actions were the result of Protestant sins, a significant shift in rhetoric, he nevertheless maintained in "On the Anniversary of the Irish Rebellion" (*Sermons on Various Subjects*, 1788) that "papal superstition" was "the great and leading cause of [the] day's calamity." But Leland and O'Conor were developing a warm friendship, and Leland assured O'Conor, in a letter of 5 January 1769, that the history must be written "with a liberal indifference to all parties English & Irish, civil & religious."

Leland's first engagement was Scottish prejudices, not Irish. His anonymous *An Examination of the Argument Contained in a Late Introduction to the History of the Ancient Irish and Scots* (1772), following O'Conor's earlier critiques, attacked the history and historiography of Scottish poet-historian James Macpherson. Macpherson had presented his poetry, inspired by Highland oral tradition, as the work of a third-century poet, Ossian. The

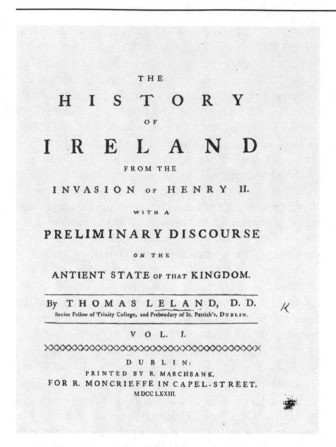

Title for Leland's 1773 history of Ireland (Eighteenth-Century Collections Online, Gale Group)

poems were extraordinarily popular throughout Europe. They were the source, too, of considerable debate. Macpherson claimed that he had only translated the poems, rather than composed them. Of more importance to historiography, he insisted on their historical veracity. The primitivism of the works fit nicely the progressive stadialism of the Scottish thought, but as O'Conor had pointed out, Macpherson failed to account for the significant changes in manners and language in the millennium that separated "Ossian" and the eighteenth century. Leland wrote *An Examination of the Argument Contained in a Late Introduction to the History of the Ancient Irish and Scots* in a more common fiction, in the guise of an unbiased observer, a native of neither Scotland nor Ireland. He both criticized Macpherson's failure to substantiate his claims and defended Irish historiography. Whereas classical writers were generally accepted as authoritative, he argued, different standards were applied to Irish annals and historians.

Leland does not seem to have told O'Conor about his role in *An Examination of the Argument Contained in a Late Introduction to the History of the Ancient Irish and Scots*. O'Conor was increasingly hopeful. With some encouragement that new sources had been found at the

university, even Curry became optimistic. He held back publication of a book on the Irish civil wars in the hope that Leland would adopt his arguments. Unlike the standard account of 1641, Curry hoped to show that Catholic actions had occurred in response to a massacre by Scottish Protestant soldiers. So eager was Curry to discover Leland's new information, he arranged independently to look at the printer's sheets being prepared for publication. He was horrified to find that Leland was arguing not with, but against, him. Leland's new discoveries seemed to confirm the chronology of Protestant accounts, if not their gross exaggeration of casualties.

In fact, Leland's *History of Ireland from the Invasion of Henry II. With a Preliminary Discourse on the Antient State of That Kingdom* (1773) pleased almost no one. In both Ireland and Britain, the work received a mixed critical reaction and generated only lukewarm sales. Learned, but long and surprisingly dull, the work appeared largely to synthesize earlier accounts. Leland acknowledged the importance of documentary sources, and the "Dissertation" preceding the work tried to establish a detached or philosophical tone. "It was scarcely possible for a writer not to share in the passions and prejudices of those around him . . . ," he wrote; "the historian of Irish affairs must be armed against censure only by an integrity which confines him to truth, and a literary courage which despises every charge but that of wilful or careless misrepresentation." The work is less noteworthy, however, for impartiality than for equivocation between previous accounts. Leland was largely indifferent to claims of a pagan high culture, but he nevertheless (citing O'Conor) supported the idea of a learned, early, though not overtly Roman, Christianity. He explained the barbarism of Irish "manners." Borrowing heavily from the canonical analysis of Sir John Davies (1569–1626), Leland explained the barbarism of Irish culture by the weakness of English government following the Anglo-Norman conquest, coupled with the failure to incorporate the native Irish into English law.

Hume, in his *History of England* (1754–1762), had mocked the Irish as having no "philosophical historian" (save the Englishman Davies). Many Irish, including O'Conor and Burke, saw Hume's portrayal of the native and Catholic Irish as uncritically repeating the more-offensive and prejudicial of past histories. Leland, in the preface to his *History of Ireland,* referred indirectly to Hume, writing that "no brain-sick monk, in days of darkness and superstition, ever betrayed such credulity as appears in these assertions. . . . But the Irish," he remarked, "have no philosophical historian." As Leland left the safety of the distant past, however, his *History of Ireland* seemed little different from Hume's, laying again the ultimate responsibility for the rebellion of 1641 on Catholic superstition. Irish Catholics–including clergy, women, and children–he wrote, "goaded [the English] forward like beasts, exulting in their sufferings." Leland acknowledged subsequent massacres of Catholics and criticized English policy but wrote in volume three that an "enthusiastic hatred of the Irish was the natural and necessary consequence" of their actions.

Thomas Leland's critique of past Irish manners, rather than of the Irish as Irish, was too fine a distinction for Catholic writers. O'Conor wrote (31 October 1772) that Leland "resign[ed] his literary merit and all credit with impartial men in favour of present advantages either within his grasp or within his expectations." Leland was answered by Sylvester O'Halloran's *Ierne Defended* (1774) and (with Curry encouraged by O'Conor) Curry's *Historical and Critical Review of the Civil Wars in Ireland* (1775). Burke was disappointed, too, and though he and O'Conor both maintained contact with Leland, Burke later wrote to his son (20 March 1792) that Leland "thought only of himself and the bookseller." Following the tepid response to his *History of Ireland,* Leland largely turned his attentions to his clerical and academic duties. He worked with O'Conor on the Antiquarian Committee of the Dublin Society, but he never published again. While he still hoped for a bishopric or university office, he transferred to the vicarage of St. Anne's, Dublin. In 1781 he resigned his university fellowship for the more lucrative rectory of Ardstraw, county Tyrone (1781–1785), and died in Dublin on 22 August 1785. Leland's *History of Ireland* represented genuine movement away from the older partisan histories, but it was a small step toward impartiality.

References:

David Berman, "David Hume on the 1641 Rebellion in Ireland," *Studies,* 65 (1976): 101–112;

Thomas W. Copeland, ed., *The Correspondence of Edmund Burke,* 10 volumes (Cambridge: Cambridge University Press, 1981);

John Patrick Delury, "Ex Conflictu Et Collisione: The Failure of Irish Historiography, 1745 to 1790," *Eighteenth-Century Ireland/Iris an dá chultúr,* 15 (2000): 9;

Francis G. James, "Historiography and the Irish Constitutional Revolution of 1782," *Éire-Ireland,* 18 (1983): 6–16;

Joep Leerssen, *Mere Irish and Fíor-Ghael: Studies in the Idea of Irish Nationality, Its Development and Literary Expression Prior to the Nineteenth Century* (Cork: Cork University, 1996);

Joseph Liechty, "Testing Thomas Leland's *History of Ireland,* 1773," *Archivum Hibernicum,* 42 (1987): 21–28;

Walter D. Love, "Charles O'Conor of Belanagare and Thomas Leland's 'Philosophical' History of Ireland," *Irish Historical Studies,* 13 (1962): 1–25;

Clare O'Halloran, "Golden Ages and Barbarous Nations: Antiquarian Debate on the Celtic Past in Ireland and Scotland in the Eighteenth Century," dissertation, University of Cambridge, 1991;

William Sullivan, "The Irish manuscripts in Case H in Trinity College Dublin Catalogued by Matthew Young in 1781," *Celtica,* 11 (1976): 229–250;

R. E. Ward, J. F. Wrynn, and C. C. Ward, eds., *The Letters of Charles O'Conor of Belanagare: A Catholic Voice in Eighteenth-Century Ireland* (Washington, D.C.: Catholic University of America, 1988).

Catherine Macaulay

(2 April 1731 – 22 June 1791)

Dale Marie Urie
University of Kansas

See also the Macaulay entry in *DLB 104: British Prose Writers, 1660–1800, Second Series.*

BOOKS: *The History of England, from the Accession of James I to That of the Brunswick Line,* 8 volumes (volumes 1 and 2, London: Printed for J. Nourse, R. & J. Dodsley, and W. Johnston, 1763, 1765);

The History of England from the Accession of James I to the Elevation of the House of Hanover (volumes 3 and 4: London: Printed for the author, 1767, 1768; volume 5: London: Printed for Edward & Charles Dilly, 1771);

Loose Remarks on Certain Positions to be Found in Mr. Hobbes's Philosophical Rudiments of Government and Society. With a Short Sketch of A Democratical Form of Government, in a Letter to Signior Paoli (London: Printed for T. Davies, Robinson & Roberts, and T. Cadell, 1767);

Observations on a Pamphlet, Entitled, Thoughts on the Cause of the Present Discontents (London: Printed for Edward & Charles Dilly, 1770);

A Modest Plea for the Property of Copyright (Bath: Printed by R. Cruttwell for Edward & Charles Dilly, London, 1774);

An Address to the People of England, Ireland, and Scotland, on the Present Important Crisis of Affairs (Bath: Printed by R. Cruttwell for Edward & Charles Dilly, London, 1775; New York: Printed by John Holt, 1775);

The History of England, from the Revolution to the Present Time in a Series of Letters to the Reverend Doctor Wilson (Bath: Printed by R. Cruttwell, 1778);

The Female Patriot: An Epistle from C---t---e M---c---y to the Rev. Dr. W-l--n [Wilson] on Her Late Marriage (London: Printed for J. Dew, 1779);

The History of England from the Accession of James I to the Revolution (volumes 6–7, London: Printed by A. Hamilton, 1781; volume 8, 1783);

A Treatise on the Immutability of Moral Truth (London: Printed by A. Hamilton, 1783);

Catherine Macaulay (Painting, c. 1778, by Robert Edge Pine, National Portrait Gallery, London)

Letters on Education, with Observations on Religious and Metaphysical Subjects (London: Printed for C. Dilly, 1790);

Observations on the Reflections of the Right Hon. Edmund Burke on the Revolution in France, in a Letter to the Earl of Stanhope (London: Printed for C. Dilly, 1790; Boston: Printed by I. Thomas & E. T. Andrews, 1791).

"It is only the democratical system, rightly balanced, which can secure the virtue, liberty and happiness of society" (*Loose Remarks on Certain Positions to be Found in Mr. Hobbes's Philosophical Rudiments of Government and Society. With a Short Sketch of A Democratical Form of Government, in a Letter to Signior Paoli* [1767]). What made this bold, antimonarchical and widely read statement surprising beyond its enlightened republican views was that its author was a woman. Catherine Macaulay ventured into contemporary politics with this broadside against Thomas Hobbes, who she believed was wrong on every point when he argued for the necessity and inevitability of monarchy. Though Macaulay's name was not on the title page, the broadside was widely known to have been written by her. She had already gained fame and admiration, as well as condemnation, for the publication of the first two volumes of her history, *The History of England, from the Accession of James I to That of the Brunswick Line* (1763, 1765). Her *History of England* was the first comprehensive, antiroyalist work of its time. When completed in 1783, it traced in detail the history of England from the ascension of James I to the Glorious Revolution of 1688. Replete with original documents and analysis, *The History of England* provided Macaulay a platform from which to debate the issues of her day.

Catherine Sawbridge was born 2 April 1731 to a wealthy country family at Olantigh, in Kent. Her father and mother, John and Elizabeth Wanley Sawbridge, came from prominent London banking families. John Sawbridge was an antimonarchist who filled his library with classical histories, literature, philosophy, and political treatises. Macaulay's mother died in 1733 after bearing four children. Her father, who became reclusive after his wife's death, supposedly saw the children rarely and refused to provide tutors for his two daughters. Catherine and her brother John seem to have developed their passion for liberty while reading the volumes in their father's library. They became intellectual and political allies for life, though most avenues of action were closed to Catherine. John became a radical Whig member of the "Bill of Rights Club" and a supporter of the policies of John Wilkes and Charles Fox. He held the offices of alderman, sheriff, Lord Mayor of London, and member of Parliament.

At twenty-nine Catherine Sawbridge married George Macaulay, a Scots physician in his mid forties, and moved to London. George Macaulay was widely acquainted with the radical Whig and Scots reform circles in London. Apparently, as an academic himself, he encouraged his intellectually gifted wife to write in the area of history. Three years after her marriage, she completed the first volume of *The History of England, from the Accession of James I to That of the Brunswick Line* (1763). Volume two followed in 1765. George Macaulay died in 1766, leaving Catherine to raise their young daughter

alone. Volume three appeared in 1767, volume four in 1768, and volume five in 1771, taking the story to the rise of the house of Hanover. However, the completion of *The History of England* had to wait another twelve years because of the exigencies of life.

Though many English women of her class were literate, Catherine Macaulay was one of the first women to write history. Her fame came partially from the novelty of her accomplishment, but it involved much more than that. Her work was important in both content and method. Historians differ in assessing the originality of her thinking, but she certainly broadened the popular interpretation of the English Civil War as having been caused by economic factors by explaining in addition the religious and sociological influences. Hers was the first history of the eighteenth century with an avowed republican outlook. She set about her task, in part, to refute David Hume's Tory interpretation of English history during that period, and she did so without falling into an ideological trap. She is highly critical of Oliver Cromwell, whom she believed betrayed the ideals of democracy. She equally abhors that Parliament ceded to William of Orange the rights it had struggled sixty years to obtain. Her narrative is rich with portraits of individuals, whom she treats as morally free agents.

In her *History of England* she omits "no anecdote that does honour to the female sex" (volume two). For example, she does not ignore the women who in 1641 petitioned the House of Commons against the Papists and prelatists. She includes the influence of wives on famous men if the documentation is reliable.

Macaulay's *History of England* examines other historical interpretations and holds no historian sacred. She is straightforward when inserting her own views, though her goal, according to the introduction of volume six, was to present "incontrovertible argument founded on fact." She does not bow to traditional republican views when the weight of facts does not support them. An example is her treatment of Charles I, in whose conduct she found much to admire, even as she supported his execution. Her research was extensive, and she let documents speak for themselves. She found and included in her analysis documents and manuscripts that previous historians had ignored.

Macaulay's *History of England* was an important achievement in eighteenth-century historiography. Her revisionist work provided an alternative to the sectarian religious accounts of the previous century and the royalist histories that dominated the field.

Macaulay was the object of much attention, both praise and scorn. Perhaps most important for a woman breaking into a male domain, she was not ignored. Sales of her volumes were high, and publishers vied for rights to future volumes. William Pitt delivered a "panegyric of the *History* to the Commons" (*Letters of Horace Walpole,* volume five [1903]). Thomas Gray reported to Horace Walpole that it was "the most sensible, unaffected and best history of England that we have had yet" (*Letters of Horace Walpole,* volume five). According to Lucy Martin Donnelly, Samuel Johnson, the "inveterate old Tory" is said to have remarked to Macaulay that she was surely aware that "there is a monarchy in heaven," to which she replied, "If I thought so, sir, I should never wish to go there."

In the mid 1760s Macaulay's life took her away from a strict focus on her *History of England.* Her celebrity gave her a platform on which to enter the debate of current affairs. In 1767 she wrote her first pamphlet, *Loose Remarks on Certain Positions to be Found in Mr. Hobbes's Philosophical Rudiments of Government and Society.* She recommended a democracy that was "rightly balanced," which meant rotation in office (effectively, term limits), the equal division of inheritance among male heirs, agrarian legal reform that placed more property in the hands of the people, a bicameral legislature, and suffrage for all men.

Her brother John Sawbridge introduced Macaulay to John Wilkes, who had been expelled from Parliament in 1763 for seditious libel against George III. Sawbridge became a leading supporter of Wilkes following his return to London in 1768. This stance placed her in the center of radical politics. Though her reputation and influence were increasing, the time-consuming work required for her *History of England* did not permit her to write another pamphlet in support of radical causes until 1770.

When she did write one, she answered Edmund Burke's *Thoughts on the Causes of the Present Discontents* (1770) with *Observations on a Pamphlet, Entitled, Thoughts on the Cause of the Present Discontents* (1770). She saw Burke's solution to monarchical corruption as replacing one evil with another. To raise up an "aristocratic faction" that governed based on self-interest was no improvement. Tyranny can be held in check only by frequent elections, rotation of officeholders, and extended suffrage. Burke himself regarded her *Observations* as the most effective reply of the many published. He described Mrs. Macaulay's pamphlet as "what he expected; there are however none of that set that can do better, the Amazon is the greatest champion among them" (from *The Correspondence of Edmund Burke* [1958]). *Observations* was recognized across the Atlantic shortly after it was published and was praised in James Burgh's *Political Disquisitions* (1763), highly regarded in the American colonies on the eve of the American Revolution.

In 1774 Macaulay wrote her least important pamphlet, *A Modest Plea for the Property of Copyright.* Authors were battling with booksellers over copyright owner-ship, and the matter was being decided that year in the courts and later by Parliament.

Macaulay became a true friend of the American cause. Many American notables who passed through London visited her. She conducted a lively correspondence with such figures as John and Abigail Adams and Mercy Otis Warren. In 1775 Macaulay published *An Address to the People of England, Ireland, and Scotland, on the Present Important Crisis of Affairs,* a pamphlet that was likely widely read in the colonies, where it was republished. She condemned the closing of the port of Boston by the British government and also the Quebec and Stamp Acts; she warned that the erosion of liberties in the colonies was simply a precursor of the rising despotism at home.

Macaulay wrote *An Address to the People of England, Ireland, and Scotland* after moving from London to Bath with her daughter in 1774. In a decision she came to regret, she moved into Alfred House, the home of Thomas Wilson, nonresident rector of St. Stephen's, Walbrook, who was more than seventy. Wilson worshiped Macaulay and deeded over his home to her, provided her with servants, and eventually had a six-foot, white marble statue made of her as Clio and placed in St. Stephen's Church. This situation provided rich fodder for gossip by Macaulay's enemies, particularly after a celebrated birthday party Wilson gave for her in 1777, in which she was eulogized in six odes, enthroned, and presented a medal. Her reputation was further injured when eighteen months later she married William Graham, then aged twenty-one. She was forty-seven. Wilson was infuriated, and Macaulay and Graham retired to Leicestershire, where she continued to work on her history. Even her friends were scandalized by this union. Only Warren, in a letter to John Adams, pointed out the obvious—that Macaulay's "independency of spirit" led her to believe that she could live with this "inoffensive youth" with the same impunity as the many old men who marry young girls without comment (quoted by Donnelly in "The Celebrated Mrs. Macaulay").

Before the scandals in her personal life, Macaulay began *The History of England, from the Revolution to the Present Time in a Series of Letters to the Reverend Doctor Wilson* (1778). She had not yet finished her original *History,* and this first volume of the series did not reflect the rigorous methods of historical research and historiographic analysis that marked *The History of England from the Accession of James I.* It was not well received and was never completed.

Between 1778 and 1783, Macaulay finished her landmark *History of England from the Accession of James I to the Revolution* with the publication of volumes six, seven, and eight. Her high standard of scholarship, insight, and analysis were again evident in these volumes. Heeding earlier criticism that her long footnotes were tedious, she wove material into the thread of the narrative wherever possible. In her preface to the sixth volume (1781) she forcefully protests that her *History of England* had been criticized for speaking truth to power. She considers the most significant contribution of the history to be its account of those who rose up to curtail royal privilege. "This, without any unconstitutional design, or any wild enthusiastic hope of being able to influence the minds of a nation in favor of a democratic form of government . . . is the grand aim of my writing. . . ." In volume eight (1783) she argues that England under the Stuarts experienced more political liberty than did the England of the 1760s. She laments the tax burden on the English people as a result of its large standing armies in Europe and elsewhere, the significant subsidies paid to German princes, and the systemic corruption throughout the administration of the empire. She goes so far in this volume as to hint that revolution may be the only way to restore to the people their constitutional right of election and the wasted finances of the country.

Macaulay turned her attention to *A Treatise on the Immutability of Moral Truth* in 1783. As a devout Anglican, she attempted to reconcile Christian thought with Enlightenment ideals. She viewed religion as the foundation of morality and reason. Without resorting to a discussion of Christ, sin, or revelation, she describes Christianity as the driving force behind all morality and the drive to perfect human institutions as the duty of all human effort. The treatise was generally well received and excited no controversy.

After completing *The History of England* Macaulay traveled to the United States with her husband. She was already well known in America, not only as an historian but also as a forceful defender of the American cause. During her fifteen-month stay, from 1784 to 1785, the "celebrated Mrs. Macaulay" met many illustrious citizens with whom she had been corresponding. Her trip culminated in a ten-day visit with George and Martha Washington at Mount Vernon. Washington wrote to General Knox that he had been "flattered" by the visit of such a literary celebrity. They remained correspondents until the end of her life. Thomas Jefferson considered her *History of England* one of his preferred authorities on the seventeenth century. He personally purchased all eight volumes, recommended them to his friends, and made sure they were a part of the University of Virginia library.

Macaulay spent two years in France after leaving the United States. She returned to London in 1787 and moved to Binfield, Berkshire, the following year, where she lived for the rest of her life. One of Macaulay's great

THE

HISTORY

OF

ENGLAND

FROM THE

ACCESSION of JAMES I.

TO THAT OF THE

BRUNSWICK LINE.

VOL. I.

By CATHERINE MACAULAY.

LONDON:

Printed for J. NOURSE, Bookseller to his Majesty, in the Strand; R. and J. DODSLEY, in Pall-mall; and W. JOHNSTON, in Ludgate-street.

MDCCLXIII.

Title page for the first edition of the initial volume in Macaulay's eight-volume work completed in 1783 (from Eighteenth Century Collections Online, Gale Group).

frustrations was her belief that the people of England were ill prepared for the democracy she envisioned. In her view, the British electorate had twice refused to elect men who would work to secure the institutions of liberty. She believed that monarchical institutions had so affected the masses that a program of education was required to prepare them for rational political behavior. She therefore turned her attention to *Letters on Education, with Observations on Religious and Metaphysical Subjects* (1790). Part 3 of this work was a revision of her earlier *A Treatise on the Immutability of Moral Truth* with an attack on the contemporary theodicies of Henry St. John, Viscount Bolingbroke, and Archbishop William King, who accepted the inevitability of evil and argued that God may even sanction it.

Parts 1 and 2 of *Letters on Education* are an evaluation and critique of the educational system with suggestions of how to improve it. Included is an insightful survey of existing literature in the field. Central to her argument is her advocacy for the equal education of women. In arguing for coeducation, Macaulay presents a comprehensive indictment of the crushing legal, political, educational, and moral disabilities with which women live. *Letters on Education* substantially influenced Mary Wollstonecraft, who reviewed it in an essay in *The Analytical Review* (November 1790). *Letters on Education* was favorably reviewed in Whig and radical publications and garnered much attention in general.

Though Macaulay died 22 June 1791, three years into the French Revolution, she did live long enough to publish a last pamphlet, *Observations on the Reflections of the Right Hon. Edmund Burke on the Revolution in France, in a Letter to the Earl of Stanhope* (1790), which criticized Burke's *Reflections on the Revolution in France* (1790). When she wrote, the excesses of the revolution had not yet occurred, and she supported the constitutional reforms enacted by the National Assembly. Her argument, based on history, was that these reforms were as likely to succeed as to fail, and thus she criticized Burke's predictions of chaos and tyranny. The French, she continued, were at least working to improve their lot, and it should not be the business of the English to interfere. Macaulay's *Observations on the Reflections of the Right Hon. Edmund Burke on the Revolution in France* was little noticed in the many published responses to Burke's pamphlet.

Catherine Macaulay's role in the development of eighteenth-century republican thought was virtually ignored until the latter half of the twentieth century. Her *History of England* lost influence in centuries subsequent to the eighteenth for the same reason it gained such fame in her own time: it was perceived as an effort to use history to support a current political position. As history carried events toward Macaulay's vision, her writings seemed less relevant. Her contribution to the historiography of English history alone is enough to secure her name. Added to that, her reasoned and influential political pamphlets and her erudite analysis of society and learning make her worthy of study. Wollstonecraft in *A Vindication of the Rights of Woman* (1792) said that Macaulay was "the woman of the greatest abilities, undoubtedly, that this country has ever produced." Wollstonecraft went on to lament the lack of respect paid to Macaulay's contribution and to her memory. She believed posterity would, however, be more just to Macaulay, remembering her as the ultimate "example of the intellectual acquirements supposed to be incompatible with the weakness of her sex."

References:

Mildred Chaffee Beckwith, "Catherine Macaulay: Eighteenth-Century Rebel," dissertation, Ohio State University, 1953;

Florence S. Boos, "Catherine Macaulay's *Letters on Education* (1790): An Early Feminist Polemic," *University of Michigan Papers in Women's Studies*, 2, no. 2 (1976): 64–78;

Florence S. and William Boos, "Catherine Macaulay: Historian and Political Reformer," *International Journal of Women's Studies*, 3, no. 1 (1980): 49–65;

Natalie Zemon Davis, "Gender and Genre: Women as Historical Writers, 1400–1820," in *Beyond Their Sex: Learned Women of the European Past*, edited by Patricia Labalm (New York: New York University Press, 1980), pp. 167–172;

Davis, "History's Two Bodies," *American Historical Review*, 93 (February 1988): 1–30;

G. M. Ditchfield, "Some Literary and Political Views of Catherine Macaulay," *American Notes and Queries*, 12 (January 1974): 70–75;

Lucy Martin Donnelly, "The Celebrated Mrs. Macaulay," *William & Mary Quarterly*, third series, 6 (April 1949): 173–207;

Claire Gilbride Fox, "Catherine Macaulay, An Eighteenth Century Clio," in *Winterthur Portfolio*, volume 4 (Charlottesville: University of Virginia Press, 1968), pp. 129–142;

Christopher and Bridget Hill, "Catherine Macaulay and the Seventeenth Century," *Welsh History Review*, 3 (December 1967): 381–402;

Caroline Robbins, *The Eighteenth-Century Commonwealthman* (Cambridge, Mass.: Harvard University Press, 1959), pp. 356–377;

Barbara Brandon Schnorrenberg, "The Brood Hen of Faction: Mrs. Macaulay and Radical Politics, 1765–1775," *Albion*, 11 (Spring 1979): 32–45;

Schnorrenberg, "*Observations on the Reflections*: Macaulay vs Burke Round Three," in *The Consortium on Revolutionary Europe 1750–1850 Proceedings 1987* (Athens, Ga.: Consortium, 1987), pp. 215–225;

Lynne E. Withey, "Catherine Macaulay and the Uses of History: Ancient Rights, Perfectionism, and Propaganda," *Journal of British Studies*, 16 (Fall 1976): 59–83.

James Macpherson

(27 October 1736 – 17 February 1796)

John E. Luebering
University of Chicago

See also the Macpherson entry in *DLB 109: Eighteenth-Century British Poets, Second Series.*

BOOKS: *The Highlander: A Poem in Six Cantos* (Edinburgh: Printed by Walter Ruddiman Jun., 1758);

Fragments of Ancient Poetry, Collected in the Highlands of Scotland, and Translated from the Galic or Erse Language (Edinburgh: Printed for G. Hamilton and J. Balfour, 1760; enlarged second edition, 1760);

Fingal, an Ancient Epic Poem, in Six Books: Together with Several Other Poems, Composed by Ossian, the Son of Fingal. Translated from the Galic Language by James Macpherson (London: Printed for T. Becket and P. A. De Hondt, 1762 [1761]);

Temora, an Ancient Epic Poem, in Eight Books: Together with Several Other Poems, Composed by Ossian, the Son of Fingal. Translated from the Galic Language by James Macpherson (London: Printed for T. Becket and P. A. De Hondt, 1763);

The Works of Ossian, the Son of Fingal: In Two Volumes. Translated from the Galic Language by James Macpherson (London: Printed for T. Becket and P. A. De Hondt, 1765); revised as *The Poems of Ossian*, 2 volumes (London: Printed for W. Strahan and T. Becket, 1773); republished as *The Poems of Ossian, the Son of Fingal: Translated by James Macpherson, Esq.* (Philadelphia: Printed by Thomas Lang, 1790);

An Introduction to the History of Great Britain and Ireland (London: Printed for T. Becket and P. A. De Hondt, 1771); revised and enlarged as *An Introduction to the History of Great Britain and Ireland; or, An Inquiry into the Origin, Religion, Future State, Character, Manners, Morality, Amusements, Persons, Manner of Life, Houses, Navigation, Commerce, Language, Government, Kings, General Assemblies, Courts of Justice, and Juries, of the Britons, Scots, Irish, and Anglo-Saxons* (London: Printed for T. Becket and P. A. De Hondt, 1772; revised and enlarged, 1773);

The History of Great Britain from the Restoration to the Accession of the House of Hannover, 2 volumes (London: Printed for W. Strahan and T. Cadell, 1775);

James Macpherson (portrait by Romney, Dawsons, Ph. Sc.; frontispiece for Thomas Bailey Saunders, The Life and Letters of James Macpherson, *1894; Thomas Cooper Library, University of South Carolina)*

Original Papers, Containing the Secret History of Great Britain from the Restoration, to the Accession of the House of Hannover: To Which Are Prefixed Extracts from the Life of James II as Written by Himself, 2 volumes (London:

Printed for W. Strahan and T. Cadell, 1775; Philadelphia: Reprinted and sold by R. Bell, 1776; enlarged edition, London: Printed for T. Cadell, 1776);

The Rights of Great Britain Asserted against the Claims of America: Being an Answer to the Declaration of the General Congress. The Sixth Edition. To Which Is Now Added, a Refutation of Dr. Price's State of the National Debt (London: Printed for T. Cadell, 1776); revised as *The Rights of Great Britain Asserted against the Claims of America: Being an Answer to the Declaration of the General Congress. The Ninth Edition. To Which Is Now Added, a Further Refutation of Dr. Price's State of the National Debt* (London: Printed for T. Cadell, 1776);

Original Papers Relative to Tanjore: Containing All the Letters which Passed, and the Conferences which Were Held, between . . . the Nabob of Arcot and Lord Pigot, on the Subject of the Restoration of Tanjore together with the Material Part of Lord Pigot's Last Dispatch to the East India Company. The Whole Connected by a Narrative and Illustrated with Notes and Observations, anonymous, likely with John Macpherson (London: Printed for T. Cadell, 1777);

A Short History of the Opposition during the Last Session of Parliament, anonymous (London: Printed for T. Cadell, 1779);

The History and Management of the East-India Company, from Its Origin in 1600 to the Present Times, anonymous, with Macpherson (London: Printed for T. Cadell, 1779).

Collections and Editions: *The Poems of Ossian, &c. Containing the Poetical Works of James Macpherson, Esq., in Prose and Rhyme: With Notes and Illustrations,* edited by Malcolm Laing, 2 volumes (Edinburgh: Printed by J. Ballantyne for A. Constable, 1805);

The Poems of Ossian and Related Works, edited by Howard Gaskill (Edinburgh: Edinburgh University Press, 1996).

OTHER: *The Iliad of Homer,* 2 volumes, translated by Macpherson (London: Printed for T. Becket and P. A. De Hondt, 1773).

SELECTED PERIODICAL PUBLICATIONS–
UNCOLLECTED: "To a Friend, Mourning the Death of Miss . . . ," *Scots Magazine* (May 1755): 246;
"On the Death of Marshall Keith," *Scots Magazine* (October 1758): 550–551;
"On the Death of a Young Lady," *Scots Magazine* (May 1759): 255;
"To the Memory of an Officer Killed before Quebec," *Scots Magazine* (October 1759): 527;

"An Ode, Attempted in the Manner of Pindar" (also called "The Earl of Marischal's Welcome to His Country," *Scots Magazine* (September 1760): 459–460.

James Macpherson remains best known for the poems in *Fragments of Ancient Poetry* (1760), *Fingal* (1761), and *Temora* (1763) and the subsequent controversy over their authenticity. Macpherson claimed he had translated these poems from ancient Gaelic sources, but his opponents argued, as Samuel Johnson did in a 20 January 1775 letter to Macpherson, that these poems were "an imposture from the beginning." Macpherson's death in 1796 sparked hope that this three-decade-long controversy could be resolved, but the Highland Society of Scotland commissioned to investigate Macpherson's methods concluded that neither Macpherson nor Johnson was correct. After seven years of research, the society found that no single existing text in Gaelic matched any of Macpherson's published poems. Likewise, the society discovered that he altered and embellished what ancient Gaelic manuscripts he did publish. Yet, those manuscripts were authentic, the society determined, and the legends of Fingal and Ossian were–in 1805, when the society's report was published–still widely told in a style resembling that of *Fingal* and *Temora*. The society's final report thus concluded that Macpherson used genuine historical documents to create semioriginal poetry in an ancient Highland style. He was, therefore, neither historian nor poet but a combination of the two. His experience with these poems deeply influenced his later work as a government polemicist and author of prose histories.

Macpherson was born 27 October 1736 at Ruthven in Inverness-shire, Scotland, to a poor farming family. His early poetry as well as the later Ossian poems show a preoccupation with Scottish history that is typically attributed, in part, to his experience of the aftermath of "The Forty-Five," the military campaigns in 1745 during which Charles Edward Stuart, a rival claimant to the British throne, and his faction, composed largely of Scottish Highlanders, were defeated during their invasion of England. Macpherson likely saw the Highlanders' destruction of the British army's barracks in Ruthven, first occupied after the Highland rising of 1715, and the return of Charles's defeated troops through the village. He also experienced the subsequent British suppression of Highland culture.

Macpherson received his first formal education at a local school in Badenoch. His father, impressed by his son's abilities, sent him to King's College in Aberdeen in the autumn of 1752 to become a minister. Macpherson matriculated in February 1753, although in 1754 (according to Fiona Stafford) or 1755 (according to Paul

J. deGategno and Thomas Bailey Saunders) he left because he could not afford a tuition increase. He then attended Marischal College, also in Aberdeen, and, briefly, the University of Edinburgh. He received no degree from any of these institutions and in 1756 returned to Ruthven. As a native Gaelic speaker, Macpherson had access to Highland literary culture and began around this time to collect Gaelic ballads in and around Ruthven. He also taught in the village charity school. He held that position until 1758, when he moved to Edinburgh, resolved to become a writer.

Of the four thousand lines of poetry Macpherson is credited with writing before 1760, his most notable poem is *The Highlander,* published in Edinburgh in April 1758. This six-canto poem is his first significant work to take ancient Scottish history as its subject: it describes an invasion by the Danes that is repelled when a fictional warrior, Alpin, rallies the Scottish army to a fierce defense of the country. In this poem Macpherson also identifies the ancient bards of Scotland as historians, an idea that became central to the Ossian project: the bards' purpose is "To keep in song the memory of the dead! / They handed down the ancient rounds of time, / In oral story and recorded rhyme." The poem sold poorly, and Macpherson wanted the print run destroyed soon after publication.

Macpherson supported his flagging literary career with copyediting and other work for publishers. Later in 1758 he turned to private tutoring. His instruction of Thomas Graham, son of the laird of Balgowan, proved to be the turning point in his career: during travels with Graham's family, Macpherson met Adam Ferguson, who, after discussing their mutual interest in Gaelic poetry, offered to introduce Macpherson to John Home, known in both Edinburgh and London by his 1756 play *Douglas.* That meeting occurred in the autumn of 1759 at Moffat, a popular resort, where Home expressed his enthusiasm for Gaelic poetry but admitted he was unable to read the language. He thus encouraged Macpherson to translate for him one of the poems the younger man had collected.

A few days later, Macpherson showed Home "The Death of Oscur," later published as Fragment VII in *Fragments of Ancient Poetry.* Home was delighted by the poem and circulated it among the literati of Scotland, including Adam Smith and David Hume. They embraced it with nationalistic fervor. Hugh Blair—who soon became Macpherson's fiercest defender—pushed Macpherson to translate and publish more fragments. Accordingly, on 14 June 1760, *Fragments of Ancient Poetry, Collected in the Highlands of Scotland, and Translated from the Galic or Erse Language* went on sale in Edinburgh. It was a slight book, with fifteen fragmentary prose poems and a brief preface by Blair, but it was an immediate success.

The opening lines of the first fragment, "Shilric, Vinvela," represent the rugged style of the collection: "My love is a son of the hill. He pursues the flying deer. His gray dogs are panting around him; his bow-string sounds in the wind." However, Blair hinted in his preface that much ancient Gaelic poetry had yet to be recovered, including a "work of considerable length, and which deserves to be styled an heroic poem." During the summer of 1760, he raised up to £200 in Edinburgh and London to allow Macpherson to collect more poetry in the Highlands. Macpherson thus left Edinburgh in August 1760 in search of an ancient Scottish epic.

Between August and October he moved through Inverness-shire, the Isle of Skye, and the Outer Hebrides. He also traveled to Argyllshire and the Isle of Mull for additional material, perhaps as late as June 1761, according to Stafford. With the help of Gaelic scholars, Macpherson acquired a substantial amount of ancient poetry, some transcribed from oral recitation and some collected in the form of manuscripts. From January 1761, in an apartment beneath Blair's in Edinburgh, Macpherson prepared what became *Fingal, An Ancient Epic Poem, in Six Books: Together with Several Other Poems, Composed by Ossian, the Son of Fingal,* published in London in December. The book built on the success of the *Fragments of Ancient Poetry,* which it closely resembled in style and content, and was praised throughout Scotland, where many welcomed the discovery of an ancient national epic.

Although Macpherson exhibited what he called the original sources of *Fingal* at his London publisher in 1762, skepticism about the authenticity of the poems began to build. In early 1763 Blair finished the first edition of his lengthy *A Critical Dissertation on the Poems of Ossian,* which defended the authenticity of the poems and which he immediately began to revise when in March Macpherson published a second Ossianic epic, *Temora.* The eight-book epic was greeted with intense criticism in England, in part because of the aggressive tone Macpherson took toward his critics in the prefatory matter of the book. The poor relations between Scotland and England during this time are also often blamed for the poor reception of *Temora,* as is the fact that the unpopular Scotsman John Stuart, third Earl of Bute, who became prime minister in 1761, funded the publication of *Temora.*

In late 1763 or early 1764, Macpherson left Great Britain for Florida. Under an appointment from Bute, Macpherson served in Pensacola as surveyor-general and secretary to George Johnstone, governor of the Western Provinces; for his service Macpherson received £200 a year. Soon bored by the work, he toured the West Indies, and in 1765 he returned to London. There

Macpherson oversaw the publication of his two-volume *The Works of Ossian* (1765), composed of slightly revised versions of *Fingal* and *Temora*. It also included revisions of the two essays Macpherson had written for earlier editions of the epics—"A Dissertation concerning the Antiquity, &c. of the Poems of Ossian," which preceded *Fingal*, and the lengthier "A Dissertation," which preceded *Temora*.

Intended to provide the historical context of the Ossian poems, these "dissertations" represent Macpherson's earliest efforts at writing historical essays. In the first he offers a brief history of what he calls "the Celtic nations," whose ancient culture, he argues, rivals those of Greece and Rome. But because Scotland lacked historians similar to Herodotus or Tacitus, the Celts "trusted their fame to tradition and the songs of the bards," which were soon lost. For Macpherson, therefore, publishing *Fingal* was an important act of both historical scholarship and bardic recitation in the new medium of print.

Macpherson's second dissertation covers much the same ground at greater length. It also relies heavily on the texts of *Fingal* and *Temora* as evidence of Scottish cultural history: "what renders Temora infinitely more valuable than Fingal," he claims, "is the light it throws on the history of the times." This light, in turn, reveals that "no kingdom now established in Europe, can pretend to equal antiquity with that of the Scots," a claim that infuriated Macpherson's English critics.

After 1765 Macpherson was employed as a writer and overseer of the government's newspapers by the Tory administrations of William Pitt the Elder, Earl of Chatham; Augustus Fitzroy, Duke of Grafton; and Frederick North, Lord North. Macpherson's most important works for the government were his *The Rights of Great Britain Asserted against the Claims of America* (1776), which went through at least ten editions in one year, and *A Short History of the Opposition during the Last Session of Parliament* (1779), which savaged the Whigs for their behavior during the American Revolutionary War.

Other writings occupied a place closer to historical scholarship than to government propaganda. Macpherson's *An Introduction to the History of Great Britain and Ireland* (1772) echoes his dissertations on Ossian in its—according to some critics—excessive focus on the Celtic nations. It received mixed reviews, but Edward Gibbon cited it as one of two sources on ancient Scotland in his *History of the Decline and Fall of the Roman Empire* (1776–1788). *The History of Great Britain from the Restoration to the Accession of the House of Hannover* (1775) and its companion volume, *Original Papers, Containing the Secret History of Great Britain from the Restoration, to the Accession of the House of Hannover* (1775), combined extensive archival work with a provocative attack on the Whigs'

"secret" role in the ousting of James II in 1688. After consulting and acquiring a broad range of historical government documents in France and Britain, Macpherson published them in *Original Papers* and made these records available for public examination. His controversial *The History of Great Britain from the Restoration to the Accession of the House of Hannover* then followed, intended to be a continuation of Hume's *The History of England, from the Invasion of Julius Caesar to the Revolution in 1688* (1754–1762). Hume was somewhat disturbed by Macpherson's work—in a 30 January 1773 letter to Adam Smith he complained that Macpherson had "the most anti-historical head in the universe"—but it sold well, and Macpherson earned £3,000 for its copyright.

Macpherson also likely collaborated on two texts with his distant relation John Macpherson, who was an agent for Muhammed Ali, Nawab of Arcot, in London—*Original Papers Relative to Tanjore* (1777) and *The History and Management of the East-India Company* (1779). Both attacked the East India Company on the nawab's behalf.

By 1780 Macpherson had replaced John Macpherson as the nawab's agent. He soon after also became a member of Parliament for Camelford, Cornwall, and was reelected in 1784 and 1790. His name appeared on a long list of poet laureate candidates in 1785. He died 17 February 1796 at his newly built villa on an estate in Badenoch and was buried at his own expense in Westminster Abbey near Poet's Corner.

James Macpherson continues to provoke controversy today. While his far-reaching influence on Romantic literature is irrefutable, analyses of his work are still marked by excessive partisanship, often tinged with moral judgments—in an echo of Johnson's well-known 1775 letter to Macpherson, scholars still find mentioning the number of Macpherson's illegitimate children hard to resist—and shot through with Scottish nationalism. Had he written only his historical texts of the 1770s, Macpherson would today be considered a minor writer. But the Ossian poems and their ambiguous straddling of the line between history and literature have made him a contested but highly important figure.

Bibliographies:

George F. Black, "Macpherson's Ossian and the Ossianic Controversy," *Bulletin of the New York Public Library*, 30 (1926): 424–439, 508–524;

John J. Dunn, "Macpherson's Ossian and the Ossianic Controversy: A Supplementary Bibliography," *Bulletin of the New York Public Library*, 75 (1971): 465–473;

Margaret M. Smith, "James Macpherson 1736–1796," *Index of English Literary Manuscripts*, volume 3:

1700–1800, part 2 (London: Mansell, 1989), pp. 179–183.

Biography:

Thomas Bailey Saunders, *The Life and Letters of James Macpherson* (London: Swann Sonnenschein, 1894).

References:

Hugh Blair, *A Critical Dissertation on the Poems of Ossian, the Son of Fingal,* second edition (London: Printed for T. Becket and P. A. De Hondt, 1765);

Paul J. deGategno, *James Macpherson* (Boston: Twayne, 1989);

Howard Gaskill, ed., *Ossian Revisited* (Edinburgh: Edinburgh University Press, 1991);

Nick Groom, "Celts, Goths, and the Nature of the Literary Source," in *Tradition in Transition: Women Writers, Marginal Texts, and the Eighteenth-Century Canon,* edited by Alvaro Ribeiro and James G. Basker (Oxford: Clarendon Press, 1996), pp. 274–296;

Groom, *The Making of Percy's* Reliques (Oxford: Clarendon Press, 1999);

Kristine Louise Haugen, "Ossian and the Invention of Textual History," *Journal of the History of Ideas,* 59, no. 2 (1998): 309–327;

Ian Haywood, *The Making of History: A Study of the Literary Forgeries of James Macpherson and Thomas Chatterton in Relation to Eighteenth-Century Ideas of History and Fiction* (Rutherford, N.J.: Fairleigh Dickinson University Press / London: Associated University Presses, 1986);

Highland Society of Scotland, *Report of the Committee of the Highland Society of Scotland, Appointed to Inquire into the Nature and Authenticity of the Poems of Ossian* (Edinburgh: University Press, 1805);

Colin Kidd, *Subverting Scotland's Past: Scottish Whig Historians and the Creation of an Anglo-British Identity 1689–1830* (Cambridge: Cambridge University Press, 1993);

Richard B. Sher, *Church and University in the Scottish Enlightenment: The Moderate Literati of Edinburgh* (Princeton, N.J.: Princeton University Press, 1985);

J. S. Smart, *James Macpherson: An Episode in Literature* (London: Nutt, 1905);

Fiona Stafford, *The Sublime Savage: James Macpherson and the Poems of Ossian* (Edinburgh: Edinburgh University Press, 1988).

Stafford and Gaskill, eds., *From Gaelic to Romantic: Ossianic Translations* (Amsterdam: Rodopi, 1998);

Derick S. Thomson, *The Gaelic Sources of Macpherson's Ossian* (Edinburgh: Oliver & Boyd, 1952);

Howard D. Weinbrot, *Britannia's Issue: The Rise of British Literature from Dryden to Ossian* (Cambridge: Cambridge University Press, 1993).

Papers:

James Macpherson's letters and personal papers are scattered across Great Britain, Ireland, and the United States. Larger concentrations are held by the National Archives of Scotland, the British Library, and several private collections in Scotland. Margaret M. Smith has compiled the most extensive list of Macpherson's papers.

Conyers Middleton

(27 December 1683 – 28 July 1750)

Philip Connell
University of Cambridge

BOOKS: *A Full and Impartial Account of All the Late Proceedings in the University of Cambridge against Dr. Bentley* (London: Printed for James Bettenham, 1719);

A Second Part of the Full and Impartial Account of All the Late Proceedings in the University of Cambridge against Dr. Bentley, anonymous (London: Printed for James Bettenham, 1719);

Some Remarks upon a Pamphlet, Entitled, The Case of Dr. Bentley Farther Stated and Vindicated, &C.: Wherein the Merit of the Author and His Performance, and the Complaint of Proctor Laughton Are Briefly Considered (London: Printed for James Bettenham, 1719);

A True Account of the Present State of Trinity College in Cambridge, anonymous (London: Printed for T. Bickerton, 1719);

Remarks, Paragraph by Paragraph, upon the Proposals Lately Publish'd by Richard Bentley, for a New Edition of the Greek Testament and Latin Version, anonymous (London: Printed by J. Roberts, 1721);

Some Farther Remarks, Paragraph by Paragraph, upon Proposals Lately Publish'd for a New Edition of a Greek and Latin Testament, by Richard Bentley (London: Printed for T. Bickerton, 1721);

Bibliothecæ Cantabrigiensis ordinandæ methodus quædam; quam domino procancellario senatuique academico considerandam & perficiendam officii et pietatis ergô proponit (Cambridge: Typis Academicis, 1723);

De medicorum apud veteres Romanos degentium conditione dissertatio; qua contra viros celeberrimos Jac. Sponium & Rich. Meadium, M.D.D. servilem atque ignobilem eam fuisse ostenditur (Cambridge: Prostant venales Cantabrigiæ apud Edmundum Jeffery Bibliopolam, 1726);

Dissertationis de medicorum Romæ degentium conditione ignobili & servili, contra anonymos quosdam notarum brevium, responsionis, atq; animadversionis auctores, defensio. Pars prima (N.p. [Cambridge]: Prostant venales Cantabrigiæ apud Edmundum Jeffery Bibliopolam, 1727); translated as *A Dissertation on the State of Physicians among the Old Romans, in Which it Is Proved to Have Been Servile and Ignoble* (London: Printed for T. Cooper, 1734);

Conyers Middleton (portrait by John Faber Jr. after John Giles Eccardt, 1751; National Portrait Gallery, London)

A Letter from Rome, Shewing an Exact Conformity between Popery and Paganism; or, The Religion of the Present Romans to Be Derived Entirely from That of Their Heathen Ancestors (London: Printed for W. Innys, 1729; enlarged edition, London: Printed for Richard Manby, 1741; Baltimore, 1835?);

A Letter to Dr. Waterland; Containing Some Remarks on His Vindication of Scripture: in Answer to a Book, Intituled, Christianity as Old as the Creation, anonymous (London: Printed for J. Peele, 1731);

A Defence of the Letter to Dr. Waterland; Against the False and Frivolous Cavils of the Author of the Reply, anonymous (London: Printed for J. Peele, 1732);

Oratio de novo physiologiæ explicandæ munere, ex celeberrimi Woodwardi testamento instituto (London: Impensis Gul. Thurlbourn Bibliopol. Canatbrigiensem. Prostant apud J. & J. Knapton, R. Knaplock & Gul. Innys, Bibliopolas Londinenses, 1732);

Remarks on Some Observations, Addressed to the Author of the Letter to Dr. Waterland, anonymous (London: Printed for J. Peele, 1732);

Some Remarks on a Reply to the Defence of the Letter to Dr. Waterland, anonymous (London: Printed for J. Peele, 1732);

A Dissertation Concerning the Origin of Printing in England. Shewing, That It Was First Introduced and Practised by Our Countryman William Caxton (Cambridge: Printed for W. Thurlbourn: and sold by Messrs. Knapton, Innys and Manby, C. Rivington, J. Clark in London; and S. Harding, Westminster, 1735);

The History of the Life of Marcus Tullius Cicero, 2 volumes (London: Printed for James Bettenham, 1741; Boston: Wells & Lilly, 1818);

Germana quædam antiquitatis eruditæ monumenta quibus Romanorum veterum ritus varii tam sacri quam profani, tum Græcorum atque Ægyptiorum nonnulli illustrantur (London: Apud Richard Manby and H. S. Cox, 1745);

An Introductory Discourse to a Larger Work, Designed Hereafter to Be Published, Concerning the Miraculous Powers Which Are Supposed to Have Subsisted in the Christian Church, from the Earliest Ages, anonymous (London: Printed for Richard Manby and H. S. Cox, 1747);

A Treatise on the Roman Senate. In Two Parts. (London: Printed for Richard Manby and H. S. Cox, 1747);

Remarks on Two Pamphlets Lately Published against Dr. Middleton's Introductory Discourse, anonymous (London: Printed for Richard Manby and H. S. Cox, 1748);

A Free Inquiry into the Miraculous Powers, Which Are Supposed to Have Subsisted in the Christian Church, from the Earliest Ages Through Several Successive Centuries (London: Printed for Richard Manby and H. S. Cox, 1749);

An Examination of the Lord Bishop of London's Discourses concerning the Use and Intent of Prophecy (London: Printed for Richard Manby and H. S. Cox, 1750; New York: Garland, 1976);

A Vindication of the Free Inquiry into the Miraculous Powers Which Are Supposed to Have Subsisted in the Christian Church, &C. From the Objections of Dr. Dodwell and Dr. Church (London: Printed for Richard Manby and H. S. Cox, 1751);

Miscellaneous Tracts (London: Printed for Richard Manby and H. S. Cox, 1752);

Letters between Lord Hervey and Dr. Middleton concerning the Roman Senate (London: Printed for W. Strahan and T. Cadell, 1778).

Editions: *Miscellaneous Works,* 4 volumes (London: Printed for Richard Manby and H. S. Cox, 1752);

The Posthumous Works (London: Printed for Richard Manby and H. S. Cox, 1753).

OTHER: *The Epistles of M. T. Cicero to M. Brutus, and of Brutus to Cicero,* edited by Middleton (London: Printed for Richard Manby, 1743).

Conyers Middleton's reputation as an historian rests most obviously upon his *History of the Life of Marcus Tullius Cicero* (1741). Yet, his notoriety, for eighteenth- and nineteenth-century readers, derived largely from his polemical theological writings. Leslie Stephen, in his *History of English Thought in the Eighteenth Century* (1876), gave succinct expression to an influential view of Middleton's intellectual character when Stephen identified Middleton with a "group of distinguished Cambridge men who, unfortunately, illustrated the truth that wide learning and elegant scholarship may be combined with controversial brutality." But Stephen's remark also suggests the degree to which, in Middleton's case, the learned classical historian and the combative religious critic need not be regarded as entirely distinct intellectual identities. Middleton's career demonstrates the degree to which the issue of religious skepticism, which had been forced into the open by the deist controversies of the late seventeenth and early eighteenth centuries, remained closely bound up with methodological questions relating to the veracity of historical testimony and the figurative interpretation of biblical narrative.

Middleton was born on 27 December 1683, the son of William Middleton, the rector of Hinderwell, near Whitby, in Yorkshire, and his second wife, Barbara Place. He entered Trinity College, Cambridge, in 1699, graduated with a bachelor of arts degree in 1703, and after being elected a fellow of Trinity in 1705, received his master of arts degree the following year. He resigned his fellowship a few years later upon his marriage to a widow, Sarah Drake, who brought with her a considerable fortune. By this time, he had embarked on a long-running dispute with the Master of Trinity College, Richard Bentley, a well-known classical scholar. On a visit to Cambridge in 1717 King George I conferred the degree of doctor of divinity on several scholars, including Middleton. Bentley, in his capacity as Regius Professor of Divinity, demanded additional fees of four guineas from each of the recipients. Middleton complained, and the affair quickly spiraled into an acrimonious legal dispute that resulted in Bentley's being temporarily deprived of all his degrees by the university and in Middleton's being found guilty of libel. Middleton's *A Full and Impartial Account of All the Late Proceedings in the University of Cambridge against Dr. Bentley* (1719) and his *A True Account of the Present State of Trinity College in Cambridge* (1719) provide striking evidence of the often rancorous nature of university politics in this period, and their polemical spirit may have vitiated some of Middleton's subsequent works. If such charges have been overstated in the past, nevertheless, the dispute with Bentley did much to refine Middleton's prose into an instrument of considerable argumentative intelligence and acute rhetorical power. His libel conviction also resulted in Middleton's compensatory appointment to the new office of "Protobibliothecarius," or Principal Library Keeper of the University, on a salary of £50 a year, a position that provided him with access to many of the bibliographical resources necessary for the pursuit of his later theological and historical researches.

Middleton set out for Italy in the early 1720s in the company of Henry Hare, third Baron Coleraine. This expedition inspired one of Middleton's most important works, *A Letter from Rome, Shewing an Exact Conformity between Popery and Paganism* (1729). *A Letter from Rome* is a sophisticated and influential example of a well-established genre of anti-Catholic argument and proceeds from the observation of similarities in the religious practices of contemporary Catholics and the ancient Romans, to the conclusion that the former is "a *Worship* formed upon the Plan, and after the very Pattern of pure *Heathenism.*" But *A Letter from Rome* also raises important methodological questions about the respective importance of human nature and cultural influence in historical explanation. The future bishop of Gloucester, William Warburton, attacked Middleton on just this point in his *Divine Legation of Moses* (1738, 1741). Warburton argues in volume two of this work that it is a mistake to assume, on the basis of superficial similarities between peoples, that "the general Customs of Men . . . are all, whether civil or religious, traductive from one another." On the contrary, it is much more likely that "the Original of this Similitude, is the Voice of one common Nature, improved by Reason, or debased by Superstition, speaking to all its Tribes of Individuals." At issue, for both Middleton and Warburton, was the place of Christianity within an historical worldview in which religious tradition was increasingly amenable to naturalistic, comparative explanation. Middleton himself suggested in a subsequent edition that traces of "pagano-papist" practice might continue to inform the English Protestant establishment, though he rather unconvincingly claimed that the truth of such an allegation "is not the part of a private man to determine, so I shall refer it, as I ought, to the Judgement of my Superiors."

After the death of his wife, Middleton was appointed Woodwardian professor in 1731 and delivered an inaugural lecture on the theological significance of the study of fossils. He resigned three years later upon his second marriage, to his cousin Mary Place. His professorial appointment coincided with the publication of *A Letter to Dr. Waterland; Containing Some Remarks on His Vindication of Scripture* (1731). The addressee of this work, Daniel Waterland, was one of the most able and influential defenders of Anglican orthodoxy at that time. Nevertheless, Middleton was unreserved in his criticisms of Waterland's *Scripture Vindicated* (1730–1732), which was itself a reply to Matthew Tindal's deistical tract *Christianity as Old as the Creation* (1730). Attacking Waterland's assertion that natural and revealed religion could not subsist separately, *A Letter to Dr. Waterland* points out that natural religion must have predated revelation. Moreover, in response to what he views as Waterland's uncompromising attachment to the literal, historical truth of biblical narrative, Middleton argues, in a discussion of the Fall, the necessity in certain cases to "desert the *outward letter,* and search for the *hidden, allegorical* sense of the story." The fabular element of biblical narrative could thus be compared, in respect to its literary form, by other ancient religions, such as the Egyptians', which similarly had recourse to *"mystical and symbolical"* signification. Middleton may not have sought thereby to impugn the peculiar status of revelation, but the conclusion to *A Letter to Dr. Waterland* carries the strong implication that deists such as Tindal should most effectively be answered by reference to the utility and antiquity of the public religion, rather than to its truth, with implications that were not lost on the more orthodox contributors to the controversy sparked by the work.

In 1741 Middleton published his *History of the Life of Marcus Tullius Cicero,* a popular and influential biography that reached eight editions by 1767. Some later readers came to regard *The Life of Cicero* as devalued by an excessively hagiographic attitude toward its subject; but Middleton's determination to represent Cicero as a moral exemplar was precisely what made the book such a success. Middleton set out to redress what he regarded as a prejudice in contemporary historiography and biography in favor of the martial heroes of classical antiquity. His Cicero, by contrast, is representative of "the pacific and civil character . . . of all others the most beneficial to mankind, whose sole ambition is, to support the laws, the rights and liberty of his citizens." Middleton also sought to excerpt and contextualize Ciceronian texts, "imagining, that it would give both a luster [*sic*] and authority to a sentiment, to deliver it in the person and the very words of *CICERO* . . . woven originally into the text, as the genuine parts of it."

Two important contexts are required for understanding Middleton's choice of subject and approach in

The Life of Cicero: one religious, the other political. Cicero was something of a hero for English deists, and his appropriation by freethinkers such as Anthony Collins had provoked the aspersions of Middleton's old antagonist, Bentley. In *The Life of Cicero,* Middleton demonstrates, once again, his predisposition to pursue a nice line between orthodoxy and free thought by seeking to rehabilitate Cicero, who, he claims, was persuaded of the immortality of the soul and a future state of reward and punishment. Middleton is careful, however, to reserve a place for revelation, and Cicero's religious beliefs are shown to vindicate the conclusion that "the most exalted state of human reason is so far from superseding the use, that it demonstrates the benefit of a *more explicit revelation.*"

Middleton's tendency to religious heterodoxy has in the past been used to identify him with a "commonwealthman" tradition of radical Whiggism. But *The Life of Cicero* has more recently been cited in opposition to this view, on the grounds that the Ciceronian inheritance was one to which Court Whigs, as well as their political opponents, could increasingly lay claim; and, more tellingly, that *The Life of Cicero* is dedicated to the vice chamberlain, Lord Hervey, one of the most important political allies of the prime minister, Robert Walpole. The significance of this dedication was not lost on novelist and playwright Henry Fielding, who parodied it at the start of his *Apology for the Life of Mrs. Shamela Andrews* (1741). Fielding ridiculed both Middleton's sycophancy and Hervey's political opportunism; but the dedication to *The Life of Cicero* also reveals something of the broader ideological framework informing Middleton's work. Middleton praises Hervey for emulating the meritocratic spirit of "old Rome" and establishes a parallel between the political virtue manifested in the age of Cicero and the similarly estimable qualities encouraged by the Whig constitution, "preserved by the provident care of our Ancestors, and the happy settlement at the Revolution." The Whiggish balance of Crown prerogative and popular rights, which had reached its perfection in the wake of the Glorious Revolution, can thus be seen to reproduce "the true balance and temperament of power between Senate and People" in republican Rome.

The Life of Cicero maintained Middleton's reputation for provoking controversy. He was not only accused (unjustly) of plagiarism but also attacked for his use of the letters of Cicero and Marcus Brutus. First, James Tunstall, then Jeremiah Markland, produced lengthy arguments for regarding these letters as ancient forgeries, and Middleton was obliged to respond in the "prefatory dissertation" to his 1743 edition of letters. Moreover, Middleton soon found himself in a friendly dispute with Hervey over the nature of the Roman Senate, in a correspondence that was later published as *A Treatise on the Roman Senate. In Two Parts* (1747) and *Letters between Lord Hervey and Dr. Middleton concerning the Roman Senate* (1778). These publications clearly

THE

HISTORY

OF

THE LIFE

OF

MARCUS TULLIUS CICERO.

In Two Volumes.

Hunc igitur spectemus. Hoc propositum sit nobis exemplum. Ille se profecisse sciat, cui CICERO valde placebit.
QUINTIL. Instit. l. x. 1.

By CONYERS MIDDLETON, D. D.
Principal Library-keeper of the University of *Cambridge.*

LONDON:
Printed for the AUTHOR.
MDCCXLI.

Title page for volume one of Middleton's 1741 biography (Eighteenth-Century Collections Online, Gale Group)

indicate that, although Middleton diverged in certain respects from traditional "country party" accounts of the Roman republic (which located its downfall in luxury, selfishness, and military corruption), his understanding of the Senate was considerably more libertarian and populist than Hervey was prepared to allow. According to Middleton in *A Treatise on the Roman Senate. In Two Parts,* "by the original constitution of the government, even under the Kings, the collective body of the people was the real soverein of *Rome,* and the dernier resort in all cases." The historical parallelism implicit in this statement offered a tacit rebuff to Hervey's belief, expressed in his *Ancient and Modern Liberty Stated and Compared* (1734), that the emergence of English constitutional liberty was of a comparatively recent historical vintage, postdating the end of Stuart despotism.

Despite his best efforts, Middleton was disappointed in his search for preferment within the church. The moderate wealth brought by his first marriage was supplemented, latterly, by private tuition (which seems to have antagonized those who felt the University should enjoy an educational monopoly in Cambridge). But although Middleton never really managed to master the patronage networks of Hanoverian England, he was certainly capable of inspiring friendship and loyalty. One of his admirers, poet Thomas Gray, claimed in 1750 that Middleton's home "was the only easy Place one could find to converse in Cambridge." According to antiquary William Cole (in a manuscript account of his life and character), Middleton was "a most regular and temperate man; never spent an evening from home, never touched a drop of wine, . . . but was one of the most sober, well-bred, easy and companionable men I ever conversed with." Middleton was also fond of music and in later life hosted regular concerts at his home.

Such personal affability was sustained in counterpoint to Middleton's continued disposition to authorial truculence. His next major work marked a return to the history of the early church and to the theological controversy that had followed *A Letter from Rome* and the attack on Waterland. *A Free Inquiry into the Miraculous Powers, Which Are Supposed to Have Subsisted in the Christian Church* was published in 1749 and immediately provoked hostile responses from Anglican critics. *A Free Inquiry* accepts the reality of scripturally attested miracles but denies those dating from the mid second century or later. The argument is couched in the anti-Catholic rhetoric that Middleton had honed in *A Letter from Rome*. The "divine and extraordinary power of working miracles" supposed to have been operative in the primitive church is thus exposed in *A Free Inquiry* as a means by which the Roman church's doctrinal and institutional authority "is rendered more persuasive and affecting to the multitude, than what the Gospel itself affords." But Middleton's argument was also clearly intended to divest Protestantism of its unhealthy attachment to a specious and corrupt historical tradition originating in the Church Fathers. Middleton's *A Free Inquiry* raises many of the same questions of testimony and proof that have made David Hume's writings on miracles so relevant to the understanding of eighteenth-century historiographical methodology. Middleton was clear, for example, in *A Free Inquiry* that historical accuracy must take priority over religious prejudice, for to "submit our belief implicitly *[sic]* and indifferently, to the mere force of authority, in all cases, whether miraculous or natural, without any rule of discerning the credible from the incredible, might support indeed the faith, as it is called, but would certainly destroy the use of all history."

The following year, 1750, Middleton published *An Examination of the Lord Bishop of London's Discourses concerning the Use and Intent of Prophecy,* a response to Thomas Sherlock's *The Use and Intent of Prophecy* (1725). The motivation for this work, Middleton's last major publication, is in some respects comparable to the earlier *Letter to Dr. Waterland,* insofar as Middleton claims once again to have been provoked by the deficiencies of Anglican apologetic and, in this case, the insufficiently subtle manner in which Sherlock's work seeks to defend biblical prophecy from the attacks of skeptical deists. Middleton argues in *An Examination of the Lord Bishop of London's Discourses concerning the Use and Intent of Prophecy* that a careful case-by-case consideration of purported prophecies is not only likely to avoid damagingly unfounded conclusions but is also sanctioned by the practice of the Evangelists themselves. Middleton moves on, however, to deny the reality of antediluvian prophecies and to argue, as in *A Letter to Dr. Waterland,* that the story of the Fall should be considered as an "Allegory, Apologue, or Moral Fable."

Middleton died on 28 July 1750 in the course of composing a reply to the critics of his *Free Inquiry.* His second wife had died in April 1745, and he had only recently been remarried, to Anne Wilkins. His widow left Middleton's unpublished papers to William Heberden, who appears to have destroyed those that he considered to be of too skeptical a tendency. A posthumous edition of less inflammatory material left unpublished at Middleton's death appeared in 1752 as *Miscellaneous Tracts* and included "An Essay on the Gift of Tongues" and "An Essay on the Allegorical and Literal Interpretation of the Creation and Fall of Man."

Middleton's *The Life of Cicero* continued to be regarded, along with his other writings, as the work of a supremely accomplished prose stylist. "No man in English literature had a clearer and more just understanding, or a style which more exactly and agreeably expressed his meaning," wrote Thomas Babington Macaulay of *A Free Inquiry.* But Macaulay also considered Middleton to be a "querulous and egotistical" controversialist, and later eighteenth- and nineteenth-century readers remembered Middleton above all as a polemical theologian of dubious religious sincerity. Yet, it was in just this role, of theological controversialist, that Middleton made some of his most important contributions to Enlightenment historiography. His *Letter from Rome, Free Inquiry,* and *Examination of the Lord Bishop of London's Discourses* played a minor but significant role in the secularization of historical narrative, not least because of the complex but vital influence of Middleton's work on Edward Gibbon's *The Decline and Fall of the Roman Empire* (1776–1788) and the resultant religious controversy over Gibbon's historical masterpiece. Gibbon not only employed Middleton's *Free Inquiry* as an ironic foil to his argument in the notorious fifteenth chapter of *The Decline and Fall,* but he also ensured its lasting notoriety by attributing to it his youthful conversion to Roman Catholicism. Although Gibbon's use of Middleton, in both *The Decline and Fall of the Roman Empire* and his autobiography, is far from straightforward, it provides some of the most striking evidence of the reputation that Middleton's writings had achieved at the close of the eighteenth century.

By this point, Conyers Middleton's reputation as a skeptic was confirmed, however much he protested, in public and private, the sincerity of his religious convictions. He had written to Hervey in 1735, of the latitudinarian Bishop Benjamin Hoadly's *Plain Account of the Nature and End of the Sacrament* (1735), recorded in John Nichols's *Literary Anecdotes of the 18th Century,* "I like both the design and the doctrine, as I do every design of reconciling Religion with Reason; or, where that cannot be, of bringing them as near together as possible." In the contested space between religion and reason Middleton, like so many of his contemporaries, found his intellectual milieu. The enduring interest of his work, according to Gibbon in the *Miscellaneous Works,* lies not so much in the extent to which he managed to bridge the gap between faith and reason as in the way in which his writings helped to define the outer limits of eighteenth-century Anglican orthodoxy, marking the edge of what Gibbon called "the precipice of infidelity."

References:

Reed Browning, *Political and Constitutional Ideas of the Court Whigs* (Baton Rouge: Louisiana State University Press, 1982);

Günter Gawlick, "Cicero and the Enlightenment," *Studies on Voltaire and the Eighteenth Century,* 25 (1963): 657–682;

Joseph M. Levine, "'Et tu Brute?' History and Forgery in Eighteenth-Century England," in *Fakes and Frauds: Varieties of Deception in Print and Manuscript,* edited by Robin Myers and Michael Harris (Winchester: St. Paul's Bibliographies, 1989);

Caroline Robbins, *The Eighteenth-Century Commonwealthman: Studies in the Transmission, Development and Circumstance of English Liberal Thought from the Restoration of Charles II until the War with the Thirteen Colonies* (Cambridge, Mass.: Harvard University Press, 1959);

Frank M. Turner, "British Politics and the Demise of the Roman Republic: 1700–1939," *Historical Journal,* 29 (1986): 577–599;

Horace Walpole, *Correspondence,* edited by W. S. Lewis and others, 48 volumes (New Haven, Conn.: Yale University Press, 1937–1983), 15: 291–315;

David Womersley, *Gibbon and the "Watchmen of the Holy City": The Historian and his Reputation 1776–1815* (Oxford: Clarendon Press, 2002);

B. W. Young, "'Scepticism in Excess': Gibbon and Eighteenth-Century Christianity," *Historical Journal,* 41 (1998): 179–199.

Papers:

Collections of Conyers Middleton's papers and correspondence are located in the British Library; Trinity College, Cambridge; and the Suffolk Record Office (Bury St. Edmunds branch).

John Millar

(22 June 1735 – 30 May 1801)

Michael Brown
University of Aberdeen

BOOKS: *A Course of Lectures on Government: Given Annually in the University,* anonymous (Glasgow, 1771);

Observations concerning the Distinction of Ranks in Society (London: Printed by W. & J. Richardson for John Murray, 1771); corrected and augmented as *The Origin of the Distinction of Ranks; or, An Enquiry into the Circumstances Which Give Rise to Influence and Authority, in the Different Members of Society* (London: Murray, 1779);

Heads of the Lectures on the Law of Scotland: In the University of Glasgow, MDCCLXXVII [1777] (Glasgow: Printed by Andrew Foulis, [1777]);

An Historical View of the English Government: From the Settlement of the Saxons in Britain to the Accession of the House of Stewart (London: Printed for A. Strahan, and T. Cadell; and J. Murray, 1787);

Letters of Crito: On the Causes, Objects, and Consequences, of the Present War (Edinburgh: Printed for J. Johnstone, and sold at the office of the *Scots Chronicle,* 1796);

Letters of Sidney, on Inequality of Property. To Which Is Added, a Treatise of the Effects of War on Commercial Prosperity (Edinburgh: Printed and sold, at the office of the *Scots Chronicle;* and by J. Debrett, London; Messrs. J. Elder, J. Robertson, and W. Berry, Edinburgh; Messrs. Brash & Reid, and Cameron & Murdoch, Glasgow, [1796]).

Editions: *An Historical View of the English Government: From the Settlement of the Saxons in Britain to the Revolution in 1688; to Which are Subjoined Some Dissertations Connected with the History of Government from the Revolution to the Present Time,* 4 volumes, edited by John Craig and James Mylne (London: Mawman, 1803);

The Origin of the Distinction of Ranks; or, An Enquiry into the Circumstances Which Give Rise to Influence and Authority, in the Different Members of Society, "To which is prefixed An Account of the Life and Writings of the Author, by John Craig Esq." (Edinburgh: Blackwood; London: Longmans, 1806).

John Millar (medallion by James Tassie [1796]; frontispiece for William C. Lehmann's John Millar of Glasgow, 1735–1801, *1960; Thomas Cooper Library, University of South Carolina)*

John Millar was the Professor of Civil Law at the University of Glasgow from 1761 to 1801. A member of the Scottish Enlightenment, he is cited as a forerunner of modern sociology and as an influence on the historical materialism of Karl Marx. He taught several significant political figures in the early nineteenth century—particularly William Lamb, second Viscount Melbourne, and James Maitland, seventh Earl of Lauderdale—often producing in them an attraction to liberal reforming politics.

Millar was born on 22 June 1735 in Shotts in Lanarkshire, Scotland, to James Millar, the local Presbyterian minister, and Anne Hamilton Millar of Westburn. Her family disapproved of the match as she was thought to be lowering herself socially as a consequence. John Millar was educated privately by his uncle, John Millar of Milheugh, before attending the local grammar school at Hamilton, under the direction of a Mr. Pillans. Millar entered the University of Glasgow in 1746. He was a student of Adam Smith, attending Smith's lectures on moral philosophy, and a close friendship developed between them. Millar also became friendly with James Watt, the engineer who greatly improved the steam engine. Although Millar began studies for the church, after graduation he lived with Henry Home, Lord Kames, for two years, acting as tutor to Home's son, on the recommendation of Smith. As during his time at the university, Millar used the opportunity to study law. Home was himself a notable jurist and author of *Essays on the Principles of Morality and Natural Religion* (1751) and the *Historical Law Tracts* (1758).

Around 1759 Millar married Margaret Craig of Glasgow, by whom he had thirteen children, five boys and eight girls, eleven of whom survived infancy. Margaret Millar died in the summer of 1795. All four surviving sons attended Glasgow University. John, the eldest, died in Pennsylvania. Millar's second son, James, became the Professor of Mathematics at Glasgow University. The third son, William, became a major in the artillery, while the fourth, Archibald, was a writer to the signet in Edinburgh. Of the daughters, Agnes married James Mylne, the Professor of Moral Philosophy at Glasgow and editor of the posthumously issued volumes of Millar's *An Historical View of the English Government*. Another daughter, Margaret, also married a professor, John Thompson, who held the chair of surgery. Of the other daughters one predeceased Millar, dying of consumption in 1791, while the others remained unmarried.

Called to the bar in 1760, Millar was appointed to the chair of civil law in Glasgow a year later. He broke from precedent by choosing to deliver his civil law lectures in English rather than Latin, building on the innovation of his predecessor and teacher, Hercules Lindesay, who had already turned to English when speaking on Scots law. While Millar still examined his students daily in Latin, this change provided a platform for him to become a celebrated and much loved teacher. His nephew John Craig wrote of Millar in his obituary in *The Scots Magazine* that "few lecturers have possessed in a more eminent degree the talents of arresting attention and commanding assent." Among many future luminaries, Millar

taught noted jurist David Hume, nephew of his more famous philosopher namesake (an extensive list of Millar's students is offered by William C. Lehmann in *John Millar of Glasgow 1735–1801*). Within the university, Millar gained a reputation as an advocate for student interests. He took several students as boarders in his house, a common enough practice, which allowed the professors to supplement an income diminished by inflation during the century. He also defended David Woodburn, a divinity student charged by college authorities with blasphemy in 1768 and repeatedly stood by students accused of impugning the reputation or impinging the authority of his colleagues.

Millar's primary task as the professor of civil law, according to John Cairns, was the instructing of students on the contents of the *Pandects* and the *Institutes* of Justinian, as arranged by Heineccius. However, in 1764 Millar decided not to repeat his course on the *Institutes* in the spring semester, as was traditionally the case, allowing him time to offer a more general course on jurisprudence. He then rearranged the order of the *Pandects* to align more fully with that of the *Institutes*. In 1765 he expanded his teaching load again, adding a course on Scots law, which he delivered three days a week. He subsequently divided this course into public and private components, the first of which had transformed into a course on government by 1771. He eventually divided the two fields into separate courses, apportioning the same hour on the remaining two days to a full course on Scots private law, which he did from 1767. Finally, Cairns says, in 1773 Millar added yet another course, on English law, which alternated with that on Scots private law.

While his duties at the university were heavy, he found time occasionally to practice law. Craig remarks in "Account of the Life and Writings of the Author" that Millar "was very frequently consulted as Counsel, previously to the commencement of a law suit, or when any difficulty occurred in conveyancing; and the time he could spare from his other employments was occupied in determining causes referred to for his arbitration." Craig also states that Millar was prone to appear as counsel in criminal law cases, thinking "that the criminal laws of this country are, in many instances, unnecessarily and unjustly severe."

In 1771 Millar published *Observations concerning the Distinction of Ranks in Society,* drawing upon his lectures on jurisprudence. He revised and amended them in 1779 under the title *The Origin of the Distinction of Ranks.* The book outlined Millar's general theory of social development. His historical methodology was in line with what Dugald Stewart, Millar's contemporary and correspondent, termed "conjectural history." This term

Title page for the 1787 edition of Millar's 1779 work in which he applied his theory of social development to the English constitution (Eighteenth-Century Collections Online, Gale Group)

meant that evidence could be drawn not only from direct accounts of the society under question but also from societies at a similar stage in development. The conjecture resided in the assumption that one society would probably share a similar structure to another, given similar conditions. Millar's acceptance of Hume's probabilistic theory of knowledge, wherein humans draw on past experience to predict the likelihood of future occurrences, underpinned this method of proceeding. Thus, in *The Origin of the Distinction of Ranks* Millar drew on a wide range of sources, from the travelogues of contemporary Jesuit missionaries to the accounts of ancient historians; from literary works, such as James Macpherson's Ossian sequence, to the Bible. Yet, Millar gave none of these sources textual authority over any other. Such a conjectural methodology was used to delineate a human society as divided into four great historical stages. These he identified with four modes of the economic organization of society. As he told his students, "by tracing the progress of wealth, we may thus expect to discover the progress of government. I shall take notice of 4 *great stages* in the acquisition of property: 1. Hunters and Fishers, or mere Savages . . . 2. Shepherds . . . 3. Husbandmen . . . 4. Commercial people" (Millar's lecture notes).

This "stadialist" (belief that human societies pass through the same stages of economic and social development) narrative was also shared by many of Millar's contemporaries, notably Smith and Adam Ferguson, although Meek has written that "Millar's great achievement was to transform the four stages theory and the more general ideas associated with it into a true *philosophy of history*," an assertion founded on Millar's emphasis upon materialist causes of social development. Yet, Millar's own concern was less with the economic history of human society per se than with the manners and mores that were generated as a result. Thus, *The Origin of the Distinction of Ranks* was largely taken up with discussions of the social and cultural results of these changes and the consequent effects upon the exercise of power. The changing place of women in society was discussed in part 1, while the authority of the father, that of the chieftain, and that of the monarch were explored in the remaining sections. Crucially, this concern with manners was prompted by Millar's belief that the narrative of human progress was reversible. He perceived in commercial society the initial indications of regression, with moral laxity and state corruption combining to undermine recent gains in personal liberty.

Millar himself rarely traveled far from industrializing Glasgow, although he regularly went to Edinburgh and may have spent time in the north of England on vacation. Only two trips took him farther afield. The first time, in 1774, he spent two months in London and visited Cambridge and Oxford. In 1792 he again visited London, where he attended Parliament and met the leader of the opposition, Charles James Fox and other members of his party. Millar had already dedicated *An Historical View of the English Government* to Fox upon its publication in 1787.

In *An Historical View of the English Government* Millar applied his general theory of social development to the specific case of the English constitution. He again identified a series of stages in the developmental narrative. In the wake of the Roman retreat from England, the society was left in the state of hunter-gatherers. Only slowly did primitive government emerge. However, from the coming of the Saxons, "the great series of events in the history of England may be divided into three parts: the first extending from the settlement of the Saxons in Britain to the Norman conquest; the second from the reign of William the conqueror to the accession of the house of Stewart; the third from the reign of James the first to the present time." These stages were identifiable through changes in the nature of government. The stages were then characterized by Millar as "feudal aristocracy," "feudal monarchy," and "commercial government." The story thus became one of the initial centralization of authority in the person of the king and the corrective measures since taken to ensure personal liberty. As he summarized the narrative at the conclusion of the second volume:

> The subsequent progress of government produced a gradual exultation of the crown; but the long, continued struggle between the king and his barons, and the several great charters which they extorted from him, contributed to ascertain and define the extent of his prerogative. While the monarchy was thus gaining ground upon the ancient aristocracy, the constitution was acquiring something of a regular form, and by the multiplication of fixed laws, provision was made against the future exertions of arbitrary power.

Indeed, he asserted that "the British government is the only one in the annals of mankind that has aimed at the diffusion of liberty through a multitude of people, spread over a wide extent of territory."

Millar accounted for this achievement through reference to Britain's "insular situation." Importantly, this location ensured that "the English were little exposed to any foreign invasion . . . and hence the king, being prevented from engaging in extensive national enterprises, was deprived of those many opportunities for signaling his military talents and for securing the admiration and attachment of his subjects." Moreover, this circumstance was added to the impact of England's climate and natural fecundity, which "by encouraging trade and manufactures, gave an early consequence to the lower order of the inhabitants." By the accession of James I in 1603, at which point Millar's initial narrative drew to a close, he was able to claim:

> upon the whole, that the English constitution, at this period, contained the essential principles of liberty, we need only attend to its operation, when the question was brought to a trial, in the reigns of the two succeeding princes . . . in the course of that struggle, it soon became evident, that parliament, without going beyond its undisputed privileges, was possessed of sufficient authority, not only to resist the encroachments of prerogative, but even to explain and define its extent and to establish a more complete, regular system of liberty.

Crucially, however, Millar did not conceive of this story of progress as inevitable or irreversible. Rather, as his actions made clear, he applied his diagnosis of commercial society's failings to British political life. Probably, however, he had undergone a significant change of heart politically following the ministerial crisis of 1784 and the rise of William Pitt. He had found little merit in the Wilkite disturbances concerning the power of the London Corporation in the 1760s, and had misgivings over the American Revolution a decade later. But with the collapse of the Fox-North administration, according to Michael Ignatieff, Millar found increasing sympathy for the idea of popular suffrage and regular elections. He became a notable campaigner for legal reform and was instrumental, according to Lehmann, in the awarding of an honorary degree in April 1791 to William Wilberforce for his work against slavery. Millar is also the most likely instigator of a petition, sent through Wilberforce the following year from the university to the House of Commons, in favor of abolition.

Despite this chronology, Alexander Carlyle of Inveresk wrote, although with significant hindsight, of his first encounter with Millar in 1768, that he had "begun to distinguish himself by his democratical principles, and that sceptical philosophy which young noblemen and gentlemen of legislative rank carried into the world with them from his law course, and, many years afterwards, particularly at the period of the French Revolution, displayed with popular zeal, to the no small perversion to all those under their influence."

He defended himself from similar denunciations in a 16 August 1784 letter to Edmund Burke explaining that

> if we are charged with *lecturing* on politics, I am afraid the charge must fall principally upon myself, as lecturing upon public law. I am certainly guilty of endeavouring to explain the principles of our own government. I know that I have been accused of including republican doctrines, but I am not conscious of having given any just ground for such an imputation. It has always been my endeavour to recommend that system of limited monarchy that was introduced at the Revolution. . . . I should think it petulance if, in the capacity of a public lecturer I were to meddle with the local and the partial.

Lecture notes taken by students indicate, however, that Millar was not always averse to such partial reflections, with remarks on the French Revolution, for example, according to Knud Haakonssen, being interpolated into the student notes on government dating from the academic session 1787–1788.

These controversial political opinions may have found their fullest expression in the fifteen *Letters of Crito,* which first appeared in *The Scots Chronicle* from 27 May to 2 September 1796. Dedicated to Fox, they are generally accepted to have been written by Millar. The only other candidate is his student, nephew, and first biographer, John Craig. Therein, the author attacked the foreign policy of Pitt, arguing that the war against revolutionary France, which had been declared in 1793, was an unjustifiable interference in the politics of another sovereign nation. The author further alleged that the war was motivated more by domestic concerns of security and state power than by fear of French expansionary tendencies. Pitt, the letters contended, was intent on reducing the scope of British liberty. Whether these were written by Millar or not, he certainly committed himself to the peace movement. He apparently signed, and allegedly even wrote, according to Lehmann, a petition signed by 40,000 Glasgow citizens requesting an end to hostilities and presented to the king in September 1793 by Millar's student and close friend, the Earl of Lauderdale. Millar also inscribed into the minute book his protest against a university grant of £300 to aid the defense of the country in 1798.

Much less certain is the ascription of the *Letters of Sidney* to Millar. Ten of the eighteen Sidney letters of both Crito and Sidney published in 1796 first appeared in that year in *The Scots Chronicle,* overlapping the correspondence from Crito. Dedicated in the pamphlet to Lauderdale, they attack the increasing inequality of property holding in eighteenth-century society and reiterate some of the criticisms of Pitt's government found in the *Letters of Crito*. Cases can be made for other items,

notably a series of reviews marked "M" in the *Analytical Review* from 1788 to 1792 or 1793, and five letters–from "A Citizen of Glasgow" to the editor of *The Scots Chronicle* in late 1796 and early 1797 on an adult-education initiative–that are in line with Millar's known views of the matter. However, these attributions remain highly conjectural.

According to Ignatieff, the depth of Millar's links to the emerging reform movements in Scotland also remains unclear. Millar was the teacher of Thomas Muir, who was sentenced to fourteen years transportation to Australia for sedition in 1793. Muir had presented an address from the United Irishmen to the General Convention of the Friends of the People held in Edinburgh in December 1792. Millar was also a member of the Scottish Association of the Friends of the People; he attended meetings in Glasgow and was a subscriber to the society's London branch as a charter member in 1792. However, according to the "Account of the Life and Writings of the Author," the level of his radical activism is uncertain. His links to the society were also personified in his eldest son, John, who was forced into emigration by poor health and the governmental crackdown in 1795. Moving to the United States of America, he died shortly after his arrival in Pennsylvania.

Millar himself died of a sudden attack of pleurisy in 1801 at Milheugh. Following Millar's death, Craig republished *The Origin of the Distinction of Ranks* and prefaced it with a lengthy account of Millar's life. Of arguably greater importance was the publication, under the stewardship of Craig and Mylne, of a new edition of *An Historical View of the English Government.* While the first two books (now two separate volumes), which had taken the story up to the accession of James I, were substantially unchanged, two further volumes were now released. The first of these surveyed the history of Scotland between 1603 and the union of the Crowns and argued that Scotland had long remained in the stage of "feudal aristocracy" rather than sharing England's precocious development of a "feudal monarchy." The volume also supplied a history of the Stuart reign up to and, briefly, including the Glorious Revolution.

The fourth and final volume was much less finished in its content. It offered a series of dissertations on a range of subjects, some of which had nothing to do with the general narrative of English governance. Thus, a history of Ireland up to the granting of parliamentary independence in 1782 jostled with a categorization of the arts and sciences. The political consequences of the Glorious Revolution also came under examination, suggesting that the revolution had instigated a steady expansion of the military power of the state, undertaken to defend its international commercial interests, and which might, if mishandled, undermine the freedom of the citizenry. In contrast, the section on commerce and manufactures was described by Francis Jeffrey of the *Edinburgh Review* as a "clear and concise abstract of the leading principles of the *Wealth of Nations*" by Millar's old teacher, Smith, although it equally emphasized Smith's own fears of the alienating power of the division of labor over the ameliorative effects of commercial practices of emulation. It also included an important essay on "the origin and progress of the sciences of law and government."

John Millar was buried at High Blantyre. His obituary in *The Scots Magazine* concluded that "by his death" his country lost "a firm and enlightened assertor of her liberty." Subsequently, Millar has somewhat fallen from view. Although Marx drew upon Millar's materialist interpretation of historical change in developing his own ideas, he rejected Millar's probabilism in favor of a philosophical determinism. More recently, Millar has been understood as a forerunner of modern sociological analysis, with particular attention given to his *Origin of the Distinction of Ranks* as a history of manners and mores. Since the 1970s, scholarly interest in the Scottish Enlightenment has led to the exploration of Millar's historical context, which has highlighted his commitment to a reform-minded brand of Whig politics. It has also shed light on his philosophical connections to Hume and Smith and underlined his use of a conjectural method and structure in writing his historical narratives.

References:

John Cairns, "'Famous as a School for Law, as Edinburgh . . . for Medicine': Legal Education in Glasgow, 1761–1801," in *The Glasgow Enlightenment,* edited by Andrew Hook and Richard B. Sher (East Linton: Tuckwell, 1997), pp. 133–159;

Alexander Carlyle, *Autobiography of Alexander Carlyle of Inveresk* (Edinburgh: T. N. Foulis, 1910);

John Craig, "Character of the Late Professor John Millar," in *Scots Magazine,* 63 (August 1801): 577–578;

Knud Haakonssen, "John Millar and the Science of a Legislator," in *Juridical Review,* 41 (1985): 41–68;

Michael Ignatieff, "John Millar and Individualism," in Istvan Hont and Michael Ignatieff, *Wealth and Virtue: The Shaping of Political Economy in the Scottish Enlightenment* (Cambridge: Cambridge University Press, 1983), pp. 317–345;

Francis Jeffrey, "Article 13," *Edinburgh Review,* October 1803;

William C. Lehmann, *John Millar of Glasgow 1735–1801: His Life, Thought and His Contributions to Sociological Analysis* (Cambridge: Cambridge University Press, 1960);

Ronald L. Meek, *Social Science and the Ignoble Savage* (Cambridge: Cambridge University Press, 1976).

Papers:

John Millar's papers are held by the National Archives of Scotland, National Library of Scotland, Edinburgh University Library, Glasgow University Library, and Aberdeen University Library.

William Mitford

(1744 – 8 February 1827)

Ian Macgregor-Morris
University of Nottingham

BOOKS: *An Essay on the Harmony of Language Intended Principally to Illustrate that of the English Language,* anonymous (London: Printed by Scott for J. Robson, 1774); second augmented edition, published as *An Essay on the Harmony of Language, and of the Mechanism of Verse, Modern and Ancient* (London: T. Cadell and W. Davies, 1804; New York: Garland, 1972);

A Treatise on the Military Force, and Particularly the Militia, of the Kingdom (1774);

Inquiry Concerning the Military Force Proper for a Free Nation of Extensive Dominion; in Which the British Military Establishments Are Particularly Considered (London: Printed for R. Blamire, 1778);

The History of Greece, volume 1(London: Printed by T. Wright for J. Murray, 1784); revisions published as *Additions and Corrections to the First Volume of the History of Greece* (London, 1789); *The History of Greece,* volume 2 (London: Printed by T. Wright for T. Cadell, 1790); fourth edition, corrected, 10 volumes, 1822; 8 volumes (Boston, T. Bedlington and C. Ewer, 1823); fifth edition, augmented and corrected, 8 volumes, edited by William King, memoir of the author by his brother, John Mitford, Baron Redesdale, third edition, 10 volumes (London: Printed by T. Cadell, 1795–1810)—comprises volumes 1–4 (1795), listed as third edition; volumes 5–6 (1797); volumes 7–10 (1810), first editions (London: Printed for T. Cadell, 1829);

Considerations upon the Opinion Stated by the Lords of the Committee of Council, in a Representation to the King upon the Corn-laws, That Great Britain Is Unable to Produce Corn Sufficient for its Own Consumption, and on the Corn-Bill Now Depending in Parliament (London: Printed for John Stockdale, 1791);

Principles of Design in Architecture Traced in Observations on Buildings . . . in a Series of Letters to a Friend (London: Printed by Luke Hansard for T. Cadell and W. Davies, 1809);

Observations on the History and Doctrine of Christianity, and, as Historically Connected, on the Primeval Religion, on the Judaic, and on the Heathen, Public, Mystical, and Philosophical: The Latter Proposed as an Appendix to the Political and Military History of Greece (London: Rodwell & Martin, 1823).

William Mitford was a leading man of letters of the late eighteenth century, a country squire, and a member of Parliament. He is best remembered as the author of a history of Greece that proved to be the standard work for two generations. When historian Arnaldo Momigliano suggested that Greek history was an invention of the British in the eighteenth century, he was primarily referring to Mitford and his contemporary John Gillies, who published a history of Greece at the same time. Mitford's history supplanted that of Gillies, however, and was much more successful: it went through many editions and was translated into French and German. Yet, its unusual style and political content made Mitford the subject of both extravagant praise and venomous criticism. Perhaps the best summation of his vices and virtues came from George Gordon, Lord Byron, who referred to the historian thus in the notes to *Don Juan* (1821):

> His great pleasure consists in praising tyrants, abusing Plutarch, spelling oddly and writing quaintly; and, what is strange, after all *his* is the best modern history of Greece in any language, and he is perhaps the best of all modern historians whatsoever. Having named his sins, it is but fair to state his virtues—learning, labour, research, wrath, and partiality. I call the latter virtues, because they make him write in earnest.

These points, references to Mitford's partiality and style on the one hand and his scholarship and expertise on the other, characterize the response his works have received, but they also testify to his importance during the early nineteenth century.

Mitford was born in London in 1744, the eldest son of John Mitford of Exbury. His mother was Philadelphia, daughter of William Revely of Newby in Yorkshire and first cousin to Hugh Percy, the Duke of

Northumberland, who changed the family surname from Smithson to Percy when he married. William Mitford's younger brother, John, later Baron Redesdale, became speaker of the House of Commons and Lord Chancellor of Ireland. William Mitford was educated at Cheam School in Surrey under William Gilpin, where he developed a taste for Greek literature and history. Since he was intended for law, however, he was encouraged to concentrate on Latin. At the age of fifteen he was forced to withdraw from school because of ill health, a problem that affected him periodically for much of his life. Soon after he withdrew, in 1761, his father died. Once William had recovered, he was sent to Queen's College, Oxford. While at Oxford he appears to have enjoyed a period of good health, and in the words of W. W. Wroth in the *Dictionary of National Biography,* he was "distinguished by his good looks and his personal strength." He continued to show a great interest in Greek literature, but at the time the subject was not considered of primary importance in the English universities, and Mitford generally studied without instruction. As he had been intended for the bar, Mitford attended the Vinerian lectures of legal historian Sir William Blackstone, which led Mitford to think at length on the role of English law in the history of the country. In the main, however, young Mitford neglected his studies, a result of what his brother described as a lack of any "parental authority," and he left Oxford without a degree. In 1763 he entered the Middle Temple, but although deeply interested in the political aspects of law, he found the reading necessary to qualify for the bar "distasteful," according to Redesdale, and soon abandoned his studies.

At the age of twenty-two, on 18 May 1766, Mitford married Frances Molloy. The marriage further strengthened Mitford's ties to the aristocracy, since Frances was a second cousin to Henry, Earl Bathurst. Mitford retired to the family seat in Exbury, Hampshire, near the New Forest, which he had inherited after his father's death. He spent the next few years in virtual seclusion with his family, continuing his study of the Greek language and literature he so loved. Mitford's brother concluded that during these years of solitude Mitford formed his passionate opinions: "In solitude, the mind, resting on itself, may form opinions which, not meeting with collision, remain strongly impressed, and are not easily abandoned." During these years, however, Mitford began to play a prominent role in local life, and in 1769 he was appointed captain in the South Hampshire Militia, wherein he made the acquaintance of Edward Gibbon, who was then a major in the regiment.

Mitford's first publication, a product of these years, was *An Essay on the Harmony of Language Intended Principally to Illustrate that of the English Language,* published anonymously in 1774. The work was intended to introduce a new and consistent system of spelling to the English language, drawing on the various languages from which English was derived, primarily Latin and Saxon. To accomplish this task, Mitford turned to ancient authorities on language, believing that language was a field in which the moderns had made no advances over the ancients: "What remains from the ancients of the subject, seems to be read, not so much with admiration as with astonishment. None seem to have thought of applying it to the consideration of the harmony of their native tongue." These ancient authorities provided the key to perfecting the English language: "The ancients have left us, interspersed in the writings, large and accurate information concerning the general harmony of human speech. I imagine that an attentive view of this information will enable us to acquire a clear insight into the particular harmony of our native tongue . . . and perfect our ideas of the general harmony of human speech."

What follows is a detailed academic study of language, drawing on ancient and modern sources. Mitford drew particularly heavily on John Foster's 1762 work, *An Essay on the Different Nature of Accent and Quantity, with Their Use and Application in the Pronunciation of the English, Latin, and Greek Languages,* which he described as "a very learned treatise." Throughout the work Mitford displays the highly critical approach and propensity to draw his own conclusions that mark all his scholarship: "The concurring authorities of Dr. Foster and Mr. Johnson are without doubt very formidable, yet, when opposed to truth, no more to be regarded than the *academiae auctoritas,* of which Dr. Foster makes so light, and which he has indeed pretty well proved to be fallible."

Mitford's first work had some limited success and was still worthy of attention when a revised edition was published in 1804 under the title *An Essay on the Harmony of Language, and of the Mechanism of Verse, Modern and Ancient.* The *Edinburgh Review* for July 1805 praised Mitford for his learning and considered the work to be "unquestionably valuable." The reviewer found Mitford boastful, however, and his style difficult: "We think that he, who proposes schemes for improving the euphony of the English language, would be heard with more deference, if he were studious of writing that language, as it now exists, with propriety and elegance." This insistence on writing in an original style, accompanied by an unusual orthography, pervaded much of Mitford's works and was the origin of Byron's accusation that Mitford spelled "oddly." Mitford eventually found, in the words of his brother's biography, that "the tide of fashion [was] too strong for him," and in his later works began to conform.

Soon after the publication of this work, Mitford's wife died (1776). He fell once more into a serious illness, which was evidently life threatening. While still convalescing, he decided to undertake a trip to the Continent, intending to spend the winter in Nice. In England he had made the acquaintance of Jean-Baptiste de Meusnier and Homeric scholar Jean-Baptiste D' Ansee de Villoison, who introduced Mitford to the Baron de Sainte-Croix. Mitford spent some time with the baron in Avignon and found that the Frenchman shared his enthusiasm for Greek literature. Some say that in the long conversations he shared with Gibbon while serving with the militia, the elder historian encouraged Mitford to write a history of Greece. These influences determined Mitford to undertake the project for which he became best known.

Mitford appears to have returned from France with a renewed sense of energy. He became more active in local affairs, becoming a county magistrate, being appointed the verderer of the New Forest in 1778, and succeeding Gibbon in 1779 as lieutenant colonel of the South Hampshire Militia; however, Mitford's main interest was his history of Greece. The first volume, *The History of Greece from the Earliest Accounts to the Death of Philip, King of Macedon,* appeared in 1784, and upon its favorable reception, Mitford was encouraged to continue, publishing a revised version of the first volume in 1789 and a second volume in 1790. Later volumes continued to appear throughout his life, with a third in 1797, a fourth in 1808, and the final volume in 1810. He had intended to continue the history down to the final conquest of Greece by the Romans (146 B.C.), but his last volume ends with the death of Alexander (323 B.C.). By this time Mitford was once more in poor health. He was suffering from failing eyesight, and, most distressing of all for a man of letters, increasing memory loss.

Mitford's *History of Greece* marks a major development in the study of Greek history. Certain important works had appeared before, such as Temple Stanyan's *Grecian History* (1707–1739) and Charles Rollin's *Histoire Ancienne* (1730–1738); both of these men had attempted, with some success, narrative histories of Greece. Stanyan and Rollin both deserve credit for establishing the history of Greece as a viable subject for study, something that few before had thought to be of importance. In the years that followed, a virtual Greek renaissance occurred, prompting a rising tide of Hellenism in almost every aspect of European culture. In literature a fashion had arisen for the classical simplicity of the Grecian style epic, epitomized by Richard Glover's *Leonidas* (1737); Johann Joachim Winckelmann's theories on art, as expounded in his *Geschichte der Kunst des Altertums* (1764), were changing the way people thought about

Greek art, a trend reflected in the huge success of James Stuart and Nicholas Revett's great studies of Athenian architecture, *The Antiquities of Athens* (1761–1830); a new wave of scholarship of Greek literature was developing, represented by such writers as Robert Wood and Johann Gottfried Herder; and in terms of political philosophy, a series of thinkers, from Adam Ferguson to Jean Jacques Rousseau and Gabriel Bonnot de Mably, were turning to Greece for radical political models. Yet, writing on Greek history had not progressed since Rollin. Claude Millot's *Elements of General History* (1761) was little read, and it failed in its self-proclaimed aim of supplanting Rollin, while Oliver Goldsmith's *History of Greece* (1774) is little more than a vulgar plagiarism of Stanyan.

In such an atmosphere Mitford published his *History of Greece*. The feature that attracted the most critical response was the attitude toward the political forms of the ancient Greek states. These responses were in the main determined by the political standpoint of the critic. Thus, *Blackwoods Magazine* (July 1819) could praise Mitford for conferring an "eminent service upon his country, by writing a history of Greece in the true English spirit," while the *Westminster Review* (1826) condemned him for "the strongest partialities; and according as these lead he is credulous or mis-trustful." Many reviewers, however, found much both to praise and to condemn. Writing in the *Edinburgh Review* (July 1808). Lord Brougham described the history as "the best that has appeared since the days of Xenophon," but lamented that "the story of the Grecian republics should have been told by one who has so many anti-republican partialities."

Certainly, Mitford was vehemently opposed to the democracy of ancient Athens, and he often finds opportunity to condemn it. The democracy is described as "tyranny in the hands of the people"; various acts are taken to show "the revengeful and unrelenting temper of democratical despotism"; while freedom of speech was curtailed by the fear of the "jealous tyranny of the Athenian democracy." While Mitford clearly prefers the Spartan system of government, describing Lycurgus's reforms as "the most extraordinary plan ever devised by man," he still expresses reservations, having harsh words to say concerning the Spartan treatment of the Helots, the state-owned slaves, who, as Mitford recognized, were crucial to the existence of the Spartan social system. As Byron claimed, Mitford did have positive words to say concerning the Greek tyrants, claiming that "History has recorded Grecian tyrants as men of extraordinary virtue." Yet, he qualifies this statement with an erudite discussion on the changing meaning of the word "tyrant."

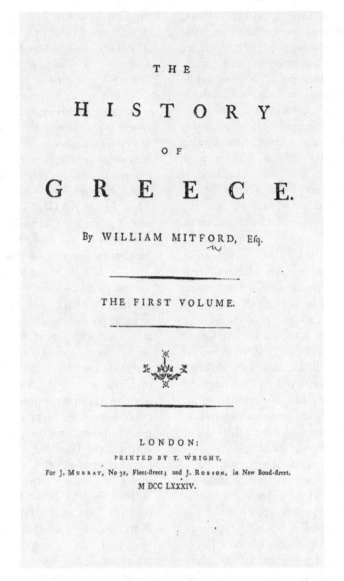

Title page for William Mitford's 1784 history (from Eighteenth-Century Collections Online, Gale Group)

Mitford saw in his history the opportunity to counteract the excessive use radical political reformers and idealists were seeking to make of ancient Greek political forms. This concern became more pressing for Mitford in the wake of the French Revolution. In contrast to their idealized visions, Mitford presented ancient Greece as he believed the sources portrayed it– a violent society in which the individual and his property were consistently at risk from others and from the state as a whole. The modern constitution of England, framed by law, was preferable. Thus, in reference to the trial of Socrates, Mitford commented that "in England no man would be put on trial on so vague a charge: no grand jury would listen to it. But in Athens, if the party was strong enough, it signified little what was the law."

In the atmosphere of growing Hellenism of the late eighteenth and early nineteenth centuries, such a picture of ancient Greece could not but attract criticism. Yet, even his critics recognized value in his work. Thomas Babington Macaulay suggests in "On Mitford's History of Greece" that Mitford's history may be a useful remedy to those who eulogized the ancient republics as models for the modern world, because they "have erred so monstrously on the other side that even the worst parts of Mr. Mitford's book may be useful as a corrective."

This highly political slant to Mitford's *History of Greece,* however, was based on a level of detailed historical research not seen before. Much of the praise focused on the belief that Mitford was the first to attempt a rigorously critical account of Greek history. Thus, Macaulay admitted that Mitford "writes of times with respect to which almost every other writer has been in the wrong; and, therefore, by resolutely deviating from his predecessors, he is often in the right." Mitford's diligent cross-referencing of sources and detailed analysis and assessment of different accounts gave his *History of Greece* an authority quickly recognized by his contemporaries. This detail of scholarship, accompanied by the sweeping range of his narrative, accounts for the huge success of his history of Greece. The scale of the undertaking discouraged any others from attempting it. Indeed, it eventually defeated even Mitford himself, who had to content himself with a history that ended in the fourth century B.C.

During these years Mitford did not concentrate on his writings alone, and he appears to have been quite conscientious about his public duties. He continued to be active in the militia, becoming full colonel of the regiment in 1805. He sat as a member of Parliament upon three occasions, initially for Newport in Cornwall, from 1785 to 1790. In 1796 he was returned to Parliament for Beeralston, on the interest of the duke of Northumberland. This occurrence reflected an ongoing family tie with the duke, since Mitford's brother, John, had represented the borough in the previous two Parliaments. Mitford represented Beeralston until 1806, and from 1812 to 1818 he sat for New Romney.

Mitford was not the most vocal member of the House of Commons; yet, he made his feelings clear on issues close to his heart. In 1791 he published *Considerations upon the Opinion Stated by the Lords of the Committee of Council, in a Representation to the King upon the Corn-laws*. This highly topical subject was the focus of many publications, and Mitford believed it was important to make a contribution. "In that state of things," he claims in this work, "no man can be indifferent to the event; no citizen can be without a right to declare his opinion." The text that follows is an erudite economic study of the situation, drawing on contemporary theory, most notably Adam Smith's *An Inquiry into the Nature and Causes of the Wealth of Nations* (1776), which he describes as the "most authoritative book the world possesses upon the very important subject of which it treats." Mitford argues against the opinions of the Lords Commission, claiming instead that Britain was quite capable of producing ample corn for her own needs.

The other main issue that drew his interest concerned the militia. Mitford believed that the militia should not be governed by the same laws as the regular army, seeing it as a counterbalance to the potential dangers of the regular army as a political force. He therefore resisted all attempts to reform the militia, most notably against the propositions of Henry Dundas, later

the first Viscount Melville, in 1798. At some point in these years, Mitford expounded his views on the matter in a short work titled *A Treatise on the Military Force, and Particularly the Militia, of the Kingdom,* although the date of this work is unclear.

His other writings of his later years covered a wide range of subjects. In 1809 he published *Principles of Design in Architecture Traced in Observations on Buildings . . . in a Series of Letters to a Friend*. This treatise examined the history of architecture and various styles and discussed current trends. It drew on a range of sources, and once again Mitford displayed a wide and critical reading. Thus, Letter XXIII, "The Revival of Grecian Architecture," provides a detailed discussion of the fashion, drawing on such contemporary sources as the earl of Sandwich, Wood, and Stuart and Revett.

In 1823 Mitford produced his final work, *Observations on the History and Doctrine of Christianity,* a survey of the history of religion. He had originally intended the work as part of his *History of Greece,* but his failing health interfered with completing the project. The *Observations on the History and Doctrine of Christianity* begins with the premise that "the variety of opinions among professors of Christianity . . . cannot be but striking to all who have any information on the subject." The ensuing discussion includes aspects of religion both Christian and pagan, throughout the ages. Mitford's partialities again emerge: the Catholic attitude toward Protestantism is based upon the "offensive and most injurious tenets, so violently hostile to the most important civil rights of individuals," while the Church of England is "the best perfection yet attained among national establishments." Both of these statements are distinctly measured, however, and they reveal that Mitford's primary concerns are political, not spiritual. More specifically, Mitford is concerned with the relationship between the individual and the institutions of state. His preference for the Anglican establishment is exactly that, a preference, not a comment of unqualified belief. Moreover, as in his history, Mitford gives credit where he believes it is due. Thus, although not praising the Athenian democracy, he still describes that city as "the great seat of science, a university for the civilised world." The resulting study is a wide-ranging discussion in which his erudition outweighs any sense of partialities.

William Mitford died on 8 February 1827 in Exbury. He had a total of seven children, six sons and a daughter, but he had the misfortune to witness the deaths of four of his sons during his lifetime. His reputation, however, survived him, and his *History of Greece* remained the standard until the Greek histories of Connop Thirlwall (1835–1847) and George Grote (1845–1856). Grote in particular attacked Mitford's history for its politics, although he clearly made use of it himself.

Moreover, the accusations made against Mitford are often unfounded. His antipathy to Athenian democracy stemmed not from a stubborn conservatism, but from a genuine belief that an excess of popular power was harmful to individual liberty. This view was widely held in the eighteenth century, and the advocates of Athens in the nineteenth century, despite their rhetoric, accepted the point. Even the radical Grote did not propose a political system based on that of Athens.

Mitford's *History of Greece* can still be useful to the historian of ancient Greece. If Mitford is at times excessive in his criticism of Athens and its institutions, the vast majority of histories since Grote are excessive in their panegyric of that city. Grote's history, just as much as Mitford's, is a product of its author's politics. In that sense, Macaulay's suggestions that Mitford can serve as a "corrective" is still relevant. In terms of the history of scholarship, Mitford's work marks a major development: *The History of Greece* is consistently supported by diligent research and a thorough knowledge of the sources, and any judgment he passes is supported by evidence from those sources. His standard of criticism and breadth of learning give the reader a sense of Greek history that more recent, and more specialized, histories find difficult to convey.

References:
Gentleman's Magazine (April 1827): 368–369;

Thomas Babington Macaulay, Baron Macaulay, "On Mitford's History of Greece," *Knight's Quarterly Magazine* (November 1824); reprinted in *The Complete Works,* 12 volumes (London: Longman, Green, 1898–1906), VII: pp. 683–703;

Brendan A. Rapple, "Ideology and History: William Mitford's *History of Greece,*" *Papers on Language and Literature,* 37 (2001): 361–381;

Rapple, "A Tory History of Ancient Greece," *Contemporary Review* (February 1995): 97–102.

Papers:
William Mitford's family papers are held by the Gloucester Records Office; the Bodleian Library holds letters to William Gilpin; the Devon Records Office holds correspondence with the first Viscount Sidmouth; and the Norfolk Records Office holds some papers among the Walsingham manuscripts.

Roger North

(3 September 1651 – 1 March 1734)

Robert W. McHenry Jr.
University of Hawaii, Manoā

BOOKS: *Arguments and Materials for a Register of Estates,* anonymous (London: Printed for Samuel Lowndes, 1698);

A Discourse of Fish and Fish-Ponds, under the Following Heads, Viz. I. Of the Situation and Disposition of the Principal Waters. II. The Manner of Making and Raising Pond-heads, with Their Dimensions, and How to Secure the Banks. III. Of Sluices, Stews, Moats, Auxiliary Waters, and the Course of Laying the Great Waters Dry. IV. Of the Breeding and Feeding of Fish, and the Manner of Stocking Waters. V. Of Disposing of Fish, of the Management for Carriage, of Nusances to Ponds and Fish, of Frosts, and the Ways to Save the Fish in Them. VI. Of the Benefits and Improvements by Fish, anonymous (London: Printed for E. Curll, 1713);

The Gentleman Accomptant: or, An Essay to Unfold the Mystery of Accompts. By Way of Debtor and Creditor, Commonly Called Merchants Accompts, and Applying the Same to the Concerns of the Nobility and Gentry of England. Done by a Person of Honour, anonymous (London: Printed for E. Curll, 1714; New York: Garland, 1986);

Examen: or, An Inquiry into the Credit and Veracity of a Pretended Complete History; Shewing the Perverse and Wicked Design of It, and the Many Falsities and Abuses of Truth Contained in It. Together with Some Memoirs Occasionally Inserted. All Tending to Vindicate the Honour of the Late King Charles the Second, edited by Montagu North (London: Printed for Fletcher Gyles, 1740);

The Life of the Right Honourable Francis North, Baron of Guilford, Lord Keeper of the Great Seal, under King Charles II, and King James II. Wherein are Inserted the Characters of Sir Matthew Hale, Sir George Jeffries, Sir Leoline Jenkins, Sidney Godolphin, and Others, the Most Eminent Lawyers and Statesmen of that Time, edited by Montagu North (London: Printed for John Whiston, 1742);

The Life of the Honourable Sir Dudley North, Knt, Commissioner of the Customs, and Afterwards of the Treasury to His Majesty King Charles the Second. And of the Honourable and Reverend Dr. John North, Master of

Roger North (portrait by Sir Peter Lely, frontispiece for General Preface and Life of Dr. John North, *edited by Peter Millard, 1984; Thomas Cooper Library, University of South Carolina)*

Trinity College in Cambridge, and Greek Professor, Prebend of Westminister, and Sometime Clerk of the Closet to the Same King Charles the Second, edited by Montagu North (London: Printed for the editor and sold by John Whiston, 1744);

A Discourse of the Poor, Shewing the Pernicious Tendency of the Laws Now in Force for their Maintenance and Settlement: Containing Likewise, Some Considerations Relating to National Improvement in General, edited by Montagu North (London: Printed for M. Cooper, 1753);

A Discourse on the Study of the Laws; Now First Printed from the Original MS. in the Hargrave Collection, with Notes and Illustrations by a Member of the Temple [i.e. Henry Roscoe] (London: C. Baldwyn, 1824);

Memoirs of Musick, edited by Edward F. Rimbault (London: George Bell, 1846);

The Autobiography of the Hon. Roger North, edited by Augustus Jessopp (London: D. Nutt, 1887);

The Musicall Grammarian, edited by Hilda Andrews (London: Oxford University Press, 1925);

Roger North on Music: Being a Selection from His Essays Written during the Years c. 1695–1728, edited by John Wilson (London: Novello, 1959);

Of Building: Roger North's Writings on Architecture, edited by Howard Colvin and John Newman (Oxford: Clarendon Press, 1981);

Roger North's "Of Sounds" and Prendcourt Tracts c. 1710–c. 1716, edited by Mary Chan and Jamie Croy Kassler (Kensington: University of New South Wales, 2000);

The Beginnings of the Modern Philosophy of Music in England: Francis North's A Philosophical Essay of Musick (1677) with Comments of Issac Newton, Roger North and in the Philosophical Transactions, edited by Kassler (Aldershot, U.K.: Ashgate, 2004; Burlington, Vt.: Ashgate, 2004).

Editions: *The Lives of the Right Hon. Francis North, Baron Guilford, Lord Keeper of the Great Seal, Under King Charles II and King James II, the Hon. Sir Dudley North, Commissioner of the Customs, and afterwards of the Treasury, to King Charles II and the Hon. and Rev. Dr. John North, Master of Trinity College, Cambridge, and Clerk of the Closet to King Charles II,* 3 volumes, edited by Henry Roscoe (London: Henry Colburn, 1826);

The Lives of the Right Hon. Francis North, Baron Guilford; the Hon. Sir Dudley North; and the Hon. and Rev. Dr. John North by the Hon. Roger North, Together with the Autobiography of the Author, 3 volumes, edited by Augustus Jessopp (London: George Bell, 1890); reprinted as *The Lives of the Norths* (Farnworth, U.K.: Gregg Press, 1972);

General Preface and Life of Dr. John North, edited by Peter Millard (Toronto, Buffalo & London: University of Toronto Press, 1984);

Roger North's Cursory Notes of Musicke (c. 1698–c. 1703): A Physical, Psychological and Critical Theory, edited by Mary Chan and Jamie C. Kassler (Kensington: University of New South Wales, 1986);

Roger North's The Musicall Grammarian, 1728, edited by Chan and Kassler (Cambridge & New York: Cambridge University Press, 1990);

The Life of Lord Keeper North by Roger North, edited by Chan, Studies in British History, volume 41

(Lewiston, N.Y. & Lampeter, Wales: Edwin Mellen Press, 1995);

Notes of Me: The Autobiography of Roger North, edited by Millard (Toronto & London: University of Toronto Press, 2000).

OTHER: "Preface," anonymous, in Sir Dudley North, *Discourses upon Trade; Principally Directed to the Cases of the Interest Coynage Clipping, Increase of Money* (London: Printed for Thos. Basset, 1691 [i.e. 1692]).

Roger North was a pioneer in the history of English biography, but because he declined to publish his most significant biographical works, he lived unknown. When many of his most important works—three detailed and unsentimental biographies of three of his brothers, his passionate historical commentary on the reign of Charles II, and his autobiography—appeared posthumously in 1740–1744, their Tory politics made them unwelcome in the Whig culture of that time. Still, scholars of the nineteenth and twentieth centuries developed a belated but spirited appreciation for North as many of his unpublished manuscripts were edited or accurately re-edited. North has come into focus as a passionate intellectual and a dramatic, if uneven, biographer. In addition to his biographies and his history, he wrote books on music, architecture, law, and science, plus essays on political and ethical issues and shorter works on accountancy and even fishponds. When his reputation was low because of his political views, he still was read for the wealth of everyday information and vivid personal experience that he provided.

North's powerful impulse to write, which led him to produce thousands of pages, arose from his loyalty to his family. He was born into a family that was large and aristocratic, but by the standards of its class not wealthy. North's grandfather, Sir Dudley, third Baron North, was a courtier during the reign of James I and an active member of the House of Lords during the reign of Charles I. Having dissipated much of the family fortune, Sir Dudley retired to his estate at Kirtling in Cambridgeshire. Because of his excesses, his son, also named Sir Dudley, had ten surviving children who had little prospect of any inheritance to support them as adults. It was clear to them, including Roger, the youngest of six sons, that all, except the heir, would have to make their own fortunes. And so they did. The three sons whose lives North records were outstandingly successful: his brother Francis, a lawyer, became Lord Keeper of the Great Seal (equivalent to Lord Chancellor) and was elevated to the rank of Baron Guilford; his brother Dudley amassed a considerable fortune as a merchant in Turkey and served as Sheriff of London; and his brother John, a scholar, became Professor of

Greek at Cambridge and Master of Trinity College, Cambridge.

Roger North, trained also in the law, enjoyed ample success, becoming an adviser to the Court of Charles II, attorney general to Queen Mary during the reign of James II, and adviser to the archbishop of Canterbury, William Sancroft. North was born on 3 September 1651 at his father's estate in Tostock, Suffolk. While early accounts often cite 1653 as North's date of birth, in 1994 Richard Grassby's research established the correct date. In *Notes of Me* (2000; first published in 1887 as *The Autobiography of the Hon. Roger North*), North gives a vivid account of a happy childhood in the country, filled with memories of his siblings and his strong, intelligent mother, Anne (daughter of Sir Charles Montague of Cranbrook). The family was enthusiastically musical, and Roger became an avid viol player. His schooling began at home under the guidance of the Reverend Ezekiel Catchpole and continued at the nearby free schools in Bury St. Edmunds and Thetford. In the fall of 1667 he entered Jesus College, Cambridge, living with his brother John. During this year in Cambridge, North discovered the delights of mathematics and fell under the spell of René Descartes. Illness ended North's studies after a year, however, and when he returned to them, it was in London, where he embarked on his legal education at the Middle Temple in 1669. He was called to the Bar in 1675. With his brother Francis's powerful patronage, North rose quickly in the legal profession, becoming a King's Counsel in 1682 and in 1683 Treasurer of Middle Temple and a Member of Parliament. He held other positions at Court in the following years and was reelected to James II's first Parliament in 1685. During the brief reign of James II, North was torn between his royalism and his unease at the king's measures to strengthen Catholicism. When the king was deposed in 1688, North refused to take the Oath of Allegiance to the new monarchs, William and Mary. Soon under attack as a Jacobite (loyal to King James II) and as a nonjuror (one refusing to swear loyalty to the king) who regarded the establishment of the new monarchs as illegal, he lost his positions at Court and as Steward to the See of Canterbury. He purchased Rougham Hall in Norfolk in 1690 and retreated there at age thirty-nine to start a new life as a country gentleman.

He entered into retirement with his usual energy, rebuilding the old house in a baroque style and improving the grounds. He also took on the guardianship of several orphaned nieces and nephews and took in his brother Montagu, who was shattered from three and a half years in a French prison. In 1696 North married Mary Gayer, daughter of Sir Robert Gayer, another Jacobite. The couple had seven children. They lived quietly, and North avoided politics. He also continued to write about his many interests—including music, art, and architecture. He turned to writing history and biography, beginning about the time of his brother Francis's death in 1685, because he grew increasingly annoyed at the Whigs' history of the reign of Charles II. To his dismay, he found that his late brother Francis was either reviled for his actions on behalf of the king or, worse, ignored. Yet, while North spent almost four decades of his long life writing, he published little and that anonymously. Sorely disappointed at the triumph of his political enemies over him, he had little desire to address a wide audience of his contemporaries, so he wrote for his family, posterity, and himself. When on 1 March 1734 he died at age eighty-two, he left a prospering estate, a large collection of books and paintings, many by his friend Sir Peter Lely, and a huge mass of his own unpublished manuscripts.

North persistently revised his works, sometimes over a period of decades. Because he habitually retained all his drafts but seldom dated them—and almost never used dates within them—editors and commentators have found it difficult to date his works or to place them in chronological order. Furthermore, records of publication are usually of little value as evidence of their times of composition, for what became his best-known books did not begin appearing in print until his son Montagu had them printed, beginning in 1740, six years after his father's death. One of North's most original works, the *General Preface* to his lives, was not published in its entirety until 1984. Scholars generally believe that North began his writing after the "Glorious Revolution" (a phrase North would have abhorred) of 1688. He seems to have continued writing and revising until the 1720s.

North's earliest written work may be the anonymous "Preface" to his brother Dudley's posthumously printed *Discourses upon Trade; Principally Directed to the Cases of the Interest Coynage Clipping, Increase of Money,* which appeared in 1692 (although dated 1691). Other anonymously published early works include *Arguments and Materials for a Register of Estates* (1698), a treatise on the need to secure titles of land.

At this time North also wrote *Notes of Me,* an autobiographical memoir. In his edition of 2000, Peter Millard estimates that the autobiography was written between 1693 and 1698. In it North always stresses the importance of his family in establishing his character. Although North's evaluation of his family is high, his account of himself is modest. He is willing to expose his weaknesses: he admits that he is not a rigorous, organized thinker, for example, and in many matters he defers to his successful brother Francis. About himself his manner is dispassionate and analytical. Critics such as Millard have defined North's contribution to life-writing as a talent for devising a kind of scientific inquiry into human character. North also sets up revealing contrasts between the difficult world of politics and law in London and the restorative world of family life in the country. He reveals a talent for delineating the distinctive attributes of his acquaintances and composing vivid, apt anecdotes that illustrate them. Some of his scenes of family life from his childhood are among the most admired in the book. They are affectionate, but not sentimental. He maintains an awareness of the folly and wickedness in human society, even among his young schoolmates.

Also from the same decade, but not published until 1753, was his *A Discourse of the Poor, Shewing the Pernicious Tendency of the Laws Now in Force for their Maintenance and Settlement: Containing Likewise, Some Considerations Relating to National Improvement in General.* In this work he criticized the Poor Laws and also composed several essays on music and on social and ethical topics, such as pride, retirement, religion, politics, and free will. North commenced work on *Of Building* (not published until 1981) at about this time. He then returned to expand his work in the 1720s. This guide to remodeling an old house is based on his own experience at Rougham. North maintained a strong amateur interest in architecture throughout his life. The gateway at the Middle Temple, on the Strand, the only one of his designs to have been built other than at Rougham, is the only one that has survived into the twenty-first century.

One of North's domestic enthusiasms resulted, in 1713, in the publication of *A Discourse of Fish and Fish-Ponds.* This treatise is memorable for its accounts of his fishing, swimming, and boating in the moat surrounding his grandfather's estate. In 1714 North published *The Gentleman Accomptant: or, An Essay to Unfold the Mystery of Accompts. By Way of Debtor and Creditor, Commonly Called Merchants Accompts, and Applying the Same to the Concerns of the Nobility and Gentry of England,* his accounting guide for the use of gentlemen managing their own estates.

North probably began composing a biography of Francis North, the Lord Keeper, soon after his brother's death in 1685. The scope of the project was comprehensive, and its multiple revisions took decades. By the time North completed it, probably about 1726, he had produced six distinct versions. The final draft is the text chosen by Mary Chan for her 1995 edition of *The Life of Lord Keeper North by Roger North,* a tome of more than five hundred pages as published, even though that edition omits the six additional manuscript volumes, including his brother's papers, that North had appended to his account. Aware that historical evidence disappears quickly, North was determined to preserve as much as he could about his brother's life.

Francis North was an important figure in the Court of Charles II who took part in several controversial legal battles connected to the Popish Plot, the Exclusion Crisis, and the Rye House Plot. He was a thoroughgoing royalist, and his efforts to support the Court's positions and undermine those of the opposition have earned him some severe criticism. In volume four of his *History of England* (1849), Thomas Babington Macaulay calls Francis North "the most ignoble of mankind." In North's loyal view, his brother is eminently wise, virtuous, and learned. North always defends his brother's public acts and his character, though he can criticize his behavior in private life. Aware that readers might repudiate this highly favorable interpretation, North seeks to confound all objections and establish his own credibility by making his account overwhelmingly factual. In the process, he creates what Chan, in her *The Life of Lord Keeper North by Roger North,* calls "one of the most fully documented conscious experiments with ways of creating the subject [of biography] to have come down to us from the early eighteenth century."

North started a second biography about 1691, shortly after his brother Sir Dudley North died. It was composed mainly between 1709 and 1720. Having made his fortune in Turkey, Dudley North returned to England in 1680, and soon he became Roger North's close companion. During the Exclusion Crisis, Dudley North agreed to serve as one of the two London sheriffs in 1682, at the king's request, to assist the Court in wresting the government of the City of London from the hands of the Whigs. Dudley North was knighted at that time and later held the posts of City Alderman and Commissioner of the Customs. This biography is notable for the affection that Roger North displays for Dudley. They shared many interests, including scientific studies and yachting. Dudley North, in his brother's view, was "a born companion, if any Ever was so, free from all manner of Morosity," who loved conversation, particularly with his brother: "And his chief delight was at Night when the work of the day was over to supp with a friend and Chirp over a bottle and so In good time as he allwaies observed to bed." Passages such as this exhibit the style that Samuel Taylor Coleridge in "The Friend" (volume one of his *Collected Works* [1969], edited by Barbara E. Rooke) praised as "the very nerve, pulse, and sinew of a hearty healthy conversational English."

Beginning also in the 1690s, North worked on a third biography, this one of his brother John, an Anglican clergyman who died in 1683 at age thirty-seven. The last of the four manuscript versions of this life, which is the basis for Millard's edition of 1984, is dated 1728. This life is much the shortest of the three. John North ordered his papers burned before his death, and

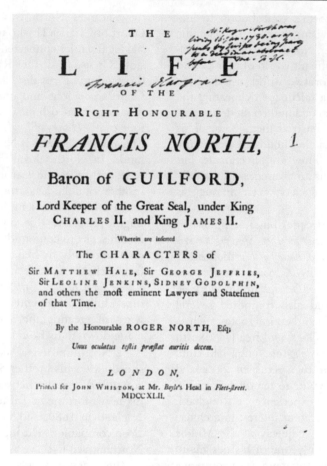

THE

LIFE

OF THE

RIGHT HONOURABLE

FRANCIS NORTH,

Baron of GUILFORD,

Lord Keeper of the Great Seal, under King
CHARLES II. and King JAMES II.

Wherein are inserted

The CHARACTERS of

Sir MATTHEW HALE, Sir GEORGE JEFFRIES,
Sir LEOLINE JENKINS, SIDNEY GODOLPHIN,
and others the moſt eminent Lawyers and Stateſmen
of that Time.

By the Honourable ROGER NORTH, Eſq;

Unus oculatus teſtis præſtat auritis decem.

LONDON,

Printed for JOHN WHISTON, at Mr. Boyle's Head in Fleet-ſtreet.
MDCCXLII.

Title page for North's 1742 biography of his brother (Eighteenth-Century Collections Online, Gale Group)

Roger North saw him less frequently throughout adulthood than he did Francis and Dudley. With fewer materials to review, North was able to produce his most tightly unified biography. He portrays John as a timid, physically frail man who seemed to become more isolated as he rose in rank. John North's life was often grim, despite his personal rectitude and academic distinction. At the age of thirty-two he became Master of Trinity College, Cambridge, but within six years, he was dying of a mysterious disease that affected his mind as well as his body. North describes it in ghastly detail. Yet, for the happier times, North recounts vivid anecdotes that illustrate his brother's virtuous nature. North makes effective use of trifling events, described with mastery of detail and a sharp comic sense, that reveal facets of his subject's temperament. While North's honesty demands that he include incidents that show his brother's physical and emotional weaknesses, he always provides a balancing emphasis upon his integrity. He inserted a lengthy discussion of Cartesian scientific principles in his manuscript of this life, but, as he recognized, it is extraneous, and no subsequent editor has printed it.

North's massive *Examen: or, An Enquiry into the Credit and Veracity of a Pretended Complete History . . . of the Late King Charles the Second* (1740) evolved from his analysis of the political crises he reviewed while drafting his life of Francis. This history of the reign of Charles II is in the form of a close, passionate critique of a Whig history published in 1706, White Kennett's third volume of the *Complete History of England*. Written between 1710 and 1722, North's *Examen* includes withering refutation, full of scorn and indignation, of Kennett's account and devastating portraits of those who opposed the king. North draws vividly upon his own recollections of these times, making his narrative one of the most important sources for firsthand observations of the tense, fearful period during the Popish Plot and Exclusion Crisis (1678–1681). This work reveals North's unrelenting Toryism. For him, the opponents of the Court were uniformly corrupt and malicious. While his point of view is anything but balanced, North's blend of detailed factuality and keen advocacy makes the *Examen* a prime source for anyone wishing to understand the political conservatism of the Restoration.

While revising the accounts of his brothers' lives, North wrote, from 1718 to 1728, the first full treatise on biography in English, the *General Preface,* largely unknown until its first complete published edition. North clearly intended it as a statement of principles; biography must not be mere "invective, or panegyric," but an attempt to do justice to a person's life. The *General Preface* also includes a methodological introduction to the three lives and a defense of the value of writing the lives of private men rather than monarchs and conquerors. In this sophisticated analysis of biography, North explores the reasons for its appeal to readers, comparing the pleasure of reading biographies to that of reading fiction, and he defends his practice of introducing trivial details into his narratives. As James L. Clifford points out, these ideas and North's insistence on the importance of including the flaws and errors of a life anticipate most of the key points made by Samuel Johnson in his influential essays on biography in the *Rambler* and *Idler* papers a generation later.

North, who clearly developed a love of the law while at the Middle Temple, also wrote *A Discourse on the Study of the Laws* (1824), in which he lays down, with rigor, advice for any student of the law who wishes to master the profession. In the 1720s North returned to the subject of music, one of his strongest enthusiasms since his youthful days at Kirtling. He wrote *Memoirs of Musick* (1846), a history of music from the ancients up to North's own day, and *The Musicall Grammarian* (1925), a study of the science of music. Both texts are now regarded as important works in the history of English music.

F. J. M. Korsten defines Roger North as a "virtuoso"—in the seventeenth-century meaning of the term, which was used for a zealous amateur who pursues learning as an avocation, often in science, but also in the arts. The word is useful in recalling North's wide and deep interests, and because it was used satirically in the Restoration and eighteenth century for dilettantish collectors of undigested facts and oddities, it can also suggest his limitations. While he is no fool, he is open to the criticism that he cannot properly organize his thoughts at times or is unable to select from the vast store of information he collects. He can delve obsessively and tediously into legal, biographical, or political details. While he can turn a phrase sharply and precisely, he often seems to need a good editor. Set against these limitations, scholars note his wide and diverse learning, his energetic style, and his capacity to grasp facts of many kinds. Even Whig readers such as Macaulay acknowledged that North's portraits of persons and events are often immediate and compelling. As a theorist of life writing, he repays study for his principles of biographical writing and for his analysis of

biography. His biographies, and his autobiography, deserve attention especially for their success at preserving the texture of the lives and the complex ideas and passions of his times. As an historical character, North commands interest as an insider who in time became a displaced person—a successful Restoration courtier who in maturity wrote in isolation against the grain of the Whig eighteenth century. His biographical works are Tory acts of defiance against the world that neglected or denigrated his brothers. They are also testaments to his humanistic faith that truth would eventually vindicate them.

Letters:

Augustus Jessopp, ed., "Letters from Roger North," in Roger North, *The Lives of the Right Hon. Francis North, Baron Guilford; the Hon. Sir Dudley North; and the Hon. and Rev. Dr. John North By the Hon. Roger North, Together with the Autobiography of the Author* (London: George Bell, 1890), III: 211–280;

Mary Chan, ed., *Life into Story: The Courtship of Elizabeth Wiseman* (Aldershot, U.K. & Brookfield, Mass.: Ashgate, 1998)—includes letters of Roger North on pp. 1–2, 9–17, 32, 51–52, 54–56, 60–67, 69–70, 75–84, 88–92, and 97.

Bibliographies:

Lois G. Schwoerer, "The Chronology of Roger North's Major Works," *History of Ideas News Letter,* 3, no. 4 (1957): 73–78;

Mary Chan and Jamie C. Kassler, *Roger North: Materials for a Chronology of His Writings. Checklist No. 1* (Kensington: University of New South Wales, 1989).

References:

T. A. Birrell, "Roger North and Political Morality in the Later Stuart Period," *Scrutiny,* 17, no. 4 (1950–1951): 282–298;

George Carver, *Alms for Oblivion* (Milwaukee: Bruce, 1946);

Mary Chan, "From Essayist to Author: Roger North and Evolving Narrative Forms," *Seventeenth Century,* 15, no. 2 (Autumn 2000): 266–282;

Chan, "Roger North's *Life* of Francis North," *Review of English Studies,* new series, 42 (May 1991): 191–211;

James L. Clifford, "Roger North and the Art of Biography," *Restoration and Eighteenth Century Literature: Essays in Honor of Alan Dugald McKillop,* edited by Carroll Camden (Chicago & London: University of Chicago Press, 1963), pp. 275–285;

Clifford, ed., *Biography as an Art* (New York: Oxford University Press, 1962);

Hamilton E. Cochrane, "Brother Against Brother: Roger North's *Life of Dr. John North*," *Biography*, 10 (Winter 1987): 59–86;

Cochrane, "The Man of Law in Eighteenth-Century Biography: The *Life of Francis North*," *Studies in Eighteenth-Century Culture*, 16 (1986): 139–148;

Cochrane, "'A Strange Bent to Traffic': *The Life of Sir Dudley North*," *Eighteenth-Century Life*, 10 (January 1986): 14–25;

Richard Grassby, *The English Gentleman in Trade: The Life and Works of Sir Dudley North 1641–1691* (Oxford: Clarendon Press, 1994);

Edgar Johnson, *One Mighty Torrent: The Drama of Biography* (New York: Stackpole, 1937);

R. W. Ketton-Cremer, "Roger North," *Essays and Studies*, new series, 12 (1959): 73–86;

F. J. M. Korsten, *Roger North (1651–1734), Virtuoso and Essayist: A Study of His Life and Ideas, Followed by an Annotated Edition of a Selection of His Unpublished Essays* (Amsterdam & Maarssen: APA-Holland University Press, 1981);

Peter Millard, "The Chronology of Roger North's Main Works," *Review of English Studies*, new series, 24 (August 1973): 283–294;

John N. Morris, *Versions of the Self: Studies in English Autobiography from John Bunyan to John Stuart Mill* (New York: Basic Books, 1966);

Roger Schmidt, "Roger North's *Examen*: A Crisis in Historiography," *Eighteenth-Century Studies*, 26, no. 1 (Fall 1992): 57–75;

Lois G. Schwoerer, "Roger North and His Notes on Legal Education," *Huntington Library Quarterly*, 22 (1958–1959): 323–343;

G. A. Starr, "Roger North and the *Arguments and Materials for a Register of Estates*," *British Museum Quarterly*, 31, nos. 1–2 (1966): 17–19;

Donald A. Stauffer, *The Art of Biography in Eighteenth-Century England* (Princeton: Princeton University Press / London: Oxford University Press, 1941);

Lytton Strachey, *Portraits in Miniature, and Other Essays* (London: Chatto & Windus, 1931; New York: Harcourt, Brace, 1931);

Richard Wendorf, *The Elements of Life: Biography and Portrait-Painting in Stuart and Georgian England* (Oxford: Clarendon, 1990), pp. 150–169.

Papers:
The largest collection of manuscripts by Roger North and other members of the North family are in the British Library. The Bodleian Library, the Cambridge University Library, the St. John's College Library (Cambridge), the Jesus College Library (Cambridge), Rougham Hall (the North residence in Norfolk), the Norfolk and Norwich Records Office, and the Hereford Cathedral Library also hold manuscripts by Roger North. A comprehensive listing may be found in F. J. M. Korsten, *Roger North (1651–1734), Virtuoso and Essayist: A Study of His Life and Ideas, Followed by an Annotated Edition of a Selection of His Unpublished Essays* (Amsterdam & Maarssen: APA-Holland University Press, 1981), pp. 317–319.

Simon Ockley

(1678 – 9 August 1720)

Julia Belian

University of Missouri, Kansas City

BOOKS: *Introductio ad linguas orientales. In qua iis discendis via munitur, et earum usus ostenditur. Accedit index auctorum, tam illorum, quorum in hoc libello mentio fit, quam aliorum, qui harum rerum studiosis usui esse possint* (Cambridge: Academic Press, at the expense of John Owen, 1706);

The Conquest of Syria, Persia, and Egypt, by the Saracens, 2 volumes (London: Printed for R. Knaplock and others, 1708, 1718); republished as *The History of the Saracens* (Cambridge: Printed for Mrs. Anne Ockley by permission of Henry Lintot, 1757);

The Dignity and Authority of the Christian Priesthood, Asserted: In a Sermon Preached at Ormond Chapel, Dec. 10, 1710 (London, 1711);

Oratio inauguralis [Inaugural Sermon] (Cambridge: Academic Press, printed by Edmund Jeffery, 1712);

An Imitation of the New Way of Writing, Introduced by the Learned Mr. Asgill (London: John Morphew, 1712);

An Account of the Authority of the Arabick Manuscripts in the Bodleian Library Controverted between Dr. Grabe and Mr. Whiston. In a Letter to Mr. Thirlby (London: H. Clements, 1712);

A Sermon on the Duty of Instructing Children in Holy Scriptures, Preached at St. Ives in Huntingdonshire (London: J. Round, 1713);

An Account of South-West Barbary: Containing What Is Most Remarkable in the Territories of the King of Fez and Morocco. Written by a Person Who Had Been a Slave There a Considerable Time; and Published from His Authentick Manuscript. To Which Are Added, Two Letters: One from the Present King of Morocco to Colonel Kirk; The Other to Sir Cloudesly Shovell: With Sir Cloudesly's Answer, &c. By Simon Ockley, B.D. Professor of Arabick, in the University of Cambridge; and Chaplain to the Most Honourable Robert, Earl of Oxford and Mortimer, Lord High-Treasurer of Great Britain (London: Printed for J. Bowyer and H. Clements, 1713); extracted and republished as *An Account of the Extream Misery of the Christian Captives in Barbary, Written by a Person Who Had Been a Slave There a Considerable Time* (London: Printed by J. Downing, 1721).

TRANSLATIONS: Leon Modena, *The History of the Present Jews throughout the World, Being an Ample Tho Succinct Account of Their Customs, Ceremonies, and Manner of Living, at this Time. To Which Are Subjoin'd Two Supplements, One Concerning the Samaritans, the Other of the Sect of the Carraites, from the French of Father Simon, with His Explanatory Notes* (London: Printed by E. Powell, 1707);

Muhammad ibn 'Abd al-Malik Ibn Tufail, *The Improvement of Human Reason, Exhibited in the Life of Hai Ebn Yokdhan with an Appendix, in Which the Possibility of Man's Attaining the True Knowledg of God, and Things Necessary to Salvation, without Instruction, Is Briefly Consider'd* (London: Printed by E. Powell, 1708; Dublin: by and for Sam. Fuller, 1731);

Second Apocryphal Book of Esdras from the Arabic (N.p., 1716);

Caliph Ali ibn Abi Talib, *Sentences of Ali Son-in-law of Mahomet, and His Fourth Successor* (London: Printed for Bernard Lintot, 1717).

British "Orientalist" Simon Ockley opened a new vista on the Islamic world with histories that read like adventure sagas and translations of Arabic sources so strange as to be nearly unbelievable to most of his countrymen. Incessant work and incessant poverty sent him to an early grave, however, and his reliance on manuscripts that were eventually discovered to be flawed made the results of his toils largely irrelevant to later Islamic historians. Thus, a scholar hailed in his day as a brilliant pioneer slipped into almost total obscurity by the end of the nineteenth century.

Ockley was born in Exeter in 1678 but raised in his father's town of Norfolk. Although his father, according to the *Dictionary of National Biography (DNB)*, was reputedly a "gentleman" of Great Ellingham, Ockley's childhood seems to have left him as penniless as he remained all his life. Although few details of his childhood are known, he undoubtedly learned Greek and Latin, as most young scholars of his era did. According to A. J. Arberry, Ockley entered Queen's College, Cambridge, at fifteen, as a sizar (an impoverished student on scholarship who serves the other students), where he studied Spanish, French, and Italian before moving on to the more difficult Hebrew and Arabic.

As Arberry relates, various friends and scholars who were impressed with his work at Cambridge, including Humphrey Prideaux, Dean of Norwich, and Richard Bentley, Master of Trinity, used their political influence to get Ockley an appointment as Hebrew lecturer at seventeen. The £10 stipend was a pittance, wholly inadequate to live on, but, according to the *DNB,* it was more than Ockley had had before. Ockley was ordained a deacon and married before he reached the age of twenty. In 1701 Simon Patrick, Bishop of Ely (another of Ockley's patrons), ordained him to the priesthood and helped him secure appointment as vicar at Swavesy, a position that gave him £80 a year. Even for its day this was not a large salary, and Ockley kept his eye on the Sir Thomas Adams endowed professorship of Arabic.

Ockley's own experience in mastering long-neglected languages prompted him to write his first book, *Introductio ad linguas orientales* (Introduction to Eastern Languages), which was published in 1706. In it he urges other students to add the Eastern languages to their university study, detailing all the ways such knowledge could benefit and further the pursuit of Christian theology. British scholars of the era generally gave Islam no more attention than was necessary to disdain it: the only English translation of the Koran then available, produced by Alexander Ross in 1649, was based upon a French manuscript and, according to Arberry, was derisive of Islam. In his *Introductio ad linguas orientales,* Ockley argued for a new study of the Koran in its original tongue, as well as renewed study of the extensive libraries and repositories of learning that were available to those versed in Arabic.

Ockley's days were full. In addition to fathering a large family, he continued with his pastoral duties while pursuing his Arabic research at both the library at Cambridge and the far superior libraries at Oxford. He was both suited and devoted, according to Arberry, to the tedium of such work, but his practical need for additional income forced him to make an effort to play politics as well. Ockley was born into the time between the Glorious Revolution of 1688 and the coronation of George I. For almost all of his productive life, Queen Anne held the throne, and in her administration the Tories, who had fallen into disfavor with the abdication of James II, found sympathy. Religious dissent was again unpopular, and conservative Anglo-Catholic the-

ology had, for a brief time, recaptured the upper hand in court politics.

Ockley did what he could to attach himself to those who might be able to help him politically—and therefore financially—even though politics was not his interest or talent. He aligned himself with Robert Harley, whom Queen Anne created earl of Oxford and named lord treasurer, one of the most influential positions in her government. Harley was closely involved with Henry St. John, later viscount Bolingbroke, who served as secretary for war and then secretary of state for Queen Anne and had the power to direct certain state projects to the translators of his choice. Bolingbroke and Harley were among those Tories constantly maneuvering for positions of power in the government and working diligently to prevent the passage of the throne to the Hanovers. These political intrigues led to the development of two distinct threads in Ockley's writings. On the one hand, his passion for Eastern languages and history propelled him to work almost feverishly on the manuscripts he located in the Bodleian Library at Oxford. On the other, he produced a stream of pamphlets, short books, potboilers, and government-commissioned translations, each of which was designed either to solicit additional work from the Crown or to disavow connections to the Whiggish Nonconformists who were so attracted to his publications on Mohammedism. He also kept up his Hebrew scholarship, publishing in 1707 a translation of Leon Modena's *The History of the Present Jews throughout the World*.

In 1707 and 1708, Ockley's attentions were diverted by an unusual brief piece of Arabic philosophy. In 1671 Edward Pococke, one of the earliest Arabic scholars in England, had translated into Latin a piece of philosophical fiction by Muhammad ibn 'Abd al-Malik Ibn Tufail called *The Improvement of Human Reason*. The story resembled an Arabic *Robinson Crusoe,* and the thesis was strikingly deist; it said that one could discover the truth about God and the world even without direct revelation. The Quakers immediately seized Pococke's Latin text and translated it in 1674 into an English version strongly suited to bolster their own theologies. Naturalist theologian George Ashwell, vicar of Banbury, completed his own English version from Pococke's Latin translation in 1686. Ockley was persuaded to make a direct translation from the Arabic, which was published in 1708, but, according to Arberry, Ockley did all he could to distance himself from those who had used the text for Nonconformist purposes. "I was not willing (though importun'd) to undertake the translating it into English," he wrote in the preface, "because I was inform'd that it had been done twice already; once by Dr. Ashwell, another time by the Quakers. However, . . . I did not question but

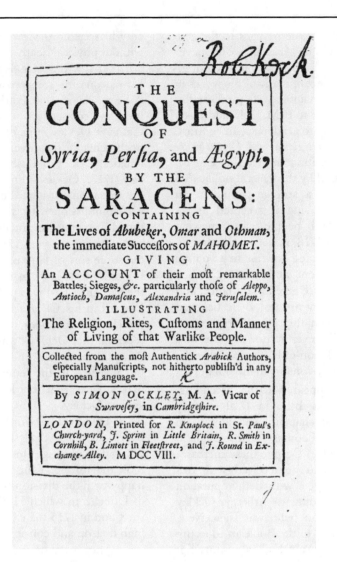

Title page for Simon Ockley's 1708 history (Eighteenth-Century Collections Online, Gale Group)

that they had mistaken the Sense of the Author in many places." He included with the volume a critical appendix outlining the doctrinal errors in the story, "Lest otherwise, that Book, which was by me design'd for the Innocent, and not altogether unprofitable Diversion of the Reader, might accidentally prove a means of leading some into Error, who are not capable of judging aright. . . ."

Throughout these early years, Ockley had been gathering materials and translating and studying them to produce his great history of the early Islamic conquests. His studies took him repeatedly to Oxford, where the collection of manuscripts at the Bodleian surpassed anything Cambridge had to offer. Oxford first admitted him as a student and finally, according to Arberry, he "was incorporated Master of Arts" in 1706. He later described to his daughter the intensity of his labors:

. . . one of the most useful and necessary authors I have is written in such a wretched hand that the very reading of it is perfect deciphering . . . for oftentimes it is so written, that a word is divided as if the former part of it was the end of another. . . . Add to this the pains of abridging, comparing authors, selecting proper materials, and the like, which in a remote and copious language, abounding least to the performing of six times so much in Greek and Latin.

Ockley told his daughter that he worked "from the time I rise in the morning till I can see no longer at night," and in his weariness he reported, "Were it not that there is some satisfaction in answering the end of my profession . . . I would sooner do almost anything than submit to the drudgery."

Once the first volume of *The Conquest of Syria, Persia, and Egypt, by the Saracens* was published in 1708, however, Ockley gained renown as the preeminent Arabic scholar of his day. Beyond that, he brought to the general public an awareness of the Arabian world never previously available. Although Pococke had used original Arabic manuscripts to prepare many of his works in the previous century, they inevitably were published in Latin, and therefore, according to P. M. Holt, addressed themselves almost exclusively to academics. In contrast, Ockley's *The Conquest of Syria, Persia, and Egypt, by the Saracens* was written in an exciting and riveting English and was immediately enjoyed by the general public as a collection of adventures by a strange people in an unknown, faraway land. Having it accepted as an authentic history of the Arab people was somewhat more difficult. Years later, in 1718, in his introduction to the second volume Ockley related how the first volume was greeted with astonishment and frank disbelief. "They say that the Arabians are given to romance; and for that reason I suppose they are not to be believed (according to Aristotle) when they speak truth. And above all, that a history will never go down in this nice age, that contains only a relation of battles, but that the very quintessence of a history consists in the politics."

Ockley's reputation appeared to be ascending. Cambridge admitted him as B.D. in 1710; Harley named him as his personal chaplain; and at last, in 1711, he was elected to the Thomas Adams Chair in Arabick Studies in Cambridge. Despite these increases in fame and the £40 stipend he received with this honor, he continued to struggle with both reputation and finances. In 1712, according to Arberry, Ockley accompanied William Whiston (who was Isaac Newton's successor at Cambridge) to the Bodleian to examine "The Doctrine of the Apostles," a manuscript connected to Second Esdras that Whiston thought would help prove that the original theology taught by Christ was Unitarian and Arian. Despite warnings and entreaties to change his dangerous course, and despite his own ignorance of Arabic, Whiston was determined to examine the manuscript in question and to put it to use in support of his position. Ockley helped Whiston with the translation work, but when Whiston persisted in his publication of Ockley's translations with his own ideas, according to the *DNB*, Ockley, in a 1712 pamphlet titled *An Account of the Authority of the Arabick Manuscripts in the Bodleian Library Controverted between Dr. Grabe and Mr. Whiston. In a Letter to Mr. Thirlby,* denied the implication that he supported Whiston's ideas, and in 1716 Ockley published his own translation of Second Esdras. Although the motivation remains obscure, in 1712 Ockley also published *An Imitation of the New Way of Writing, Introduced by the Learned Mr. Asgill,* a tract attacking John Asgill, a Nonconformist thinker admired by Daniel Defoe (in *An Essay upon Projects* [1697]) but excluded from the House of Commons for his suppos-

edly blasphemous views on the possibility of salvation without physical death.

At this time Ockley continued to search among his patrons for some manner of increasing his living. Arberry claims that Harley, long a supporter of Ockley's, had connections to Secretary of State Bolingbroke that gave Ockley hope of securing a position translating documents for the government. In demonstration of his abilities, Ockley published *An Account of South-West Barbary* (1713). Ockley admitted he had no idea who wrote the sensationalist item, but his efforts paid off when he was commissioned to translate two official letters from the Moroccan government.

During the year 1714, Ockley apparently committed some sort of faux pas while dining with the earl of Oxford. Much later, in 1859, the letter Ockley wrote to the earl afterward was published in its entirety by Isaac Disraeli in his *Calamities and Quarrels of Authors*. Among the effusive apologies is a denial of a charge someone repeated that Ockley "was a very sot." Whether it was the quantity drunk or his behavior while indulging is not revealed in the letter, but further correspondence makes clear that Harley did not hold any grudge against Ockley.

The earl of Oxford's patronage became comparatively worthless that same year, however, when the Tory-sympathizing Queen Anne died and George I took the throne. King George I was not particularly happy with the division of Europe effected by the Peace of Utrecht, to which Harley contributed in great measure, and in 1715 the earl was impeached on charges of high treason and consigned to the Tower of London.

After a few more attempts to gain some translation work, Ockley resigned himself to finding a new patron, according to Arberry, which he did in the person of Thomas Freke. At Freke's request, Ockley published the small book *Sentences of Ali Son-in-Law of Mahomet, and His Fourth Successor* (1717). The niceties of the request out of the way, he settled in to complete his history, *The Conquest of Syria, Persia, and Egypt, by the Saracens*. Ockley's financial troubles caught up with him at last, however, and he was imprisoned in Cambridge Castle for a debt of approximately £200. Ockley continued to work from prison, even claiming in the introduction to the second volume of the history that "I have enjoyed more true solid Repose in six Months here, than in thrice the same Number of Years before." The introduction to volume two, which was published in 1718, reveals the combined effects on the author of solitude and society's ingratitude. Out of seven pages of introductory text, Ockley uses three full pages to address the supposed critics of volume one (and to address them none too admiringly) and another three to bemoan his situation and the lack of support he continually faced. Moreover, Ockley had begun to mention in letters to friends that he was beset by an evil spirit ("cacodaemon") that distracted his days and disrupted his nights.

His friends—at long last—collected together the funds necessary to free him, but aside from some incidental annotations to William Wotton's *Miscellaneous Discourses,* Ockley never published another thing after the second volume of his history. Letters written later from Swavesy indicate that when he walked out of Cambridge Castle after eighteen months in prison, he brought the demon with him. Ockley seemed never to recover, and in fact died a short time later, on 9 August 1720.

Edward Gibbon, author of *The History of the Decline and Fall of the Roman Empire* (1776–1788), much admired Ockley's work and, according to Arberry, relied on Ockley heavily in those chapters devoted to the Arabians. Nevertheless, less than a hundred years after Ockley's death, Leiden University professor H. A. Hamaker demonstrated that Ockley's primary source for *The Conquest of Syria, Persia, and Egypt, by the Saracens* was much older than Ockley thought and far less reliable. Ockley's scholarly work, therefore, became useless within a few generations. His true innovation, however, was to hold apparently earlier manuscripts to be the more authoritative, combined with a new voice, one that allowed the Arabian conquerors to use their own natural speech to tell their story. Simon Ockley was the first English historian to attempt such a feat, and it secured his place as a great historian long after the accuracy of his history had been disproven. Ockley knew he was in

uncharted territory, and in the introduction to his second volume, specifically warned that ". . . no one ought to wonder if I have accommodated my style to the humour of the people of whom I write. To write of men in their circumstances, who were all humorists, bigots, and enthusiasts, in the same style as becomes the sedateness and gravity of the Greeks and Romans, would be most unsuitable and unnatural. In such a case you put them in a dress which they would no more thank you for than a Roman senator would for a long periwig, or Socrates for a pair of silk stockings." The combination of native voice with his own gift for storytelling made Ockley's history the standard text long after more accurate sources had been discovered.

References:

A. J. Arberry. *Oriental Essays: Portraits of Seven Scholars* (New York: Macmillan, 1960);

Daniel Defoe, *Essay upon Projects, Blackmask Online, Provider of Internet Literature* <http://etext/adelaide.edu.au> [accessed 26 January 2007];

Isaac Disraeli, *Calamities and Quarrels of Authors* (London: Frederick Warne, 1859);

P. M. Holt, "The Study of Islam in Seventeenth- and Eighteenth-Century England," *Journal of Early Modern History,* 2 (May 1998);

"Letters to Simon Ockley, 1699 [i.e. 1700]–1718," Beinicke Library, Yale University (Gen. Mss. 90);

"Simon Ockley," *Dictionary of National Biography,* edited by Sir Leslie Stephen and Sir Sidney Lee (London: Humphrey Milford, 1937–1938).

Charles O'Conor of Belanagare

(1 January 1709/1710 – 1 July 1791)

Seán Patrick Donlan
University of Limerick

BOOKS: *Dissertations on the Antient History of Ireland: Wherein an Account Is Given of the Origine, Government, Letters, Sciences, Religion, Manners and Customs, of the Antient Inhabitants,* anonymous (Dublin: Printed by J. Hoey, for the editor, M. Reilly, 1753); second edition, enlarged and republished as *Dissertations on the Antient History of Ireland: Wherein an Account Is Given of the Origine, Government, Letters, Sciences, Religion, Manners and Customs, of the Antient Inhabitants. To Which Is Subjoined a Dissertation on the Irish Colonies Established in Britain with Some Remarks on Mr. Macpherson's Translation of Fingal and Temora* (Dublin: George Faulkner, 1766);

The Case of the Roman-Catholics of Ireland: Wherein the Principles and Conduct of That Party Are Fully Explained and Vindicated (Dublin: Printed for P. Lord, 1755);

The Principles of the Roman-Catholics Exhibited in Some Useful Observations on a Pamphlet Intituled Plain Matters of Fact Humbly Recommended to the Consideration of the Roman-Catholics of Ireland (Dublin: Printed for and sold by P. Lord, 1756);

Statistical Account of the Parish of Kilronan in Ireland and of the Neighbouring District. 1773 (Dublin: N.p., 1773; Edinburgh: N.p., 1798);

Observations on the Popery Laws, by O'Conor and John Curry (Dublin, 1774).

SELECTED PERIODICAL PUBLICATION–
UNCOLLECTED: "Letter to David Hume, on Some Misrepresentations in His History of Great Britain," *Gentleman's Museum* (April–May 1763): 55–64, 65–78.

OTHER: "A Dissertation on the Origin and Antiquities of the Ancient Scots," in Roderic O'Flaherty, *The Ogygia Vindicated: Against the Objections of Sir George Mackenzie, King's Advocate for Scotland in the Reign of King James II,* edited by O'Conor (Dublin: George Faulkner, 1775).

The last of the Gaelic Catholic aristocracy, Charles O'Conor of Belanagare was at the center of

Charles O'Conor of Belanagare (photograph of miniature by permission of the Royal Irish Academy © RIA; Royal Irish Academy)

Irish historiography for much of the eighteenth century. His status permitted him to move freely among both Catholic and Protestant Irish literati. His scholarship, especially the two editions of the *Dissertations on the Antient History of Ireland* (1753, 1766) linked Irish bardic history to eighteenth-century enlightenment. O'Conor was, however, never able to write a comprehensive historical narrative and was equally unsuccessful in finding a moderate Protestant to write a "philosophical history" of Ireland, free of confessional prejudice. His own faith was linked to his works and to his historical writings; he added many political pamphlets critiquing the ethical and economic costs of the Irish penal (or "Popery") laws then imposed, to varying degrees, on Catholics and dissenters.

O'Conor was born on 1 January 1709/1710 at Knockmore, county Sligo, son of Donnchadh Liath O'Conor and Máire Ní Ruairc (Mary O'Ruark). The O'Conors descended from the last nominal high king of Ireland, Ruaidhrí O Conchobhair, defeated in the Anglo-Norman conquest. Because of their loyalty to the Jacobite cause in the seventeenth century, much of the family's land had been confiscated. By 1720, however, the O'Conors were able to reclaim a small Roscommon estate at Belanagare, held—as was the necessary fiction under the penal laws—through a Protestant family. The family continued the Gaelic tradition of patronage of the arts, and the famous poet-harpist Turlough O'Carolan dedicated songs to both Charles and his father. A native Irish speaker, O'Conor studied Irish history as well as the classics under a variety of teachers. Among these was his uncle, Tadhg Ó Ruairc (Thaddeus O'Rourke), the Catholic bishop of Killala, clergy often being ignored, if not sanctioned, under the penal laws. O'Conor also studied in Dublin. Through historian John Fergus (Seán mac Macraith Ó Fearghusa), he was introduced to the circle of poet-teacher Tadhg Ó Neachtáin and began his first translations of Irish texts. On O'Conor's marriage to Catherine O'Hagan (1731), he returned to Belanagare and the life of an "improving" gentleman farmer. With his wife's death a decade later (1741), O'Conor returned to his studies, amassing what became a considerable library of ancient and Enlightenment materials.

During this period, O'Conor's reputation as a scholar had already begun to grow, and he associated with both Catholic and Protestant thinkers. His first essay into history was a proposed collaboration with Irish Protestant playwright and pamphleteer Henry Brooke. While the truth remains unclear, Brooke seems to have attempted to use O'Conor's material as his own. The two men remained linked, however, as adversaries and allies, for two decades. O'Conor also began a lifelong friendship with John Curry, a Catholic physician with whom he shared both political and historical interests. In the following decades, the two wrote or sponsored many pamphlets criticizing the restrictions of the penal laws on religious practice, education, and property ownership. Curry wrote several historical works on the Irish rebellion of 1641 and engaged in debate with Protestant historian Walter Harris. Among other events, the rebellion remained significant to eighteenth-century Ireland. Coming as it did at the eclipse of Gaelic Ireland, confiscation and settlement, it confirmed a shift from colonial to confessional divisions. Portrayed

as a series of Catholic atrocities, Protestant alarm and triumphalism set the tone for the next century.

O'Conor's first significant historical work was the anonymous *Dissertations on the Antient History of Ireland,* drawing materials perhaps from his aborted collaboration with Brooke. *Dissertations on the Antient History of Ireland* may have been prepared and out of his hands in the years before publication, and he was always somewhat apologetic about its quality. In the assorted essays that make up the work, O'Conor wavered between a history of "manners" (or, anachronistically, "culture") and a chronology of kings. To substantiate the accounts of Irish medieval chronologists, he compared them with Isaac Newton's *Chronology of Ancient Kingdoms Amended* (1728). Newton appeared to validate the Irish writers, a similarity more accurately explained by common sources. O'Conor also made extensive use of bardic sources, following them in portraying the existence of a civil and literate culture in pre-Christian Ireland, developed independently of Greek and Roman civilization.

But *Dissertations on the Antient History of Ireland* is unquestionably "enlightened" in spirit, and O'Conor displays a genuine concern for source materials. He shows a familiarity, and some sympathy, with John Toland's critical portrayal of the Druids and stresses an ancient, balanced constitution of church and state. Employing contemporary language of commonwealth and republican thought, in the 1766 edition he projected English models of government, complete with "glorious revolutions" and "patriot kings," into the Irish past. "The contrast between liberty and faction," he wrote, "can be found in no history better illustrated than in that of Ireland." With the introduction of Christianity, Ireland's primacy in European scholarship and theology was secured. Its civilization and unwritten constitution were not without internal disorders. Both, O'Conor notes, were significantly undermined by successive assaults of the Scandinavian-Viking ancestors of the Anglo-Normans.

Dissertations on the Antient History of Ireland garnered notice both at home and abroad—mentioned, for example, shortly after its publication by the Abbé James MacGeoghan in his *Histoire d'Irlande* (1758–1762). Irish printer George Faulkner, founding member of Dublin's Physico-Historical Society and friend of O'Conor, sent a copy of the work to Samuel Johnson, English Tory writer and wit. With many others, Johnson unsuccessfully pressed O'Conor to write a comprehensive narrative of Irish history, ancient and modern. (His letters were included in James Boswell's *The Life of Samuel Johnson, LL.D.* [1791].) For his part, O'Conor hoped to have Johnson write in defense of Irish Catholics, perhaps the first of his many attempts to enlist Protestants in public critiques of the penal laws. He also assisted

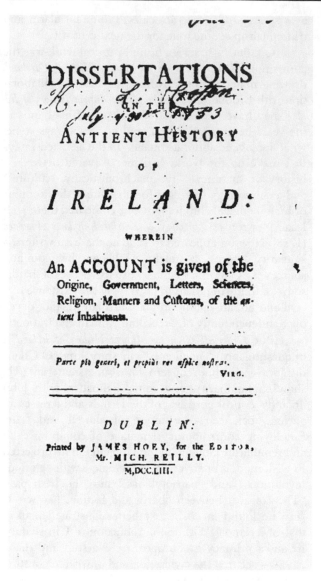

DISSERTATIONS

ON THE

ANTIENT HISTORY

OF

I R E L A N D:

WHEREIN

An ACCOUNT is given of the
Origine, Government, Letters, Sciences,
Religion, Manners and Customs, of the antient Inhabitants.

Parte plù generi, et propriù res aspice nostras.
　　　　　　　　　　　　　　VIRG.

D U B L I N:

Printed by JAMES HOEY, for the EDITOR,
Mr. MICH. REILLY.
M,DCC,LIII.

Title page for the first edition of O'Conor's 1753 history of Ireland (Eighteenth-Century Collections Online, Gale Group)

historian and English Whig statesman George, fourth Baron Lyttleton, whose *The History of the Life of King Henry II and of the Age in Which He Lived* (1767) included the invasion of Ireland. O'Conor's political activities continued, too, and with Curry he founded the Catholic Association (later the Catholic Committee) in 1756 to underline Catholic loyalty and to press for reform. Surprisingly, O'Conor and the Catholic Committee arranged for Brooke, now sympathetic to the Catholic cause, to argue that the penal laws were against both the general and Protestant interests. While Brooke again proposed a joint history, O'Conor declined.

Shortly after publication of the *Dissertations on the Antient History of Ireland,* Scottish historian and philosopher David Hume began publishing the volumes of his

History of England (1754–1762). O'Conor saw Hume's portrayal of the native and Catholic Irish as uncritically repeating the more offensive and prejudicial of the histories of Ireland, especially in discussing the Irish Brehon Laws and the rebellion of 1641. He unfavorably contrasted Hume's "declamation" against the traditional Irish laws with contemporary penal statutes. Similarly, Hume's account of the rebellion of 1641 followed the most prejudiced sources, grossly exaggerating the number of Protestants killed by Catholics (to several hundred thousand instead of several thousand). O'Conor spent a considerable amount of energy trying to convince Hume of this error, sending both Curry's works and his own. Increasingly frustrated by his efforts, O'Conor finally published a public "Letter to David Hume" in an obscure English monthly. Notable for his skepticism toward religious sources, O'Conor wrote of Hume: "you carry credulity to all the excesses of monastic faith in the darkest period of its resignation." In these efforts, he had important allies—not least, Scottish historian Tobias Smollet and fellow Irishman Edmund Burke, the latter sharing many of O'Conor's views. Despite these efforts, Hume made only minor adjustments in future editions. In this intellectual context, O'Conor wrote Burke (25 April 1765), comparing "the Ages of Barbarism and Ignorance" to their "own enlightened Days of Good Sense and Sound Policy."

Disagreements between Irish and Scottish historians were not new but had developed additional importance at mid century. Earlier, Scottish priest Thomas Innes had, for example, in his *Critical Essay on the Ancient Inhabitants of the Northern Parts of Britain or Scotland* (1729), challenged the ancient Irish civility presented by the bardic traditions and the idea that Ireland was originally settled by migration from Scotland. The poems of James Macpherson, presented as the work of a third-century poet, Ossian, revised these debates. O'Conor did not initially take the poems seriously, but the popularity of Macpherson's works and claims of their historical veracity made a critique necessary. While the primitivism of the "Ossian" poems fit nicely the progressive stadialism of Scottish thought, it was a challenge to O'Conor's portrayal of an early, literate Irish civilization. His first response was simply to assist English ecclesiastical writer Ferdinando Warner, whose nationality suggested neutrality. O'Conor provided materials for Warner's *Remarks on the History of Fingal* (1762), his critique of Macpherson, and his *History of Ireland* (1763).

On the basis of these debates, the second edition of O'Conor's *Dissertations on the Antient History of Ireland* was far more detailed, scholarly, and skeptical than the first. While he never relinquished his focus on the succession of Irish kings, O'Conor repeatedly underscored the relationship of "manners" to political and legal institutions. Given the failure of the Anglo Normans to bring the Irish under a uniform system of law after the conquest of Ireland, according to the 1766 *Dissertations on the Antient History of Ireland,* only these native manners prevented the nation from "sinking into absolute barbarism." He also notes, in line with Charles-Louis de Secondat, baron de Montesquieu, the historical appropriateness of different laws to diverse societies and historical periods. The Brehon Laws most criticized by writers such as Hume, according to O'Conor, "never prevailed more, than when this country became the prime seat of literary knowledge to all Christendom." Drawing together his historical and political themes, O'Conor wrote:

> Who could imagine, that men, in whom our Tanist and Agrarian Laws excite so much horror, should themselves be the inhabitants of a country, wherein two-thirds of the people live in a state of despondency and invincible poverty! What Tanistry Law, in the days of anarchy, could produce more politic evil, than such men experience in days of the profoundest repose.

For O'Conor, there was no little irony in the critique of the Brehon Laws on the basis of prohibiting social and economic progress in Ireland when the penal laws did so by design.

To the second edition, O'Conor also appended a "Dissertation on the First Migrations and Final Settlement of the Scots in North Britain; with Occasional Observations on the Poems of *Fingal* and *Temor.*" In it, he discussed long-standing disagreements with Scottish historians. Generations of writers, he wrote, had "persuaded themselves, and endeavored to persuade others, that the Irish . . . so celebrated through all Europe . . . were natives of the Highlands of North-Britain . . .!" With Warner and Samuel Johnson, he was also sharply critical of Macpherson. O'Conor noted his amazement that the poems of an "illiterate bard" could be preserved "through the clear stream of oral tradition, through so short a period as eleven hundred years" without considerable changes in language and manners. "The modern *sentiments, manners, customs* and *allusions,* they contain," he wrote, "affix them to *modern* times. . . ." In his correspondence of 4 July 1781, he added, in agreement with modern historiography, that "it may for the future pass for what it really is, an ingenious forgery, which as it proved entertaining to many, can be injurious to none, except to those who believe it useful in their researches concerning British antiquities."

O'Conor continued to encourage others to write against the Irish penal laws. He was largely responsible for ghostwriting Nicholas, Viscount Taaffe's *Observations on Affairs in Ireland, from the Settlement of 1691 to the Present Time* (1756). He also attempted to find writers to translate Irish annals, an idea he invariably ascribed to Burke. He provided materials to Francis Stoughton Sullivan, an Irish speaker, Protestant, and first Professor of Feudal and English law at the University of Dublin. Sullivan's early death and the apparent reluctance of the Dublin gentry to fund the project ensured that little progress was made. Again with Burke, O'Conor attempted throughout the 1760s to find sympathetic Protestant writers to take up the challenge of an impartial or "philosophical" history of Ireland. Through Faulkner, O'Conor met Thomas Leland—writer, professor of oratory, and librarian at the University of Dublin. O'Conor believed Leland "would fill such a post with Dignity" (*Letters,* 13 June 1767), and the two developed a warm friendship. Leland collected Irish manuscripts for the university and arranged for O'Conor to have access to the library, a privilege otherwise denied him as a Catholic.

O'Conor in turn assisted Leland with translations of manuscripts provided by Burke, but along with Burke and Curry, he was deeply disappointed with Leland's subsequent *History of Ireland* (1773) and even encouraged Curry to issue a critique. O'Conor continued, however, to move in both Catholic and Protestant circles. Through the efforts of the eccentric, enthusiastic Charles Vallancey, an English army officer then in Ireland who sought to link the Irish with Phoenician culture, the Dublin Society established a "Select Committee" to encourage the study of Irish antiquities. The committee provided a real opportunity to establish common ground between the communities. Through Leland, O'Conor was invited to join as an honorary member. The committee also became affiliated with Irish Catholic antiquarians in Paris, and even John Carpenter, the Catholic archbishop of Dublin, was introduced to and warmly received by its members. Among its first projects was the 1775 translation of Roderic O'Flaherty's (Ruarí Ó Flaithearta) *Ogygia Vindicated,* a seventeenth-century defense, published posthumously, of the Irish origins of the Scots of "North-Britain." O'Conor included notes and another essay underlining his critique of Macpherson.

In the 1770s and 1780s, O'Conor remained in contact with a wide variety of historians. He corresponded with the Chevalier Thomas O'Gorman, Sylvester O'Halloran, and Scottish historian John Pinkerton. When the members of the newly-formed Hibernian Antiquarian Society (1779) attempted to revive antiquarian study, the ever-present Vallancey offered his series, the *Collectanea de rebus hibernicis,* as their official publication. O'Conor submitted several minor pieces. But the journal quickly became the site of historiographical disagreement. O'Conor, and in more exaggerated forms, Vallancey and O'Halloran, continued to defend an ancient, civilized Ireland whose distant ancestors had come by way of Spain. A new generation of Protestant historians, especially Edward Ledwich and William Beauford, suggested instead that Ireland was populated by Scandinavian barbarians. Along with Thomas Campbell, they argued that Irish civility had only come with the Anglo-Norman conquest.

O'Conor was repeatedly distracted from his attempts to respond to these attacks. His youngest brother, Hugh, a convert (at least temporarily) to Protestantism, filed a bill under the penal laws against him (1777). Hugh sued for the whole of the family estate, leading to a prolonged series of lawsuits and a brief period of house arrest for O'Conor in Dublin (1779). Settled out of court six years later, the suit also exacted great financial and physical costs from him. Vallancey, now involved in the creation of the Royal Irish Academy (1785), arranged for an annual pension for the elderly O'Conor with the promise to leave his manuscripts to the academy. Charles O'Conor continued to assist other Protestant writers turning to the Gaelic past, most notably Joseph Cooper Walker and Charlotte Brooke, daughter of Henry Brooke. He continued, too, to work on a comprehensive history, but it remained incomplete at his death on 1 July 1791. On his instructions, his unfinished works were destroyed.

Although he never completed a comprehensive history of Ireland, Charles O'Conor of Belanagare was at the center of Irish historiography for much of the eighteenth century. His life and writings are essential for understanding Irish Catholic life in the period.

Letters:

R. E. Ward, J. F. Wrynn, and C. C. Ward, eds., *The Letters of Charles O'Conor of Belanagare: A Catholic Voice in Eighteenth-Century Ireland* (Washington: Catholic University of America, 1988).

References:

David Berman, "David Hume on the 1641 Rebellion in Ireland," *Studies,* 65 (1976): 101–112;

John Patrick Delury, "Ex conflictu et collisione: The Failure of Irish Historiography, 1745 to 1790," *Eighteenth-Century Ireland/Iris an dá chultúr,* 15 (2000): 9–37;

Ann De Valera, "Antiquarian and Historical Investigations in Ireland in the Eighteenth Century," thesis, University College, Dublin, 1978;

Hilary Larkin, "'A Dull Nation amidst the Great'?: An Irish Voice in the European Enlightenment," thesis, University College, Dublin, 2001;

Joep Leerssen, *Mere Irish and Fíor-Ghael: Studies in the Idea of Irish Nationality, its Development and Literary Expression Prior to the Nineteenth Century* (Cork: Cork University, 1996);

Walter D. Love, "Charles O'Conor of Belanagare and Thomas Leland's 'philosophical' history of Ireland," *Irish Historical Studies,* 13 (1962): 1–25;

Diarmuid Ó Catháin, "Charles O'Conor of Belanagare: Antiquary and Irish Scholar," *Journal of the Royal Society of Antiquaries of Ireland,* 119 (1989): 136–163;

Clare O'Halloran, "Golden Ages and Barbarous Nations: Antiquarian Debate on the Celtic Past in Ireland and Scotland in the Eighteenth Century," dissertation, University of Cambridge 1991;

Nessa Ní Shéaghdha, "Irish Scholars and Scribes in Eighteenth-Century Dublin," *Eighteenth-Century Ireland/Iris an dá chultúr,* 4 (1989): 41–54.

Papers:

The papers of Charles O'Conor of Belanagare are located in the Ashburnham Collection at the Royal Irish Academy, Dublin, and at the Clonalis House, Castlrea, county Roscommon in the O'Conor Don papers.

Sylvester O'Halloran

(31 December 1728 – 11 August 1807)

Mercy Cannon
Stephen F. Austin State University

BOOKS: *A New Treatise on the Glaucoma: or Cataract* (Dublin: Printed by S. Powell, 1750);

A Critical Analysis of the New Operation for a Cataract (Dublin: Printed by S. Powell, 1755);

A Complete Treatise on Gangrene and Sphacelus: With a New Method of Amputation (Dublin: P. Wilson / London: Paul Vaillant, 1765);

Insula Sacra; or, The General Utilities Arising from Some Permanent Foundation, for the Preservation of our Antient Annals Demonstrated, and the Means Pointed Out (Limerick: Printed by T. Welsh, 1770);

An Introduction to the Study of the History and Antiquities of Ireland: In Which the Assertions of Mr. Hume and Other Writers Are Occasionally Considered (Dublin: Printed by Thomas Ewing, 1772; London: Printed for J. Murray, 1772);

Ierne Defended; or, A Candid Refutation of Such Passages in the Rev. Dr. Leland's and the Rev. Dr. Whitaker's Works as Seem to Affect the Authenticity and Validity of Antient Irish History (Dublin, 1774);

A General History of Ireland, from the Earliest Accounts to the Close of the Twelfth Century, Collected from the Most Authentic Records. In Which New and Interesting Lights Are Thrown on the Remote Histories of Other Nations as Well as of Both Britains, 2 volumes (London: Printed by A. Hamilton for the author, 1778);

A New Treatise on the Different Disorders Arising from External Injuries of the Head (London: Printed by J. J. & G. Robinson, 1793; Dublin: Printed by Zachariah Jackson for W. Gilbert, 1793).

SELECTED PERIODICAL PUBLICATIONS–
UNCOLLECTED: "The Poems of Ossine, the Sone of Fionne Mac Comhal, Reclaimed: By a Milesian," as Miso-Dolos, *Dublin Magazine* (January 1763).

Although he is categorized with major Irish historians such as Charles O'Conor, Charles Vallancey, and John Cutter, Sylvester O'Halloran is regarded as a minor figure in the field of history. His most notable

Sylvester O'Halloran (from <http://www.clarelibrary.ie/eolas/coclare/ genealogy/ohalloran_family.html>)

achievements were actually in the medical profession, in which his surgical innovations and medical treatises received much approbation both in his lifetime and in future generations. Minor though O'Halloran may be, modern critics often mention his notable part in the nationalist movement that worked to recover a heroic Gaelic past, striving against cultural representations of the Irish as barbaric, savage, and wild. This change in representation was registered primarily in literary endeavors rather than in political and social fields. Clare O'Halloran explains that O'Halloran and other eighteenth-century antiquarians "invented a glorious pre-colonial past which contrasted with their present perceived situation as colonial subjects." While O'Halloran's historical accuracy has since been largely discredited, he retains an important place in the national mythmaking efforts of eighteenth-century Irish patriots.

O'Halloran was born on 31 December 1728 to Michael and Mary O'Halloran of Caherdavin, County Clare, Ireland. While there is little record of O'Halloran's childhood, critics view his family connection to Gaelic poet Sean Claragh McDonnell (Sean Clarach MacDomhnaill) as significant. McDonnell taught young O'Halloran the Gaelic language and apparently left him with a passionate interest in ancient Ireland. In addition to his education by McDonnell, O'Halloran attended a Limerick school run by a Protestant minister. Ronan Sheehan suggests that by age eleven O'Halloran had already decided to become a physician. Although his aptitude for medical study made him an excellent candidate for the university, O'Halloran's Catholicism hampered his professional aspirations. Because Catholics in Ireland were denied access to universities, O'Halloran studied and trained abroad, attending Catholic universities in Leyden and Paris.

O'Halloran returned to Limerick in 1749 to begin practicing medicine. Throughout the 1750s and 1760s he concentrated on building his medical practice and gained much admiration for his publications. He wrote several medical treatises—including *A New Treatise on the Glaucoma* (1750), *A Critical Analysis of the New Operation for a Cataract* (1755), *A Complete Treatise on Gangrene and Sphacelus: With a New Method of Amputation* (1765), and later, *A New Treatise on the Different Disorders Arising from External Injuries of the Head* (1793). His personal life also seemed prosperous and agreeable. In 1752 he married Mary O'Casey, whom he described in his diary as "amiable in her person, of the sweetest, and most human disposition possessed of the most exalted principles of Religion"; they had one daughter and four sons. O'Halloran contributed to civic life by participating in such organizations as the Free Debating Society and the Citizens of Limerick Committee and by founding the Limerick Infirmary in 1760. His role in creating the Royal College of Surgeons, however, is considered his most meaningful and lasting achievement. His "Proposals for the Advancement of Surgery in Ireland," appended to the 1765 *A Complete Treatise on Gangrene and Sphacelus,* mapped out a series of professional and organizational reforms that were adopted by the medical community. His reputation was secured when the Dublin Society of Surgeons, founded in 1780, and the Royal College of Surgeons, founded in 1784, both elected him an honorary member of their associations. A successful professional man and an active citizen, O'Halloran represented a new order—the Catholic middle class, which, like the English middle class, rose in the eighteenth century.

Among O'Halloran's many correspondents, O'Conor was the most considerable. O'Conor, a prominent eighteenth-century historian, published the influential *Dissertations on the Antient History of Ireland* in 1753 and continued to shape the field of historical scholarship for decades. As O'Halloran began to devote his leisure time to the study of Irish history, his warm professional relationship with O'Conor seems to have facilitated his efforts. Letters between the two indicate O'Conor's support and approval of O'Halloran's work, and O'Halloran appeared grateful for this encouragement, even answering O'Conor's request for medical advice on eye problems.

O'Halloran began his historical work partially in response to the Ossian debate, which began in the 1760s. Between 1760 and 1763, James MacPherson published three volumes that he claimed were translations of poems by Ossian, a third-century Scottish bard. Enthusiastically received by European literary circles, these poems chronicled the battles of Fingal, king of Morvan and Ossian's father, and demonstrated the innocent, Irish primitivism of a lost age. Some critics, however, were suspicious of MacPherson's claims. O'Conor in particular challenged the authorship of the poems, and his exchanges with O'Halloran on the subject influenced the latter's opinion. O'Halloran, who wrote the first Irish response to the Ossian poems in January 1763, initially thought that the poems were authentic, if corrupted by time and translation. His primary goal was to attribute the poems to Irish rather than Scottish sources. After corresponding with O'Conor, O'Halloran wrote a second article, in August 1763, which was much more critical of MacPherson's historicism; yet, O'Halloran remained convinced that Ossian was in fact the author of the poems until O'Conor finally persuaded him otherwise. Several years later, with the publication of his first history, O'Halloran forcibly repudiated MacPherson's poems. O'Halloran's participation in the Ossian debates marked not only the beginning of his engagement with Irish history but also his particular approach to Irish history as chivalric and noble.

Insula Sacra; or, The General Utilities Arising from Some Permanent Foundation, for the Preservation of our Antient Annals Demonstrated, and the Means Pointed Out (1770) was a transition work for O'Halloran. The Ossian articles he had written several years previously were published under the psuedonym "Miso-Dolos," but O'Halloran claimed *Insula Sacra* with his own name. At this point, he was prepared to accept either praise or criticism as he expressed his beliefs and arguments regarding Irish history. The title refers to the "Sacred Island" of Ireland

and indicates O'Halloran's deep reverence for its national past. In this work he argues for the preservation of Irish annals, citing their valuable role in establishing the ancient culture of Ireland. Ever practical, O'Halloran suggested the possibility of establishing an institution responsible for storing, categorizing, and protecting the documents. This proposal met with little interest and was eventually abandoned, although many scholars shared his passion for the manuscripts. Because *Insula Sacra* does not provide much historical information, however, it is generally viewed as a precursor to O'Halloran's more-significant volumes.

O'Halloran's major historical works were published in the 1770s. These chronicles of Ireland followed what is now called the Oriental system of ancient Irish history. With this approach O'Halloran joined Roderic O'Flaherty, John Toland, Vallancey, and O'Conor in their assertions of a sophisticated pre-Christian Ireland. In his first full-length study, *An Introduction to the Study of the History and Antiquities of Ireland* (1772), O'Halloran presented his claims that the Milesians, the first settlers in Ireland, came through Spain, bringing with them the highest achievements of literate eastern civilizations. Although little archeological evidence was available to O'Halloran and other historians, at least several medieval manuscripts provided some support for this theory. According to *An Introduction to the Study of the History and Antiquities of Ireland,* the peaceful Milesians followed a pagan natural religion that was ultimately compatible with the Christian teachings of St. Patrick. In fact, argued O'Halloran, their Druidic faith rendered their minds so receptive to Christianity that the transition developed with little conflict or divisiveness. Such continuity signified the stability of Irish culture as well as the inherent rationality that prevented unruly responses to historical changes.

An Introduction to the Study of the History and Antiquities of Ireland also discusses the development of Irish linguistics. This interest may initially appear disconnected from O'Halloran's historical scholarship, but in the context of nationalism such work takes on immediate relevance. O'Halloran explained that the Gaelic language was but one indication among many that the Milesian culture neither originated from, nor was influenced by, Roman and Greek civilizations. After studying the Milesians' scientific terminology, O'Halloran concluded that "they borrowed little from, whatever they have lent to, other nations." O'Conor and O'Halloran exchanged letters on the subject, and O'Conor certainly advanced this thesis in his own works. Although modern scholars dismiss O'Halloran's claims about the Irish language as wildly inaccurate, the picture that emerges from his description of the ancients is one of a complex, cultured, and intellectual people—a civilization to rival that

A

GENERAL HISTORY

OF

IRELAND,

FROM THE

EARLIEST ACCOUNTS

TO THE

CLOSE of the TWELFTH CENTURY,

COLLECTED FROM THE

MOST AUTHENTIC RECORDS.

IN WHICH

New and interesting Lights are thrown on the remote Histories of other Nations as well as of both BRITAINS,

BY Mr. O'HALLORAN,

Author of an Introduction to the History and Antiquities of Ireland.

IN TWO VOLUMES.

VOL. I.

LONDON,

Printed for the AUTHOR, by A. HAMILTON:

And sold by G. ROBINSON, Pater-noster-Row; J. MURRAY, N° 32, Fleet-street; J. ROBSON, New Bond-street: and by Mess. FAULKNER, HOEY, and WILSON, in Dublin.

MDCCLXXVIII.

Title page for O'Halloran's 1778 history (from Eighteenth-Century Collections Online, Gale Group)

of Greece or Rome. Charlotte Brooke, in *Reliques of Irish Poetry* (1789), describes *An Introduction to the Study of the History and Antiquities of Ireland* as "a work fraught with learning, rich with the treasures of ages, and animated by the very soul of Patriotism, and of genuine Honor!"

In 1774 O'Halloran published *Ierne Defended,* which challenged Thomas Leland's *History of Ireland* (1773). Leland's stated goal was impartiality, since he believed objectivity was lacking in many historical accounts. Nevertheless, his depiction of the Irish Rebellion of 1641 was as emotionally charged and subjective as any eighteenth-century antiquarian's work. Since discussions of the Rebellion provoked much passion among patriots, even more than a century later, Leland's anti-Catholic account antagonized many. In "Edmund Burke and an Irish Historiography Controversy" Walter D. Love claims that the Rebellion "most often was urged against the Irish as historical proof of their incorrigible treachery." No wonder, then, that

O'Halloran vehemently opposed Leland's *History of Ireland,* which cast the Irish—and especially Irish Catholics—as bloodthirsty hooligans. O'Halloran's defense included many of the same themes that occur in all his histories: the Irish descended from a civilized, learned people who valued a peaceful, orderly life. Although his scholarly works typically remained within the medieval period, he understood the political implications of historical representation. For the Irish, to be portrayed as wild, savage primitives in any era undermined their heritage, their national identity, and ultimately their political power. Viewed as incapable of governing themselves, the Irish would be permanently colonized and regulated by the English. Thus, O'Halloran had a compelling motive to write *Ierne Defended,* as well as his other histories.

A *General History of Ireland* (1778) reemphasized and expanded the arguments of *An Introduction to the Study of the History and Antiquities of Ireland.* According to John Patrick Delury in "Ex Conflictu, Et Collisione," the romantic and emotional tone of this work made O'Halloran "the antiquarian of exclamation points." *A General History of Ireland,* O'Halloran's largest historical work, presented the religious, political, and social structure of the Milesian civilization. In addition to their natural—though pagan—religion, the ancient Milesians practiced a form of constitutional government that enabled its citizens to prosper economically, commercially, intellectually, and artistically. Their social structure included ranks of nobles, officials, merchants, artisans, scholars, and scientists, indicating once more an illustrious culture rather than a barbaric tribalism.

The Milesians also distinguished themselves by carefully recording historical events: each province had an official recorder who offered his accounts every three years to a national assembly that would confirm or deny the veracity of the history. Such a methodical system for preserving the past surely appealed to an historian, and O'Halloran implied in *A General History of Ireland* that any hint of fabrication in historical scholarship deserved the greatest of punishments. Further, by detailing the Milesians' historical preservation, he verified the reliability of his source material. O'Halloran attributed a kind of purity and merit to the native record against the new systems of history and philosophical inquiry that distorted the truth of the past.

Some critics have suggested that O'Halloran is properly categorized as an antiquarian—one who rarely offers solid proof of events and persons—rather than an historian. Indeed, O'Halloran's often biased and speculative histories lack the scholarly rigor that characterized later works on the past of Ireland. The problems with O'Halloran's histories reflect a problem with Irish historiography in general. Scholars agree that eighteenth-century Irish historians struggled with a deep need to gloss over social divisions and historical discontinuities in order to show the glorious past of contemporary Ireland. Historians such as Vallancey and O'Conor stressed the continuity of Irish history as a means to solidify national identity. Because historical narratives were often subject to political agendas, many of these Irish scholars and antiquarians felt obligated to promote positive versions of the development of Ireland. Political tension and social insecurity rendered objectivity difficult and impracticable, especially when recording events of the sixteenth and seventeenth centuries. O'Halloran's failure as an historian, it seems, assured his success as a nationalist. In *The History of Limerick* (1789), John Ferrar celebrates this bias: O'Halloran "not only appears skillful in his profession [medicine], but learned in the Irish language and ancient laws, and a warm advocate for the honour and interests of his native country."

The impact of Sylvester O'Halloran's vision of Irish history was substantial. Joseph Walker, for example, utilized O'Halloran's historical works as he completed *Historical Memoirs of the Irish Bards* (1786). O'Halloran was also a significant influence on Brooke, particularly in her *Reliques of Irish Poetry,* for which he wrote an introduction. Clare O'Halloran in "Irish Re-Creations" further notes that Lady Morgan's novel *The Wild Irish Girl* (1807) "presented the O'Halloran case for Gaelic Ireland as the home of European chivalry and learning." Maria Edgeworth's assessment of O'Halloran's *A General History of Ireland* was less than flattering. In *An Essay on Irish Bulls* (1802), Edgeworth hinted that "the incensed irish [sic] historian, Mr. O'Halloran" was "violently anxious" to prove the superiority and autonomy of ancient Ireland, while she found such arguments "a matter of indifference." Nevertheless, one of the characters in her later novel *The Absentee* (1856) was named after O'Halloran: Count O'Halloran is an apparently positive figure who, according to Robert Tracy, is closely linked to Irish tradition and its Catholic past, both of which Edgeworth supported. O'Halloran's work also indirectly influenced the national literature of the nineteenth and twentieth centuries. Standish James O'Grady, whose historical volumes prompted the Irish literary revival, described *A General History of Ireland* as his greatest inspiration. Reading this work, O'Grady declared in an essay, "governed the general trend of my life, and through me that of others."

On 11 August 1807 O'Halloran died at home in Limerick. The obituary that ran in *The Dublin Journal* four days later commemorated his accomplishments in medicine and history and noted his kind disposition. While his historical work now simply provides modern scholars with an example of eighteenth-century thought and politics, O'Halloran's scientific legacy continues to be honored, as his name distinguishes conferences and medical buildings. His work in both fields attests to his boundless energy and interest in human life.

Letters:

"The Letters," 2 parts, edited by John B. Lyons, *North Munster Antiquarian Journal*, 9, no. 1 (1962): 169–181; no. 2 (1963): 25–50; republished as *The Letters,* edited by Lyons (1962?).

References:

D. George Boyce, *Nationalism in Ireland* (Baltimore: Johns Hopkins University Press, 1982);

Charlotte Brooke, *Reliques of Irish Poetry* (Dublin, 1789);

John Patrick Delury, "Ex Conflictu, Et Collisione: The Failure of Irish Historiography, 1745 to 1790," *Eighteenth-Century Ireland,* 15 (2000): 9–37;

Maria Edgeworth, *An Essay on Irish Bulls* (New York: Garland, 1979);

John Ferrar, *The History of Limerick, Ecelesiastical, Civil and Military: From the Earliest Records, to the Year 1787 . . .* (Limerick: A. Watson, 1787);

Jacqueline R. Hill, "Popery and Protestantism, Civil and Religious Liberty: The Disputed Lessons of Irish History 1690–1812," *Past and Present,* 0, no. 118 (1988): 96–129;

Colin Kidd, "Gaelic Antiquity and National Identity in Enlightenment Ireland and Scotland," *English Historical Review,* 109, no. 434 (1994): 1197–1214;

Joep Leerssen, *Studies in the Idea of Irish Nationality, Its Development and Literary Expression Prior to the Nineteenth Century* (Cork: Cork University Press, 1996);

Walter D. Love, "Edmund Burke and an Irish Historiography Controversy," *History and Theory,* 2, no. 2 (1962): 180–198;

J. B. Lyons, "Sylvester O'Halloran, 1728–1807," *Eighteenth-Century Ireland,* 5 (1989): 65–74;

W. J. McCormack, *Ascendancy and Tradition in Anglo-Irish Literary History from 1798 to 1939* (Oxford: Clarendon Press, 1985);

R. B. McDowell, *Ireland in the Age of Imperialism and Revolution 1760–1801* (Oxford: Clarendon Press, 1979);

T. W. Moody and W. E. Vaughan, eds., *A New History of Ireland,* volume 4 (Oxford: Clarendon Press, 1986);

Clare O'Halloran, "Irish Re-Creations of the Gaelic Past: The Challenge of Macpherson's Ossian," *Past and Present,* 0, no. 124 (1989): 69–95;

Robert Tracy, "Maria Edgeworth and Lady Morgan: Legality Versus Legitimacy," *Nineteenth-Century Fiction,* 40, no. 1 (1985): 1–22;

Vaughan, ed., *A New History of Ireland,* volume 5 (Oxford: Clarendon Press, 1989);

Robert E. Ward, John F. Wrynn, and Catherine Loogan Ward, eds., *Letters of Charles O'Conor of Belanagare: A Catholic Voice in Eighteenth-Century Ireland* (Washington: Catholic University of America Press, 1988).

John Oldmixon
(1673? – 9 July 1742)

Judith Dorn
St. Cloud State University

BOOKS: *Poems on Several Occasions, Written in Imitation of the Manner of Anacreon* (London: Richard Parker, 1696);

Reflections on the Stage, and Mr. Collyer's Defence of the Short View in Four Dialogues (London: Richard Parker & P. Buck, 1699);

The Grove, or, Love's Paradice, libretto by Oldmixon, music by Daniel Purcell (London: Richard Parker, 1700);

Amores Britannici: Epistles Historical and Gallant, in English Heroic Verse (London: J. Nutt, 1703);

The Governour of Cyprus (London: Printed by R. Tookey for Richard Parker, 1703);

Iberia liberata: A Poem. Occasion'd by the Success of Her Majesties Arms in Catalonia, Valentia, &C. under the Command of . . . Charles, Earl of Peterborough and Monmouth (London: Printed for Anthony Barker, 1706);

The British Empire in America, Containing the History of the Discovery, Settlement, Progress and Present State of All the British Colonies on the Continent and Islands of America, 2 volumes (London: Printed for John Nicholson and Benjamin Tooke, 1708; second corrected edition, London: Printed for J. Brotherton, 1741; reprint of the 1741 second edition, New York: Augustus M. Kelley, 1969);

The History of Addresses (London, 1709);

The History of Addresses: With Remarks Serious and Comical. In Which a Particular Regard Is Had to All Such as Have Been Presented since the Impeachment of Dr. Sacheverell, part 2 (London: Printed for J. Baker, 1711);

The Dutch Barrier Our's; or, The Interest of England and Holland Inseparable, anonymous (London, 1712);

Reflections on Dr. Swift's Letter to the Earl of Oxford, about the English Tongue, anonymous (London: Printed for A. Baldwin, 1712);

The Secret History of Europe: Shewing That the Late Greatness of the French Power Was Never So Much Owing to the Number or Goodness of Their Troops, . . . as to the Treachery and Corruption of the Ministers Abroad, 2 vol-

umes, anonymous (London: Printed for the booksellers of London and Westminster, 1712);

The Life and History of Belisarius: Who Conquer'd Africa and Italy . . . and a Parallel between Him and a Modern Heroe, anonymous (London: Printed for A. Baldwin, 1713);

Arcana Gallica: or, The Secret History of France, for the Last Century, anonymous (London: Printed for A. Bell, N. Cliff, and D. Jackson, 1714);

The Court of Atalantis (London: J. Roberts, 1714); republished as *The Amorous Statesmen; or, Wanton Tories*, 1715;

The Secret History of Europe: The Whole Collected from Authentick Memoirs, as Well Manuscript as Printed, part 3, anonymous (London: E. Curll & J. Pemberton, 1715);

Memoirs of the Life of the Most Noble Thomas Late Marquess of Wharton (London: Printed for J. Roberts, 1715);

Memoirs of North-Britain, anonymous (London: Printed for J. Baker and John Graves, 1715);

The Secret History of Europe, part 4, anonymous (London: E. Curll & J. Pemberton, 1715);

The Catholick Poet; or, Protestant Barnaby's Sorrowful Lamentation (London: Printed for J. Morphew, J. Roberts, R. Burleigh, J. Baker, and S. Popping, 1716);

Memoirs of Ireland from the Restoration, to the Present Time (London: Printed for J. Roberts, 1716);

Memoirs of the Life of John Lord Somers, anonymous (London: Printed for J. Roberts, 1716);

Nixon's Cheshire Prophecy at Large, anonymous (London: Printed for J. Roberts, 1716);

The Critical History of England: Ecclesiastical and Civil: Wherein the Errors of the Monkish Writers, and Others before the Reformation, Are Expos'd and Corrected, 2 volumes (London: Printed for J. Pemberton, 1724, 1726);

A Review of Dr. Zachary Grey's Defence of Our Ancient and Modern Historians (London: Printed for J. Roberts, 1725);

Clarendon and Whitlock Compar'd (London: J. Pemberton, 1727);

An Essay on Criticism as It Regards Design, Thought, and Expression, in Prose and Verse (London: Printed for J. Pemberton, 1728);

The History of England, During the Reigns of the Royal House of Stuart (London: Printed for J. Pemberton, 1730);

The History of England during the Reigns of King William and Queen Mary, Queen Anne, King George I (London: Printed for Thomas Cox, Richard Ford, and Richard Hett, 1735);

The History of England during the Reigns of Henry VIII. Edward VI. Queen Mary. Queen Elizabeth (London: Printed for Thomas Cox, and Richard Hett, 1739);

Memoirs of the Press, Historical and Political, for Thirty Years Past, from 1710 to 1740 (London: Printed for T. Cox, 1742).

OTHER: *The Muses Mercury: or, The Monthly Miscellany,* prefaces to volume 1, no. 1, and volume 2, no. 1, by Oldmixon, edited by Oldmixon (1707–1708);

The Medley, edited by Oldmixon and Arthur Maynwaring (London: Printed by A. Baldwin, 1710–1712);

The Life and Posthumous Works of Arthur Maynwaring, Esq., edited by Oldmixon as J.O. (London: A. Bell, 1715);

Court Poems, by Mary Wortley Montagu and others (London: J. Roberts, 1716).

TRANSLATIONS: Torquato Tasso, *Amintas: A Pastoral Acted at the Theatre Royal* (London: Richard Parker, 1698);

The History of Doctor Sacheverell, anonymous (London: A. Baldwin, 1711);

Dominique Bouhours, *The Arts of Logick and Rhetorick* (London: Printed for John Clark and Richard Hett, John Pemberton, Richard Ford, and John Gray, 1728).

Credit for making John Oldmixon's name represent a caricature of the early-eighteenth-century professional writer largely goes to Alexander Pope, whose satirical poem *The Dunciad* (1728–1743) featured Oldmixon prominently among the writers competing for lucre and fame—or for something to eat—by holding pissing contests or diving into sewage (1743, II, ll. 283–290). Pope converted Oldmixon's enormous productivity into the mark of a "dunce." Publishing almost as much as Daniel Defoe did in sheer quantity of words, especially in his enormous national histories, Oldmixon came under attack by men of letters, who saw him, according to J. P. W. Rogers, as violating the literary standards that they were trying to refine ("The Whig Controversialist as Dunce"). The more Oldmixon

attempted to win prestige with each of the available literary forms, including many kinds of history, according to Rogers, the more he exposed himself to criticism and attack. Although he protested his own innocence, Oldmixon became an emblem of the scurrility of the English book trade, seen as degrading the literary world by serving profit and political manipulation.

Oldmixon was born near Bridgwater near Somerset, probably in 1673. His father's name was also John; his mother's name was Elinor. What is known of the Oldmixon family finances does not suggest that young John had many advantages beyond his talents as a writer. His father may have died bankrupt when the boy was six, and by the age of twelve Oldmixon lived with a family closely related to Robert Blake, a renowned admiral. He later moved to the home of his uncle Sir John Bawden, who, according to Rogers and the *Dictionary of National Biography (DNB),* had been a substantial merchant and plantation owner in Barbados. In his mid teens Oldmixon was orphaned. Never attending university but showing promise as a writer, young Oldmixon received encouragement and committed himself to his drive to write, seeking support from patrons with occasional success. His London literary career began in the traditional way with poetry and drama, and then his ambitions turned toward the steady writing of voluminous historical works. He worked on his histories alongside many shorter projects, usually political works that served the Whig Party's efforts to sway public opinion.

First publishing poems individually, including some for the literary magazine *Gentleman's Journal,* he issued a volume collection of Anacreontic poems in 1696, and then contributed the one-act play *Thyrsis, a Pastoral* to Peter Anthony Motteux's production *The Novelty* in 1697. Another pastoral play, *Amintas,* followed the next year, without success. Turning critic in response to the cultural warfare over the theater, he published *Reflections on the Stage* (1699) to defend William Congreve's plays against Jeremy Collier's attack on the theater world. In 1700 Oldmixon produced an opera at Drury Lane with music by Daniel Purcell and an epilogue by George Farquhar, *The Grove, or, Love's Paradice.* The tragedy *The Governour of Cyprus* appeared in 1703, the year he married Elizabeth Parry; the couple eventually had five children. In the same year, he also produced his revision of Michael Drayton's heroic epistles imagining the love lives of England's national heroes, *Amores Britannici.*

How Oldmixon interpreted his own career by the end of his life can be gathered from his autobiographical *Memoirs of the Press, Historical and Political, for Thirty Years Past, from 1710 to 1740,* published after his death in 1742. As in many of his works, he justifies publishing as necessary to correct hostile public opinion. This work stands as a last attempt to clear his name. An unfounded reputation as a "court" writer had made even booksellers sharing his affiliation with the Whig political party unwilling to publish his writings because of his reputation as a hireling. He contends that he has spent his entire life writing in the Whig cause, often taking a financial loss, with a loyalty not shared by the powerful politicians who employed him without paying him. These claims fit the evidence provided by his record of publication, and indeed, according to Rogers, Oldmixon's accuracy as a reporter of fact has stood up well under investigation.

Although men of letters typically wrote in a variety of genres on many subjects, Oldmixon stretched himself further than most, his writing ranging from traditional genres such as "lives" (biographies) to marketable "prophecy" and court gossip. In the English world of polite letters that writers such as John Dryden, Pope, Jonathan Swift, and many others sought to refine, only indefinable brilliance and wit counted. Merely to write well amounted to failure, a standard that placed power in the hands of critics. Oldmixon sought to create his own literary circle by publishing a quarto periodical, *The Muses Mercury: or, The Monthly Miscellany,* from January 1707 to January 1708 with contributions from writers including Richard Steele, Sir Samuel Garth, Pierre Motteux, as well his own. His inability to bring the periodical out regularly turned the venture into a failure in addition to his failed plays.

In the meantime, he had taken on more remunerative long-term projects. During the late seventeenth century, diplomat Sir William Temple had pointed out in print that England had no grand national history to match the productions of France and other continental nations. Temple also made the practical suggestion that a national history could be assembled out of the accounts of individual kings and queens already written by some of the great writers of England. These narratives—by such men as Samuel Daniel, Sir Francis Bacon, Sir Thomas More, and William Camden—needed only the addition of recent Stuart reigns to present a complete history of England. A consortium of publishers fulfilled this design in large folio volumes in 1706, with John Hughes and Oldmixon serving as editors for the first two volumes. White Kennett, bishop of Peterborough, prepared the third to bring the narrative through the recent death of William III. All of the Whig-leaning participants attempted to remain anonymous, according to Joseph M. Levine, because of the current political sensitivity of national history, both ancient and contemporary.

Oldmixon already had a more ambitious project under way, *The British Empire in America,* which totaled almost 1,100 pages in two volumes and appeared in 1708. This history provides a survey of all the British colonies in America in terms of their usefulness to British interests. His introduction defends the colonies against detractors by calculating the enormous profits they brought to England, and his discussion of each colony points out opportunities for economic development. Oldmixon spoke accurately in his later *Memoirs of the Press, Historical and Political* when he described his career as wholly serving the Whig cause. His Whiggish optimism about trade displays no utopian illusions, however, and he rehearses the Whig theme of resisting tyranny and injustice. Surveying many colonies allows him to exhibit a range of examples of injustice and "dishonor," including the enslavement of "Indians." His chapter on Barbados in volume two declares, "For the *Charibbeans* hating Slavery as much as any Nation in America, abhorred the English for imposing their Yoke upon them." On the other hand, uprisings by Negro and Creole slaves are "folly" that "good laws" could prevent. He makes a point of observing the process by which colonies create laws to deal with exigencies. The second edition of 1741 is dedicated to the attorney general of Barbados, apparently a personal friend with a reputation for having defended "the Rights and Properties of the People."

Oldmixon's upbringing with Humphrey Blake and Bawden, two men who established themselves in the new world, may have motivated him to write *The British Empire in America.* Diligent in amassing materials, Oldmixon established in this work the method he later pursued in most of his historical writing. Enormous numbers of narratives representing every part of the British colonies and schemes for turning them to profit had been published in previous decades. Oldmixon combed these for vivid detail, consulted experienced travelers, and checked official records. Digesting as many of the available sources on a subject as possible, he wrote a narrative that arbitrates among these competing accounts with ample interjection of commentary. In this case, the approach mitigates Oldmixon's never having been to the Americas, since he demonstrates his method of evaluating sources and weighing evidence. The result is lively and also provides readers with a model of critical historical judgment. New England and Barbados receive the lengthiest treatments. Volume one works from Newfoundland southward to Georgia, except that Oldmixon describes Hudson's Bay last, as he explains, because the insignificance of the colony made it an inappropriate beginning point for a history. Volume two covers the British islands of the Caribbean.

Intensifying party conflict drew Oldmixon into a series of works justifying the Whigs and attacking the Tories. His first effort at party warfare appeared in two installments of *The History of Addresses,* 1709 and 1711, an exposé of Tory manipulation of the "addresses," or declarations of loyalty, that various constituencies presented to Queen Anne. At stake in the matter were partisan claims regarding the evident power of public opinion. Collecting examples from the time of Oliver Cromwell to the present, Oldmixon explodes Tory exaltation of royal authority by quoting from addresses declaring loyalty to opposite sides of an issue–often made by the same official bodies, such as municipalities, at different times. To discredit Tory claims to serve the people's interests, he quotes officials who describe petitions from ordinary people as disruptive.

As the Whigs fell from power and Sarah, Duchess of Marlborough, lost her position as Queen Anne's confidante while Robert Harley rose to head the government, a paper called the *Examiner* appeared, which featured the wit of Swift in defense of Queen Anne's government and of making peace with France by discrediting Queen Anne's general, John Churchill, first Duke of Marlborough. After Joseph Addison's *Whig Examiner* lapsed, the role of providing a weekly rebuttal fell to Arthur Maynwaring, who asked Oldmixon to write and edit *The Medley* as a Whig opposition paper between 5 October 1710 and August 1711, when Swift's *Examiner* ceased. Oldmixon had a large share in the writing of *The Medley,* and contributions also came from Kennett and Steele. The heat of factional debate drew political pamphlets from Oldmixon in a torrent. For example, he rebutted Tory arguments–such as Swift's *Conduct of the Allies* (1711)–against the participation of England in the War of the Spanish Succession by maintaining that England needed Holland for defense against France (*The Dutch Barrier Our's; or, The Interest of England and Holland Inseparable,* 1712).

According to Oldmixon in *Memoirs of the Press,* Maynwaring talked him into republishing the *Medley* papers as a complete collection, only to scrap the volume when the political tide turned, so that Oldmixon had to assume the costs of the whole publication. Nor had Oldmixon received the £100 installments he had been promised for the original *Medley* essays, and the death of Maynwaring shortly thereafter lost Oldmixon his best-placed backer. *The Life and Posthumous Works of Arthur Maynwaring, Esq.* appeared in 1715, valuable because of Oldmixon's direct knowledge of his subject.

With the publication of four installments of *The Secret History of Europe* between 1712 and 1715, Oldmixon and his collaborators sought to demonstrate that only Whig policies could defend the English constitution amid the sweep of international events. These "secret histories" revealed the hidden agenda of the opposing faction–conspiracy with France to return England to Catholicism and a state of slavery. Old-

mixon viewed all Tories as Jacobites who conspired to return the Catholic heirs of James II to the throne and overturn the 1688 revolution by which William and Mary had confirmed the English Constitution and Protestant rule. Drawing parallels between political conditions during the last years of Queen Anne and the perilous times under Charles II and James II, who had secretly allied themselves with French power, Oldmixon presaged doom for English liberty from the secret counsels of ministers and the principles of kings' divine right and high church authority. Instead of providing a continuous narration of events, he claimed to bring to light pivotal examples of politicians endangering England, based on recently available memoirs and documents.

Oldmixon may have modeled his "secret histories" on those published immediately after William and Mary took the throne in 1688. These Whig publications demonstrated the importance of "transparent" government by describing the Stuart kings' behind-the-scenes betrayals of the English people. Many of these episodes, such as Charles II's secret treaty with France, reappear in Oldmixon's works. His acquaintance with the original *Secret History* by the sixth-century historian Procopius led to *The Life and History of Belisarius* (1713). This political allegory draws a parallel between the fall of the great general who had given the Byzantine emperor Justinian many victories and the unjust demotion of the heroic duke of Marlborough.

In his *Memoirs of the Press* Oldmixon conveys his awareness of literary standards by grouping the works from the middle period of his career into "secret histories" and "critical histories." He lists his *Arcana Gallica* (1714), *Memoirs of North-Britain* (Scotland) (1715), and *Memoirs of Ireland from the Restoration, to the Present Time* (1716)–an anecdotal rundown of power plays by the leading kings and cardinals of France–as the fifth, sixth, and seventh parts of his secret history, as though dignifying them by the classification. *Clarendon and Whitlock Compar'd* (1727) counts as an extension of *The Critical History of England: Ecclesiastical and Civil* (1724, 1726). Since secret history and critical history had only dubious standing in the eyes of readers, and since Oldmixon's style and method often seemed immoderate, he jeopardized his reputation by allying himself with these forms.

This period fixed the character of Oldmixon as a "Grub Street" hack, his name becoming associated with the writers who scribbled for a living in the seamier quarters of London. Writing to assert a worldview less nuanced than that held by many Whig leaders, he also damaged his reputation by association with Edmund Curll, a bookseller notorious for profiting from pirated and scandalous publications. Oldmixon published without permission a poem by Pope, whom he also criti-

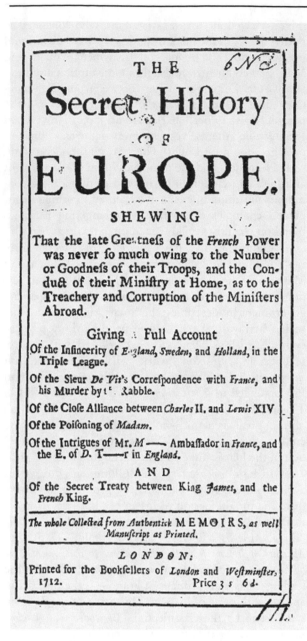

THE
Secret History
OF
EUROPE.

SHEWING

That the late Greatness of the *French* Power
was never so much owing to the Number
or Goodness of their Troops, and the Conduct of their Ministry at Home, as to the
Treachery and Corruption of the Ministers
Abroad.

Giving a Full Account

Of the Insincerity of *England*, *Sweden*, and *Holland*, in the
Triple League.

Of the Sieur *De Vit*'s Correspondence with *France*, and
his Murder by t' Rabble.

Of the Close Alliance between *Charles* II. and *Lewis* XIV

Of the Poisoning of *Madam*.

Of the Intrigues of Mr. *M——* Ambassador in *France*, and
the E. of *D. T——r* in *England*.

AND

Of the Secret Treaty between King *James*, and the
French King.

The whole Collected from Authentick MEMOIRS, as well
Manuscript as Printed.

LONDON:

Printed for the Booksellers of *London* and *Westminster*,
1712.   Price 3 s 6 d.

*Title page for volume one of John Oldmixon's history of Europe, in
which he reveals a Tory plan to return England to Catholic rule
(from Eighteenth-Century Collections Online, Gale Group)*

cized in *The Catholick Poet* (1716) and other works.
Always sensitive about his reputation, Oldmixon published an "advertisement" to insist that he was innocent
of purveying the politically sensitive *Court Poems* (1716),
written by Pope, Lady Mary Wortley Montagu, John
Gay, and others. However, according to Ralph Straus,
these likely passed through his hands. Lives of Thomas
Wharton and John, first Baron Somers appeared during
these years along with the gossiping *The Court of Atalantis*
(1714). After unsuccessfully appealing to Whig leaders

for financial support, Oldmixon accepted the post of
Collector of the Customs at remote Bridgwater in 1716,
but the profits turned out to be half of what he had
been told to expect. He served James Brydges, first
Duke of Chandos, briefly as a political agent and twice
got into trouble with the authorities in 1718, getting
reported for attending conventicles and undergoing
questioning by authorities seeking names of protestors
in 1718.

During his "exile" from London, Oldmixon
assumed the role of critic while working steadily on historical projects. The announced purpose of his *Critical
History of England* was to counter the magisterial authority of *The History of the Great Rebellion* (1702–1704) by
Edward Hyde, Earl of Clarendon. Clarendon's style
and testimonial authority so overawed readers, Oldmixon claimed, that he was obliged to show readers
that alternative accounts of the Civil Wars could possibly be true. Likewise, Laurence Echard had earned
renown by singlehandedly writing a folio *History of
England* (1707, 1718). Oldmixon had been hired to prepare the index for this work, a task that apparently
stoked his antipathy to every detail of the narrative.
The index he prepared consists of one-line descriptors
that twist interpretation of each event to counter
Echard's representation of it. This stratagem did not
escape the notice of the political press, and a pamphlet
called *The Index-Writer* (1729) denounced each of Oldmixon's tendentious index entries.

With a drive that bordered on obsession, Oldmixon devoted hundreds of pages over more than
twenty years to explicit attacks on the histories written
by Clarendon and, especially, Archdeacon Echard.
Indeed, Oldmixon's need to correct their influence on
English historical memory pervaded all of his subsequent histories of England as well as his critical histories. The purpose of his *Critical History of England* (1724)
was to prepare the reading public to accept his ultimate
project, folio histories of England that would rival Clarendon's and Echard's and promote Whig views. Cham-
pioning the memoirs and documentary compilations
prepared by John Rushworth, Bulstrode Whitlock, and
Bishop Gilbert Burnet, Oldmixon was unable to recognize Echard as a Whig historian, according to Deborah
Stephan, because of Echard's reverence for High
Church principles and monarchs.

Ultimately, Oldmixon's unwavering adherence to
a set of principles did not gain him legitimacy as a historian and critic. His historical writings proceed out of
interpretations of key English historical characters and
events that he believed could not be controverted. In
the preface to the second volume of his *Critical History of
England* (1726), he lists the opposites of these tenets and
defies anyone to support these points. In keeping with

the fixity of his convictions, he seized on a colleague's letter that voiced suspicion about the editing of Clarendon's *History of the Rebellion* and went public in the preface to *Clarendon and Whitlock Compar'd* with the charge that Oxford editors had altered Clarendon's text. A minor pamphlet war over this issue drew his responses for the rest of his life. Robert Burton in 1744 definitively dismissed the two or three substantive charges on which the entire debate had been based.

Notably, Oldmixon did not write his histories of England so as to establish them as methodologically distinct from his secret histories and critical histories. The three volumes of *The History of England* comprise thousands of folio pages and attempt a comprehensive story of events but resemble his other writings in commenting on—or railing at—existing histories throughout. All of Oldmixon's longer works appear to have been written in counterpoint to several books lying open on the table before him, without much time available for revision. This method allowed him to fill many pages with long quoted passages from his sources. He guided his readers to assemble a comprehensive narrative understanding of history for themselves by selecting and interpreting materials for them.

Oldmixon's historical writings reveal a contradiction between his philosophy of history and his practice. On the one hand, Oldmixon champions neoclassical principles in *An Essay on Criticism as It Regards Design, Thought, and Expression, in Prose and Verse* (1728) and other critical works: histories ought to create a transparent, substantive narration, without digressing, pursuing a middle way between abstract, general ideas that explain events and the minute, material details on which those ideas are based. Oldmixon cites Jesuit René Rapin as his principal guide, an odd choice for an antipapist Francophobe to make. Rapin's authority, nevertheless, allows Oldmixon to denounce his rival English historians. The language of histories must emphasize material events rather than distract common readers with a style that is ornamental and "puffy," as Oldmixon liked to call it. According to Oldmixon, Clarendon was guiltiest of this style. Since history comprises material events rather than lofty and mystifying ideas, any heightening of the language "by words rather than by things" is a mystification and violates neoclassical principles. Neoclassical history achieves linear, instructive storytelling without digressing. Like Echard and other current historians, he acknowledged both neoclassical and scholarly—"erudite"—principles and professed to make use of both, legitimizing his narratives by pointing toward their reliance on original documents while announcing the linearity and perspicuity of his narrative style.

On the other hand, Oldmixon's narratives violate these principles. His heavy citation of sources can count

as scholarly documentation, but it also weighs down the clarity of the storytelling. Zachary Grey, writing a book-length *Defence of Our Antient and Modern Historians* (1725), demonstrates that when Oldmixon attacks a rival with the line "almost every Sentence of his Book executes itself," the charge could apply to Oldmixon himself, who commits every fault he finds in others. What is also telling is that Grey devotes ninety-five pages, or almost half of his *Defence of Our Antient and Modern Historians,* to the single chapter in Oldmixon's *Critical History of England* on the most ancient parts of Britain's history. At issue was the Whig claim that the ancient Britons and Saxons held parliaments representing the people's rights over their kings.

The last fifteen years of his life Oldmixon spent in writing the three volumes of his *History of England,* with a dedication that supports his claim in his memoirs not to be mercenary. In order to complete the last two volumes, he risked leaving his post in Bridgwater in the hands of a deputy and set up a second household in London, where he could do research. According to the memoirs, he received notice while writing volume two that official review of Bridgwater accounts revealed debt of £1,100. Oldmixon's protests reduced the amount to £360, which he had to pay out of the £100 pension he had received through the influence of Queen Caroline. Resigning his post, he wrote on under increasing burdens of gout and then blindness, his enormous productivity never in his lifetime catching up with his debts.

While many historians found publishing contemporary history too great a risk, John Oldmixon started with the controversial recent periods of history. The first volume of his *History of England* covers "the reigns of the Royal House of Stuart" (1730), and the second takes the narrative through George I's reign (1735). The third (1739) turns back to the Tudor reigns in order to present Reformation history from a view supporting religious dissenters and to demonstrate how little the people ought to trust their liberty to the generosity of monarchs. Sales of his critical history had called for extra editions, but his worsening reputation, according to Rogers, forced Oldmixon to publish his third volume of *The History of England* by private subscription. Oldmixon died 9 July 1742.

Any effort to define Oldmixon's achievement in letters begs the question of criteria for measuring that achievement, since other eighteenth-century writers used him as a bad example that illustrated their superior literary standards. By referring to him in the *Dunciad* as "Oldmixon, the Poet" (1728, II, l. 199), Pope meant to deride Oldmixon's poetic achievement. Since Oldmixon had written both heroic epistle and pastoral before Pope did, according to Rogers, Pope needed to negate Oldmixon. The long footnote to this reference in the *Dunciad Variorum* enumerates Oldmixon's failings: his labored verse, his poor judgment in criticizing greater writers than himself, and his character as "a Perverter of History" and "a virulent Party-writer for hire." Pope presents Oldmixon as memorable mainly for accusing three eminent persons of fabricating parts of Lord Clarendon's great history, and merely names Oldmixon's *Critical History of England* in order to discredit him.

References:
John Burton, *The Genuineness of Ld. Clarendon's History of the Rebellion Printed at Oxford, Vindicated. Mr. Oldmixon's Slander Confuted* (Oxford: J. Fletcher, 1744);

Frank H. Ellis, ed., *Swift vs. Maynwaring: The Examiner and The Medley* (Oxford: Clarendon Press, 1985);

Zachary Grey, *A Defence of Our Antient and Modern Historians, Against the Frivolous Cavels of a Late Pretender to Critical History,* second edition (London: Charles Rivington, 1725);

Philip Hicks, *Neoclassical History and English Culture* (New York: St. Martin's Press, 1996);

Joseph M. Levine, *The Battle of the Books* (Ithaca & London: Cornell University Press, 1991);

J. P. W. Rogers, *Grub Street: Studies in a Subculture* (London: Methuen, 1972);

Rogers, "The Whig Controversialist as Dunce: A Study of the Literary Fortunes and Misfortunes of John Oldmixon," dissertation, Cambridge University, 1968;

Deborah Stephan, "Laurence Echard–Whig Historian," *Historical Journal,* 32, no. 4 (1989): 843–866;

Ralph Straus, *The Unspeakable Curll* (New York: Augustus M. Kelley, 1927; revised, 1970).

Papers:
Some letters of John Oldmixon are located in the British Library, the Hartfordshire Archives and Local Records, the National Archives, and Edinburgh University Library.

John Pinkerton
(17 February 1758 – 10 March 1825)

Jean Culp Flanigan
East Tennessee State University

BOOKS: *Craigmiller Castle: An Elegy,* anonymous (Edinburgh: Privately printed, 1776);

Rimes (London: Printed for Charles Dilly, 1781; second edition, enlarged, 1782);

Scottish Tragic Ballads (London: Printed by and for James Nichols, 1781); enlarged as *Select Scotish Ballads,* 2 volumes (London: Printed by and for John Nichols, 1783);

Tales in Verse (London: Printed for James Dodsley, 1782);

Two Dithyrambic Odes: I. On Enthusiasm. II. To Laughter, by the author of *Rimes* (London: Printed for Charles Dilly, 1782);

An Essay on Medals, anonymous (London: Printed for James Dodsley, 1784); revised, enlarged, and illustrated with plates (London: Printed for J. Edwards & J. Johnson, 1789); revised and enlarged (London: Printed for T. Cadell & W. Davies, 1808);

Letters of Literature, as Robert Heron, Esq. (London: G. G. J. & J. Robinson, 1785);

A Dissertation on the Origin and Progress of the Scythians or Goths: Being an Introduction to the Ancient and Modern History of Europe (London: Printed by John Nichols for George Nicol, 1787); republished in *An Enquiry into the History of Scotland Preceding the Reign of Malcolm III* (London: Printed by John Nichols and sold by B. & J. White, 1794); two volumes, revised and enlarged (Edinburgh: Printed by James Ballantyne for Bell & Bradfute, 1814);

Vitae antiquae sanctorum qui habitaverunt in ea parte Britanniae nunc vocata Scotia vel in ejus insulis, as Johannes Pinkerton (London: Printed by John Nichols, 1789); translated from the Latin by W. M. Metcalfe as *Ancient Lives of Scottish Saints* (Paisley, U. K.: Alexander Gardner, 1895);

An Enquiry into the History of Scotland Preceding the Reign of Malcolm III. Or the Year 1056. Including the Authentic History of That Period, 2 volumes (London: Printed by John Nichols for George Nicol and John Bell, Edinburgh, 1789; London: Printed by John Nichols, 1794; revised and enlarged, Edinburgh:

John Pinkerton (<www.geocities.com/Heartland/Prairie>)

Printed by James Ballantyne for Bell & Bradfute, 1814);

The Medallic History of England to the Revolution, anonymous (London: Printed for Edwards and Faulder, 1790);

The History of Scotland from the Accession of the House of Stuart to that of Mary. With Appendixes of Original Papers, 2 volumes (London: Printed by Bye & Law for Charles Dilly, 1797);

Iconographia Scotica; or, Portraits of Illustrious Persons of Scotland, with Biographical Notes (London: Printed for I. Herbert; Barrett, 1797);

The Scottish Gallery; or, Portraits of Eminent Persons of Scotland: Many of Them After Pictures by the Celebrated Jameson, at Taymouth, and Other Places. With Brief Accounts of the Characters Represented, and an Introduction on the Rise and Progress of Painting in Scotland (London: Printed for E. Harding, 1799);

Modern Geography: A Description of the Empires, Kingdoms, States, and Colonies, with the Oceans, Seas, and Isles in All Parts of the World, 2 volumes, astronomical introduction by the Rev. S. Vince (London: T. Cadell & W. Davies / T. N. Longman & O. Rees, 1802; abridged to one volume with an added catalogue of maps and books of travels and voyages, 1803); 2 volumes, corrected and essay "America" enlarged by Dr. Barton (Philadelphia: John Conrad, 1804); republished as *Pinkerton's Geography, Epitomised for the Use of Schools* by David Doyle (Philadelphia: Printed for Samuel F. Bradford, 1805); republished with the original title and enlarged by the author, 3 volumes (London: T. Cadell & W. Davies, 1807);

Recollections of Paris in the Years 1802-3-4-5 (London: Longman, Hurst, Rees & Orme, 1806);

Petralogy. A Treatise on Rocks, 2 volumes (London: Printed by S. Hamilton for White, Cochrane, 1811).

PLAY PRODUCTION: *The Heiress of Strathearn: or, the Rash Marriage,* 24 March 1813, Royal Theatre, London.

OTHER: *Ancient Scotish Poems, Never Before in Print. But Now Published from the MS. Collections of Sir Richard Maitland . . . ; Comprising Pieces Written from about 1420 till 1586. With Large Notes, and a Glossary; Prefixed Are an Essay on the Origin of Scotish Poetry, A List of All the Scotish Poets,. . . and an Appendix Is Added, Containing, . . . an Account of the Contents of the Maitland and Bannatyne MSS* (London: Printed for Charles Dilly, 1786; Edinburgh, Printed for William Creech, 1786);

The Treasury of Wit; Being a Methodical Selection of about Twelve Hundred, the Best, Apophthegms and Jests; from Books in Several Languages, as H. Bennett, M.A. (London: Charles Dilly, 1786);

John Barbour, *The Bruce; or, The History of Robert I, King of Scotland. Written in Scotish Verse. . . . The First Genuine Edition, Published from a MS. Dated 1489; with Notes and a Glossary by J. Pinkerton,* translated and edited by Pinkerton (London: Printed by H. Hughs for George Nicol, 1790);

Scotish Poems, Reprinted from Scarce Editions . . . with Three Pieces before Unpublished, 3 volumes, collected by Pinkerton (London: Printed by and for John Nichols, 1792);

Horace Walpole, *Walpoliana,* 2 volumes, compiled and edited by Pinkerton (London: Printed by T. Bensley for R. Phillips, 1799); previously printed serially in *Monthly Magazine* (March 1798–May 1799);

"Dissertation on the Gowrie Conspiracy," in Malcolm Laing, *The History of Scotland, from the Union of the Crowns on the Accession of James VI, to the Throne of England, to the Union of the Kingdoms in the Reign of Queen Anne,* 2 volumes (London: Printed by A. Strahan for T. Cadell Jun. and W. Davies / Edinburgh: Manners & Miller, 1800);

A General Collection of the Best and Most Interesting Voyages and Travels in all Parts of the World; Many of Which Are Now First Translated into English. Digested on a New Plan, 17 volumes, compiled by Pinkerton (London: Longman, Hurst, Rees & Orme, 1808–1814; volumes 1–6, Philadelphia: Kimber & Conrad, 1810–1812);

A Modern Atlas, from the Latest and Best Authorities, Exhibiting the Various Divisions of the World, with Its Chief Empires, Kingdoms, and States, in Sixty Maps, compiled and edited by Pinkerton (London: Printed by T. Bensley for T. Cadell & W. Davies, 1809–1815; Philadelphia: Printed by William Fry for Thomas Dobson, 1818).

The eighteenth-century fascination with ancient Scottish history reached its popular peak in the novels of Sir Walter Scott, whose third *Waverley* novel, *The Antiquary* (1816), deals directly with the topic. Scott's fictional characters, Jonathan Oldbuck (the antiquary of the title) and his friend Sir Arthur Wardour, represent two competing views of the latter half of the eighteenth century, with Oldbuck claiming that the Picts were of Gothic origins and Wardour asserting that their language was Celtic:

> "Why, man, there was once a people called the Piks—"
>
> "More properly Picts," interrupted the Baronet.
>
> "I say the Pikar, Pihar, Piochtar, Piaghter, or Peughtar," vociferated Oldbuck; "they spoke a Gothic dialect—"
>
> "Genuine Celtic," again asseverated the knight.
>
> "Gothic! Gothic, I'll go to death upon it!" counter-asseverated the squire. ". . . I have the learned Pinkerton on my side."

Oldbuck's "learned Pinkerton" is John Pinkerton, born 17 February 1758 in Edinburgh. His father, James Pinkerton, was one of several children of Walter Pinkerton, a small farmer of Dalserf, Lanarkshire. James established himself as a successful dealer in wigs in Somerset, after which he returned to Edinburgh in

1755. There he increased his modest fortune by marrying a widow, Mrs. Bowie, the daughter of an Edinburgh merchant named Heron. John, the third of their sons, received his earliest education at a small school in a village near Edinburgh. In 1764 he was sent to the grammar school at Lanark, where he studied for six years. As a young student he had a reputation for being a skilled classicist and a hypochondriac like his father.

He returned to Edinburgh in 1770 hoping to attend the university, but his father disapproved. For the next few years Pinkerton was tutored at home by a French teacher. He studied Latin on his own, achieving considerable mastery. For two or three years he also studied mathematics under Mr. Ewing, a respected teacher in Edinburgh. About 1775 Pinkerton undertook the traditional five-year apprenticeship to William Ayton, a prominent Edinburgh writer to the signet (a Scottish lawyer similar to a solicitor).

In 1776, still in his apprenticeship, he anonymously published a poem, *Craigmiller Castle: An Elegy.* On this small scale at age seventeen, Pinkerton began his career as a tireless researcher and prodigious writer on a variety of subjects.

Pinkerton finished his apprenticeship in 1780, and his father died the same year. Pinkerton's inheritance allowed him financial independence with £300 per year. He visited London that same year to buy books, and the abundance available there was the basis of his decision to move to London permanently in late 1781.

In quick succession, in 1781 and 1782, he published four volumes of poetry: *Rimes* (1781), *Scottish Tragic Ballads* (1781), *Tales in Verse* (1782), and *Two Dithyrambic Odes on Enthusiasm and to Laughter* (1782). The following year he expanded *Scottish Tragic Ballads* to two volumes, adding *Ballads of the Comic Kind* and publishing all the ballads under the title *Select Scotish Ballads* (1783). The poems included in these volumes were presented as traditional ballads in the Lowland Scots language, the merits of which Pinkerton claims to be on a par with the poetry of Homer. Among the *Tragic Ballads* is "Hardyknute," a supposedly ancient ballad commemorating the victory of Scots king Alexander III over Haakon Haakonsson of Norway at Largs in 1283. In addition to the previously known ballad, Pinkerton added part 2, which he supposedly had just discovered. His additions to "Hardyknute" were exposed as a forgery by Joseph Ritson, an English antiquary who became Pinkerton's chief nemesis. Pinkerton admitted to the forgery as well as to having composed other poems which he had claimed to be newly discovered traditional works. Further, the original "Hardyknute" was revealed to be the 1719 composition of Lady Wardlaw of Pitreavie.

As a boy Pinkerton was given a rare coin from the reign of the Emperor Constantine, which the giver had mistaken for a farthing. This coin triggered Pinkerton's interest in numismatics. He developed tables of coins for his own use and in 1784, with the assistance of Richard Southgate and Francis Douce of the British Museum, anonymously published *An Essay on Medals.* It resulted in Pinkerton's introduction to Horace Walpole, who in turn introduced him to Edward Gibbon, who praised Pinkerton to London booksellers. The work was well received and was revised, illustrated, and expanded into two volumes for the second and third editions.

Perhaps because of embarrassment over the "Hardyknute" affair, Pinkerton published his next work under the pseudonym "Robert Heron, Esquire," borrowing his mother's maiden name. *Letters of Literature* (1785) is presented as fifty-seven letters on various topics of literary criticism. The proposed innovations in English spelling and deprecating assessments of classical writers set forth in this work provoked outrage among most critics.

In 1786 Pinkerton published *Ancient Scotish Poems,* which he claimed to be from the Maitland manuscripts in the Pepsyian Library at Cambridge. Probably because of his previous deceptions, many critics assumed that these poems were also forgeries. Robert Chambers says that "the forgery was one of the most audacious recorded in the annals of transcribing." More recent authority has established that the poems are genuine and are still to be found in the Pepsyian Library.

Pinkerton's collection *The Treasury of Wit* (1786) was a deviation from his accustomed subject matter and, according to Chambers, may have been solicited by a bookseller. It appeared under a pseudonym, "H. Bennett, M.A." The same year Pinkerton published under his own name his first real historical treatise, *A Dissertation on the Origin and Progress of the Scythians or Goths* (1787). The central thesis of this work is his historical theory that the Goths were a race superior to the Celts and that both the Greeks and the Romans were of Gothic origins. He claims that the "Piks" were a Gothic tribe who came to Scotland via Scandinavia. The work brims with classical references to Thucydides, Pliny, Tacitus, Herodotus, Strabo, and others to support what Pinkerton asserts as "Historic Truth."

In 1788 Walpole recommended Pinkerton for the position of librarian at the British Museum, writing Sir Joseph Banks, a great botanist and the president of the Royal Society, asking his support for Pinkerton. Banks replied that his support was

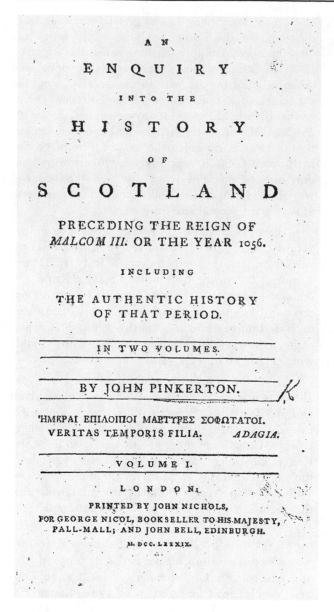

AN
ENQUIRY
INTO THE
HISTORY
OF
SCOTLAND
PRECEDING THE REIGN OF
MALCOM III. OR THE YEAR 1056.

INCLUDING

THE AUTHENTIC HISTORY
OF THAT PERIOD.

IN TWO VOLUMES.

BY JOHN PINKERTON.

ΉΜΚΡΑΙ ΕΠΙΛΟΙΠΟΙ ΜΑΡΤΥΡΕΣ ΣΟΦΩΤΑΤΟΙ.
VERITAS TEMPORIS FILIA.   *ADAGIA.*

VOLUME I.

LONDON,
PRINTED BY JOHN NICHOLS,
FOR GEORGE NICOL, BOOKSELLER TO HIS MAJESTY,
PALL-MALL; AND JOHN BELL, EDINBURGH.
M. DCC. LXXXIX.

Title page for Pinkerton's work that established his reputation as an historian (Eighteenth-Century Collections Online, Gale Group)

Barbour's *The Bruce,* an old Scots poem about the history of Robert I.

Pinkerton's reputation as an historian was firmly established with the publication of *An Enquiry into the History of Scotland Preceding the Reign of Malcolm III. Or the Year 1056* (1789). The two-volume work is bound with *A Dissertation on the Origin and Progress of the Scythians or Goths* and expands on the ideas first set forth in the earlier work. Pinkerton opines that the racially superior Picts—or "Piks," as he calls them—conquered the Celtic Scots from Ireland and that the northern kingdom was misnamed in the writings of Irish monks. Pinkerton refers to ancient Scotland as "Pikland," a name he feels is more apt. He asserts that the Picts were Goths rather than Celts, that they are the ancestors of modern-day Lowland Scots, and that the Scots language is "modern Pikish." He contends that the Celtic people were absorbed by the Picts in all but the Highland regions, where they retain their inferior characteristics. Of considerable value to historians is the extensive bibliography he provides on the ancient history of Britain, Scotland, and Ireland.

Pinkerton then returned to his former subject of coins, publishing *The Medallic History of England to the Revolution* in 1790. Two more years lapsed before his final venture into the collection of Scots poetry with his three-volume *Scotish Poems, Reprinted from Scarce Editions* (1792).

In 1793 Pinkerton was once again unsuccessfully trying to organize his friends to influence his appointment as librarian of the British Museum. In the same year, he married Henrietta Burgess, a woman in possession of a respectable fortune and the sister of Thomas Burgess, Bishop of Salisbury. That this was not a love match is strongly suggested in Pinkerton's letter of 23 September 1793 to David Steuart Erskine, the eleventh earl of Buchan, assigning his delay in corresponding "partly to domestic disquiets, which have forced me to change my former mode of life, and to enter into the holy state of matrimony." The marriage was not a happy one, and the couple separated after producing two children, ultimately divorcing on the grounds of Pinkerton's infidelity. He may have married yet another woman before the divorce was final. Pinkerton also provided for the education of three illegitimate children.

In December 1794 he initiated a subscription series that came to be known as *Iconographia Scotica; or, Portraits of Illustrious Persons of Scotland, with Biographical Notes.* The serial publication was not successful, but the whole was expanded and republished as a book in 1797.

already pledged, and nothing more came of the matter.

About this time, at age thirty, Pinkerton began to suffer severe eye trouble. His intense and constant research in old documents must have added to vision problems which plagued him for the rest of his life.

Pinkerton's next book was in Latin—*Vitae antiquae sanctorum qui habitaverunt in ea parte Britanniae nunc vocata Scotia* (1789). This work was edited from ancient printed and manuscript writings of Scottish monks. Only one hundred copies were printed. In 1790 Pinkerton also published his translation of John

Meanwhile, Pinkerton was finishing the research and writing of his continuing history of Scotland, *The History of Scotland from the Accession of the House of Stuart to that of Mary. With Appendixes of Original Papers* (1797). According to Gordon Donaldson and Robert Morpeth in *Who's Who in Scottish History* (1973), the state papers appended to the two-volume work make it valuable still for studying the reign of James V. But preparation of the work resulted in Pinkerton's being sued by William Anderson, an Edinburgh lawyer whom he had hired to transcribe the public records and documents from the Advocates Library. The lawyer's bill was more than £12, which Pinkerton found excessive and refused to pay. The lawyer successfully sued to compel payment of the fee plus the cost of the suit, garnisheeing some of Pinkerton's rents in Scotland. He also published a pamphlet: *An Answer to an Attack Made by John Pinkerton, Esqr., of Hampstead, in His "History of Scotland"* (1797).

Walpole's friendship with Pinkerton continued until Walpole's death in 1797. Pinkerton must have enjoyed his contacts with the literati and Whig politicians of the late eighteenth century at Strawberry Hill, the extravagant Gothic home of Walpole, Earl of Orford. When Walpole died, Pinkerton assembled a collection of reminiscences of his friend and published them as a series in the *Monthly Magazine* from March 1998 to May 1799. He then published them under the title *Walpoliana* in two volumes in 1799.

Pinkerton's other 1799 book, *The Scottish Gallery; or, Portraits of Eminent Persons of Scotland,* was along the same lines as *Iconographia Scotica.* The fifty-two "eminent persons" are arranged chronologically, beginning with Robert I, crowned king of Scotland on 27 March 1306, and ending with Colin Maclaurin, a distinguished mathematician.

Pinkerton next turned his attention to geography, publishing *Modern Geography: A Description of the Empires, Kingdoms, States, and Colonies, with the Oceans, Seas, and Isles in All Parts of the World* in 1802. About this time he moved to Paris for a few years, reporting on his experiences there in *Recollections of Paris in the Years 1802-3-4-5* (1806), which was not well received by the critics.

By the summer of 1803 Pinkerton had entirely lost the sight of one eye. In spite of the progressive degeneration of his vision, he continued to be a tireless researcher. Between 1808 and 1814 he compiled a seventeen-volume work on geography, *A General Collection of the Best and Most Interesting Voyages and Travels in all Parts of the World; Many of Which Are Now First Translated into English* followed by *A Modern Atlas, from the Latest and Best Authorities, Exhibiting the Various Divi-sions of the World, with Its Chief Empires, Kingdoms, and States, in Sixty Maps* (1809-1815). In between, intrigued by his association in Paris with several eminent geologists, he turned his attention to rocks, publishing the two-volume *Petralogy. A Treatise on Rocks* in 1811.

For a period in the early nineteenth century Pinkerton edited *The Critical Review,* which was experiencing a decline from its previous prominence. In late 1812 he moved to Edinburgh, where he produced a play he had written, *The Heiress of Strathearn; or, The Rash Marriage,* at the Theatre Royal on 24 March 1813. When he failed to be appointed to a position in the Register House overseeing Scotland's public records, he left Edinburgh for Paris in 1814, where he spent the rest of his life in ill health and reduced circumstances. In 1819 Francis Douce visited him in Paris and wrote to G. J. Thorkelin, describing Pinkerton as "a banished man . . . , living in mean lodgings, and [existing] partly by gleaning scarce books on the Parisian stalls, and supplying some of the London dealers in that article." For the last five years of his life, Pinkerton was totally blind. He died in poverty on 10 March 1825 at the age of sixty-seven. According to Chambers, he was "a very little and very thin old man, with a very small, sharp, yellow face, thickly pitted by the small-pox, and decked with a pair of green spectacles."

John Pinkerton was a prodigious researcher and productive writer with a passionate interest in the history of his native Scotland. His talents brought him in contact with some of the great men of his age, but his focus on the merits of the Picts and the defects of the Celts made him an oddity among his fellow historians. His younger contemporary, Sir Walter Scott, summed him up with this assessment: "A man of considerable learning and some severity as well as acuteness of disposition." In spite of the personal prejudices and temperament that biased his writings, Pinkerton made positive contributions to historiography. In 1872, Scottish historian W. F. Skene described him as "the only historian who has estimated correctly the value and superior claims of the earlier documents, and saw somewhat of their true bearing upon the early history."

Letters:

The Literary Correspondence of John Pinkerton, Esq.: Now first Printed from the Originals in the Possession of Dawson Turner (London: Henry Colburn & Richard Bentley, 1830);

The Percy Letters, edited by Harriet Harvey Wood, *Volume VIII: The Correspondence of Thomas Percy & John Pinkerton,* edited by Cleanth Brooks and A. F. Falconer (New Haven, Conn. & London: Yale University Press, 1985).

References:

S. Austin Allibone, *A Critical Dictionary of English Literature and British and American Authors, Living and Deceased, from the Earliest Accounts to the Latter Half of the Nineteenth Century,* 3 volumes (Philadelphia: J. B. Lippincott, 1872); republished (Detroit: Gale Research, 1965), II: 1598–1599;

William Anderson, *The Scottish Nation; or, The Surnames, Families, Literature, Honours, and Biographical History of the People of Scotland by William Anderson,* 3 volumes (Edinburgh: A. Fullarton, 1864), III: 286–288;

Bertrand H. Bronson, "Ritson's Bibliographia Scotia," *PMLA* (March 1937): 122–159 <http://jstor.org/>;

William Ferguson, *The Identity of the Scottish Nation* (Edinburgh: Edinburgh University Press, 1998);

John Nichols and John Bowyer Nichols, *Illustrations of the Literary History of the Eighteenth Century. Consisting of Authentic Memoirs and Original Letters of Eminent Persons. To Which Are Appended Additions to the Literary Anecdotes and Literary Illustrations,* 8 volumes (London: Printed for the author by Nichols & Bently, 1817–1858);

Sir Walter Scott, *The Antiquary* (Edinburgh: Printed by James Ballantyne for Archibald Constable, Edinburgh; London: Longman, Hurst, Rees, Orme & Brown, 1816).

Papers:

A collection of John Pinkerton's papers is in the Manuscripts Division of the National Library of Scotland. Correspondence from Pinkerton is also found in the Beinecke Library and in the Lewis Walpole Library at Yale University, in the Fitzwilliam Museum at Cambridge, in the Bodleian Library at Oxford, and in the British Library.

Joseph Priestley
(13 March 1733 – 6 February 1804)

Alan Tapper
Edith Cowan University

See also the Priestley entry in *DLB 252: British Philosophers, 1500–1799*.

BOOKS: *The Rudiments of English Grammar; Adapted to the Use of Schools. With Observations on Style* (London: Printed for R. Griffiths, 1761);

The Scripture Doctrine of Remission Which Showeth That the Death of Christ Is No Proper Sacrifice nor Satisfaction for Sin: But That Pardon Is Dispensed Solely on Account of Repentance or A Personal Reformation of the Sinner (London: Printed for C. Henderson and R. Griffiths & P. A. De Hondt, 1761);

A Course of Lectures on the Theory of Language and Universal Grammar (Warrington: W. Eyers, 1762);

No Man Liveth to Himself. A Sermon Preached Before an Assembly of Protestant Dissenting-Ministers, of the Counties of Lancaster and Chester, Met at Manchester, May 16, 1764, to Carry into Execution a Scheme for the Relief of Their Widows and Children (Warrington, 1764);

A Description of a Chart of Biography: With a Catalogue of All the Names Inserted in It, and the Dates Annexed to Them, second edition (Warrington: Printed for the author and sold by himself, and by J. Bowles, London, 1765; revised, 1772);

An Essay on a Course of Liberal Education for Civil and Active Life. With Plans of Lectures on I. The Study of History and General Policy. II. The History of England. III. The Constitution and Laws of England. To Which Are Added, Remarks on a Code of Education, Proposed by Dr. Brown, in a Late Treatise, Intitled, Thoughts on Civil Liberty, &c. (London: Printed for C. Henderson, T. Becket & P. A. De Hondt, and J. Johnson & Davenport, 1765);

A Syllabus of a Course of Lectures on the Study of History (Warrington: Printed by William Eyres, 1765);

A Catechism for Children and Young Persons (London, 1767); abridged as *Extracts from Dr. Priestley's Catechism for Children and Young Persons* (Salem, Mass.: Printed by Samuel Hall, 1785);

Joseph Priestley (steel engraving from a portrait by Gilbert Stuart; The Joseph Priestley Collection, Rare Books and Manuscripts, Special Collections Library, Penn State University)

The History and Present State of Electricity, with Original Experiments (London: Printed for J. Dodsley, J. Johnson & B. Davenport, and T. Cadell, 1767; corrected and enlarged, 1769; corrected and enlarged again, 2 volumes, London: Printed for C. Bathurst & T. Lowndes, J. Rivington & J. Johnson, and T. Becket & T. Cadell, 1775);

An Essay on the First Principles of Government; and on the Nature of Political, Civil, and Religious Liberty (London: Printed for J. Dodsley, T. Cadell, and J. Johnson, 1768; corrected and enlarged edition, London: Printed for J. Johnson, 1771);

A Familiar Introduction to the Study of Electricity (London: Printed for J. Dodsley, T. Cadell, and J. Johnson, 1768);

Considerations on Church-Authority; Occasioned by Dr. Balguy's Sermon, on That Subject; Preached at Lambeth Chapel, and Published by Order of the Archbishop (London: Printed for J. Johnson & J. Payne, 1769);

Considerations on Differences of Opinion among Christians: With a Letter to the Reverend Mr. Venn, in Answer to His Free and Full Examination of the Address to Protestant Dissenters, on the Subject of the Lord's Supper (London: Printed for J. Johnson & J. Payne, 1769);

A Free Address to Protestant Dissenters, as Such, as A Dissenter (London: Printed for G. Pearch, 1769; enlarged edition, London: Printed for J. Johnson, 1771);

A Free Address to Protestant Dissenters, on the Subject of the Lord's Supper (London: Printed for J. Johnson, 1769);

The Present State of Liberty in Great Britain and her Colonies, as an Englishman (London: Printed for J. Johnson & J. Payne, 1769);

Remarks on Some Paragraphs in the Fourth Volume of Dr. Blackstone's Commentaries on the Laws of England, Relating to the Dissenters (London: Printed for J. Johnson & J. Payne, 1769; Philadelphia: Printed by Robert Bell, 1772);

A Serious Address to Masters of Families, with Forms of Family-Prayer (London: Printed for J. Johnson & J. Payne, 1769);

A View of the Principles and Conduct of the Protestant Dissenters, with Respect to the Civil and Ecclesiastical Constitution of England (London: Printed for J. Johnson & J. Payne, 1769);

Additions to the Address to Protestant Dissenters, on the Subject of the Lord's Supper, with Some Corrections on It; and A Letter to the Author of the Protestant Dissenter's Answer to It (London: Printed for Joseph Johnson, 1770; Boston: Printed by Thomas & John Fleet, 1774);

An Answer to Dr. Blackstone's Reply to Remarks on the Fourth Volume of Commentaries on the Laws of England (Dublin: Printed by James Williams, 1770; Philadelphia: Printed by Robert Bell, 1772);

An Appeal to the Serious and Candid Professors of Christianity. On the Following Subjects, viz. I. The Use of Reason in Matters of Religion. II. The Power of Man to Do the Will of God. III. Original Sin. IV. Election and Reprobation. V. The Divinity of Christ. And, VI. Atonement for Sin by the Death of Christ, anonymous (Leeds, 1770; Philadelphia: Printed and sold by Robert Bell, 1784);

A Description of a New Chart of History, Containing a View of the Principal Revolutions of Empire, That Have Taken Place in the World, second edition (London: Printed

for J. Johnson, 1770; New Haven, Conn.: Printed by T. & S. Green for Amos Doolittle, 1792);

A Familiar Introduction to the Theory and Practice of Perspective (London: Printed for J. Johnson & J. Payne, 1770);

A Free Address to Protestant Dissenters, on the Subject of Church Discipline; With a Preliminary Discourse, concerning the Spirit of Christianity, and the Corruption of It by False Notions of Religion (London: Printed for J. Johnson, 1770);

Letters to the Author of Remarks on Several Late Publications Relative to the Dissenters, in a Letter to Dr. Priestley (London: Printed for J. Johnson, 1770);

Letters and Queries Addressed to the Anonymous Answerer of An Appeal to the Serious and Candid Professors of Christianity; to the Rev. Mr. Tho. Morgan, and to Mr. Cornelius Caley (Leeds: Sold by J. Binns, 1771);

Directions for Impregnating Water with Fixed Air; in Order to Communicate to It the Peculiar Spirit and Virtues of Pyrmont Water, and Other Mineral Waters of a Similar Nature (London: Printed for J. Johnson, 1772);

A Familiar Illustration of Certain Passages of Scripture: Relating to the Power of Man to Do the Will of God, Original Sin, Election and Reprobation, the Divinity of Christ, and Atonement for Sin by the Death of Christ, as A Lover of the Gospel (London: Printed for J. Johnson, 1772); as Priestley (Philadelphia: Printed by Thomas Dobson, 1794);

The History and Present State of Discoveries Relating to Vision, Light and Colours (London: Printed for J. Johnson, 1772);

Institutes of Natural and Revealed Religion. Vol. I. Containing the Elements of Natural Religion; To Which Is Prefixed, An Essay on the Best Method of Communicating Religious Knowledge to the Members of Christian Societies (London: Printed for J. Johnson, 1772);

Observations on Different Kinds of Air (London: Printed by W. Bowyer & J. Nichols, 1772); revised as volume 1 of *Experiments and Observations on Different Kinds of Air* (2 volumes, London: Printed for J. Johnson, 1774, 1775; enlarged, 3 volumes, 1777–1781);

An Address to Protestant Dissenters, on the Subject of Giving the Lord's Supper to Children (London: Printed for J. Johnson, 1773);

Institutes of Natural and Revealed Religion. Vol. II. Containing the Evidences of the Jewish and Christian Revelations (London: Printed for J. Johnson, 1773);

A Letter of Advice to Those Dissenters Who Conduct the Application to Parliament for Relief from Certain Penal Laws. With Various Observations Relating to Similar Subjects, as The Author of the *Free Address to Protestant Dissenters, as Such* (London: Printed for J. Johnson, 1773);

A Sermon, Preached Before the Congregation of Protestant Dissenters at Mill-Hill-Chapel in Leeds, May 16, 1773. By

Joseph Priestley, LLD. F.R.S., on Occasion of His Resigning His Pastoral Office among Them (London: Printed for J. Johnson, 1773);

An Address to Protestant Dissenters of All Denominations: On the Approaching Election of Members of Parliament, with Respect to the State of Public Liberty in General, and of American Affairs in Particular (London: Printed for J. Johnson, 1774; Philadelphia: Printed and sold by James Humphreys Jr., 1774);

An Examination of Dr. Reid's Inquiry into the Human Mind on the Principles of Common Sense, Dr. Beattie's Essay on the Nature and Immutability of Truth, and Dr. Oswald's Appeal to Common Sense on Behalf of Religion (London: Printed for J. Johnson, 1774);

Institutes of Natural and Revealed Religion. Vol. III. Containing a View of the Doctrine of Revelation (London: Printed for J. Johnson, 1774);

A Letter to a Layman, on the Subject of the Rev. Mr. Lindsey's Proposal for a Reformed English Church, upon the Plan of the Late Dr. Samuel Clarke (London: Printed for J. Wilkie, 1774);

Considerations for the Use of Young Men and the Parents of Young Men (London: Printed for J. Johnson, 1775);

Philosophical Empiricism: Containing Remarks on a Charge of Plagiarism Respecting Dr. H---s, Interspersed with Various Observations Relating to Different Kinds of Air (London: Printed for J. Johnson, 1775);

Observations on Respiration, and the Use of the Blood . . . Read at the Royal Society, Jan. 25, 1776 (London, 1776);

A Course of Lectures on Oratory and Criticism (London: Printed for J. Johnson, 1777);

Disquisitions Relating to Matter and Spirit. To Which Is Added the History of the Philosophical Doctrine concerning the Origin of the Soul, and the Nature of Matter; With its Influence on Christianity, Especially with Respect to the Doctrine of the Pre-Existence of Christ (London: Printed for J. Johnson, 1777; second edition, improved and enlarged, 2 volumes, Birmingham: Printed by Pearson & Rollason for J. Johnson, 1782);

The Doctrine of Philosophical Necessity Illustrated; Being an Appendix to the Disquisitions relating to Matter and Spirit. To Which Is Added an Answer to the Letters on Materialism, and on Hartley's Theory of Mind (London: Printed for J. Johnson, 1777); enlarged as *The Doctrine of Philosophical Necessity Illustrated; Being an Appendix to the Disquisitions relating to Matter and Spirit. To Which Is Added, an Answer to Several Persons Who Have Controverted the Principles of It* (Birmingham: Printed by Pearson & Rollason for J. Johnson, London, 1782);

A Free Discussion of the Doctrines of Materialism and Philosophical Necessity, in a Correspondence between Dr. Price and Dr. Priestley. To which are added, by Dr. Priestley, an Introduction Explaining the Nature of the Controversy, and Letters to Several Writers Who Have Animadverted on His Disquisitions Relating to Matter and Spirit, or his Treatise on Necessity (London: Printed for J. Johnson and T. Cadell, 1778);

Miscellaneous Observations Relating to Education. More Especially, as It Respects the Conduct of the Mind. To Which Is Added, an Essay on a Course of Liberal Education for Civil and Active Life (Bath: Printed by R. Cruttwell for J. Johnson, London, 1778; New London, Conn.: Printed by J. Springer for T. C. Green, S. Green, and J. Trumbull, Norwich, 1796);

The Doctrine of Divine Influence on the Human Mind: Considered, in a Sermon, Published at the Request of Many Persons Who Have Occasionally Heard It (Bath: Printed by R. Cruttwell, 1779; Northumberland, Pa.: Printed by John Binns, 1804);

Experiments and Observations Relating to Various Branches of Natural Philosophy with a Continuation of the Observations on Air, 3 volumes (London: Printed for J. Johnson, 1779–1786);

A Letter to the Rev. Mr. John Palmer, in Defence of the Illustrations of Philosophical Necessity (Bath: Printed by R. Cruttwell, London, 1779);

A Harmony of the Evangelists in English; With Critical Dissertations, an Occasional Paraphrase, and Notes for the Use of the Unlearned (London: Printed for J. Johnson, 1780);

A Letter to Jacob Bryant, Esq. in Defence of Philosophical Necessity (London: Printed by H. Baldwin for J. Johnson, 1780);

Letters to a Philosophical Unbeliever, Part I. Containing an Examination of the Principal Objections to the Doctrines of Natural Religion, and Especially Those Contained in the Writings of Mr. Hume (Bath: Printed by R. Cruttwell, London, 1780);

A Second Letter to the Rev. Mr. John Palmer, in Defence of the Doctrine of Philosophical Necessity (London: Printed by H. Baldwin for J. Johnson, 1780);

Two Letters to Dr Newcome, Bishop of Waterford, on the Duration of Our Saviour's Ministry (Birmingham: Printed by Pearson & Rollason for J. Johnson, London, 1780);

A Sermon, Preached December the 31st, 1780 at the New Meeting in Birmingham, on Undertaking the Pastoral Office in That Place (Birmingham: Printed by Pearson & Rollason for J. Johnson, London, 1781);

A Scripture Catechism, Consisting of a Series of Questions: With References to the Scriptures Instead of Answers (London: Printed for J. Johnson, 1781);

A Third Letter to Dr Newcome, Bishop of Waterford, on the Duration of Our Saviour's Ministry (Birmingham: Printed by Piercy & Jones for J. Johnson, London, 1781);

Additional Letters to a Philosophical Unbeliever, in Answer to Mr. William Hammon (Birmingham: Printed by Pearson & Rollason for J. Johnson, London, 1782);

An History of the Corruptions of Christianity, 2 volumes (Birmingham: Printed by Piercy & Jones, for J. Johnson, London, 1782; Boston: Printed by William Spotswood, 1797);

The Proper Constitution of a Christian Church, Considered in a Sermon, Preached at the New Meeting in Birmingham, November 3, 1782. To Which Is Prefixed, a Prefatory Discourse, Relating to the Present State of Those Who Are Called Rational Dissenters (Birmingham: Printed by Pearson & Rollason, 1782);

Two Discourses; I. On Habitual Devotion; II. On the Duty of Not Living to Ourselves: Both Preached to Assemblies of Protestant Dissenting Ministers, and Published at Their Request (Birmingham: Printed by Piercy & Jones for J. Johnson, London, 1782);

A General View of the Arguments for the Unity of God: And Against the Divinity and Pre-existence of Christ, from Reason, from the Scriptures, and from History (Birmingham: Printed by Piercy & Jones for J. Johnson, London, 1783; Philadelphia: Printed by Robert Bell, 1784);

A Reply to the Animadversions on the History of the Corruptions of Christianity, in the Monthly Review for June, 1783: With Additional Observations Relating to the Doctrine of the Primitive Church, Concerning the Person of Christ (Birmingham: Printed by Piercy & Jones for J. Johnson, London, 1783);

Letters to Dr. Horsley, in Answer to His Animadversions on the History of the Corruptions of Christianity. With Additional Evidence That the Primitive Christian Church Was Unitarian (Birmingham: Printed by Pearson & Rollason for J. Johnson, London, 1783);

Letters to Dr. Horsley, Part II.: Containing Farther Evidence That the Primitive Christian Church Was Unitarian (Birmingham: Printed by Pearson & Rollason for J. Johnson, London, 1784);

Remarks on the Monthly Review of the Letters to Dr. Horsley; in Which the Rev. Mr. Samuel Badcock, the Writer of That Review, Is Called upon to Defend What He Has Advanced in It (Birmingham: Printed by Pearson & Rollason for J. Johnson, London, 1784);

The Importance and Extent of Free Inquiry in Matters of Religion: A Sermon, Preached Before the Congregations of the Old and New Meeting of Protestant Dissenters at Birmingham. November 5, 1785. To Which Are Added, Reflections on the Present State of Free Inquiry in this Country (Birmingham: Printed by M. Swinney for J. Johnson, London, 1785);

An History of Early Opinions Concerning Jesus Christ, Compiled from Original Writers; Proving That the Christian Church

Was at First Unitarian (Birmingham: Printed for the author by Pearson & Rollason and sold by J. Johnson, London, 1786);

Letters to Dr. Horsley, Part III. Containing an Answer to His Remarks on Letters, Part II. To Which Are Added Strictures on Mr. Howe's Ninth Number of Observations on Books Ancient and Modern (Birmingham: Printed by Pearson & Rollason for J. Johnson, London, 1786);

Letters to the Jews; Inviting Them to an Amicable Discussion of the Evidences of Christianity (Birmingham: Printed by Pearson & Rollason and sold by J. Johnson, London, 1786); republished in *Letters from Dr. Priestley to the Jews; Inviting Them to an Amicable Discussion of the Evidences of Christianity* (New York: Printed by J. Harrison for Benjamin Gomes, 1794);

An Account of a Society, for Encouraging the Industrious Poor: With a Table for Their Use. To Which Are Prefixed, Some Considerations on the State of the Poor in General (Birmingham: Printed by Pearson & Rollason, 1787);

Discourses on Various Subjects, Including Several on Particular Occasions (Birmingham: Printed for the author by Pearson & Rollason, London, 1787);

A Letter to the Right Honourable William Pitt, First Lord of the Treasury, and Chancellor of the Exchequer; On the Subjects of Toleration and Church Establishments; Occasioned by His Speech Against the Repeal of the Test and Corporation Acts, on Wednesday the 28th of March, 1787 (London: Printed for J. Johnson and J. Debrett, 1787; corrected and enlarged, 1787);

Letters to a Philosophical Unbeliever. Part II.: Containing a State of the Evidence of Revealed Religion, with Animadversions on the Two Last Chapters of the First Volume of Mr. Gibbon's History of the Decline and Fall of the Roman Empire (Birmingham: Printed by Pearson & Rollason for J. Johnson, London, 1787);

Letters to Dr. Horne, Dean of Canterbury: To the Young Men, Who Are in a Course of Education for the Christian Ministry, at the Universities of Oxford and Cambridge; To Dr. Price; and To Mr. Parkhurst; on the Subject of the Person of Christ (Birmingham: Printed for the author by Pearson & Rollason, 1787);

Letters to the Jews. Part II. Occasioned by Mr. David Levi's Reply to the Former Letters (Birmingham: Printed for the author by Pearson & Rollason, 1787); republished in *Letters from Dr. Priestley to the Jews; Inviting Them to an Amicable Discussion of the Evidences of Christianity* (New York: Printed by J. Harrison for Benjamin Gomes, 1794);

Defences of Unitarianism for the Year 1786. Containing Letters to Dr. Horne, Dean of Canterbury; To the Young Men, Who Are in a Course of Education for the Christian Ministry at the Universities of Oxford and Cambridge; To the

Rev. Dr. Price; and To the Rev. Mr. Parkhurst; on the Subject of the Person of Christ, 3 volumes (Birmingham: Printed for the author by Pearson & Rollason, 1788);

Defences of Unitarianism for the Year 1787. Containing Letters to the Rev. Dr. Geddes, to the Rev. Dr. Price, Part I, and to the Candidates for Orders in the Two Universities; Part II, Relating to Mr. Howes's Appendix to His Fourth Volume of Observations on Books, A Letter by an Undergraduate of Oxford, Dr. Croft's Bampton Lectures, and Several Other Publications (Birmingham: Printed for the author by Pearson & Rollason, 1788);

Lectures on History, and General Policy to Which Is Prefixed, An Essay on a Course of Liberal Education for Civil and Active Life, 2 volumes (Birmingham: Printed by Pearson & Rollason for J. Johnson, London, 1788; Philadelphia: Printed for P. Byrne, 1803);

A Sermon on the Subject of the Slave Trade: Delivered to a Society of Protestant Dissenters, at the New Meeting, in Birmingham; and Published at Their Request (Birmingham: Printed for the author by Pearson & Rollason, 1788);

The Conduct to Be Observed by Dissenters in Order to Procure the Repeal of the Corporation and Test Acts, Recommended in a Sermon Preached Before the Congregations of the Old and New Meetings at Birmingham, November 5, 1789 (Birmingham: Printed by J. Thompson, 1789);

Defences of Unitarianism for the Years 1788 & 1789. Containing Letters to Dr. Horsley, Lord Bishop of St. David's, to the Rev. Mr. Barnard, the Rev. Dr. Knowles, and the Rev. Mr. Hawkins (Birmingham: Printed by J. Thompson for J. Johnson, London, 1790);

Dr. Priestley's Letters to the Candidates for Orders in Both Universities on Subscription to Articles of Religion, with an Address to Conforming Arians, &c. (Cambridge: Sold by J. & J. Merrill and J. Bowtell, Cambridge, D. Prince, Oxford, and J. Johnson, London, 1790);

Familiar Letters, Addressed to the Inhabitants of the Town of Birmingham, in Refutation of Several Charges, Advanced against the Dissenters, by the Rev. Mr Madan, Rector of St. Philip's, in His Sermon, Entitled "The Principal Claims of the Dissenters Considered." Preached at St. Philip's Church, on Sunday February 14, 1790 (Birmingham: Printed by F. Thompson, 1790);

A General History of the Christian Church to the Fall of the Western Empire (2 volumes, Birmingham: Printed by Thomas Pearson and sold by J. Johnson, London, 1790; 4 volumes, Northumberland, Pa.: Printed for the author by Andrew Kennedy, 1803);

Letter to the Rev. Edward Burn, of St. Mary's Chapel, Birmingham, in Answer to His on the Infallibility of the Apostolic Testimony, concerning the Person of Christ (Birmingham: Printed by J. Thompson, 1790);

Reflections on Death. A Sermon, on Occasion of the Death of the Rev. Robert Robinson, of Cambridge, Delivered at the New Meeting in Birmingham, June 13, 1790 (Birmingham: Printed by J. Belcher, 1790);

A View of Revealed Religion; a Sermon, Preached at the Ordination of the Rev. William Field of Warwick, July 12, 1790 (Birmingham: Printed by J. Thompson, 1790);

An Appeal to the Public, on the Subject of the Riots in Birmingham. To Which Is Added, Strictures on a Pamphlet, Intitled "Thoughts on the Late Riot at Birmingham" (Birmingham: Printed by J. Thompson, 1791);

A Discourse on Occasion of the Death of Dr. Price: Delivered at Hackney, on Sunday, May 1, 1791 (London: Printed for J. Johnson, 1791);

The Duty of Forgiveness of Injuries: A Discourse Intended to Be Delivered Soon after the Riots in Birmingham (Birmingham: Printed by J. Thompson, 1791);

The Evidence of the Resurrection of Jesus Considered: In a Discourse First Delivered in the Assembly-room, at Buxton, on Sunday, September 19, 1790. To Which Is Added, An Address to the Jews (Birmingham: Printed by J. Thompson, 1791);

Letters to the Members of the New Jerusalem Church, Formed by Baron Swedenborg (Birmingham: Printed by J. Thompson, 1791);

Letters to the Right Honourable Edmund Burke: Occasioned by His Reflections on the Revolution in France, &c (Birmingham: Printed by Thomas Pearson, 1791; New York: Printed by Hugh Gaine, 1791);

A Particular Attention to the Instruction of the Young Recommended, in a Discourse, Delivered at the Gravel-pit Meeting, in Hackney, December 4, 1791, on Entering on the Office of Pastor to the Congregation of Protestant Dissenters, Assembling in That Place (London: Printed for J. Johnson, 1791);

The Proper Objects of Education in the Present State of the World: Represented in a Discourse, Delivered on Wednesday, the 27th of April, 1791, at the Meetinghouse in the Old-Jewry, London, to the Supporters of New College at Hackney (London: Printed for J. Johnson, 1791);

Letters to a Young Man: Occasioned by Mr. Wakefield's Essay on Public Worship; to Which Is Added, a Reply to Mr. Evanson's Objections to the Observance of the Lord's Day (London: Printed for J. Johnson, 1792);

Letters to a Young Man, Part II. Occasioned by Mr. Evanson's Treatise on the Dissonance of the Four Generally Received Evangelists (London: Printed for J. Johnson, 1793);

Experiments on the Generation of Air from Water; To Which Are Prefixed, Experiments Relating to the Decomposition of Dephlogisticated and Inflammable Air (London: Printed for J. Johnson, 1793);

Letters to the Philosophers and Politicians of France, on the Subject of Religion (London: Printed for J. Johnson, 1793; Boston: Printed and sold by Samuel Hall, 1793);

A Sermon Preached at the Gravel Pit Meeting, in Hackney, April 19th, 1793, Being the Day Appointed for a General Fast (London: Printed for J. Johnson, 1793);

An Answer to Mr. Paine's Age of Reason, Being a Continuation of Letters to the Philosophers and Politicians of France, on the Subject of Religion; And of the Letters to a Philosophical Unbeliever (Northumberland, Pa., 1794; London: Printed for J. Johnson, 1795);

A Continuation of the Letters to the Philosophers and Politicians of France, on the Subject of Religion; And of The Letters of a Philosophical Unbeliever; In Answer to Mr. Paine's Age of Reason (Northumberland, Pa.: Printed by Andrew Kennedy, 1794);

Discourses on the Evidences of Revealed Religion (London: Printed for J. Johnson, 1794; Boston: Printed and sold by William Spotswood, 1795);

Heads of Lectures on a Course of Experimental Philosophy: Particularly Including Chemistry, Delivered at the New College in Hackney (London: Printed for J. Johnson, 1794);

The Present State of Europe Compared with Antient Prophecies: a Sermon, Preached at the Gravel Pit Meeting in Hackney, February 28, 1794: Being the Day Appointed for a General Fast . . . with a Preface Containing the Reasons for the Author's Leaving England (London: Printed for J. Johnson, 1794); republished in *Two Sermons Viz. I. the Present State of Europe Compared with Antient Prophecies; Preached on the Fast-day in 1794; With a Preface, Containing the Reasons for the Author's Leaving England. II. The Use of Christianity, Especially in Difficult Times; Being the Author's Farewell Discourse* (Philadelphia: Printed by Thomas Dobson, 1794);

The Use of Christianity, Especially in Difficult Times: A Sermon, Delivered at the Gravel Pit Meeting in Hackney, March 30, 1794. . . . Being the Author's Farewell Discourse to His Congregation (London: Printed for J. Johnson, 1794); republished in *Two Sermons Viz. I. the Present State of Europe Compared with Antient Prophecies; Preached on the Fast-day in 1794; With a Preface, Containing the Reasons for the Author's Leaving England. II. The Use of Christianity, Especially in Difficult Times; Being the Author's Farewell Discourse* (Philadelphia: Printed for Thomas Dobson, 1794);

Observations on the Increase of Infidelity. First Prefixed to the American Edition of Letters to the Philosophers and Politicians of France on the Subject of Religion, but Now Much Enlarged (Northumberland, Pa.: Printed by Andrew Kennedy, 1795; London: Printed for J. Johnson, 1796);

Considerations on the Doctrine of Phlogiston, and the Decomposition of Water (Philadelphia: Printed by Thomas Dobson, 1796);

Discourses Relating to the Evidences of Revealed Religion: Delivered in the Church of the Universalists at Philadelphia, 1796 (Philadelphia: Printed by Thomas Dobson, 1796); republished as *Discourses Relating to the Evidences of Revealed Religion. Vol. II, Being the First Delivered at Philadelphia in 1796* (London: Printed for J. Johnson, 1796);

Unitarianism explained and defended in a discourse delivered in the Church of the Universalists at Philadelphia, 1796 (Philadelphia: Printed by John Thompson, 1796; London: Printed for J. Johnson, 1796);

An Address to the Unitarian Congregation at Philadelphia, Delivered on Sunday, March 5, 1797 (Philadelphia: Printed by Joseph Gales, 1797);

The Case of Poor Emigrants Recommended: in a Discourse, Delivered at the University Hall in Philadelphia, on Sunday, February 19, 1797 (Philadelphia: Printed by Joseph Gales, 1797);

Letters to Mr. Volney: Occasioned by a Work of His Entitled Ruins, and by His Letter to the Author (Philadelphia: Printed by Thomas Dobson, 1797);

Observations on the Doctrine of Phlogiston and the Decomposition of Water. Part the Second (Philadelphia: Printed by Thomas Dobson, 1797);

An Outline of the Evidences of Revealed Religion (Philadelphia: Printed by Thomas Dobson, 1797; London: Printed for the British and Foreign Unitarian Association, 1833);

Discourses Relating to the Evidences of Revealed Religion: Delivered in Philadelphia . . . Vol. II (Philadelphia: Printed by Thomas Dobson, 1797); republished as *Discourses Relating to the Evidences of Revealed Religion. Vol. III, Being the Second Delivered at Philadelphia in 1797* (London: Printed for J. Johnson, 1799);

A Comparison of the Institutions of Moses with Those of the Hindoos and Other Ancient Nations: With Remarks on Mr. Dupuis's Origin of All Religions, the Laws and Institutions of Moses Methodized, and an Address to the Jews on the Present State of the World and the Prophecies Relating to It (Northumberland, Pa.: Printed for the author by A. Kennedy, 1799);

The Doctrine of Phlogiston Established, and That of the Composition of Water Refuted (Northumberland, Pa.: Printed for the author by A. Kennedy, 1800);

Sermons, by Priestley and Richard Price (London: Printed by J. Davis, 1800);

An Inquiry into the Knowledge of the Antient Hebrews Concerning a Future State (London: Printed for J. Johnson, 1801);

Letters to the Inhabitants of Northumberland and its Neighbourhood on Subjects Interesting to the Author and to Them: to

Which Is Added a Letter to a Friend in Paris, Relating to Mr. Liancourt's Travels in the North American States (Philadelphia: Printed by John Bioren for John Conrad, 1801);

A General History of the Christian Church, from the Fall of the Western Empire to the Present Time, 4 volumes (Northumberland, Pa.: Printed for the author by Andrew Kennedy, 1802);

A Letter to an Antipædobaptist (Northumberland, Pa.: Printed by Andrew Kennedy, 1802);

A Letter to the Reverend John Blair Linn, A.M: A Pastor of the First Presbyterian Congregation in the City of Philadelphia, in Defence of the Pamphlet, Entitled, Socrates and Jesus Compared (Northumberland, Pa.: Printed by Andrew Kennedy, for P. Byrne, Philadelphia, 1803);

A Second Letter to the Revd. John Blair Linn, D.D., Pastor of the First Presbyterian Congregation in the City of Philadelphia: A Reply to His Defence of the Doctrines of the Divinity of Christ and Atonement (Northumberland, Pa.: Printed by Andrew Kennedy for P. Byrne, Philadelphia, 1803);

Notes on All the Books of Scripture, for Use of the Pulpit and Private Families, 4 volumes (Northumberland, Pa.: Printed for the author by Andrew Kennedy, 1803–1804);

The Originality and Superior Excellence of the Mosaic Institutions Demonstrated (Northumberland, Pa.: Printed by Andrew Kennedy, for P. Byrne, Philadelphia, 1803);

Socrates and Jesus Compared (London: Printed for J. Johnson, 1803);

The Doctrine of Heathen Philosophy: Compared with Those of Revelation (Northumberland, Pa.: Printed by John Binns, 1804);

Index to the Bible in Which the Various Subjects Which Occur in the Scriptures Are Alphabetically Arranged, with Accurate References to All the Books of the Old and New Testaments (Philadelphia, 1804; London: Printed for J. Johnson, 1805);

Discourses on Various Subjects: Intended to Have Been Delivered in Philadelphia; To Which Are Added, Some Others, Selected from the Same Author (Northumberland, Pa.: Printed by John Binns, 1805);

Four Discourses: Intended to Have Been Delivered in Philadelphia (Northumberland, Pa.: Printed by John Binns, 1806);

Memoirs of Dr. Joseph Priestley, to the Year 1795, Written by Himself: With a Continuation, to the Time of His Decease, by His Son, Joseph Priestley and Observations on His Writings, by Thomas Cooper, President Judge of the 4th District of Pennsylvania, and the Rev. William Christie (Northumberland, Pa.: Printed by J.

Binns, 1806; London: Printed for J. Johnson, 1806);

The Theological and Miscellaneous Works of Joseph Priestley, LL.D. F.R.S. &c., 25 volumes, edited by John Towill Rutt (London: Printed by George Smallfield, Hackney, 1817–1831).

Editions: Priestley's Writings on Philosophy, Science and Politics, edited by John A. Passmore (New York: Collier, 1965);

Autobiography of Joseph Priestley, edited by Jack Lindsey (Bath: Adams & Dart, 1970);

Political Writings, edited by Peter N. Miller (Cambridge: Cambridge University Press, 1993);

Theological and Miscellaneous Works of Joseph Priestley, 26 volumes, with an introduction by John Stephens (Bristol: Thoemmes Press, 1999);

Memoirs and Correspondence of Joseph Priestley (Bristol: Thoemmes Press, 2002).

OTHER: Hartley's Theory of the Human Mind, on the Principle of the Association of Ideas; With Essays Relating to the Subject of It, edited, with an introduction, by Priestley (London: Printed for J. Johnson, 1775).

Ars longa, vita brevis ("Art is long, life short") was one of Joseph Priestley's favorite mottoes. In fact, his life was relatively long (he lived to be seventy-one), and in it he mastered many "arts." By any standard he was a leading scientist, though he practiced his science only in his spare time. His preferred vocation was that of Unitarian clergyman and theologian. He made contributions to various branches of philosophy, from metaphysics to political philosophy. He also wrote on education, rhetoric, grammar, psychology, and political affairs. Science, theology, and philosophy were, in his eyes, all part of one great system of knowledge. The unity of this system was not always as clear to his contemporaries as it was to him, but, as his biographer Robert E. Schofield has observed in his introduction to the 1966 edition of Priestley's The History and Present State of Electricity, Priestley was "inclined throughout his life to approach intellectual problems in an historical manner," and in doing so he became a significant historian. His historical writings make up the largest part of his voluminous output. They fall into four main categories: historian of science, historian of religion and philosophy, an educator and guide to the craft of history, and a theorist of historical progress.

Priestley was born on 13 March 1733 in a village a few miles outside Leeds. His family were Yorkshire Calvinists, or "Independents." His father was a cloth dresser. His mother died when Joseph was six years old, and he was sent to live with a childless aunt, Sarah Keighley, who, although herself a strict Calvinist, made

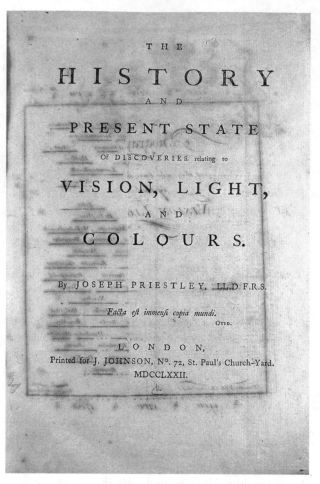

T H E

HISTORY

A N D

PRESENT STATE

OF DISCOVERIES relating to

VISION, LIGHT,

A N D

COLOURS.

By JOSEPH PRIESTLEY, LL.D. F.R.S.

Facta est immensi copia mundi.
OVID.

LONDON,
Printed for J. JOHNSON, Nº. 72, St. Paul's Church-Yard.
MDCCLXXII.

Title page for Priestley's work commonly known as The History
of Optics *(Thomas Cooper Library, University
of South Carolina)*

her home a center for Dissenting ministers of all persuasions. Priestley's experience of tolerant debate in that household formed him for life. According to *Memoirs of Dr. Joseph Priestley, to the Year 1795, Written by Himself* (1806), his experience at Daventry Academy in 1752–1755, where he trained to become a Dissenting minister, was similar. There, he said, "the students were about equally divided upon every question of much importance, such as liberty and necessity, the sleep of the soul, and all the articles of theological orthodoxy and heresy; in consequence of which, all these topics were the subject of continual discussion." His education at Daventry ranged across theology, philosophy, ancient (but not modern) history, classical and modern languages, and the sciences. That wide range of interests marked his whole career.

Already by this period Priestley had begun to depart from Calvinist orthodoxy on original sin. His deviation led to a rift with his family that was never

fully healed. For a time he tended toward Arminianism. He came to reject the doctrine of atonement, and for about fifteen years he was an Arian. His heterodoxy hampered his early career as a minister at Needham Market and Nantwich, the first two of the five congregations that he served. But his rejection of orthodoxy in no way lessened his faith in divine Providence or in the Christian promise of a future life. He remained a Christian while rejecting strenuously the divinity of Christ. He eventually became a leading Rational Dissenter and by the 1780s was the main champion of Unitarianism in Britain.

In 1761 Priestley was happy to be appointed tutor in languages and literature at Warrington Academy, where he lectured on history, rhetoric, literary criticism, and aesthetics, and where he first made his name as an author with three works: a textbook on English grammar, a study of the theory of language, and an essay on the aims and practice of education. He moved quickly to design a new liberal arts curriculum, which had at its heart the study of modern history, along with English, Latin, French, and mathematics. The lectures he gave on history were written up for publication but did not appear until 1788. In 1762 Priestley was ordained as a Presbyterian minister, and in that same year he married Mary Wilkinson, the sister of a Welsh iron master. They eventually had three sons and a daughter.

Priestley published an account of his modernized curriculum in 1765 in *An Essay on a Course of Liberal Education for Civil and Active Life*. The essay demonstrates a broad conception of historiography: the historian's task is to encompass not only politics, religion, war, and law, but also manners, arts, trade, manufacturing, technology, cities, education, and arts. The study of history equips young men for a public role in business, industry, and government. It involves the study not just of good and bad character or wise and unwise statesmanship; history also teaches the basic principles of social progress, particularly the liberal ideals of toleration and limited government. His idea of history was always bound up with a conception of and concern for progress.

An Essay on a Course of Liberal Education and the much later *Lectures on History, and General Policy to Which Is Prefixed, An Essay on a Course of Liberal Education for Civil and Active Life* (1788) are writings on the craft and educational value of history, not works of historical scholarship. One practical contribution to the subject while Priestley taught at Warrington was his *Chart of Biography*, published in 1765 and updated in 1772 as *The New Chart of Biography*. The main purpose of the chart was pedagogical; it attempted to date about two thousand persons and a hundred empires, dynasties, and societies, from 1200 B.C. to the present. Its main sources were

Isaac Newton's chronology and the multivolume *An Universal History, from the Earliest Account of Time* (compiled from many authors), published between 1736 and 1765.

In his spare time at Warrington in 1765 (while also teaching for five hours a day in the liberal arts) Priestley began work on a history of discoveries in electricity, for which he also conducted many of his own experiments. The result, his *History and Present State of Electricity, with Original Experiments,* was published in 1767, and is still well regarded by historians of science. It is a remarkable achievement both personally, since he had to teach himself the theory of electricity while writing its history, and professionally, since the project of writing a complete account of the development of a scientific subdiscipline had few predecessors.

The project arose in part through chance connections. He had studied some chemistry at Daventry and taught some science at Nantwich. But he was little more than an interested amateur with no special knowledge of electricity when he began the book. Scholars have assumed that the spark that ignited his interest came from his meeting with John Canton and Benjamin Franklin in London in 1765, but Schofield has shown that Priestley likely had a substantial manuscript in hand before he met those scientists, whose interest and assistance—aided also by William Watson and Richard Price—then helped him considerably.

Priestley's narrative begins in the seventeenth century with Gilbert and Boyle. Francis Hauksbee, Charles Du Fay, Stephen Gray, and John Theophilus Desaguliers take the story down to 1745. The key event in Priestley's history is the invention of the Leyden jar in 1745. Most of *The History and Present State of Electricity* traces the consequences of that invention, mainly in the work of Franklin (including a well-known description of his kite experiment), Abbe Jean-Antoine Nollet, Franz Aepinus, Watson, Canton, Giambattista Beccaria, and Robert Symmer. Some might say that his account is dominated by the work of his advisers. He was sensitive to the objection and tried to avoid Anglo-American bias. In the second edition, 1775, he incorporated more fully the work of the German electricians.

The History and Present State of Electricity is important in several ways. Priestley's account is rigorously based on original sources scrupulously footnoted, thus setting a high standard of historical accuracy. He is careful to describe and document the technical details of scientific work, the exact apparatus, and the precise techniques used, with all their potential pitfalls. He attended carefully, moreover, to the circumstances, both accidental and methodological, that led to discoveries and sometimes to dead ends. Thus, he sought to explain as well as to describe scientific progress. The work was important also in Priestley's career. It led him to membership

in the Royal Society and to a lifelong friendship with Franklin. It also set him on the path toward his experimental career. And it gave him an international reputation, involving many scientific correspondents, even before his own discoveries were published.

In 1767 Priestley left Warrington to pursue his main vocation as a Dissenting minister at Mill Hill Chapel, Leeds, a prosperous congregation in a lively city. In 1768 he published his most important work on political philosophy, *An Essay on the First Principles of Government; and on the Nature of Political, Civil, and Religious Liberty.* The essay is strongly Lockean in character. It makes a clear distinction between civil and political liberties. Priestley always thought civil liberty more important than political liberty. His later political radicalism is based upon his apprehension that the British government was encroaching on vital civil liberties.

In his six years at Leeds he carried on his history of science. Pleased with the reception of his *History and Present State of Electricity,* he had conceived the ambitious idea, according to a letter he wrote to Hugh Percy, second Duke of Northumberland, of writing "the history of all the other branches of experimental philosophy," in six or eight quarto volumes. As the second stage in this task, he completed in 1772 *The History and Present State of Discoveries Relating to Vision, Light and Colours,* usually known as *The History of Optics.* The subject took him further back into the previous century than had been necessary in the case of electricity. He chronicled the work of the leading scientists in this field, before and after Newton, such as René Descartes, Christiaan Huygens, Pierre de Fermat, Leonhard Euler, Pierre-Louis Moreau de Maupertuis, and Gottfried Wilhelm Leibniz. However, Priestley did not handle the mathematical and theoretical dimensions of the subject with the ease he showed when describing experimental and qualitative inquiries. The work was hastily carried out and required extensive corrections, many errors the result of carelessness. Schofield observes that "it was to be the only history of optics in English for 150 years and the only one in any language for more than fifty."

Priestley's brave plan to write the first general history of science foundered on financial difficulties. Access to the Royal Society's library did not obviate the need to purchase a considerable library of his own, and the expense proved to be more than he could bear. His *History of Optics* did not sell well, and many subscribers defaulted.

In 1773 he was employed as the librarian and companion of William Petty-Fitzmaurice, Lord Shelburne, a position that led to a considerable improvement in Priestley's financial situation and brought him from the provinces into the heart of the intellectual and political life of London. He mixed with fellow scientists at the Royal Society and fellow Whigs at the London coffeehouse St. Paul's, all supporters of American independence. He helped his friend Theophilus Lindsey establish the liberal-minded Essex Street chapel, where Priestley sometimes preached. With his new freedom, his interests shifted from the chronicling to the practice of "experimental philosophy." In this six-year period with Shelburne he made his greatest chemical discoveries, especially those reported in his *Experiments and Observations on Different Kinds of Air* (1774, 1775).

At Leeds in 1767 Priestley quietly abandoned Arianism and adopted what was then called "Socinianism," now known as Unitarianism, committing himself to complete denial of Christ's divinity. He thought the doctrine of the Trinity internally contradictory; he denied that it had any basis in Scripture or early (first-century) church teaching; what is more, he thought belief in Christ's divinity a species of idolatry. As he first put this point in volume two of his *Institutes of Natural and Revealed Religion* of 1773:

> Upon the very same principles, and in the very same manner, by which dead men came to be worshipped by the ancient idolaters, there was introduced into the Christian church, in the first place, the idolatrous worship of Jesus Christ, then that of the Virgin Mary, and lastly that of innumerable other saints, and of angels also; and this modern Christian idolatry has been attended with all the absurdities, and with some, but not all the immoralities, of the ancient heathen idolatry.

This statement was a declaration of intellectual war on his fellow religionists. It committed him to becoming the historian of how Christianity suffered a "decline and fall" from its simple and rational beginnings to its irrational medieval "corruptions." For Priestley, however, the long-run history of Christianity is also one of recovery and revival in modern times, aided by the advent of the Reformation and, even more, by the Enlightenment. To understand fully his work on church history, which occupied him for two decades, one has to see its connection with his philosophical writings.

In 1774 Priestley visited Paris with Shelburne and met some of the leading philosophes. He found himself almost as incredulous at their atheism—some were bishops—as they were at his religious beliefs. Faced with a divide between English Christian conservatism and French radical atheism, he sought a path between (as he saw it) credulity and irrational skepticism. Portrayed this way, Priestley may seem an idiosyncratic figure. He thought that he had behind him all the authority and force of "science." Natural science after Newton, he thought, achieved sufficient self-definition to furnish a methodology applicable to both theology and the human mind. This Newtonianism drove both his philosophical thought and his heterodox religion.

The search for a consistent worldview led Priestley in the 1770s into the metaphysical disputes of his day. In the *Institutes of Natural and Revealed Religion* (1772–1774) he sets out the standard eighteenth-century argument for natural religion, based on the Argument from Design. He sees nature as everywhere exhibiting order, and yet as not in any way self-ordering, since nothing seen in nature shows order arising naturally. The order must come from "outside," and since it resembles human productions, it must derive from intelligence, indeed a supreme intelligence. He was thus never tempted to reject theism, and he later replied to the attack on the Design theory in David Hume's *Dialogues concerning Natural Religion* (1779).

Priestley's next move in philosophy shocked his English contemporaries. In *Disquisitions Relating to Matter and Spirit* (1777) he argued for materialism, denying what he called "the hypothesis of the soul" on the grounds that no evidence for the soul exists, nor does any coherent theoretical rationale for it. Newton's "rules of reasoning" forbid acceptance of any idle hypotheses ("we are to admit no more causes of things than such as are both true and sufficient to explain appearances"). All the "appearances" of the mind can be accounted for by supposing that they are a function of brain activity. One underpinning of mind/matter dualism was the supposition that matter is inherently passive and powerless, but Priestley—inspired in part by his discussions with John Michell while writing his *History of Optics,* in part by his reading of the works of Jesuit physicist R. J. Boscovich—saw Newtonian physics as moving toward the idea of matter as made up of powers of attraction and repulsion, what later came to be thought of as field theory.

Disquisitions Relating to Matter and Spirit includes a long appendix on "The History of the Philosophical Doctrine concerning the Origin of the Soul, and the Nature of Matter; With its Influence on Christianity, Especially with Respect to the Doctrine of the Pre-Existence of Christ." In this appendix he foreshadows the program of historical research that he was about to undertake. Metaphysical materialism may seem remote from issues in church history, but at least in Priestley's mind there were two immediate connections.

First, he thought that the conception of matter as passive had come to dominate modern philosophy, in part through the influence of Gnostic religion. Gnostic religion could only be a remote influence on modern ideas, but it was no less real an influence. Matter, he claimed, has been the victim of prejudice, religious in origin, and this prejudice has had an adverse influence on the church and on Western culture more generally.

Even philosophers as modern as his friend Richard Price and his Scottish adversary Thomas Reid held that matter possessed no powers of its own. For them and for most other thinkers, mind and matter had no common properties.

Second, he thought that the doctrine of Christ's pre-existence—a doctrine accepted by both Trinitarians and Arians—depended upon the supposition of an immaterial soul. But if that supposition is flawed, then so, too, is Christian orthodoxy. As he observes, "if no man has a soul distinct from his body, Christ, who, in all other respects, appeared as a man, could not have had a soul which had existed before his body; and the whole doctrine of the pre-existence of souls (of which the opinion of the pre-existence of Christ was a branch) will be effectually overturned" (Priestley, *Works* [1817–1831], edited by John Towill Rutt, volume three).

In 1780 Priestley moved to Birmingham, where he became minister at the New Meeting chapel, said to be the most liberal pulpit in England. He took his duties seriously, but he was still able to devote himself to a mixture of scientific and historical researches. He threw himself into the activities of the Lunar Society, where he mixed and debated with Matthew Boulton, James Watt, Erasmus Darwin, Josiah Wedgwood, and other leading figures at the heart of the industrial, scientific, technological, and commercial transformation of Britain. He deeply valued this company, in which political and religious differences were of no account.

In 1782 he published his two-volume *An History of the Corruptions of Christianity*. This was followed in 1786 by *An History of Early Opinions Concerning Jesus Christ, Compiled from Original Writers; Proving That the Christian Church Was at First Unitarian,* in four volumes. In 1790 his third and widest-ranging study appeared as *A General History of the Christian Church to the Fall of the Western Empire.* Finally, in 1802, two years before his death, he completed the series with *A General History of the Christian Church, from the Fall of the Western Empire to the Present Time.* Since his materialistic Unitarianism was a rarity, his research program could hardly fail to be original. Even so, and even though he "found it necessary to have recourse [in this work] to the original authorities in every thing of consequence," he was dependent in many ways on the work of others. He lists his sources, also in this work, as Samuel Clarke, Nathaniel Lardner, John Jortin, Jacques Basnage, Isaac de Beausobre, Jean Le Clerc, Hugo Grotius, Louis Ellies Du Pin, Abbé Claude Fleury, Johann Lorenz von Mosheim, and Pietro Giannone. Of these, perhaps Mosheim and Beausobre are particularly significant. The Lutheran scholar Mosheim's *Ecclesiastical History* of 1726 pioneered the secular study of church tradition. The French Protestant Beausobre's *Histoire Critique du Manichee et du Man-*

icheisme of 1734 and 1739 suited Priestley's interests in philosophical and Gnostic influences on Christian tradition. His later volumes also made use of the works of Johann Salomo Semler.

By "Gnosticism" Priestley meant not so much a body of esoteric lore ("gnosis") that offers salvation from the forces of evil, but rather the metaphysical dualism that underlies this doctrine of salvation. The essential features of Gnosticism, in his account, are that it regards the mundane material world as evil, and it believes the soul to be celestial in origin and destiny. Belief in the natural eternity of the soul was the common denominator of the Eastern doctrine of reincarnation, the Platonic doctrine of pre-existence, and the Christian doctrine of Christ's pre-existence. His historical claim, baldly stated, is that Hindu and Persian philosophy had influenced Platonism, and that these philosophies had jointly led to the formation of Gnosticism, which in turn had intertwined itself with early Christianity to produce the doctrines of Nicaea and Chalcedon. Its long-term legacy is the mind/matter dualism of modern philosophy. Such a dualism, he contends, must be embarrassed to explain why matter has been created at all. If matter can only confine, limit, or encumber the soul's powers, as some of his contemporaries claimed, then, according to his 1777 *Disquisitions Relating to Matter and Spirit,* the Christian "resurrection of the body" can only be, at best, "barely no disadvantage."

The essence of Christianity, according to what Priestley says in his *History of the Corruptions of Christianity* (1782), is that "the Universal Parent of mankind commissioned Jesus Christ to invite men to the practice of virtue, by the assurance of his mercy to the penitent, and of his purpose to raise to immortal life and happiness the virtuous and good, but to inflict adequate punishment on the wicked." Trinitarian Christology is no part of this essence, but the miraculous physical resurrection of Christ is indispensable divine confirmation of this message, since its truth could not be known by natural means. Even in the time of Tertullian, he thinks, "the greater part of Christians . . . were Unitarians, and exceedingly averse to the doctrine of the Trinity."

As a thinker deeply committed to the idea of progress, for Priestley to regard the intellectual struggles of the early church as the progressive unfolding of the latent rational content of the original revelation might seem natural. In fact, he takes the opposite view, regarding all the patristic doctrinal developments—Original Sin, Incarnation, Atonement, and Trinity—as "corruptions," mere human additions and incumbrances obscuring the simple, original truth. This Protestant primitivism appears quite at odds with his more general progressivism. His objection to doctrinal development, however, is not to development as such, but to those particular developments, each of which seemed to him to involve logical contradictions or some other offense against the requirements of reason.

In the modern world, he contends, secular advances have usually tended to further the cause of religious progress. Renaissance scholarship assisted the Reformation; the invention of the printing press made the Bible generally available; and modern prosperity has fostered the literacy and education required to understand it. International trade helped to spread the Christian message around the globe; John Locke's political philosophy supports the cause of religious toleration; Newtonian science, and modern science generally, have deepened the foundations of theism; and David Hartley's associationistic psychology culminates in "theopathy," the love of God. In the course of these changes an important transition occurs. According to the 1788 *Lectures on History of the Corruptions of Christianity,* at the beginning of modern history Providence works secretly

> rather by an accidental concurrence of circumstances, than by any efforts of human wisdom and foresight. We see the hand of Divine Providence in those revolutions which have gradually given a happier turn to affairs, while men have been the passive and blind instruments of their own felicity. . . . But the situation at present is vastly different. . . . Reflection upon our present advantages, and the steps by which we have arrived to the degree of power and happiness we now enjoy, has shewn us the true sources of them. . . .

Priestley's philosophical and theological position struck many of his contemporaries as paradoxical. One of them was his fellow historian Edward Gibbon, who remarked in his *Autobiography* (1827) that "the dauntless philosopher of Birmingham continued to fire away his double battery against those who believed too little, and those who believed too much." Against, that is, the skeptic, who rejects the hope and larger vision of rational religion and the orthodox Christian, encumbered by doctrines of the soul, free will, and Christ's divinity. The latter category included Samuel Horsley, then Archdeacon of St. Alban's, fellow member and former secretary of the Royal Society and editor of Newton's works. The controversy between Horsley and Priestley was acrimonious and too often ad hominem; intellectually, it was soon bogged down in minor details. The tone was captured in Horsley's remark that "The conviction of the orthodox Trinitarian, that his philosophy is Plato's and his creed St John's, will alleviate the mortification he would otherwise feel in differing from Dr. Priestley."

The category of those who "believed too little" included Gibbon himself. Curiously, the basic structure of Priestley's church history (from primitive truth and simplicity to subsequent decline and then—many centuries later—modern revival and recovery) has a parallel in the structure of Gibbon's secular history (from republican virtue to imperial corruption, followed finally by the progressive modern world of European states). Priestley also expressed that he was grateful to Gibbon because Gibbon's attacks on Christianity contributed toward its purification from error. Much that Gibbon had said in *The History of the Decline and Fall of the Roman Empire* (1776–1788) about otherworldly or all-too-worldly tendencies in the early church was restated by Priestley in his own terms. Where he mainly differed from Gibbon was about Christian origins. Gibbon had sought to give a secular account of the rise of the new religion, while hedging on the question of whether or not this account is sufficient to explain that rise. Priestley insisted that it was far from sufficient and that only supposing the truth of the original Christian message could complete the explanation. Gibbon, in a 1783 letter to Priestley, contrasted "the historian"—himself—who "has delivered a simple narrative of authentic facts," with "the disputant, who proudly rejects all natural proof of the immortality of the soul, overthrows (by circumscribing) the inspiration of the Evangelists and Apostles, and condemns the religion of every Christian nation as a fable less innocent, but not less absurd, than Mahomet's journey to the third Heaven." The sentence might have been written by Horsley; disingenuously, it made Priestley, and not Gibbon, seem the religious skeptic. Gibbon declined any further controversy.

Priestley's sensitivity to methodological issues is evident in the list of seventeen "Maxims of historical criticism" with which he concludes his *An History of Early Opinions Concerning Jesus Christ, Compiled from Original Writers.* The maxims are criteria for assessing the value of testimony. Two can be mentioned by way of illustration: one is "Great changes in opinion are not usually made of a sudden, and never by great bodies of men. That history, therefore, which represents such changes as having been made gradually, and by easy steps, is always the more probable on that account"; the other is "The common or unlearned people, in any country, who do not speculate much, retain longest any opinions with which their minds have been much impressed; and therefore we always look for the oldest opinions in any country, or any class of men, among the common people, and not among the learned." He shows how these maxims have guided his account of the early church.

Priestley's church history is in obvious ways a partisan work—it is history written to prove a highly controversial thesis. Yet, while he was never one to seek controversy, he did not always avoid it, and he could write in a mode that is collaborative and consensus-seeking. His *Lectures on History,* published in 1788, is written in such a mode. His main purpose is educative; the text began as lectures he gave at Warrington Academy and were designed to "enlarge the minds of young men, and to give them liberal views of many important subjects." He intends something more like a guide to the study of history than a study of history itself. "Many of the observations . . . are, as far as I know, original; but it is not in my power to distinguish those that are so from those which I collected from other writers." (If published today, several sections of the *Lectures* would be regarded as plagiarism.) There is an extended discussion of historical sources, the list of which includes not just official records and the works of contemporary historians but also oral tradition, mythology, names, monuments, coins and medals, languages, laws, and astronomy. Another set of lectures discusses briefly a long list of ancient, medieval, and modern historians and chroniclers.

The largest part of the *Lectures,* however, is a synthesis of Enlightenment historical, social, political, and economic thought, and its concerns are almost wholly secular. His modern authorities and sources include Charles-Louis de Secondat, Baron de Montesquieu; Henry St. John Bolingbroke; Hume; William Robertson; Voltaire; Anne-Robert-Jacques Turgot, Baron d' Aulne; Marie-Jean-Antoine-Nicolas de Caritat Condorcet; Pierre-Francois-Xavier Charlevoix; Adam Smith; Sir James Stewart; Henry Home, Lord Kames; Cesare Beccaria; and Price. Of these thinkers, Montesquieu is most often cited.

Priestley believed that the systematic study of social progress belongs to the historian, and especially to the modern historian. Real history, he says, "resembles the experiments made by the air pump, the condensing engine and electrical machine, which exhibit the operations of nature, and the God of nature himself, whose works are the noblest subject of contemplation to the human mind, and are the ground-work and materials of the most extensive and useful theories." The study of history shows that in the "battle" between the Moderns and the Ancients, the Moderns have indeed triumphed. According to the *Lectures,* what is evident is that "the state of the world at present, and particularly the state of Europe, is vastly preferable to what it was in any former period." All the achievements of modern Europe—in exploration, trade, finance, technology, science, medicine, social organization, scholarship, and religion—are seen as converging toward human betterment and happiness. He knew well enough that European prominence was mostly a modern phenomenon. From the time of Charlemagne to the late fifteenth cen-

Title page for Priestley's history of Christianity
(The British Library)

tury, he said, Europe "would scarce attract the notice of a spectator of the affairs of men, who had no European connexions. . . . Asia exhibited the most inviting spectacle." Nevertheless, his Western self-confidence extended easily to the assumption not just that Europe leads the rest of the world, but that the rest of the world would willingly follow that lead.

By contrast with this celebration of modernity, Priestley's account of the distant past is almost unrelievedly dismal. Ancient societies are depicted as ignorant, superstitious, and barbaric. In religion, they are ignorant of all the essentials—the unity of God, his goodness, his final judgment, and the promise of a future life. In moral matters he considered that matters are no better: "Idleness, treachery and cruelty are predominant in all uncivilized countries; notwithstanding the boasts which the poets make of the *golden age* of mankind, before the creation of empires." Even the Greeks, generally accounted the most civilized of ancient societies, condoned infanticide, suicide, sodomy, and adultery; the Egyptians and Persians permitted incest. Such political liberty as they enjoyed was purchased at the expense of the personal liberty of many slaves—ancient slavery far exceeding the scope of the modern slave trade. Ancient governments, for all their harshness, provided little security against banditry. Nor did the "primitive" societies discovered by European explorers offer an alternative to the European world. Such societies were still effectively in a state of nature, no further advanced than Europe's ancient forerunners, not yet having discovered the benefits of rational cooperation in a division of labor. "From generation to generation every man does the same that every other does, or has done, and no person begins where another ends; at least, general improvements are exceedingly slow and uncertain" (as he observed in his 1768 *Essay on the First Principles of Government*).

Priestley believed that both conquest and commerce were the drivers of progress. He (like Turgot and Charlevoix) speculates that war and hostilities first stirred men out of primeval indolence, spurring their inventiveness, the by-product of which has been "many of the most useful arts of civil life." In the modern era commerce has assumed this role, with even greater economic and moral benefits. The radicals of his day tended to regard prosperity ("luxury") as destructive of liberty, but his view was that it can present no great danger. He allows that, by creating great inequalities of wealth, commerce can sometimes endanger the commonwealth, giving rise to a Medici-style dynasty. He can even remark that commerce, "which never fails to introduce luxury and inequalities into men's circumstances, does not perfectly suit with the true spirit of a commonwealth." But this hint of "republican" sentiment is out of character: on the whole he maintains that commercial prosperity is favorable to liberty. "When men, by the practice of the arts [of luxury], acquire property, they covet equal laws to secure that property."

Nor does luxury endanger liberty by opening the commonwealth to the threat of external aggressors. It does not make men effeminate and cowardly: "surely more spirit and courage may be expected from a man who has had good nourishment, and who has something to defend, than from one who is almost starved, and who has little or nothing to fight for." Besides, he adds, modern knowledge is itself a source of power for the defense of the state. The real danger to modern society comes, he thought, from the militarism that results from the enforced idleness of Europe's aristocracies, leading as it did to fiscal disaster and, subse-

quently, to revolutions. The remedy, he thought, is the gradual abolition of the privileges of birth.

It is this remedy that, just a year after the *Lectures on History* appeared, Priestley expected from the French Revolution. The outcome of that revolution severely tested the Enlightenment reforming optimism that pervades the *Lectures*. Nevertheless, as Schofield observes in *The Enlightenment of Joseph Priestley* (1997), the *Lectures on History* "were republished eight times by 1826, including Dutch and French translations, were used as texts at Princeton and Harvard universities in the United States and, after John Symonds and Matthew Arnold rescued the Regius professorships in modern history, were recommended for use in the English universities."

In 1791 Priestley was driven out of his beloved Birmingham by the mob riots that made him their chief target and that destroyed his library and laboratory. He was resented, even hated, on both religious and political grounds, being heterodox in religion and supportive of the French Revolution, at least in its early phases. Edmund Burke's *Reflections on the Revolution in France* (1790) had attacked him with considerable vehemence; Burke carried on the attack ever more furiously as the French Revolution worsened. In this period Priestley doubted, according to *Letters to the Inhabitants of Northumberland* (1801), "whether any person in England (the prime minister for the time being excepted) ever had so much of what is commonly called abuse" as he experienced. "Neither Mr. Hume nor Mr. Gibbon was a thousandth part so obnoxious to the clergy as I am," he remarked in *An Appeal to the Public, on the Subject of the Riots in Birmingham* (1791). He was, however, a hero to the young English radicals of the time—Samuel Taylor Coleridge, William Wordsworth, Charles Lamb, William Hazlitt, William Godwin, Mary Wollstonecraft, Jeremy Bentham, and James Mill. With the Reign of Terror and the rise of Romanticism, this hero worship soon faded.

After a few unsettled years in London, in 1794 Joseph Priestley and his wife left England to settle in Northumberland, Pennsylvania, where he lived out the last ten years of his life. He continued to write prolifically to the end, completing his *General History of the Christian Church*. Plans to set up a utopian community on the banks of the Susquehanna River fell apart, and the difficulties of life in this remote outpost were mitigated only by continued correspondence with his friends; included among them was Thomas Jefferson. In his last years Priestley kept track of Napoleon Bonaparte's conquests and wondered whether Europe was witnessing the millenarian drama prophesied in the book of Daniel: the "great troubles" of the end times, the fall of "the ten crowned heads of Europe," and the final restoration of the Jews. He lived long enough to see that the millennium had not arrived, when Napoleon concluded a concordat with the Pope, restoring the alliance between church and state.

At his death on 6 February 1804 Priestley had few followers committed to carrying on his version of Rational Dissent. His complete nonscientific works, including all his historical writings, were published in 1817–1831 in twenty-five volumes. Little is known of his influence on later historians, such as Macaulay. Certainly, his progressive and liberal outlook lived on to play a large role in the Victorian era.

Today he is well-regarded as a pioneering historian of science, if only for his *History and Present State of Electricity.* His historical theology is almost entirely disregarded by modern scholars. As Schofield says (in *The Enlightened Joseph Priestley*), he "wrote, compiled, and commented, in more than a dozen volumes and some fifteen thousand pages, on biblical criticism, the higher criticism, and the study of the ante-Nicene church fathers. All of this is next to forgotten, even in historical studies." The recent revival of interest in the great Enlightenment philosophical historians–Hume, Gibbon, Robertson, Adam Ferguson, Smith, John Millar–has rarely included Priestley in their ranks, though he was clearly engaged in the same kind of enterprise.

Letters:

A Scientific Autobiography of Joseph Priestley (1733–1804). Selected Scientific Correspondence, edited by Robert E. Schofield (Cambridge, Mass.: MIT Press, 1966);
Memoirs and Correspondence of Joseph Priestley, 2 volumes, edited by John Towill Rutt (Bristol: Thoemmes Press, 2003).

Bibliography:

Ronald E. Crooke, *A Bibliography of Joseph Priestley, 1733–1804* (London: Library Association, 1966).

Biographies:

F. W. Gibbs, *Joseph Priestley: Adventurer in Science and Champion of Truth* (London: Thomas Nelson, 1965);
Robert E. Schofield, *The Enlightened Joseph Priestley: A Study of His Life and Work from 1733 to 1804* (University Park, Pa.: Pennsylvania State University Press, 2004);
Schofield, *The Enlightenment of Joseph Priestley. A Study of His Life and Work from 1733 to 1773* (University Park, Pa.: Pennsylvania State University Press, 1997).

References:

R. G. A. Anderson and Christopher Lawrence, eds., *Science, Medicine and Dissent: Joseph Priestley (1733–1804)* (London: Wellcome Trust/Science Museum, 1987);
Ira V. Brown, "The Religion of Joseph Priestley," *Pennsylvania History,* 24 (1957): 85–100;
Margaret Canovan, "The Irony of History: Priestley's Rational Theology," *Price–Priestley Newsletter,* no. 4 (1980): 16–25;
Dan Eshet, "Rereading Priestley: Science at the Intersection of Theology and Politics," *History of Science,* 39 (2001): 127–159;
Jack Fruchtman Jr., *The Apocalyptic Politics of Richard Price and Joseph Priestley: A Study in Late Eighteenth-Century English Millenialism* (Philadelphia: American Philosophical Society, 1983);
Knud Haakonssen, ed., *Enlightenment and Religion. Rational Dissent in Eighteenth-Century Britain* (Cambridge: Cambridge University Press, 1996);
James J. Hoecker, "Joseph Priestley as an Historian and the Idea of Progress," *Price–Priestley Newsletter,* no. 3 (1979): 29–40;
Lester Kieft and Bennett R. Willevord, eds., *Joseph Priestley: Scientist, Theologian, and Metaphysician* (Lewisburg, Pa.: Bucknell University Press, 1980);
John G. McEvoy and J. E. McGuire, "God and Nature: Priestley's Way of Rational Dissent," *Historical Studies in the Physical Sciences,* 6 (1975): 325–404;
Robert E. Schofield, "Joseph Priestley: Theology, Physics and Metaphysics," *Enlightenment and Dissent,* 3 (1983): 69–82;
A. Truman Schwartz and McEvoy, eds., *Motion Toward Perfection: The Achievement of Joseph Priestley* (Boston: Skinner House, 1990);
Earl Morse Wilbur, *A History of Unitarianism* (Cambridge, Mass.: Harvard University Press, 1947).

Papers:

Many of Joseph Priestley's nonscientific papers and letters were destroyed in the Birmingham Riots. Collections are to be found in the Dr. Williams Library, London; Dickinson College, Pennsylvania; the American Philosophical Society Library, Pennsylvania; and the Royal Society, London. See also the careful "Select Bibliography" in Robert E. Schofield, *The Enlightenment of Joseph Priestley. A Study of His Life and Work from 1733 to 1773* (University Park: University of Pennsylvania Press, 1997).

William Robertson

(19 September 1721 – 4 June 1793)

Russell M. Lawson
Bacone College

See also the Robertson entry in *DLB 104: British Prose Writers, 1660–1800, Second Series.*

BOOKS: *The Situation of the World at the Time of Christ's Appearance, and Its Connexion with the Success of His Religion, Considered. A Sermon* (Edinburgh: Printed by Hamilton, Balfour & Neill, 1755);

The History of Scotland, during the Reigns of Queen Mary and King James VI, till His Accession to the Crown of England (London: A. Millar, 1759; revised edition, London: Printed for T. Cadell, 1787);

The History of the Reign of the Emperor Charles V, 3 volumes (London: Printed by W. & W. Strahan for W. Strahan, T. Cadell, and J. Balfour, Edinburgh, 1769); republished as *The History of the Reign of Charles the Fifth, Emperor of Germany and of All the Kingdoms and States in Europe, during His Age,* 3 volumes (Philadelphia: Sold by Robert Bell, 1770 [i.e., 1771]); revised edition, *The History of the Reign of Emperor Charles V,* 4 volumes (London: Printed for A. Strahan, T. Cadell, and J. Balfour, Edinburgh, 1787);

The History of America, 2 volumes (London: Printed for W. Strahan; T. Cadell; and J. Balfour, Edinburgh, 1777 / Dublin: Whitestone, 1777); revised edition, 3 volumes (London: Printed for A. Strahan, T. Cadell, and J. Balfour, Edinburgh, 1788; 2 volumes, New York: Printed by R. Wilson for Samuel Campbell, 1798);

An Historical Disquisition concerning the Knowledge Which the Ancients Had of India and the Progress of Trade with That Country, Prior to the Discovery of the Passage to It by the Cape of Good Hope (London: Printed for A. Strahan, T. Cadell, and E. Balfour, Edinburgh, 1791; Philadelphia: Printed by William Young, 1792);

The History of America. Books IX and X: Containing the History of Virginia to the Year 1688, and New England to the Year 1652, edited by William Robertson, secundus (London: Printed for A. Strahan, T. Cadell Jun., and W. Davies and E. Balfour, Edin-

William Robertson (frontispiece for his History of Scotland during the Reigns of Queen Mary and King James VI, till His Accession to the Crown of England, *1791, twelfth revised edition; Eighteenth-Century Collections Online, Gale Group)*

burgh, 1796; Philadelphia: Printed by J. Humphreys, 1799);

An Index, Drawn up about the Year 1629, of Many Records of Charters Granted by the Different Sovereigns of Scotland Between the Years 1309 and 1413, Most of Which Records Have Been Long Missing: with an Introduction, Giving a State, Founded on Authentic Documents Still

Preserved, of the Ancient Records of Scotland, Which Were in That Kingdom in the Year 1292 to Which Is Subjoined, Indexes of the Persons and Places Mentioned in Those Charters (Edinburgh: Murray & Cochrane, 1798).

Editions and Collections: *The Works of William Robertson*, 12 volumes, edited by Richard Sher (London: Routledge/Thoemmes Press, 1996);

The Progress of Society in Europe, edited by Felix Gilbert (Chicago: University of Chicago Press, 1972).

William Robertson was one of the foremost eighteenth-century British historians, eclipsed only by Edward Gibbon. Gibbon's inquiry focused on the fall of a great ancient civilization. Robertson wrote the more contemporary history of sixteenth-century Europe and America. Although Gibbon's topic was more dramatic, Robertson's erudition was equal to Gibbon's. Both were, as well, superb writers employing English prose in the service of writing traditional didactic history.

Whereas Gibbon looked to a declining civilization as a basis for significant interpretation, Robertson chose the crucial sixteenth century, the time of the Renaissance, the age of exploration and discovery, the Protestant Reformation, the emergence of European nation-states, the beginnings of diplomacy on the principle of balance of power, and urban commercial centers increasingly focused on capitalism, manufacturing, and a growing middle class.

Robertson was a Scot who lived most of his life in Edinburgh. He was born on 19 September 1721 in the small village of Midlothian, where his father served as minister of the local Presbyterian kirk. His parents were William and Eleanor Pitcairne Robertson. Young William was educated at a local school until 1733, when his family moved to Edinburgh, and William matriculated at the University of Edinburgh. The university was the premier institution of higher learning in Scotland and one of the forces behind the intellectual achievements of the Scottish Enlightenment.

The son followed in the profession of the father. William became a minister upon graduation from the university in 1741. Robertson served at Dalkeith and East Lothian before moving to Edinburgh in 1758 to take up duties at Old Greyfriar's Church, where his own father had once served. During these years (1741–1758) Robertson became the guardian for half a dozen of his siblings, left orphaned by the deaths of their parents. Robertson married Mary Nisbet in 1751; the couple had three sons.

Robertson's life as a Presbyterian minister was hardly mundane. One of his best sermons was published, per the custom of the time, in 1755. It was *The Situation of*

the World at the Time of Christ's Appearance, which combined study of Scripture and ancient Greek and Roman writers to answer the question: why did Jesus, the son of God, become incarnate and appear on earth at the time of Rome's Augustan Age? Such a question implies that faith is just as important as reason in historical inquiry. Indeed, Robertson held the customary belief that a minister's duties went beyond church services and sermons. A minister must be an historian for several reasons. First, an historical inquiry is a natural function of the minister's role, since the minister is necessarily an historian of the local kirk and community: he collects historical data—records of births, baptisms, marriages, and deaths—on a regular basis. Second, history is a tale of morality. The minister's role as teacher requires an historical record of good deeds and bad, examples of the good to imitate and of evil to avoid. Third, who else but a minister can trace the role of providence in human history? God's will, Robertson thought, is present throughout time; history is a religious as well as a secular record of human experience.

Even with such a commitment to faith, Robertson was by the 1750s an emerging voice in the Scottish Enlightenment. He came to know David Hume, historian and philosopher, and joined with Adam Smith, economist, to found the *Edinburgh Review* in 1754. Robertson was heavily influenced by the French Enlightenment, particularly the writings of the philosophes. He disagreed with Voltaire's religious beliefs but not his approach to uncovering the historical truth. Robertson agreed with the political theories of Charles-Louis de Secondat, Baron de Montesquieu. As Robertson was not monolithic in his historical interpretations, combining secular and religious history, likewise he was eclectic in his political views. He assumed, as did the Whigs, that liberty and the rights of Englishmen under the law were of supreme importance. He was against the oppression of people in any form. Yet, he had an aristocrat's sensibilities, and he believed in duty, decorum, polished manners, and correct morality. He was a distant man, known intimately by few. Often he appeared haughty and arrogant. This demeanor was particularly evident after the publication of his first major history.

The publication of Robertson's *The History of Scotland, during the Reigns of Queen Mary and King James VI* (1759) solidified his growing leadership of the Scottish literati. The book explored the civil and religious conflict of sixteenth-century Scotland. Robertson sorted through the myths and legends of early Scotland, bringing the story up to the Renaissance and the emergence of the modern state based on commerce and Protestantism. During the sixteenth century, the Catholicism of Mary Queen of Scots clashed with the growing Protestant claims upon the Scottish people. James VI, King of Scotland, succumbed to the influence of the English-

THE

HISTORY

OF

SCOTLAND,

DURING THE REIGNS OF

Queen M A R Y and of King J A M E S VI.

TILL

His ACCESSION to the Crown of ENGLAND.

WITH A

REVIEW of the SCOTCH HISTORY previous to that Period;
And an APPENDIX containing ORIGINAL PAPERS.

IN TWO VOLUMES.

By W I L L I A M R O B E R T S O N, D. D.

V O L U M E I.

·L O N D O N:
Printed for A. MILLAR in the Strand.
MDCCLIX.

*Title page for Robertson's history of sixteenth-century Scotland
(Eighteenth-Century Collections Online, Gale Group)*

backed Scottish Protestants. During the latter half of the sixteenth century, the General Assembly of the Kirk (Church of Scotland) began meeting, and the courts of the Scottish Presbyterians gained legal standing. Robertson clearly felt a personal commitment to the history of Scotland; as a Protestant minister he felt strongly the repercussions of the historical conflict between Catholicism and Protestantism as it played out in Europe, England, and especially Scotland.

The History of Scotland was successful both financially and critically. Robertson received accolades from Scottish thinkers such as Hume and notable English writers such as Horace Walpole and Gibbon (who remarked that he hoped to write history as remarkably as did Robertson). The book earned the author £600. Robertson received other material accolades from aristocrats and royalty. He became the "Principal of the University of Edinburgh" and the "Historiographer Royal of Scotland." Under his leadership the University of Edinburgh became a major leader not only in the Scottish but also in the European academic worlds.

Living and working within the consequences of the battle for religious authority during the reigns of

Mary and James of the 1500s and 1600s, Robertson was a moderate in religious and social matters. He became a leader of the General Assembly of the Scottish Kirk. He advocated tolerance toward Catholics and a continuation of aristocratic patronage in the selection of ministers. Robertson argued that such preferment was more apt to result in stability and order in religious affairs, providing similar benefits in civil affairs. Besides, he had benefited from aristocratic preferment himself and was not so inconsistent as to argue against it.

During the 1760s Robertson went against the advice of his friends to research, write, and publish a book on sixteenth-century Europe. He realized that such a topic would not enlist as much support as something more popular, such as Gibbon's treatment of the decline and fall of the Roman Empire; yet, Robertson was heavily influenced by what he thought was the utility of history. Historical inquiry was the means by which a person could examine human experience and make his own decisions regarding humans and their form of government and social institutions. Robertson was convinced as well that the sixteenth century was the watershed in human history regarding human progress, just as the fall of Rome was a watershed in human degeneracy.

When *The History of the Reign of the Emperor Charles V* appeared in bookshops in 1769, eager readers were treated to a massive tome, in three quarto volumes, that provided something akin to a universal history of Europe, at least for the sixteenth century. Robertson prefaced the book with "A Historical Outline from the Subversion of the Roman Empire to the Beginning of the Sixteenth Century," in which he provided an outline of his philosophy of history and his views on Rome's fall, the dawn of the Middle Ages, and how the darkness of Medieval Europe was vanquished by the light of learning, science, and commerce during the Renaissance.

The History of the Reign of the Emperor Charles V reveals Robertson's philosophy of history. His account of the Roman Empire relied heavily on Greek and Roman literary sources; Roman historian Tacitus was a favorite author. Indeed, one can see in Robertson's work the clear influence of ancient Roman historians. Livy and Tacitus were moralists who believed that history was the means to shape character and influence behavior. The historian, through the historical narrative of the actions, victories, and tragedies of famous men, teaches the reader what behaviors to imitate and what to avoid. This didactic function of history marks eighteenth-century historiography, particularly the work of Robertson.

Robertson also believed that history provides the clearest account of what it means to be civilized, and how civilization came to be from distant, darker eras when savage and barbarian peoples ruled Europe. He made a fine distinction between the savage and the barbaric; the latter was at least informed by some of the accoutrements of civilization, such as writing and towns; the former was subject to the whims of nature, living a nomadic existence of utter ignorance. Rome was one of the great civilizations of all time. Robertson, like Gibbon, was duly impressed by Rome's achievements in government, law, culture, and society. Yet, he also showed how this great civilization became corrupt and declined. Presenting a theory of history that explained Rome's fall according to the barbarization of its peoples, Robertson argued that as Rome expanded in power and conquered the outlying peoples of Gaul, Britain, North Africa, the Near East, the Rhine Valley, and the Danube Valley, it imposed an oppressive, unfair, and degenerative rule on the provinces. Taxes were too high and governors too rapacious. The people resented the exploitation of their resources by Rome. Rome itself seemed far away; Roman culture and society were growing more meaningless in a cosmopolitan, diverse society. Provincials increasingly cared less whether Rome survived or not. Traditional Roman virtue—manly courage—was vanishing in the face of effeminacy. Roman piety toward Roman traditions, ancestors, family, and Roman genius—a system of beliefs that made Rome great—was also disappearing. Economic decline and disruption of trade inhibited cultural advance and stable government. These problems added to a despotic regime of emperors, and an increasingly disloyal and indolent army combined with other problems to bring the Western Roman Empire to its knees by the fifth century.

Western Europe's increasing barbarism, political conflict, intellectual decline, and moral disintegration resulted in the worst period in the history of mankind and the advent of feudalism in Europe. Robertson, like most of his contemporaries, condemned feudal Medieval Europe for its lack of enlightenment, for its superstition, primitive economy, chaotic government, and abandonment of science, taste, decorum, and civility—all the characteristics that made the eighteenth-century Enlightenment one of the great times in human history. For centuries Europeans lacked "sanctity and virtue," "order, equal laws, and humanity." Not until the Renaissance of the fourteenth, fifteenth, and sixteenth centuries did Europe again resurrect its civilization. Stability in government resulted in expanded and more-sophisticated commerce. Order in government and success in trade inspired the revival of science, literature, art, and urbanity.

Robertson was unusual for his time and an inspiration for other historians in his focus on "Proofs and Illustrations" to provide concrete data to support his assertions and interpretations. He provided copious quotations and references from extant literary sources, the primary documentary sources upon which history is based. His research was exhaustive, a fact that gave support to his narrative and explanations. Setting the stage for modern scholarship, Robertson used his "Proofs and Illustrations" to discuss historical issues that were too intricate or unclear for the main narrative. Readers could choose to read only the narrative, which was gracefully written, without consulting the evidence, or supplement the narrative with additional information through a perusal of the appendices.

In *The History of the Reign of the Emperor Charles V* Robertson purposely omitted a full discussion of Spanish conquests and involvement in the Americas. He planned a full, erudite narrative at a later date on the Americas, which was published in 1777 as *The History of America*. Robertson hoped his book would help to substantiate and defend the British Empire by presenting a polished narrative of Britain's American colonies. The book appeared soon after the American Declaration of Independence and the beginning of war between the American colonies and the British Empire. If Robertson's *History of America* failed to convince American rebels of the value of staying a part of the British Empire, the book nevertheless was (and is) considered a masterpiece of historical narrative. Americans, even Patriots, were as apt to read the history as Loyalists and other supporters of the British Empire. Jeremy Belknap, for example, one of the foremost American historians of the latter eighteenth century and a Patriot, used Robertson's work in a variety of ways. Belknap imitated his style, purpose, and erudition in his works *The History of New-Hampshire* (1784) and *American Biography* (1792). Belknap did not always agree with Robertson, but through his treatment of the historian and references to his books Belknap showed deference toward the admitted master of the historical narrative.

Robertson's *History of America* is divided into five parts: early voyages, particularly of Columbus; the conquest of Mexico; the conquest of Peru; a description of the Native Americans; and a narrative of colonial New England and colonial Virginia. He hypothesized in *The History of America,* as in his earlier work, a dichotomy of savagery/barbarism and civilization. The American civilizations of Mexico and Peru represented barbarism; the less sophisticated aborigines of North America represented savagery. They were indolent and immoral like the European savages of Northern Europe and Asia before the invasion of Rome. Indeed, all humans spring from the same source, Robertson argued, but they change over time according to the environment in which they live—particularly the climate and geography. Regarding the origin of Native Americans, he said that they could not be from

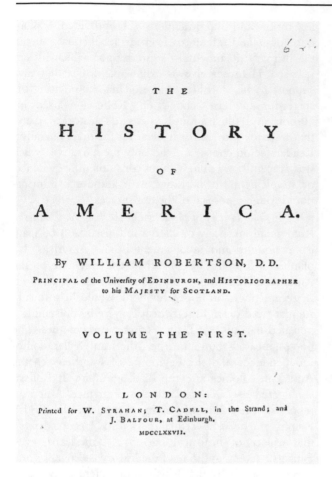

T H E

HISTORY

O F

A M E R I C A.

By WILLIAM ROBERTSON, D.D.

PRINCIPAL of the Univerfity of EDINBURGH, and HISTORIOGRAPHER
to his MAJESTY for SCOTLAND.

V O L U M E T H E F I R S T.

L O N D O N:
Printed for W. STRAHAN; T. CADELL, in the Strand; and
J. BALFOUR, at Edinburgh.
MDCCLXXVII.

*Title page for Robertson's history that begins with Columbus's earliest
voyages to the New World (Eighteenth-Century
Collections Online, Gale Group)*

the Old World because they lacked iron tools and weapons; therefore, they derived from a savage and barbaric, not a civilized, people. Robertson hypothesized that Native Americans came from Siberia by means of the Bering Strait. He discounted the story (as described in Herodotus's *Histories* [circa 430 B.C.]) gaining popularity in America to explain the origins of the Native Americans, that the Phoenicians, having circumnavigated Africa in 600, also had the knowledge and the ability to sail across the Atlantic.

Robertson was aware of the limited sources with which to trace Native American history. He relied on literary sources supplied by Europeans. Some of the great passages of *The History of America* are about great Europeans, not great Americans. True to the didactic aim of traditional history, Robertson wrote about public events as detailed by important people, the proceedings of dignified characters—for example, Christopher Columbus.

Columbus emerged from the pages of *The History of America* as a completely confident and competent character, a great man. Not only was Columbus a

superb sailor, able to trace the path and speed of his ship over unknown, unexplored waters, but he also knew how to prevent mutiny and accomplish his destiny. The following lines could have been written by Livy or Tacitus eulogizing a heroic Roman of the past: "Happily for himself, and for the country by which he was employed, he joined to the ardent temper and inventive genius of a projector, virtues of another species, which are rarely united with them. He possessed a thorough knowledge of mankind, an insinuating address, a patient perseverance in executing any plan, the perfect government of his own passions, and the talent of acquiring an ascendant over those of other men" (book 2, *The History of America,* quoted in J. R. Hale's *The Evolution of British Historiography*).

Columbus was for Robertson the representative Enlightenment man, one who used science and reason to accomplish great goals of empire, trade, and the enrichment of his kingdom and people. The sailors under Columbus were like the barbarians of America, like the typical commoner in England: superstitious, credulous, easily swayed, and unstable. They wanted to destroy Columbus, at least to mutiny and turn the ships back to Spain. But then they spied land, and their entire demeanor changed.

> They threw themselves at the feet of Columbus, with feelings of self-condemnation mingled with reverence. They implored him to pardon their ignorance, incredulity, and insolence, which had created him so much unnecessary disquiet, and had so often obstructed the prosecution of his well-concerted plan; and passing, in the warmth of their admiration, from one extreme to another, they now pronounced the man, whom they had so lately reviled and threatened, to be a person inspired by Heaven with sagacity and fortitude more than human, in order to accomplish a design, so far beyond the ideas and conception of all former ages (book 2, *The History of America,* quoted in Hale's *The Evolution of British Historiography*).

The reader familiar with classical literature can see in these words a description not unlike what Arrian wrote of the Macedonians' admiration for Alexander the Great or what Julius Caesar wrote about the loyalty of the legions under his charge in the conquest of Gaul. Robertson's history, unlike history written today, was personal, focusing on distinct characters, individuals, and great men. Sometimes he might write of the English people or the Spanish Empire, but he always wrote from the standpoint of human reason, actions, successes, and mistakes. When gold flooded Spain after the conquest of Mexico and Peru, the Spanish Empire went through a slow decline, not just in power but in morality, manners, and industry. Wealth corrupts was

Robertson's moral lesson, unless one knows how to use it, mitigating its negative consequences. A standard of right and wrong exists among men, clarity on what constitutes good and evil. Such are the requirements of classical didactic history, and such were the assumptions that Robertson brought to historical research and writing.

After the success of his three great works—*The History of Scotland, The History of the Reign of the Emperor Charles V,* and *The History of America*—Robertson's later years were spent largely in quiet. He continued to serve as a Presbyterian pastor, though he retired from the Assembly of the Kirk and from leadership at the University of Edinburgh. He served in several honorary scientific societies. He wrote *An Historical Disquisition concerning the Knowledge Which the Ancients Had of India; and the Progress of Trade with That Country, Prior to the Discovery of the Passage to It by the Cape of Good Hope* (1791). He watched his sons and daughters mature and marry. His oldest son became involved in the law; his two youngest sons had important careers in the military; and his two daughters married successful men. Robertson slowly declined as he reached his seventieth year. He died on 4 June 1793 at age seventy-one.

Contemporaries described Robertson as dignified, reserved, grave, quiet, condescending, studious, and sometimes pompous; his writing as concise, factual, and usually just; and his research as erudite and exhaustive. Gibbon expressed his obligation to Robertson's work. Thomas Carlyle the biographer recalled his youth reading Robertson's histories. Catherine the Great claimed to be unable to put down *The History of the Reign of the Emperor Charles V.* Scotsman James Mackintosh in the early 1800s summed up Robertson's writing style: "His merit consists in a certain even and well-supported tenour of good sense and elegance. There is a formality and demureness in his manner; his elegance has a primness, and his dignity a stiffness which reminds one of the politeness of an old maid of quality, standing on all her punctilios and propriety and prudery" (quoted in Thompson, *History of Historical Writing*).

Robertson was a typical elite Englishman during the reign of George III. Unlike most historians of his time and since, Robertson gained fame and honor through writing history. He earned enough wealth from his three books to live a life of ease. He was confident that his type of history, based on his moral assumptions, was best, an important contribution to individuals, England—indeed, to the world.

Robertson's histories had a profound impact on subsequent historians, biographers, and writers. Modern scholars laud Robertson's literary style, his impact on the Scottish Enlightenment, and his pioneering work in cultural anthropology.

Bibliography:

E. Adamson Hoebel, "William Robertson: An Eighteenth Century Anthropologist-Historian," *American Anthropologist,* 62 (1960): 648–655.

References:

J. B. Black, *The Art of History: A Study of Four Great Historians of the Eighteenth Century* (London: Methuen, 1926);

S. J. Brown, ed., *William Robertson and the Expansion of Empire* (Cambridge: Cambridge University Press, 1997);

J. R. Hale, *The Evolution of British Historiography, from Bacon to Namier* (Cleveland: Meridian Books, 1964);

Karen O'Brien, *Narratives of Enlightenment: Cosmopolitan History from Voltaire to Gibbon* (Cambridge: Cambridge University Press, 1997);

Jeffrey Smitten, "Impartiality in Robertson's *History of America,*" *Eighteenth-Century Studies,* 19 (1985): 56–77;

Smitten, "Robertson's *History of Scotland:* Narrative Structure and the Sense of Reality," *Clio,* 11 (1981): 29–47;

James E. Thompson, *A History of Historical Writing,* volume 2 (New York: Macmillan, 1942);

David J. Womersley, "The Historical Writings of William Robertson," *Journal of the History of Ideas,* 47 (1986): 497–506.

Papers:

William Robertson's papers, especially his letters, are widely scattered. The primary holdings are in the National Library of Scotland, the Edinburgh University Library, and the British Library. The National Library of Scotland houses the Robertson-McDonald papers, a large collection of letters and other documents from Robertson's family, including the unfinished translation of Marcus Aurelius, the manuscript of the 1788 sermon, the manuscript of the unfinished history of British America, the manuscript of *An Historical Disquisition concerning the Knowledge Which the Ancients Had of India,* and the questionnaires used for *The History of America.* The library also has many other manuscript letters by and to Robertson in other collections. The Edinburgh University Library houses many letters. The British Library has a large collection of letters as well as manuscript materials used in writing *The History of the Reign of the Emperor Charles V.* Other important collections of letters are to be found in the Scottish Record Office, the Bute papers at Mount Stuart, and Duke University Library.

Owen Ruffhead

(1723 – 25 October 1769)

Juilee Decker
Georgetown College

BOOKS: *Ministerial Usurpation Displayed: and The Prerogatives of the Crown, with the Rights of Parliament and of the Privy Council, Considered. In an Appeal to the People,* anonymous (London: Printed for R. Griffiths, 1760);

Reasons Why the Approaching Treaty of Peace Should Be Debated in Parliament: as a Method Most Expedient and Constitutional. In a Letter Addressed to a Great Man, (Dublin: Printed for James Hoey Jr., 1760);

A Digest of the Poor Laws: In Order to Their Being Reduced into One Act: With References to the Statutes, and Marginal Observations (London: Printed for P. Uriel, 1768);

The Life of Alexander Pope, Esq. Compiled from Original Manuscripts; With a Critical Essay on his Writings and Genius (London: Printed for C. Bathurst, H. Woodfall, W. Strahan, J. & F. Rivington, W. Johnston, 1769);

A Complete Index to the Statutes at Large: from Magna Charta to the Tenth Year of George III Inclusive (London: Printed by His Majesty's Statute and Law Printers for P. Uriel, 1772).

Editions: *The Life of Alexander Pope* (Hildesheim: G. Olms, 1968);

The Life of Alexander Pope (New York: Garland, 1974).

OTHER: *The Con-Test,* edited by Ruffhead (London: Printed for C. Corbett, 23 November 1756–6 August 1757; reprinted in the United States by Garland);

Matthew Bacon, *A New Abridgment of the Law. By a Gentleman of the Middle Temple,* 5 volumes (London: Printed by E. & R. Nutt, and R. Gosling for H. Lintot, 1736–1766)–fourth and fifth volumes by Ruffhead and Joseph Sayer;

Volumes 7–9, in *The Statutes at Large; From Magna Charta, to the Thirtieth Year of King George II,* 9 volumes (London: Printed by Thomas Baskette, 1758–1773);

Giles Jacob, *A New Law-Dictionary: Containing the Interpretation and Definition of Words and Terms Used in the Law; As Also the Law and Practice, under the Proper Heads and Titles,* edited and enlarged by Ruffhead and John Morgan (London: Printed by Strahan & Woodfall for J. Beecroft; W. Strahan; J. & F. Rivington, and others, 1772).

SELECTED PERIODICAL PUBLICATIONS– UNCOLLECTED: Review of *The History of England, under the House of Tudor,* in *Monthly Review,* 20 (April–May 1759): 344–364, 400–417;

Review of *The History of England, from the Invasion of Julius Caesar,* in *Monthly Review,* 25 (December 1761): 401–414; 26 (February 1762): 81–95.

From the eighteenth century onward, authors and essayists catered to the fascination for biographical and anecdotal details that consumed the fields of politics, literature, and law. The characteristics of these fields of study became less distinct, and this blurring of boundaries enabled historians to gain access to a variety of materials. Historians such as Owen Ruffhead felt called upon not only to comment on the present but also to make connections between the present and the past. Ruffhead's career as an historian also bears witness to his legal training and experience in the thriving fields of politics and literature as well as his capacities as an historian. As a writer, he developed his skills as a reviewer and editor of political tracts, essays, and reference works and his significant editions of legal reference volumes, including an edition of *The Statutes at Large; From Magna Charta, to the Thirtieth Year of King George II* (1758–1773) and his editing of Giles Jacob's *A New Law-Dictionary: Containing the Interpretation and Definition of Words and Terms Used in the Law; As Also the Law and Practice, under the Proper Heads and Titles* (1772). The former presented the laws in a straightforward, clear manner unencumbered by the irregularity of earlier statutes, while the latter reduced the perplexing language of the law to a plain and easy format.

Ruffhead was born in Piccadilly in 1723. Lottery ticket winnings of £500 as a child afforded him the opportunity to enroll as a member of the Honourable Society of the Middle Temple, part of the Inns of Court, in 1742. Obtaining his law degree there in 1747, Ruffhead undertook a consulting practice; his entry into the world of British politics came in 1756, when he established *The Con-Test,* a weekly periodical published in thirty-eight issues from November 1756 to August 1757. As a vehicle of political partisanship, these issues largely supported the previous successes of William Pitt and called for Pitt's return to office. Pitt sought independent testimonials and appraisals that came in the form of gold or silver boxes bestowed upon him. Thus, according to Horace Walpole, "for some weeks it rained gold boxes" from all over the country, thus using the presence of gold boxes as an embodiment of national opinion in support of Pitt. Dismissed from the government the previous year, Pitt had the role of prime minister in all but name by the end of 1756 in the Duke of Devonshire's government. Pitt's chief opponent was Henry Fox, first Baron Holland, whose periodical *The Test* served as his vehicle of self-promotion.

Ruffhead's periodical, *The Con-Test,* became less a vehicle of support for Pitt and more a register of the disdain for the current political situation. Covert remarks referred to the controversies and political instabilities of George III's reign. A comment on 4 June 1757 went so far as to call for Pitt's return: "The nation have unanimously declared their dislike to their administration, and expressed their wishes for the return of the late ministry." If dislike of the present administration was enthusiastic, at times praise of Pitt was less so.

Ruffhead's authority as editor of the weekly periodical marked an alliance with Pitt that was not without criticism. More important, however, is the role that the periodical played as an agent of print culture, for Ruffhead aimed *The Con-Test* to be a response to *The Test.* The tensions between *The Con-Test* and *The Test* may be viewed as a microcosm of the changing political situation during 1756 and 1757. On Pitt's side were *The Con-Test, The Monitor,* and *The Crab-Tree;* on Fox's were *The Test* and *The Constitution.* The existence of these publications, moreover, demonstrates the importance of the press as an instrument of propaganda and an index of popular opinion.

As a reviewer, Ruffhead wrote historical as well as biographical accounts. In 1758 he commented on John Jortin's *Life of Erasmus* (1758), a work based on Jean Le Clerc's life of Erasmus. In *The Monthly Review,* Ruffhead commented on the sad results of indiscriminate publication: "as the business of biographical writing, however, consists principally in the art of *compiling,* the seeming facility of the employment, has induced many laborious drones to commence biographers, who have neither been blest with genius, taste, or learning." Ruffhead

THE

LIFE

OF

ALEXANDER POPE, Efq.

COMPILED FROM

ORIGINAL MANUSCRIPTS;

WITH A

CRITICAL ESSAY

ON HIS

WRITINGS AND GENIUS.

By OWEN RUFFHEAD, Esq.

LONDON:

Printed for C. Bathurst, H. Woodfall, W. Strahan, J. and F. Rivington, W. Johnston, B. White, T. Caslon, T. Longman, B. Law, Johnson and Payne, S. Bladon, T. Cadell, and the Executors of A. Millar. MDCCLXIX.

Title page for Owen Ruffhead's only book on a literary topic (Eighteenth-Century Collections Online, Gale Group)

also reviewed David Hume's *The History of Great Britain,* which was published in four installments from 1754 until 1762. As the title of the work suggests, the historical emphasis was central to Hume's work. While Hume's fame today rests on both his philosophical and his historical contributions, in its time *The History of Great Britain* marked Hume's role as an historian and the significance of this work, which achieved considerable fame early on and by the end of the following century had been published in more than one hundred editions and reprintings.

From 1758 to 1760 Ruffhead was engaged as principal contributor to the annual *The Grand Magazine of Universal Intelligence, and Monthly Chronicle of Our Own Times,* which served as a compendium of news, reviews, public events, American news, selections from literature, and excerpts from published books. Despite the short run of these periodicals, political controversy ensued. Immersing oneself in the role of a writer for the opposition press was a duty that many pamphleteers, including Ruffhead, upheld. As a crucible of the political argument and public opinion of the eighteenth century, pamphlets and tracts were important, despite their ephemeral nature, and remain historical documents that indicate the viability and controversy surrounding British politics of the era.

In 1760 Ruffhead's attention turned once again to Pitt. Ruffhead wrote a letter to Pitt regarding the Treaty of Peace to end the Seven Years War. The Pitt-Newcastle administration was ambitious in its war aims, conquering French possessions in two continents; yet, the price of continued conflict was too high for the taxpayers to support. George III moved to secure peace and thus broke up the administration, with Pitt's departure in 1761 and Newcastle's the following year. George III then installed John Stuart, third Earl of Bute, in the position of Prime Minister. This act was criticized in the press throughout the nation. Among the most outspoken opinions was that printed in *The North Briton,* which included the writings of John Wilkes.

Ruffhead expounded upon Lord Bute's loyalty to his fellow Scots in politics. Bute had served in the previous decade as an intermediary to Pitt and, as prime minister under George III, resolved the Seven Years War with the signing of the Treaty of Paris. His favor with George III stemmed from Bute's early role as tutor to him and, in 1760, his appointment as privy councilor and later secretary of state. Ruffhead charged that Bute patronized Scots to an unfair advantage; thus, Ruffhead anonymously published *Considerations on the Present Dangerous Crisis,* a single-sheet pamphlet that pointed out Bute's seemingly injudicious act. In the larger scheme, the earl's opponents charged him with the "scourge" of Scottish migration and a transfer of power from Englishmen to Scots and, by extension, fanning hostility toward the Scots with hatred of Bute. Having applied opprobrious national characteristics to Bute, Ruffhead and a host of other political pamphleteers were spurred to action. Other pamphlets include *An Ode to Lord B***, on the Peace. By the Author of the Minister of State, a Satire,* Henry Howard's essay on the "Political Bagpiper," and John Almon's review of Bute's administration.

Ruffhead's next significant project as an historian was a departure from political history; it focused instead on legal discourse. He began work on Matthew Bacon's *A New Abridgment of the Law. By a Gentleman of the Middle Temple,* a five-volume publication of the laws. Bacon died before completing his survey, however, and many of the later entries in *A New Abridgment of the Law* were added by Joseph Sayer and Ruffhead. Thus, the publication dates span three decades (1736–1766).

Ruffhead's work on Bacon's project was helpful for his compilation of *The Statutes at Large.* For this work, Ruffhead assembled the statutes from the Magna Carta to the present, including recent laws, such as the Currency Act of 1751, which was enacted as a means of regulating the monetary affairs of the colonies by restraining the use of paper bills of credit. Ruffhead's task was the continuation of scattered efforts at compiling laws over the centuries. As early as the fifteenth century there was need for an official edition of the law; manuscript material "Readings on Early Statutes of England" was drawn up from serial lectures given in one of the Inns of Court. By 1607 the "Companie of Stationers" had printed *Institutions or Principale Grounds of the Lawes and Statutes of England.* Published in quarto volumes, the first five books of Ruffhead's compilation were published in 1763 and the remaining three the following year. An advertisement in the text of volume eight indicates that "at the request of many of the subscribers" the series would be brought up to date and completed by a ninth volume. Charles Runnington completed this task by publishing an expanded ten-volume set in 1786. New, expanded editions were published as updates to Ruffhead's original series.

Ruffhead's edition of *The Statutes at Large* was praised for its thoroughness and regarded as a necessity at home or abroad, as noted in a letter from William Samuel Johnson to his son Samuel William Johnson in 1786; a passage relays the exchange of books between father and son across the ocean. The father inquires, "Would not the British Statutes be of Use to you? If they will I can send you Ruffheads Edit. of them." Runnington's 1786 edition was followed by an extended eighteen-volume edition. Ruffhead's edition served as a standard until the publication of *Statutes of England* by Hardinge Stanley Giffard, first Earl of Halsbury, the following century.

Toward the end of the 1760s, Ruffhead's interests shifted toward literary criticism. As a biographer, Ruffhead is known for his work on Alexander Pope, a project undertaken at the request of Bishop Warburton. Ruffhead was not the first to comment on Pope's life and times. Critical commentary on Pope's translations of Homer were offered by Joseph Spence and John Dennis early on and later by Samuel Johnson, Percival Stockdale, William Wordsworth, Samuel Taylor Coleridge, and William Hazlitt. Often cited among these,

Samuel Johnson's "Life of Pope," which appeared in his edition of the *Lives of the English Poets* (1779–1781), is a helpful starting point for understanding Ruffhead's treatment of Pope.

Johnson's *Lives of the Poets* is filled with commentary on many authors. Johnson's interest, however, was less with the authors' writings than with their conversation, causing him to lament of Pope that "so near his time, so much should be known of what he has written, and so little of what he has said." By contrast, Ruffhead chose to dedicate a single volume to Pope, whose heroicomical cantos were at once public and private satires. A well-documented life, Pope's biography offered Ruffhead the opportunity to sift through the author's papers and manuscripts, including his *Works,* which appeared in many editions; translations of Homer; and Pope's contributions to *The Spectator.* With these sources at hand and with respect for Pope as a distinctive contributor to English eighteenth-century verse as a guide, Ruffhead provided quotations from Pope's works and his letters as a vehicle "fully and candidly to exemplify the beauties and blemishes of his compositions." Ruffhead, in his lengthy volume, wove together the threads of Pope's character as a person and his authority as an author. Ruffhead concludes his biography by addressing the public:

> I submit the foregoing sheets, in which I have endeavoured to do justice to Mr. Pope's character, whether he is considered as an author, or as a man. If I have been mistaken in my judgment of his *literary* capacity, his writings are in every body's hands, and the reader's better taste will correct me. In the delineation of his *moral* character, I have been more attentive to preserve a faithful likeness, than to draw a graceful picture. The work, such as it is, will not, I trust, be altogether without its use: One of the most instructive gifts to posterity, being the Life of a Man of Genius and Virtue.

In later centuries, Pope, and Ruffhead's edition of Pope's life, were sources of commentary by authors. For example, George Gordon, Lord Byron, called for Pope's exaltation as "the national poet of mankind," and Victorian writer John Ruskin praised Pope's works as having "inestimable value." By the end of the nineteenth century, Victorian sympathies for Pope exalted his work; meanwhile, Ruffhead's edition of Pope's life seemed dull and lifeless in comparison to this heightened praise. By 1889 Ruffhead's edition was relegated, in the words of Whitwell Elwin, to the work of "an uncritical transcriber." Ruffhead completed the five-volume manuscript on 1 January 1769 and lived to see the early success of this work. It was reprinted in four editions in its first year, including a two-volume format in Dublin. Ruffhead died later that year on 25 October 1769.

While Ruffhead's biography of Pope was his last completed work, he had begun work on two final projects, which his death cut short. The first was his role as compiler of Jacob's *A New Law-Dictionary.* Originally published in 1729, the work combined the attributes of a dictionary, an abridgement, and a book of English etymology. The ninth edition, which appeared in 1772, was edited by Ruffhead and John Morgan. *A New Law-Dictionary* carried on the tradition of legal history begun two centuries earlier by John Rastell, whose *Exposiciones Terminorum Legum Anglorum* (1525, The Exposition of the Terms of the Laws of England, later known as the *Termes de la Ley*), included definitions of words in alphabetical order and served as a model for Jacob's work and Ruffhead's later compilation of it.

While at work on the edition of Pope's life and Jacob's *A New Law-Dictionary,* Ruffhead was commissioned to supervise a new edition of the *Cyclopedia: or, An Universal Dictionary of Arts and Sciences* of English mapmaker Ephraim Chambers. Originally published in 1728, Chambers's work was based upon a format established by theologian John Harris, who presented all articles alphabetically, used articles contributed by specialists, and included bibliographies. Ruffhead's work on *Cyclopedia* ended upon his death; a new edition was edited by Abraham Rees and was printed from 1780 to 1786 by William Strahan.

Concerned with systems of classification and designation and aimed at clarifying them for the reader, Owen Ruffhead poured his creative energies into the bourgeois public sphere as an historian who also worked in the biographical, literary, political, and legal genres. In this way, he seems to have nourished Samuel Johnson's notion of a "nation of readers" described in the preface to his *Lives of the Poets.* Ruffhead witnessed and capitalized upon the new areas of public responsibility relative to authorship, including the growing interest in the lives of authors and the relation of their lives to their work, the classification of legal statutes, and an interest in authentication of authorship. His roles as pamphleteer, biographer, and compiler held singular as well as national importance by virtue of their broad appeal and their historical significance. Undeniably, Ruffhead was positioned as an historian and arbiter of national taste in the spheres of politics, literature, and legal affairs.

References:

John Brewer, "The Misfortunes of Lord Bute: A Case-Study in Eighteenth-Century Political Argument and Public Opinion," *Historical Journal,* 16, no. 1 (March 1973): 3–43;

John D. Cowley, *A Bibliography of Abridgments, Digests, Dictionaries and Indexes of English Law, to the Year 1800* (London: Quaritch, 1932);

Whitwell Elwin, *The Works of Alexander Pope,* 10 volumes (London: J. Murray, 1871–1889);

James Fieser, ed., *Early Responses to Hume's History of England,* 2 volumes (Bristol: Thoemmes Press, 2002);

Henry Fox, Lord Holland, and A. Murphy, *Test* (6 November 1756–9 July 1757) (London: S. Hooper at Gay's Head near Beaufort Buildings in the Strand);

Paul Langford, "William Pitt and Public Opinion, 1757," *English Historical Review,* 88 (January 1973): 54–80;

Maynard Mack, *Collected in Himself: Essays Critical, Biographical and Bibliographical on Pope and Some of His Contemporaries* (Newark: University of Delaware Press, 1982);

J. G. Marvin, *Legal Bibliography; or, A Thesaurus of American, English, Irish, and Scotch Law Books* (Philadelphia: T. & J. W. Johnson, 1847);

John Nichols, *Literary Anecdotes of the Eighteenth Century; Comprizing Biographical Memoirs of William Bowyer, Printer, F.S.A., and Many of His Learned Friends; An Incidental View of the Progress and Advancement of Literature in this Kingdom during the Last Century; and Biographical Anecdotes of a Considerable Number of Eminent Writers and Ingenious Artists; With a Very Copious Index,* 9 volumes (London: Printed for the author by Nichols & Bentley, 1812–1815), IV: 97 and V: 633;

Nichols, *Literary Anecdotes of the Eighteenth Century,* edited by Colin Clair (Carbondale: Southern Illinois University Press, 1967);

Judith O'Neill, *Critics on Pope* (Coral Gables, Fla.: University of Miami Press, 1968).

Thomas Rymer

(1643? – 13 or 14 December 1713)

John E. Luebering
University of Chicago

See also the Rymer entry in *DLB 101: British Prose Writers, 1660–1800, First Series.*

BOOKS: *The Tragedies of the Last Age Consider'd and Examin'd by the Practice of the Ancients, and the Common Sense of All Ages. In a Letter to Fleetwood Shepheard, Esq.* (London: Richard Tonson, 1678 [August 1677]);

Edgar, or the English Monarch; An Heroick Tragedy (London: Richard Tonson, 1678 [1677]);

A General Draught and Prospect of Government in Europe, and Civil Policy. Shewing the Antiquity, Power, Decay of Parliaments. With Other Historical and Political Observations Relating Thereunto. In a Letter, anonymous (London: Printed for Tho. Benskin, 1681);

An Epistle to Mr. Dryden (N.p., 1688);

A Poem on the Prince of Orange, His Expedition and Success in England (London: Printed for Awnsham Churchill, 1688);

A Poem on the Arrival of Queen Mary. February the 12th. 1689 (London: Printed for Awnsham Churchill, 1689);

A Short View of Tragedy; It's Original, Excellency, and Corruption. With Some Reflections on Shakespear, and Other Practitioners for the Stage (London: Richard Baldwin, 1693 [Dec. 1692]);

Letters to the Right Reverend the Ld. Bishop of Carlisle: Occasioned by Some Passages in His Late Book of the Scotch Library. Wherein Robert the Third Is Beyond All Dispute Freed from the Imputation of Bastardy. A Particular Account Is Given of King David's Ransom, and of the Hostages for the Payment of the Same. With Several Original Papers Relating to the Scotch Affairs: and a Grant of the Liberties of Scotland. Letter I, anonymous (London: James Knapton, 1702); *To the Right Reverend the Ld. Bishop of Carlisle. Containing an Historical Deduction of the Alliances Between France and Scotland . . . to Which Is Added, a Notable Piece of Church-History. . . . Letter II* (London: Tho. Hodgson, [1703?]); *To the Right Reverend the Ld. Bishop of Carlisle. Containing a Third Vindication of Edward the*

Thomas Rymer *(frontispiece for Rymer,* The Tragedies of the Last Age Consider'd and Examin'd, *1678; Thomas Cooper Library, Microforms Collection, University of South Carolina)*

Third. Letter III (London: Printed by Thomas Bowyer, 1706).

Collections and Editions: Selections, in volume 2, *Critical Essays of the Seventeenth Century,* 3 volumes, edited by J. E. Spingarn (Oxford: Oxford University Press, 1908–1909);

The Critical Works of Thomas Rymer, edited by Curt A. Zimanky (New Haven, Conn.: Yale University Press, 1956);

A Short View of Tragedy, introduction by John Valdimir Price (London: Routledge/Thoemmes, 1994).

OTHER: *Epithalamia Cantabrigiensia in Nupitas Auspicatissimas Serenisssimi Regis Caroli II, Britanniarum Monarchae, et Illustrissimae, Principis Catherinae, Potentissimi Regis Lusitaniae Sororis Unicae* (Cambridge: John Field, 1662)–includes a Latin poem by Rymer;

Thomae Hobbes Angli Malmesburiensis Philosophi Vita . . . (London: Wm. Cooke, 1681)–contributions likely by Rymer;

Bulstrode Whitlocke, *Memorials of the English Affairs: or, An Historical Account of What Passed from the Beginning of the Reign of King Charles the First, to King Charles the Second His Happy Restauration* (London: Nathaniel Ponder, 1682)–preface likely by Rymer;

"To Dorolissa, On Her Being Like My Lord Dorset," in *Poems by Several Hands* (London, 1685);

Thomas Hobbes, *Historia Ecclesiastica Carmine Elegiaco Concinnata,* Latin preface by Rymer (London, 1688);

Poems to the Memory of that Incomparable Poet Edmond Waller Esquire (London: Joseph Knight and Francis Saunders, 1688)–includes several poems by Rymer, pp. 4–9, 10, 26–27;

John Wilmot, Earl of Rochester, *Poems, &c. on Several Occasions: With Valentinian, a Tragedy,* preface by Rymer (London: Jacob Tonson, 1691);

Foedera, Conventiones, Literae, et Cujuscunque Generis Acta Publica, inter Reges Anglicae, et Alios Quosvis Imperatores, Reges, Pontifices, Principes, Vel Communitates, ab Ineunte Saeculo Duodecimo . . . , volumes 1–15 edited by Rymer, materials for volume 16 compiled by Rymer and edited by Robert Sanderson, volumes 17–20 by Sanderson (London: A. & J. Churchill, 1704–1735);

Curious Amusements: Fitted for the Entertainment of the Ingenious of Both Sexes: Writ in Imitation of the Count De Roche Foucault, and Render'd into English from the 15th Edition Printed at Paris, poems by Rymer (London: D. Browne, W. Mears, and J. Browne, 1714), pp. 133–192;

Paul Rapin de Thoyras, *Acta Regia: Being the Account Which Mr. Rapin De Thoyras Published of the History of England, by Authority of the Lords the States-General; and Grounded upon Those Records Which, by Order of the Late Majesties King William, Queen Anne, and King George, Are Collected in That Inestimable Fund of History Mr. Rymer's Foedera . . .* (London: Printed for J. & J. Knapton, 1731);

Edmund Waller, *The Works of Edmund Waller, Esq; in Verse and Prose* (London: Printed for J. & R. Tonson and S. Draper, 1744)–includes "Epitaph on Waller's monument by Mr. Rymer."

TRANSLATIONS: René Rapin, *Reflections on Aristotle's Treatise of Poesie, Containing the Necessary, Rational, and Universal Rules for Epick, Dramatick, and the Other Sorts of Poetry . . .* (London: Printed by T. N. for H. Herringman, 1674);

Ovid, "Penelope to Ulysses," in *Ovid's Epistles* (London: Jacob Tonson, 1680), pp. 169–176;

Plutarch, "The Life of Nicias," in *Plutarch's Lives,* 3 volumes (London: Jacob Tonson, 1683–1686): III: 437–499;

Ovid, from *Amores,* 3, 6, in *Miscellany Poems. Containing a New Translation of Virgill's Ecologues, Ovid's Love Elegies . . .* (London: Jacob Tonson, 1684), pp. 150–153.

Since the 1690s, Thomas Rymer has attracted a mix of scorn and pity. Despite early success as the translator of an influential French treatise on poetry, he later wrote a play considered one of the worst of the seventeenth century and launched a vitriolic attack on William Shakespeare's *Othello* that dogged his reputation for centuries. The conclusions of that attack (in *A Short View of Tragedy* [1693])–that Othello is a "Jealous Booby" and the play "a Bloody Farce"–encouraged historian Thomas Macaulay to declare him "the worst critic that ever lived." Macaulay's verdict represents the culmination of two centuries of growing anti-Rymer sentiment; as that sentiment subsided during the twentieth century, Rymer became a literary curiosity, variously described as an author, dramatist, literary critic, and archaeologist and reluctantly credited (by some, as George Watson) with being one of the first practitioners of modern English literary criticism. Because of his literary reputation, Rymer's supervision of one of the most important collections of medieval government documents–the twenty-volume *Foedera, Conventiones, Literae, et Cujuscunque Generis Acta Publica, inter Reges Anglicae, et Alios Quosvis Imperatores, Reges, Pontifices, Principes, Vel Communitates, ab Ineunte Saeculo Duodecimo* (1704–1735)–has also been disparaged: he is today more often identified as a collector of historical documents than as an historian. Yet, Rymer deserves the title of historian, not just for the *Foedera* but for the historical scholarship that runs throughout his literary criticism and other published work.

The place and date of Rymer's birth are unknown. Rymer's biographer, Curt A. Zimansky, suggests that he was likely born at Yafforth, near Northallerton, Yorkshire. Estimates of Rymer's birth have ranged from 1638 to 1643, with 1642 or 1643 most probable.

Rymer may have had three siblings, but only an older brother, Ralph, and older sister, Mary, have been identified. Almost nothing is known of his mother.

Rymer's father, Ralph, was a prominent supporter of the Parliamentary cause during the English Civil War: he was active throughout the 1640s and 1650s supplying local troops, and he moved up in Yorkshire's government from justice of the peace to treasurer. He accumulated enough wealth and power during the war to acquire two estates—at Yafforth and nearby Wickmore—that he had previously rented from a Royalist landlord at £200 a year. Additional land acquisitions at Helpersby and Brafferton came in 1656.

Against this background of prosperity Rymer began his education in 1649. He attended Northallerton Free School, where he was taught by Thomas Smelt, a Royalist. Ten years later, on 29 April, he was admitted to Sydney Smith College at Cambridge.

The Restoration in 1660 reversed the Rymers' fortunes: Rymer's father was removed from local government and lost the estates at Yafforth and Wickmore. Rymer achieved some personal success at Cambridge during this time: in 1662 he published a thirty-eight-line poem in Latin on the marriage of Catherine of Braganza to Charles II. But that accomplishment was offset the following year when his father and brother were among ninety people accused of involvement with an attempted armed uprising on 12 October at Farnley Woods, near Leeds. The elder Ralph Rymer, who denied all charges, was convicted of leading the plot. After his execution in 1664, according to David C. Douglas, Ralph Rymer's head was left on display at Doncaster. The younger Ralph Rymer confessed his involvement and implicated his father; he was sentenced to life imprisonment but was released in July 1666.

Rymer seems to have left Cambridge without a degree, and by 1666 he was in London, where on 2 May he entered Gray's Inn. On 16 June 1673 he was admitted to the bar, but a year later he launched his career as a writer with *Reflections on Aristotle's Treatise of Poesie,* an anonymous translation of a tract by French critic René Rapin. Rymer's translation was one of the earliest to introduce Rapin's French formalism to an English audience, and he drew considerable praise for it. Rymer's brief preface sounds a complaint that he made for the next two decades: English playwrights fail because they do not follow the model of ancient drama. But most of his preface is devoted to sketching a history of English heroic poetry. This genre history ranges widely, citing from, for example, Apollonius Rhodius, Virgil, Tasso, Abraham Cowley, and John Dryden, praising or dismissing them with a colloquial, sharp tone.

In 1677 (the title page is postdated to 1678), Rymer continued his career as a critic with *The Tragedies of the Last Age Consider'd and Examin'd.* Again, he finds

modern playwrights lacking, and he uses extended critiques of several popular plays by Francis Beaumont and John Fletcher to prove his case. The primary fault of these plays is that they diverge from the dictates of probability and decorum, which for Rymer are built on a combination of ancient tragedy, French formalist theory, and common sense. In this text Rymer also invokes what he calls "Poetical Justice"—that the guilty should come to a bad end and the righteous to a good one—a concept Rymer has traditionally been credited with inventing.

But perhaps more important are the opening pages of the text, in which Rymer outlines a brief history of Greek drama. Maintaining his earlier assertion that poetry must instruct, Rymer argues that the ancients turned to drama because it was a better instructor than past events: "in History, the same *end* happen[ed] to the *righteous* and to the *unjust*" and he observes, with since "*vertue* often opprest, and *wickedness* [was] on the Throne"; therefore, a description of the past could not teach morality, nor was it particularly pleasing to an audience. According to Rymer, the ancients found that "*History,* grossly taken, was neither proper to *instruct,* nor apt to *please; . . .* therefore they would not trust History for their examples, but refin'd upon the History; and thence contriv'd something more *philosophical,* and more *accurate* than *History.*" That something was dramatic tragedy.

The Tragedies of the Last Age drew a mixture of reactions. William Wycherly savaged it in an August 1677 letter, while at about the same time, Dryden (according to James Anderson Winn) called it "very learned, & the best piece of Criticism in the English tongue." But Rymer's other work in 1677 (the title page is postdated) drew no such mixture. Rymer explained in a preface that his history play, *Edgar, or the English Monarch* (published but never acted), was intended as a demonstration of "that Verse . . . I take to be most proper for Epic Poetry." The play was (and still is) universally ridiculed.

During the 1680s, Rymer likely split his time between London and the surrounding countryside. He continued to churn out translations—from Ovid in 1680 and 1684, and from Plutarch in 1684. He also likely contributed to a 1681 collection of Latin biographies of Thomas Hobbes. Rymer again tried his hand at poetry in English during this period, often without success: the ungainly "To Dorolissa" appeared in a collection by multiple authors in 1685, and an attack on Dryden called *An Epistle to Mr. Dryden* can be dated to 1688.

Rymer's most important work during this period was *A General Draught and Prospect of Government in Europe, and Civil Policy,* a survey of the history of European parliamentary government, published in 1681 and reprinted at least five times. As in his previous literary histories, Rymer ranges widely: his primary focus is medieval and contemporary Europe, with the governments of France, Germany, and England his foremost examples. But he also incorporates quotation-laden discussions of Venice, ancient Greek and Roman literature, and the Bible.

Throughout, he emphasizes his support for a parliamentary form of government and for England's Parliament in particular: "It is in *England* onely that the ancient, generous, and manly Government of *Europe* survives," he writes, "and continues in its original lustre and perfection." He also articulates his approach to historical research: he argues that "We must not be confin'd to the Writers of this or that Age, or Countrey; but consult the Universal reason and sense of humane kind, where Civil Government has been exercised." Rymer rejects, however, the authority of official government historians—"You are not to expect truth from an *Historiographer Royal;* it may drop from their pen by chance, but the general herd understand not their business"—and cautions against reliance on government records, which "themselves are not always accurately worded." What Rymer does analyze are "the Customs and particular Laws of every Nation," which indicate, he argues, that political power should rest in a parliament.

Having thrown his support behind Parliament long before the so-called Glorious Revolution of 1688–1689, Rymer was well positioned to benefit from the accession of William and Mary of Orange. After several more years of published work similar to that of the 1680s—a preface to the poems of John Wilmot, Earl of Rochester, poems praising William and Mary, more Latin translations—Rymer's Whig loyalty was rewarded: after Thomas Shadwell, poet laureate and historiographer royal, died in November 1692, the appointments were split, with Nahum Tate taking the laureateship and Rymer the position of historiographer royal.

Rymer was emboldened by his new position and pushed into print his most notorious work of literary criticism, *A Short View of Tragedy.* Published in 1692, the text has long been considered a hasty and ill-developed work. It is today remembered almost exclusively for its attack on *Othello:* using lengthy quotations from the play, Rymer dismisses Othello as a "Jealous Booby" and denounces Shakespeare's play as "none other than a Bloody Farce, without salt or savour." He criticizes its improbablity and violations of decorum, complains of Shakespeare's wordiness, and asks with indignation, "Why was this not call'd the *Tragedy of the Handerkchief ?*"

Often overlooked is the history of tragedy that fills five of the eight chapters of the book. Again, as with his earlier histories, Rymer's range of analysis is sweeping, ranging from Greek drama to medieval Passion plays to modern French theater. While his scholarship is shaky by modern standards, Rymer accomplished something that few had tried before him: a nearly book-length analysis of a literary genre, with an especial focus on line-by-line analysis of texts. Historian J. E. Spingarn grudgingly concedes that with this work Rymer became "a pioneer in England" in literary history.

Among his English contemporaries, however, Rymer's method of critical analysis—largely unchanged after twenty years—was out of favor, and his attack on Shakespeare turned many against him. After *A Short View of Tragedy,* Rymer did not write another work of literary history or criticism.

A royal warrant issued on 26 August 1693 made Rymer responsible for a collection of all documents related to Britian's agreements with foreign powers. According to Douglas, Charles Montagu, Earl of Halifax, and John Somers were most likely behind the project. The plan for such a collection was not unique: Rymer closely followed the pattern of the *Codex Juris Gentium Diploamticus* (1693) of Gottfried Wilhelm Leibnitz, with whom, according to Douglas, Rymer corresponded after 1694. Elsewhere in Europe similar but smaller collections had been made, especially in France. Throughout the seventeenth century many Englishmen had also been compiling private collections of such documents, and James I decreed in the early 1600s that his treaties with Spain and France be published. What was unusual was the project's massive scale: as the warrant stated, Rymer was "to transcribe and publish all the leagues, treaties, alliances, capitulations, and confederacies which have at any time been made between the Crown and any other kingdoms, princes, and states." He was thus given unprecedented access to government records.

Financial difficulties constantly plagued what came to be known as the *Foedera:* as early as 1698, according to the *Dictionary of National Biography,* Rymer complained he had spent £1,253 on the project but had received only £500 in compensation. Douglas says that although Rymer began work in September 1693, he did not publish the first volume until November 1704; it reproduced documents from 1101 to 1273 across its 900 folio pages. The subsequent fourteen volumes followed at a quicker rate: the second appeared in 1706; the seventh, eighth, and ninth in 1709; the fifteenth in 1713, the year Rymer died. Rymer collected additional material that was published in 1715 as the sixteenth volume, which was compiled by Robert Sanderson, Rymer's assistant since 1696. Sanderson completed four more volumes by 1735. Despite some instances of misdating and the inclusion of some forgeries, historians have generally found Rymer's judgment and accuracy to be laudable.

Aside from several published letters on Scottish history, Thomas Rymer devoted the last twenty years of his life to the *Foedera*. He died poor and in relative obscurity on 13 or 14 December 1713 in London.

Shakespeare scholar Gary Taylor has observed that, after *A Short View of Tragedy*, Rymer "became at once, and has remained, the bogeyman of Shakespeare idolatry." His attack on *Othello* has generated a seeming obsession among recent literary critics and historians, who have produced at least three facsimile editions of the book since 1970. But efforts to mainstream Rymer are unlikely to succeed as long as Shakespeare remains an unassailable cultural icon. Because he is so indelibly linked to Shakespeare, Rymer's significant contributions to the practice of literary and political history will most likely continue to be overlooked or, at best, acknowledged with reluctance. Literary historian George Watson has best summed up the current state of Rymer's legacy: after he notes that *Tragedies of the Last Age* is "the first critical book in English" to analyze English literary texts and that *A Short View of Tragedy* is "the first pure example of literary history in English," he explains that "It is an astonishing Double First which the conscientious historian, however regretfully, is bound to record."

Biographies:

Thomas Duffus Hardy, *Syllabus (in English) of the Documents Relating to England and Other Kingdoms Contained in the Collection Known as "Rymer's Foedera,"* 3 volumes (London: Longmans, Green, 1869–1885);

Curt A. Zimansky, "Introduction," in *The Critical Works of Thomas Rymer,* edited by Zimansky (New Haven: Yale University Press, 1956).

References:

Paul D. Cannan, "*A Short View of Tragedy* and Rymer's Proposals for Regulating the English Stage," *Review of English Studies,* new series, 52 (May 2001): 207–226;

David C. Douglas, *English Scholars 1660–1730,* second edition (London: Eyre & Spottiswoode, 1951);

Earl Miner, "Mr. Dryden and Mr. Rymer," *Philological Quarterly,* 54 (Winter 1975): 137–151;

James Osborne, "Thomas Rymer as Rhymer," *Philological Quarterly,* 54 (Winter 1975): 152–177;

Gerard Reedy, "Rymer and History," *Clio,* 7 (Spring 1978): 409–422;

Scott Cutler Shershow, "'Higlety, Piglety, Right or Wrong': Providence and Poetic Justice in Rymer, Dryden, and Tate," *Restoration: Studies in English Literary Culture, 1660–1700,* 15 (Spring 1991): 17–26;

Gary Taylor, *Reinventing Shakespeare: A Cultural History from the Restoration to the Present* (New York: Oxford University Press, 1989), pp. 33–39, 134–136;

George Watson, *The Literary Critics,* enlarged edition (London: Hogarth Press, 1986);

James Anderson Winn, *John Dryden and His World* (New Haven: Yale University Press, 1987).

Papers:

Few manuscripts of Thomas Rymer's original work have survived. The British Library owns at least fifty-eight volumes of manuscript documents generated during research for the *Foedera*. Several of Rymer's letters are held at the National Library of Scotland and Christ Church Library, Oxford. Several of Rymer's poems in manuscript have been deposited in the Yale University Library.

Anthony Ashley Cooper, Third Earl of Shaftesbury

(26 February 1671 – 15 February 1713)

Christine Owen
University of Melbourne

See also the Shaftesbury Entry in DLB 101: *British Prose Writers, 1660–1800, First Series.*

SELECTED BOOKS: *An Inquiry concerning Virtue, in Two Discourses* (London: Printed for A. Bell . . . , E. Castle . . . , and S. Buckley . . . , 1699);

Paradoxes of State, Relating to the Present Juncture of Affairs in England and the Rest of Europe: Chiefly Grounded on His Majesty's Princely, Pious, and Most Gracious Speech, anonymous (London: Printed for Bernard Lintot, 1702);

The Moralists, a Philosophical Rhapsody. Being a Recital of Certain Conversations upon Natural and Moral Subjects (London: Printed for John Wyat, 1709);

Sensus Communis: An Essay on the Freedom of Wit and Humour. In a Letter to a Friend, anonymous (London: Printed for E. Sanger, 1709; New York: Garland, 1971);

Soliloquy, or Advice to an Author, anonymous (London: Printed for John Morphew, 1710);

Characteristicks of Men, Manners, Opinions, Times, 3 volumes (London: N.p., 1711; second edition, corrected, London: Printed by J. Purser, 1714; Indianapolis: Liberty Fund, 2001);

A Letter Concerning the Art or Science of Design: Written from Italy on the Occasion of the Judgment of Hercules to My Lord **** (London? 1712);

A Notion of the Historical Draught; or, Tablature of the Judgment of Hercules (London, 1714);

Several Letters Written by a Noble Lord to a Young Man at the University (London: Printed for J. Roberts, 1716)—written by the third Earl of Shaftesbury to Michael Ainsworth;

Letters from the Right Honourable the Late Earl of Shaftesbury, to Robert Molesworth, Esq; Now the Lord Viscount of That Name (London: Printed by W. Wilkins, 1721);

Second Characters; or, The Language of Forms, edited by Benjamin Rand (Cambridge: Cambridge University Press, 1914; New York: Greenwood Press, 1969).

Editions: *An Inquiry Concerning Virtue, in Two Discourses,* edited by Joseph Filonowicz (New York: Delmar, 1991);

Anthony Ashley Cooper, Earl of Shaftesbury (from volume one of the 1727 edition of Characteristicks of Men, Manners, Opinions, Times; *Eighteenth-Century Collections Online, Gale Group)*

Characteristicks of Men, Manners, Opinions, Times, edited by Philip J. Ayres (Oxford: Oxford University Press, 1999).

OTHER: Benjamin Whichcote, *Select Sermons of Dr. Whichcot[e]*, edited by Shaftesbury (London: Printed for Awnsham and J. Churchill, 1698).

Anthony Ashley Cooper, Third Earl of Shaftesbury, was an author whose writings on Greek and Roman history, contemporary and ancient morality, politics, theology, aesthetics, and the arts were highly influential in eighteenth-century England and Europe. His historically based writings are important to understanding the intellectual climate of the period following the death of James II in 1688 when the High Church and the royal court were becoming less significant than commerce and Parliament. Drawing on his historical investigations into Roman and Greek societies, Shaftesbury argues for virtuous behavior based on an innate moral sense as the basis for polite and civil society. His views implicitly criticize the ideas of John Locke and seventeenth-century philosopher Thomas Hobbes as well as religion and the monarchy. As a result of the influence of Greek and Roman thought on his work, he is also regarded as a key thinker in the field of aesthetics and art criticism.

Shaftesbury was born in Exeter House, his grandfather's home in London, on 26 February 1671, only a few years after the Great Plague and the Great Fire had devastated London. His family's forty thousand acres of property in Dorset in the south of England reflected a long and successful family tradition of representing their country as soldiers and politicians. Robert Voitle, in his biography of the third Earl of Shaftesbury, says that the third earl's great-grandfather Sir Anthony Ashley had been a scholar and soldier as well as a baronet and clerk of the Privy Council, and his grandfather, Anthony Ashley Cooper, the first Earl of Shaftesbury, as well as Lord Chancellor, was also Lord Proprietor of the Carolina Colony, a position that the third Earl of Shaftesbury eventually inherited. Shaftesbury's father, also an Anthony Ashley Cooper, was the second Earl of Shaftesbury, and his mother was Lady Dorothy Manners, daughter of John, Earl of Rutland. Locke, renowned English philosopher, was a close political ally, friend, and physician to the first Earl of Shaftesbury. The fourth Earl of Shaftesbury said that he thought that Locke had introduced his parents.

When Shaftesbury was three years old, his grandfather became his guardian because of his father's weak health. Although he died when Shaftesbury was only twelve years old, he was a significant influence on Shaftesbury's life. The first Earl of Shaftesbury, a Protestant, had been unsuccessful in preventing the Catholic James II from succeeding to the throne. The first earl's actions had brought about the Whig Party, but his opposition to the monarchy led to his exile and death in Holland in 1683.

James II eventually came to the throne in 1685, only to be deposed in 1688. Influenced by his grandfather, support for Parliament became the third Earl of Shaftesbury's creed throughout his life. Laurence Klein argues that the consideration of what kind of civil society would take the place of the monarchy was enormously influential in Shaftesbury's writings, and to this end, he made an extensive study of the past: "Shaftesbury spent much time analysing past and present cultures to illustrate that, while literature and art were invariably hobbled by ecclesiastical or courtly influences, contemporary Britain was ready for a cultural take-off that would attest to as well as strengthen the moral and civic virtue of its elite." When Shaftesbury was three, his education came under the influence of Locke, and their friendship as adults continued throughout their lives in spite of an eventual divergence in their philosophies. Locke's influence led to the appointment of Elizabeth Birch, the daughter of a Nonconformist teacher, as tutor when Shaftesbury was four. The education Shaftesbury received under Birch led to the classics being enormously important to him, as Birch was conversant with Latin and Greek and taught him through the practice of dialogue, which had been so influential in the development of Greek and Roman ideas.

Shaftesbury left his private tutorship at the age of twelve to attend the pro-Tory (and therefore pro-monarchy) Winchester College in 1683. He left what was likely to have been a difficult schooling at fifteen and undertook the Grand Tour of the Continent, the final stage of education for a young person of his rank. For two years, between July 1686 and May 1689, he traveled with another tutor, Daniel Denoune, and his friend Sir John Cropley. In Holland, Shaftesbury visited Locke, who had been in exile since the first Earl of Shaftesbury's death. The two-year Grand Tour included an eight-month stay in Paris, even though for most of Shaftesbury's life, England and France had been at war. Then, according to Phillip Ayres, they visited the courts of Vienna, Dresden, and Berlin. In the latter, Shaftesbury dined with the grandfather of Frederick the Great before finally returning home via Hamburg and Holland. His unpublished journal gives a day-by-day account of his travels at this time. Voitle suggests that the landscapes and vistas he experienced in nature and in art influenced later writings such as *The Moralists, a Philosophical Rhapsody* (1709) as well as forming a lifelong love of art and aesthetics.

Because of the war in Europe, Shaftesbury was obliged to return to London via Austria and Germany. While he was away from London, the Interregnum had begun, the period between the short Catholic rule of James II and that of the new Protestant rulers, William and Mary. Shaftesbury returned to find his mother distressed. Voitle even suggests she had become mentally unstable and his father bedridden, giving Shaftesbury early responsibility for his six brothers and sisters. His mother's family eventually took her away from the St. Giles house in Dorset. She did not return for seven years, a period of negotiation and financial squabbles, in which, Voitle says, Shaftesbury tried not to be involved.

On his return, Shaftesbury, inspired by the sights and sounds of Europe, resisted family pressure to sit in the House of Commons, instead choosing to spend the next six years studying and writing. The period Shaftesbury lived through is sometimes referred to as the time of the Battle between the Ancients and Moderns, and his writings exemplify both. Among the Moderns he read Niccolò Machiavelli and mid-seventeenth-century author and republican James Harrington. In this period Shaftesbury also studied the classics, developing ideas from Plato and his followers, as well as Xenophon and the Stoics. Shaftesbury's major unfinished historical work was a life of Socrates, provisionally titled "Socratick History"; Benjamin Rand published the notebook that included Shaftesbury's preparations for this work in *Life, Unpublished Letters, and Philosophical Regimen* (1900).

Shaftesbury's scholarly ambitions were interrupted in 1693 when he inherited the position of Lord Proprietor of the Carolina Colony, a position that brought responsibilities and expenses but no profit. Voitle shows, drawing on Shaftesbury's letters from this period, that he intervened to support the French Huguenot immigrants and to try to stop the mistreatment of the Indians in Carolina.

Voitle suggests that around 1694, Shaftesbury's contact with Locke lessened, based almost certainly on the divergence in their ideas, although the two remained in touch until Locke died in 1704. Shaftesbury was highly critical of Locke's ideas, saying that they constituted a threat to moral virtue: "Twas Mr Locke that struck at all fundamentals, threw all order and virtue out of the world."

Shaftesbury finally entered politics as a Whig in 1695, becoming a member for the town of Poole. He was twenty-four years old and sat in the House of Commons for the next three years when, because of ill health caused by asthma, he declined to continue. England and France ended their war in 1697, the year of his mother's death, and at about this time, Shaftesbury left for his second visit to Holland, the publishing center of Europe. On this visit, which lasted for twelve months, he probably wrote the "private notebooks" that Rand published as the "Philosophical Regimen" in *Life, Unpublished Letters, and Philosophical Regimen*. The notebooks reveal Shaftesbury's extensive historical study of classical stoicism as well as his historical research on individual Greek and Roman thinkers.

Many studies of Shaftesbury's version of stoicism have been published. Klein suggests that Shaftesbury's *An Inquiry Concerning Virtue, in Two Discourses* (1699) emphasizes solidarity, while the notebooks emphasize the stoic traits of a love of isolation and tranquillity. Voitle shows that Shaftesbury himself oscillates continually between public activity and scholarly retreat. In this regard Voitle suggests that Shaftesbury's third visit to Europe was brought about by an emotional crisis precipitated by his family and political responsibilities.

A Cambridge follower of Plato, Benjamin Whichcote, was the subject of Shaftesbury's first solo venture into writing. Shaftesbury edited and wrote the preface to a collection of Whichcote's sermons in 1698. Voitle suggests that this work demonstrates the result of years of Shaftesbury's research into the writings of the Ancients and Moderns as well as his earlier contacts with Socinians, deists, and Quakers. The preface announces Shaftesbury's preoccupation with the essential goodness of human beings, an idea directly in opposition to the beliefs of Hobbes, who thought that greed was an innate human trait. Shaftesbury's ideas are essentially of his time, though he was anti–High Church and believed in human goodness rather than in original sin. His emphasis on sociability, as he himself observed in *Sensus Communis: An Essay on The Freedom of Wit and Humour* (1709), was being practiced in the new coffeehouses, where tradesmen gathered to trade and exchange gossip about the latest deals and news from the colonies. His criticisms of the Church led to his being referred to as a deist, as his writings were understood to be critical of Christian doctrine such as the Scriptures and the idea of the Revelation.

Pantheist writer John Toland did not have permission to publish Shaftesbury's *An Inquiry Concerning Virtue*. In Rand's *Life, Unpublished Letters, and Philosophical Regimen*, the fourth Earl of Shaftesbury states that, although Toland was a close friend, the book was published without permission, so Shaftesbury immediately bought up every copy before finishing the work and republishing. The book encapsulates Shaftesbury's moral philosophy that human beings are naturally benevolent and that happiness, arising out of pursuing what is natural, is linked to the promotion of the public interest because the human system is related to all other systems, including the galaxy. In this respect, benevolent behavior is ultimately rewarded. According to Joseph Filonowicz, in his *Free Thoughts in Defense of a Future State* (1700), Robert Day objected to the idea that "to do good in the hopes of Reward hereafter, increases the vitious [sic] Principle of Selfishness." For Day, according to Filonowicz, the *Inquiry Concerning Virtue* was "ingenuous, subtle, erroneous, and dangerous."

Between 1700 and 1701 Shaftesbury served in the House of Lords, where he had inherited his father's seat. His term ended on the death of King William (1702), to whom he had given support. The accession of Anne to the throne effectively brought Whig influence to an end. During his time in Parliament, Shaftesbury was one of those who campaigned successfully for a bill giving the right to counsel to those accused of treason. Consistent with his beliefs, Voitle states that Shaftesbury fought for "tolerance for Dissenters, for parliamentary authority, [and] against measures that might lead to a Catholic hegemony in Europe." Throughout his time in politics he maintained his writing and cared for his family.

In 1703 Shaftesbury returned to Holland once more. Between 1698 and 1706 he communicated with many European intellectuals, including Huguenot philosopher Pierre Bayle and Locke's translator, Pierre Coste, as well as the writers Gottfried Liebniz and Denis Diderot. At this time, Shaftesbury also developed his interest in European, particularly Italian, art. In 1706 Shaftesbury made one of the earliest uses of the metaphor of light to describe the growth in knowledge and ideas that became known as the Enlightenment when he wrote to theologian and editor Jean Le Clerc saying, "There is a mighty light which spreads it's [sic] self over the whole world, especially in those two free Nations of England and Holland; on whome the affairs of all Europe now turn."

Shaftesbury focused on humor in his *Sensus Communis*. In this text Shaftesbury argued, according to Preben Mortensen, that historically the human desire for pleasure had led to the development of communities with a "social feeling or sense of partnership with human kind." Shaftesbury's argument is developed against Hobbes's and Locke's ideas of a social contract. Shaftesbury's belief that basic human nature was innocent contradicted religious ideas of the day, which argued that the Fall of Man indicated that the individual was evil and corrupt. Shaftesbury's theory that people naturally knew right from wrong was contrary to Locke's idea that without belief in an omnipotent God, people were incapable of acting morally. Klein states that in *Sensus Communis*, in keeping with the growing commercial basis of society, Shaftesbury lays out the ideal of freethinking, yet polite and sociable, conversation as the basis for a rational society.

The Moralists, a Philosophical Rhapsody is partly a complaint against a perceived disregard for philosophy, or "the study of happiness" in the period. It rehearses Shaftesbury's key themes: natural order in society and in the cosmos and natural goodness in the individual. Shaftesbury's style of philosophy was not only historically based but also inherently social and practical,

CHARACTERISTICKS, &c.

VOLUME I.

I. A Letter concerning ENTHUSIASM.

II. *Senfus Communis*, or an Effay on the Freedom of Wit and Humour.

III. *Soliloquy*, or Advice to an Author.

MVSEVM BRITANNICVM

Printed in the Year 1711.

Title page for the collection of Shaftesbury's works, which are more historical and sociological than philosophical (Eighteenth-Century Collections Online, Gale Group)

imbued with the style of the conduct books that advised readers in the period how to behave in order to live a better life. The study of happiness, in Shaftesbury's view, was necessary for complete participation in the world. His ideas were deeply engaged in an historical approach that led him, according to Klein, to "locate antique origins for his project" in order to "recuperate language, history and culture." His historical research of Ancient Greece led him to support one of the locations for his advocated "politeness" or "refined sociability"—the new coffeehouses of London, which he saw as "potential sites of rational discussion."

In 1709 Shaftesbury married Jane Ewer from Hertfordshire, reputedly to produce an heir. On 9 February 1710, at Reigate, in Surrey, his wife produced a son, the fourth Earl of Shaftesbury.

The Moralists, a Philosophical Rhapsody was followed in 1710 by *Soliloquy, or Advice to an Author.* This work again follows the style of the then-fashionable conduct or advice book. It is directed at the role of the author, which Shaftesbury understood to be that of an adviser. In this work, Klein states, Shaftesbury points out that advice is actually rarely heeded and mainly serves to give the adviser power over the advised. His main message is that "diversity of opinion" is the hallmark of civilization. On this basis, he thought Greek society to be exemplary, in spite of its slavery, of which, Voitle states, Shaftesbury did not approve. In *Soliloquy, or Advice to an Author,* Shaftesbury attacks Jonathan Swift's *Tale of a Tub* (1704), probably because he was galled when *A Letter Concerning Enthusiasm* had earlier been attributed to Swift.

The total of Shaftesbury's life work was eventually published in three large volumes as *Characteristicks of Men, Manners, Opinions, Times* in 1711. It was not only a collected edition of his writings but also a book of art, including many "immaculate and polished engravings with references to relevant passages in the text." In his introduction to *Characteristicks of Men, Manners, Opinions, Times,* Klein suggests that it is a work more historical and sociological than philosophical, as it differs in its conception from philosophical treatises both in its own period and in the present. As was common in the period, none of Shaftesbury's works were printed either with his name or his initials, and knowledge of his authorship comes mainly from correspondence, cited references, and published criticism from the period. Apart from the works already discussed, the third volume of *Characteristicks of Men, Manners, Opinions, Times* includes *Miscellaneous Reflections,* in which Shaftesbury takes the opportunity to respond to criticism, in particular to defend his use of the Greek dialogic form.

European thinkers greeted the publication of *Characteristicks of Men, Manners, Opinions, Times* positively, and major criticisms did not occur in England until a year after Shaftesbury's death, when Bernard Mandeville, a doctor and philosopher, published a major rebuff in *The Fable of the Bees* (first published in pamphlet form in 1714). In this work, itself much criticized, Mandeville, influenced by the growing dominance of commercialism, allies himself with the ideas of Hobbes, with whose ideas Shaftesbury had taken issue.

Shaftesbury, plagued by chronic asthma all his life, went abroad again in the summer of 1711. He set sail from Dover on 3 July 1711, and, after traveling through Paris, Turin, and Rome, he arrived in Naples where, though sick, he industriously wrote a second edition of *Characteristicks of Men, Manners, Opinions, Times. A Notion of the Historical Draught; or, Tablature of the Judg-*

ment of Hercules first appeared in French in the *Journal des Scavans* in November 1712, three months before Shaftesbury's death. The work refers to *Choice of Hercules,* a Roman story related by Prodicus and recorded by Xenophon, in which Hercules chooses between Pleasure and Wisdom. According to Ronald Paulson, the Hercules story was later addressed in William Hogarth's drawings, in which Hogarth opposes Shaftesbury's perspective, basing his work on a philosophy more closely akin to that of Mandeville and Hobbes. *The Letter concerning Design* addresses popular taste, which Shaftesbury links to the current politics of the period, arguing that freedom was necessary in order for aesthetic taste to develop. According to Rand, Shaftesbury also produced the draft of a new work, titled *Second Characters; or, The Language of Forms.* Voitle states that this work was to include *The Letter concerning Design, A Notion of the Historical Draught of Hercules, An Appendix Concerning the Emblem of Hebes,* and *Plasticks; or, The Original Progress and Power of Designatory Art,* but Shaftesbury had only finished the first two before he died on 15 February 1713 at age forty-two. Voitle states that *Plasticks; or, The Original Progress and Power of Designatory Art,* an unfinished work consisting of notes, was a work on aesthetics based on "Shaftesbury's theory of history."

The Utrecht Treaty, which brought about peace in Europe, was concluded a month after Shaftesbury's death in 1713. His body was taken back by sea to England and buried at St. Giles, the Dorsetshire family seat. His only son, Anthony Ashley Cooper, succeeded him as fourth earl, and his great-grandson, the seventh earl, became a well-known English philanthropist.

Several of Shaftesbury's letters were published posthumously, including fourteen letters from Shaftesbury to politician and long-time friend Robert Molesworth, edited by Toland in 1721. The letters of moral instruction Shaftesbury wrote to Michael Ainsworth, a young man from his hometown of Wimborne St. Giles, whom he had sent to Oxford, became *Several Letters Written by a Noble Lord to a Young Man at the University,* published in 1716.

The writings of Anthony Ashley Cooper, Earl of Shaftesbury, were extremely popular in England for almost a century after his death. Voitle even describes this popularity as "a remarkable popular adulation." During the eighteenth century, the *Characteristicks of Men, Manners, Opinions, Times,* encompassing the main body of his work, went through thirteen editions before its final edition was published in Basel in 1790. His work influenced the ideas of many thinkers, including Frances Hutcheson and the Scottish philosophers, as well as historian David Hume, economist Adam Smith, and theologian Joseph Butler, Bishop of Durham. Ayres states, however, that after the final English publication in 1773 interest in Shaftesbury declined. *Characteristicks of Men, Manners, Opinions, Times* was not published in England again until 1900.

In contrast, during this period in Europe, Le Clerc and Leibnitz published major interpretations of Shaftesbury's ideas. In 1745 Diderot reproduced the *Inquiry concerning Virtue* as his *Essai sur le mérite et la vertu* (1745). All of Shaftesbury's works were translated into French in 1769, and German translations appeared from 1738. In 1776–1779, a complete German translation of the *Characteristicks of Men, Manners, Opinions, Times* appeared. Shaftesbury's writings now inform literary histories as well as histories of politics and ideas.

Letters:

Benjamin Rand, *The Life, Unpublished Letters, and Philosophical Regimen of Anthony, Earl of Shaftesbury* (London: Swan, Sonnenchein, 1900).

Biography:

Robert Voitle, *The Third Earl of Shaftesbury, 1671–1713* (Baton Rouge: Louisiana State University Press, 1984).

References:

Alfred Owen Aldridge, "Shaftesbury and the Deist Manifesto," *Transactions of the American Philological Society*, 41 (1951): 297–385;

Aldridge, " Shaftesbury's Earliest Critic," *Modern Philology*, 44, no. 1 (1946);

Mary Astell, *Bart'lemy Fair; or, An Enquiry after Wit* (London: R. Wilkin, 1709)–Library of Congress Pre-1801 Imprint Collection;

Rex A. Barrell, "Anthony Ashley Cooper, Earl of Shaftesbury (1671–1713) and *Le Refuge Francais*

Correspondence," *Studies in British History,* volume 15 (New York: Edwin Mellen Press, 1989);

R. L. Brett, *The Third Earl of Shaftesbury: A Study in Eighteenth-Century Literary Theory* (London & New York: Hutchinson's University Library, 1951);

Stephen Darwall, *The British Moralists and the Internal 'Ought'* (Cambridge: Cambridge University Press, 1995);

Thomas Forster, ed., *Original Letters of Locke, Algernon Sidney, and Anthony Lord Shaftesbury* (London: J. B. Nichols, 1830);

Edward Fowler, *Reflections upon a Letter Concerning Enthusiasm, to My Lord XXXX. In Another Letter to My Lord* (London: H. Clements, 1709);

Michael B. Gill, "Shaftesbury's Two Accounts of the Reason to Be Virtuous," *The Journal of the History of Philosophy,* 38, no. 4 (2000): 529–548;

Lawrence Klein, *Shaftesbury and the Culture of Politeness: Moral Discourse and Cultural Politics in Early Eighteenth-Century England* (Cambridge: Cambridge University Press, 1994);

John Christian Laursen, *Religious Toleration: "The Variety of Rites" from Cyrus to Defoe* (New York: St. Martin's Press, 1999);

Preben Mortensen, *Art in the Social Order: The Making of the Modern Conception of Art* (Albany: State University of New York Press, 1997);

Ronald Paulson, *The Beautiful, Novel, and Strange: Aesthetics and Heterodoxy* (Baltimore: Johns Hopkins University Press, 1996).

Papers:

The Public Record Office in England houses several memoranda, letters, and rough drafts by Anthony Ashley Cooper, Third Earl of Shaftesbury.

Adam Smith

(5 June 1723 – 17 July 1790)

Elizabeth Purdy

See also the Smith entries in *DLB 104: British Prose Writers, 1660–1800, Second Series* and *DLB 252: British Philosophers, 1500–1799.*

BOOKS: *The Theory of Moral Sentiments* (London: Printed for A. Miller and A. Kincaid & J. Bell, Edinburgh, 1759; revised, 1761); revised and enlarged as *The Theory of Moral Sentiments. To Which is Added A Dissertation on the Origin of Languages* (London: Printed for A. Miller and A. Kincaid & A. Bell, Edinburgh, 1767); republished as *The Theory of Moral Sentiments; or, An Essay towards an Analysis of the Principles by which Men Naturally Judge concerning the Conduct and Character, First of Their Neighbours, and Afterwards of Themselves* (London: Printed for W. Strahan, J. & F. Rivington, W. Johnston, T. Longman, and T. Cadell, and for W. Creech, Edinburgh, 1774; revised, 1781; enlarged and corrected edition, 2 volumes, London: Printed for A. Strahan and A. Cadell; and W. Creech and J. Bell, Edinburgh, 1790; Philadelphia: Anthony Finley, 1817; Boston: Wells & Lilly, 1817);

An Inquiry into the Nature and Causes of the Wealth of Nations, 2 volumes (London: W. Strahan & T. Cadell, 1776; revised, 1778; revised and corrected edition, 3 volumes, 1784; Philadelphia: Dobson, 1789);

Essays on Philosophical Subjects (London: Printed for T. Cadell Jun. and W. Davies, and W. Creech, Edinburgh, 1795; Indianapolis, Ind.: Liberty Classics, 1982);

Lectures on Rhetoric and Belles Lettres, Delivered in the University of Glasgow by Adam Smith, Reported by a Student in 1762–1763, edited by John M. Lothian (London & New York: Thomas Nelson, 1963).

Editions: *The Works of Adam Smith. With an Account of his Life and Writings by Dugald Stewart,* 5 volumes (London: T. Cadell & W. Davies and W. Creech, Edinburgh, 1811–1812);

The Glasgow Edition of the Works and Correspondence of Adam Smith, 6 volumes (Oxford: Clarendon Press, 1976–1983; second edition, Oxford: Clar-

ADAM SMITH.
Né à Kirkaldy en 1723. mort à Edimbourg
Age de 67. ans.

Adam Smith (frontispiece for the second edition [1822] of Smith's Recherches sur la nature et les causes de la richesse des nations; from <http://www.liberaalarchief.be/archief4.html>)

endon Press; New York: Oxford University Press, 1987–   ).

The influence of Adam Smith—historian, political economist, writer, rhetorician, astronomer, and social philosopher—continues centuries after his death. Since for scholars to study a range of subjects was common practice in the eighteenth century, Smith was also a student of mathematics, the natural sciences, classical literature, politics, and law. His interdisciplinary approach provided a comprehensive view of the eighteenth-century world in which he lived, and his views of the period were presented in language so simple that any reader with average intelligence could understand it. As a result, Smith's frank criticism of the policies of European governments reached many people, both domestically and internationally. Even those who had not read Smith's work soon came to know him as the originator of the idea that an "invisible hand" controls the market. Within a relatively short time after the publication in 1776 of Smith's seminal work, *An Inquiry into the Nature and Causes of the Wealth of Nations,* commonly referred to simply as *The Wealth of Nations,* Smith's views on the role of government in economics replaced those of his contemporaries.

At the time that Smith wrote about the eighteenth century, the industrial revolution was in its early stages in Great Britain. Government policies were controlled by mercantilists, who convinced politicians to establish policies that furthered the self-interested goals of capitalists, including the accumulation of individual wealth, protectionist policies for domestic agriculture and industry, and the establishment of foreign trading monopolies. While the European economic system was relatively stable by eighteenth-century standards, Smith perceived it as unwisely restrictive and believed that, ultimately, it worked to the detriment of national interests.

Contrary to prevailing eighteenth-century views, Smith suggested that the role of government in economics should be to maintain equilibrium by allowing the market to regulate itself without government interference. Like most classical liberals, Smith accepted only the basic roles of government: protection for the nation from foreign invasion, protection of the lives and basic rights of citizens from domestic interference, and provision of public works that citizens could not obtain for themselves and that promoted the prosperity of nations as a whole. Smith's views were often visionary. For example, he argued that teachers should be paid according to how well they performed their jobs. This idea did not become popular until well into the twentieth century, when the idea of the "master teacher" surfaced.

Smith rejected the mercantilist view that governments would prosper if economic policies benefited the many rather than the few. He had observed firsthand the negative effects of restrictive mercantilist policies on the eighteenth-century British economy, which in just a few years had turned Great Britain from an exporter of grain to an importer. This change in status resulted in large part from the Navigation Acts that mercantilists had succeeded in passing in 1660 and that had been extended through various acts until 1696. These acts, also known as the British Acts of Trade, stipulated that only British ships were to be used to transport goods from other countries into Great Britain and banned British colonies from exporting goods to any but the mother country.

While mercantilist policies ignored the rights of laborers to aspire to a basic standard of living, Smith understood that workers who were hungry, uncomfortable, and miserable were unlikely to be productive. He spent a good deal of time talking to workers as well as to capitalists, and he witnessed the effect of mercantilist-orchestrated legislation on workers. He believed that workers were unfairly punished by legislation such as that passed in 1768 and 1776, which placed controls on the wages and hours of journeymen, tailors, and silk workers. Subsequent legislation placed restrictions on other industries. However, by the beginning of the nineteenth century, Smith's theories were so widely accepted that all such restrictions on wages and hours were repealed. Because of Smith, the British government also abolished the parish apprentice system, in which the government had forced orphans and foundlings of young ages to become little more than slaves of industry.

Smith published only two major works in his lifetime, but each served to define the disciplines with which they were concerned and chronicled for posterity eighteenth-century politics, economics, and society. *The Theory of Moral Sentiments,* first published in 1759, established a new paradigm in moral philosophy. Smith endorsed the notion of what was defined later as "business ethics," believing that the moral views of the business world, both individually and collectively, had an enormous impact on the lives of workers and on society as a whole. The publication of *An Inquiry into the Nature and Causes of the Wealth of Nations* proved to be a watershed in political economy for both Europe and the United States, and the work continues to be perceived as one of the most influential works of all time. Smith, who became known as the architect of capitalism, was fortunate enough to witness his impact on the world in which he lived. Yet, he could not have known that his insight into the development of capitalism would continue to form a foundation for the study of economic thought from that point forward.

Smith was one of the leaders of the Scottish Enlightenment, as was his mentor, David Hume, and both had a major influence on the French and American Enlightenments as well. Smith and Hume approached

Manuscript for an early draft of Smith's An Inquiry into the Nature and Causes of the Wealth of Nations, *1776, sheet 3, p. iii, with marginal addition and alterations in the text in Smith's hand (from William Robert Scott,* Adam Smith as Student and Professor, *1937; Thomas Cooper Library, University of South Carolina)*

the economic order according to the classical liberal perspective, which was based on the idea that individuals were capable of making rational choices for themselves without government interference. In consequence, Smith and Hume rejected any limits on trade that interfered with the normal equilibrium of an unregulated market.

In 1776, the same year that *An Inquiry into the Nature and Causes of the Wealth of Nations* was published, Smith's friend Hume died; Jeremy Bentham, the founder of Utilitarianism, published *Fragments on Government;* American radical Thomas Paine wrote *Common Sense;* and the American colonies declared themselves independent from English rule in the Declaration of Independence and followed up with the American Revolution. Smith took up Hume's mantle and became the voice of the classical liberals who were dedicated to dis-

crediting the economic theories of the mercantilists. The American Revolution paved the way for the writing of the United States Constitution in 1787 and led to the implementation of many of Smith's theories, including the emphasis on laissez-faire or limited government.

No one has been able to pinpoint the exact day on which Smith was born, but records show that he was baptized in Kirkcaldy, Scotland, on 5 June 1723. Smith's father, Adam Smith Sr., died five months before his son was born. Adam Smith Sr. was a lawyer and a customs collector in the small port town of Kirkcaldy. Adam Smith's mother, Margaret Douglas Smith, remained a major influence on Smith throughout his life. From an early age, Smith showed great potential as a student, particularly in math and physics. He began his studies at the University of Glasgow in 1737 at the age of fourteen. Of all his teachers there, Smith was most heavily influenced by Francis Hutcheson, his professor of moral philosophy. By age seventeen, Smith had won a Snell Exhibition, a scholarship to study at Balliol College of Oxford University in England.

In 1739 Oxford was not the center of learning that it later became, and Smith studied a good deal on his own. He later wrote in *An Inquiry into the Nature and Causes of the Wealth of Nations* that the professors at Oxford had given up all pretense of teaching. Intellectual pursuits were encouraged as long as students did not stray into what school authorities considered "dangerous" material. Despite the shortcomings of his professors, Smith availed himself of the extensive library at Balliol and read Greek and Latin classics, French literature, and modern philosophers. Smith was almost expelled for reading Hume's *A Treatise on Human Nature* (1739–1740), which was perceived as atheistic and immoral.

Smith remained at Oxford for six years. Once his studies were completed, he returned to Scotland and began to give a series of public lectures on rhetoric and literature; later he added lectures on civil law. These lectures formed the core of those he later gave in a more formal classroom setting. Most of Smith's students at the early lectures were law and theology students, but as word spread, many prominent townspeople began to attend. Smith conducted the lectures over a period of years, earning £100 annually.

In 1750, at age twenty-seven, Smith became a professor at the University of Glasgow, where he taught logic, metaphysics, rhetoric, and literature. When the professor of moral philosophy died, Smith assumed that position. Under Smith's guidance, the moral philosophy classes included theology, ethics, economics, and the general principles of law and government. Smith also continued to cover the classes on rhetoric and literature. He worked hard at keeping his students interested, and he was a popular teacher. His normal practice was to give a lecture followed by lively discussion or a written examination. He also tutored students individually. Never content with a single focus, Smith became an administrator, serving as the treasurer of the university for six years. At various times, he acted as dean of faculty, vice rector, and the chairman of many committees. Politically astute, Smith was designated by the university as liaison with the Edinburgh town council. He joined the Political Economy Club, a local business club, which gave him firsthand knowledge of capitalism and trade. The experience he gained through this club later proved invaluable to Smith and gave added weight to the theories he proposed in *An Inquiry into the Nature and Causes of the Wealth of Nations*.

In 1759 Smith published *The Theory of Moral Sentiments,* which received accolades from many noted writers and thinkers, including Hume, Edmund Burke, and Immanuel Kant. During Smith's lifetime, *The Theory of Moral Sentiments* was published in six separate English editions and was translated into both French and German. Students were sent from all over Europe to study with him at the University of Glasgow. After reading *The Theory of Moral Sentiments,* Charles Townshend, third Viscount Townshend, developed a deep respect for Smith and lured him away from the University of Glasgow to tutor his stepson, Henry Scott, third Duke of Buccleuch, and to accompany him on a European tour. (Townshend later become the Chancellor of the Exchequer and promoted the notorious Tea Act of 1773, which led to the Boston Tea Party.) At the University of Glasgow, professors were paid directly by their students, and when Smith resigned in the middle of the school year to travel with Townshend's stepson, he refunded tuition fees to his students, who were chagrined to see him leave.

On the European tour, Smith was able to mingle with prominent thinkers and writers of his day. In France he met Voltaire and social-contract theorist Jean-Jacques Rousseau. Smith also spent time with François Quesnay, the architect of physiocracy, a new method of analyzing the economic system through the core belief that agriculture is the only true source of wealth. Smith also spent a good deal of time with the ladies in the Paris salons. As the tutor of a rich young duke, he made more money than he had ever had and was able to live a life well suited to his intellectual abilities and to his natural inclinations. In addition to his salary, Smith received a lifetime pension of £300 per year. After the duke's younger brother joined them in Europe, both young men became ill. Smith was devastated when the duke's brother died and offered to give up the pension that Townshend had bestowed on him. The tour was abandoned, and Smith returned to Scotland.

The Theory of Moral Sentiments established the foundation for *An Inquiry into the Nature and Causes of the Wealth of Nations.* In *The Theory of Moral Sentiments* Smith was concerned with the ways in which individuals made moral decisions. He examined the propriety of action, the objects of reward and punishment, the character of virtue, and the practice of philosophy. Even though he acknowledged that humans were self-interested, he believed that virtue should be the standard by which a person lived. Smith was not interested in morals in a religious sense and did not see virtue as a way to achieve heaven. Instead, he saw morals as a way for human beings to live peacefully together in a mutual search for happiness and as a means of promoting the general good. According to Smith, humans owed respect to both God and nature. Contending that his views on morals were scientific, Smith attempted to

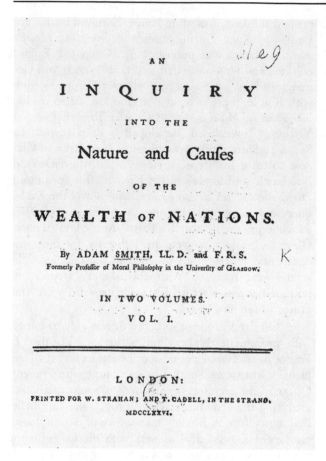

*Title page for the first volume of Smith's work on economic theory
(Eighteenth-Century Collections Online, Gale Group)*

combine Hume's atheistic, utilitarian philosophy with the view of virtue taught by the Stoics. While Smith was not a Stoic in the traditional sense, he accepted the Stoic idea that God guides the world, although he rejected the Stoic tendency toward fatalism and unconcern for the external world. Smith saw no reason that individuals should cultivate their souls while neglecting the nurturing of their intellects.

The Theory of Moral Sentiments identifies four essential virtues: self control, which is based on Plato's theory of moderation; prudence, which Smith saw as a rational result of understanding cause and effect; justice, which he saw as the foundation of society; and beneficence, which he saw as closely akin to justice because it encouraged individuals to look out for one another. Smith argued that humans have a natural inclination toward justice, a tendency that makes individuals able to give up certain rights in exchange for living in society under a government that promises a certain level of security.

Lectures on Jurisprudence (1976), Smith's university lectures from 1662 to 1666, focuses on the constitu-

tional and cultural implications of the moral code that he presented in *The Theory of Moral Sentiments*. During his lectures on jurisprudence, Smith discussed with his students justice, the history of law and government, legal authority, taxes, and the arms issue; he invited them to examine the issues individually and then to place them within an overall context. Smith believed that none of these subjects could be dealt with or understood as separate entities. He based his own understanding of jurisprudence within the context of natural law, a tradition that began with Cicero and spanned the periods from medieval times to post-Renaissance Europe and continued into his own period, the Enlightenment.

Smith endorsed John Locke's notion of inalienable rights. Locke, the father of classical liberalism, maintained that humans were created by God and given certain rights that could never be taken away by any government. Locke's theory was written into the Declaration of Independence in 1776, establishing the right of Americans to life, liberty, and the pursuit of happiness. To Locke, the pursuit of happiness meant the right to own property, which gave one a stake in government and in the society in which one lived. Smith believed that human nature predestined individuals to be conflicted about the choices they made. Because of self-interest, human beings were inclined toward bad choices, but rationality and an innate sense of justice caused most people to reject the bad in favor of the good. Economically, free competition employed rational choice to produce a healthy and wealthy economy. Smith believed that if society were not tempered by justice, the bad decisions would gain prominence, and vast inequalities could lead to immoral decisions.

When Smith began to write *The Wealth of Nations* in 1766, Western European economic thought was still dependent on the philosophy of Aristotle to a great extent. Since Smith saw Aristotelian thought as an obstacle to economic growth, he set out to replace it with a new worldview that embraced the realities of industrialization and recognized its potential for changing the world while uniting Christianity with Greek philosophy. Rejecting the classical notion that individuals were born into a particular mold that fitted them for certain occupations, Smith contended that a person's natural abilities were heavily influenced by his or her overall upbringing in conjunction with whatever education and training he or she received. *The Wealth of Nations* presented Smith's systemic explanation of an economic system in which moral codes affected jurisprudence, which, in turn, influenced economic growth.

Once Smith returned from his European tour in 1766 to his mother's home in Scotland, he left home only to see his publisher in London. While in London,

Smith frequented the coffeehouses and joined the Literary Club, where he came into contact with such notables as Burke, Samuel Johnson, James Boswell, Oliver Goldsmith, and other well-known writers of the day. Smith may also have been somewhat in the intellectual debt of American thinkers, particularly that of Benjamin Franklin. Franklin and Smith met in London, where Smith had traveled to meet with his publisher William Strahan. In February 1759 Franklin traveled to Scotland to receive an honorary degree from St. Andrews University. While Franklin was in Scotland, he and Smith met once in Edinburgh and once in Glasgow. When Smith returned to London, where he remained from the spring of 1773 until the publication of *The Wealth of Nations* in March 1776, he and Franklin spent a great deal of time together. Records indicate that Smith rewrote whole chapters during that time, and Franklin told friends that Smith brought them to him to read. Both Smith and the American thinkers were heavily influenced by Locke and classical liberalism, which formed the basis for Smith's worldview and proved to be the foundation for all American political thought. At this point Smith wrote, rewrote, and polished *An Inquiry into the Nature and Causes of the Wealth of Nations.*

The two-volume book was published on 9 March 1776. Upon completion of the work, Smith sent a copy to Hume, who responded that he was much pleased with Smith's work. Other scholars echoed Hume, maintaining that *An Inquiry into the Nature and Causes of the Wealth of Nations* had presented Western society with a new understanding of itself. Despite his praises, Hume saw the work as purely scholarly and thought it unlikely to sell well. However, the first edition sold out in the first six months.

The work received a good deal of attention from other contemporaries of Smith, such as Bentham and Georg Friedrich Wilhelm Hegel, but important figures besides scholars and writers were impressed with *The Wealth of Nations.* The government of Scotland asked Smith to be the Commissioner of Customs in Edinburgh at a salary of £600 a year, and he accepted. Smith again offered to give up his lifetime pension, but the Duke of Buccleuch rejected his request. For the first time in his life, Smith considered himself a rich man.

According to Smith in *The Wealth of Nations,* history was made up of stages, beginning with a primitive stage in which individuals supported themselves through hunting or fishing. Other stages followed as humans learned to grow food and then progressed to using the surplus food to barter for additional goods. The final stage, and the one that was most desired, was the stage of industrialization, in which specialization became the order of the day, and trade provided the

necessities as well as the luxuries. Each of the stages of history had its own specific social structure derived from the system of production. Karl Marx, the father of socialism, later drew on Smith's view of history as the basis for his explanation that society is defined by the mode of production.

Smith was concerned with justice and injustice. He believed that justice was the foundation of government, providing accountability and stability. He was a master of persuasion, and he used *The Wealth of Nations* to deliver his call for major political, economic, and social reform. For Smith, the utilitarian notion of the greatest good for the greatest number meant that a growing economy in which free competition was encouraged was more likely to produce a "wealthy" nation than a mercantilist economy that satisfied the appetites of a few capitalists but treated great portions of society as tools of the trade.

Self-interest was an essential element in classical liberalism, and Smith believed that self-interested capitalists set out to corner as large a share of the market as possible. Because unfettered competition was inherent in a free market, capitalists greedy for increased profits and consumers greedy for goods checked one another, working for the common good. Workers who asked for more than the current wage were unlikely to find jobs, while employers who tried to hire workers for wages lower than market value ended up without employees. In Smith's view, society benefited from both the capitalist, who expanded the market by investing his profits in other enterprises, and from the consumer, who helped to support different aspects of the market through the purchase of various goods. Smith believed that all the different elements of a free market worked together to produce a perfect balance. In the classical liberal view, government policies that interfered with this process of self-interested accumulation were detrimental to society and were certain to upset the equilibrium of the market. By placing obstacles in the way of free trade, mercantilists had promoted their own interests to the detriment of others. Like other classical liberals, Smith accepted the minimal roles of legitimate government as promoting national defense, guaranteeing a nonviolent domestic environment, preventing injustice and oppression, and providing public works and necessary institutions.

In Smith's view, the government should also nurture new industries and the economies of developing countries. Smith argued that the wealth of a nation was derived from unchecked competition, free trade, and the division of labor. He and several other classical economists that followed him, such as David Ricardo, used their writing to argue against the British Corn Laws, which placed high tariffs on imported goods in order to protect Britain's wheat products. The Corn

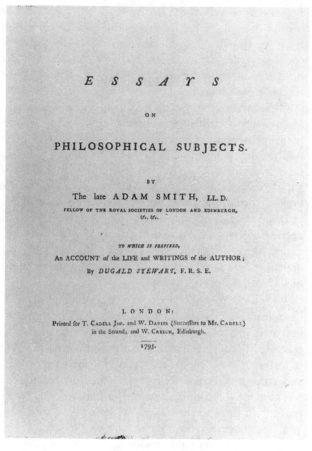

Title page for Smith's collection of his philosophical essays
(Bibliopoly, Hamish Riley-Smith)

support government. He foresaw that excessive capitalism was dangerous and destructive, and he believed that free competition was the remedy. In Smith's time, for the king or queen of England to grant monopolies to certain individuals to repay them for service to the crown was common practice. Smith deplored this practice, arguing that the state should give monopolies to no one but should encourage the creation of as many as possible, dispersing the risks throughout the system.

According to Smith, the most efficient markets were those in which labor was developed to the highest degree so that each worker became expert at performing a particular task. To explain the benefits of specialization, Smith used the analogy of a pin factory in which "One man draws out the wire, another straightens it, a third cuts it, a fourth points it, a fifth grinds it at the top for receiving the head; to make the head requires two or three distinct operations; to put it on is a peculiar business, to whiten the pin is another, it is even a trade by itself to put [the pins] into the paper" (Smith, *The Wealth of Nations*, book one, chapter one, paragraph one). Smith saw this division of labor as the key to greater efficiency, drawing on the individual's innate "propensity [to] truck, barter, and exchange one thing for another" (Smith, *Wealth of Nations*, book 1, chapter 2, paragraph 1).

The downside of efficient production, in Smith's view, was that performing the same task over and over led to negative effects on the minds of those engaged in mass production. Smith was especially appalled at the conditions of boys, some as young as ten years old, who were put to work in factories. At a time when education was generally the province of the wealthy, Smith proposed educating the boys as a way of freeing their minds. In *The Wealth of Nations* Smith wrote that capitalists were unconcerned with the well-being of their workers. Despite Smith's dislike of government regulation, he recognized the need for government protection of workers to check the abuses of capitalism. Smith also directed his attention to other social causes. He saw a direct correlation between the high infant and child mortality rate in Great Britain and the low wages paid to workers. Smith contended that if wages rose to beyond subsistence level, families could purchase food of higher quality, and infants and children would be healthier. As a result, mortality rates would decline, and more children would grow up to become productive workers who would to help stimulate the economy.

The Wealth of Nations undoubtedly influenced the writing of both the Declaration of Independence and the United States Constitution. By 1789 the book was in its fourth American printing. Franklin's connection with the book was significant and predated its publication. John Adams, who was a major force in the writing

Laws were finally repealed in 1846, seventy years after Smith's call for repeal in *The Wealth of Nations*.

In addition to unfettered competition, Smith saw the division of labor that resulted in specialization as the key to an industrial economy. In a just political economy, according to Smith, the majority of workers were allowed to follow their natural inclinations toward a particular kind of employment. This pursuit meant using strength, skill, imagination, labor, and ingenuity to perform the assigned tasks successfully. If a person were successful at a particular job, then opportunities for purchasing property were increased, and both the individual and society benefited.

Although Smith never saw industrialization fully developed, he recognized the inherent inequities of capitalism. In direct contrast to the mercantilist, who saw the worker as a tool, Smith recognized that "No society can surely be flourishing and happy of which the far greater part of the members are poor and miserable" (Smith, *The Wealth of Nations*. Because life under government was inherently unequal, Smith contended that the people should be taxed according to their ability to help of both the Declaration of Independence and the United States Constitution, had been Ambassador to France in 1778 and owned both a British second edition and a French edition. A biographer of Alexander Hamilton has documented that Hamilton, who had a part in the early history of the United States, read *The Wealth of Nations*. Records also show that James Madison, James Monroe, and James Wilson—all of whom were delegates to the Constitutional Convention—had read *The Wealth of Nations* by 1785. Around 1791 Thomas Jefferson praised Smith's work, calling it the best book in existence.

As early as 1777, Smith's economic theories had influenced the budget passed by the British House of Commons. Smith was also asked to offer recommendations on British policy toward the American colonies. Unasked, Smith proffered his views that free trade should be established in Ireland. More than a decade after *The Wealth of Nations* was published, Prime Minister William Pitt the Younger told the British House of Commons in a budget speech on 17 February 1792 that Smith's work would ultimately answer all pertinent questions about political economy. Reactions to *The Wealth of Nations* were not all positive. The religious community was outraged with Smith's assertion that one could be virtuous without being a Christian.

Five additional British editions of *The Wealth of Nations* were published within Smith's lifetime. A revised edition was published in 1778. This edition was followed by an expanded third version in 1784. Smith again revised the work in 1789. The first German edition was published in 1776, followed by French and Danish editions in 1779, an Italian edition in 1780, and a Spanish edition in 1794. The first American edition was published in 1789, but many Americans, including many of the founders, had already read the book.

The last months of Smith's life were spent working on an expanded version of *The Theory of Moral Sentiments* and a philosophical history of literature and philosophy. He never finished either. He asked his literary executors, Joseph Black and James Hutton, to burn sixteen volumes of his unfinished work. Smith died on 17 July 1790 at the age of sixty-seven. Five years after Smith's death, Black and Hutton published his *Essays on Philosophical Subjects,* which included "The Principles Which Lead and Direct Philosophical Enquiries Illustrated by the History of Astronomy."

Many Smith scholars have maintained that a good deal of theoretical inconsistency existed between *The Theory of Moral Sentiments* and *An Inquiry into the Nature and Causes of the Wealth of Nations*. More recent analyses, however, have concluded that the problems were in interpretations of Smith's works rather than in the content of the two books. Only when Smith's work is taken as a whole does a true understanding of his contributions emerge. This understanding must begin with acknowledging Smith's grounding in the thinking of the Scottish Enlightenment, which developed into an overall view of social and political thinking. Smith was a product of a time when scholars were not restricted to a single discipline but were allowed to draw in elements from several fields. For Smith, writing in rhetoric, political science, law, history, or economics was simply a consequence of his own interests and studies. Modern scholars have recognized that understanding Smith as a rhetorician is essential to comprehending Smith as an economist.

An Inquiry into the Nature and Causes of the Wealth of Nations has been studied by scholars from around the world, continuing to reverberate for more than two centuries. Since it was first published in 1776, it has never been out of print. After Smith's death, three economists emerged who built on his work to develop a clearer understanding of classical economic theory, although at times they intensely disagreed with Smith's conclusions: they were John Baptiste Say, Thomas Robert Malthus, and Ricardo. Say believed that Smith's work was a disorganized collection of work supported by examples that were applicable only in Smith's view. Yet, Say used Smith's theories as a starting place for what became known as Say's Law, the belief that demand would always rise to meet the supply of available goods. Like Smith, Malthus saw the ugly side of capitalism and its exploitation of the working poor. However, the conclusions that they drew were drastically different. While Smith saw free trade and unfettered competition as a way of improving the economy and providing greater economic opportunities for all people, Malthus believed that overpopulation was detrimental to society and argued that natural selection should rid the world of those who are too weak to survive. Ricardo remained closest to the spirit of Smith. Ricardo's "iron law of wages" stated that wages tend to stabilize around the subsistence level, ensuring that workers are never able to break the cycle of poverty. Like Smith, Ricardo was interested in international trade and developed the concept of comparative advantage, maintaining that each country should manufacture and export only those goods that provided the greatest efficiency and profit.

Almost two centuries after the publication of *An Inquiry into the Nature and Causes of the Wealth of Nations,* scholars of the Chicago School of Economics, such as arch-conservative economist Milton Friedman, argue that Adam Smith is more relative to today's economic thought than to his own in 1776. In 1990 people all over the world held celebrations to honor the bicentennial of Smith's death. An exhibition at the Royal Museum of

Scotland, called "Morals, Motives, and Market of Adam Smith, 1723–1790," was opened by ten economists who had won the Nobel Prize in economics. The historian, writer, rhetorician, political economist, astronomer, and social philosopher who saw himself as plain in looks but beautiful in his use of rhetoric used the power of his writing skills to send a moral message that changed perceptions of the ways in which simple values affect the mighty institutions that govern the world.

Biography:

Ian Simpson Ross, *The Life of Adam Smith* (Oxford: Clarendon Press, 1995; New York: Oxford University Press, 1995).

References:

Maurice Allais, "The General Theory of Surpluses As a Formalization of the Underlying Thought of Adam Smith, His Predecessors, and His Contemporaries," in Michael Fry, *Adam Smith's Legacy: His Place in the Development of Modern Economics* (London & New York: Routledge, 1992), pp. 29–62;

Vivienne Brown, *Adam Smith's Discourse: Canonicity, Commerce, and Conscience* (London & New York: Routledge, 1994);

J. C. Bryce, "Lectures on Rhetoric and Belles Lettres," in *Adam Smith Reviewed,* edited by Peter Jones and Andrew S. Skinner (Edinburgh: Edinburgh Press, 1991), pp. 1–20;

Athol Fitzgibbons, *Adam Smith's System of Liberty, Wealth, and Virtue: The Moral and Political Foundations of an Inquiry into the Nature and Causes of the Wealth of Nations* (Oxford: Clarendon Press, 1995);

John Kenneth Galbraith, *Economics in Perspective* (Boston: Houghton-Mifflin, 1987);

Fred R. Glahe, ed., *Adam Smith and the Wealth of Nations: 1776–1976 Bicentennial Essays* (Boulder: Colorado Associated University Press, 1978);

Charles L. Griswold, Jr., *Adam Smith and the Virtues of the Enlightenment* (Cambridge: Cambridge University Press, 1999);

Robert L. Heilbroner and Lester C. Thurow, *Economics Explained* (New York: Simon & Schuster, 1982);

Steven Horowitz, "From Smith to Menger to Hayek," *Independent Review,* 6 (2001): 81–97;

Peter Jones and Andrew S. Skinner, eds., *Adam Smith Reviewed* (Edinburgh: Edinburgh Press, 1991);

Henry Kaufman, "If Adam Smith Were Alive Today," *Vital Speeches of the Day,* 67 (2001): 12–16;

J. Ralph Lindgren, *The Early Writings of Adam Smith* (New York: A. M. Kelley, 1967);

G. Warren Nutter, *Adam Smith and the American Revolution* (Washington, D.C.: American Enterprise Institute, 1976);

Alvin Rabushka, *From Adam Smith to the Wealth of America* (New Brunswick, N.J.: Transaction, 1985);

D. D. Raphael, "Smith," in *Three Great Economists* (Oxford & New York: Oxford University Press, 1997), pp. 1–104;

Razeen Sally, "David Hume, Adam Smith, and the Scottish Enlightenment," *Society,* 36 (1999): 41–45;

Adam Smith, *Wealth of Nations* (http://www.econlib.org/library/Smith/smWN.html);

W. P. D. Wightman and Bryce, *Essays on Philosophical Subjects* (Indianapolis: Liberty Press, 1982).

Papers:

Glasgow University Library holds the largest and most important collection of manuscripts related to Adam Smith. Several dozen other worldwide locations of original documents are listed in the bibliography of Ian Simpson Ross's *The Life of Adam Smith.* Most of the books that made up Smith's personal library are now split between the Edinburgh University Library and the Faculty of Economics Library at the University of Tokyo Graduate School of Economics.

John Strype
(1 November 1643 – 11 December 1737)

Rory Thomas Cornish
Winthrop University

BOOKS: *A Sermon Preached at the Assizes at Hertford, July VIII, 1689* (London: Printed for Richard Chiswell, 1689);

Memorials of the Most Reverend Father in God, Thomas Cranmer, Sometime Lord Archbishop of Canterbury (London: Richard Chiswell, 1694);

David and Saul: A Sermon Preached on the Day of National Thanksgiving for God's Gracious Deliverance of the King's Majesty from an Assassination and the Kingdom from a French Invasion (London: Printed for B. Aylmer, 1696);

The Life of the Learned Sir Thomas Smith, Kt. Doctor of the Civil Law (London: Printed for A. Roper and R. Basset, 1698);

Lessons Moral and Christian, for Youth and Old Age: in Two Sermons Preach'd at Guildhall Chappel, London (London: Printed for John Wyat, 1699);

Some Genuine Remains of the Late Pious and Learned John Lightfoot, D.D. (London: Printed by R. J. for J. Robinson . . . and John Wyat . . . , 1700);

Historical Collections of the Life and Acts of the Right Reverend Father in God, John Aylmer, Lord Bishop of London (London: Printed by W. Bowyer for Brabazon Aylmer, 1701);

The Life of the Learned Sir John Cheke, Kt. (London: John Wyat, 1705);

Annals of the Reformation and Establishment of Religion and Other Various Occurrences in the Church of England during the First Twelve Years of Queen Elizabeth's Happy Reign, 4 volumes (London: Printed for John Wyat, 1709–1731);

Lessons Proper for Fallible Man: In a Sermon Preached at the Lecture at St. Augustins Hackney. Sept. the 21. 1707 (London: Printed for John Wyat, 1709);

History of the Life and Acts of the Most Reverend Father in God, Edmund Grindal. The First Bishop of London and the Second Archbishop of York and Canterbury Successively in the Reign of Queen Elizabeth, 2 volumes (London: John Hartley, 1710);

John Strype (frontispiece for volume 1 of Ecclesiastical Memorials; Chiefly Relating to Religion, *1721; Eighteenth-Century Collections Online, Gale Group; original portrait in the British Library)*

The Life and Acts of Matthew Parker, the First Archbishop of Canterbury in the Reign of Queen Elizabeth (London: John Wyat, 1711);

The Thankful Samaritan: A Sermon Preached at the Cathedral Church of S. Paul, Before the . . . Lord Mayor, and the

Aldermen . . . September the 16th. 1711 (London: Printed for John Wyat . . . , 1711);

The Life and Acts of the Most Reverend Father in God, John Whitgift D.D. The Third and Last Lord Archbishop of Canterbury in the Reign of Queen Elizabeth (London: Printed for T. Horne, J. Knapton, R. Knaplock, John Wyat, and others, 1718);

Ecclesiastical Memorials; Chiefly Relating to Religion and the Reformation of It, and the Emergence of the Church of England under King Henry VIII, King Edward VI and Queen Mary the First, 3 volumes (London: Printed for John Wyat, 1721);

Short Rules for Christian Practice: Delivered at Hackney Church on Sunday, May 31. 1724. Being the Farewel Sermon of the Lecturer There (London: Printed for T. Edlin, 1724).

OTHER: John Lightfoot, *The Works of the Reverend and Learned John Lightfoot D.D.,* 2 volumes, edited by Strype (London: Printed by W[illiam]. R[awlins]. for Robert Scot; Thomas Basset; Richard Chiswell; and John Wright, 1684);

Richard Hooker, *The Works of That Learned and Judicious Divine, Mr. Richard Hooker: In Eight Books of the Laws of Ecclesiastical Polity, Compleated out of His Own Manuscripts,* edited by Strype (London: Printed for R.C., S.S., B.W., M.W., G.C., 1705);

John Hughes and White Kennett, *A Complete History of England: With the Lives of All the Kings and Queens Thereof; From the Earliest Account of Time, to the Death of His Late Majesty King William III,* notes by Strype (London: Printed for B. Aylmer, 1706);

John Stow, *A Survey of the Cities of London and Westminster: Containing the Original, Antiquity, Increase, Modern Estate and Government of Those Cities,* 2 volumes, enlarged by Stow, Strype, Henry Dyson, and Anthony Munday, edited by, and with a life by, Strype (London: Printed for A. Churchill, 1720).

John Strype, a noted antiquarian, was an important early-eighteenth-century ecclesiastical and metropolitan historian who stressed the importance of basing historical writing upon primary manuscript sources. His own voluminous output on the English Reformation includes vast transcribed documental material, often without comment or interpretation. Consequently, his works are perhaps deservedly unread today: they are considered inaccurate by contemporary historians, and Strype himself is seen as more of a collator than an historian in the modern sense. Nonetheless, his important 1720 edition and extension of John Stow's *A Survey of London* (1598) is still considered an essential record of early Georgian London and is regularly consulted by contemporary urban historians.

Strype was born on 1 November 1643 in his parents' house in present-day Strype Street, East London. His parents, John and Hester Bonnel Strype, were Dutch immigrants with strong Nonconformist religious beliefs. Strype's father relocated to London to follow his uncle Abraham Van Strype in his prosperous silk-weaving business in Spitalfields, London, a business venture the senior John Strype inherited. Before his early death when his son was only four years old, John Strype Sr. had become a naturalized English citizen, a freeman of the City of London, and master of the Silk Throwers Company. Educated at St. Paul's School, the younger Strype was influenced by John Johnson, his brother-in-law and a dedicated Presbyterian minister. Having matriculated at Jesus College, Cambridge, on 5 July 1662, and under Johnson's influence, he later transferred to the more amenable St. Catherine's Hall in 1663. At the university Strype was tutored by John Lightfoot, an early Presbyterian who later conformed to the Anglican Church. Lightfoot clearly had a great influence on the young Strype, who not only took holy orders in the established church, becoming one of its strongest supporters, but also published *The Works of the Reverend and Learned John Lightfoot D.D.* (1684). This first work set a trend in Strype's historical writing, for Strype came to believe that biographies of great men could have a "considerable influence upon the manners of men" and that their virtuous example could "do work more powerfully than the most subtle reasonings, and the most elaborate arts of persuasion."

Having graduated with a B.A. in 1665 and with an M.A. in 1669, Strype was appointed curate at Theydon Bois, Essex, on 14 July 1669. In November 1669 he became rector of St. Mary the Virgin, Leyton, Essex, later becoming the vicar of Leyton. Strype's association with this parish, now part of East London, lasted for sixty-eight years, and here Strype married Susanna Lowe in 1681 and raised a family. It was fortunate that Strype's family were prosperous, for the living at Leyton was small, and Strype, who found both the ancient church and the vicarage in great disrepair, spent a great deal of his own money in repairing both. His appointment also proved fortunate for his career, as it brought him into contact with Sir William Hicks of Rucholt Manor, one of his parishioners and grandson of the Sir William Hicks who had been the secretary of William Cecil, first Baron Burghley, Queen Elizabeth's secretary of state. Sir William provided Strype with access to Burghley's papers, which launched Strype on a career as an ecclesiastical historian and collector of manuscripts. Strype's own collection became so large that after his death its purchase interested Robert Harley, first Earl of Oxford, though it was finally sold to William Petty, second Earl of Shelburne, in 1772, becoming part of the British Library's Lansdowne Manuscripts.

Strype's only biographer, A. P. Wire, may have been correct in asserting that Strype might have preferred to spend a quiet life in his rural parish writing his books, an activity Strype himself considered the "main delight of my life," but the temper of the times and Strype's own religious orthodoxy embroiled him in opposition to the religious policy of the Catholic James II. In supporting the Bishop of London, Henry Compton (suspended because he refused to suspend antipapal writer John Sharp, rector of St Giles's-in-the-Fields), Strype clandestinely published tracts opposing the king. Strype openly supported the Glorious Revolution of 1688 in his sermons, which well into the eighteenth century displayed a strong anti-Catholic, anti-Jacobite position. A grateful Bishop Compton rewarded Strype in 1689 with a lectureship at Hackney and the position of rural dean of Barking, Essex. The latter appointment further involved Strype in Essex county politics in the troubled first decade of the eighteenth century, and his support for the church, together with his growing reputation as an ecclesiastical historian, an activity strongly supported by the church hierarchy, led to his further preferment when Archbishop Thomas Tenison secured for him in 1711 the sinecure of West Tarring, Sussex.

In 1694, ten years after his first book on Lightfoot, Strype published his *Memorials of the Most Reverend Father in God, Thomas Cranmer*. Thomas Cranmer was the archbishop whose break with Rome vindicated the "crown from a bale dependence upon a foreign jurisdiction." In his preface Strype confessed that he had "been for a long time not a little addicted to read whatsoever I could of the Reformation of this famous church [the Anglican]." This work initiated Strype's thorough study of the Tudor bishops who carried out the reform of the Anglican Church. Strype followed the work on Cranmer with the life and works of Bishop John Aylmer (1701), Archbishop Edmund Grindal (1710), Archbishop Matthew Parker (1711), and Archbishop John Whitgift (1718). During these years Strype had also been working on two of his major works, the four-volume *Annals of the Reformation and Establishment of Religion and Other Various Occurrences in the Church of England during the First Twelve Years of Queen Elizabeth's Happy Reign* (1709–1731), a review of religious policy during the first twelve years of the reign of Elizabeth I, and his three-volume *Ecclesiastical Memorials* (1721), an account of the emergence of the Anglican Church in the reigns of Henry VIII, Edward VI, and Mary I. The stamp of religious orthodoxy was particularly strong in this latter project, for an impressive list of subscribers accompanied the work, including the archbishops of Canterbury and York, as well as leading contemporary politicians–

Harley; Wriothesley Russell, fourth Duke of Bedford; and the Speaker of the House of Commons, Spencer Crompton. All of these works included extensive appendixes of transcripts of manuscripts, sometimes a third of each volume, and Strype's labors were undertaken so such important documents would "not be lost forever" to posterity.

This prodigious output itself was considered so important historically that the Clarendon Press of Oxford University reprinted all of Strype's works in twenty volumes between 1812 and 1824; an index to the works was completed by R. F. Laurence in 1828. The works were reprinted, however, with all of Strype's original mistakes and the misattributions common in early-eighteenth-century histories, an unfortunate occurrence that led more-professional and more-modern historians to be critical of the value of Strype's labors. In 1848 Samuel R. Maitland, librarian of Lambeth Palace Library from 1832 to 1849, lamented that the Clarendon Press had published Strype's work unedited, reproducing Strype's own inaccurate plagiarism of his sources. Considering Strype's works crucial reading for any English churchman who wished to investigate the origins of the national church, Maitland, nonetheless, was critical of Strype's "notorious laxity" in accuracy and despaired that many of his misinterpretations would influence future church histories.

In his *Memorials of the Most Reverend Father in God, Thomas Cranmer* Strype hoped his work would fill a gap in the historiography of English national development. While previous historians–such as Charles Pratt, first Earl Camden, and Edward Herbert, first Baron Herbert of Cherbury–had contented themselves in considering temporal developments, Strype considered their treatment of spiritual matters less than satisfactory, for religious developments have a "more special benefit" to the reader of history as they are "weightier by far, and concern us more a great deal than temporal matters." In recognizing the contribution made to this particular field by Gilbert Burnet, Bishop of Salisbury, and Thomas Fuller, Strype emphasized that he had not based his work on previously published histories, but primary source material, "manuscripts, whether registers, records, letters, instruments and such like: a great sort of which by Providence fell into my hands." Aware that his approach and use of language may even have been archaic by the late seventeenth–early eighteenth century, he made no apologies, for a lover of history should love also the "language and phrases of antiquity." In his *The Life and Acts of Matthew Parker*, perhaps Strype's fullest biography of a religious leader, he made a statement important for all historians; if people disliked his interpretation and ordering of the documents in the work, he should be forgiven as he was only an

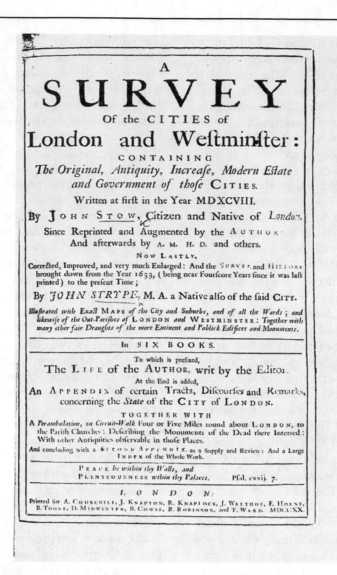

Title page for Strype's 1720 revision and update of John Stow's survey of London (Eighteenth-Century Collections Online, Gale Group)

historian who related "passages and events, and matters of fact, as I find them, without any design of favoring or exposing any side." Nor was Strype afraid to be open and honest in displaying the negative side of the men he wrote about, for, as Bishop Parker had said, all the best men have their imperfections.

In his major work, *Annals of the Reformation and Establishment of Religion,* Strype was even more forthright as an historian, saying that having gone "as near the fountain head as possible" in his primary research, he had recorded things that would earn him censure. However, it was not the historian's role to use "discretion in concealing things" then unacceptable to modern society. While he may have served the church better in burying certain discoveries in oblivion, such a practice "becomes not a just historian; nor ought he to assure

such power to himself." Whatever the supposed consequences of historical research, in a published work the historian should not consciously omit facts from the record or "alter or misrepresent what he pleaseth; when by taking liberty, the History becomes defective, actions and events are not fully related." Although Strype's massive tomes are somewhat short on interpretation, he nonetheless also held that historians should be oblivious to the interest of political party and be indifferent as to whether their work "betray some imperfection in government, or the like." While a modern historian would disagree that his main role is that of a recorder of events only, few would disagree with Strype's dictum that in recording primary sources the writer should attempt to present his research in the context and sense that the original "writer meant it." Strype himself did not always succeed in such objectivity; nor, of course, was he free from individual interpretation in his writing. Strype, as a firm upholder of orthodox Anglicanism, undertook his extensive writing career not only to support the church but also to provide a moral lesson for his readers.

In a long life he had witnessed the many political and social traumas that had rocked the English state. Only six years old when Charles I was executed, he witnessed the Restoration as an eighteen-year-old, lived through the Great Plague and the Fire of London, supported the overthrow of James II, lived through the party squabbles of the reign of Queen Anne and the French Wars of William and Mary, and not only witnessed the Hanoverian succession of George I but also survived into the eleventh year of the reign of George II. Having welcomed the Glorious Revolution of 1688 as the harbinger of a new reformed age, Strype had begun his ecclesiastical biographies at the age of fifty in 1693. By the late 1690s, however, he had become disillusioned with the growing materialism of his own age, and in 1699 he delivered two sermons at the Guildhall Chapel in London. His *Lessons Moral and Christian, for Youth and Old Age* was designed "to reclaim, if possible, this degenerate age of ours."

While he continued to work on his ecclesiastical biographies in this period, he also completed his only two secular biographies of the secretaries of state during the reign of Edward VI—*The Life of the Learned Sir Thomas Smith, Kt. Doctor of the Civil Law* (1698) and *The Life of the Learned Sir John Cheke, Kt.* (1705). Believing that biographies of the great and good would provide important historical lessons for his contemporaries, Strype hoped that these two accounts of scholar-politicians "brought to court by the fame of their learning" would inspire contemporary statesmen to transcend party and restore "good learning and true religion to this Kingdom." As the nation entered the eighteenth century, Strype, having experienced the disruptions of the seventeenth century, perhaps romantically looked back to the great Tudor age, hoping that in this new century his contemporaries would learn to curb their "desires of earthly things," believing it unbecoming for those who were going into another world "to be griped and scraping for things of this" world. This hope was what motivated Strype to undertake his 1720 monumental edition of Stow's *A Survay of London*, first published in 1598—a work that linked Stow's Tudor city to the growing Georgian metropolis of more than one and a half million inhabitants, the largest city in Europe.

Stow, a tailor by trade, had displayed a strong literary bent during his lifetime. Before he published *A Survay of London*, he had edited the works of Geoffrey Chaucer, and following Stow's death in 1605, new edi-

tions of his *Survay of London* had regularly appeared as London histories became popular at the end of the seventeenth century. Contacted by the publisher Richard Blome in 1694 to edit a newly corrected and updated edition of *A Survay of London*, Strype began to collate material for a modern account of London, a city that had emerged from the plague years and the Great Fire of London to become a sprawling metropolis of more than two thousand streets covering more than 250 square miles. Conceived as a commercial venture, the project was dropped when Edward Hatton published his *A New View of London* (1708). When Hatton's work proved to be inaccurate and unscholarly, however, Strype continued work on his edition, finally published in six books in large folio volumes including many important engravings of the Georgian city and based upon a new walking map survey undertaken by Blome and William Leybourn.

Historically, the most important of all of Strype's published works, his new edition, *A Survey of the Cities of London and Westminster*, remains monumental for several reasons. Not only does it portray the growth of the Georgian city since the 1660s, but it also includes accounts of the growing suburban expansion of the city into the neighboring counties. While based upon more than 180 books noted in Strype's bibliography, it nonetheless remains true to Stow's original work as Strype, as an editor, wished to preserve the description of the Elizabethan city as described by Stow himself. Strype preserved all the original text while adding his own new material clearly marked by marginal annotations. A reader of Strype's eighteenth-century edition is thus presented with a multidimensional work—an enlarged account of London, which portrays a dynamically growing city as well as one that retains the old ward system of Stow's period, which had long disappeared. Consequently, not only is the reader presented with a description of a city seen as a whole, a concept many of Strype's contemporaries would have been unfamiliar with given London's growth, but also with a strong sense of historical continuity. Concerned as Strype was with questions of morality and the influence growing wealth had on traditional values, the work also mirrors eighteenth-century preoccupations with the effect urbanization had on the lives of London's inhabitants.

While pages upon pages include statistics and tables, a great portion of new material presents evidence of religious concern for the poor, a growing feature of urban growth in the eighteenth century. Strype's preoccupation with forms of social control and moral reform is clearly evident in his detailed discussions of schools, hospitals, and workhouses, as well as such organizations as the Society for the Reformation of Manners. Of particular interest in this context is

Strype's preoccupation in listing eighteen pages of the "Honourable Acts of Citizens," to be followed by three pages of contemporary "Honourable Acts of Ladies" and another twenty-five pages of "Honourable Citizens" in book 2. Although a large and expensive work, Strype's *A Survey of the Cities of London and Westminster* went through six editions between 1720 and 1755. Increasingly, as the eighteenth century progressed, the size of London was something wealthy Londoners read about rather than experienced themselves. While Stow would not have recognized Strype's 1720 London, similarly today Strype would not recognize his own Leyton, once a "pleasant village washed on its west side by the sweet River Lea," which by the 1880s was overtaken by Victorian urban development.

In old age, decayed in both sight and reason, Strype went to live with his granddaughter, Susan Harris, the wife of Thomas Harris of Hackney. Having "done writing books," he hoped that his histories would be of lasting "use to the Church and the true religion." On 11 December 1737, Strype died at the age of ninety-four and was buried in the chancel of St. Mary the Virgin, Leyton. Unlike the Victorians, few readers today are passionately interested in ecclesiastical history, and even professional historians would find Strype's densely packed works a daunting task to interpret. As an amateur eighteenth-century historian, however, John Strype remains an important contributor to the development of the study of history.

Biography:
A. P. Wire, *John Strype. The Leyton Antiquary and Historian* (Leyton: New Era Press, 1902).

References:
Samuel R. Maitland, *Remarks on the First Volume of Strype's Life of Archbishop Cranmer* (London: John Petheram, 1848);

J. F. Merritt, *Imagining Early Modern London. Perceptions and Portrayals of the City from Stow to Strype, 1598–1720* (Cambridge: Cambridge University Press, 2001).

Papers:
John Strype's papers are in the Lansdowne Manuscripts, British Library, London.

Gilbert Stuart
(9 November 1743 – 13 August 1786)

Jaime Ramon Olivares
Houston Community College–Central

BOOKS: *An Historical Dissertation Concerning the Antiquity of the English Constitution* (Edinburgh: Printed for A. Kincaid & J. Bell / London: Printed for W. Sanby, J. Dodsley, E. Dilly, and T. Cadell, 1768); second edition, corrected (London: Printed for T. Cadell, successor to Mr. Millar / Edinburgh: Printed for A. Kincaid & John Bell, Edinburgh, 1770; corrected, 1771);

An Address to the Citizens of Edinburgh, Relative to the Management of George Heriot's Hospital (Edinburgh, 1773);

Considerations of the Management of George Heriot's Hospital (London, 1774);

Faction Displayed; or, A Genuine Relation of the Representation of the Trades, and of the late Political Contentions in the City of Edinburgh, anonymous (Edinburgh, 1778);

A View of Society in Europe, in Its Progress from Rudeness to Refinement; or, Inquiries concerning the History of Law, Government, and Manners (Edinburgh: Printed for John Bell / London: J. Murray, 1778);

Character of a Certain Popular Historian, Now Ministerial Agent, for Reconciling Our Complaisant Clergy to the Church of Rome (Edinburgh, 1779);

Observations concerning the Public Law, and the Constitutional History of Scotland (London: J. Murray / Edinburgh: W. Creech, 1779);

The History of the Establishment of the Reformation of Religion in Scotland (London: Printed for J. Murray / Edinburgh: Printed for John Bell, 1780);

Critical Observations Concerning the Scottish Historians Hume, Stuart, and Robertson: Including an Idea of the Reign of Mary Queen of Scots, as a Portion of History, Specimens of the Histories of this Princess, by Dr. Stuart and Dr. Robertson, and a Comparative View of the Merits of These Rival Historians (London: Printed for T. Evans, 1782);

History of Scotland, from the Establishment of the Reformation, till the Death of Queen Mary (London: Printed

Gilbert Stuart (*frontispiece for* The History of the Establishment of the Reformation of Religion in Scotland, *1780; Eighteenth-Century Collections Online, Gale Group*)

for J. Murray / Edinburgh: Printed for John Bell, 1782).

OTHER: "A Discourse Concerning the Laws and Government of England," in Francis Stoughton Sullivan, *Lectures on Constitution and Laws of England; with a Commentary on the Magna Charta and Illustrations of Many of the English Statutes* (Edinburgh: Printed for E. and C. Dilly [etc.], 1776; Portland, Me.: Printed by Thomas B. Wait, 1805).

TRANSLATION: J. L. DeLolme, *The Constitution of England, or an Account of the English Government; In Which It is Compared with the Republican Form of Government and Occasionally with the Older Monarchies in Europe* (London, 1777).

Gilbert Stuart was renowned for his many works and abilities. He integrated English history with Scottish history. In both monographs and serial forms, moreover, he related the tribulations of the Scottish people to the travails of the Romans and Greeks. This approach shaped Stuart into one of the best of the early Scottish historians.

On 9 November 1743 Gilbert Stuart—historian, scholar, and political philosopher—was born in the booming town of Edinburgh, Scotland. Stuart was the eldest child of George Stuart and Jean Duncanson Stuart. A native of Edinburgh, George Stuart was a professor of Humanity, or Latin, at the University of Edinburgh. Thus, the elder Stuart provided an environment for intellectual development, both at home and in public. George Stuart also was acquainted with all of the major figures of the Scottish Enlightenment, such as Francis Hutchinson, Adam Ferguson, William Robertson, and Dugal Stuart, as well as David Hume. Consequently, Gilbert Stuart's adolescence was filled with intellectual stimulation.

Gilbert was the eldest of the six Stuart children, two of whom died in infancy. The other children were born between 1746 and 1750. Gilbert thus assumed definite parental duties that forced an accelerated maturity upon him. Throughout his early years, he had a tendency to be temperamental in both education and personal behavior. As a youth, he was known for walking the streets of Edinburgh in an intoxicated state. Since his father was teaching constantly, Gilbert lived at the college. With the patronage of his father and Robertson, Gilbert became an assistant in the University of Edinburgh library. Once again he was surrounded not only by great intellectuals but also by the masterpieces of literature and history. By the early 1760s Stuart had matriculated at the university to attain a degree in political philosophy and law. In 1764 Stuart studied under influential Scottish historian and philosopher Ferguson, who had been a professor since 1759. Two years later, Stuart attained additional training at the University of Edinburgh. Stuart studied at the university for a total of eight years, though he did not receive any type of degree. He did, however, receive a distinct brand of historical training under the auspices of Ferguson, who taught him the intricacies and fallacies of the natural theory of history.

By 1766 Stuart had terminated his education at the University of Edinburgh. Forced by his father to work, Gilbert became an apprentice at one of the local law firms. Shortly afterward, however, after seemingly interminable working days at the firm and the "Outer House" (the part of the court of session consisting of twenty-four Lords Ordinary either sitting alone or with a civil jury), Stuart decided to conclude his apprenticeship and seek other employment opportunities.

He decided to become involved in local writing and publishing. He joined the prestigious local firm of William McKenzie, where he served as an apprentice. In late 1766 twenty-three-year-old Stuart, who now imbibed six to eight bottles of wine daily, completed his apprenticeship. While still an apprentice, and influenced by his father, Stuart wrote *An Historical Dissertation Concerning the Antiquity of the English Constitution* (1768). This work is essentially a summary history of England, tracing the roots of the English political system to the Romans and the Germanic tribes. He posited a revolutionary idea, prevalent in the ideals of the Scottish Enlightenment, that liberty originated with the people, living in a perfect state of nature. Essentially, his work created a nexus between English and German history. Most Scottish historians were critical of his theories. The notion that English republicanism was not an English invention invariably denigrated English culture. Stuart had the audacity to send a copy of the work to Hume, whose theories were publicly challenged by Stuart. In addition, many argued that Stuart's ideas were not original and, as a result, were inconsequential. Despite Stuart's notoriety and his continued faith in his own abilities, no prospects for employment existed for Stuart in Edinburgh. With help from his father, Stuart tried to obtain a position as a professor of Public Law at Edinburgh University. Because the position was a sinecure, or one that must be paid for by the applicant, Stuart did not receive it. The cost was too excessive. Stuart decided to set out for London in January 1769 to seek a better life and possible employment.

When Stuart arrived in London, he immediately became enthralled by the new "Grub Street" literature that was popular in the working-class corridors of London. He opened a business that distributed what was called "Grub" literature. Specifically, in 1770 he established a periodical, *The Repository; or, Treasury of Politics and Literature*. The main focus was on politics, specifically the major issues of the day, such as the letters of

Junius (a pseudonym for their unknown writer) about the controversial trial of John Wilkes. In addition, Stuart became an innovative literary critic, as he reviewed popular political histories of the era. For example, he wrote a critical review of fellow Scotsman Robertson's *History of the Reign of the Emperor Charles V* (1769). In addition, Stuart compiled many journalistic accomplishments when he contributed to *The Monthly Review,* in which he published more than 250 reviews of prominent books and scholarly publications. Stuart's economic situation was deteriorating to the point at which he was forced to earn additional income through the editing of Nathaniel Hooke's *Roman History, from the Building of Rome to the Rise of the Commonwealth* (1756) and Richard Rolt's *The History of the Isle of Man* (1773), which needed to be completed for publication. In 1773, after many years of updating older and contemporary historical works, Stuart decided to return to his native homeland of Scotland and to Edinburgh.

Upon his arrival in Scotland in 1773, Stuart was imbued by the reformist tendency that prevailed in Scottish politics and government. When he returned to Edinburgh, Scotland was in the midst of an intense political conflict, especially over the nature of British power in Scotland (as well as overseas in the North American colonies) and the reform of the Scottish political system. Beginning that same year, Stuart compiled a series of historical articles and book reviews for *The Edinburgh Magazine and Review* (1773–1776). In this magazine Stuart found an expression for his opinions on religion, politics, and literature. Each issue had fifty-six pages of text. Initially, Stuart, William Smellie, and William Creech distributed 2,500 copies, and the journal was circulated to the Continent and the American colonies. Thematically, Stuart focused upon Scottish emigration and architecture. Eventually, he turned his sights toward writing biographies of eminent Scots, such as Mary, Queen of Scots; Scottish statesman William Carstairs; Scottish statesman Duncan Forbes; and Scottish religious reformer John Knox. Stuart also included more than 150 poems, as well as political articles dealing with the American Revolution. In the early 1770s, however, Stuart's health began to deteriorate because of his excessive drinking and reckless living.

In 1777 Stuart returned to a topic that had always fascinated him—the Middle Ages. In *A View of Society in Europe, in Its Progress from Rudeness to Refinement* (1778) Stuart provided a study of Europe during the medieval period. He glorified the feudal system in its original condition by implying that men had work and a stable social system. The feudal system of the Middle Ages thus provided Europeans with an earthly form of paradise, without wants or needs. In addition, the work had the secondary impact of praising the Scottish legal sys-

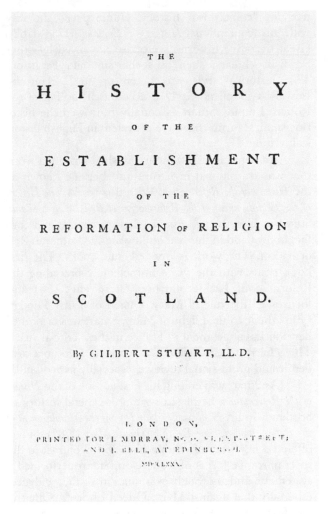

THE

HISTORY

OF THE

ESTABLISHMENT

OF THE

REFORMATION OF RELIGION

IN

SCOTLAND.

By GILBERT STUART, LL.D.

LONDON,
PRINTED FOR J. MURRAY, N°. 32, FLEET-STREET;
AND J. BELL, AT EDINBURGH.
MDCCLXXX.

Title page for Stuart's 1780 history (Eighteenth-Century Collections Online, Gale Group)

tem. Despite the importance of the argument, the book sold few copies. Nevertheless, the publication, which was a criticism of Robertson's work, led to a duel with Robertson's son. The work provided a stepping stone, though, in Stuart's historical writing.

Stuart's work clearly fit within the historiographical realm of the newly emergent Scottish Enlightenment. In the writing of history, the Scots tended to view the development of European civilization from a meta-sociological account of the natural progress of civilization. Hume started this form of "natural history." Prominent Scottish philosophers such as Ferguson, John Millar, and Adam Smith echoed Hume's philosophical tendencies. Smith, for example, visualized history as progressing through four economic stages, attended by political and social structures. This form of stadial history was a prominent basis of philosophical influence by many Scottish historians.

The Scottish scholars also pursued a decidedly different form of history, otherwise known as "narrative" or "conjectural" history. Hume paved the way with his contentious *History of England* (1754–1762). Great narrative histories were also advanced by other Scottish scholars, such as Robertson and Ferguson. This historical style was taken up in England by Edward Gibbon in his 1776 account of the fall of the Roman Empire. Stuart essentially borrowed the historiographical forms that were prevalent in English historical writing.

In February 1780 Stuart finished writing a work that was transitional in nature and became known as the *History of the Reformation.* With this work, *The History of the Establishment of the Reformation of Religion in Scotland,* Stuart tackled the process of religious change and conflict in Scotland in the years following the Lutheran Reformation. The work is divided into books. The first book deals with the years immediately preceding the Reformation. The second book starts after 1561 and focuses on the rule of Mary, Queen of Scots. Though sympathetic to the plight of Mary, Stuart was critical of her political attachment to France in these crucial years. The *History of the Reformation* received favorable academic and professional reviews, especially in Scotland.

As Stuart was editing his first edition of the *History of the Reformation,* he began writing a general history of Scotland. In his *History of Scotland, from the Establishment of the Reformation, till the Death of Queen Mary* (1782), Stuart offered a new way of writing history. In contrast to the strict narrative forms of Robertson, Stuart performed a systematic and thorough examination of the evidence, especially that against Mary, Queen of Scots. Offering an alternative to Robertson's version of the Marianist legend, in which Mary is presented as an evil woman, Stuart offers a sympathetic portrayal of her. He argues that Mary was a victim until her death in 1587. In addition, he argues that rather than being the seducer of James Hepburn, fourth Earl of Bothwell, Mary was, indeed, the seduced party. This argument was significant in that Stuart identified his historical writing with tragedy, and he believed that he championed women's rights in general. In addition, Stuart identified Mary as a rebel. He, too, was rebelling—against the traditional Marianist historiography, which analyzed Mary from the English (and hence the Elizabethan) perspective.

From 1783 to 1786 Stuart remained in London. In January 1783 an old acquaintance, John Murray, published a new magazine called *The English Review; or, An Abstract of English and Foreign Literature.* Murray's goal was to present this magazine as a complementary publication, not to compete with established journals such as *The Monthly Review.* Thus, Murray decided to hire Stuart, known to be one of the best local writers. Stuart,

however, had other visions. He was enthusiastic about the volatile political situation in London. He wanted to work for a journal to pay bills but also to offer solutions to the crisis. In 1783 three prominent Englishmen—Charles James Fox, Edmund Burke, and Richard Brinsley Sheridan—approached Stuart for a new periodical, one that would analyze daily politics. Concomitantly, in July 1785 Stuart began to organize and publish *The Political Herald and Review; or, A Survey of Domestic and Foreign Politics.* Stuart was able to disseminate his message in this journal. Specifically, he used the magazine as a factional vehicle to emphasize the need to exploit public opinion in shaping government policy. A total of twelve numbers were published between July 1785 and the summer of 1786. Stuart then suffered a decline in health.

In the spring of 1786 Gilbert Stuart deteriorated physically. He was jaundiced and weak. In addition, he suffered from severe arthritis. He also was having trouble breathing. Clearly, years of alcoholism had caught up to the hard-living Stuart. He decided to leave London and return to his beloved Edinburgh. Upon his return to that city, he lived with his parents. In the summer of that same year, his condition worsened. On 13 August 1786 Stuart, considered one of the most significant Scottish historians of his time, died in Edinburgh. He was buried at Inversk Churchyard.

Biography:

William Zachs, *Without Regard to Good Manners: A Biography of Gilbert Stuart, 1743–1786* (Edinburgh: Edinburgh University Press, 1992).

References:

Julian Goodare, *State and Society in Early Modern Scotland* (Oxford: Clarendon Press, 1999);

Roger A. Mason, *Kingship and the Commonweal: Political Thought in Renaissance and Reformation Scotland* (East Lothian, Scotland: Tuckwell Press, 1998);

R. R. Palmer, *The Age of the Democratic Revolution: A Political History of Europe and America, 1760–1800,* 2 volumes (Princeton, N.J.: Princeton University Press, 1959);

Arthur H. Williamson, *Scottish National Consciousness in the Age of James VI* (Edinburgh: John Donald, 1979);

William Zachs, *The First John Murray and the Late Eighteenth-Century London Book Trade* (London: British Academy and the Museum, 1998).

Papers:

Letters from Gilbert Stuart to John Murray are held by the Bodleian Library, Oxford University.

William Stukeley
(7 November 1687 – 3 March 1765)

Walter H. Keithley
Arizona State University

BOOKS: *An Account of a Roman Temple, and Other Antiquities, near Graham's Dike in Scotland* (London, 1720);

Of the Roman Amphitheater at Dorchester (London? 1723);

Of the Spleen, Its Description and History, Uses and Diseases, Particularly the Vapors, with Their Remedy. Being a Lecture Read at the Royal College of Physicians, London, 1722 (London: Printed for the author, 1723 [1724]);

Itinerarium curiosum; or, An Account of the Antiquitys and Remarkable Curiositys in Nature or Art, Observ'd in Travels thro' Great Brittan (London: Printed for the author, 1724);

Asiæ antiquissime tabula ([London: Thomas Bowles & John Bowles, 1726]);

A Letter to Sir Hans Sloan, Bart. President of the College of Physicians, London, and of the Royal Society; about the Cure of the Gout, by Oils Externally Apply'd (London: Printed by J. Roberts, 1733);

Of the Gout; In Two Parts. First a Letter to Sir Hans Sloan, Baronet, about the Cure of the Gout, by Oils Externally Apply'd: Secondly, a Treatise of the Cause and Cure of the Gout (London: Printed for J. Roberts, 1734); republished as *A Treatise on the Cause and Cure of the Gout: With a Letter to Sir Hans Sloane, Bart. On the Cure of the Gout by Oils Externally Applied* (London: Printed for J. James, 1739);

An Account of a Large Silver Plate, of Antique Basso Relievo, Roman Workmanship, Found in Derbyshire, 1729. Read before the Antiquarian Society of London, 8 April, 1736 (London: Printed for G. Vander Gucht, 1736);

Geographia classica: The Geography of the Ancients So Far Describ'd as Is Contain'd in the Greek and Latin Classicks in the Maps of the Old World and Its Several Kingdoms and Provinces (Dublin: G. Grierson, 1736);

Palæographia sacra; or, Discourses on Monuments of Antiquity That Relate to Sacred History. Number I. a Comment on the Ode of Horace, Shewing the Bacchus of the Heathen to Be the Jehovah of the Jews (London: Printed for William Innys & Richard Manby, 1736);

William Stukeley (frontispiece from volume two of Itinerarium curiosum; or, An Account of the Antiquitys and Remarkable Curiositys in Nature or Art, *1724; Eighteenth-Century Collections Online, Gale Group)*

Stonehenge: A Temple Restor'd to the British Druids (London: Printed for William Innys & Richard Manby, 1740);

National Judgments on the Consequence of a National Profanation of the Sabbath. A Sermon Preached Before the Honorable House of Commons, at St. Margaret's, Westminster; on the 30th Day of January, 1741–2 (London: Printed for T. Cooper, 1742);

Abury, a Temple of the British Druids, with Some Others Described, volume 2 (London: Printed for the author, 1743)–companion volume to *Stonehenge;*

Palæographia Britannica: or, Discourses on Antiquities in Britain, 3 volumes (London: Printed for Richard Manby, 1743–1752);

The Healing of Diseases, a Character of the Messiah. Being the Anniversary Sermon Preached Before the Royal College of Physicians, London: on September 20, 1750 (London: Printed for Charles Corbet, 1750);

The Philosophy of Earthquakes, Natural and Religious; or, An Inquiry into Their Cause, and Their Purpose (London: Printed for Charles Corbet, 1750);

Observations on the Sanctuary at Westminster. . . . Read at the Society of Antiquaries, Oct. 30, 1755 (London, 1755);

An Account of Richard of Cirencester, Monk of Westminster, and of His Works: with an Ancient Map of Roman Britain; . . . Read at the Antiquarian Society, March 18, 1756 (London: Printed by Richard Hett, 1757);

The Medallic History of Marcvs Avrelivs Valrivs Caravsivs, Emperor in Britain (London: Printed for Charles Corbet, 1757–1759);

A Letter . . . to Mr. Macpherson, on His Publication of Fingal and Temora. With a Print of Cathmor's Shield (London: Printed by Richard Hett, 1763);

The Family Memoirs of the Rev. William Stukeley, M.d.: and The Antiquarian and Other Correspondence of William Stukeley, Roger & Samuel Gale, Etc. Series: Publications of the Surtees Society, 73, 76, 80 (Durham, U.K.: Andrews, 1882–1887);

Memoirs of Sir Isaac Newton's Life, 1752: Being Some Account of His Family and Chiefly of the Junior Part of His Life, edited by A. Hastings White (London: Taylor & Francis, 1936);

The Commentarys, Diary, & Common-Place Book & Selected Letters of William Stukeley (London: Doppler Press, 1980);

Stukeley's "Stonehenge": An Unpublished Manuscript, 1721–1724, edited by Aubrey Burl and Neil Mortimer (New Haven & London: Yale University Press, 2005).

Edition: *Palæographia Britannica; or, A Discourse on Antiquities in Britain. In Which Is Given a Particular Account of Lady Roisia (Foundress of Royston) and Her Family: With a Description of Her Cave There, Discovered in 1742* (Cambridge: Printed by F. Hodson/I. Deighton, 1795)–definitive eighteenth-century edition.

After he was restored to the throne of England in 1660, Charles II made broad steps toward making sci-

ence a public institution by granting the Royal Society of London charters in 1661 and 1662. The Royal Society was the first public scientific society in England, and it aroused a great deal of curiosity from the public. Though the members of the Royal Society saw such activities as closely examining insects, roaming around the countryside gathering leaves, and building collections of antiquities as important steps in the Baconian empirical-inductive methodology, many saw their activities as pointless and even ridiculous activities for grown men. The members of the Royal Society were often ridiculed in public and were derisively referred to as the "virtuosi," a term intended to ridicule their seemingly unfocused and directionless activities. As much as this criticism might have stung, however, the agenda of the virtuosi did not change. Through the rest of the seventeenth and throughout the eighteenth century, the Royal Society not only survived but also helped to revolutionize conceptions of history, time, and space, as well as all of the disciplines that are now referred to as "hard sciences."

If nothing else, William Stukeley was a prototypical virtuoso. Like many of his brethren, Stukeley was not content to focus on any particular area of natural philosophy (a term that in the seventeenth and eighteenth centuries broadly referred to all natural sciences). He was a medical doctor and was interested in botany, physiology, astronomy, and chemistry. Also, like many of his fellow virtuosi, Stukeley had a range of interests that were considered supplemental to (if not part of) the study of natural philosophy, such as cartography, antiquarian studies, and history. The relatively recent emphasis that has been placed on strict disciplinarity of the sciences has sometimes made it hard to understand what these latter areas of inquiry had to contribute to the study of the more "scientific" aspects of natural philosophy. In the seventeenth and eighteenth centuries, however, all of Stukeley's interests ran together into a single body of knowledge. Thus, to understand the life and work of William Stukeley, virtuoso, is, in many ways, to understand the early history of modern science.

Stukeley was born on 7 November 1687 in Holbeach, Lincolnshire. He was the eldest of the five children born to attorney John Stukeley and his wife, Frances Bullen. From the age of five, Stukeley was educated by Edward Kelsall at the Free School, Holbeach. In 1700 he left school and was apprenticed as a clerk in his father's local law firm, occasionally journeying with his father to the law courts in London. Despite these early experiences, Stukeley showed no real interest in the law. He was admitted to Corpus Christi College, Cambridge, in 1703. There, Stukeley first studied medicine, the vocation that sustained him for nearly thirty years. Because of financial difficulties incurred after the deaths of his father and uncle, he was forced to leave Cambridge in 1708, but only after receiving a bachelor of medicine degree. He moved to London and subsequently studied anatomy at Chancery Lane and medicine with Richard Mead at St. Thomas's Hospital in Southwark. In 1710 he moved to Boston, Lincolnshire, where he had a practice, but he returned to London in 1717. Stukeley took his M.D. degree from Cambridge in 1719 and was named a fellow of the Royal College of Physicians on 30 September 1720. In 1726 he left his house on Ormond Street in London for a rural setting in Grantham, Lincolnshire, where he practiced until 1729. There he met his first wife, Frances Williamson, whom he married in 1728. They had three daughters before Frances died in 1737.

An accomplished and competent physician, Stukeley gave the Goulstonian Lecture to the College of Physicians in 1722. Additionally, he published several pieces on the topic of medicine, including *Of the Spleen, Its Description and History, Uses and Diseases* (1723); *Of the Gout* (1734), probably occasioned by Stukeley's own struggles; and *The Healing of Diseases, a Character of the Messiah* (1750). Like many other virtuosi, however, Stukeley was interested in more than medicine. As early as 1720 he began a serious study of theology and was initiated into Freemasonry, believing it to be the remains of the mysteries of the ancients; in December 1721 he was invested as a grand master. After his move to Grantham, however, Stukeley became even more drawn to the study of religious history. With the encouragement of his friend William Wake, Archbishop of Canterbury, Stukeley was ordained in the Church of England in 1729 and took a position at All Saints in Stamford. There he worked until November 1747, when John Montagu offered him the living of St. George the Martyr in Queen Square, Bloomsbury, where he served until his death in 1765.

In addition to his two primary vocations, Stukeley throughout his life showed tremendous skill in natural philosophy. Though he had been interested in nature since his early years at the Free School, Stukeley first had an opportunity to explore natural philosophy during his studies at Cambridge. There he displayed an interest in botany and astronomy and with Stephen Hales built an early form of an orrery. After the deaths of his father and uncle, Stukeley nurtured these interests further while living in Ormond Street. There he counted as friends some of the best-known natural philosophers of his day, including astronomers Edmund Halley, William Whiston, and Mead, and antiquarians Martin Folkes and Hans Sloane, with whom Stukeley dissected an elephant. (The results of this dissection were published as an appendix to *Of the Spleen.*) Stukeley

became a fellow of the Royal Society of London in 1718 and was subsequently elected to its council, standing as a candidate for Halley's successor as secretary in 1721. Early in his fellowship, Stukeley presented several papers to the Society. On one of these occasions, Stukeley argued that the practice of natural philosophy as a whole was effective in defending religious orthodoxy. Just as had Robert Woodward before him, Stukeley argued that increasing knowledge of the origin and placement of fossils could provide evidence of the biblical deluge. Unlike Woodward, Stukeley did not publish his work on fossils and the Flood. The nature of his presentation, however, demonstrates the variety of his interests and effectively illustrates his belief in their interconnection.

During this early part of Stuckley's career, one of his most significant influences was certainly Sir Isaac Newton. Newton, the president of the Royal Society, was author of one of the best-known and most influential books of his time, *The Principia* (1687), which described his theory of gravitation. Stukeley privately discussed astronomy, physiology, and history with Newton on several occasions, and in one such conversation with Stukeley, Newton explained for the first time the story of how he had come to his theory of gravity. Newton's version did not mention an apple striking him in the head; it simply described a realization occasioned by Newton's curiosity as to why an apple that fell from a tree did not fall from side to side, but instead toward the center of the earth. Stukeley endorsed Newton's belief that the ancients were the first to embrace the concept of a heliocentric universe and that they had also understood the inverse-square rule of gravity. Part of the benefit for Stukeley of moving to Grantham, along with his love of the countryside and some relief for his gout, was that he was able to acquire important biographical materials on the early life of Newton, who had grown up in the town. Stukeley's material was published posthumously as *Memoirs of Sir Isaac Newton's Life* (1936).

Stukeley spent much of his time in Stamford investigating its topographical features. He was frustrated by the loneliness of the place, and in the summer of 1736 he assembled a group of intellectuals and formed the Brazen Nose Society. At a basic level, the meetings mimicked those of the Royal Society, including demonstrations of "philosophical experiments" by Whiston with air pumps, a microscope, and a magic lantern. After Stukeley moved back to Bloomsbury in London, he spent the final years of his life regularly attending meetings of the Royal Society. He attempted to explain, in terms of electricity, the earthquake that struck London in 1750. He presented several papers on the topic to the Royal Society, and these were reprinted

STONEHENGE

A

TEMPLE

RESTOR'D

TO THE

British DRUIDS.

By *WILLIAM STUKELEY*, M. D.

Rector of *All Saints* in STAMFORD.

———*Deus est qui non mutatur in ævo.*   MANILIUS.

LONDON:

Printed for W. INNYS and R. MANBY, at the West End
of St. Paul's.

MDCCXL.

Title page for Stukeley's 1740 publication (Eighteenth-Century Collections Online, Gale Group)

in the *Philosophical Transactions* (volume 46) and were presented to his parishioners in a sermon at St. George's. Stukeley gave some credit for his argument to the work on electricity done by Benjamin Franklin, with whom he had been a correspondent.

Despite his fascination with natural philosophy, however, Stukeley is now best remembered as an antiquarian. He was a founder of the reestablished Society of Antiquities in 1718 and was appointed its first secretary. Through his participation in this society he met two lifelong friends, Roger and Samuel Gale, with whom he traveled to Avenbury in Wiltshire in 1719. He traveled the entire length of Hadrian's Wall with Roger Gale in 1725, and he brought the destruction of the wall by military road builders to the attention of the society in 1757. At the same time that he was a living on Ormond Street and keeping regular company with Hal-

ley, Newton, and Mead, Stukeley was a regular at the meetings of the society, presenting both papers and antiquities that he had gathered during his travels around England. These collections provided the material for his book *Itinerarium curiosum* (1724). Stukeley subsequently formed the Society of Roman Knights, which placed a strict emphasis on classical studies. The group had notable members, including Henry Herbert, ninth Earl of Pembroke; Daniel Finch, eighth Earl of Winchilsea; Samuel Buck; Fowlkes; and Roger and Samuel Gale. This society is more notable still because it was the first English antiquarian society to include women among its members.

After the death of Frances, while he was still living in Grantham, Stukeley finished two of his most significant publications: *Stonehenge: A Temple Restor'd to the British Druids* (1740) and *Abury, a Temple of the British Druids* (1743), both detailed descriptions based on notes, sketches, and measurements that he compiled from 1718 to 1724. He had previously also proposed the publication of four volumes on the Celts but was rebuffed; the likely cause was the expense of printing the heavily illustrated *Itinerarium curiosum*. Stukeley's marriage to Elizabeth Gale (sister of Roger and Samuel) in 1739, however, brought him a large enough portion to see future projects through the press without worrying about earnings.

Stonehenge and *Abury, a Temple of the British Druids* are significant for their emphasis on fieldwork. Stukeley was the first to discover the astronomical arrangement of Stonehenge, and he was the first to discover and name the neighboring earthwork avenue and the cursus. At Avenbury he made important observations and surveys while the stone circles were being harvested for building materials, and he identified the site as a serpent-temple, an erroneous conception informed by his recollection of Egyptian hieroglyphs depicting a serpent passing through a circle. Though Stukeley was proven to be incorrect on this count, he certainly had a better understanding than many of his contemporaries, who had suggested Roman, Danish, and Anglo-Saxon origins for the temples. For the rest of his time in Grantham, Stukeley continued to publish heavily on British antiquities, and the first volume of his massive *Palæographia Britannica* (1743–1752) contained his description of Royston Cave, which was discovered in 1742.

Although he had moved to the countryside voluntarily, Stukeley missed the intellectual stimulation that he received at the Royal Society and the Society of Antiquities. His association with the Brazen Nose Society helped to alleviate this problem somewhat. Eventually, however, membership in the society waned, and, despite an attempt at revival in 1745, it finally disappeared completely. In 1738 he started a clergymen's book club but was soon disappointed that his fellow members were more interested in wine and tobacco than in the genuine discussion of antiquities. During his 1741 winter visit to London, Stukeley participated in the founding of the Egyptian Society by John Montagu, the Earl of Sandwich. During the meetings of this short-lived club, Montagu became a close friend and patron, who eventually arranged for Stukeley to move back to London to take up the living of St. George the Martyr. Back in London, Stukeley was able again to become a regular participant in the Royal Society and the Society of Antiquaries.

In 1747 Stukeley unwittingly became part of an antiquity fraud. He was contacted by one Charles Bertram, who informed him of the discovery of a copy of a previously unknown Roman map of Britain, *De Situ Britanniae,* made by a fourteenth-century monk of Westminster. Stukeley took Bertram at his word and attempted to purchase the map for the British Museum. Despite his failure to acquire the map, Stukeley used his correspondence with Bertram as a basis for *An Account of Richard of Cirencester, Monk of Westminster, and of His Works* (1757). Bertram also capitalized on the correspondence, publishing his own book, *Britannicarum gentium historiae antiquae scriptores tres* (1757). Bertram's forgery was a success; *De Situ Britanniae* was considered an authentic source (it was even used by Gibbon) and was not discounted until 1869. Stukeley's involvement with *De Situ Britanniae* only damaged his reputation as an historian posthumously. Moreover, it was not the only controversial issue in which he was involved. In 1763 Stukeley stepped to the defense of James Macpherson, who claimed to have published three authentic translations of the work of an ancient Gaelic poet named Ossian. Though public opinion was split, Samuel Johnson voiced his skepticism, and Stukeley's reputation was permanently tarnished. Stukeley suffered a stroke of the palsy at his rectory on 27 February 1765 and, after lying

in a coma for four days, died on 3 March 1765. He was buried in East Ham Churchyard, Essex.

In the last years of his life, William Stukeley was known to be increasingly eccentric. He talked openly about his patriarchal druids, and he took the nickname of "Arch Druid" for himself. Despite these eccentricities and his involvement with the *De Situ Britanniae* and Ossian controversies, however, Stukeley made some lasting contributions to his several fields of interest. His work with Stonehenge and Avenbury added significant insight into their respective histories, and his work on stone circles was instrumental in settling their true antiquity. He was a respected physician, and though he never achieved the status of some of his contemporaries in the Royal Society, Stukeley made important contributions with his elephant dissection and his use of natural philosophy to dispute religious heterodoxy. Most important, however, Stukeley is a significant historical figure because reviewing his career as a virtuoso lends important insight into the development of early modern scientific process as well as the generation of protoscientific knowledge before rigid definition of scientific disciplines.

References:
D. B. Haycock, *William Stukeley: Science, Religion and Archeology, in Eighteenth Century England* (Woodbridge, U.K.: Boydell, 2002);
Stuart Piggot, *William Stukeley: An Eighteenth Century Antiquary* (London: Thames & Hudson, 1985).

Papers:
William Stukeley's personal papers, drawings, journals, and correspondence are held by the British Library, the Bodleian Library, the Cardiff Central Library, and the Devizes Museum. Extant papers relating to archeology are held at the British Library, the Bodleian Library, the National Library of Wales, the Society of Antiquaries, the Wellcome Library, and the Wiltshire Archaeological and Natural History Society, who also hold his notes on medical subjects.

Nicholas Tindal

(25 November 1688 – 27 June 1774)

Clare Callaghan
University of Maryland

BOOKS: *The History of England, as Well Ecclesiastical as Civil,* volumes 16–28 (London: Printed for James and John Knapton, 1727–1747)—volumes 16–28 by Tindal; republished as *The History of England . . . from the Revolution to the Accession of King George II,* 4 volumes in 5 (London: John & Paul Knapton, 1744–1747)—volumes 1 and 2 are by Paul de Rapin-Thoyras; volumes 3 and 4 are by Tindal; *The History of England,* 12 volumes, fourth edition, corrected (London: Printed by Mr. Knapton for T. Osborne and others, 1757);

The History of Essex, 2 volumes (London: Printed by H. Woodfall, 1732);

A Copy of the Will of Matthew Tindal, with an Account of What Pass'd Concerning the Same between Mrs. Lucy Price, Eustace Budgell, Esq., and Mr. Nicolas Tindal (London: T. Cooper, 1733).

TRANSLATIONS: Augustin Calmet, *Antiquities Sacred and Profane; or, A Collection of Curious and Critical Dissertations on the Old and New Testament,* translated as "by a clergyman of the Church of England" (London: Printed for J. Roberts, 1724);

Isaac de Beausobre and Jacques L'Enfant, *A New Version of the Gospel According to Saint Matthew: With a Liberal Commentary on All the Difficult Passages; To Which Is Prefixed an Introduction of the Reading of the Holy Scriptures, Intended Chiefly for Young Students in Divinity,* translated by Tindal and Philip Morant (London, 1726)—earliest extant copy (Cambridge: Printed by J. Archdeacon for J. Nicholson, 1779);

Paul de Rapin-Thoyras, *The History of England, as Well Ecclesiastical as Civil,* 15 volumes (London: Printed for James and John Knapton, 1725–1731);

Demetrius Cantemir, Prince of Moldovia, *The History of the Growth and Decay of the Othman Empire* (London: James, John & Paul Knapton, 1735).

OTHER: Joseph Spence, *A Guide to Classical Learning; or, Polymetis Abridged. . . . Being a Work Absolutely Necessary, Not Only for the Right Understanding of the Clas-*

Nicholas Tindal (portrait by George Knapton, circa 1726–1744; from <http://www.nmm.ac.uk>)

sics, but Also for Forming in Young Minds a True Taste for the Beauties of Poetry, Sculpture, and Painting, edited by Tindal (London: J. Dodsley, 1764); second edition, corrected and enlarged (London: R. Horsfield & J. Dodsley, 1765).

Nicholas Tindal is significant in the field of history not only as an historian in his own right but also as a translator of major contemporary historical works. His works, both translations and original, are significant as well because of what they demonstrate about how historical works were presented to the public during his times. While today people who primarily translate are not typically considered scholars in the fields in which they are translating, Tindal was considered an historian by his contemporaries, as evidenced by the membership lists of the Society of Antiquaries in William Bowyer's memoirs: inscribed therein is a certain "Mr. Tindal the Historian."

Tindal was born at Plymouth on 25 November 1688, the only son of cleric John Tindal of Cornwood, Devonshire, and Elizabeth Prideaux Tindal. His father's brother was Matthew Tindal, a noted figure in the religious controversies of the prior generation. Nicholas enrolled at Exeter College, Oxford, when he was nineteen. He studied to be a clergyman and was awarded his bachelor's degree in 1710 and his master's degree in 1713. Three years later, in 1716, he became the rector of Hatford, Berkshire. While there, he married his first wife, Anne, daughter of a local gentleman. They had three sons; one became a rector in Essex; one became a captain in the Royal Navy; and the last became a captain in the dragoons.

In 1721 Tindal was given the parish of Great Waltham, Essex. This parish was one of the largest in Essex, and under the patronage of Trinity College, Oxford, of which Tindal was a fellow, but it was not a particularly remunerative post. The *Essex Review* reports that the vicar's salary was less than £50 per year, rising to £80 only in 1751, more than a decade after Tindal had left. Writing and tutoring were the two primary opportunities for an eighteenth-century cleric to earn additional income without disrupting his parish obligations. Tindal chose writing, and in Essex Tindal began preparing the histories and translations for which he is well known.

In 1724 J. Warwick in London, S. Wilmot in Oxford, and C. Crownfield in Cambridge published Tindal's serialized, annotated translation of *Antiquities Sacred and Profane; or, A Collection of Curious and Critical Dissertations on the Old and New Testament*. The work, initially published in French by Augustin Calmet, became successful in Britain. According to R. M. Wiles, four of its serial installments had to be reprinted, demonstrating a demand unanticipated by the printers. This work by Tindal set out the hallmarks of his later translations—supplemented with his notes, translated both accurately and elegantly, and serialized. One marked difference, though, is attribution. The publicity for this translation referred to Tindal simply as a Church of England clergyman.

Just as the serialization of his translation of Calmet was completed, Tindal published a translation of Isaac de Beausobre and Jacques L'Enfant's *A New Version of the Gospel According to Saint Matthew* in 1726 (extant copy, 1779), and, almost simultaneously, his best-known

work began to appear. His translation and extension of Paul de Rapin-Thoyras's *History of England* became the standard British history for about fifty years. This work was first published in French at The Hague in 1723, and Tindal's translation, supplemented by his annotations, appeared in London starting in 1725, the year of Rapin-Thoyras's death.

James and John Knapton published the first edition of Tindal's translation as a monthly serial between 1725 and 1732. As the last volume was completed, a rival printer, James Mechell, began issuing a cheaper edition in weekly installments by a different translator, John Kelly. The Knaptons immediately prepared a second edition of Tindal's translation, also to be published weekly. The Knaptons won this publishing war not only by heavily advertising their edition as being cheaper and better but also because Tindal's translation was genuinely regarded as superior to Kelly's. Tindal's own continuation volumes, updating the work from 1688 through the accession of George I and then of George II, were released by the Knaptons starting in 1736.

This sustained success lay both in Rapin-Thoyras's content and in Tindal's translation. Rapin-Thoyras was a Huguenot who had left France after the revocation of the Edict of Nantes, which had provided religious toleration to the French Protestants. Rapin-Thoyras went to England briefly, then to Holland, from which he accompanied William of Orange on his entrance into England in 1688. After leaving William's service, Rapin-Thoyras first returned to The Hague, where he became a tutor to a nobleman's son. After that engagement ended, he settled in Wesel in the German principality of Cleves, where he wrote his history, among other works. He was particularly captivated by Thomas Rymer's compendium of all the treaties England had engaged in since 1066, and Rymer's work shaped Rapin-Thoyras's own. Rapin-Thoyras's *History of England* became hugely successful in England because his sense that English liberty was rooted in centuries of political development was mirrored in the ideology of the Whig Party, who came to power after Queen Anne's death in 1713 and dominated British politics under both George I and George II. Rapin-Thoyras's approach to British history and Tindal's translation of it captured the contemporary British mood.

Tindal began his translation of Rapin-Thoyras in 1725, but dedications of individual volumes demonstrate that he did continue his work elsewhere. First, in 1726 he completed volume two while serving as the chaplain of the *Torbay*, stationed in the Bay of Revel in the Gulf of Finland under the captaincy of Sir Charles Wager. Second, he completed volume four and rejoined the *Torbay* in 1727 while it was stationed in Gibraltar

Bay. Finally, he dedicated volume six, published in 1728, to the men of a Lisbon factory, whom he had met while officiating for five months for their regular chaplain, Joseph Sims, who was absent on a trip to England.

Although there are no other records of Tindal's travels, he did retain his connections with the navy. Later, in 1739, Wager appointed Tindal as chaplain to the royal naval hospital in Greenwich; he held this position for the rest of his life. Tindal also served as a chaplain to a marine regiment in 1740, and Wager later served both as an admiral and as a member of Parliament.

Rapin-Thoyras's original work concluded with the Glorious Revolution of 1688, which he had personally witnessed in the company of William of Orange. Tindal provided two continuation volumes, one from the revolution through the accession of George I, and the second up through the accession of George II. Ultimately, after Tindal's death, Tobias Smollett prepared a third continuation of Rapin-Thoyras's work, updating it through the end of George II's reign. Before that time, though, the *History of England* had fallen out of favor both stylistically and politically, so Smollett's version was only moderately successful.

All of the editions translated by Tindal were immensely successful. John and James Knapton, sometimes with Paul Knapton, published all the Tindal translations. According to the reminiscences of Bowyer, a contemporary printer, the first edition succeeded so far beyond their expectations that they gave Tindal a bonus of £200. Such a reward was unusual for a publisher, who would typically pay an author or translator only a fixed, small fee for his work. The second edition also yielded a reward for Tindal. Bowyer notes that Tindal received a gold medallion from Frederick, Prince of Wales, to whom the edition was dedicated.

Tindal also attempted his own original historical work. In 1725, just as the Knaptons published his first translation, he proposed a three-volume history of the county of Essex, a comprehensive examination of all of its manors from the time of the Norman Conquest in 1066 up to Tindal's time. Only the first two volumes appeared, in 1731 and 1732. These were based largely on materials already compiled by William Holman, whose work had been given to Tindal upon Holman's death in 1730. The two published volumes covered only about five of the manors in Essex, showing that the three volumes initially planned would be insufficient for the project. Philip Morant, a friend of and assistant to Tindal, later recalled in Bowyer's memoirs that the work would have been "too bulky and tedious." That realization, and the lack of demand for the first two volumes, dissuaded the publishers from commissioning the third volume.

Title page of Tindal's translation of Paul de Rapin-Thoyras's history of England, which Tindal extended (Eighteenth-Century Collections Online, Gale Group)

Tindal did not restrict himself to his historical or church work. He was appointed head of the Royal School at Chelmsford in 1731. The following year, he was made a chaplain in ordinary at Chatham. In 1733 his uncle Matthew Tindal, the controversial religious thinker, died. Nicholas had expected to inherit his uncle's estate, but Sir Eustace Budgell presented a will that left everything to him instead. Nicholas Tindal disputed Budgell's claim, but even though most people thought the second will was forged, Tindal was not successful in his suit. This dispute led Tindal to publish *A Copy of the Will of Matthew Tindal, with an Account of What Pass'd Concerning the Same between Mrs. Lucy Price, Eustace Budgell, Esq., and Mr. Nicolas Tindal* (1733), a pamphlet to bring attention to the situation.

In 1738 Tindal was appointed chaplain to the Greenwich Hospital, which was known for its service to those who had served in the Royal Navy. His wife Anne died during this period, and in 1753 Tindal married Elizabeth Gugelman, whose father was on the hospital staff. In 1740 he was given the livings of Calbourne, on the Isle of Wight, and Alverstoke, in Hampshire, the latter by itself a living, according to Wiles, of more than £400 per year. In addition, Tindal remained in-residence at the hospital.

Historiographic trends in the second half of the century diminished the luster of Tindal's translation. For example, David Hume and Edward Gibbon both prepared their respective histories as deliberately opposed to the Rapin-Thoyras approach. Also, in 1757 an anonymous critique of Tindal's translation style was published. Tindal remained involved with publishing, although he did change his focus.

In 1764 Tindal edited Joseph Spence's *A Guide to Classical Learning; or, Polymetis Abridged*. This was a popular handbook for the public-school system. This work is unique because it draws together both his extensive educational background and his experiences as the master of the Royal School at Chelmsford. Its aim was not to educate the mind with facts but to shape the aesthetic sensibilities of students by providing them with classical references.

Tindal died at Greenwich Hospital on 27 June 1774 and was buried in the grounds of the hospital. His portrait was painted by George Knapton some time after his translation of Rapin-Thoyras became well known. This portrait is now in the National Maritime Museum in London because of his long-standing relationship with the British navy, both under Wager and as chaplain at Greenwich Hospital.

Because his greatest contributions were as a translator of a significant work, Nicholas Tindal's accomplishments in the field of history defined historical learning for at least two generations in the eighteenth century. Rapin-Thoyras's overarching view of British history, accessible through Tindal's translations, shaped the contemporary British sense of its national heritage. Tindal's translation style was well regarded for both its adherence to the original and its own elegance. His annotations to Rapin-Thoyras were considered so authoritative that they were translated into French and included in French-language editions of the history. Ultimately, Tindal demonstrated to his audience that an effective translator of history is, and must also be, an effective historian.

References:

Alumni Oxenienses: The Members of the University of Oxford, 1500–1714, volume 4 (London: Parker, 1891–1892);

"Great Waltham," *Essex Review,* 2 (1893): 168;

Philip Hicks, *Neoclassical Culture and English History* (London: Macmillan, 1996);

John Nichols, *Literary Anecdotes of the Eighteenth Century; Comprising Biographical Memoirs of William Bowyer, Printer, F.S.A., and Many of His Learned Friends* (London: Nichols & Bentley, 1812–1816);

Hugh Trevor-Roper, "A Hugeunot Historian: Paul Rapin," in *Hugeunots in Britain and their French Background, 1550–1800,* edited by Irene Scouloudi (Hong Kong: Macmillan, 1992), pp. 3–19;

R. M. Wiles, *Serial Publication in England Before 1750* (Cambridge: Cambridge University Press, 1957);

D. R. Woolf, *Reading History of Early Modern England* (Cambridge: Cambridge University Press, 2000).

John Toland

(30 November 1670 – 11 March 1722)

Michael R. Hutcheson
Landmark College

See also the Toland entry in *DLB 252: British Philosophers, 1500–1799.*

BOOKS: *Two Essays Sent in a Letter from Oxford to a Nobleman in London,* as L. P. (London, 1695);

Christianity Not Mysterious; or, A Treatise Shewing, That There Is Nothing in the Gospel Contrary to Reason, Nor above It: and That No Christian Doctrine Can Be Properly Call'd a Mystery, anonymous (London, 1696; revised edition, London: Samuel Buckley, 1696);

An Apology for Mr. Toland, in a Letter from Himself to a Member of the House of Commons in Ireland, Written the Day Before his Book was Resolv'd to be Burnt by the Committee of Religion: To Which is Prefix'd a Narrative Containing the Occasion of the Said Letter (London, 1697);

A Defence of Mr. Toland, in a Letter to Himself (London: E. Whitlock, 1697);

The Militia Reform'd; or, An Easy Scheme of Furnishing England with a Constant Land-Force, anonymous (London: Printed by John Darby, 1698);

The Danger of Mercenary Parliaments (London, 1698);

The Life of John Milton, Containing, I. A Catalogue of above Fourscore Books . . . Attributed in the Primitive Times to Jesus Christ, His Apostles, &C. With Several Important Remarks and Observations Relating to the Canon of Scripture; II. A Compleat History of the Book Intituled Icon Basilike, Proving Dr. Gauden, and Not King Charles the First, to Be the Author of It; III. Reasons for Abolishing the Observation of the 30th of January (London: Booksellers of London and Westminster, 1699);

Amyntor; or, A Defence of Milton's Life Containing I. A General Apology for All Writings of That Kind, Ii. A Catalogue of Books Attributed in the Primitive Times to Jesus Christ, His Apostles and Other Eminent Persons . . . , Iii. A Complete History of the Book Entitul'd Icon Basilike, Proving Dr. Gauden and Not King Charles the First to Be the Author of It, with an Answer to All the Facts Alledg'd by Mr. Wagstaf to the Contrary, and to the Exceptions Made Against My Lord Anglesey's Memorandum, Dr. Walker's Book or Mrs. Gauden's Narrative, Which Last Piece Is Now the First Time Publish'd at Large (London:

John Toland (from U. G. Thorschmid, Versuch einer Vollständige Engländische Freydenker-Bibliothek, *1766; <http://www.luminade.com/toland.htm>)*

Printed by the Booksellers of London and Westminster, 1699);

Clito: A Poem on the Force of Eloquence (London: Printed by the Booksellers of London and Westminster, 1700);

Anglia Libera; or, The Limitation and Succession of the Crown of England Explain'd and Asserted; as Grounded on His Majesty's Speech; the Procedings in Parliament; the Desires of the People (London: Bernard Lintott, 1701);

Anglia Libera; or, The Limitation and Succession of the Crown of England Explained and Asserted, Etc. (London: Bernard Lintott, 1701);

The Art of Governing by Partys: Particularly in Religion, in Politics, in Parlament, on the Bench, and in the Ministry . . . , anonymous (London: Bernard Lintott, 1701);

Propositions for Uniting the Two East-India Companies in a Letter to a Man of Quality, Who Desir'd the Opinion of a Gentleman Not Concern'd in Either Company . . . (London: Printed for Bernard Lintott, 1701);

I. Reasons for Addressing His Majesty to Invite into England Their Highnesses, the Electress Dowager and the Electoral Prince of Hanover: and Likewise, II. Reasons for Attainting and Abjuring the Pretended Prince of Wales, and All Other Pretending Any Claim, Right, or Title from the Late King James and Queen Mary: with Arguments for Making a Vigorous War against France (London: Printed by John Nutt, 1702);

Vindicius Liberius; or, M. Toland's Defence of Himself Against the Late Lower House of Convocation and Others . . . (London: Bernard Lintott, 1702);

Letters to Serena Containing, I. The Origin and Force of Prejudices. II. The History of the Soul's Immortality among the Heathens. III. The Origin of Idolatry, and Reasons of Heathenism, as Also, IV. A Letter to a Gentleman in Holland, Showing Spinosa's System of Philosophy to Be Without Any Principle or Foundation. V. Motion Essential to Matter; an Answer to Some Remarks by a Nobel Friend on the Confutation of Spinosa. To All Which Is Prefixed, VI. A Preface; Being a Letter to a Gentleman in London (London: Bernard Lintot [i.e. Lintott], 1704);

An Account of the Courts of Prussia and Hanover; Sent to a Minister of State in Holland by Mr. Toland (London: Printed by John Darby, 1705);

The Memorial of the State of England in Vindication of the Queen, the Church, and the Administration, anonymous (London: Booksellers of London and Westminster, 1705);

Socinianism Truly Stated, anonymous (London, 1705);

Some Plain Observations Recommended to the Consideration of Every Honest English-Man (London, 1705);

Adeisidaemon, sive Titus Livius a superstitione vindicatus (The Hague: Thomas Johnson, 1709);

The Jacobitism, Perjury, and Popery of High-Church Priests, by Toland, Daniel Defoe, and Matthew Tindal (London: Printed for J. Baker, 1710);

Mr. Toland's Reflections on Dr. Sacheverell's Sermon Preach'd at St. Paul's, Nov. 5, 1709 in a Letter from an English-man to an Hollander (London: Printed by F. Baker, 1710);

The Description of Epsom, with the humors and politicks of the place: in a letter to Eudoxa . . . There is added a Translation of Four Letters out of Pliny, as Britto-Batavus (London: A. Baldwin, 1711);

High-Church Display'd: Being a Compleat History of the Affair of Dr. Sacheverel, in its Origin, Progress, and Consequences: In Several Letters to an English Gentleman at the Court of Hanover (London, 1711);

Her Majesty's Reasons for Creating the Electoral Prince of Hanover a Peer of this Realm: or, The Preamble to his Patent as Duke of Cambridge (London: A. Baldwin, 1712);

An Appeal to Honest People against Wicked Priests; or, The Very Heathen Laity's Declarations for Civil Obedience and Liberty of Conscience, Contrary to the Rebellious and Persecuting Principles of Some of the Old Christian Clergy . . . , as Hierophilus (London: Printed for Mrs. Smith, 1713);

Dunkirk or Dover; or, The Queen's Honour, the Nation's Safety, the Liberties of Europe, and the Peace of the World, All at Stake till That Fort and Port Be Totally Demolish'd by the French (London: Printed for A. Baldwin, 1713);

Reasons for Naturalizing the Jews in Great Britain and Ireland on the Same Foot with All Other Nations, anonymous (London: James Roberts, 1714);

The Grand Mystery Laid Open: Namely, by Dividing of the Protestants to Weaken the Hanover Succession, and by Defeating the Succession to Extirpate the Protestant Religion . . . (London: Printed for James Roberts, 1714);

The Art of Restoring; or, The Piety and Probity of General Monk in Bringing about the Last Restoration . . . (London: Printed for James Roberts, 1714);

The Reasons and Necessity of the Duke of Cambridge's Coming to and Residing in Great Britain . . . (London: Printed for J. Baker, 1714);

The State Anatomy of Great Britain, as Patricola (London: Printed for John Phillips, 1717);

The Second Part of the State Anatomy, as Patricola (London: Printed for John Phillips, 1717);

Nazarenus; or, Jewish, Gentile and Mahometan Christianity (London: Sold by J. Brown, James Roberts & J. Brotherton, 1718);

The Destiny of Rome; or, The Probability of the Speedy Destruction of the Pope, as X. Z. (London: James Roberts & A. Dodd, 1718);

Tetradymus Containing I. Hodegus; or, The Pillar of Cloud and Fire, That Guided the Israelites in the Wilderness, Not Miraculous . . . (London: J. Brotherton & W. Meadows, 1720);

Pantheisticon, written in Latin, as Janus Junius Eoganesius (Cosmopoli [i.e. London], 1720); translated anonymously as *Pantheisticon; or, The Form of Celebrating the Socratic-Society* (London: Printed for Sam Paterson, 1751);

Anthony Ashley Cooper Shaftesbury, Earl of; Robert Molesworth, Viscount Molesworth; John Cropley, Sir; Letters from the Right Honourable the Late Earl of Shaftesbury, to Robert Molesworth, Esq; Now the Lord Viscount of That Name. With Two Letters Written by the Late Sir John Cropley. to Which Is Prefix'd a Large Introduction by the Editor (London: Printed by W. Wilkins, 1721);

A Collection of Several Pieces of Mr. John Toland, Now First Publish'd from His Original Manuscripts, 2 volumes (London: John Peele, 1726); republished as *The Miscellaneous Works of Mr. John Toland,* 2 volumes (London: J. Whiston, 1747);

The Sentiments of the Old Whigs upon a Place-Bill in Two Parts: Containing, First, Considerations on the Nature of P----ts, and Elections, and Secondly, the Danger of Mercenary P----ts: to Which Is Prefix'd an Introduction (London: Printed by and for T. Gardner, 1740);

A Critical History of the Celtic Religion and Learning, Containing an Account of the Druids (London: Lackington, Hughes & Harding, [1740?]).

Editions and Collections: *Letters to Serena, 1704,* British Philosophers and Theologians of the 17th and 18th Centuries, no. 58 (New York & London: Garland, 1976);

Pantheisticon, British Philosophers and Theologians of the 17th and 18th Centuries, no. 59 (New York: Garland, 1976);

John Toland's Christianity Not Mysterious: Text, Associated Works and Critical Essays, edited by Philip McGuinness, Alan Harrison, and Richard Kearney (Dublin: Lilliput, 1997);

Nazarenus, edited by Justin Champion, British Deism and Free Thought, no. 1 (Oxford: Voltaire Foundation, 1999).

TRANSLATIONS: Bernardo Davanzati, *A Discourse upon Coins* (London: Printed by J. D. for Awnsham & John Churchill, 1696);

Pierre de Boissat, *The Fables of Aesop: With the Moral Reflections of Monsieur Baudoin,* translated, with a preface, by Toland (London: Printed for Thomas Leigh & Daniel Midwinter, 1704);

The Ordinances, Statutes, and Privileges of the Royal Academy, Erected by his Majesty the King of Prussia, translated by Toland (London: John Darby, 1705);

Marcus Tullius Cicero, *Cicero illustratus, dissertatio philologico-critica: sive consilium de toto edendo Cicerone, alia plane methodo quam hactenus unquam factum* (London: J. Humfreys, 1712);

Quintus Tullius Cicero, *The Art of Canvassing at Elections* (London: Printed for J. Roberts, 1714).

OTHER: Algernon Sidney, *Discourses concerning Government,* edited by Toland (London, 1698);

John Milton, *A Complete Collection of the Historical, Political and Miscellaneous Works of John Milton . . . ,* edited by Toland (Amsterdam, 1698);

Daniel Defoe, *A Letter to a Member of Parliament, Shewing, That a Restraint on the Press Is Inconsistent with the Protestant Religion, and Dangerous to the Liberties of the Nation,* edited by Toland (London: Printed by John Darby, 1698);

Denzil Holles, *The Memoirs of Denzil, Lord Holles, Baron of Ifield in Sussex from the year 1641, to 1648,* edited by Toland (London: Printed for Tim. Goodwin, 1699);

Memoirs of Lieutenant General Ludlow, The Third and Last Part, edited, with a preface, by Toland (London: John Darby, 1699);

James Harrington, *The Oceana of James Harrington and His Other Works; Som[e] Whereof Are Now First Publish'd from His Own Manuscripts,* edited by Toland (London: Printed by the Booksellers of London and Westminster, 1700);

Mathäus Schinner, Cardinal, *A Philippick Oration to Incite the English against the French; but Especially to Prevent the Treating of a Peace with Them Too Soon after They Are Beaten: Offer'd to the Privy-Council of England, in the Year of Christ, 1514,* edited by Toland (London: Printed for Egbert Sanger and John Chantry, 1707);

Sophia Charlotte, Queen Consort of Frederick I King of Prussia, *A Letter against Popery* (London: Printed for A. Baldwin, 1712)—prefatory letter by Toland, as J. Londat.

John Toland was one of the earliest and most radical Deists, a group of thinkers who sought to recast Christianity in light of modern scientific and rationalist thought. He coined the term *pantheist* to describe his adherence to a natural religion free of superstition. Politically, Toland aligned himself with the Radical Whigs, an affiliation that led to several polemical works promoting republicanism. Toland's historical research was often undertaken to inform and buttress his religious and political agenda, and, consequently, his reputation is more as a polemical freethinker than as an historian.

Toland was born on 30 November 1670. He stated his birthplace as Inishowen, County Donegal, Ireland, although an alternative tradition claims that he was born in France of Irish parents and was brought to Ireland as a child. Other speculation, repeated by

Jonathan Swift, is that his father was a Catholic priest. Further obscuring the circumstances of Toland's birth is the question of his name: he may initially have been given a Gaelic name, likely Seán Ó Tuathhalláin, although in his 1720 work *Pantheisticon* Toland maintained that his given name was Janus Junius. Toland was brought up as a Catholic but attracted a Protestant sponsor to pay his tuition at the Redcastle school. He converted to Protestantism by age sixteen and received patronage to study at Glasgow University in 1686. Having alienated the archbishop of Glasgow within his first year there, Toland cast his lot with the Presbyterian leadership. The need to secure patronage and the loss of it because of his outspokenness became constants in Toland's career.

Toland received his M.A. in 1690 from Edinburgh University. It is unclear whether he completed his academic work there or whether Edinburgh simply awarded the degree, a custom extended to Glasgow University students who refused to take the oath of allegiance. According to F. H. Heinemann, when Toland left Scotland for London that year, he carried with him a certificate from the magistrates declaring that he was "ane trew protestant and loyal subject."

In London, Toland became a protégé of Daniel Williams, an influential Presbyterian minister and author of *Gospel Truth Stated and Vindicated* (1692). Williams raised money in late 1692 to fund Toland's matriculation at Leiden University in the Netherlands. Leiden was a hotbed of dissenting religion; it was where René Descartes had taught; Baruch Spinoza had found relief from persecution; and John Locke had studied. Despite the congenial intellectual atmosphere, Toland remained at Leiden less than a year, resided briefly at Utrecht, and moved to Oxford at the end of 1693.

At Oxford, Toland may have written "The Fabulous Death of Atilius Regulus" (1694), debunking myths about a Roman consul and general of the First Punic War. He likely wrote *Two Essays Sent in a Letter from Oxford to a Nobleman in London* (1695), a libertine's critique of institutional Christianity. If these were Toland's first works, they were a mere prelude to his first great subject. In *Christianity Not Mysterious; or, A Treatise Shewing, That There Is Nothing in the Gospel Contrary to Reason, Nor above It: and That No Christian Doctrine Can Be Properly Call'd a Mystery* (1696) Toland joined the chorus of voices asserting that the teachings of Jesus were completely compatible with reason, an idea stated by Locke in book 4 of his *Essay concerning Human Understanding* (1690). Toland moved from Oxford to London at this time to seek Locke's favor and patronage.

The first half of Toland's *Christianity Not Mysterious* follows Locke's philosophical critique of superstition as contrary to the foundations of human understanding. In Toland's words, "what is evidently repugnant to clear and distinct Ideas, or to our common Notions, is contrary to Reason." In the second half of the book, however, Toland adds an historical dimension to the argument by reading the Bible as an unfolding revelation. Thus, what may have been described as "Mystery" in the Old Testament was later unveiled by the teachings of Jesus: "some Doctrines of the Gospel are more particularly call'd *Mysteries,* because they were hid from God's peculiar People under the *Mosaick* Oeconomy. . . [and] were not clearly and fully revealed till the *New Testament* Times." Toland also assigns historical responsibility for the infusion of superstition into Christianity, faulting early proselytizers and "Church Fathers" such as Paul, Justin Martyr, and Origen of Alexandria for appealing to Gentiles' taste for mystery and ritual. The institutionalizing of Christianity under the Church of Rome established these Christian apologists as "Authorities" and therefore beyond critical scrutiny. The result, Toland concludes, was the enshrinement of ritual ceremonies that "take off the Mind from the Substance of *Religion*" and obscure Jesus' message.

Toland, who moved to Dublin in early 1697, did not foresee how much attention *Christianity Not Mysterious* would bring. Locke, already offended by Toland's using his name to gain entry into intellectual circles in Dublin, criticized the book as subversive of Christianity. Swift repeatedly satirized Toland, most pointedly in *An Argument against Abolishing Christianity* (1711), in which Toland is called "the great oracle of the Anti-Christians." More dangerous to Toland was the ordering, by the Irish House of Commons, that the book be publicly burned by the hangman in 1697, an action prompting Toland's hasty return to England. Toland defended himself in two pamphlets, *An Apology for Mr. Toland* and *A Defence of Mr. Toland* (both 1697).

The uproar over *Christianity Not Mysterious* did not deter Toland from stoking religious controversy. In *The Life of John Milton* (1699), Toland focused more on Milton's defense of freedom and religious heterodoxy than his achievements as a poet. Consequently, Toland treats Milton's plea for freedom of the press in *Areopagitica* (1644) far more extensively than he does *Paradise Lost* (1667). In discussing the religious controversies of Milton's time, Toland expressed doubts about the authorship of some Christian texts. This statement unleashed another storm of attacks, with Toland accused of denying the validity of the Gospels. Toland responded in *Amyntor; or, A Defence of Milton's Life* (1699) with an expanded list of works "falsely ascribed to Jesus, his Apostles, and other eminent persons" by the Church Fathers. Toland again was embroiled in religious controversy, increased even further by the publication of

Ch... anity not Mysterious:

OR, A

TREATISE

Shewing,

That there is nothing in the

GOSPEL

Contrary to

REASON,

Nor ABOVE it:

And that no Christian Doctrine
can be properly call'd

A MYSTERY.

John Toland

*We need not desire a better Evidence that any Man is in the
wrong, than to hear him declare against Reason, and thereby
acknowledg that Reason is against him.* ABp Tillotson.

London, Printed in the Year 1696.

Toland's philosophical work expressing his attitude toward historical
events (Rare Book and Special Collections Division, Library of
Congress <http://www.loc.gov/exhibits/religion/obj-list.html>)

*Vindicius Liberius; or, M. Toland's Defence of Himself Against
the Late Lower House of Convocation and Others* (1702), in
which he claimed to recant his controversial religious
ideas but largely restated them.

Partly to avoid further accusations of atheism,
partly because of a sincere Ciceronian belief that politics offered the best hope for moral improvement, and
partly because of the continuing need to secure patronage, Toland began at the turn of the century to concentrate on writing political works and currying political
favor. While some commentators see this period as a
new stage in Toland's career, he had in fact written earlier political works. After leaving Ireland in 1697,
Toland became part of a circle of Radical Whigs—
including John Trenchard and Walter Moyle—who met
at the Graecian Coffee-house in London. This group
produced many pamphlets on the standing-army controversy, freedom of the press, and the East India Com-

pany scandals. During this period Toland prepared
editions of key works by the Radical Whigs' republican
forebears: Algernon Sidney's *Discourses concerning Government* (1698), *The Memoirs of Denzil, Lord Holles* (1699), and
The Oceana of James Harrington (1700). Toland also wrote
The Militia Reform'd (1698), which offered a compromise
between the supporters of a standing army, such as
Daniel Defoe, and the Radical Whigs, who called for a
citizen militia. While Toland couched his argument in
terms of "reason," the solution he proposed—for the
standing army to become the backbone of a militia distributed throughout England—was more an attempt to
ingratiate himself with the "country Whigs" in Parliament. In fact, the leader of the "country" faction, Robert Harley, first Earl of Oxford, may have
commissioned Toland's pamphlet.

Toland's mix of political principle and practical
tactics is fully visible in two works published in 1701:
*The Art of Governing by Partys: Particularly in Religion, in Pol-
itics, in Parlament, on the Bench, and in the Ministry* and
*Anglia Libera; or, The Limitation and Succession of the Crown
of England Explained and Asserted,* . . . The first criticizes
the rise of parties in British politics, blaming the machinations of the Stuart kings for the rise of faction. The
result, Toland argues, has been "a sort of Civil War"
between "Pensioners, Officers, and Tories on this [side]. . .
Republicans, Whigs, and Dissenters on the other" that
has crept into every branch of government. Toland also
savages William III's ministers, branding them "Evil
Counsellors, Cormorants, Bloodsuckers, and Harpies."
Anglia Libera, written in praise of the Act of Settlement
(1701), takes a more positive view of British politics.
Toland saw the stipulation of a Protestant monarch as
an important step in relegating "papist" superstitions to
the past, and the new provisions on ministerial responsibility and the judiciary as reducing the role of "party."

Thanks to these writings, Toland enjoyed a brief
period of political favor among the Whigs. He was
named a member of the delegation to Hanover that
delivered the Act of Settlement to Princess Sophia,
mother of the future King George I. Sophia arranged
for Toland to meet her daughter, Queen Sophie Charlotte of Prussia, known as "Serena." This introduction
led to one of Toland's most important philosophical
works, *Letters to Serena* (1704). The Queen maintained
an early Enlightenment salon and corresponded regularly with Toland and German philosopher Gottfried
Wilhelm Leibniz. In his letters Toland gave full expression to the philosophical materialism hinted at in his
earlier works. Most startling in the context of the times
was Toland's idea that motion was inherent in matter. A
commonplace of Augustan religious thought was that
motion was evidence of God's continuing intervention
in Creation. If God were not responsible for motion,

then, in the words of Richard Bentley's Boyle Lectures of 1692, the physical world was ruled by "mere Chance and Accident." Toland's argument that motion was simply a property of matter, therefore, was tantamount to denying God's existence, or more accurately in Toland's case, identifying God with nature rather than as transcendent over nature.

In the ten years following *Letters to Serena,* Toland wrote mainly short, polemical works. Among these works, *Socinianism Truly Stated* (1705) is noteworthy for its antitrinitarianism and for including the first use in English of the term "pantheist." Toland's main publication of this decade was *Adeisidaemon, sive Titus Livius a superstitione vindicatus* (1709), the main title of which translates as "man without superstition." This defense of the Roman historian Titus Livy against charges of superstition is typical of Toland's historical methods. He demonstrates an impressive command of Livy and other Latin writers but treats Rome as an analogue for eighteenth-century Britain. As in all of Toland's work, historical, religious, and political analysis is intertwined to promote his vision of a rational civic religion free of mystery and irrationality.

Between 1714 and 1720, Toland experienced one final period of producing major works. This stage was inaugurated by a radical plea for toleration, *Reasons for Naturalizing the Jews in Great Britain and Ireland on the Same Foot with All Other Nations* (1714). Although Toland did not extend his principle of toleration to the Catholics of his native Ireland, he was in his day, according to Defoe, "the most extreme for toleration." Toland's anti-Catholicism, visible in virtually all of his work, was given full voice in *The Destiny of Rome; or, The Probability of the Speedy Destruction of the Pope* (1718).

The major political work of this final stage was *The State Anatomy of Great Britain* (1717), published in two parts. These volumes affirm "Court Whig" policy, presenting the Whigs in such phrases as "friends of the Crown," "asserters of Liberty," and "civil and friendly to foreigners" while casting the Tories as "enemies of the Crown," "abettors of tyranny," and "declared enemies" of foreigners. Beyond the partisan plumping, *The State Anatomy of Great Britain* also synthesizes Toland's earlier ideas on freedom of the press and of conscience, and the need for a standing army.

The other major works of Toland's late years are theological, although his interest in civic religion meant that political considerations were ever present. The impetus for *Nazarenus; or, Jewish, Gentile and Mahometan Christianity* (1718) was an Italian manuscript with Arabic notations that Toland had seen in Holland. Toland believed it was evidence of an early Arabic version of the "lost gospel" of Barnabas. He was later proved wrong—the document was, in fact, written by an Italian

Muslim no earlier than the fifteenth century—but other elements of this book remain of interest, particularly Toland's expansion of two ideas first expressed in *Christianity Not Mysterious.* The first was that the Nazarene Christians were closest to the original teachings of Jesus and therefore models for a reformed Christology. The sections on these "Jewish Christians" comprise some of Toland's most sustained historical inquiry. By placing Christianity within its Jewish context and incorporating philology, Toland anticipated nineteenth-century "higher criticism," which applied the same analytical methods to the Bible as to other historical texts." The second, even more provocative assertion was imbedded in the title. The reference to "Jewish, Gentile, and Mahometan Christianity" indicated that since all three traditions believed in a single God revealed through scripture, one could speak of Muslim Christianity. Since theologians considered Islam the antithesis of Christianity, Toland could not have been more inflammatory.

Toland's last major work was *Pantheisticon,* published in Latin under the name Janus Junius Eoganesius (that is, of Inishowen), which Toland claimed was his baptismal name. Partly a parody of Catholic ritual, *Pantheisticon* is also a manual for the civic, pantheistic religion Toland envisioned. It begins with Toland's most extended statement of pantheistic beliefs, relying heavily on Classical, especially Stoic, sources. God is defined by Toland as "the Force and Energy of the Whole, the Creator and Ruler of All. . . whom you may call the Mind, if you please, and Soul of the Universe." The "Ethereal Fire" that burns in each human being, Toland argues, is part of that whole, linking God, nature, and human life. The style and structure of the remainder of *Pantheisticon* mirror Toland's religious leveling, mixing classical rhetoric with vernacular parody and treating canonical sources equally with esoterica. In its call for Socratic Clubs and its elaborate rubrics, *Pantheisticon* became an important source for the early Masonic movement, especially in France.

In his final years, Toland also outlined ideas about the early history of Ireland, especially Druidic culture. This historical sketch was combined with notes Toland had made at Oxford almost thirty years earlier to produce the posthumous *A Critical History of the Celtic Religion and Learning, Containing an Account of the Druids* (1740). It includes groundbreaking work in Celtic linguistics, comparing phrases from the Irish and Breton languages to demonstrate that Ireland was a colony of the Gauls. The sections on Druidism demonstrate that Toland was to the end fascinated by religion and its role in shaping human society.

Toland's repeated alienation of patrons and his financial losses in the South Sea Bubble of 1720 led to impoverishment at the end of his life. He spent his final two years living in Putney, outside London, in a room so small that his library of 155 books had to be stacked on chairs. Toland, who had long suffered from asthma and rheumatism, contracted jaundice in early March of 1722 and died on 11 March.

In his self-written epitaph, John Toland characterizes himself as "an assertor of liberty, a lover of all sorts of learning, a speaker of Irish, but no man's follower or dependent." It is as "an assertor of liberty," a freethinker, that Toland is remembered. As with his fellow promoters of republicanism, Toland's opinions had little impact on British politics or institutions. Unlike Trenchard and Gordon, Toland had little discernible influence on American revolutionary ideals; his radical Whiggism was too alloyed with support for the post-Stuart monarchy to appeal to the revolutionary leaders. However, Toland did influence the development of French Enlightenment thought. Paul-Henri Thiry, Baron d'Holbach, was especially indebted to Toland's writings, and Voltaire characterized Toland as "a proud and independent soul: born in poverty, he could have risen to fortune had he been more moderate." Traces of Toland's pantheism can be seen in the French Masonic movement and in the experiment in civic religion undertaken in 1793–1794 under the revolutionary leadership of Maximilien-François-Marie-Isidore de Robespierre.

References:

S. H. Daniel, *John Toland: His Methods, Manner and Mind* (Montreal: McGill-Queen's University Press, 1984);

Daniel, "The Subversive Philosophy of John Toland," in *Irish Writing: Exile and Subversion,* edited by Paul Hyland and Neil Sammells (London: Macmillan, 1991), pp. 1–12;

Thomas Duddy, *A History of Irish Thought* (London & New York: Routledge, 2002);

Robert Rees Evans, *Pantheisticon: The Career of John Toland,* American University Studies, series 9: History, volume 98 (New York: Peter Lang, 1991);

F. H. Heinemann, "John Toland and the Age of Enlightenment," *Review of English Studies,* 20, no. 78 (1944): 125–146;

Margaret C. Jacob, *The Radical Enlightenment* (London: Allen & Unwin, 1981);

Phillip McGuinness, "The Peculiar Contradictions of John Toland," *Times Literary Supplement,* 27 September 1996, pp. 14–15;

Caroline Robbins, *The Eighteenth-Century Commonwealthman: Studies in the Transmission, Development and Circumstance of English Liberal Thought from the Restoration of Charles II until the War with the Thirteen Colonies* (Cambridge, Mass.: Harvard University Press, 1959);

J. G. Simms, "John Toland (1670–1722), a Donegal Heretic," *Irish Historical Studies,* 16, no. 63 (1968–1969): 304–320;

Robert E. Sullivan, *John Toland and the Deist Controversy: A Study in Adaptations* (Cambridge, Mass.: Harvard University Press, 1982);

Jonathan Swift, *Satires and Personal Writings,* edited by William Alfred Eddy (London: Oxford University Press, 1932).

Papers:

Manuscript material by John Toland is located in the British Library; the Bodleian Library, Oxford; Lambeth Palace Library; the Public Record Office, London; and the National Austrian Library, Vienna.

Joseph Towers

(31 March 1737 – 20 May 1799)

Juilee Decker

Case Western Reserve University

BOOKS: *A Review of the Genuine Doctrines of Christianity. Comprehending Remarks on Several Principal Calvinistical Doctrines* (London: Printed for W. Sandby, 1763);

An Enquiry into the Question, Whether Juries Are, or Are Not, Judges of Law, as Well as of Fact; With a Particular Reference to The Case of Libels (London: Printed for J. Wilkie, 1764);

Observations on Public Liberty, Patriotism, Ministerial Despotism, and National Grievances: With Some Remarks on Riots, Petitions, Loyal Addresses, and Military Execution (London: Printed for Joseph Towers, 1769);

A Letter to the Rev. Mr. John Wesley; In Answer to His Late Pamphlet, Entitled, "Free Thoughts on the Present State of Public Affairs" (London: Printed for Joseph Towers, 1771);

A Dialogue between Two Gentlemen, concerning the Late Application to Parliament for Relief in the Matter of Subscription to the Thirty-nine Articles and Liturgy of the Church of England, anonymous (London: Printed for Joseph Towers, 1772);

A Letter to the Rev. Dr. Nowell . . . Occasioned by His Very Extraordinary Sermon, Preached Before the House of Commons on the Thirtieth of January, 1772 (London: Printed for Joseph Towers, 1772);

An Examination into the Nature and Evidence of the Charges Brought against Lord William Russel, and Algernon Sydney, by Sir John Dalrymple, Bart. In His Memoirs of Great Britain (London: Printed for the author, 1773);

Funeral Reflections; or, Conscience the Loudest Knell: A Satyr. Occasioned by Several Complaints . . . of the Too Long and Frequent Tolling of the Bells at Deaths and Burials (London: Printed for Joseph Towers, 1773); republished with additions as *La Cloche De L'ame; or, Conscience the Loudest Knell. A Satyr. Occasioned by Several Late Complaints from Places of Public Resort, of the Too Long and Frequent Tolling of the Bells at Deaths and Funerals. To Which Is Added, Vigiliana Novissima; or, The Reformed Watchman* (London: Printed for Joseph Towers, 1774);

A Letter to Dr. Samuel Johnson: Occasioned by His Late Political Publications. With an Appendix, Containing Some Observations on a Pamphlet Lately Published by Dr. Shebbeare (London: Printed for Joseph Towers, 1775);

The Professors of the Gospel under the Strongest Obligations to Labour to Distinguish Themselves by an Eminent Degree of Piety and Virtue: a Sermon Preached at St. Thomas's, January 1, 1777, for the Benefit of the Charity-school in Gravel-lane, Southwark (London: Printed for J. Johnson and J. Buckland, 1777);

Observations on Mr. Hume's History of England (London: Printed by H. Goldney for G. Robinson, 1778);

A Vindication of the Political Principles of Mr. Locke: In Answer to the Objections of the Rev. Dr. Tucker, Dean of Glocester (London: Printed for G. Robinson, 1782);

Observations on the Rights and Duty of Juries in Trials for Libels (London: J. Debrett, 1784);

Dialogues concerning the Ladies. To Which Is Added, an Essay on the Antient Amazons (London: Printed for T. Cadell, 1785);

An Essay on the Life, Character, and Writings of Dr. Samuel Johnson (London: Printed for Charles Dilly, 1786);

An Oration Delivered at the London Tavern, on the Fourth of November, 1788, on Occasion of the Commemoration of the Revolution, and the Completion of a Century from That Great Event (London: Printed for Charles Dilly, 1788);

Memoirs of the Life and Reign of Frederick the Third, King of Prussia, 2 volumes (London: Printed for Charles Dilly, 1788);

Thoughts on the Commencement of a New Parliament: with an Appendix, Containing Remarks on the Letter of the Right Hon. Edmund Burke, on the Revolution in France (London: Printed for Charles Dilly, 1790);

A Dialogue between an Associator and a Well-informed Englishman, on the Grounds of the Late Associations, and the Commencement of a War with France (London: Printed for Thomas Evans, 1793);

The History of Philip Waldegrave, 2 volumes, anonymous (London: Printed for T. Evans, 1793);

Remarks on the Conduct, Principles, and Publications, of the Association at the Crown and Anchor, in the Strand, for Preserving Liberty and Property Against Republicans and Levellers, anonymous (London: Printed for T. Evans, 1793);

An Address to the Electors of Great Britain, anonymous (London: Printed for J. Johnson, T. Evans, and J. Debrett, 1796);

Tracts on Political and Other Subjects Published at Various Times and Now First Collected Together (London: T. Cadell & W. Davies, 1796).

OTHER: *British Biography; or, An Accurate and Impartial Account of the Lives and Writings of Eminent Persons, in Great Britain and Ireland; from Wickliff, Who Began the Reformation by His Writings, to the Present Time,* 7 volumes, compiled by Towers (London: Printed for R. Goadby, 1766–1772);

The Moral and Entertaining Magazine. Or a Miscellany of Literary Instruction and Amusement: To Which Is Added a Display of the Universe, or a Survey of the Wonderful Works of Creation, and the Various Customs & Inventions of Men, Adorned with Beautiful Copper Plate Cuts (London: Printed for R. Goadby, 1777–1780);

Biographia Britannica; or, The Lives of the Most Eminent Persons Who Have Flourished in Great Britain and Ireland, from the Earliest Ages, down to the Present Times: Collected from the Best Authorities, Printed and Manuscript, and Digested in the Manner of Mr. Bayle's Historical and Critical Dictionary, second edition, 5 volumes, volumes 2–5 by Andrew Kippis, assisted by Towers and others (London: Printed by W. and A. Strahan, for C. Bathurst, W. Strahan [etc.], 1778–1793).

Joseph Towers was a biographer, political commentator, historian, and dissenting minister. Perhaps his best-known work was *British Biography; or, An Accurate and Impartial Account of the Lives and Writings of Eminent Persons, in Great Britain and Ireland; from Wickliff, Who Began the Reformation by His Writings, to the Present Time* (1766–1772). It was an encyclopedic work in its approach, and Towers treated his subject (England, Ireland, and their constituents) carefully, with attention paid to individual contributions as well as to those of the entire culture. The entries, therefore, take historical as well as biographical points of view. Careful to distance himself from the artificiality that had dominated biography for several decades, Towers proclaimed disinterestedness on the part of the author/compiler. His *British Biography* was unlike the streams of events recorded in other biographies, which served only as recollections of behavior and speech.

Towers was born in Southwark on 31 March 1737. The son of a secondhand-book seller, Towers was immersed in literary culture from his early childhood. Publishing and books became a familiar milieu for him. In addition to his familial connection with books, he worked as an errand boy for a stationer by the age of twelve and a decade later (1754) was apprenticed to Robert Goadby, who ran a circulating library in Sherborne. The working relationship between the two men flourished for twenty years.

While under Goadby's tutelage, Towers assisted his mentor with the printing of *An Address to Those Who Consider the Holy Scriptures as a Rule of Conduct Given Them by God, as a Display of His Perfections, and a Manifestation of His Will.* Although written by Goadby in 1762, the publication line indicates that the work was printed for R. Goadby and J. Towers. The following year, Towers tried his own hand at writing and wrote a seventy-four-page religious treatise, *A Review of the Genuine Doctrines of Christianity. Comprehending Remarks on Several Principal Calvinistical Doctrines.* Religious works appeared in the 1760s and 1770s—that is, while Towers worked with Goadby and following Towers's taking up a role as dissenting minister. This interest may have come from his training with Goadby in ancient languages and philosophy.

Goadby sought Towers's editing skills in 1766 for the first seven volumes of *British Biography.* As the title suggests, the work claimed both accuracy and impartiality—traits that seemed to have appeared with less frequency in modern biographies. Writing historical entries that spanned the four centuries since the age of the British pre-reformer John Wycliffe captured Towers's interest until 1772. During these six years, Towers used much of the literature in *Biographia Britannica* (1747–1766) in addition to original research that he pursued in the British Museum. He learned the trade of a researcher by combing for facts and making original discoveries there.

In addition to historical works such as *British Biography,* Towers was also interested in politically charged events from history. In 1773 he published an essay that examined Sir John Dalrymple's *Memoirs of Great-Britain & Ireland from the Dissolution of the Last Parliament of Charles II* (1771), a work that was vehemently attacked by William Russel and Algernon Sydney. By 1774 Towers had given up his proprietorship and had become a dissenting minister of Unitarian theology, taking up the pastorate of a Presbyterian congregation in Highgate. In 1778 he left Highgate to become preacher at Stoke Newington Green as assistant to Richard Price, and the following year he obtained his law licentiate from Edinburgh University. Despite giving up his business and ordination as a minister, Towers continued to write responses to current debate. In his pamphlets and writings, Towers took into account earlier writings and incorporated a tradition of narratives as the structure for his own texts. He served as critic of David Hume's *History of England* (1754–1762) in *Tracts on Political and Other Subjects* (1796). By the time Hume composed his work, a considerable tradition of English historical writing had evolved. Towers praised Hume's neutrality regarding the Reformation and the model his work set for other classical historical writing.

Public liberties became a concern of Towers during the last four decades of the eighteenth century. In *An Enquiry into the Question, Whether Juries Are, or Are Not, Judges of Law, as Well as of Fact; With a Particular Reference to The Case of Libels* (1764) Towers proclaimed the liberty of the English press. He observed that "the freedom of the Press may, and sometimes does, degenerate into licentiousness, cannot be disputed; but the laws against sedition and libeling are already amply sufficient and much too strong to be left to the arbitrary decision of any Lord Chief Justice. The liberty which this nation enjoys, has rendered it the admiration and the envy of Europe; the man who is insensible of its value and its importance, is unworthy to live in a free country." In his essay *Observations on Public Liberty, Patriotism, Ministerial Despotism, and National Grievances* (1769) Towers insisted that the Dissenters adhere to "old Whig principles," but he admitted that they were a stigmatized group who were seen as "factious, seditious, disaffected, and even rebellious." The Dissenters, however, made a major contribution to the evolving autonomy of the voter by insisting that voters should be able to elect whomever they wished. Towers observed that "When we reason only speculatively, it appears rational to suppose, that men in good circumstances, and of affluent fortunes, would be less liable to be influenced by corrupt motives, than those whose inferior situation seems to expose them more naturally to temptation." He hoped that "inferior ranks" of people could be politically engaged as an effort to incite change.

Part of Towers's role as a political historian may be gauged by his writings, which served as a microcosm of the political disputes among supporters and disputers of Lockean principles. *A Treatise Concerning Civil Government,* published in 1781 by economist and clergyman Josiah Tucker, D.D., indicated conservative hostility toward Lockeanism and was the most sustained critique of Lockean politics during the eighteenth century. Tucker's treatise, however, was based upon earlier essays and tracts that he prepared as early as 1775 and printed in a draft version, *The Notions of Mr. Locke, and his Followers,* in 1779. Towers published *A Vindication of the Political Principles of Mr. Locke: In Answer to the Objections of the Rev. Dr. Tucker, Dean of Glocester* in 1782. The two works and their authors (Tucker and Towers) indicate

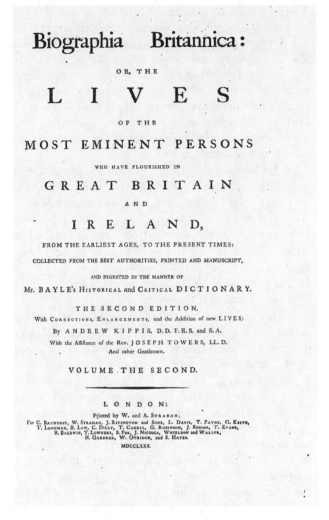

Title page for the corrected second edition (1778–1793) of Joseph Towers's best-known work (Eighteenth-Century Collections Online, Gale Group)

opposition between a clergyman of the Establishment, who favored absolutism, and a Unitarian, who supported rational dissent. Towers's essay, while supporting Locke first and foremost, served to criticize Tucker's writings as well as the principles expounded by Sir Robert Filmer, an absolutist and pamphleteer of the previous century, who believed in the unlimited power of the sovereign.

In *A Vindication of the Political Principles of Mr. Locke* Towers championed John Locke's case against absolutism, particularly in his support of the parliamentary reform movement and, by extension, legitimization of the Glorious Revolution. A century earlier, however, that revolution and the current political situation in England had heralded Locke's notions of constitutionalism, fair franchise, and denial of unlimited absolute power. The connection to Locke was not only historical but also a real part of the present political debate; thus,

Towers sought to vindicate Locke and those who supported his ideals at the present time. Refuting Tucker, Towers noted "that the general maxims of government, laid down by that celebrated writer, are highly rational and just, and calculated, so far as they are attended to for the promotion of the great interests of mankind." Further into the essay, Towers refers to the followers of Locke's philosophy as "his disciples," thereby suggesting a mentoring relationship that would have promoted close alignment in doctrine.

Locke spurred activity by other pamphleteers, including a rebuttal by Tucker, who refueled his attack on Locke by publishing in 1783 *Four Letters on Important National Subjects . . . Addressed to the Earl of Shelburne.* Defenders of Locke included John Towill Rutt, a Unitarian political activist and author of "Defense of Locke against Lord Eldon" (1807). Towers's *A Vindication of the Political Principles of Mr. Locke* was republished in 1796 in the first volume of his collected tracts.

Towers's concern for the dissolution of absolute power was supplemented with his hope for parliamentary reform–issues that were of interest over the course of the next two decades. Towers's *Observations on the Rights and Duty of Juries in Trials for Libels* (1784) recognized the right of trial by jury as being "of infinite importance to the liberty of the subject. It cannot be guarded with too much vigilance, nor defended with too much ardour." Towers considered his audience to be people other than those in the legal profession. In *Observations on the Rights and Duty of Juries in Trials for Libels* he claimed that since he was writing "not for lawyers, but chiefly for men of other professions and employments, he thought it best to make use of language that should be generally intelligible." Towers was quick to note those in the legal profession who had done well by it and those who had not. Two essays by Towers and one by Francis Maseres (1792) explained the right of a defendant, especially in criminal libel cases, to have a jury decide the laws and facts that would determine his or her fate. This approach conformed to the Camdenian doctrine of jury process (named for Charles Pratt, first Earl of Camden) as opposed to the Mansfieldian doctrine, named for William Murray, first Earl of Mansfield.

In contrast to these lengthy accounts, Towers wrote more than twenty known pamphlets of a few pages each. These pamphlets are historical documents that, many times, merit considerable attention because they encouraged rigorous philosophical and political exchange between an author and one member (perhaps speaking for many) in his audience. While this relationship can be compared to the modern academic conception of a discussant and reader of a paper at a conference, historically, this exchange confirms the strength and vitality of Jürgen Habermas's notion of "Offentlichkeit" or the "public sphere."

In 1785 Towers published, anonymously, *Dialogues concerning the Ladies. To Which Is Added, an Essay on the Antient Amazons.* Seven essays offer transcriptions of a dialogue regarding female dress; literary characters; marriage; miscellaneous observations; virtues such as politeness, gentleness, and meekness; and distinguished literary talents. Following the dialogues, an essay on the Amazons concludes the volume.

In considering the advantages of men over women in terms of education, dialogue two recounts that "Men undoubtedly possess advantages much superior to women in point of education, and especially with respect to the acquisition of antient literature; and in an inquiry into the comparative intellectual powers of the sexes, this certainly ought to be considered." Despite strides taken in education, the speaker suggests that an inequality would still exist, "Great has been the number of those ladies, whose advantages of education have been exceedingly superior to those of Shakespeare; and yet, I believe, no literary lady will venture to produce against him a female competitor."

The essay on the Amazons was undertaken as "a matter of literary curiosity." Towers traced the mention of this society by Greek writers, including Homer and Herodotus. The writings of Herodotus recount the battle between Greeks and Amazons on the river Thermodoon, which resulted in a Greek victory and the capture of the Amazons. Upon their seizure, the Amazons were discovered to be women. The story did not end there, however, and the Amazons on board the three ships of captives conspired against the men and, upon arrival in the territories of the Scythians, killed them.

The essay ends, thus, with Samuel Johnson's assessment of the Amazons as a violent people: "The character of the antient Amazons was rather terrible than lovely; the hand could not be very delicate that was only employed in drawing the bow, and brandishing the battleaxe; their power was maintained by cruelty, their courage was deformed by ferocity, and their example only shews, that men and women live best together." Towers's essay on the Amazons and the collection of dialogues on, about, and by women make plain that women over history had been and were secondary to men.

Shortly after writing his *Dialogues,* Towers turned again to biographical works and chose to recount the histories of King Frederick of Prussia and a lesser-known work about Philip Waldegrave. *Memoirs of the Life and Reign of Frederick the Third, King of Prussia* (1788) was reviewed in *European Magazine* in March 1789 by John Watkins, LL.D., a former dissenter who had contributed more than one hundred reviews for that periodical. In consideration of Towers's entire career, then, biographies form an opening and a close to his career as an historian and author. He died on 20 May 1799 at his house on St. John's Square.

As an author, Joseph Towers's literary career may be marked by the presence, at varying times, of three distinct subjects: religion; history and biography; and politics and law. Towers's *British Biography* served as a model for a new type of biography, which treated individuals through alphabetical entry rather than chronology. His significance as a writer and political historian is evidenced by his defense of Locke, which marked the beginning of an association—even, vindication—of Locke by fellow Unitarians for his ideals. Towers's writing is also important for more literary forms, including the biographical dictionary entries for *British Biography* and his contributions to the second edition of *Biographia Britannica* (1778–1793), in which he used the signature "T."

References:

Gregory Claeys, ed., *Political Writings of the 1790s: French Revolution Debate in Britain,* 8 volumes (London: Pickering & Chatto, 1995);

James Fieser, ed., *Early Responses to Hume's History of England,* 2 volumes (Bristol: Thoemmes Press, 2002);

Mark Goldie, ed., *The Reception of Locke's Politics from the 1690s to the 1830s* (London: Pickering & Chatto, 1999);

Knud Haakonssen, ed., *Enlightenment and Religion: Rational Dissent in Eighteenth-Century Britain* (Cambridge: Cambridge University Press, 1996);

Jürgen Habermas, *The Structural Transformation of the Public Sphere: An Inquiry into a Category of Bourgeois Society,* translated by Thomas Burger with the assistance of Frederick Lawrence (Cambridge, Mass.: MIT Press, 1991);

Mark Salber Phillips, *Society and Sentiment: Genres of Historical Writing in Britain, 1740–1820* (Princeton, N.J.: Princeton University Press, 2000);

Mark Philp, "Vulgar Conservatism, 1792–3," *English Historical Review,* 110 (February 1995): 42–69;

John Seed, "Gentlemen Dissenters: The Social and Political Meanings of Rational Dissent in the 1770s and 1780s," *Historical Journal,* 28 (June 1985): 299–325;

Kathleen Wilson, "Inventing Revolution: 1688 and Eighteenth-Century Popular Politics," *Journal of British Studies,* 28 (October 1989): 349–386.

Papers:

Joseph Towers's notebook including lists of persons and books, extracts, and prayers is held by the Bodleian Library, Special Collections, at Oxford University.

John Trenchard

(1662 – 17 December 1723)

Michael R. Hutcheson
Landmark College

BOOKS: *A Sermon Preached Before the Right Honourable the Lord-Mayor, and Court of Aldermen, of the City of London, at St. Mary Le Bow, on the 29th of May, 1694,* Early English Books, 1641–1700 (London: Printed for Richard Baldwin, 1694);

An Argument, Shewing That a Standing Army Is Inconsistent with a Free Government, and Absolutely Destructive to the Constitution of the English Monarchy, by Trenchard and Walter Moyle (London: [John Darby], 1697);

A Letter from the Author of the Argument Against a Standing Army: To the Author of the Balancing Letter, anonymous (London, 1697);

Some Remarks upon a Late Paper, Entituled, an Argument, Shewing, That a Standing Army Is Inconsistent with a Free Government, and Absolutely Destructive to the Constitution of the English Monarchy, anonymous, by Trenchard and Moyle ([London], 1697);

A Short History of Standing Armies in England, anonymous (London: Printed for A. Baldwin, 1698);

The Secret History of the Trust; With Some Reflections upon the Letter from a Souldier, to the House of Commons, in a Familiar Discourse Between J. Truncheon Esq., and Mr. Inquisitive, anonymous (London, 1702);

The Natural History of Superstition, anonymous ([London]: Sold by A. Baldwin, 1709);

Some Reflections upon a Pamphlet, called The Old Whig (London: Printed for J. Roberts, 1719);

Some Considerations upon the State of Our Publick Debts in General, and of the Civil List in Particular, anonymous (London: Printed by J. Roberts, 1720);

A Collection of Letters to the Editor of The London Journal, as Cato, by Trenchard and Thomas Gordon (London: Printed for J. Roberts, 1720);

A Comparison Between the Proposals of the Bank and the South-Sea Company: Wherein Is Shewn, That the Proposals of the First Are Much More Advantageous to the Publick, than Those of the Latter, anonymous (London: Printed by J. Roberts, 1720);

The Second Collection of Cato's Political Letters in the London Journal, Continued to the End of January, 1720, as Cato, by Trenchard and Gordon (London: Printed for J. Roberts, 1720 [1721]); revised and enlarged as *Cato's Letters,* 4 volumes (London: W. Wilkins, T. Woodward, J. Walthoe & J. Peele, 1723–1724);

A Collection of Tracts by the Late John Trenchard, Esq., & Thomas Gordon, Esq., 2 volumes (London: F. Cogan, 1751);

Essays on Important Subjects, by the Late John Trenchard, Esq; Never before Published (London: Printed for A. Miller, 1755).

Editions and Collections: *The English Libertarian Heritage: From the Writings of John Trenchard and Thomas Gordon in "The Independent Whig" and "Cato's Letters,"* edited by Donald L. Jacobson (Indianapolis: Bobbs-Merrill, 1965);

An Argument, Shewing That a Standing Army Is Inconsistent with a Free Government, and Absolutely Destructive to the Constitution of the English Monarchy (Exeter, U.K.: The Rota, 1971)—facsimile reprint;

Cato's Letters; or, Essays on Liberty, 2 volumes, edited and annotated by Ronald Hamowy (Indianapolis: Liberty Fund, 1995).

OTHER: *The Independent Whig,* anonymous, edited by Trenchard and Thomas Gordon (London: Printed for J. Peele, 1721; corrected and expanded, 2 volumes, 1732).

John Trenchard was a political essayist whose writings developed the English "radical Whig" ideology of the period after the "Glorious Revolution" of 1688. In a series of pamphlets and periodical essays, Trenchard criticized standing armies, licensing of the press, and governmental corruption, while commending citizen militias, freedom of expression, and parliamentary reform. He often supported his arguments with historical examples, primarily from Roman history. His writings are most significant for providing eighteenth-century liberal constitutionalists with key ideas and phrases.

Trenchard was born in 1662 to Anglo-Irish parents, William and Ellen (Norton) Trenchard. Little is known of his early life. He enrolled at Trinity College, Dublin, where his tutor was Edward Smith, later the Church of Ireland bishop of Down and Conor. He then studied law in London and was called to the bar; however, his marriage to Anne Blackett and the death of an uncle gave Trenchard the financial security to give up the practice of law and devote himself to writing. Trenchard also held two political offices during his life. The first was as a commissioner of Forfeited Estates in Ireland. In this position, he contributed to several reports to Parliament between 1699 and 1703. This appointment also provided Trenchard with many encounters with political corruption, including his discovery that Crown officials had transferred to their own control some 1,700,000 acres of land in Ireland. In the last two years of his life, Trenchard also served as a Member of Parliament for Taunton, Somerset.

Trenchard's published works comprise pamphlets and reprints of works originally published in periodicals. His first publication is disputed; he may have written *Remarks on the Proceedings of the Commissioners for Putting in Execution the Act . . . for the Establishing of a Land Bank* (1696), or the credit may belong to John Asgill, a cofounder of the Land Bank, who also holds the distinction of having been expelled from both the Irish Parliament (in 1703) and the Parliament at Westminster (in 1707) for a pamphlet judged blasphemous.

The first publication in which Trenchard unquestionably had a hand is *An Argument, Shewing That a Standing Army Is Inconsistent with a Free Government, and Absolutely Destructive to the Constitution of the English Monarchy* (1697), co-authored with Walter Moyle. This short pamphlet was reprinted (with slight changes) four times in the next ten years and was followed by three more works by Trenchard on the same topic; the most substantial of these works was *A Short History of Standing Armies in England* (1698). This work, too, proved popular and went through twelve English editions (two of them abridged) between 1698 and 1782.

All of Trenchard's works on standing armies emphasize the threat to individual liberty posed by a permanent military and the preferability of a citizen militia. Surveying historical nations that had fallen into tyranny in *An Argument, Shewing That a Standing Army Is Inconsistent with a Free Government,* Trenchard and Moyle state, "And if we enquire how these unhappy Nations have lost that precious Jewel *Liberty,* and we as yet preserved it, we shall find . . . That their Necessities or Indiscretions have permitted a standing Army to be kept amongst them, and our Situation rather than our Prudence, hath as yet defended us from it. . . ." The safeguard against tyranny, they continue, is "making

The SECOND

COLLECTION

OF

CATO's
Political Letters

IN THE

LONDON JOURNAL,

Continued to the End of
January, 1720.

LONDON:

Printed for J. ROBERTS in *Warwick-Lane,* 1720.

Title page for the second volume in the series of essays by John Trenchard and Thomas Gordon in defense of individual liberty (Eighteenth-Century Collections Online, Gale Group)

the Militia to consist of the same Persons as have the Property." This view was apparently shaped by Trenchard's reading of the Roman historian Tacitus, and of *Oceana* (1656) by James Harrington. However, Trenchard never produced historical scholarship to match that of his co-author Moyle, whose *Democracy Vindicated: An Essay on the Constitution of the Roman State* (published posthumously, 1726) supported its republican argument with greater erudition. Trenchard's early writings on standing armies set off a heated pamphlet debate, with Daniel Defoe joining the fray on the opposing side in his *A Brief Reply to the History of Standing Armies in England. With Some Account of the Authors* (1698).

Tracing the development of Trenchard's ideas is challenging, because his writings were published anonymously or under assumed names, sometimes with uncredited contributions from other radical Whigs. In the first edition of *An Argument, Shewing That a Standing Army Is Inconsistent with a Free Government,* for instance, the author is listed as "A.B.C.D.E.F.G." Adding to the confusion was Trenchard's taking on multiple identities to stoke the fires of pamphlet debates. For example, in 1719 Trenchard anonymously published *Some Reflections upon a Pamphlet, called The Old Whig.* Authorship of *The Thoughts of a Member of the Lower House* is usually attributed to Trenchard, but sometimes to Robert Walpole. Similarly, Trenchard was apparently the author of *A Letter from a Souldier to the Commons of England, Occasioned by an Address Now Carrying on by the Protestants of Ireland . . .* (1702). He then responded to his own letter, adding a fictional disputation, *The Secret History of the Trust; With Some Reflections upon the Letter from a Souldier, to the House of Commons, in a Familiar Discourse between J. Truncheon Esq., and Mr. Inquisitive* (1702), with "Truncheon" clearly a pun on Trenchard's own surname. Such elaborate obfuscations were also typical means of avoiding political persecution and libel charges in the eighteenth century.

In spite of such difficulties concerning attribution, Trenchard's work consistently demonstrates concern for individual liberty. Trenchard saw the abuse of religion as a second major threat to this liberty, either through the state church gaining excessive power or through the propagation of superstition. Trenchard's fullest early exploration of the latter topic was *The Natural History of Superstition* (1709), which demonstrates some tenets of deism. This pamphlet begins with a portrayal of a mechanistic creation and the claim that recent scientific advances should lead one "to admire and adore the Power of God, who has given being and motion to such vast Machines." Despite that mankind lives in a perfectly ordered cosmos, superstitions arise, Trenchard claims, from several causes. Like the deists, Trenchard believes that some organized religions promote superstition: "the Fables of Heathens, the Alchoran of *Mahomet,* the more gross and impious forgeries of the Papists, and the Frauds and Follies of some who call themselves Protestants, have so far prevailed over genuine Christianity." Superstitions also appear when the natural human inclination to understand seeks causes hidden from mankind, and when humans confuse dreams, melancholy, and hypochondria for religious experience. Trenchard even approaches philosophical materialism in his contention that "everything in Nature is in constant Motion, and perpetually emitting Effluviums and minute Particles of its Substance, which operate upon, and strike other Bodies." However, Tren-

chard's deism is limited by his beliefs that God actively hides causes from human view and that humans share a fallen nature: "But as there is no perfection in this frail State, nor any excellency without some defect accompanying it, so those noble faculties of the Mind have misled and betrayed us into Superstition."

Trenchard had firmly established his radical Whig credentials by 1719, when he met Thomas Gordon, some thirty years his junior. Gordon, who later produced translations of Roman historians Tacitus and Sallust, supplied youthful energy and scholarship to their working relationship, while Trenchard acted as political mentor. From January 1720 to January 1721, they issued a weekly political newspaper, *The Independent Whig.* The fifty-three essays published therein were collected in a 1721 volume with the same title—eighteen by Trenchard, twenty-two by Gordon, and three co-authored. The remaining ten are identified with the letter "C," which may indicate the authorship of Arthur Collins. Significant among the eight English editions of *The Independent Whig* that appeared between 1721 and 1753 was the fifth edition (1732), in which Gordon indicated the authorship of individual entries and appended the subtitle *Defence of Primitive Christianity and of our Ecclesiastical Estates against the Exorbitant Claims and Encroachments of Fanatical and Disappointed Clergymen.*

As this subtitle implies, the authors' primary target in these essays is church hierarchy, especially in Catholicism and "High Church Toryism." Their latitudinarian arguments are framed in the language of individual liberty, as in Essay No. 30: "Religion is a voluntary Thing; it can no more be forced than reason, or Memory, or any Faculty of the Soul." Beyond the political principles, many of the essays in the *Independent Whig* are strongly anti-Catholic. The authors believed that Roman Catholicism was one of the greatest threats to individual liberty as was Jacobitism, the movement to restore the Stuart monarchs, who had produced rebellion in 1715, to the British throne. That some participants in the rebellion were Anglican leaders confirmed in Trenchard's and Gordon's minds the conflation of High Church Toryism and Roman Catholicism.

The Independent Whig was the first of Trenchard's works to be published in North America (Philadelphia [1724]), and it also influenced French Enlightenment thought through the translation by Baron d'Holbach, *Esprit du clergé, ou le Christianisme primitif vengé des entreprises et des excès de nos Prêtres modernes* (1767). Although d'Holbach also claimed that his *La Contagion sacrée ou l'Histoire naturelle de la Superstition* (London [that is, Amsterdam], 1767) was a translation of Trenchard's *The Natural History of Superstition,* the atheism of the French work bears little relation to Trenchard's Protestant deism.

Along with *The Independent Whig,* the work by Trenchard that had the greatest impact was *Cato's Letters,* also co-authored with Thomas Gordon. Writing under the name of the Roman defender of Republican government who opposed Julius Caesar, Trenchard and Gordon began contributing letters to the *London Journal* on 5 November 1720. The last of the original letters appeared in the *British Journal* on 27 December 1723. The letters also began to be published separately in 1720, the first edition, under the title *A Collection of Letters to the Editor of The London Journal.* Seven "continuation" volumes appeared in 1720–1722, and a complete four-volume set in 1724. In 1733 Gordon added six essays, a table of contents, and a revised introduction, and he identified authorship of each of the letters.

The Cato letters were prompted by the South Sea Bubble crisis of 1720, when the collapse of several speculative investment schemes led to financial panic. Nine of the first ten letters concern the "Bubble," which was also the subject of four pamphlets written anonymously by Trenchard in 1720. *Cato's Letters* often arise from such contemporary political issues and then propose solutions supported by classical history and modern social-contract theory, particularly that of Locke.

Locke's influence is apparent whenever an essay in *Cato's Letters* discusses the basis of government, as in Letter No. 59, in which government is described as "a departure from the state of nature, and a union of many families forming themselves into a political machine for mutual protection and defence." In such a system, magistrates owe their authority to the consent of the governed, and, Trenchard continues, "if the persons thus interested will not act at all, or act contrary to their trust, their power must return of course to those who gave it."

The best way to discourage tyranny and assure natural rights, argues *Cato's Letters,* is a mixed constitution. In Letter No. 59 Trenchard argues that the primary characteristic of a government that ensures liberty is that "in free governments there are checks and restraints appointed and expressed in the constitution itself." The "ancient constitution" of England embodied this balance, in part because, as Trenchard states in Letter No. 60, "Our kings had neither revenues large enough, nor offices gainful and numerous enough in their disposal, to corrupt any considerable number of members." As a result, English subjects had true individual liberty until the "Norman yoke" and modern tax revenues began to tip this traditional balance in favor of the monarch, creating opportunity for corruption and abuse of power.

Trenchard and Gordon favored a broad oligarchy of landowners to balance the power of the Crown, as stated in Letter No. 62. However, despite their warnings against monarchical tyranny, Trenchard and Gordon did not claim that merely transferring power from monarch to Parliament guaranteed political liberty. Human nature is too fallible, and the available inducements of the Crown too great, to assume that representatives will always act in the public interest. Avoiding corruption necessitated residency requirements, the elimination of "rotten boroughs," and "rotation of magistracy" through frequent elections (as stated in Letter No. 61).

The defense of individual liberty against the predations of government, not government itself, is the main subject of *Cato's Letters.* As in Trenchard's other writings, Republican Rome repeatedly serves as an historical reference point, as in Letter No. 18, which draws extensively on Sallust. However, the historical references are secondary to the arguments based on English constitutional tradition. In this context, *Cato's Letters* argues for freedom of the press and against all but the most minimal libel laws. As Trenchard writes in Letter No. 100, "What are usually called libels, undoubtedly keep great men in awe, and are some check upon their behaviour, by shewing them the deformity of their actions, as well as warning other people to be on guard against oppression." Far more important for the public good is to "preserve the advantages of liberty of speech, and liberty of writing (which secures all other liberties)."

The ideas of natural right, limited monarchy, parliamentary reform, and freedoms of conscience and the press expressed in *Cato's Letters* resonated powerfully with those American colonists beginning to chafe at British control. As Clinton Rossiter states in his study of colonial American ideas of political liberty, *The Seedtime of the Republic,* "No one can spend any time in the newspapers, library inventories, and pamphlets of colonial America without realizing *Cato's Letters* rather than Locke's *Civil Government* was the most popular, quotable, esteemed source of political ideas in the colonial period."

Trenchard, never physically hearty, fell ill in November 1723 with what his friend Gordon, in the preface to the 1733 edition of *Cato's Letters,* called "an Ulcer in the Kidneys" and died the following month. He was survived by his wife, but their union had produced no children. Trenchard named Gordon as his executor, and Gordon in turn added to the estate by issuing a complete edition of *Cato's Letters.* In his remembrance of Trenchard that prefaces the 1733 edition, Gordon adds an oblique coda to the story of the two authors' relationship: "The Day before his Death, he talked to me much and often of an Affair which regarded myself, and which, were I to mention it, would shew the great Concern and Tenderness that he had for me." Trenchard had asked Gordon to marry his widow, Anne Blackett Trenchard, and to oversee her financial affairs. This marriage produced several children and provided Gordon with the wherewithal to complete his translations and commentaries on Roman historians.

John Trenchard was important mainly as a transmitter of "radical Whig" principles to American colonial political thinkers and revolutionaries rather than as an historian per se. In the words of Gordon, "He was very knowing, but not learned; that is, he had not read many Books." Nevertheless, his writings had a profound impact on the shaping of early American political ideals. Copies of Trenchard and Gordon's works were to be found in the personal libraries of many American revolutionary leaders; in fact, Thomas Jefferson's copies of *Cato's Letters* and *The Independent Whig* were part of his bequest to the Library of Congress. As Bernard Bailyn states in *The Ideological Origins of the American Revolution*, "the writings of Trenchard and Gordon ranked with treatises of Locke as the most authoritative statement of the nature of political liberty and above Locke as an exposition of the social sources of the threats it faced."

Bibliography:

J. A. R. Seguin, *A Bibliography of John Trenchard (1662–1723)* (Jersey City, N.J.: Ross Paxton, 1965).

References:

Bernard Bailyn, *The Ideological Origins of the American Revolution* (Cambridge, Mass.: Harvard University Press, 1967);

Ronald Hamowy, "Cato's Letters, John Locke, and the Republican Paradigm," *History of Political Thought,* 11 (1990): 273–294;

William T. Laprade, *Public Opinion and Politics in Eighteenth Century England, to the Fall of Walpole* (New York: Macmillan, 1936);

J. G. A. Pocock, "Machiavelli, Harrington, and English Political Ideologies in the Eighteenth Century," *William and Mary Quarterly,* 22 (1965): 549–583;

Charles B. Realey, "*The London Journal* and its Authors, 1720–1723," *Bulletin of the University of Kansas,* 36, no. 23 (1935): 1–34;

Caroline Robbins, *The Eighteenth-Century Commonwealthman: Studies in the Transmission, Development and Circumstance of English Liberal Thought from the Restoration of Charles II until the War with the Thirteen Colonies* (Cambridge, Mass.: Harvard University Press, 1959);

Clinton Rossiter, *The Seedtime of the Republic: The Origin of the American Tradition of Political Liberty* (New York: Harcourt, Brace, 1953);

Lois G. Schwoerer, *"No Standing Armies!" The Antiarmy Ideology in Seventeenth-Century England* (Baltimore: Johns Hopkins University Press, 1974).

Thomas Warton the Younger

(9 January 1728 – 21 May 1790)

Shannon Schedlich-Day
Flinders University of South Australia

See also the Warton entries in *DLB 104: British Prose Writers, 1660–1800, Second Series* and *DLB 109: Eighteenth-Century British Poets, Second Series.*

BOOKS: *Five Pastoral Eclogues: The Scenes of Which Are Suppos'd to Lie among the Shepherds Oppress'd by the War in Germany* (London: Printed for R. Dodsley, 1745);

The Pleasures of Melancholy. A Poem (London: Printed for R. Dodsley, 1747);

Verses on Miss C----s and Miss W----t (London: Printed for W. Owen, 1749);

The Triumph of Isis, a Poem. Occasioned by Isis, an Elegy (London: Printed for W. Owen, 1750);

A Description of the City, College, and Cathedral of Winchester (London: Printed for R. Baldwin, 1750; revised, 1760); third edition published as *The Winchester Guide* (Winton, U.K.: Printed and sold for T. Blagden, 1796);

New-Market, A Satire (London: Printed for J. Newbery, 1751);

Ode for Music, as Performed at the Theatre in Oxford, on the Second of July 1751 (Oxford: Printed for R. Clements & J. Barrett / Cambridge: W. Thurlbourne; London: R. Dodsley, 1751);

Observations on the Faerie Queene of Spenser (London: R. & J. Dodsley, 1754; 2 volumes, second edition corrected and enlarged, 1762; New York: Haskell House, 1969);

A Companion to the Guide and Guide to the Companion: Being a Complete Supplement to All the Accounts of Oxford Hitherto Published (London: Printed for H. Payne, 1760; second edition, corrected and enlarged, 1762?)

Mons Catharina; prope Wintoniam. Poema (London: R. & J. Dodsley, 1760);

The Life and Literary Remains of Ralph Bathurst, 2 volumes (London: Printed for R. & J. Dodsley and C. Bathurst; and J. Fletcher, Oxford, 1761);

The Life of Sir Thomas Pope, Founder of Trinity College Oxford (London: Printed for T. Davies, T. Becket, T.

Thomas Warton the Younger (portrait by Charles Howard Hodges, after Sir Joshua Reynolds, 1784; National Portrait Gallery, London)

Walters, R. Newbery; and J. Fletcher, Oxford, 1772; revised edition, London: Printed for Thomas Cadell, 1780);

The History and Antiquities of Winchester, 2 volumes (Winton, U.K.: Printed by J. Wilkes, 1773);

The History of English Poetry, from the Close of the Eleventh to the Commencement of the Eighteenth Century, 3 volumes (London: Printed for and sold by J. Dodsley, J. Walter, T. Becket, J. Robson, G. Robinson, J. Bew, and Messrs. Fletcher, Oxford, 1774–1781); 88 pages of volume 4 (N.p., [1789?]);

Poems. A New Edition (London: Printed for T. Becket, 1777; third edition, corrected, 1779; fourth edition, corrected and enlarged, London: Printed for G. G. J. & J. Robinson, 1789);

An Enquiry into the Authenticity of the Poems Attributed to Thomas Rowley (London: Printed for J. Dodsley, Oxford, 1782);

Specimen of a Parochial History of Oxfordshire. Kiddington ([1782?]); corrected and enlarged as *Specimen of a History of Oxfordshire* (London: Printed for J. Nichols, J. Robson, and C. Dilly; Messrs. Fletcher, D. Prince & J. Cook, Oxford; J. Merrill, Cambridge, 1783); third edition, *The History and Antiquities of Kiddington* (London: J. Nichols & Bentley, 1815);

Verses on Sir Joshua Reynold's Painted Window at New-College Oxford (London: Printed for J. Dodsley and sold by Messrs. Fletcher, Oxford, 1782);

A History of English Poetry: An Unpublished Continuation, edited by Rodney M. Baine, Augustan Reprint Society Publication no. 39 (Los Angeles: William Andrews Clark Memorial Library, 1953).

Collections: *The Poems on Various Subjects, of Thomas Warton . . . Now First Collected* (London: Printed for G. G. J. & J. Robinson, 1791);

The Poetical Works of the Late Thomas Warton, B.D., 2 volumes, edited by Richard Mant (Oxford: Oxford University Press, for W. Hanwell and J. Parker, 1802).

OTHER: *The Union; or Select Scots and English Poems,* edited by Warton (Edinburgh [i.e., Oxford]: Printed for Archibald Monro and David Murray [i.e., Printed by William Jackson], 1753);

Inscriptionum Romanarum Metricarum Delectus, edited by Warton (London: Apud R. & J. Dodsley, 1758);

The Oxford Sausage; or, Selected Poetical Pieces Written by the Most Celebrated Wits of the University of Oxford, edited by Warton (London: Printed for J. Fletcher, 1764);

Anthologiae Graecae à Constantino Cephala condita libri tres, edited by Warton (Oxford: E typographeo Clarendoniano, prostant venales apud Jacobum Fletcher; J. Nourse, P. Vaillant, and J. Fletcher, London, 1766);

Theocriti Syracusii Quae Supersant, 2 volumes, edited by Warton (Oxford: E typographeo Clarendoniano, 1770);

Poems upon Several Occasions, English, Italian, and Latin, with Translations, by John Milton, edited by Warton (London: Printed for J. Dodsley, 1785; revised edition, London: Printed for G. G. J. & J. Robinson, 1791).

SELECTED PERIODICAL PUBLICATIONS– UNCOLLECTED: Essays 51 and 57, *Adventurer* (1753)–probably cowritten with Joseph Warton;

Essay 33, "Journal of a Senior Fellow," *Idler* (2 December 1758);

Essay 93, "Sam Softly," *Idler* (26 January 1760);

Essay 96, "Hacho, King of Lapland," *Idler* (16 February 1760).

Thomas Warton the Younger was an important intellectual of eighteenth-century Oxford University. Not only outstanding in the area of literary history and criticism, Warton had a successful career as a poet, an occupation that he shared with both his father, Thomas the Elder, and his brother, Joseph. Warton's *The History of English Poetry, from the Close of the Eleventh to the Commencement of the Eighteenth Century* (1774–1781) was the only cultural history completed by a university don in the eighteenth century. While it includes many errors, this work should not be overlooked. *The History of English Poetry* was the first systematic approach to the study of literary history in any depth. It paved the way for subsequent studies of English literary history, and in his research for the text Warton uncovered many manuscripts of early English literature that had faded into obscurity.

Warton was born on 9 January 1728 to Thomas and Elizabeth Warton of Basingstoke, Hampshire. His mother was the second daughter of Joseph Richardson, rector of Dunnsfold, Surrey. His father, Thomas the Elder, had been elected Professor of Poetry at Oxford in 1718 and reelected five years later. His position as professor ended in the same year as his younger son's birth, and the family were residing at the vicarage of Basingstoke. A brother, Joseph (born 1722), and a sister, Jane (born 1724), preceded Thomas.

The Warton family were close, and Thomas enjoyed a warm relationship with both his brother and his sister. He and his father also shared a firm friendship, although the younger Thomas always maintained respect for his father. The son Thomas showed a love of learning and reading and was known to withdraw from the family group so that he could read in peace. He also had a fondness for music from a young age.

Thomas's early education was supervised by his father. While Joseph studied at Winchester College, Thomas the Younger was being taught Latin, poetry, and the classics at home by his father. In March 1744 young Thomas transferred his studies to Trinity College, Oxford University. The cost of educating two sons put a strain on the family's finances, but the importance of a good education was paramount to the elder Thomas.

Not long after Thomas the Younger entered Trinity College, Thomas the Elder died. The family was left with little more than a few debts, but among his father's possessions Joseph found some unpublished poems by his father's hand. He set about getting them published and relied on his father's wide circle of friends to purchase copies, which they duly did. Joseph was then able to send some money to his younger brother, Thomas, at Trinity College.

Warton gained a bachelor of arts in 1747 and a master's degree in 1750. He was involved in the social life of Oxford and had a great affinity with the university. Oxford did not enjoy the academic standing in the eighteenth century that it had in the past (and that it has subsequently regained), but Warton stands out as one of the leaders of academic thought within the university in the eighteenth century. He became a probationary fellow in 1752 and a fellow of Trinity College in 1753. He remained a fellow and tutor at the college for the rest of his life.

By the time that Warton was made a fellow of Trinity College, he had started to establish a name for himself as a poet. His first collection, *Five Pastoral Eclogues: The Scenes of Which Are Suppos'd to Lie among the Shepherds Oppress'd by the War in Germany* appeared in 1745. In 1750 he became the toast of Oxford with *The Triumph of Isis*, which defended the repuation of Oxford as a center of learning. The 1748 poem *Isis, an Elegy*, by William Mason, had criticized Oxford for no longer holding up the high standards that it had in the past. Warton's response was much appreciated throughout the university.

In 1754 Warton published *Observations on the Faerie Queene of Spenser*. This work is significant in the development of Warton into a British literary historian. Warton did not follow the previously accepted methods of historical criticism but, rather, created his own. He recognized that historical method was needed to study and critically analyze poetry of ages gone by. Not only did Warton look at Edmund Spenser's *Faerie Queene*, but he also included digressions that placed the work into its historical context and gave an overview of the history of English poetry. Although the work did receive some criticism, it was, on the whole, well received. A second edition of *Observations on the Faerie Queene of Spenser* was released in 1762. The work retained the majority of the history included in the original, with some alterations. Warton also expanded on the sketch of the history of English poetry to include later history. Literary historian Richard Hurd wrote to Warton on 10 October 1762 that *Observations on the Faerie Queene of Spenser* had the "noble design of giving a history, in form, of English poetry."

After the publication of the original work on Spenser, Samuel Johnson went to Oxford and was entertained by Warton. The two remained friends throughout their lives, although there were periods when they were not so close. Johnson encouraged Warton to write the edition Warton was planning on Spenser's other works, but to no avail. Other interests and tutorial work got in the way of this project's ever being completed.

By the mid 1750s, thanks to the success of *Observations on the Faerie Queene of Spenser*, Warton had established himself as a literary historian. Sometime around Johnson's initial visit to see Warton at Oxford in 1754, Warton began considering the possibility of writing a full history of English poetry. This project was delayed for years, though, because of Warton's other commitments for his time.

One such commitment was his role within the clergy. He received his first placement within the clergy in 1755 when he was placed at the curacy of Woodstock, a position that he held until 1774. At other times he received the preferment of Shalfield, Wiltshire (1768), a living at Kiddington Park (1771), and the donative of Hill Farrance in Somersetshire (1782). Both the vicarage of Shalfield and Hill Farrance were gifts of Trinity College. As Warton got older, he became less and less interested in his duties within his role in the clergy.

Following in his father's footsteps, Warton was elected Professor of Poetry at Oxford. His tenure as professor began in 1756, and he was in the position for ten years. He used the opportunity of his lectures (which were delivered in Latin) to encourage classical poetry. At the end of his tenure as Professor of Poetry, Warton was interested in a position of professorship in modern history, but the position was ultimately given to Thomas Nowell, who held the position until his death in 1801.

Much has been made of Warton's apparent lack of direct relation between his teaching and research. Such claims, however, do not agree with the prodigious output of Warton's work. A look at his bibliography shows a wide variety of works on a broad range of subjects. What many have taken as laziness was actually a patient, methodical approach to his work and duties. While he did discourage student attendance to lectures, he would set aside his own work when students needed his assistance.

Throughout his life, Warton was known for his boyish nature and mischievous sense of fun. He was a regular visitor to his brother's home and spent time with his brother's students at Winchester, often playing pranks. He was known, at times, to write essays for the students, complete with typical schoolboy errors. He enjoyed smoking and drinking ale. He presented a slovenly figure and did not care about his appearance. Frances Burney wrote in 1778 that Warton was "the greatest clod I ever saw, and so vulgar a figure with his clunch wig that I took him for a shoemaker at first." Warton's lack of pride in his appearance and his roguish behavior added to the notion that he did not take his job seriously when, in fact, the opposite was true.

In 1764 Warton edited *The Oxford Sausage*, a lighthearted collection of verse. *The Oxford Sausage* included much of Warton's own verse, as well as that of many of Warton's contemporaries. Although Warton was serious about his work, he was still able to poke fun at himself.

THE

HISTORY

OF

ENGLISH POETRY,

FROM THE

CLOSE of the ELEVENTH

TO THE

COMMENCEMENT of the EIGHTEENTH CENTURY.

TO WHICH ARE PREFIXED,

TWO DISSERTATIONS.

I. ON THE ORIGIN of ROMANTIC FICTION IN EUROPE.
II. ON THE INTRODUCTION OF LEARNING INTO ENGLAND.

VOLUME THE FIRST.

By THOMAS WARTON, B.D.
FELLOW OF TRINITY COLLEGE OXFORD, and of the SOCIETY OF ANTIQUARIES.

LONDON:

Printed for, and sold by J. DODSLEY, Pall Mall; J. WALTER, Charing Cross; T. BECKET,
Strand; J. ROBSON, New Bond-Street; G. ROBINSON, and J. BEW, Pater-noster-Row;
and Messrs. FLETCHER, at Oxford.   M.DCC.LXXIV.

*Title page for the only history of English poetry written in the eighteenth
century (from Eighteenth-Century Collections Online, Gale Group)*

From early in his academic career, Warton had a vast knowledge of Old English literature. When Thomas Percy sought to publish a collection of old ballads, he requested Warton's assistance in finding old manuscripts. Percy also relied on Warton's vast knowledge of old literature to provide him with leads. Not only did Warton find many manuscripts, but he also compared manuscripts from different sources to try to find the most authentic versions of the ballads. Percy's collection was published in 1765.

The 1772 study of Trinity College's founder, *The Life of Sir Thomas Pope, Founder of Trinity College Oxford,* had begun with a much shorter piece in *Biographia Brittanica* in 1760. Warton expanded on this original piece to write a more thorough history of the founder of the college. This work, which was republished with additions in 1780, used fabricated sources as documents. Some people have suggested that Warton himself was responsible for the forgeries, but the evidence does not support this conclusion. Rather, it seems to have been either the fault of a research assistant or an honest mistake.

The reputation that Warton had begun as a literary historian with *Observations on the Faerie Queene of*

Spenser in the 1750s was solidified with the publication in 1774 of the first volume of *The History of English Poetry, from the Close of the Eleventh to the Commencement of the Eighteenth Century.* Previously, Thomas Gray had attempted a similar project, working mainly between 1657 and 1754, but Gray had given up by the time that Warton came to write his *History of English Poetry.* As early as 1765 Warton had written, "My materials are almost ready." Not, however, until July 1769 did Warton find the time to sit down and work on the history. Gray sent Warton a copy of his plan for the history that he had been working on, but Warton did not use it much.

Warton was hoping to achieve what had not been attempted before–a thorough history of poetry. His aim was to show the improvement of poetry over time along with the progression of the language. He wrote in the preface, "The object being to faithfully record the features of the time, and preserve the picturesque representation of manners. . . . I have chose to note but the history of our poetry in a chronological sense." In this endeavor, Warton was not entirely successful, but the work–for all of its deviations, errors, and omissions–became a significant part of eighteenth-century English cultural history.

Like the first volume, the subsequent volumes of the work were delayed for many reasons. Volume two was published in 1778, while volume three was not published until 1781. Volume four was not completed before Warton's death in 1790. While Warton was trying to write a history of English poetry, the completed work was first and foremost an anthology and bibliography, and secondarily a history. The work included extremely long quotes–sometimes running to three hundred lines. It also included the most thorough analysis of Geoffrey Chaucer's work that had been done up to that date. Moreover, it included a discussion of the Thomas Rowley/Thomas Chatterton poems, which were popularly believed to be genuine fifteenth-century poems. Warton found that they were not authentic fifteenth-century poems, but he felt that because of the interest surrounding them, he had to include reference to them in his work. He concluded that they were forgeries and included his findings in his history. *The History of English Poetry* did not include much on Middle English, and Warton ignored the Anglo-Saxon period. The Elizabethans were presented as the focal point in English literary history, and Warton showed respect for classicism and an interest in primitivism. He unearthed the medieval and Renaissance roots in English literature.

In 1782 Joseph Ritson, an antiquarian, published anonymously *Observations on the Three First Volumes of the History of English Poetry. In a Familiar Letter to the Author.* In this work Ritson pointed out 116 mistakes that Warton had made in *The History of English Poetry*. Despite mistakes and omissions, though, Warton's work was a success. Although his work was broad and, some suggested, more antiquarianism than history, and although Warton did not fully explore the social influences of the literature that he was writing about, it was the first time that such a history had been attempted. Many readers found it unpalatable, with Horace Walpole writing after reading volume two: "antiquary as I am, it is a tough achievement. He has dipped into an ocean of dry and obsolete authors of the dark ages, and has brought up more rubbish than riches."

Warton's work was the first reference for centuries to some early manuscripts that might have been lost if it were not for his research. Although not a perfect history, it created a much greater understanding of medieval and Renaissance poetry than ever before. The work was wide-ranging and became a sourcebook for subsequent poets.

Drawing on his popularity after the publication of the first volume of *The History of English Poetry*, Warton wrote *Poems. A New Edition*, published in 1777. Another edition of the work, which included *The Triumph of Isis*, was published in 1779. Both editions were successful.

After the publication of volume three of *The History of English Poetry*, Warton was elected to the most influential literary society of the second half of the eighteenth century. Established in 1764 at the suggestion of Sir Joshua Reynolds, the group (which included Samuel Johnson) met at the Turk's Head in Soho. Originally begun as an informal meeting of intimates, the Club grew and became known as The Literary Club.

In 1782 Warton waded deeper into the Rowley/Chatterton controversy when he printed *An Enquiry into the Authenticity of the Poems Attributed to Thomas Rowley*. Over the course of 125 pages, Warton systematically listed the obvious signs that these poems were fakes. This approach convinced many scholars that the poems were not genuine fifteenth-century poems, but some still disagreed. The controversy was not totally ended until the second half of the nineteenth century, with W. W. Skeat's 1871 work on the subject.

In 1785 George III appointed Warton poet laureate. Whether the appointment was made as a result of the King's wishes or because of the suggestion of Sir Joshua Reynolds is unclear. Either way, it was not an appointment that Warton sought, and he was often ridiculed after the appointment for not being able to produce high-quality poems on royal subjects. Warton did publish another edition of his poems in 1789, which included the laureate odes; it was subsequently reprinted in 1791.

In the same year as his appointment as poet laureate, Warton was also appointed Camden Professor of Ancient History at Oxford in recognition of his contribution to the university. Warton was not particularly interested in the position, and he does not appear to have given any lectures after his inaugural one.

Until 1788 Warton had enjoyed good health. In 1788, however, he contracted gout. He spent some time in Bath recovering after his illness, and he seemed to be regaining his health. In 1790, however, he suffered from two strokes, the second of which proved fatal. He died on 21 May and was buried in the antechapel of Trinity College with highest academic honors, a fitting tribute considering that he had spent the greatest part of his life at Trinity. At the time of his death, Warton apparently had ready for publication a history of Saxon and Gothic architecture. Despite extensive searching, no one ever found it. Eighty-eight pages of volume four of *The History of English Poetry* were also ready for publication, and publishers clamored to be the ones who got to publish the work. Many people thought that Warton's brother, Joseph, might take on the responsibility of completing the final volume, but Thomas's notes were far too brief for Joseph to finish it.

Even though Thomas Warton's *The History of English Poetry* had many errors and omissions, its significance as a work of history was not diminished. *The History of English Poetry* introduced the concept of literary history, and all subsequent histories of English literature have built upon the base Warton established. His work was imperfect, but it was far beyond what anybody else had been able to achieve until that point. As René Wellek pointed out in his 1929 study, Warton's *History of English Poetry* determined the future of English literary history. Warton's work as a tutor, poet, critic, and historian shows the wide range of his talents. For all of its deficiencies, *The History of English Poetry* was a significant and influential work of cultural history and shaped all literary history that succeeded it.

Letters:

Clarissa Rinaker, "Twenty-Six Unedited Letters from Thomas Warton to Jonathon Toup, John Price, George Stevens, Isaac Reed, William Mavor, and Edmond Malone," *Journal of English and Germanic Philology*, 14 (1915): 96–118;

"Correspondence of Thomas Warton," *Bodleian Quarterly Record*, 6 (1931): 303–307;

The Correspondence of Thomas Percy and Thomas Warton, edited by M. G. Robinson and Leah Dennis (Baton Rouge: Louisiana State University Press, 1951);

David Fairer, "The Correspondence of Thomas Warton," doctoral thesis, Oxford University, 1975;

The Correspondence of Thomas Warton, edited by David Fairer (Athens: University of Georgia Press, 1995).

Bibliographies:

Clarissa Rinaker, *Thomas Warton: A Biographical and Critical Study* (Urbana: University of Illinois Press, 1916), pp. 233–238;

John A. Vance, *Joseph and Thomas Warton: An Annotated Bibliography* (New York: Garland, 1983).

Biographies:

Richard Mant, "Memoir of Warton," in *The Poetical Works of the Late Thomas Warton, B.D.,* 2 volumes (Oxford: Oxford University Press, 1802);

Alexander Chalmers, "Thomas Warton," in *The Works of the English Poets,* volume 18 (London: Johnson, 1810), pp. 145–153;

Clarissa Rinaker, *Thomas Warton: A Biographical and Critical Study* (Urbana: University of Illinois Press, 1916).

References:

John Brewer, *The Pleasures of the Imagination: English Culture in the Eighteenth Century* (London: HarperCollins, 1997);

W. P. Ker, "Warton Lecture on English Poetry; 1. Thomas Warton," *Proceedings of the British Academy* (London: Published for the British Academy by Henry Frowde, Oxford University Press, [1910?]);

Gwin J. Kolb and Robert DeMaria Jr., "Thomas Warton's 'Observations on the "Faerie Queene" of Spenser,' Samuel Johnson's 'History of the English Language,' and Warton's 'History of English Poetry': Reciprocal Indebtedness?" *Philological Quarterly,* 74 (Summer 1995): 327–336;

Eric Partridge, ed., *The Three Wartons: A Choice of Their Verse* (London: Scholartis Press, 1927);

David Nichol Smith, "Warton's History of English Poetry," *Proceedings of the British Academy,* 15 (1929): 73–99;

John A. Vance, *Joseph and Thomas Warton* (Boston: Twayne, 1983);

René Wellek, *The Rise of English Literary History* (Chapel Hill: University of North Carolina Press, 1941), pp. 166–201.

Papers:

The largest collections of Thomas Warton the Younger's papers are held in the British Library and in the Bodleian Library at Oxford University.

Browne Willis

(14 September 1682 – 5 February 1760)

Jean Culp Flanigan
East Tennessee State University

BOOKS: *Queries Addressed by B.W. to Persons in the Different Parishes of Buckinghamshire to Elicit Information for a History of the County* (London? 1712);

The Case of the Borough of Buckingham (On the Qualifications of Certain Burgesses to Exercise the Franchise) (London, 1713);

Notitia Parliamentaria; or, An History of the Counties, Cities, and Boroughs in England and Wales, 2 volumes (London: Printed for Robert Gosling, 1715, 1716; second edition, enlarged, 3 volumes, 1730);

A Survey of the Cathedral-Church of St. David's, and the Edifices Belonging to It, as They Stood in the Year 1715, collected by Willis (London: Printed for Robert Gosling, 1717);

A History of the Mitred Parliamentary Abbeys and Conventual Cathedral Churches, 2 volumes (London: Printed by W. Bowyer for Robert Gosling, 1718, 1719);

A Survey of the Cathedral-Church of Landaff (London: Printed for Robert Gosling, 1719);

A Survey of the Cathedral-Church of St. Asaph (London: Printed for Robert Gosling, 1720);

A Survey of the Cathedral Church of Bangor; and the Edifices Belonging to It (London: Printed for Robert Gosling, 1721);

The Whole Duty of Receiving Worthily the Blessed Sacrament (London: Printed by and for T. Norris, 1723);

A Survey of the Cathedrals of York, Durham, Carlisle, Chester, Man, Lichfield, Hereford, Worcester, Gloucester, and Bristol, 3 volumes (London: Printed for Robert Gosling, 1727);

A Survey of the Cathedrals of Lincoln, Ely, Oxford, and Peterborough (London: Printed for Robert Gosling, 1730);

Parochiale Anglicanum; or, The Names of all the Churches and Chapels within the Dioceses of Canterbury, Rochester, London, Winchester, Chichester, Norwich, Salisbury, Wells, Exeter, St. David's, Landaff, Bangor, and St. Asaph (London: Printed for Robert Gosling, 1733);

Browne Willis (*from <http://clutch.open.ac.uk/schools/eaton-fenny00/ st_martins.htm>*)

A Table of the Gold Coins of the Kings of England: by B.W. Esq; a Member of the Society of Antiquaries, London 1733 (London, 1733);

A Modest and Serious Defence of the Author of the Whole Duty of Man, from the False Charges and Gross Misrepresentations of Mr. Whitefield, and the Methodists His Adherents, as by a presbyter of the Church of England (London: Printed for J. Roberts, 1740);

Notitia Monastica; or, An Account of All the Abbies, Priories and Houses of Friers, Heretofore in England and Wales; and Also of All the Colleges and Hospitals Founded Before

A.D. MDXL, by Willis, John Tanner, and Thomas Tanner (London: Printed by William Bowyer, 1744);

To the Patrons of Ecclesiastical Livings (London? 1753?);

The History and Antiquities of the Town, Hundred, and Deanry of Buckingham (London: Printed for the author, 1755).

OTHER: Richard Allestree, *The Whole Duty of Man: Necessary for All Families with Private Devotions for Severall Occasions;* abridged by Willis as *The Whole Duty of Man, Abridged for the Benefit of the Poorer Sort,* anonymous (London: Robert Gosling, 1717);

John Stow, *Survey of London,* edited by John Strype with the assistance of Willis (London, 1720);

John Ecton, *Thesaurus Rerum Ecclesiasticarum,* revised by Willis (London: Printed for J. & P. Knapton and others, 1754).

Antiquary, ecclesiastical historian, parliamentary historian, church builder and restorer, intrepid traveler, coin collector, philanthropist, Member of Parliament, squire of Whaddon, and eccentric—Browne Willis was known in all of these roles in eighteenth-century England. He was also known, both affectionately and derisively, as "Old Wrinkle-Boots" and "Old Chariot." But he was not always known by such names.

The portrait of the young Willis that serves as the frontispiece for J. G. Jenkins's biography of him, *The Dragon of Whaddon,* was painted by Michael Dahl, a fashionable London portraitist in the reign of Queen Anne. An etching of the original painting was commissioned by Willis's good friend and protégé, William Cole, more than twenty years after Willis's death. The portrait shows a distinguished, bewigged young gentleman of about twenty-five. It was probably painted about the time of Willis's marriage. Sending a copy of the etching to their mutual friend Andrew C. Ducarel, Cole writes in a letter dated 22 December 1781:

You will probably object that it is not like Mr. Willis: agreed, and God forbid it should! But no doubt it was like him in his best days, in Queen Anne's time, when Dahl drew him; and no one that reveres Mr. Willis would wish to have a caricature of him, such as he made of himself, when you and I were acquainted with him.

The caricature he made of himself may have resulted partly because of poverty, for he spent his fortune on church building, antiquarian research, publishing his works, coin collecting, and philanthropy. But it probably indicated his preoccupation with those interests to the exclusion of all other matters. Catherine Talbot, granddaughter of the bishop of Salisbury and a London acquaintance of the family, wrote to a friend on 2 January 1739 that while Willis had "one of the honestest hearts in the world, he has one of the oddest heads that ever dropt from the moon." She goes on to say,

I have told you before that he is the dirtiest creature in the world; so much so that it is quite disagreeable to sit by him at table; yet he makes one suit of clothes serve him at least two years; and then his great-coat has been transmitted down, I believe, from generation to generation, ever since Noah.

Cole described him as having "the appearance more of a mumping beggar than of a gentleman." He detailed Willis's strange garb:

He then, as always, was dressed in an old slouched hat, more brown than black, a weather-beaten large wig, three or four old-fashioned coats, all tied round by leathern belt, and over all an old blue cloak, lined with black fustian, which he told me he had new made when he was elected member for the town of Buckingham, about 1707. I have still by me, as relicks, this cloak and belt, which I purchased of his servant.

This genuine eccentric and dedicated antiquary was born 14 September 1682 at Blandford St. Mary, Dorsetshire, the home of his mother's family. His father, Thomas Willis, was from Bletchley, Buckinghamshire, and Willis spent most of his life in that county.

His earliest education was in Beachampton, Buckinghamshire, at the school of the Reverend Abraham Freestone. In about 1695 Willis was sent to the prestigious Westminster School on the grounds of Westminster Abbey. Perhaps it was there that Willis became infatuated with antiquities, Gothic architecture, and church history. According to Jenkins, evidence in Willis's manuscripts reveals that as a pupil at Westminster, he helped fight the fire that destroyed most of Whitehall Palace in 1697.

Thomas Willis died in 1699 at the age of forty-one, and his wife, Alice, a few months later in January 1700 at the young age of thirty-six. Following his mother's death, young Willis left Westminster School, and in March he entered Christ Church College, Oxford. Later that year he was admitted to the Inner Temple as a student of law. His tutor at Oxford was mathematician and geographer Edward Wells, who later became rector of Bletchley. While at Oxford, Willis showed a deep interest in the preservation of the manuscripts of John Leland's *Itinerary* (published by Thomas Hearne in 1710). Remarkably, Willis was able to persuade the officials of the Bodleian Library to permit him to take the manuscripts to his rooms at Christ

Church in order to work on his transcriptions. According to his own note prefacing the transcript of the first three and a half volumes, he achieved the task in nine consecutive days, omitting one Sunday. The transcriptions are among Willis's own manuscripts in the Bodleian.

In 1704 Willis left Oxford without taking a degree. His early departure from the university he obviously loved may have resulted from ill health. His younger brother, John, wrote that the death of their parents so afflicted Browne that he thereafter suffered from "the falling sickness," or epilepsy, and throughout his life, people referred to his having "spells."

For the next three years Willis lived and studied with theological scholar William Wotton, rector of Milton Keynes. Wotton was the author of *Reflections upon Ancient and Modern Learning* (1694), and his position in favor of the "moderns" was satirized by Jonathan Swift in "The Battle of the Books." Wotton had lived in Wales and studied the language, and it was undoubtedly from him that Willis became interested in the history of the Welsh cathedrals.

In 1705 Willis stood as the Tory candidate for Buckingham in a hotly contested parliamentary election. The right of election was vested in the twelve burgesses and the bailiff. The vote was tied six to six, and when the thirteenth elector was sought, he was found to be in prison. He was brought out to the marketplace, where he declared his vote for Willis. The Parliament of 1705–1708 was a significant one, financing the campaigns of John Churchill, first Duke of Marlborough (general against the French at the Battle of Blenheim), and enacting the Union of England and Scotland. Willis was regular in attendance and served on committees, but he apparently made no speeches. He politely declined the offer of reelection.

Upon his father's death, Willis had become the owner of a significant estate, including not only his father's share of Whaddon Hall, Water Hall, and other Buckinghamshire properties but also an estate in Herefordshire. When he came of age, he began taking a serious interest in using his inheritance. He began in 1702 by reviving the market of the town of Fenny Stratford, and the following year he repaired the damaged chancel at Little Brickhill. Between 1704 and 1709 he spent more than £800—a small fortune in those days—toward the repair and improvement of St. Mary's Church at Bletchley as a memorial to his parents, who were buried there. In 1712 he had a peal of eight bells made for St. Mary's at the Rudhall foundry in Gloucester.

His interest in churches was not just architectural and antiquarian. Willis was a staunch believer in the High Anglican tradition. In 1711 he had a dissenters' chapel in Fenny Stratford pulled down to prevent congregations from meeting there. He transported the materials to nearby Whaddon, where he used them to build the new servants' hall, having purchased the entire property in 1710 and undertaken its renovation.

In 1707 Willis married Catherine Eliot of Cornwall. As her father's only child and heir, her considerable marriage portion was between £6,000 and £8,000. Although even noblewomen of the period received little formal education, Catherine was sufficiently educated and independent minded to write two theological pamphlets, which her husband scorned. According to Cole, Willis made a marginal note in his copy of his wife's book, saying, "All the connexion in this book is owing to the book-binder." But George Ballard, a noted Oxford scholar, judged differently, writing to the Reverend Francis Wise on 18 April 1743 his opinion of her as "a gentlewoman of excellent sense, sound judgment, and well versed in theological studies."

The Willises had ten children, eight of whom survived their mother, who died 2 October 1724 and was buried in the north chapel of Bletchley church. Only the eldest, twin daughters Gertrude and Catherine, outlived their father. In his wife's epitaph, Willis notes, "Both she and her husband were descended from the antient lords of this and the adjoining parish of Whaddon." This reference is indicative of one of Willis's concerns of antiquarian research—personal genealogy.

Having a distinguished pedigree was of great importance to Willis. A visitor to Whaddon Hall described it as containing "the most copious registers of marriages, births and burials, that is to be found in the world." Willis traced his lineage and that of his wife to "'Walter Giffard Earl of Buckingham under the reign of William the Conqueror, who died seised of Whaddon and Blechley parishes AO.1104." This genealogy established an ancient hereditary link between Willis and his estates in Buckinghamshire. It indicated he was not a Johnny-come-lately to the squirearchy, and it may have been authentic, since Willis had the lengthy pedigree approved by John Anstis, Garter King at Arms.

April 1712 marked Willis's first official publication, *Queries Addressed by B.W. to Persons in the Different Parishes of Buckinghamshire to Elicit Information for a History of the County,* closely followed by *The Case of the Borough of Buckingham* (1713). According to S. Austin Allibone in *A Critical Dictionary of English Literature* (1871), these questionnaires were for the purpose of obtaining information for *Notitia Parliamentaria; or, An History of the Counties, Cities, and Boroughs in England and Wales,* first published in 1715, but they were more likely the early efforts to gather data for his planned history of the County of Buckingham, which was never fully realized. A nonantiquarian work, *The Whole Duty of Man, Abridged*

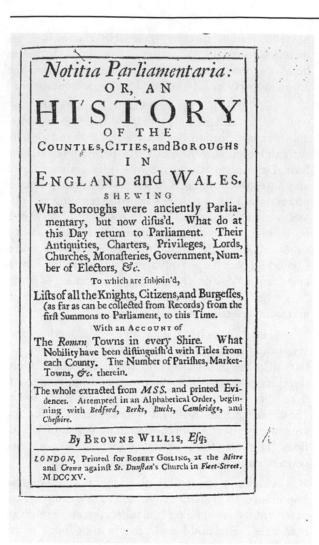

Title page for Willis's 1715 two-volume history based on questionnaires (Eighteenth-Century Collections Online, Gale Group)

Cathedrals of York, Durham, Carlisle, Chester, Man, Lichfield, Hereford, Worcester, Gloucester, and Bristol in 1727, followed by a third volume covering the cathedrals of Lincoln, Ely, Oxford, and Peterborough in 1730. His "Old Chariot" must have accumulated a great many hard miles during those years, because Willis made what he called "pilgrimages" to every cathedral in England and Wales, except for Carlisle, during a period when travel in Great Britain was extremely difficult, as the roads had not been routinely maintained since Roman times.

In spite of Willis's firsthand visits and research based on original documents, his works are criticized for being full of errors and careless in detail. The errors may have resulted in part from the sense of haste that seemed to motivate him to produce a large volume of work in a relatively short time. But many of the errors were undoubtedly attributable to his unreliable amanuensis, William Sliford. (Willis spells it "Slyford.") Often drunk, Sliford was nonetheless indispensable to Willis for transcribing the original records. Willis routinely fired Sliford but just as regularly rehired him. Cole cites a typical example of Sliford's failings: an inscription correctly copied by Willis read "Pray for the soul of Will: Thomas of the Overweld and Jane his wife, the which decessid the Xth day of Iuly in the yere of our Redeemer 1496, on whose soul Iesu have mercy." Sliford's version of the same inscription read "Pray for the sowls of William of Okynfield and Ione his wife which William decessid the X day of Iuly in the yere of God MCCCCLXXXXVI."

In spite of these shortcomings, Willis's cathedral surveys were valuable additions to scholarship because of his interest in medieval architecture at a time when classical architecture was the vogue and because of his concern for the preservation of the ancient buildings, which were often sadly in need of repair. His written accounts were accompanied by plans and copperplate engravings by John Harris, an architectural and topographical artist, who often provided the first accurate drawings of the buildings.

Willis became the victim of a bookseller's misrepresentation in 1742. The three volumes of his 1727–1730 survey of fourteen cathedrals had been published by Robert Gosling. When Gosling closed his business, he sold the unbound remainders to Thomas Osborne, who issued them with a new title page claiming that Willis had expanded the survey to all twenty-six cathedrals. The author took out an advertisement in the *London Evening Post* for 5–8 March to correct the error.

In 1733 Willis did address some of the cathedrals not included in his earlier surveys in *Parochiale Anglicanum: or, The Names of all the Churches and Chapels within the Dioceses of Canterbury, Rochester, London, Winchester, Chichester, Norwich, Salisbury, Wells, Exeter, St. David's, Lan-*

for the Benefit of the Poorer Sort, appeared anonymously in 1717.

That same year he began his series of histories of the Welsh cathedrals with *A Survey of the Cathedral-Church of St. David's* (1717), followed in quick succession by *A Survey of the Cathedral-Church of Landaff* (1719), *A Survey of the Cathedral-Church of St. Asaph* (1720), and *A Survey of the Cathedral Church of Bangor* (1721). The first two were probably written at least partially by Wotton and may have been undertaken by Willis to complete or expand his mentor's unfinished work. Also in 1720 Oxford University honored Willis with an M.A. by diploma.

Having found his calling, he continued with his cathedral histories, publishing the two volumes of *A History of the Mitred Parliamentary Abbeys and Conventual Cathedral Churches* in 1718 and 1719. It took him eight more years to complete two volumes of *A Survey of the daff, Bangor, and St. Asaph.* The same year he turned his attention to another of his passions in his *Table of the Gold Coins of the Kings of England.* For several years thereafter he occupied himself with interests other than writing, until the undated *To the Patrons of Ecclesiastical Livings,* which appeared sometime before 1753. It was shortly followed in 1754 by his revision of John Ecton's *Thesaurus Rerum Ecclesiasticarum,* a list of the ecclesiastical benefices, patrons, and values of the holdings in all the dioceses of England.

From 1712 Willis had tried to collect material to write a history of the entire county of Buckinghamshire, but he apparently received sufficient responses for only one of the eight hundreds (divisions) within the county. This material was finally published in 1755 as *The History and Antiquities of the Town, Hundred, and Deanry of Buckingham.* Its poor reception prompted the author to write to Ducarel on 21 August 1755: "I ought to have done with Antiquity, as I am like to be such a loser by my present undertaking, having only sold two books since my return from London the 6th of this instant; and one of my best and oldest friends excusing his buying the book, when I carried it him six miles off." He ultimately sold sixty-nine copies of the work. On 20 December 1756, suffering from rheumatism and gout, he wrote to Ducarel, "I have worked for nothing; nay, except in one book, have been out of pocket, and at great expence in what I printed." The one book that brought him profit was *Notitia Parliamentaria,* from which he claims to have made £15.

The popular failure of Willis's books did not result from their subject matter, inaccuracies of content, or lack of substance, but from his poor narrative style. Fellow antiquary Thomas Hearne wrote in his diary: "Mr. W. is a poor writer of history and antiquities, unless he gets somebody to do it for him, at least to cook and adjust his papers." Willis may have been painfully aware of his lack of talent, and that may have been the motivation behind his appointment of Cole as rector of Bletchley. Shortly before his death, Willis persuaded Cole to accept five quarto volumes of research notes for the histories of the Newport and Cottesloe hundreds of Buckinghamshire. Cole completed the work of transcribing and methodizing the material before turning over Willis's manuscripts to Oxford University in keeping with Willis's will. He described his efforts as "downright and tedious work." In spite of Cole's labors, the completed histories were never published, although John Nichols was interested in the project. So Cole's manuscripts of Willis's research languish in the British Library as Willis's do in the Bodleian.

In addition to his genealogical pursuits, cathedral surveys, and investigations into the history of Buckinghamshire, Willis amassed an amazing collection of coins. His quest went so far as to have pitted the grounds of Whaddon in search of Roman coins and other relics. In 1849, however, a ploughman turned up a cache of four hundred British gold coins in Whaddon Chase; in 1857 some 140 Roman coins were discovered in the same vicinity; and in 1858 three gold guineas minted in the reign of Charles II were found buried in a brass box, also in Whaddon Chase. These treasure troves would have belonged to Willis as lord of the manor had they been discovered in his lifetime.

Nonetheless, his collection of coinage was extensive. He was one of the earliest systematic collectors of tokens or tradesmen's farthings—nongovernmental currency issued between 1649 and 1672 to meet the necessity of small change for local business. He began his serious collecting as a young man at Oxford, when he had a cabinet of twenty-eight tables made up to hold his growing collection. Because his children were no more interested in his coins than in any other of his antiquarian interests, he gave the entire collection and cabinet to Oxford University in 1742, where it may still be seen in the Ashmolean Museum. Although offered freely as a gift, the University paid him 150 guineas in compensation for the 167 gold coins in the collection, which still made it an incredible bargain at the rate of 4 guineas per ounce of gold. For the rest of his life, Willis visited the collection on St. Frideswide's Day (19 October). He continued to accumulate coins and to donate them to Oxford, a magnificent gift of more than 2,400 coins of all types. In 1749 Oxford honored his generosity to the university and his dedication to scholarship by awarding him the degree LL.D.

At the same time as he was compiling his cathedral surveys, Willis undertook his greatest charitable and church-building project, St. Martin's Church in the village of Fenny Stratford. Dedicating the structure to the memory of his grandfather, Thomas Willis, a physician, Willis tirelessly raised money, dictated architectural plans, and arranged for the annual commemoration on St. Martin's Day (11 November). To finance the annual celebrations, Willis gave two cottages, the rent from which would pay a preacher's fee and cover the following secular entertainments. To this day, these celebrations include the firing of a peculiar kind of fireworks, the Fenny Poppers. The poppers are brass vessels that look like beer steins. St. Martin's website describes them thus: "The poppers each weigh about 19 pounds (8.5 kilos). The bore, 6" by 1 3/4" will take up to 1/4 pound of gunpowder, which is plugged with well-rammed newspaper. They are fired three times on St. Martin's Day; 12 Noon, 2:00 pm and 4:00 pm precisely."

Willis's further church benevolences include the repair and restoration of Bow Brickhill Church in 1756 and a monument in Christ Church Cathedral, Oxford, to Thomas Iles, a canon of the cathedral for whom his grandfather Thomas Willis was a retainer while he was a student at the university. Browne Willis's philanthropic nature was described after his death by John Gibberd, curate of Whaddon:

> He appeared to me to have no greater regard to money than as it furnished him with an opportunity of doing good. He supported yearly three charity schools at Whaddon, Bletchley, and Fenny Stratford; and, besides what he constantly gave at Christmas, he was never backward in relieving his poor neighbours with both wine and money when they were sick, or in any kind of distress. He was a faithful friend where he professed it, and always ready to contribute what lay in his power to their advantage.

After a period of declining health, Willis died at Whaddon on 5 February 1760 in the presence of his friend and curate Gibberd, who described Willis's passing as "with great ease and without the usual agonies of death." On 11 February Willis was buried beneath the altar at St. Martin's, Fenny Stratford.

His good friend Ducarel immediately proposed writing an eulogy on his life and reading it before the Society of Antiquaries, which Willis had helped to reestablish in 1717. Having received the approbation of the members of the society, Ducarel gathered information about Willis from those who knew him best, composed and printed the eulogy, distributed copies to many of Willis's friends and family, and read the work to the society on 15 May 1760. He described Willis as "indefatigable in his researches" and praised him for being "the first who placed our ecclesiastical history and antiquities upon a firm basis, by grounding them upon records and registers." This distinction still merits appreciation of Browne Willis, antiquary.

Biography:

J. G. Jenkins, *The Dragon of Whaddon: Being an Account of the Life and Work of Browne Willis (1682–1760), Antiquary and Historian* (High Wycombe, U.K.: Bucks Free Press, 1953).

References:

The Anglo-Catholic Parishes of Milton Keynes & Buckinghamshire <http://mkanglocatholic.org.uk.>;

John Nichols, *Illustrations of the Literary History of the Eighteenth Century. Consisting of Authentic Memoirs and Original Letters of Eminent Persons; and Intended as a Sequel to the Literary Anecdotes,* 8 volumes (London: John Nichols, 1822), III: 532; IV: 226;

Nichols, *Literary Anecdotes of the Eighteenth Century; Comprizing Biographical Memoirs of William Bowyer, Printer, F.S.S. and Many of His Learned Friends,* 9 volumes (London: J. Nichols & Bentley, 1812), VI: 186–211; VIII: 217–223;

H. B. Walters, *The English Antiquaries of the Sixteenth, Seventeenth and Eighteenth Centuries* (London: Edward Walters, 1934), pp. 44–49.

Papers:

Browne Willis's manuscripts, 112 volumes, are in the Bodleian Library, Oxford. His coin collection is now at the Ashmolean Museum, Oxford, having been moved there from the Bodleian in 1921.

Francis Wise

(3 June 1695 – 6 October 1767)

Craig A. Hanson
Calvin College

BOOKS: *Annales Rerum Gestarum Ælfredi Magni, Auctore Asserio Menevensi* (Oxford, 1722);

Epistola ad V[irum] Cl[arissimum] Joannem Masson de Nummo Abgari Regis (Oxford: Sheldonian Theatre, 1736);

A Letter to Dr Mead Concerning Some Antiquities in Berkshire: Particularly Shewing That the White Horse, Which Gives Name to the Vale, Is a Monument of the West Saxons, Made in Memory of a Great Victory Obtained over the Danes A.D. 871 (Oxford: Printed for Thomas Wood, 1738);

Further Observations upon the White Horse and Other Antiquities in Berkshire. With an Account of Whiteleaf-Cross in Buckinghamshire. As also of the Red Horse in Warwickshire, and some other Monuments of the Same Kind (Oxford: Printed for Thomas Wood, 1742);

Nummorum Antiquorum Scriniis Bodleianis Reconditorum Catalogus cum Commentario, Tabulis Aeneis, et Appendice (Oxford: Sheldonian Theatre, 1750);

Some Enquiries Concerning the First Inhabitants, Language, Religion, Learning, and Letters of Europe, by a Member of the Society of Antiquaries in London, as F.W.R.L. (Oxford: Printed at the [Sheldonian] Theatre, 1758);

The History and Chronology of the Fabulous Ages, Considered: Particularly with Regard to the Two Ancient Deities, Bacchus and Hercules, by a Member of the Society of Antiquaries in London, as F.W.R.L. (Oxford: Printed at the [Sheldonian] Theatre, 1764).

Antiquary and cleric Francis Wise established his reputation as a scholar on the grounds of his research into Anglo-Saxon history and his love for coins. He is best remembered for his edition of John Asser's "Life" of King Alfred and his speculative theories on the ancient topographical features around Oxford, particularly the White Horse of Uffington, which he mistakenly identified as a monument to Alfred's military success in 871. Prior to his appointment as Radcliffe Librarian in 1748, Wise served as underkeeper of the Bodleian Library and then keeper of the university archives. He was also a fellow of the Society of Antiquaries in London, and his acquaintances included many of the most important scholars in eighteenth-century Britain.

In 1754 Samuel Johnson paid several visits to Wise at his modest estate at Ellsfield, just outside of Oxford, and in a letter the following year, Johnson memorably described the antiquary's home as a "nest of British and Saxon Antiquities." In the absence of any portraits of Wise (a point made to William Huddesford by Wise's sister), the estate provides a material point of entry into the scholar's life and work. An ordained priest, Wise was granted curacy of the nearby village of Ellsfield in 1726 and in the 1730s and 1740s paid careful attention to the development of his garden there. Huddesford's "Memoirs" describe the grounds as being laid out "in a whimsical but pleasing manner," complete with "ponds, cascades, seats, a triumphal arch, the tower of Babel, a Druid temple, and an Egyptian pyramid," all resembling "the structures of antiquity" and "erected in exact scale and measure, to give, as far as miniature would permit, an idea of the edifices they were intended to represent." One of two contemporary prints of the estate shows a pool of water and a cascade pouring from a ruined archway, a classical folly that repeats the arch motif, and Wise's house to the far left. The other depicts the countryside looking toward Oxford, with the foliage of the trees framing the spires of Oxford University, and the dome of the newly built Radcliffe Library given pride of place. The landscape echoes Wise's scholarly allegiances both to the distant world of antiquity and to the intellectual life of eighteenth-century Oxford. That the two prints, designed and engraved by John Green, appeared in Wise's most ambitious work, *Nummorum Antiquorum Scriniis Bodleianis Reconditorum Catalogus* (1750, A Catalogue of the Ancient Coins in the Bodleian Library), suggests the antiquary himself saw them as an important gesture of self-presentation.

Named after his father, a cloth merchant in Oxford, Wise was born in the parish of All Saints, Oxford, on 3 June 1695. Upon completing his initial education under James Badger at New College school, he proceeded to Trinity College in January 1711, taking his M.A. on 16 October 1717. A week after his twenty-third birthday he was elected a probationer fellow of Trinity and in 1719, an actual fellow. He took his B.D. in 1727 after having been ordained deacon and priest in September 1721.

Toward the end of 1719, Wise had replaced John Fletcher as sublibrarian at the Bodleian (to the angry consternation of Thomas Hearne, who had been forced to resign from the same position in 1716 for refusing to pledge his loyalty to the new Hanoverian king). The scant salary of £10 a year, however, led Wise also to take on students, and in this capacity he met Francis North (later third Baron and then Earl of Guilford, as well as Lord of the Bedchamber to Frederick, Prince of Wales). North soon became Wise's most important patron, and the two remained friends until Wise's death. In 1723 North presented Wise with the curacy of Wroxton in Oxfordshire and in 1726 with the donative of Ellsfield.

Wise's first publication, the *Annales Rerum Gestarum Ælfredi Magni, Auctore Asserio Menevensi* (Chronicles of the Deeds of Alfred the Great by John Asser), appeared in 1722. His edition of the Latin text—generally believed to have been written by Bishop Asser in 893—was based on Otho A.xii, an early-eleventh-century manuscript belonging to the Cotton library that was destroyed by fire in 1731. The *Annales Rerum Gestarum Ælfredi Magni* marks the third time the text appeared in print and the first attempt at a scholarly edition. The provenance of the manuscript points to many of the leading antiquaries of England. After the death of John Leland, who apparently acquired the manuscript during the dissolution of the monasteries, it entered the possession of Matthew Parker, Archbishop of Canterbury. Parker produced the first printed edition in 1574 but made many unfounded additions. These were retained by William Camden in his edition of 1602 and supplemented with the spurious tale of Alfred's founding the university at Oxford. Encouraged by Arthur Charlett, Master of University College, Wise sought to produce an authoritative text with the help of Humphrey Wanley and James Hill, who collated the first two editions against the manuscript itself. By modern standards, Wise's efforts were wanting, and he continued to favor Parker's transcript over the manuscript. Still, these faults do not occlude his intentions, which at least marked a step toward the creation of a critical edition. He did, for instance, question the role of Alfred as founder of Oxford University, and the most valuable sources for information about the now-lost manuscript come from this publishing venture. Wanley's letter to Wise describing Otho A.xii and the inclusion in *Annales*

Rerum Gestarum Ælfredi Magni of an engraved facsimile of the opening page of the manuscript provide the material foundation for all subsequent Asser scholarship. While the facsimile does not permit scholars to date the script, it has, nonetheless, proved useful for making judgments based on layout and demonstrates an increasing awareness of the value of visual evidence, even for textual studies.

Wise also included in the Asser volume Alfred's Old English preface to Pope Gregory the Great's *Pastoral Care* (sixth century A.D.), which the king translated from the original Latin and had distributed across the kingdom. A lament over the decline of learning and a call to renewed scholarship, the preface must have resonated with Wise's view of the intellectual climate of his own era, for throughout his lifetime he routinely bemoaned the lack of esteem granted historical studies. Wise, in fact, was working in the aftermath of Oxford's golden age of Anglo-Saxon scholarship, which dawned in the last quarter of the seventeenth century and came to a close with the deaths of two of its most important contributors, Edward Thwaites in 1711 and George Hickes in 1715. In a letter to Charles Lyttelton, Wise himself confessed to a "superficial" knowledge of the language. Yet, just as Old English studies were starting to decline, the figure of King Alfred became an increasingly visible component of British culture, more generally as a symbol of the just and benevolent monarch. In particular, associations were drawn between Prince Frederick and Alfred. The best-known example comes from Thomas Arne's musical account of the king, which was first performed for the prince at his house at Cliveden in 1740 and which continues to give shape to British patriotism through its anthem *Rule Britannia*.

On the whole, the 1720s proved a fruitful period for Wise. In addition to the appointments from Lord North and the publication of Asser's "Life," Wise's status within the Oxford community continued to rise through his appointment as Keeper of the Archives in April 1726. He filled the position for the rest of his life, and the annual salary of £40 resulted in a substantial boost to his income. Yet, countering this record of mounting success, Wise's first professional setback came in the final month of this otherwise rewarding decade. His application to become the principal librarian of the Bodleian was rejected in December 1729 with the position going to Robert Fysher instead. It was another eighteen years before Wise was installed in a comparable position at a library that in 1730 did not yet exist.

In 1736 Wise published his *Epistola ad V[irum] Cl[arissimum] Joannem Masson de Nummo Abgari Regis* (A Letter to the Most Distinguished Gentleman John Masson Regarding the Coin of King Abgar). Adopting a comparative approach, the treatise on a single coin from the collection of Thomas Herbert, the eighth Earl of Pembroke, serves as a vehicle for Wise to demonstrate his knowledge of ancient numismatics more generally. As such, the text can be seen as a fitting preliminary exercise for his *Nummorum Antiquorum Scriniis Bodleianis Reconditorum Catalogus,* and to the extent that Wise attempts to elucidate an obscure example against the backdrop of familiar, canonical sources, the *Epistola ad V[irum] Cl[arissimum] Joannem Masson de Nummo Abgari Regis* also prefigures Wise's last two publishing ventures on the relationship between fable and history.

At this same time, Wise resumed his interests in King Alfred and extended his antiquarian studies to the topography of the nearby Berkshire downs. In *A Letter to Dr Mead Concerning Some Antiquities in Berkshire,* published toward the end of 1738, Wise argued that the White Horse of Uffington, a giant Bronze-Age figure cut in the chalky hillside, was created as a monument to commemorate Alfred's seminal victory over the Danes in 871. (As a result of the 1974 reorganization of county boundaries, it is now in Oxfordshire.) Matching a surplus of speculation with pronounced self-assurance, Wise was convinced he had at last pinpointed the location of Ashdown, the site of the battle that resulted in the death of Alfred's brother, King Æthelred, and Alfred's own ascendancy to the throne. Wise attempted to coordinate the textual record with various forms of material and visual evidence, including the natural landscape, the monument itself, and the iconography of Anglo-Saxon battle standards.

Wise's correspondence (letter to Andrew C. Ducarel, 17 December 1738) offers a glimpse of the practical aspects of this publishing endeavor, from his own initial ambitions to his growing frustration and disappointment over the lackluster reception of the book. The cost of the project came to £58–in Wise's own words, "a sum vastly too great for a private scholar to expend upon a public work." And because Wise was determined to market the books himself rather than relying upon a bookseller, sales remained sluggish. Of the six to eight hundred copies Wise had printed, he seems to have sold only around three hundred, at a cost of eighteen pence each. Writing to Ducarel in May 1739, Wise promised to destroy the remaining copies, making the "book as good a bargain as" he could for "those who have purchased it."

Yet, for all of the personal expense Wise assumed from the project, he did receive financial assistance from two patrons. Physician Richard Mead and William Craven, third Baron Craven, covered the cost of the two plates for the book engraved by George Vertue. In the opening paragraphs of *A Letter to Dr Mead Concerning Some Antiquities in Berkshire,* Wise praises Mead's erudi-

Title page for Francis Wise's published letter about a Bronze-Age white horse cut into a chalky hillside, which Wise believed was created much later (Eighteenth-Century Collections Online, Gale Group)

tion, noting that he follows the "illustrious patterns" of the ancients in that "after being thoroughly versed in the learning of other nations, you have not thought it beneath you, to search the antiquities of your own." Lord Craven's involvement was to be expected, since the Uffington Horse was on his land, just a short distance from his house at Ashdown Park.

Unfortunately for Wise, not only did *A Letter to Dr Mead Concerning Some Antiquities in Berkshire* not sell well, it also occasioned a scathing response from one "Philalethes Rusticus" (William Asplin) in 1740. *The Impertinence and Imposture of Modern Antiquaries Displayed; or, A Refutation of Rev. Wise's Letter to Dr Mead* challenged not only Wise's conclusion about the White Horse but also took issue with every methodological move he made along the way–arguing, for instance, that the color of the figure can hardly be used in iconographical arguments, since the chalk is natural to the downs, and noting that based on the numismatic evidence, one should attribute the monument to the ancient Britons rather than the Anglo-Saxons (a line of reasoning certainly available to Wise, given his love of coins). More seriously, the anonymous writer subtly called into question Wise's loyalty to the reigning Hanover line. As Huddesford notes, this latter accusation caused Wise particular concern, as he feared it would obstruct future appointments. He was thus naturally delighted to see *The Impertinence and Imposture of Modern Antiquaries Displayed; or, A Refutation of Rev. Wise's Letter to Dr Mead* in turn countered with *An Answer to a Scandalous Libel, Entitled The Impertinence and Imposture of Modern Antiquaries Displayed* (1741), written by George North, though published anonymously. And indeed, Wise himself returned to the topic shortly after, in 1742, with his *Further Observations upon the White Horse and Other Antiquities in Berkshire. With an Account of Whiteleaf-Cross in Buckinghamshire,* in which he restates his initial argument and extends it to include several additional sites.

The timing of Wise's *Letter to Dr Mead* and his *Further Observations* is itself noteworthy. Even more than would normally be the case, Wise looked to these texts to help establish himself as a respected man of learning, since it was at this point he first began lobbying for the position of Radcliffe Librarian. John Radcliffe, upon his death in 1714, had provided funds for the construction and outfitting of a new library at Oxford University, and though the trustees of his estate had been slow in executing the wish, finally a design by James Gibbs was accepted and the first stone laid in 1737. As a protégé of the fashionable physician, Mead had taken over much of Radcliffe's practice and certainly had some degree of influence in the appointment. In a letter to John Ward of Gresham College, Wise voiced concerns over Mead's support, and Wise's decision to structure his first study of the White Horse as a letter to Mead can hardly have been coincidental, though *The Impertinence and Imposture of Modern Antiquaries Displayed; or, A Refutation of Rev. Wise's Letter to Dr Mead* must have caused Wise to second-guess the strategy since "Rusticus" took several satirical shots at Mead in addition to criticizing Wise. In any event, Wise's bid for the job proved successful; he resigned his position at the Bodleian and officially became the Radcliffe librarian in May 1748.

Throughout this period, Wise had also been busy with his *Nummorum Antiquorum Scriniis Bodleianis Reconditorum Catalogus,* begun perhaps as early as the 1720s. Writing to Ducarel in November 1738, however, he admitted progress on the catalogue had "been much retarded by this affair of the Horse." As subscribers' patience wore thin, Wise increasingly wondered whether he would ever complete the project, largely because of economic restraints, and as Strickland Gib-

son observes, it was ultimately the substantial annual salary of £150 from the new librarian position that financed the project (he suggests Wise lost as much as £250 altogether, with the plates alone costing £200). At last, the *Nummorum Antiquorum Scriniis Bodleianis Reconditorum Catalogus* was available in 1750. As is often the case with such works of reference, its performance in the marketplace bore little relation to its scholarly value, and it ranks as one of the outstanding numismatic accomplishments of the period. (Appropriately, Wise donated many coins to the Bodleian's collection during his lifetime, and after his death his sister gave others to the Radcliffe, which also eventually ended up in the Bodleian.)

The Radcliffe appointment, too, helped pave the way for Wise's election to the Society of Antiquaries in London in April 1749, and by the middle of the century Wise's circle had come to comprise many of Britain's leading scholars and patrons, including, in addition to those already mentioned, Sir Andrew Fountaine, William Stukeley, John Burton of York, Joseph Ames, and Browne Willis. Wise, together with Thomas Warton, was largely responsible for Johnson's first academic degree: Oxford granted the M.A. in February 1755—just in time for it to be noted on the title page of his *Dictionary* (1755)—at the request of Wise and Warton, with Wise arguing the diploma would honor Oxford more than it would Johnson.

Wise's last two publications—*Some Enquiries Concerning the First Inhabitants, Language, Religion, Learning, and Letters of Europe* (1758) and *The History and Chronology of the Fabulous Ages* (1764), both signed F.W.R.L. (for "Francis Wise Radcliffe Librarian")—attempted to trace strands of European culture and history back to ancient classical sources of the Mediterranean. Obscure or mythic peoples and divinities such as the Cabiri, Cimbri, Cimmerians, Pelasgians, and Scythians are placed front and center. Starting from the belief that for "an age or two after the Flood, the whole world was of *One Speech,*" Wise aims in the former text to trace the diversities of language and culture back as far as possible to the "fountain head." In particular, he argues that the first people to populate Europe, including Western Europe, were Scythians, and as a way of validating the historical importance of the Continent, he associates these early inhabitants with key characters from classical mythology. He argues, for instance, that Atlantis must have been located in the North (though he disagrees with Olaf Rudbeck, who identified the isle with Sweden) and that the Amazons were in fact the wives and daughters of Scythian warriors. He asserts that the Titans were Scythians and that Greece came to prominence only with Jupiter's triumph. He argues that science began in Europe rather than Egypt and claims

Apollo and Diana as Northern deities "connecting the Scythian and Grecian history." Likewise, he posits "a vast empire, comprehending all Europe and a great part of Asia" that "existed long before those petty kingdoms in Greece, that boasted of the greatest antiquity."

Similarly, in *The History and Chronology of the Fabulous Ages,* Wise aims to establish historical truth by tracing "things back to their first beginnings" and sees the fables of Antiquity as one way of uncovering vestiges of "real facts, times, and persons." Toward this end, he looks to Bacchus and Hercules, both of whom he sees as extremely old deities whose cult followings extended beyond Greece. In particular, he proposes that the "true" Bacchus—not to be confused with the later "fictitious and counterfeit" variations—first appeared in India and only later was worshiped throughout the Mediterranean world. Bringing the heathen mythology to bear on the biblical account, Wise suggests Bacchus "may be one of the best arguments to prove that India and China were planted by Noah and part of his family." He similarly argues "that the exploits of the true Hercules were performed in India" as well, though he goes on to describe the hero as a Scythian, a connection that allows him again to address the "spirit of the northern nations" to which he once more attributes the "beginning and progress of science." While these two works evince a deep belief in the potential of mythology to elucidate history—and in this sense might be seen as a precursor to comparative anthropology—above all they demonstrate the divide between Wise's engagement with the past and current historical studies.

Suffering from gout and often ill, Wise spent most of his latter years at Ellsfield, to the frustration of would-be library users, who were forced to arrange their schedules around that of Wise. Gibson notes that Wise went so far as to padlock the doors of the Radcliffe, a particularly ironic action considering that the librarian continued to bemoan the decline of learning up until his final days. Wise died on 6 October 1767 and was buried in the garden he loved so much.

As an historian, Francis Wise was an active figure in the late stage of the flowering of Anglo-Saxon studies at Oxford, and throughout his lifetime he argued for the importance of antiquarian research. He was a knowledgeable numismatist and diligently sought to expand the study of the past to include cultures beyond those of ancient Greece and Rome. From a twenty-first-century perspective, these attempts failed because of basic methodological problems, and yet Wise's insistence on the importance of comparative approaches to language, religion, and mythology eventually yielded rich rewards when undertaken by the more critically

nuanced approaches of subsequent academic disciplines, including comparative religion, anthropology, linguistics, archaeology, and art history.

Letters:

Illustrations of the Literary History of the Eighteenth Century Consisting of Authentic Memoirs and Original Letters of Eminent Persons, edited by John Nichols, 8 volumes, (London: John Nichols, 1817–1858), III: 632–637, IV: 171, 433–452, 686;

The Correspondence of Thomas Warton, edited by David Fairer (Athens: University of Georgia Press, 1995).

References:

Eleanor Adams, *Old English Scholarship in England from 1566–1800* (New Haven: Yale University Press, 1917);

Asser's Life of King Alfred and Other Contemporary Sources, translated, with an introduction and notes, by Simon Keynes and Michael Lapidge (New York: Penguin Books, 1983);

Herbert Blakiston, "Thomas Warton and Machyn's Diary," *English Historical Review,* 11 (1896): 282–300;

Boswell's Life of Johnson, edited by George Birkbeck Hill, revised by L. F. Powell, 6 volumes (Oxford: Clarendon Press, 1934–1964), I: 273–283;

David Fairer, "Anglo-Saxon Studies," in *The History of the University of Oxford, V: The Eighteenth Century,* edited by L. S. Sutherland and L. G. Mitchell (Oxford: Clarendon Press, 1986), pp. 807–829;

Strickland Gibson, "Francis Wise, B.D.: Oxford Antiquary, Librarian, and Archivist," *Oxoniensia,* 1 (1936): 173–195;

William Huddesford, "Memoirs of the Rev. Francis Wise, B.D.F.S.A. Communicated to Dr. Ducarel, May 23, 1771," in *Illustrations of the Literary History of the Eighteenth Century Consisting of Authentic Memoirs and Original Letters of Eminent Persons,* edited by John Nichols, 8 volumes (London: John Nichols, 1817–1858), IV: 479–480;

Simon Keynes, "The Cult of King Alfred the Great," *Anglo-Saxon England,* 28 (1999): 225–356;

Stuart Piggott, "Antiquarian Studies," in *The History of the University of Oxford, V: The Eighteenth Century,* edited by Sutherland and Mitchell (Oxford: Clarendon Press, 1986), pp. 757–777.

Papers:

Collections of Francis Wise's correspondence are in the British Library, the Society of Antiquaries in London, and the Bodleian Library in Oxford.

Robert Wodrow

(1679 – 21 March 1734)

Ralph Stewart
Acadia University

BOOKS: *The Oath of Abjuration, Considered: In a Letter to a Friend* ([Edinburgh, 1712]);

The History of the Sufferings of the Church of Scotland, from the Restauration to the Revolution (Edinburgh: Printed by J. Watson, 1721–1722); republished as *The History of the State and Sufferings of the Church of Scotland, from the Restoration to the Revolution,* 2 volumes, abridged by William Crookshank (London: Oswald, 1749); original reprinted as *The History of the Sufferings of the Church of Scotland from the Restoration to the Revolution,* 4 volumes, edited by R. Burns (Glasgow: Blackie, Fullarton, 1828–1830);

Life of James Wodrow, A.M., edited by John Campbell (Edinburgh: William Blackwood, 1828);

Collections upon the Lives of the Reformers and Most Eminent Ministers of the Church of Scotland, 3 volumes, edited by W. J. Duncan and Matthew Leishman (Glasgow: Maitland Club, 1834–1848);

Analecta; or, Materials for a History of Remarkable Providences; Mostly Relating to Scottish Ministers and Christians, 4 volumes, edited by Matthew Leishman (Edinburgh: Maitland Club, 1842–1843);

Sermons by the Rev. Robert Bruce, Minister of Edinburgh: Reprinted from the Original Edition of MDXC and MDXCI, with Collections for His Life by the Rev. Robert Wodrow, edited by W. Cunningham (Edinburgh: Printed for the Wodrow Society, 1843);

Selections from Wodrow's Biographical Collections: Divines of the North-east of Scotland, edited by Robert Lippe (Aberdeen: New Spalding Club, 1890).

Robert Wodrow was an important collector of historical documents, a diarist who remains a useful primary source and the biographer of many Scottish clergymen. But he is best known as the historian of the "sufferings" of the Scottish Presbyterian Church during the period it was suppressed, from 1660 to 1688.

Wodrow was born in the country town of Glasgow in 1679, the second son of James Wodrow, an outlawed Presbyterian minister, and Margaret Hair. His mother was first cousin to Sir George Maxwell of Pollock, whose son John later became Robert's patron. (She was also descended from the Stuart kings through an illegitimate son of Robert III, but this relationship does not seem to have modified her disapproval of the later Stuarts, who had disestablished Presbyterianism.) His father's family descended from a priest who married after the Reformation. Robert's uncle fought for the rebel Presbyterians in the Pentland Rising of 1666 and was captured and executed after it. His first cousin fought in the second rebellion, at the battle of Bothwell Bridge in the year of Robert's birth; he was also captured and was drowned in a ship taking prisoners to America.

James Wodrow had a mild disposition, though after 1673 he preached illegally as a Presbyterian minister and was obliged to live secretly to avoid arrest. He managed to see his wife just after Robert was born, but soldiers were waiting outside to arrest him, and he escaped only by disguising himself as the doctor's assistant. Despite this beginning, Robert's own life was uneventful, at least externally, except for the early deaths in his family that were then almost inevitable. The family, including Robert (or "Robin") and his elder brother Sandy, went to live in James's home village of Eaglesham, ten miles south of Glasgow, but settled in town early in 1688 at the time of an "indulgence" for Presbyterian ministers. The boys' mother died soon after. Robert went to the public grammar school and later to a private school set up by his father. His father married again in 1692 and about the same time became Professor of Divinity at Glasgow University, which Robert had begun attending. After completing his M.A. and spending a year at the house of his second cousin, Sir John Maxwell, Robert Wodrow returned to the university in 1697 to study divinity under his father and for the next six years was also the university librarian (then a fairly junior post). In 1702 he became chaplain to Sir John—now a high court judge, known as Lord Pollock—and the next year became minister of the small parish of Eastwood, five miles south of Glasgow, where Sir John was the main landowner. Here, despite pressing "calls" from other larger parishes, including Glasgow, Wodrow spent the rest of his life. His brother, Sandy, who had been expected to succeed his father as Professor of Divinity, died suddenly in 1706, and his father the next year. In 1708 Wodrow married Margaret Warner, daughter and granddaughter of covenanting (illegal Presbyterian) ministers. His letters to her, usually from the Church's General Assembly in Edinburgh, suggest a happy marriage and a community of interests. They had sixteen children, of whom nine survived Wodrow and three became ministers.

Wodrow was a conscientious and popular minister who sometimes preached to combined congregations of 1,200 people. Although not one of the leaders of the Scottish Church, he was influential. He advised on the implications of the Union with England in 1707, on the dangers of unqualified oaths of allegiance to the sovereign (publishing on this point his only pamphlet, in 1712), and on the abortive negotiations with George I in 1714 to abolish patronage. He was also a member of the committee that recommended the deposition of the Professor of Divinity at Glasgow (his father's successor), which was carried out in 1727 on the grounds of unsound dogma and, four years later, on the committee that pronounced on the "Marrow" controversy (another doctrinal dispute).

Wodrow was deeply religious, but also, as he frequently said, an "Athenian"—interested in almost everything. In youth he was fascinated by antiquity and natural history, and amassed large collections of coins and fossils; and he was always a collector of documents relating to the Scottish Church. He followed politics, at home and abroad, and especially the effects of the Union, which he deplored, and the schemes of the Jacobites to bring back the Stuart kings, which he feared. He wrote interesting accounts of the most dangerous uprising in his lifetime, in 1715, and particularly of the situation shortly before the critical battle of Sherrifmuir, in which he defends the tactics of John Campbell, Duke of Argyll, commander of the small pro-government army. All these interests and many others appear in Wodrow's letters and in *Analecta; or, Materials for a History of Remarkable Providences; Mostly Relating to Scottish Ministers and Christians* (both eventually published in 1842–1843), the latter a journal he kept from 1701 until almost the end of his life. Few of the "remarkable providences" of the subtitle are actually supernatural, although Wodrow fully believed in witches and ghosts. They are rather the experiences, religious and secular, of notable Presbyterians—what may be termed the internal history of the Church of Scotland.

Apart from his pamphlet against the "Oath of Abjuration" of 1712—and even it, he claimed, was not intended for publication—the only work Wodrow published in his lifetime was *The History of the Sufferings of the Church of Scotland, from the Restauration to the Revolution* (1721–1722), which includes most of the information he was able to gather about the disestablished and partly outlawed Presbyterian church. Wodrow had begun concentrating on this work by 1713. He was reacting to the assertions—notably by the chief government prosecutor of the period, Sir George Mackenzie, in his *Vindication of the Government in Scotland* (1691)—that no one then suffered for his/her religion. Wodrow wished to disprove this assertion and also to record all the people, most of them humble, who did indeed suffer for their religious beliefs, from fines to torture and execution. Admittedly, the dispute was largely one of interpretation. The Presbyterians believed that they should not be constrained by the state in what they considered religious matters. The government and, in general, the Episcopalian clergy believed that anyone refusing to swear an oath of loyalty to the government, whatever his/her motives, might reasonably be treated as a traitor and executed. Some later historians agreed. Mark Napier describes the edict that women in this situation were to be drowned (rather than hanged) as "a humane order" (*The Case for the Crown in re the Wigtown Martyrs,* 1863). In *Scotland: James V to James VII* (1971) Gordon Donaldson says that, even in a period of conciliation toward the Presbyterians, the penalty of death for any Presbyterian minister holding an outside (illegal) service "had to be" introduced.

Wodrow originally intended *The History of the Sufferings of the Church of Scotland* to be a collection of documents linked by brief commentaries, in the manner of many sixteenth- and seventeenth-century histories, such as his predecessor David Calderwood's *History of the Kirk of Scotland* (1842–1849). However, although the final version of Wodrow's history of the Scottish church includes a great many documents, it is largely in his own words. The main exception is at the beginning, where the letters of James Sharp—who went from negotiator for the Presbyterians to Episcopal Archbishop—are reproduced to demonstrate his treachery. Wodrow's history is, like Calderwood's and many other early-modern histories, primarily a year-by-year chronicle, with so much mass and detail that discerning a pattern is difficult. (The edition of 1828, the main one now in use, makes understanding somewhat harder by converting Wodrow's appendixes to footnotes, which has the effect of fragmenting the text.) Yet, the history also includes long sections of continuous narrative, notably the book-length treatment of the causes, course, defeat, and consequences of the second rebellion of 1679. It also includes analyses of events, though admittedly most are based on James Kirkton's account, *A History of the Church of Scotland, 1660–1679* (1693), and typically reuse Kirkton's words, with some expansion and extra detail.

Wodrow was disappointed in the initial reactions to his work. Much less information was volunteered than he had hoped, and then the subscriptions necessary to fund the publication came in rather slowly, and most ministers seemed to him uninterested. However, the King's acceptance of a dedication gave *The History of the Sufferings of the Church of Scotland* some official status, and interest seems to have increased after publication. (Later, in 1725, the King gave Wodrow 100 guineas.) There were some contemporary attacks on the book, principally on matters of interpretation. Episcopalian pamphlets, probably by Alexander Bruce and David Symson, complained that Wodrow was far too sympathetic to the extreme Presbyterians. From the other side, John McMain and Patrick Walker attacked him for not being sympathetic enough to the extremists. So far, this balance between the attacks tends to endorse Wodrow's stance. However, Bruce does make other points that resurfaced in later criticism of Wodrow, that what written evidence he is using is often unclear and that his oral evidence is heavily biased because it comes from "rebels." Wodrow replies in a letter of June 1722 that his documents are available to anyone who wants to see them and that he checks oral evidence as far as possible.

The History of the Sufferings of the Church of Scotland was not reprinted entire in the eighteenth century, although a condensed version appeared three times. Interest revived in the nineteenth century, perhaps because the issue of how far a church could be independent of the state had again become important. The history was finally reprinted in 1828–1830, with an introduction noting the historians who had praised its author. But there was also strong criticism of Wodrow's work, by William Ayton in 1849, and most notably by Napier in three books written between 1858 and 1870. Like earlier Episcopalian critics, he disagrees strongly with Wodrow's politics, but his main contention is that much of what Wodrow says is simply untrue: "a calumnious tissue of monstrous fables." Napier's reasons for asserting this point are rather hard to sort out. He gives a list of Wodrow's "outrageous calumnies" in the index to *Memorials and Letters Illustrative of the Life and Times of James Graham of Claverhouse, Viscount Dundee* (1859–1862), but most of these misrepresentations come down to matters of interpretation. His general points seem to be that most of Wodrow's history is based on oral testimony, which is inherently unreliable, and that Wodrow was credulous and uncritical about sifting his evidence. Historians understandably prefer written records, which can be rechecked and circulated, but these records are usually based on oral reports—as Philip Sidney points out in his "Apology for Poetry [Literature]"—

and it therefore seems unreasonable to dismiss oral testimony per se. As regards Wodrow's critical abilities in determining what was likely to be true, he does search extensively for written records and uses oral testimony as an addition and not a substitute. As he points out in his preface, soldiers are unlikely to report what they have plundered or whom they may have injured unfairly, and much of the information about "sufferings" could only be obtained orally and from the sufferers. Also, although he believed his accounts to be "well attested," he acknowledges at various points in *The History of the Sufferings of the Church of Scotland* that there will be "in such a Multitude of Facts almost unavoidable mistakes" (preface to volume two), and he solicits further testimonies and corrections, while suggesting that some mistakes do not affect the "general truth" of *The History of the Sufferings of the Church of Scotland,* the overall pattern of persecution. And, as he points out, the memoirs of Bishop Gilbert Burnet, which appeared soon after *The History of the Sufferings of the Church of Scotland,* corroborate Wodrow in almost all points where they intersect. Since Burnet had been a leading Episcopal minister in Scotland through the 1660s, his memoirs provide strong confirmation of Wodrow's account.

However, Napier scores on his main specific point, on which he wrote two complete books, that Wodrow was wrong on the "Wigton Martyrs." Napier argues convincingly that, although two women were indeed condemned to be drowned at Wigton (on the south coast of Scotland) for refusing an oath of allegiance to the government—as Wodrow says—they were finally pardoned because they took the oath. Wodrow does note that he has found a letter of reprieve (postponement) of the executions, but he believed that they had eventually taken place because the local minister, Robert Rowan, had told him so, and indeed had given a graphic account of the drownings. The "Wigton martyrs" are one of the most dramatic (apparent) instances of martyrdom, and showing that they actually recanted and lived does throw some doubt on Wodrow's judgment and also on the accuracy of the oral testimony he drew on. Yet, after all, Wodrow points to both the order for execution and the letter of reprieve, and he is guilty only of believing one report that turned out to be untrue. Since his history of the Presbyterian church records literally tens of thousands of alleged atrocities, undermining only one of them does not disprove either the value of oral testimony or Wodrow's theme that the Presbyterians were cruelly persecuted.

Wodrow's time was limited by pastoral duties, church controversies, and—after 1725—illness, but he did draw up many biographies, based on the material in *Analecta,* between 1723 and 1731. Almost all the biographies remained in manuscript until the nineteenth century. The longest are the life of his father, James, one of Robert Bruce (1554–1631), and a long life, or at least—as its title suggests—collection of records on, Robert Boyd of Trochrig (1578–1627). For periods before 1625, Calderwood's *History of the Kirk of Scotland* is a major source of information. Typically, half or more of each biography consists of long quotations from contemporary letters and official documents, in the manner of Calderwood's *History of the Kirk of Scotland*. Wodrow approved of this traditional method of writing—or assembling—history, as it gave readers greater freedom to make their own judgments. Near the end of his life of Bruce, Wodrow says that he will not sketch Bruce's character: "The reader will be able, in some measure, to form it from facts; which, in my opinion, is the best way of forming a judgment of persons." The "facts" are the documents provided. This way of proceeding is reasonable, and Wodrow should not be judged as a weak historian or biographer when he is in fact acting as an editor, in the manner of many early-modern historians.

Yet, his diffidence about making judgments and tendency to follow traditional patterns do limit most of the biographies. All have an element of hagiography: they provide examples of pious men who should be imitated and not much pattern beyond this assessment. Wodrow does not give a vivid sense of personality (unlike Kirkton and Burnet on their contemporaries). When he tells the reader that his stepmother was "a religious, virtuous, grave, and worthy person," he probably feels that he has said all that is relevant: an indication of the type is enough. Yet, the biographies are valuable because Wodrow indicates sources clearly and frequently analyzes and judges them, as he does in Bruce's biography: "This is Mr. Calderwood's account of the matter. I wish he had been a little more particular as to the oversights, as he terms them." Wodrow is especially cautious about oral sources. At the end of Bruce's biography, he draws on these for some details, but tentatively and as needing further verification. "I set them down here rather for preservation, and further inquiry, than for present publication, till they be further considered." And, when Wodrow had health and time, he often developed more-coherent narratives. His lives of James Wodrow and Bruce (and one or two of the shorter lives) are indeed biographies in the modern sense, if rather heavily freighted with long quotations.

In 1725 Wodrow was confined to his house for months with sciatica; he recovered, but he was never again in good health. Worse followed: in letters to friends, he briefly expressed his grief at the death of his eldest boy, James, aged nineteen, and of "my dear Sandy," aged fifteen, the next year. These were heavier blows than the deaths of young children, which were expected at this period. Wodrow himself was seriously

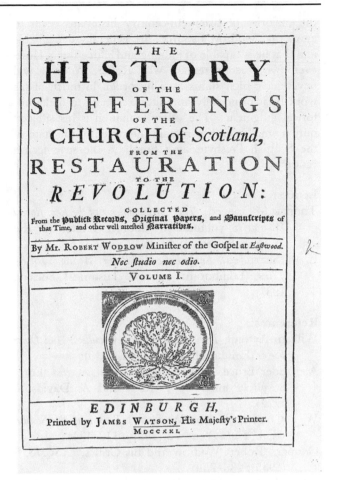

Title page for Robert Wodrow's history of the partly outlawed Presbyterian church (Eighteenth-Century Collections Online, Gale Group)

ill from 1731. He managed to attend his last Kirk Session in October 1733 and died on 21 March 1734. Twentieth-century attitudes toward his work are rather mixed. At the beginning of the twentieth century, Henry Grey Graham described him as "an inquisitive, garrulous, credulous man whose ears were erect at every tale of wonder," but he was referring to the *Analecta* and letters and not to the biographies and history. A century later, Edward J. Cowan distinguished between the "somewhat uncritical" folklorist and the "scrupulous" historian, and this distinction is important for understanding and evaluating Wodrow. *Analecta* is intended as a collection of largely unsifted material: in *The History of the Sufferings of the Church of Scotland*, critical standards are applied. In the twentieth and twenty-first centuries, most historians agree on Wodrow's good faith and on the usefulness of the material he gathered. There are a few dissident voices: Rosalind Mitchison complains that much of Wodrow's material "is hearsay which does not even bear the name of the teller." Yet, the majority of twentieth-century historians seem to agree that Wodrow's sources are generally dependable and that he is capable of judging and sifting them. However, two reasons remain why Robert Wodrow will never have high status as a historian. In much of his work he is principally an editor, reluctant to make historical judgments. The other limitation is his subject: only a small minority remain interested in the state of the Scottish Presbyterian Church in the seventeenth century.

Letters:

Thomas M'Crie, ed., *The Correspondence of the Rev. Robert Wodrow,* 3 volumes (Edinburgh: Printed for the Wodrow Society, 1842–1843);

L. W. Sharp, ed., *Early Letters of Robert Wodrow, 1698–1709* (Edinburgh: Scottish Historical Society, 1937).

References:

William Aytoun, *Lays of the Scottish Cavaliers: And Other Poems* (Edinburgh: Blackwood, 1849);

Alexander Bruce, *The Scottish Behemoth Dissected* (Edinburgh: Printed by J. Ross and A. Davidson, 1722);

W. J. Couper, "Robert Wodrow," *Records of the Scottish Church History Society,* 3 (1929): 112–134;

Couper, "Robert Wodrow and his Critics," *RSCHS,* 5 (1935): 238–250;

Edward J. Cowan, "The Covenanting Tradition in Scottish History," in *Scottish History: The Power of the Past,* edited by Cowan and Richard J. Finley (Edinburgh: Edinburgh University Press, 2002), pp. 121–145;

Gordon Donaldson, *Scotland: James V to James VII* (Edinburgh: Oliver & Boyd, 1971);

William Ferguson, *Scotland: 1689 to the Present* (Edinburgh: Mercat Press, 1965);

Henry Grey Graham, *The Social Life of Scotland in the Eighteenth Century* (London: Black, 1906);

George Mackenzie, *A Vindication of the Government in Scotland, during the Reign of King Charles II* (London, 1691);

John McMain, ed., Introduction, in Alexander Shields, *The Life and Death . . . of Mr. James Renwick* (Edinburgh, 1724);

John Millar, *Scottish Prose of the Seventeenth and Eighteenth Centuries* (Glasgow: James Maclehose, 1912);

Rosalind Mitchison, *A History of Scotland* (London: Methuen, 1970);

Mark Napier, *The Case for the Crown in re the Wigtown Martyrs* (Edinburgh: Edmonston & Douglas, 1863);

Napier, *History Rescued (A Recapitulation of the Case for the Crown)* (Edinburgh: Edmonston & Douglas, 1870);

Napier, *Memorials and Letters Illustrative of the Life and Times of James Graham of Claverhouse, Viscount Dundee,* 3 volumes, including an index (Edinburgh: Stevenson, 1859–1862);

David Symson, *A True and Impartial Account of the Life of . . . James Sharp* (Edinburgh? 1723);

Patrick Walker, *Six Saints of the Covenant,* 2 volumes, edited by D. Hay Fleming (London: Hodder & Stoughton, 1901);

Walker, *Some Remarkable Passages . . . J. Semple . . . with Remarks upon . . . Mr. Wodrow's History* (Edinburgh: P. Walker, 1727).

Papers:

Manuscripts of Robert Wodrow's works and correspondence are held by the universities of Glasgow and Edinburgh, and at the Scottish National Library and the British Library.

Books for Further Reading

Anderson, Matthew Smith. *Historians and Eighteenth-Century Europe, 1715–1789*. Oxford: Clarendon Press, 1979.

Ayres, Philip J. *Classical Culture and the Idea of Rome in Eighteenth-Century England*. Cambridge: Cambridge University Press, 1997.

Black, J. B. *The Art of History: A Study of Four Great Historians of the Eighteenth Century*. New York: Russell & Russell, 1965.

Black, Jeremy. *Eighteenth-Century Britain: 1688–1783,* History of Britain. Basingstoke, U.K.: Palgrave-Macmillan, 2001.

Borsay, Peter. *The Image of Georgian Bath 1700–2000: Towns, Heritage, and History*. Oxford: Oxford University Press, 2000.

Bracken, James K., and Joel Silver, eds. *Dictionary of Literary Biography 154: The British Literary Book Trade, 1700–1820*. Detroit: Gale Research, 1995.

Braudy, Leo. *Narrative Form in History and Fiction: Hume, Fielding & Gibbon*. Princeton, N.J.: Princeton University Press, 1970.

Brom, Frans. *English Catholic Books, 1701–1800: A Bibliography*. Aldershot, U.K.: Scolar, 1996.

Brown, Lucy M., and Ian R. Christie. *Bibliography of British History, 1789–1851*. Oxford: Clarendon Press, 1977.

Christie. *British History Since 1760: A Select Bibliography*. London: Historical Association, 1970.

Collini, Stefan, Richard Whatmore, and Brian Young, eds. *Economy, Polity, and Society: British Intellectual History, 1750–1950*. Cambridge: Cambridge University Press, 2000.

Collini, Whatmore, and Young, eds. *History, Religion, and Culture: British Intellectual History, 1750–1950*. Cambridge: Cambridge University Press, 2000.

Cordasco, Francesco. *A Register of Eighteenth-Century Bibliographies and References: A Chronological Quarter-Century Survey Relating to English Literature, Booksellers, Newspapers, Periodicals, Printing & Publishing, Aesthetics, Art & Music, Economics, History & Science; A Preliminary Contribution*. Chicago: V. Giorgio, 1950.

Cragg, Gerald R. *Reason and Authority in the Eighteenth Century*. Cambridge: Cambridge University Press, 1964.

Cubitt, Geoffrey, ed. *Imagining Nations,* York Studies in Cultural History. Manchester: Manchester University Press, 1998.

Davies, Godfrey, and Mary Frear Keeler, eds. *Bibliography of British History: Stuart Period, 1603–1714,* second edition. Oxford: Clarendon Press, 1970.

Davis, Leith. *Acts of Union: Scotland and the Literary Negotiation of the British Nation, 1707–1830*. Stanford, Cal.: Stanford University Press, 1998.

Douglas, David Charles. *English Scholars, 1660–1730,* second revised edition. Westport, Conn.: Greenwood Press, 1975.

Elton, G. R. *Modern Historians on British History, 1485–1945: A Critical Bibliography.* London: Methuen, 1970.

Furber, Elizabeth Chapin, ed. *Changing Views on British History: Essays on Historical Writing Since 1939.* Cambridge: Harvard University Press, 1966.

Grose, Clyde L. *A Select Bibliography of British History, 1660–1760.* New York: Octagon Books, 1967.

Hannam, June, Ann Hughes, and Pauline Stafford, comps. *British Women's History: A Bibliographical Guide.* Manchester & New York: Manchester University Press, 1996.

Haywood, Ian. *The Making of History: A Study of the Literary Forgeries of James Macpherson and Thomas Chatterton in Relation to Eighteenth-Century Ideas of History and Fiction.* Rutherford, N.J.: Fairleigh Dickinson University Press, 1986.

Hicks, Philip Steven. *Neo-Classical History and English Culture: From Clarendon to Hume,* Studies in Modern History. New York: St. Martin's Press, 1996.

Horwitz, Barbara Joan. *British Women Writers, 1700–1850: An Annotated Bibliography of Their Works and Works about Them.* Lanham, Md.: Scarecrow Press / Pasadena: Salem Press, 1997.

Kelley, Donald R., and David Harris Sacks, eds. *The Historical Imagination in Early Modern Britain: History, Rhetoric, and Fiction, 1500–1800,* Woodrow Wilson Center Series. Washington, D.C.: Woodrow Wilson Center Press, 1997.

Kenyon, J. P. *The History Men: The Historical Profession in England Since the Renaissance.* London: Weidenfeld & Nicolson, 1983.

Kidd, Colin. *Subverting Scotland's Past: Scottish Whig Historians and the Creation of an Anglo-British Identity, 1689–c. 1830.* Cambridge & New York: Cambridge University Press, 1993.

Langford, Paul, ed. *The Eighteenth Century, 1688–1815,* The Short Oxford History of the British Isles. Oxford & New York: Oxford University Press, 2002.

Levine, Joseph M. *The Battle of the Books: History and Literature in the Augustan Age.* Ithaca, N.Y.: Cornell University Press, 1991.

Levine. *Dr. Woodward's Shield: History, Science, and Satire in Augustan England.* Berkeley: University of California Press, 1977.

Levine. *Humanism and History: Origins of Modern English Historiography.* Ithaca, N.Y.: Cornell University Press, 1987.

Looser, Devoney. *British Women Writers and the Writing of History 1670–1820.* Baltimore, Md.: Johns Hopkins University Press, 2000.

Lynch, Jack. *The Age of Elizabeth in the Age of Johnson.* Cambridge: Cambridge University Press, 2002.

McIntosh, Carey. *The Evolution of English Prose, 1700–1800: Style, Politeness, and Print Culture.* Cambridge: Cambridge University Press, 1998.

Myers, Robin, and Michael Harris. *Sale and Distribution of Books from 1700.* Oxford: Oxford Polytechnic Press, 1984.

O'Connell, Sheila, Roy Porter, Celina Fox, and Ralph Hyde. *London, 1753.* Boston: Godine, 2003.

O'Gorman, Frank. *The Long Eighteenth Century: British Political and Social History, 1688–1832,* Arnold History of Britain Series. London & New York: Arnold, 1997.

Okie, Laird. *Augustan Historical Writing*. Lanham, Md. & London: University Press of America, 1991.

Pargellis, Stanley, and D. J. Medley, eds. *Bibliography of British History: The Eighteenth Century, 1714–1789*. Oxford: Clarendon Press, 1951.

Patterson, Annabel. *Nobody's Perfect: A New Whig Interpretation of History*. New Haven, Conn.: Yale University Press, 2002.

Peardon, Thomas Preston. *The Transition in English Historical Writing, 1760–1830*. New York: Columbia University Press / London: P. S. King, 1933.

Peltz, Lucy, and Martin Myrone, eds. *Producing the Past: Aspects of Antiquarian Culture and Practice, 1700–1850*. Aldershot, U.K.: Ashgate, 1999.

Phillips, Mark Salber. *Society and Sentiment: Genres of Historical Writing in Britain, 1740–1820*. Princeton, N.J.: Princeton University Press, 2000.

Pocock, J. G. A., ed. *Virtue, Commerce, and History: Essays on Political Thought and History, Chiefly in the Eighteenth Century*, Ideas in Context. Cambridge: Cambridge University Press, 1985.

Roy
Porter. *The Creation of the Modern World: The Untold Story of the British Enlightenment*. New York: Norton, 2000.

Porter. *English Society in the Eighteenth Century*, Pelican Social History of Britain. London: Allen Lane, 1982.

Porter. *The Enlightenment*, second edition. Basingstoke, U.K. & New York: Palgrave, 2001.

Porter. *London: A Social History*. Cambridge, Mass.: Harvard University Press, 1995.

Porter. *Rewriting the Self: Histories from the Renaissance to the Present*. London: Routledge, 1997.

Rawlings, Philip. *Drunks, Whores, and Idle Apprentices: Criminal Biographies of the Eighteenth Century*. London: Routledge, 1992.

Richardson, R. C., and W. H. Chaloner, comps. *British Economic and Social History: A Bibliographic Guide*, third edition. Manchester: Manchester University Press, 1996.

Shapiro, Barbara. *A Culture of Fact: England, 1550–1720*. Ithaca, N.Y.: Cornell University Press, 2000.

Sharpe, Kevin, and Steven Zwicker, eds. *Refiguring Revolutions: Aesthetics and Politics from the English Revolution to the Romantic Revolution*. Berkeley: University of California Press, 1998.

Smith, R. J. *The Gothic Bequest: Medieval Institutions in British Thought, 1688–1863*. Cambridge: Cambridge University Press, 1987.

Smith, Robert A. *Late Georgian and Regency England, 1760–1837*. Cambridge: Cambridge University Press, 1984.

Spector, Robert Donald, comp. *Backgrounds to Restoration and Eighteenth-Century English Literature: An Annotated Bibliographical Guide to Modern Scholarship*. New York: Greenwood Press, 1989.

Swedenberg, H. T., ed. *England in the Restoration and Early Eighteenth Century: Essays on Culture and Society*. Berkeley: University of California Press, 1972.

Sweet, Rosemary. *Antiquaries: The Discovery of the Past in Eighteenth-Century Britain*. London: Hambledon & London, 2004.

Sweet. *The Writing of Urban Histories in Eighteenth-Century England,* Oxford Historical Monographs. Oxford: Oxford University Press, 1997.

Ward, William Smith. *British Periodicals & Newspapers, 1789–1832.* Lexington: University Press of Kentucky, 1972.

Watson, Charles A. *The Writing of History in Britain: A Bibliography of Post-1945 Writings about British Historians and Biographers.* New York: Garland, 1982.

Winks, Robin W., ed. *The Historiography of the British Empire–Commonwealth: Trends, Interpretations and Resources.* Durham, N.C.: Duke University Press, 1966.

Woolf, Daniel. *The Social Circulation of the Past: English Historical Culture 1500–1730.* Oxford: Oxford University Press, 2003.

Contributors

Annamarie E. Apple . . . . *University of Pittsburgh*
Julia Belian. . . . . *University of Missouri, Kansas City*
Troy Bickham . . . . *Texas A&M University*
Tania Boster . . . . *University of Pittsburgh*
Michael Brown . . . . *University of Aberdeen*
Clare Callaghan. . . . . *University of Maryland*
Mercy Cannon . . . . *Stephen F. Austin State University*
Philip Connell . . . . *University of Cambridge*
Rory Thomas Cornish . . . . *Winthrop University*
Juilee Decker . . . . *Georgetown College*
H. T. Dickinson. . . . . *University of Edinburgh*
Seán Patrick Donlan . . . . *University of Limerick*
Judith Dorn . . . . *St. Cloud State University*
Jean Culp Flanigan . . . . *East Tennessee State University*
Patrick Gill . . . . *Johannes Gutenberg University*
Michael Griffin . . . . *University of Limerick*
Aneilya Hancock-Barnes . . . . *University of Arkansas*
Craig A. Hanson . . . . *Calvin College*
Robert W. Haynes . . . . *Texas A&M International University*
Michael R. Hutcheson . . . . *Landmark College*
Walter H. Keithley . . . . *Arizona State University*
Russell M. Lawson . . . . *Bacone College*
Anthony W. Lee . . . . *Kentucky Wesleyan College*
Jeannine M. Loftus . . . . *Salem State College*
John E. Luebering . . . . *University of Chicago*
Ian Macgregor-Morris . . . . *University of Nottingham*
Robert W. McHenry Jr.. . . . . *University of Hawaii, Manoā*
James Moore . . . . *University of London*
Jaime Ramon Olivares. . . . . *Houston Community College–Central*
Christine Owen . . . . *University of Melbourne*
Charles W. A. Prior . . . . *University of Hull*
Elizabeth Purdy . . . . *LaGrange, Georgia*
Carey M. Roberts . . . . *Arkansas Tech University*
Gareth Sampson . . . . *University of Manchester*
Shannon Schedlich-Day. . . . . *Flinders University of South Australia*
Mark G. Spencer . . . . *Brock University*
Ralph Stewart . . . . *Acadia University*

Alan Tapper... *Edith Cowan University*

Dale Marie Urie .... *University of Kansas*

Rowland Weston .... *University of Waikato*

Jeffrey R. Wigelsworth .... *Dalhousie University*

Cumulative Index

Dictionary of Literary Biography, Volumes 1-336
Dictionary of Literary Biography Yearbook, 1980-2002
Dictionary of Literary Biography Documentary Series, Volumes 1-19
Concise Dictionary of American Literary Biography, Volumes 1-7
Concise Dictionary of British Literary Biography, Volumes 1-8
Concise Dictionary of World Literary Biography, Volumes 1-4

Cumulative Index

DLB before number: *Dictionary of Literary Biography*, Volumes 1-336
Y before number: *Dictionary of Literary Biography Yearbook*, 1980-2002
DS before number: *Dictionary of Literary Biography Documentary Series*, Volumes 1-19
CDALB before number: *Concise Dictionary of American Literary Biography*, Volumes 1-7
CDBLB before number: *Concise Dictionary of British Literary Biography*, Volumes 1-8
CDWLB before number: *Concise Dictionary of World Literary Biography*, Volumes 1-4

D

H

K

L

M

R

W

Cumulative Index

ISBN-13: 978-0-7876-8154-8
ISBN-10: 0-7876-8154-7